I0751227

Hudson Park — On the Lower West Side.

THE TENEMENT HOUSE PROBLEM

INCLUDING THE REPORT OF THE NEW YORK STATE TENEMENT HOUSE COMMISSION OF 1900

BY VARIOUS WRITERS

EDITED BY

ROBERT W. DeFOREST AND LAWRENCE VEILLER

IN TWO VOLUMES

VOL. II

New York
THE MACMILLAN COMPANY
LONDON: MACMILLAN & CO., Ltd.
1903

Set up, electrotyped, and published November, 1903.

Norwood Press
J. S. Cushing & Co. — Berwick & Smith Co.
Norwood, Mass., U.S.A.

CONTENTS

VOLUME II

APPENDICES

LIST OF ILLUSTRATIONS

VOLUME II

LIST OF ILLUSTRATIONS

VOLUME II

PARKS AND PLAYGROUNDS FOR TENEMENT DISTRICTS

BY LAWRENCE VEILLER

PARKS AND PLAYGROUNDS FOR TENEMENT DISTRICTS

ATTENTION was first called to the great need of parks in tenement districts by the Tenement House Commission appointed in 1884. In the report which they submitted to the legislature in the early part of 1885, they called attention to this need, suggesting the opening of Leonard Street through to Pell Street, so as to do away with "The Mulberry Bend," a notorious block of tenements. This plan, it appears, was recommended forty years previously, but had never been carried out. In 1887, through the efforts of the Hon. Abram S. Hewitt, a law was passed known as the Small Parks Act, being Chapter 320 of the Laws of that year, authorizing and empowering the Board of Street Opening and Improvement of New York City "to select, locate and lay out such and so many public parks in the City of New York south of 155th Street, as the said Board may from time to time determine." The act also provided that not more than the sum of $1,000,000 should be expended or be authorized to be expended in any one year for this purpose. Notwithstanding the fact that this law had been on the statute-books for six years, as late as 1893 no action had been taken under it except proceedings commenced in 1887 to have the notorious Mulberry Bend torn down and converted into a small park. The commissioners appointed by the Supreme Court to determine the assessments and the award of damages did not, however, present their report to the court until five years later, in 1892, and not until 1896, nine years after the resolution was passed, was Mulberry Bend Park finally finished.

The Tenement House Commission of 1894 devoted much time and thought to the subject of small parks, and had bills introduced in the Legislature requiring the laying out of two small parks in the tenement quarters of the city, below 14th Street. These laws were passed in 1895. One of these parks, the Hamilton Fish Park, located at Houston and Sheriff Streets, was turned over to the public in the summer of 1900, after five years. The other park, known as the W. H. Seward Park, located at Canal and Jefferson Streets, has not yet been completed. The old tenement houses have been torn down for a number of years, and about two years ago the land was levelled off at the urgent request of the Outdoor Recreation League, a private society, which has since equipped this park with gymnastic apparatus and has maintained and still maintains a public playground there at its own expense. Since the Commission of 1894 made its report, the only park located in tenement districts, which has been completed and turned over to the public, in addition to the one above mentioned, has been that known as Hudson Park, located at Hudson and Leroy Streets, upon the site of the old St. John's graveyard. Three other tenement house parks are reported by the Department of Parks to be in process of condemnation, one located at 27th and 28th Streets, from Ninth to Tenth Avenue, another at 52d to 54th Streets and the North River, and the third at 74th to 76th Streets and the East River. No work, however, has been commenced on any of these parks.

The Tenement House Commission of 1894 recommended, in regard to the subject of neighborhood parks, that the mayor should appoint a Commission to locate park spaces and other improvements contemplated; the decisions of this Commission to be subject to ratification by the legislature by an act based upon their recommendations. Or, as an alternative, that the mayor should appoint an unofficial advisory committee or board of private citizens, whose conclusions and recommendations on this subject should be laid before the existing official agencies for action. In accordance with this suggestion, Mayor W. L. Strong appointed, in the month of June in the year 1897, a special committee known as the Small Parks Committee. The Hon. Abram S. Hewitt was chairman of this committee and Mr. Jacob A. Riis, secretary. The other members were De Witt J. Seligman, John B. Devins, Myer S. Isaacs, James J. Higginson, William R. Stewart, Joseph D. Bryant, Charles G. Wilson, *ex officio*, and Samuel McMillan, *ex officio*.

This Committee made an exhaustive report upon the subject, making fourteen distinct recommendations to the city authorities, providing for parks to be located in tenement districts in nearly all of the different wards of the city. This report stated the needs in each ward at that time in great detail, and presented in the form of tables the acreage of the ward, the population, the density of population per acre, the number of children under fifteen years of age, the density per acre of such child population, the death-rate of the ward in 1896, the general death-rate of the city for that year, and the death-rate of children under five years of age. Accompanying this report was a map showing the existing parks in the city at that time, the parks that were in process of construction, the new schools, the areas of turbulence where arrests had been especially heavy, the areas of overcrowding and playground destitution; also the sites recommended by the committee for the establishment of small parks. The report of this committee also included a statistical statement of the death-rate in New York from 1865 to 1896 inclusive, with the population of the city by wards during the same period, as well as the text of the Small Parks Act (Chapter 320 of the Laws of 1887). Notwithstanding this valuable report, embodying, as it did, the careful study and recommendations of experts upon this subject, nothing has been done to carry out any of these recommendations.

PRESENT PARK AREAS IN THE CITY

The city of Greater New York has at present a total park area, exclusive of parkways, of 6776 acres, distributed as follows: 1343 acres in the Boroughs of Manhattan and Richmond; 1573 acres in the Boroughs of Brooklyn and Queens; and 3849 acres in the Borough of the Bronx. That is, the Borough of the Bronx contains practically three times the park area of Manhattan and Richmond combined. The large parks in Manhattan, however, are all located in the upper portions of the city, away from the tenement house quarters, at too great a distance to be of much use, either as a breathing spot or as recreation grounds at ordinary times, being of value to the poorer classes chiefly as a place of pilgrimage on Sundays and holidays.

Of the 1141 acres of park area in the Borough of Manhattan, the greater part is located in two large parks, Central Park and Riverside Park, situated in the residential quarters of the city, leaving the small amount of 157 acres to be distributed throughout the rest of Manhattan Island. At present there are only a very small number of tenement district parks, and these are nearly all very small in size. On the lower East Side Corlears Hook Park has an acreage of 8.30; a small triangle at Grand Street and East Broadway has an acreage of 0.630; Hamilton Fish Park, at Sheriff and Houston Streets, comprises 3.673 acres; Tompkins Square, located at Avenue A and 7th Street, contains 10.508 acres; and on the upper East Side the East River Park, at 86th Street and the East River, comprises 12.546 acres. Also, in other parts of the tenement districts are the following parks: Hudson Park, located at Hudson and Leroy Streets, comprising 1.70 acres; Mulberry Bend Park, comprising 2.750 acres; Paradise Park, a little triangle of open space comprising 0.114 acre; making a total of actual park area of 40.221 acres for the entire tenement house population of the island of Manhattan. When one realizes that the tenement house population in Manhattan is 1,585,000 persons, and that at least two-thirds of these people live in the ordinary type of tenement house, it becomes evident that a park area of forty acres to over 1,000,000 persons is not what might be termed a liberal allowance by the city. It would seem that the time had come when the needs of the tenement house dwellers in this respect should be met. It is a duty that the city owes, not only to its citizens, but to itself. The propriety of expending additional money each year for additional parks in the Borough of the Bronx and for the maintenance of Bronx Park, Van Cortlandt Park, Pelham Bay Park, and other parks in this portion of the city is not questioned. If such appropriations, however, are to be made at the expense of the lower portions of the city and are to deprive the tenement dwellers of needed opportunities for recreation and for fresh air, it would seem that further appropriations for large parks in these districts should for a while be discontinued. The value of a small park in a tenement quarter is so well understood that it seems unnecessary at this time to present any arguments for the expansion of this work. The history of the old Five Points and Mulberry Bend has shown that the creation of a park in such quarters means a total change in the character of the neighborhood. Both the old Five Points and Mulberry Bend, with the letting in of the sunlight and fresh air, changed completely from the haunts of criminals to quiet and peaceful sections of the city. The effect upon the death-rate of such quarters is also equally apparent.

THE PRESENT NEEDS OF NEW YORK

New York at present needs a number of additional small parks in tenement neighborhoods. When it is borne in mind that the streets in our tenement house districts, originally laid out for three-story dwelling houses, each house containing one family, or about five persons, are now occupied on both sides by tall tenement houses, usually five or more stories in height, containing from 22 to 26 families in each, with a population of from two to three thousand persons in each block, with no back yards in which the children may play, it is evident that some method must be adopted of meeting the needs of this great and rapidly increasing population. If the city permits builders of tenement houses to encroach so upon the yard space as to leave practically no back yard to the building, the city will have to pay for it in other ways by condemning whole blocks for park purposes. Such action will be wise economy. The police records show that where a small park has been established the number of arrests for juvenile crime has greatly diminished. It would hardly seem to need argument to convince any one that it is essential that children should have opportunity for physical exercise, to work off their abundance of animal spirits in the natural form of play. Just as sure as such

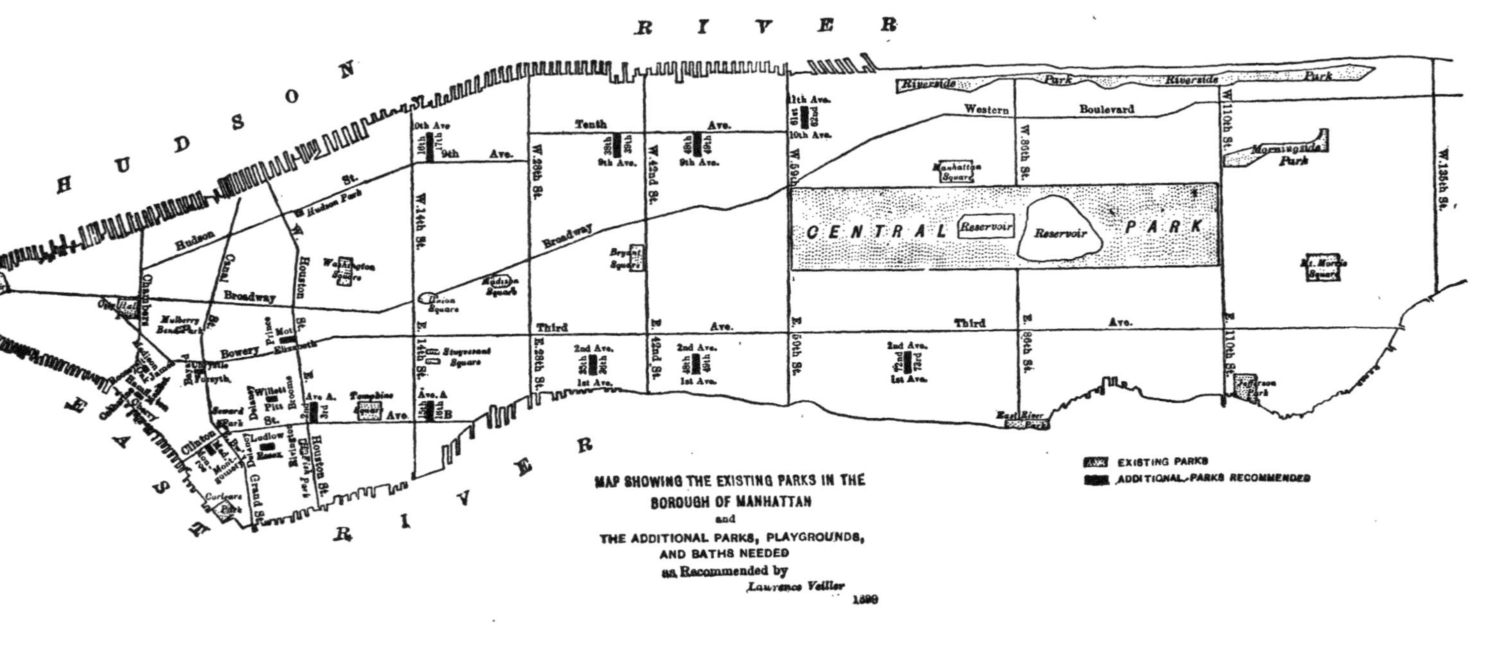

MAP SHOWING THE EXISTING PARKS IN THE BOROUGH OF MANHATTAN and THE ADDITIONAL PARKS, PLAYGROUNDS, AND BATHS NEEDED as Recommended by *Laurence Veiller* 1899

opportunity is denied them will this excess of physical energy find vent in other channels. If our future citizens are to be good citizens, they must have opportunity to lead a rational human existence when they are young. Nothing better can be urged in this connection than the following extract from the report of the Small Parks Committee of 1897: —

"In the original plan of the city of New York the children seem to have been forgotten. Doubtless this oversight was due to the extensive area of unoccupied land which was available for the games and sports in which the youth of that day were wont to indulge. But as the city has grown in population, and especially within the last thirty years, this unoccupied space has been covered by improvements which have left to the children no other opportunity for play but such as can be found in the streets. The streets themselves have been largely occupied by car tracks and new servitudes, so that it is dangerous as well as obstructive to traffic for the children to use them for games of any kind, without incurring the interference of the police. A sense of hostility between the children and the guardians of public order is thus engendered, leading to the growth of a criminal class and to the education of citizens who become enemies of law and order. Nothing can be worse or more to be deplored than this state of affairs, whether regarded from a moral or economic point of view. The outlay for police, courts, reformatories, hospitals, almshouses, and prisons is thus largely increased, while outside of these safeguards against poverty and crime is bred a general feeling of discontent, which is the cause of much misery, poverty, and danger to society. Your Committee are convinced from the careful examination which they have been enabled to make, and especially by the marvellous improvement in the neighborhood of the new small parks, which have recently been brought into use, that the failure to provide for the reasonable recreation of the people, and especially for playgrounds for the rising generation, has been the most efficient cause of the growth of crime and pauperism in our midst."

THE NEEDS IN EACH TENEMENT WARD

THE FOURTH WARD

The fourth ward is located on the lower East Side, and is the district bounded by Peck Slip on the south, the East River on the east, Catherine Street on the north, and Park Row on the west and north. It contained in 1900 a tenement house population of 19,335 persons, of which 1661 were children under five years of age. Notwithstanding this fact, there are no parks whatsoever in the ward.

The ward comprises 83.3 acres, and in 1896 the death-rate[1] of the entire ward was 36.31, 15 points higher, or more than half as much again, as the general death-rate of the city, while the death-rate of children under five years of age in the ward was 123.5. The death-rate in this ward is the highest of any ward in the city, and next to the fourteenth ward it had the highest infant death-rate in 1896. The Small Parks Committee of 1897 recommended that a proper playground be established on Cherry Hill, on the site of "Gotham Court," now demolished. A few years ago, an act was passed in the legislature making it mandatory for the city authorities to establish a public park in this ward. The bill was vetoed by the mayor on the ground that it interfered with home rule and that the city authorities had full power to lay out such park. Nothing, however, has been done since then by the city authorities. Not only are there no parks in the fourth ward, but the nearest park of any kind is City Hall Park in one direction and the proposed Seward Park in the other direction. Neither of these can be of use as parks to the children of the fourth ward. Parks to be of use must be located at not too great a distance. It has at different times been urged against the establishment of a park in this ward that the ward is losing its tenement characteristics and that the tenement houses are gradually being displaced by business buildings. Statistics, however, do not bear out this belief. In the past forty years the change that has taken place in the ward is hardly noticeable, the number of tenement houses having decreased in all that time from 486 to 471, or only 3 per cent, while the tenement house population has increased from 17,611 to 19,335. It is also interesting to note that the tenement house population in this ward at the present day is greater than the entire population of the ward in 1896, four years ago. To those familiar with the conditions in the ward, it is evident that it will continue to be a crowded tenement house district for many years to come, and that the establishment of a small park in this district is urgently needed.

THE SEVENTH WARD

This ward is located on the lower East Side of the city, being bounded by Catherine Street on the south, Division and Grand Streets on the north, and the East River on the east and south. The ward contains 206 acres. Forty years ago it was one of the fashionable residential quarters of the city; to-day it is distinctively a tenement house district, and the tenement house population alone amounts to 72,466 persons, of which 11,473 are children under five

[1] Death-rates given in this paper have been based on statistics of 1896, because these are the latest accurate statistics available.

Mulberry Bend Park — The Site of a Notorious Slum.

years of age. The only park in the ward is Corlears Hook Park, located at the extreme eastern end by the water front. Investigations show that in tenement districts few children are apt to travel a greater distance than four or five blocks to use a park, and that indeed it is not possible for little children to go any greater distance from home. It is apparent, therefore, that Corlears Hook Park, at the eastern end of the district, can be of very little service to the very large tenement house population living in this ward.

THE TENTH WARD

The tenth ward is one of the Jewish quarters of the city, and, while one of the smallest wards, it is the most densely crowded one. It contained in 1900 a tenement population of 76,073 persons, of which 10,633 were children under five years of age. There are no parks wholly within the ward, the only park at all within the ward being the proposed park known as Seward Park and located at the extreme southeast section, near Canal and Jefferson Streets. In considering this question of small parks, natural and artificial boundaries must be borne in mind. For instance, a park to the west of the Bowery is absolutely of no value to people living on the east side of that thoroughfare, even if it were only two blocks away, as the children would not dare run the risk of crossing this street. Similarly, a park located below Grand Street on the east side would be seldom used by persons living above Grand Street. It is a line they seldom cross. For this reason, if for no other, Seward Park is little used by the inhabitants of the tenth ward, being too far away for the children.

THE THIRTEENTH WARD

This ward is bounded on the south by Division and Grand Streets, and on the east by the East River, on the north by Rivington Street, and on the west by Norfolk Street, and contains 109 acres. The tenement house population is 55,564, of which 9414 are children under five years of age. There are no parks whatsoever in the ward. When one considers that in the district between Rivington and Grand Streets, from the Bowery to the East River, there is not one park, and that in 1896 there were 85,949 persons living in this district, it becomes apparent that the need of a park is urgent.

THE FOURTEENTH WARD

The fourteenth ward is bounded on the south by Canal Street, on the east by the Bowery, on the north by Houston Street, and on the west by Broadway, and contains 108 acres. The tenement house population is 35,250. It comprises the chief Italian quarter of the city. It has been a popular belief for some time that business has been crowding out the tenement houses in this district; statistics, however, do not bear out these facts. Also, a number of new tenement houses have been recently erected in the district. During the last 40 years the number of tenement houses has increased 17 per cent, while the total tenement house population has increased from 20,008 to 35,250, or 76 per cent. There are no parks whatsoever in the ward. In 1896 there were 10,182 children under fifteen years of age living there.

THE SIXTEENTH WARD

This ward is bounded on the south by 14th Street, on the east by Sixth Avenue, on the north by 26th Street, and on the west by the Hudson River. It contains 318 acres, with a tenement house population of 43,467. There is not a single park in the ward, the nearest park to the south being just above Canal Street, while to the east the nearest park is Union Square, and to the north Central Park, none of which is of any use to the inhabitants of this ward.

THE SEVENTEENTH WARD

The seventeenth ward is located on the East Side of the city, and is bounded on the south by Rivington Street, on the east by Avenue B and Clinton Street, on the north by 14th Street, and on the west by the Bowery and Fourth Avenue. It contains 266 acres, and has a tenement house population of 114,559 persons, of which 13,519 are children under five years of age. It has within its boundaries one large park known as Tompkins Square, which years ago, before it was made into a park, was the scene of the "Bread and Blood" riots. While this park is able to meet the needs of the northern end of the ward, it is not sufficient to meet the requirements of the people living in the other portions.

THE EIGHTEENTH WARD

The eighteenth ward extends from 14th to 26th Street, and from Sixth Avenue to the East River. It contains 500 acres. While there are a number of parks in this ward, namely, Madison Square, Union Square, and Stuyvesant Square, comprising all together 13 acres of park area, yet none of these parks are situated within the tenement house district of the ward. The ward has a tenement house population of 40,724. The nearest park is Tompkins Square, which is too far away to be of use to most of the people in this ward. In the district north of Tompkins Square, from 11th Street to 26th Street, and from First Avenue to the East River, there is a population of 44,330 persons, without sight of grass or trees, or any green thing.

THE NINETEENTH WARD

The nineteenth ward is located on the upper East Side and extends from 40th Street to 86th Street, and from Sixth Avenue to the East River. That portion of the ward east of Third Avenue is distinctively a tenement house district. The ward contains a total tenement house population of 203,815, of which 24,794 are children under five years of age.

THE TWENTIETH WARD

This ward is located on the West Side of the city, and extends from 26th to 40th Street, and from Sixth Avenue to the Hudson River. It contains 418.7 acres. The tenement house population of the ward is 79,732, and this population is on the increase. There is not a park in the whole ward, although the ward is large in area and contains a very large population, having in 1896 a population of 94,969. The nearest park on the south is just above Canal Street, while the nearest park on the north is Central Park, and on the east Bryant Park, all too far away to be of use to the tenement dwellers in this district. It is especially desirable that a park should be established in this neighborhood, which for many years has received the unfortunate appellation of "Hell's Kitchen," and has attained recent notoriety in the public mind through the race riots which took place there in the summer of 1900. No one can doubt that the establishment of a park in this district would be of the greatest benefit to the community.

THE TWENTY-FIRST WARD

This ward extends from 26th to 40th Street and from Sixth Avenue to the East River. It contains 380 acres, and has at the present time a tenement house population of 42,818 persons. There is not a park in the ward.

THE TWENTY-SECOND WARD

The twenty-second ward extends from 40th Street to 86th Street and from Sixth Avenue to the Hudson River, and contains 1681 acres. The most densely populated block in the entire city is located in this ward, containing a population of about 4000 persons at the present time; and there is in the ward a total tenement house population of 182,508 persons, of which 15,651 are children under five years of age. When one considers that the nearest park to the south is Canal Street, miles away, and the nearest park to the east is Central Park, it would seem essential that a park should be at once established in this ward.

GENERAL CONSIDERATIONS

In selecting sites for proposed parks in the different tenement house districts of the city, the following considerations should be taken into account: the death-rate of the block chosen as compared with the general death-rate of the city; the character of the tenement houses now erected upon the site; the nearness to public schools and other educational agencies in the districts; the distance away from other parks or from new proposed parks; and especial consideration should be given to the density of population in neighboring blocks.

In locating new parks in tenement districts, it is essential, not only that these open spaces should be created, but that in them there should be full opportunity for play and for healthful recreation. Merely a park with grass and walks is not sufficient to meet the needs of our tenement districts. What is needed is a playground, above all other things; that is, a place where the children and young people of the neighborhood can play without restraint. In such playgrounds provision should be made for children of all ages.

The work done by the Outdoor Recreation League, a private society of this city, has demonstrated so fully the advantages of this form of recreation, that a description of the work carried on by them conveys, better than anything else, the right impression of the results to be obtained in this way.

This society in 1898 obtained from the Stryker Estate the use of some vacant land at 53d Street and Eleventh Avenue. It secured private funds to fence in this lot and equipped it with outdoor gymnastic apparatus, consisting of parallel bars, ladders, vaulting-bucks and horses, horizontal bars, rings, running-track, etc.; as well as, for the younger children, swings, sand-boxes, shelter tent for kindergarten games, etc. The great success achieved by this playground led the Outdoor Recreation League, in the spring of 1898, to petition the Board of Estimate and Apportionment to appropriate the sum of $12,000 to fill in, level off, and fence the vacant land at Canal and Jefferson Streets, which was in process of conversion into a small park to be known as Seward Park. This work was done in the spring of that year, and the Outdoor Recreation League then set to work and raised funds for the equipment and maintenance of an outdoor playground at this place. A full gymnastic equipment, including running-track and all sorts of gymnastic apparatus, has been placed in Seward Park, and thousands of children now enjoy the use of this spot. The accompanying illustrations give but a faint idea of the value of playgrounds of this kind in crowded districts. No one who has not personally visited the Seward Park playground can appreciate

A Corner of Seward Park.

what this opportunity for natural play means to the anæmic, underfed, and mentally overdeveloped young people of the East Side.

In addition to the playgrounds at 53d Street and Eleventh Avenue, known as Hudson Bank playground, and to the Seward Park playground, other similar playgrounds maintained by private means have been established in different parts of the city; among these may be mentioned the playgrounds at 68th Street and Broadway, Amsterdam Avenue and 99th Street, at 35th Street and First Avenue, known as Kip's Bay playground; also the playground at the foot of East 76th Street maintained by the East Side Settlement.

As the needs of New York in regard to bathing facilities in our tenement house districts are very great, it would seem to be desirable in establishing new parks in tenement districts to provide at the same time for public baths. This can be done in a very simple way and at a very greatly reduced expense. In the past, it has been customary, when creating a park in a tenement district, to tear down the old tenement houses just a little below the sidewalk level, leaving the foundations, old pipes, and débris of every kind, filling in with brick and all kinds of material, and then sprinkling over this a number of loads of soil. Aside from the point of view of danger to health involved in this method, the method is also a wasteful one. It is suggested, therefore, that in establishing every park or playground in the future, such an area be excavated down to a distance of about 12 or 14 feet below the sidewalk, and that a portion of the space below the sidewalk be given up to the use of public baths. In this way the city will get the use of its land for baths practically without expense, and the very great needs of tenement dwellers for ample bathing facilities will be met.

As at present there are only 40 acres of park area for the tenement house population of New York, which amounts to 1,585,000 persons, of which at least two-thirds, or 1,000,000, are living in the ordinary type of tenement house, it would seem that the city should at once make provision for the needs of these people by establishing parks, playgrounds, and public baths in the different tenement districts of the city.

PROSTITUTION AS A TENEMENT HOUSE EVIL

BY JAMES B. REYNOLDS

PROSTITUTION AS A TENEMENT HOUSE EVIL

THE subject of immorality in the tenement houses was forced upon the attention of the Commission by complaints and appeals made to it from many sources. In its consideration of the subject the Commission was hampered because of the lack of adequate and authoritative literature upon the general question of prostitution. In view of the extent of the evil in the cities of our country, and the necessity of the application of special laws for its control, it seems surprising that so little attempt has been made to accurately ascertain the exact working of the evil, its causes and its results. An investigation of the whole subject is greatly needed, but such a general investigation could not be undertaken by us and did not come within the scope of our authority. It could properly be undertaken only by some body specially constituted for the purpose.

In the investigation of our special subject we found, however, many witnesses prepared to testify, and many felt deeply that, whatever the solution of the general problem of prostitution, it ought to be possible to drive the evil from the tenement houses and thereby prevent enforced contact with it in the homes of those whose poverty made it impossible for them to change their dwelling place and so escape contamination.

The special statements made to the Commission by Dr. Felix Adler and Mrs. Charles Russell Lowell, and summarized from their testimony, are herewith presented.

The verdict that the conditions which at present, 1900, exist are unendurable is unanimous. That the landlord should be cognizant of the character of his tenants was the universal opinion of all the witnesses who have appeared before us, and equally unanimous was the opinion that the landlord should be held far more strictly responsible for the character of his tenants, so that reputable occupants of tenement houses should be protected from enforced association with women of immoral character, and from all the evils attendant upon such companionship. This unanimity of opinion appears to the Commission remarkable, and to afford ample justification for the legislative propositions presented in its report.

STATEMENT PRESENTED BY DR. FELIX ADLER

As to the causes of immorality in the tenement houses, it seems to me that one would naturally divide them under different heads. For instance, in any proper, careful consideration of the subject I should think that the economic causes would be mentioned first, especially the evils of the sweat shop system on the East Side, which produce a condition of things that render these poor unfortunate girls more susceptible — far more susceptible to temptation than they otherwise would be. I have known directly of cases where young women refused to share the poverty of their families, saying that life at best under the prevailing conditions was a continuous series of privations, and that if they could, even for a short time, escape from this horror of the tenement house and of the poverty-stricken home in the tenement house, to the streets, or to the gay saloon, or to the company of such companions as they had access to, they preferred the latter. I think that in the second place there is, of course, the great question of what might be done through the enforcement of the laws already existing; and then the question of the extent to which the laws now existing might be improved; and finally the question of the best means of redeeming those who have already fallen. It seems to me these would naturally be the four heads under which the whole subject might be considered, and I should think it would be a mistake if the community received the impression, through the effort now being made to secure a better enforcement of the law — that that is all that is necessary, and that if the political conditions have been improved the conscience of the city may go to sleep. It seems to me that the manufacturers of the city have a responsibility in the matter, and that all efforts made to break up this congestion of pauper labor of the East Side, and transfer if possible the sweat shops to the rural districts, to the suburbs, to factories, would be a great step in the solution of our problem.

As to the enforcement of the law, I have nothing special to add to what has been said on other occasions, but as to the matter of improving the laws, I should think that some such action as has been contemplated of more easily getting access to the landlord would greatly help the situation. At present the landlord often escapes because the *onus probandi* — the burden of proof — is on the complainant. The complainant must show that the landlord had knowledge of these evil conditions, and it is very often difficult to establish the fact of such knowledge on his part. If, however, the onus was shifted upon the landlord, if when the whole neighborhood is aware that a house is used for illegal purposes, after a certain period has elapsed in which this condition can be proved to have continued, if then the presumption is that the landlord knows, because he ought to know, what is being done with his property, it would be very much easier to punish him. I have thought sometimes that we might take an attitude toward the tenement house that the halls and the stairs are to some extent to be likened to public highways, and that the police power of the State, which is not permitted to intrude into the house, might on that ground be introduced into the interior of the tenement houses. The apartment resembles the street, and just as the power of the State is exercised over a public street, so we might claim it would be right to extend this power into the interior of the tenement houses so as to establish laws and regulations concerning what is permissible and what is not in the public part of the tenement house. The tenement, with its often vast population, is becoming a kind of public institution, which cannot properly be dealt with from the point of view of regarding it as a private house. The English principle, that one's house is one's castle, would then apply to the apartments occupied by the separate families, while all that part of the tenement house which is devoted to the traffic of the various inmates of the apartments would rather be dealt with from the point of view of the highway. If this were done, then I should think it would be possible to prevent such deplorable occurrences as are now frequent: the assembling in the halls and on the stairways of numbers of lewd persons, men and women; the crowding on the stairways, and also improper exhibitions from the windows and from the open doors. These evils that go together with the particular vice that you are considering I think could be suppressed if that point of view can be fairly taken. I am not a lawyer, and may be therefore not able to say whether the legal mind would sustain that conception; but I merely mention it here as a suggestion, and in connection with the improvements in the law. Besides an attempt to shift the burden of proof upon the landlord as to the matter of knowledge, it occurs to me that if penalties were inflicted upon the housekeeper in case of a violation of these rules of propriety; if not only the landlord, but the housekeeper, as his representative, were held responsible, that probably instead of finding the housekeeper an obstacle, as she often is, in the way of enforcement of the law, we should then have a means of compelling the housekeeper, through fear of the penalty to be inflicted, to carry out the law. I am not sure whether there is such a law; but would it not be possible to provide that every tenement house, every house harboring more than three families, should be required to have a housekeeper representing the landlord on the premises? Whether we should go on further and adopt the European method of registration, I am not sure. If we could obtain a register, containing the names, the age, the sex, and if possible the occupations, of all the inmates of the different apartments of a tenement house, such a register to be kept and duly corrected from time to time by the housekeeper, it would be much easier than it is now to prevent overcrowding, and to prevent the lodging of infamous vice in the tenement houses.

STATEMENT PRESENTED BY MRS. CHARLES R. LOWELL.

As to the present conditions, of course there is no question that they are very bad in every way. The immoral women in the houses directly tempt young girls to join them. They also indirectly present the strongest temptations, for they are the only women who have good food, fine clothes, and an easy life in these houses. A girl who is earning $2 or $3 a week by standing behind a counter, running errands 10 hours a day (and 14 or 15 hours at what is called the "holiday season") cannot but compare her own life with that of one of these girls, who seems to have all she wants and to do nothing to earn it.

As to the causes of the conditions, the foundation cause is the corruption of the Police Department. Other causes are the temptations so freely offered to girls and boys, the shows all around the neighborhood, for instance, which stimulate evil imagination; the saloons, etc. This is only another symptom of police rottenness.

The low moral tone of both landlords and tenants is notorious, the former being ready to share in the profits of the vice, the latter being unwilling to protest against it.

Still another cause of existing conditions is the failure of police magistrates to deal rightly with men and women when arrested. The men arrested in raids are all discharged, upon giving false names and addresses. If they were taken into court and subjected to the public disgrace they deserve, many who perhaps are more foolish than depraved would no doubt fear to run the risk of entering such places, and would thus be saved from both temptation and sin, and the trade would consequently be less lucrative to the women and their masters.

The women are also wrongly dealt with. Fining only forces them to continue in the same life, when the object should be to remove them from it and to reform them if possible. To fine them is to bind them to it. They have only the one means of earning money, and if they pay for their fines by past sin, or if some one pays for them, they become enslaved to bad men more irrevocably. I think it would be better to make no arrests at all than to arrest and fine these women as at present. Commitment for six months to the workhouse would at least be a punishment. Judge Mott has the honorable distinction of sentencing to the workhouse instead of fining, and when he is sitting, these women shun his district for that reason. That we have heard constantly. I belong to a committee that visits the station-houses, and in going month by month to the places the police matrons have said, "We have not had many women this month." "Why not?" "Judge Mott is on the bench." That is constantly what different members of the committee visiting different station-houses hear.

It is not necessary to commit to the workhouse, however, if the women themselves can be persuaded to enter some of the "homes" which are ready to receive them, and where they will be helped to reform, and later to find employment. The Magdalen Asylum, the House of the Good Shepherd, The House of the Holy Family, the Salvation Army Home, are some of these.

As to the remedies, the first is to reform the Police Department. Dr. Parkhurst has always been right in saying that that is the first step. A corrupt police can and will render unavailing any and every system which might be adopted.

Assuming that to be understood, there are many steps to be taken, all dependent upon an aroused moral public opinion.

The police magistrates, the institutions, should all join in trying to deliver the women from the life of sin, and in trying to reform them. The following plan has been suggested: that probation officers and court officers (all women) should be nominated by the various institutions interested in such work to go with the police when arrests are made, and try on the spot to persuade the women to go into one of the homes named; that the magistrate should in such cases suspend sentence, and allow the institutions the opportunity to deal freely with such women.

When they refuse such offers, they should be committed to the workhouse for six months, and later, when the reformatory at Bedford is opened, to that institution.

I think the fining for vagrancy, for misdemeanors, and for disorderly conduct should be forbidden by law; also that such part of Section 318 of the City Charter as authorizes the entry of the police to houses supposed to be used for such purposes, solely on the statement of a police officer, should be repealed. It facilitates blackmail.

Another amendment to the law should be to make it a felony to keep or to let rooms for immoral purposes in a tenement house, it being now only a misdemeanor in any case.

I think if that distinction were made, it being a misdemeanor to let such rooms in a private house, if it were made a felony to let such rooms, or to carry on such immorality in a tenement house, it would emphasize the greater sin, the greater wrong of the sin in a tenement house, and the recognition by law that it was a worse sin would have a good influence on public opinion.

The experience of the city of Glasgow is one that is encouraging in the highest degree, and I believe the same results could be very readily attained here, provided that our Police Department was established on the right foundation, and was an honorable body of decent men.

I should like to quote just a few extracts from testimony about Glasgow, because it is very remarkable and ought to be known. This is a summary of what has happened since 1870.

"The Glasgow administration, which, as we have seen, includes repressive law, municipal vigilance, and organized beneficence, has been carried on since 1870. Its results may be noted under the seven following heads: —

"First — The streets have been cleared of the disreputable business of solicitation and assignation, and left free for their legitimate use as safe and decent thoroughfares.

"Second — The number of brothels has been steadily and largely decreased, notwithstanding the growing population.

"Third — Clandestine prostitution, judging from the most careful observation possible, has decreased generally in the same ratio as the brothels.

"Fourth — There has been a slight decrease in illegitimacy.

"Fifth — An increased desire to reform has been shown by fallen women.

"Sixth — Crime, always connected with vice, has diminished.

"Seventh — Disease which arises from promiscuous intercourse has decreased."

This was written in 1881. It is called the "Wrong and Right Methods of Dealing with the Social Evil, as shown by lately published Parliamentary Evidence, by Dr. Elizabeth Blackwell." I am sorry to say it is out of print. It begins by showing the evils of the "Let Alone" system in London, and then the regulations of the registration system in Paris, and shows how each is bad, and third, the Glasgow system, which was the maintaining of public order with the assistance of a body of private citizens who helped in this work, and the help of the magistrates.

"The facts in relation to brothels, and the effect of law and public opinion upon them, is noteworthy. In 1849, with a population of 314,000, and an inert public opinion, there were 211 brothels, with 538 inmates. In 1870, with a population of 510,816, and a public opinion gradually awakening to the evil, there were 204 brothels. After nine years of vigorous measures required by the citizens, the brothels were reduced to less than one-seventh of the original number. This remarkable result shows the power of public opinion when it demands and supports the enforcement of law.

"The great mischievous error, that vigorous repression of the public manifestations of vice is necessarily productive of an increase of secret vice, is entirely disproved by carefully recorded facts in the municipal experience of this great city of Glasgow."

The Chief of Police himself says: "Notwithstanding the frequently expressed opinion of well-meaning people, who take, as they state, a philosophical view of prostitution and brothel-keeping, and from their mode of reasoning arrive at the conclusion that both are necessary evils, and incapable of being either eradicated or greatly diminished, I consider myself justified in the opinion that the results indicated above, and which have been brought about by a steady and persistent application of the law by the authorities, have been of very great advantage to this community. Viewed from no higher standpoint than that of profit and loss in property, the benefits are apparent and tangible; but when the social and moral advantages are taken into account, the removal of seductive temptations from the youthful and thoughtless, and not infrequently from the intoxicated and foolish adults, the results, though they cannot be expressed in figures, are far more precious. While the reduction in the number of brothels has been so considerable, and the streets have been to a great extent cleared of abandoned women who used to frequent them, I am to the present time without one single complaint from a respectable citizen that prostitution has gone into more secret or private channels, or that the repressive measures of the authorities have inflicted the slightest hardship upon any one."

A recent report of the Glasgow Chief of Police states also, that the brothels in 1892 were 7; in 1893, 9; in 1894, 11; and in 1895, 9; in 1896, 13, when the population was 707,000. When the population was 500,000 there were 204, and they say in 1896, when the population was 707,000, there were only 13 brothels known to the police at that time in Glasgow.

It is to be remembered, likewise, that the protection of the character of the individual police officer is one of the most important things to be provided for in any plan of dealing with the subject of prostitution. The methods heretofore employed in this city, and all systems of license, whether legal or by the use of the fining system, are absolutely demoralizing to the men who enforce them.

POLICY — A TENEMENT HOUSE EVIL

BY F. NORTON GODDARD

POLICY — A TENEMENT HOUSE EVIL

IN the course of attending to a large number of cases of eviction in the 20th Assembly District, an effort was made to determine the immediate cause of the inability to pay the rent, and it was found that more cases of destitution seemed to be referable to policy playing than to drink. Policy is a real evil of very considerable proportions — nor are its evil effects confined to the economic consequences. It is also a great moral evil: children in great numbers are frequenters of the policy shop; their patronage is solicited, and the minimum stake is fixed at two cents with a special view to their means. Women become "fiends," as the habitual player is termed; they play away their husband's earnings and pawn the household possessions, even, in some cases, putting their children to bed to have their clothes to sell.

The prevalence of policy playing in this city and the openness with which the sale of policy slips is conducted is, as a result of some attention that the newspapers have been giving to the subject, beginning to be understood. Most people when they read these newspaper articles probably do not know what policy consists of, or how it is played, or who plays it. The greater number of people who have heard the name of the game mentioned simply know that it is some form of gambling, in which numbers figure, and the belief is general that the patrons of the game are negroes. The following quotation from an article in the *New York Sun*, published in November, 1899, is significant as to the extent of this evil: —

"The fact is that fully half a million white persons in this city have become infatuated with the game and play it daily. Many of the players are women who live in the tenement districts and spend almost every cent they earn in playing 'gigs,' 'horses,' and 'saddles,' the terms applied to combinations of numbers in the policy shops. People who are in a position to know say that there are at least fifteen hundred policy shops in Greater New York, and that they are known to the majority of school children."

Policy shops are almost invariably located in tenement house districts, the exception being that there are one or two located near the Stock Exchange for the special benefit of office boys and young clerks in brokers' offices. Policy is, therefore, distinctly a tenement house evil. Following is a description of the game, as published in the newspaper article above referred to. It must be understood, however, that this description of the game proceeds on the theory that the game is honestly conducted and is actually what it purports to be. This, however, is a supposition absolutely contrary to fact. The description that follows is, therefore, merely a description of how the player sees the game. Actually there is no game. The backers, in the time that elapses between the closing of the "books" and the announcing of the drawings, figure out to suit themselves what numbers they will announce.

"It should be understood that policy is an alleged lottery in which only the numbers from one to seventy-eight are made use of. The lottery is supposed to be operated out of town. Every day, excepting Sunday, there is supposed to be a drawing in Kentucky and another in Louisiana. In the morning, as the story goes, thirteen numbers are drawn from a wheel containing the entire seventy-eight. These thirteen are placed in a column, one beneath the other, and they may be any numbers from one to seventy-eight. Then alongside of the column of the Kentucky drawings comes a similar column of numbers supposed to be drawn in Louisiana. These two columns are printed on slips of paper and distributed among persons who have played the game for that particular drawing. The numbers supposed to be drawn turn up in the policy shop after two o'clock and are known as the morning draw, although posted in the shop at two o'clock in the afternoon. After seven o'clock in the evening, the numbers supposed to be drawn in the evening appear in the shop, and then the policy fiends get at work. To be more explicit, the player enters the shop and selects any three numbers he desires, provided they are from one to seventy-eight. He writes these three numbers on a slip of paper, and then bets any amount of money from one cent up to $1000, with the understanding that in case his numbers appear in the column of figures drawn, he receives odds of 100 to 1. For instance, take three numbers and write them on a slip of paper in this style: 19–46–62. These three numbers constitute a gig. If the player bets ten cents on that gig he simply writes the ten beneath the three numbers selected and hands it over to the policy writer, who writes the three numbers on a carbon sheet, making a copy for the player and a copy for himself. Then the writer takes a rubber stamp and stamps the date upon the piece of paper he gives to the player, and he keeps that in his pocket as a receipt. When he gets his ticket he has made his play and goes out. He returns to the shop again any time after two o'clock, to see whether he has been lucky. He goes into the place and finds a crowd of persons like himself, looking over the list that has been given out as the list of numbers that has been drawn that morning. There are many of these lists lying around the place, having been printed with a rubber stamp, and copied from a list sent out by the backers of the policy game. This list of numbers is referred to by the player as the slip. If it contains the numbers he played, no matter what part of the slip they are on, so long as they were in the same column, he would consider himself a winner of $10, or, in policy language, he would have made a $10 'hit.'

"The backers of the game work it so that they just feed out enough money to dupe people into playing it. There is really no drawing, such as is supposed to occur. One man attends to that end of it, and simply makes up the slip after he has a copy of all the plays made in the city. He makes up the slip so as to pay out as little money as possible. Of course he has to keep putting out bait to keep the game going. People who play two or three cents on a gig and play lists of thirty or forty gigs every morning and night, are likely to make one hit in two days. They may invest $4.80 in four days and then win back $2, which is not a very profitable investment."

It is not necessary, for the purpose of this report, to describe all the different variations of the game, such as "saddles" and "horses," which are merely different ways of betting.

It may be stated that, arithmetically figured out, the player has about 200 chances out of about 76,000 of winning, and in case of a "hit," that is, in case he wins, is paid 100 for 1. It is thus apparent that if the game were played fairly the player stands no chance, and that the game is therefore a robbery. It is in addition a swindle, as already pointed out.

Every possible combination of three numbers, that is, every gig, has a name. There is the dead gig, the washwoman's gig, the medicine gig, the corpse gig, the father gig, the divorced gig, etc., etc., and superstition plays a large part in the player's selection of what gig to bet his money on. If a policy fiend's father died, he would probably play the dead gig and the father gig. The two most famous gigs are the three numbers 4–11–44, known as the washwoman's gig, and the numbers 9–19–29, known as the dead gig. The infatuation of men, women, and children for policy is probably largely due to the immense amount of superstition that is interwoven with it.

The vogue of the game, however, is chiefly due to the fact that it is within the power of the poorest to play it, inasmuch as any policy shop will take as low as two cents, and many of them will take bets of one cent. It will thus be seen that policy, under the guise of being a lottery, is really a scheme devised by unscrupulous men for robbing the ignorant poor. If conducted honestly, the chances against the player are enormous; but the game is not conducted honestly, but is operated as a swindle by the "backers," who are united in a syndicate, and are, some of them, millionnaires.

All that the player knows of the game is that he puts up his money in the hands of the writer, and some hours afterward is told whether he has won or lost. Each writer must send to headquarters at a fixed hour a list of every play made with him, and then an hour and a half later a list of the winning numbers is sent out; it is not hard to imagine that the numbers that are issued are those that a careful calculation shows involve the smallest cost to the backer. It is a small policy shop that takes in only $25 in a day; some take in $100,—the average is probably $35 or over. In the 20th Assembly District there were recently twelve policy shops, and as the amount paid out as winnings to the players does not average $15 a week by each shop, a simple calculation shows that $2240 is taken out of that district each week; nor is that district the worst by any means.

Policy is a veritable gold mine to the backers, as the expenses are small. The writer gets about $12 to $15 a week, and then there are heat and gas and rent to pay, which are small items, although the rent exacted by the landlord of a policy shop is higher than a legitimate business would have to pay for the same accommodation.

The fascination that the game exerts on its victims is hard to understand, for it is entirely lacking in any features of diversion that belong with most methods of gambling; but policy is not gambling, it is larceny. Perhaps the fact that the winner is paid one hundred times the amount of his investment may account in some degree for the hold this game has on its devotees, who are unable to figure out the odds against them.

Policy should be abolished, and will be abolished when the legislature decides to make the possession of policy paraphernalia a felony, just as the possession of burglars' tools and knock-out drops is now a felony. The legislature should also, by an enactment of a drastic law, make it easier to get at the landlord and punish him.

Some headway is being made against policy, under the law as it now stands, and more headway can be made, especially if the judges will inflict sentences of imprisonment in the State prison in cases where a conviction is secured; to fine a convicted policy writer is an encouragement to him, because the backer, who can well afford it out of his stealings, pays the fine, and the writer has the personal experience that no harm comes to him.

Policy is protected by the police; a police captain in his stationhouse, where a citizen had gone to complain against two shops, called his wardman to him and in the presence of the person who made the complaint, told the officer to "put on his hat and go around and tell

'Jack' and 'Tim' that they must close up." It is gratifying to be able to state that that captain was tried and convicted. The punishment inflicted on him was, however, inadequate. The backer pays the police captain a fixed amount monthly for every policy-shop in the captain's district. There is not a single shop in the city that does not pay its quota of blackmail to the captain of the precinct in which it is located. It is impossible, therefore, to get any assistance whatever from the police in suppressing policy.

Policy is a tenement house evil and policy shops are the scourge of tenement house districts. Policy may well be called The Poor Man's Burden.

PUBLIC BATHS

BY FRANK TUCKER

Buffalo's Free Public Bath-house No. 1.

PUBLIC BATHS

SINCE the People's Baths were opened to the public by the New York Association for Improving the Condition of the Poor, in August, 1891, the movement for public bathing facilities has spread to many other cities. At the present time there are public baths in New York, Chicago, Philadelphia, Boston, Buffalo, San Francisco, Pittsburg, Rochester, Syracuse, Yonkers, Brookline, Mass., Baltimore, Newark, and St. Paul. In Worcester, New Haven, St. Louis, Minneapolis, and Louisville the question is being investigated and agitated. In Kansas City, Albany, and Troy contracts for the erection of bath buildings have been let.

The only public baths considered in this report are those conducted all the year round by municipalities and private organizations without charge, or for a fee not exceeding five cents for each bather.

Leaving New York for subsequent consideration, the following is a summary of the progress made in other cities: —

CHICAGO

During the year 1901 Chicago will have four public baths in operation. They are owned and maintained by the municipality.

The first bath, known as the Carter H. Harrison Bath, was opened in January, 1894. It is situated at 192 Mather Street. The cost of the building is given as $7825, and of the plumbing and heating apparatus as $2511. The number of baths taken has been as follows: —

1894, 91,379; 1895 (closed 68 days), 92,798; 1896 (closed 73 days), 90,695; 1897 (closed 70 days), 106,233; 1898 (closed 141 days), 78,746.

The cost of maintenance has been as follows: —

1894, $3469.65; 1895, $3525.73; 1896, $3777.59; 1897, $4434.72; 1898 (including repairs), $5759.35.

When this bath was constructed it was thought necessary to provide a swimming pool, "in order to entice the children of the community into the bath." Experience demonstrated that it was difficult and expensive to heat the water for the swimming pool; that it made great delay in the use of the showers, and that its care took too much of the attendants' time. During the year 1898 the swimming pool was removed and the entire bath remodelled. The bath now has 34 showers, double its former capacity.

The second bath, known as the Martin B. Maden Bath, was opened April 17, 1897. It is situated at 39th Street and Wentworth Avenue. It has 31 shower-baths and 1 tub bath. Its cost is given as $13,500.

The number of baths taken has been as follows: 1897 (208 days), 84,559; 1898 (288 days), 108,922.

The cost of maintenance has been as follows: 1897, $4044.91 1898, $4040.31.

Public Bath No. 3 was opened on May 26, 1900. The building and ground cost $7200. It has 15 showers.

The fourth bath, known as the R. A. Waller Bath, was completed in 1900. It has cost about $8500. It has 18 showers.

The Chicago baths are entirely free, soap and towel being furnished. Each bath has its own heating plant to heat water for the showers and the building. Each bath also has its own laundry where the towels are washed. The baths are under the jurisdiction of the Department of Health. The city authorities are evidently proceeding on the right theory in developing their bath system, viz. inexpensive buildings, conveniently located and sufficient in number to meet the needs of the population.

The total number of baths taken during 1900 is shown by the following table: —

BATHS TAKEN DURING YEAR 1900

	Men	Women	Boys	Girls	Total
Carter H. Harrison Bath	72,395	28,344	85,015	33,286	219,040
Martin B. Maden Bath	58,287	9,323	49,726	20,600	137,936
[1] Public Bath No. 3	19,611	2,971	24,656	16,262	63,500
Totals	150,293	40,638	159,397	70,148	420,476

PHILADELPHIA

The only public bath in Philadelphia is operated by a private organization known as The Public Baths Association of Philadelphia. It is situated on the corner of Gaskill and Leithgow Streets. The fee charged bathers is five cents for soap and towel. The plant,

[1] Open 7 months only.

PHILADELPHIA'S PUBLIC BATHS.

including land, building, and equipment cost $29,903.70. It was opened for business in May, 1898. The building is plain and substantial, but complete in every detail and designed to give its patrons every modern convenience. The men's department is on the first floor. It contains 26 showers and 1 tub. The baths are separated by iron partitions painted white. Each bath has a dressing-room. There is a separate entrance for women. The entrances for men and women are separated as widely as possible, which is most desirable. From the women's entrance there are two stairways; one leads to the baths above, and the other descends to the laundry in the basement. In the women's bathing department there are 14 showers and 3 tubs. The laundry is fitted with 6 sets of tubs, 12 drying closets, ironing boards, a laundry stove, soap boiler, power washer, and wringer. In this laundry the towels used in the baths are also washed. They come down in towel chutes, and are thrown into a disinfecting tank before being washed. The number of baths taken during 1899 was 34,680. The cost of maintenance was $4338.77. The total number of baths taken in 1900, to December 1, was 46,644. This would indicate the remarkable increase for the year of about 14,000 baths taken.

The total number of washers using the laundry in 1898 was 1333. The total number of washers in 1900, to December 1, was 1677. This would indicate an increase for the year of about 375 washers. The cost of maintaining the laundry is included in the figures given above. The income during 1899 was derived from the following sources: Contributions, $2127; receipts from bathers, $1,760.25; laundry receipts, $167.20; interest on deposits, $2.42; total, $4,056.87.

The history of the Philadelphia bath is a duplication of the history of the People's Baths of New York. Each year there is an increase in patronage, and the receipts more nearly approximate the cost of maintenance. There is no reason to doubt that the Philadelphia bath will be self-supporting within a few years.

BOSTON

The Boston all-the-year-round bath, known as the Dover Street Bath, was opened to the public on October 14, 1898. It is a handsome building with beautiful appointments. The dimensions of the building are about 43 feet by 110 feet. The cost of the building is given as $75,000, and the cost of the site as $15,000. The bath has 50 bathing compartments, of which 17 are for women. There are living apartments in the building for the superintendent. Soap and towel are furnished at a cost of 1 cent. The cost of maintenance is approximately $10,000 per annum. Steam is obtained from the fire department repair shop, which adjoins the bath building, but the cost is included in the total given above. The bath is under the jurisdiction of the Department of Baths, which has under its authority all the baths and gymnasiums of the city.

The number of baths taken at the Dover Street Bath since its opening is shown by the following table: —

1898	Men	Women	Boys	Girls	Total
October	4,156	669	1,460	518	6,803
November	6,877	2,465	3,907	2,323	15,572
December	7,559	2,812	3,812	2,535	16,718
Total	18,592	5,946	9,179	5,376	39,093
1899	**Men**	**Women**	**Boys**	**Girls**	**Total**
January	7,646	2,633	3,780	2,988	17,047
February	7,733	2,641	3,664	2,354	16,392
March	9,796	3,791	4,341	2,866	20,794
April	12,535	4,414	5,637	4,017	26,603
May	13,338	4,441	4,081	2,912	24,772
June	15,684	5,039	2,276	3,000	25,999
July	18,660	5,774	497	5,281	30,212
August	15,349	4,860	1,090	5,452	26,751
September	14,959	4,309	2,205	3,709	25,182
October	12,869	3,783	1,418	2,564	20,634
November	10,718	3,266	1,516	2,527	18,027
December	10,910	4,034	1,377	2,775	19,096
Total	150,197	48,985	31,882	40,445	271,509

PITTSBURG

The only public bath in Pittsburg is maintained by a private association, the Civic Club of Allegheny County. The building was erected by Mrs. William Thaw, Jr., as a memorial to her husband. It is located on the corner of Sixteenth Street and Penn Avenue. It contains 22 showers and 2 tubs. It was opened to the public on December 1, 1897. A fee of 5 cents is charged, for which soap and towel are furnished. From December 1, 1897, to October 1, 1898, 10 months, the baths taken numbered 27,947; from October 1, 1898, to October 1, 1899, they numbered 41,424; from October 1, 1899, to October 1, 1900, they numbered 55,378. Although built in two sections and originally intended for both men and women, so many men patronized the baths that both sections were turned

View of Showers.

Waiting their Turn.

BOSTON'S PUBLIC BATHS.

over to the use of men, with the exception of one section on Tuesday, when women are permitted to use it.

The bath is not only self-supporting, but earns a surplus. The receipts and expenditures are shown by the following table : —

DISBURSEMENTS

	Salaries	Fuel and Gas	Lighting	Soap	Printing	Repairs	Supplies	Improvements	Towels
1899									
Oct.	$ 95.00	$14.70	$4.10		$6.00		$2.24	$10.00	
Nov.	100.00	16.80	6.48				2.07		
Dec.	100.00	22.20	7.92				4.75		
1900									
Jan.	100.00	24.15	7.56			$5.40	4.60		
Feb.	112.00	24.20	5.80				5.05		
Mar.	130.00	28.80	5.60	$24.41					$95.71
April	130.00	28.50	5.20						
May	150.00	13.20	3.30	60.33			5.78		
June	150.00	10.35	3.00	113.37			5.99		
July	148.00	9.90	2.80		7.15		11.00		
Aug.	150.00	8.70	2.70				4.89		
Sept.	150.00	8.40	3.00				2.24		
	$1,515.00	$209.90	$57.46	$198.11	$13.15	$5.40	$48.61	$10.00	$95.71

Total disbursements for the year $2,153.34

DISBURSEMENTS AND RECEIPTS BY MONTHS

Month	Disbursements	Receipts
October, 1899	$132.04	$204.00
November, 1899	125.35	144.00
December, 1899	134.87	138.00
January, 1900	141.71	150.00
February, 1900	147.05	122.00
March, 1900	284.52	154.00
April, 1900	163.70	265.00
May, 1900	232.61	280.00
June, 1900	282.71	315.00
July, 1900	178.85	337.00
August, 1900	166.29	322.00
September, 1900	163.64	243.00
Total	$2,153.34	$2,674.00

BROOKLINE, MASSACHUSETTS

The public bath of Brookline was opened on January 1, 1897. Its creation is a fine example of public spirit supporting energetic action and thoughtful consideration for social betterment. Brookline has a population of only 20,000, and yet it has in a way taken the lead in developing public bathing facilities. The bath is perhaps more a natatorium than a bath for cleansing purposes only. The inscription over the entrance reads "The Health of the People the Beginning of Happiness." The building and equipment cost $43,000. It is a beautiful building architecturally, and stands detached, with the grounds about it artistically laid out. The main tank is 80 feet by 26 feet; there is a smaller tank 22 feet by 10 feet. There are 15 showers in various parts of the building, and 3 tubs. The fee for the use of the showers, including soap and towel, is 5 cents, except on Wednesday and Saturday, when they are free; 10 cents is charged for the tubs, and they are also free on Wednesday and Saturday. The fee charged for the swimming pool varies from 5 cents to 50 cents, with certain hours reserved for the free instruction of school-boys. The use of towel and bathing suit are included in the fee. The number of baths taken during the thirteen months from January 1, 1897, to February 1, 1898, was 47,793. During the year February 1, 1898, to February 1, 1899, 46,147 baths were taken. During the year February 1, 1899, to February 1, 1900, 49,391 baths were taken. It is stated that the expense of maintenance during the present fiscal year will be about $8000, and that about $6000 will be received from fees, leaving only $2000 to be provided by the taxpayers. The bath is under the care of a special committee of nine citizens appointed by the selectmen of the town. The committee has recorded itself in its reports as in favor of the fee system.

ROCHESTER

The Rochester public bath-house was opened to the public on July 27, 1899. It is located on the east side of South Avenue, near Howell Street. The building and land cost $15,000. The bath contains 17 showers. Soap and towel are provided each bather. The bath is entirely free. The cost of maintenance is about $2500 per year. The bath is under the jurisdiction of the Department of Public Works. During the five months of 1899 that the bath was open, 19,089 baths were taken. During the ten months of 1900 to November 1, 46,950 baths were taken. The largest number on any one day was 879 on August 13, 1900. A report to the Common Council by its Committee on Public Baths, under date of November 19, 1900, states that during June, July, and August a large number of people were obliged to go away on account of lack of room. The committee recommends that two additional bath-houses be erected on sites chosen after a statistical record has been made of the homes of the patrons of the existing bath. On the recommendation of the committee a resolution was passed by the Common Council requesting the proper officers of the city to take such steps as might be necessary to secure the erection of an additional bath-house.

SYRACUSE

The Syracuse public bath was formerly a resort known as White Oak Springs. There are several wooden buildings, containing a swimming pool, tubs, and showers. The baths are entirely free, except tub baths, which are supplied with natural sulphur water, and for these a fee of 25 cents is charged. Soap and towel are furnished without charge to all bathers. The cost of buildings, land, and equipment was $12,400. The bath is under the jurisdiction of the Commissioner of Public Works. The yearly cost of maintenance is shown by the following table: —

Superintendent	$ 600.00
Matron	600.00
Engineer	912.00
Watchman	730.00
Two laundresses	365.00
Two attendants	1,095.00
Coal	534.00
Lighting	44.08
Towels	108.46
Soap	50.15
Ice	64.20
Miscellaneous	641.37
Total	$5,444.76

The number of baths taken and the receipts from bathers is shown by the following table: —

		Free		Paid		
1900	Total	Male	Female	Male	Female	Receipts
January	165	129	7	29	0	$ 7.25
February	295	197	1	92	5	24.25
March	401	299	19	80	3	20.75
April	1,179	916	49	212	2	53.50
May	9,626	9,053	360	300	13	78.25
June	22,768	21,612	733	406	17	105.75
July	22,193	20,887	916	367	23	97.50
August	16,652	15,131	1,126	363	32	98.75
September	6,993	6,474	297	208	14	55.50
October	3,611	3,135	263	206	7	53.25
November	1,357	1,195	74	86	2	22.00
December	1,706	1,611	26	66	3	17.25
Total	87,046	80,639	3,871	2,415	121	$634.00

BUFFALO

The following account of the public baths in the city of Buffalo has been written by William A. Douglas and Williams Lansing: —

The tenement houses in the city of Buffalo are practically, and always have been, without bathing facilities. In the winter of 1894–1895 a subcommittee of the Buffalo Charity Organization Society, which had, through personal investigation of the tenement house districts, become familiar with the need of bathing facilities, undertook to procure the erection of a free bath by the city authorities. With the coöperation of the Health Department the matter was brought before the Common Council and pressed to a point where such a free bath-house was assured, when the following act, known as the Brown Law, establishing free baths in cities, villages, and towns, was passed by the State Legislature: —

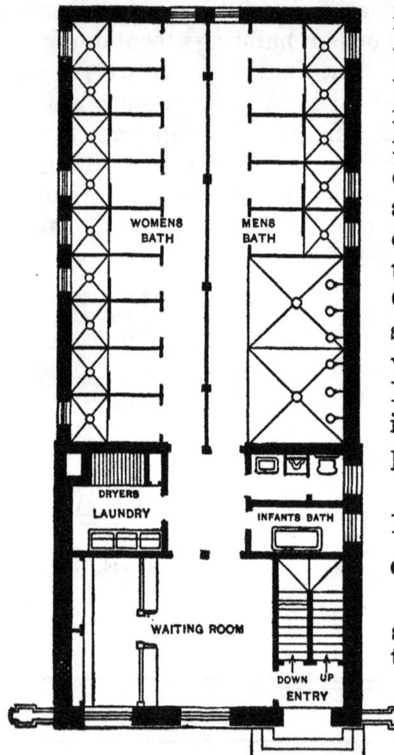

Ground Plan.
Buffalo Free Public Bath-house No. 1.

An Act to establish Free Public Baths in Cities, Villages, and Towns: —

Chapter 351.—Laws of New York State, 1895.

Sec. 1. All cities of the first and second class shall establish and maintain such number of public baths as the local Board of Health may determine to be necessary; each bath shall be kept open not less than fourteen hours for each day, and both hot and cold water shall be provided. The erection and maintenance of river or ocean baths shall not be deemed a compliance with the requirements of this section. Any city, village or town having less than 50,000 inhabitants may establish and maintain free public baths, and any city, village or town may loan its credit or may appropriate its funds for the purpose of establishing such free public baths.

Sec. 2. This act shall take effect immediately.

Under this authority financial provision was immediately made by the city of Buffalo, and by January 1, 1897, the first free municipal bath-house was established and put into operation. It is officially known as Public Bath-house No. 1. The plans for the house, having been made before the enactment of the Brown Law, were somewhat experimental, it being considered an experiment, which, if successful, might be further extended thereafter. It is located in Precinct No. 1, which according to the census of 1895 had a population of 20,587, and which precinct includes the Italian tenement district. The lot on which the bath-house is located is triangular in shape, having a frontage on the terrace of 50 feet. The building is of brick, two stories in height, with living apartments for tenants in the upper story. The interior arrangement of the building consists of a waiting room, wash room, toilet room, and infants' bath-room, with tub and 14 separate rain baths. There are besides 6 rain baths in one large open space, so that there is a total, including the bath-tub, of 21 baths. The wash-room contains three laundry tubs of concrete and a patent drying closet, which permits the bather who has but one suit of clothes to wash and dry them himself, and thus not only go away with a clean body, but clean clothing.

The following table shows the cost of the land, building, equipment, the cost of maintenance, and the number of baths per month for each year since the bath opened: —

FREE PUBLIC BATH-HOUSE No. 1, BUFFALO, N.Y.

Cost of land	$6,500
Cost of building	8,000
Cost of equipment	300
	$14,800

COST OF MAINTENANCE

	1897	1898	1899	1900
Salary of keeper	$500.00	$500.00	$500.00	$500.00
Salary of matron	400.00	400.00	400.00	400.00
Salary of assistant keeper	200.00[1]	480.00	480.00	480.00
Cost of soap	232.77	141.56	102.74	165.85
Cost of coal	275.35	330.30	300.00	300.00
Cost of furnishing and laundering towels	384.37	400.02	406.18	410.77
Cost of incidentals	—	48.05	182.00	222.23
Total	$1,992.49	$2,299.93	$2,370.92	$2,478.85
Towel estimate for December				20.00
				$2,498.85

NOTE. — The low cost of fuel is accounted for by the fact that steam for heating is supplied from the "Municipal Building," the charge being an approximate one. There being no expenditure for engineer's salary further reduces cost of maintenance.

[1] For five months.

TABLE OF BATHS TAKEN

Month	1897	1898	1899	1900
January	3,851	5,918	4,045	5,396
February	4,357	4,219	3,919	4,060
March	6,612	6,633	6,389	5,411
April	6,984	6,356	8,094	7,671
May	7,206	7,406	8,057	8,701
June	9,291	9,860	9,627	11,662
July	9,536	10,221	10,398	10,802
August	8,773	9,319	10,829	11,712
September	7,064	7,372	5,661	7,146
October	5,720	5,138	6,172	6,365
November	3,576	3,261	4,576	3,539
December	3,903	3,678	4,026	4,000 [1]
Total	76,873	78,481	81,793	86,465

Of the number of baths taken in 1897, 55,051 were taken by men, 1395 by women, and 20,427 by children.

Of those using the bath in 1898, 58,832 were men, 1841 were women, and 17,808 were children.

There is also a wash-room in connection with the bath-house for the convenience of the bathers, enabling them to wash and dry their underclothing.

In 1897, 1542 persons took advantage of this privilege, while in 1898, 2821 persons accepted this same privilege.

Of those using the bath during 1899, 60,029 were men, 2588 women, and 19,176 children ; 3166 persons made use of the laundry.

In 1900, eleven months, 59,699 men, 2821 women, and 19,973 children; 2205 used the laundry during eleven months.

From this table it appears that, beginning with the year 1897, in four years there have been given, in Bath-house No. 1, 323,510 baths at a total cost for all items, except depreciation, of $9162.19, or an average rate per bath of slightly over 2.8 cents.

In 1898 steps were taken for the erection of another bath-house on the east side of the city in the midst of the Polish quarter. The land was purchased on the corner of Woltz Avenue and Stanislaus Street, a bath-house was erected, and was opened for use on January 1, 1901. The site for this bath-house cost $2600, the building cost $15,802.19, and the equipment $500, making a total of $18,902.19. This bath-house has 18 separate rain baths, with 9 rain baths in 3 apartments, and 1 bath-tub, or a total of 28 baths. It is, unlike Bath-house No. 1, divided into two departments, one for men and one for women, so that both may bathe at the same time. Both bath-

[1] Estimated.

Public Bath No. 2 — Buffalo.

houses are absolutely free, that is, without charge whatever for soap, attendants, or towels.

YONKERS

Public Bath No. 1 is situated on the corner of Vark and Jefferson Streets. It was opened on October 10, 1896. The building is 25 feet by 63 feet and built on a lot 25 feet by 90 feet. The lot cost $2000 and the building and equipment $9350, making a total cost of $11,350. The building contains 18 showers and 2 tubs. There are living quarters for the superintendent.

Public Bath No. 2 is situated at No. 27 Vineyard Avenue. It was opened on July 14, 1898. The building is 25 feet by 67 feet and built on a lot 25 feet by 100 feet. The lot cost $1200 and the building and equipment $9765, making a total cost of $10,965. The building contains 22 showers and 2 tubs. There are living quarters for the superintendent.

The baths are under the jurisdiction of the Department of Public Works. A fee of 5 cents is charged for soap and towel. Each bathing compartment is divided into two sections, one containing the shower and the other a dressing room. The compartments are divided by sheet steel partitions painted with white enamel paint.

The annual cost of operating each bath is estimated at $1200, exclusive of laundry work. The towels are furnished and washed by a laundry company at a cost of 75 cents per hundred. The entire work of each bath is done by a superintendent and his wife, who receive a salary of $750 per annum. Each superintendent is competent to keep the plumbing and heating apparatus in order. There is no steam plant, the water and building being heated by hot water heaters.

The number of baths taken at Public Bath No. 1 and the receipts for the same are shown by the following table: —

PUBLIC BATH No. 1

1900	Men	Women	Total	Receipts
January	652	230	882	$44.10
February	592	193	785	39.25
March	844	250	1,094	54.70
April	1,099	356	1,455	72.75
May	1,102	433	1,535	76.75
June	2,095	815	2,910	145.50
July	1,683	891	2,574	128.70
August	1,627	842	2,469	123.45
September	1,314	605	1,919	95.95
October	820	427	1,247	62.35
November	643	290	933	46.65
December	709	261	970	48.50
Total	13,180	5,593	18,773	$938.65

NOTE. — The number of children using the baths is not kept.

NEW YORK

The needs of New York in the matter of public bathing facilities were thoroughly investigated by the "Mayor's Committee" appointed by Mayor Strong in July, 1895. That committee transmitted its report to the legislature on April 9, 1897. The report is entitled "Report on Public Baths and Public Comfort Stations, being a Supplementary Report to the Inquiries into the Tenement House Question in the City of New York, pursuant to Chapter 479 of the Laws of 1894." It is an elaborate document and covers the subject so thoroughly that there is little to add to its findings. Interest centres in what has been done to carry out the recommendations of the committee by the municipal authorities.

At the time the committee filed its report with the legislature the municipal authorities had decided to build a bath on Tompkins Square, one of six sites recommended by the committee. Opposition to the site developed and it was abandoned. Later the present site on Rivington Street, near the East River, was chosen, not because it was an ideal location, but because the city owned the land.

Apparently the New York officials did not consider Chapter 351, Laws of New York State, 1895, under which the Buffalo bath was built and which is quoted in full in that section of this report treating of Buffalo, sufficient authority for them to do the same things in this city. The law under which the Rivington Street bath was built was passed March 25, 1896. It reads as follows: —

An Act to provide for the construction in the City of New York of certain buildings for the promotion of public health and comfort.

CHAPTER 122. — Passed March 25, 1896.

Sec. 1. The Commissioner of Public Works in the City of New York, with the consent and approval of the Board of Estimate and Apportionment of said city, expressed as hereinafter provided, is hereby authorized and empowered to erect such and so many buildings for Free Public Baths, and such and so many structures for the promotion of public comfort within said City of New York as in the opinion of said Commissioner of Public Works and of said Board of Estimate and Apportionment shall be necessary and proper.

Sec. 2. Before proceeding to erect or construct any building or structure as authorized by the last preceding section the said Commissioner of Public Works may, from time to time, present to the said Board of Estimate and Apportionment a statement of any work proposed to be done, with plans and specifications therefor, and an estimate of the proximate probable cost therefor, whereupon the said Board of Estimate and Apportionment may, by resolution, authorize said work to be done wholly or in part, and may approve of the plans and specifications therefor, or may return the same to said Commissioner of Public Works for modification or alteration, whereupon said Commissioner of Public Works shall resub-

Shower Baths of the Association for Improving the Condition of the Poor—New York.

mit said plans and specifications, and after having modified or altered the same shall again submit them to said Board of Estimate and Apportionment, who may then approve the same or again return them to the said Commissioner of Public Works for further modification or alteration, and said plans and specifications may be so returned to said Commissioner of Public Works and resubmitted to said Board of Estimate and Apportionment until the said Board of Estimate and Apportionment shall, by resolution, approve said plans and specifications and authorize the work to be proceeded with accordingly.

SEC. 3. When any work provided for by this act shall have been authorized and the plans and specifications therefor approved by the Board of Estimate and Apportionment, the said Commissioner of Public Works shall proceed to execute and carry out said work, which shall be done by contract, made at public letting to the lowest bidder, pursuant to the general provisions of law and ordinances regulating the letting, execution and performance of public contracts in the City of New York. The Commissioner of Public Works, with the approval of the Board of Estimate and Apportionment first had and obtained, is hereby authorized and empowered, with the consent in writing of the contractor and his sureties, to alter any plans, and the terms and specifications of any contract entered into by authority of this act, provided that such alteration shall in no case involve or require an increased expense greater than five per centum of the whole expenditure provided for in said contract.

SEC. 4. The Commissioner of Public Works is authorized and empowered with the consent and approval of the Board of Estimate and Apportionment, to locate any or all of the structures for the promotion of public comfort to be erected under the authority of this act to be so erected in any public park of the City of New York, and for that purpose the Commissioner of Public Parks shall permit the said Commissioner of Public Works, his officers and agents and the contractors to enter upon said park or parks and therein to perform the work so authorized. Any such structure which may be erected in any public park of said city shall, after its erection and completion, be under the care, custody, and control of the Department of Public Parks in said City, who are hereby authorized and empowered to make proper and necessary rules for the use and management thereof.

SEC. 5. For the purpose of carrying out the work authorized by this act, including compensation of any architect or architects employed by said Commissioner of Public Works to prepare plans and specifications and to supervise the work done thereunder, and of any architect employed by the Board of Estimate and Apportionment to examine any plans and specifications, and including also the cost of such furniture and fixtures for any building hereby authorized as shall be approved and consented to by the Board of Estimate and Apportionment, the Comptroller of the City of New York is hereby directed, from time to time, when thereto directed by the Board of Estimate and Apportionment, to issue consolidated stock of the City of New York in the manner now provided by law to an amount not exceeding in the aggregate the sum of two hundred thousand dollars.

SEC. 6. This act shall take effect immediately.

The query naturally arises, Why is not a law that is sufficient authority for Buffalo also sufficient authority for New York? They are both first-class cities. The Act of 1895 is simple and mandatory. It places the responsibility of deciding the necessity upon the Board of Health and the duty of carrying out that decision upon the executive of the city.

The Act of 1896 in its first section is general in its provisions: it says that the Commissioner of Public Works in the City of New York, with the consent and approval of the Board of Estimate and Apportionment of said city, expressed as hereinafter provided, is hereby authorized and empowered to erect such and so many buildings for free public baths and such and so many structures for the promotion of public comfort within said City of New York as in the opinion of said Commissioner of Public Works and of said Board of Estimate and Apportionment shall be necessary and proper. Section 5 reads as follows: "For the purpose of carrying out the work authorized by this act, including compensation of any architect or architects employed by said Commissioner of Public Works to prepare plans and specifications and to supervise the work done thereunder, and of any architect employed by the Board of Estimate and Apportionment to examine any plans and specifications, and including also the cost of such furniture and fixtures for any building hereby authorized as shall be approved and consented to by the Board of Estimate and Apportionment, the Comptroller of the City of New York is hereby directed, from time to time, when thereto directed by the Board of Estimate and Apportionment, to issue consolidated stock of the City of New York in the manner provided by law to an amount not exceeding in the aggregate the sum of two hundred thousand dollars."

It is obvious that no general system of public bath-houses and public comfort stations as provided for in Section 1 could be erected in this city for the sum of $200,000, the amount allowed by Section 5. It is equally obvious that unless the officials of the city are willing to proceed under the Act of 1895, there will be no additional public baths without additional legislation.

Of the $200,000 appropriated by the Act of 1896, $100,000 was set aside to build the bath-house on the Rivington Street site. Ground was broken in December, 1897, and in December, 1900, three years after, workmen were working upon the building and it was unfinished.

By operation of the charter of Greater New York the building came under the jurisdiction of the Commissioner of Public Buildings, Lighting, and Supplies. In October, 1900, the incumbent of the office, Henry S. Kearny, appeared before the Board of Estimate and Apportionment and asked for the following appropriation to maintain the Rivington Street Bath during the fiscal year 1901: —

SALARIES

One janitor	$1,200.00	
Two engineers at $1200 each	2,400.00	
Four firemen, 365 days at $2.50 per day each	3,650.00	
One oiler, 365 days at $2.50 per day	912.50	
Two clerks at $1000 each	2,000.00	
Ten male bath attendants, 365 days at $2.50 per day each	9,125.00	
Sixteen female bath and laundry attendants at $50 per month each	9,600.00	
One electrician, 365 days at $4 per day	1,460.00	
Five male cleaners, 365 days at $2 per day	3,650.00	
		$33,997.50

REPAIRS AND SUPPLIES

General repairs to building, including water, steam, electric plant, etc.	$2,000.00	
Fuel	4,500.00	
Ice	200.00	
Window shades and awnings	150.00	
Office and other furniture	250.00	
Telephone service	250.00	
Janitor's, cleaners', and engineers' supplies	400.00	
Gas and electric lighting	10,100.00	
Sundry items not included in above	100.00	$17,950.00
Total asked for		$51,947.50

The Board of Estimate and Apportionment granted the sum of $35,000.

Under date of December 19, 1900, the New York Association for Improving the Condition of the Poor, which built and operates the People's Baths at No. 9 Centre Market Place, the first public bath built in this country, addressed a communication to the Hon. Robert A. Van Wyck, mayor of the city, protesting against the expenditure of so large a sum for the maintenance of a single bath-house and offering to conduct the bath for $17,500, one-half of the sum allowed. In its communication the Association says: —

"It is the belief of the Board of Managers of this Association, founded upon eight years' practical knowledge of the matter, that the expenditure of any such sum as $35,000 for one year's maintenance of the Free Public Bath in Rivington Street, is unnecessary, unwarranted, and prejudicial to progress in extending the public bath system.

"The Commissioner's estimate calls for an independent engineering force of 2 engineers, 4 firemen, 1 oiler, and 1 electrician with salaries aggregating $8422.50 per annum, and for $4500 for fuel, yet, notwithstanding these large estimates, the enormous sum of $10,100 is asked for gas and electric lighting. Although this is a new building, presumably to be turned over to the City in complete working order,

$2000 is also asked for 'general repairs to building, including water, steam, electric plant, etc.'

"Moreover, a further examination of the items of the appropriation asked reveals the singular omission of a most important item of expense. Nowhere in the statement of items necessary to conduct the Rivington Street Bath, footing up the large total of $52,000, is a single cent asked for to provide soap and towels.

"If it should be considered that the law does not require the bath management to furnish soap and towels free, provision should be made for furnishing them at the smallest possible price.

"Bathers must have towels; they should have soap. It is our experience that almost all bathers demand both. These articles should, therefore, be furnished by the City. They should not be left to individual enterprise and profit, and the smallest possible price for them should be charged.

"The People's Baths were built and conducted by this Association for the purpose of demonstrating the existence of a public need, and the possibility of meeting it at a moderate cost. Its history has proved both of these facts. The very first step taken by the City in a similar experiment in social betterment should not be endangered by unnecessary cost of maintenance, nor should money sufficient to run two bath-houses for the public's use be needlessly expended on one.

"The People's Baths during their last fiscal year gave about 131,000 baths at a cost of $5775. The sum of $52,000, or nine times as much, was asked for the Rivington Street Baths, and $35,000, or over six times as much, was allowed; the difference in capacity of the two establishments being that the People's Baths have twenty-six compartments, and the Rivington Street Bath has seventy-seven, or about three times as many.

"In order to prevent, if possible, the failure or abuse of a commendable attempt to improve the living condition of those forced to live in overcrowded tenements under unsanitary conditions, this Association submits for your consideration the following proposition: —

"If the City will turn over the Rivington Street Bath in good working order to this Association for administration, it will undertake the management of said Bath and conduct the same according to the high standard which has made the People's Baths at No. 9 Centre Market Place so successful, and will guarantee that the cost to the City of operating said Rivington Street Bath during the fiscal year 1901 shall in no event exceed the sum of $17,500, exclusive of the cost of supplying water. If the cost of operating said Bath during said fiscal year according to the above standard, including a fresh piece of soap and a newly laundered towel to each bather, shall exceed the said sum of $17,500 the Association will meet such excess from its own funds. As a protection to the city authorities, the Association will give a bond for the faithful performance of such agreement.

"The Association further offers, in case it should be decided by the City's legal advisers that the term 'free public bath' does not contemplate that soap and towel should be furnished, to make a charge of five cents to each bather for soap and towel and to turn the entire sum so received into the City Treasury."

Up to January 1, 1900, the mayor had taken no action upon the Association's offer, except to refer it to the Commissioner of Public Buildings, Lighting, and Supplies.

In May, 1900, limited bathing facilities were opened to the public in Hamilton Fish Park. They consist of three showers for men and three for women. These baths are entirely free and are under the jurisdiction of the Department of Parks.

On August 1, 1900, the Board of Education awarded a contract for installing shower-baths in Public School No. 1, Henry, Catherine, and Oliver Streets.

While official action in New York on this important public need has been characterized by delay and lack of interest, private effort has not been inactive. The remarkable success of the People's Baths is shown by the following tables: —

STATEMENT OF BATHS TAKEN AT PEOPLE'S BATHS

DURING THE FISCAL YEAR COMMENCING OCTOBER 1, 1899, AND ENDING SEPTEMBER 30, 1900

MONTH	MEN	WOMEN	CHILDREN	TOTAL
October, 1899	7,342	849	956	9,147
November, 1899	6,066	556	808	7,430
December, 1899	6,029	489	893	7,411
January, 1900	5,849	439	820	7,109
February, 1900	4,289	318	689	5,296
March, 1900	6,423	542	892	7,857
April, 1900	7,976	840	1,232	10,048
May, 1900	8,685	1,196	1,430	11,311
June, 1900	12,340	2,759	2,566	17,665
July, 1900	12,116	3,110	2,577	17,803
August, 1900	11,767	3,038	2,319	17,124
September, 1900	9,118	1,669	1,490	12,277
Total	98,000	15,805	16,672	130,477

SUMMARY OF THE WORK OF THE PEOPLE'S BATHS

The work of the People's Baths since starting in 1891 is shown by the following table: —

	Expenses	Receipts from Bathers	Deficit	Credit Balance	Number of Baths taken
1891 (Aug.-Sept.)	$667.81	$424.55	$243.29		10,504
1891-1892 . .	5,077.75	2,794.00	2,283.75		59,440
1892-1893 . .	5,106.85	3,266.10	1,840.76		68,629
1893-1894 . .	5,293.31	3,801.00	1,492.31		80,537
1894-1895 . .	5,152.91	4,165.25	987.66		88,734
1895-1896 . .	5,061.17	4,391.95	669.22		93,808
1896-1897 . .	5,977.83	4,768.65	1,209.18		101,023
1897-1898 . .	5,875.65	5,489.30	386.35		115,685
1898-1899 . .	5,571.99	5,709.00		$137.01	120,347
1899-1900 . .	5,775.35 [1]	6,203.05		427.70	130,477

The cost of a bath is five cents, including soap and towel. The city furnishes the water free of charge.

DISBURSEMENTS AND RECEIPTS OF PEOPLE'S BATHS FOR FISCAL YEAR COMMENCING OCTOBER 1, 1899, AND ENDING SEPTEMBER 30, 1900

Disbursements

Salaries	$4,153.75
Fuel	622.45
Gas	151.90
Soap	327.11
Printing and stationery	13.30
Repairs	171.92
Engineer's supplies	14.29
Incidentals	259.43
Towels	61.20
Total	$5,775.35

Receipts

Received from bathers, at 5 cents per bath $6,203.05

The People's Baths represent an investment of $30,000 for the building and equipment. The building is erected on land owned by a kindred organization for which no ground rent is charged. There are 17 sprays for men, 6 sprays for women, and 3 tubs for old women and children. The largest number of baths taken on any one day was on July 22, 1899, when 1175 men, women, and children were cared for. The largest number taken in any one month was in July, 1900, 17,803.

[1] This does not include the sum of $1518.40 paid for the installation of a new steam plant.

WAITING-ROOM OF THE PEOPLE'S BATHS — NEW YORK.

During May, June, July, August, and September, the baths are open daily from 6 A.M. to 9 P.M.

During October, March, and April, from 8 A.M. to 8 P.M.

During November, December, January, and February, from 9 A.M. to 8 P.M.

The Baths are open on Sunday morning from 6 to 9.30 A.M. Holidays from 7 to 11 A.M.

Public baths were placed in the basement of the De Milt Dispensary, 23d Street and Second Avenue, in 1893. There are 12 showers and 2 tubs. The baths are open daily; on Sunday mornings until twelve o'clock. A charge of 5 cents is made for soap and towel. The largest number of baths taken in any one day has been 437; in any one month, 5318.

The baths of the Riverside Association, 259 West 69th Street, were opened in 1894. There are 13 showers. The baths are open daily; on Sunday morning until half past eleven o'clock. A charge of 5 cents is made for soap and towel. The largest number of baths taken in any one day has been 435; in any one month 5685. Women are no longer admitted to these baths, in order to accommodate the larger number of men.

During the summer of 1900 public baths were installed in the building of the University Settlement, corner of Rivington and Eldridge Streets. There are 10 showers and 3 tubs. These baths became popular immediately, for in the month of August 4919 baths were taken. During the months of August, September, October, and November a total of 11,529 baths were taken. The baths are open daily; on Sundays until one o'clock. A charge of 5 cents is made for soap and towel.

The new settlement house at 50th Street and Tenth Avenue conducted under the auspices of the Fifth Avenue Baptist Church has a number of shower baths for public use.

THE NEEDS OF NEW YORK

Experience has shown that in a tenement house containing a large number of families and without proper supervision, as is usually the case, common bathing facilities are not feasible. An adequate supply of hot water cannot be furnished at reasonable cost, nor is there the constant care and attention which are necessary to keep baths used by many people in a sanitary condition. Once common bathing facilities in a tenement house fall into disuse for their proper purposes, they come into use for improper purposes, which often leads to the hasty and unwarranted conclusion that tenement house dwellers do not want to bathe.

The large patronage of all public baths in this city where a fee no larger than 5 cents per bath is charged, leaves no room for doubt as to the need for such facilities on an extensive scale. The history of the People's Baths demonstrates that sufficient patronage may be developed to make a bathing establishment self-supporting on a fee of 5 cents per bath. The history of the Buffalo baths shows that a municipality can furnish bathing facilities without charge all the year round to a large number of people at a very small cost. The history of these baths also proves that, given an interested and energetic city official or department, public bath buildings can be erected at such moderate cost as to disarm opposition on the part of taxpayers.

The need exists. It is clearly the duty of the municipality to meet the need, because the health of the whole community is concerned. The frightful congestion of humanity that exists in sections of our city, resulting in physical conditions that lead to degeneracy, poverty, and crime, should at least be alleviated by opportunity for cleanliness.

New York should have a comprehensive system of public baths. The spirit governing any official or department in charge of the development of such a system should be economy in construction and economy in administration. Private enterprise has paid for experience in details. The requisites for success in construction and administration are well known and are at the service of the city.

Before any further progress can be made in developing such a system for New York, there must be further legislation or an acceptance of the provisions of the mandatory Act of 1895. Under this act it is the duty of the Board of Health to determine the number of public baths necessary. It is evidently left optional with the chief executive officer of the municipality to determine which department of the city government shall exercise authority over the construction and maintenance of the baths. Buffalo has settled the question most satisfactorily by placing the whole matter under the control of her Department of Health.

No progress can be made under the special Act of 1896, because that act, while general in its provisions for establishing a system of public baths, automatically stops progress because it appropriates a sum obviously inadequate to construct a system of bath buildings, and one half of which in fact has been used in constructing the Rivington Street bath.

The report of the mayor's committee recommended six bath buildings as necessary to meet the needs existing at the time of its investigation; two may well be added now for the Borough of Manhattan and two for the Borough of Brooklyn. If only two a year were constructed, it would take five years to meet the present needs of the city. Should any further legislation on the subject be enacted, it should provide for the construction of at least two buildings a year for five years.

The question as to whether any existing department or official of the city government should have jurisdiction over the construction and maintenance of a system of municipal bath-houses, or whether such a system should be in charge of a special commission, either multiple or single-headed, is an open question. Boston has a Department of Baths which controls its baths of all kinds. Chicago and Buffalo have placed their baths under the Department of Health. Other cities have placed them under the Department of Public Works.

It is certain that the development of an adequate system of municipal baths will require serious thought, close attention, and energetic action. It is doubtful whether all these can be expected from any existing city department with other duties to perform. As years go on the necessity for all-the-year-round baths will increase. It is doubtful whether the system of summer floating baths can be maintained many years longer on account of the vast amount of sewage deposited in our rivers. Last summer a serious outbreak of a disease affecting the eyes alarmed the officials of the Health Department. Energetic investigation traced the cause to a floating bath in Brooklyn which was anchored near the outlet of a large sewer. One who has given the subject of public baths much study has advanced the opinion that it is not advisable to repair or renew any floating bath; that it is wiser policy to invest the money in permanent all-the-year-round bath buildings.

The situation in this city in the matter of municipal baths may be summed up as follows: private enterprise has met the cost of demonstrating the public need for them; it has also paid for acquiring the knowledge necessary to build, equip, and conduct them economically; there is ample legislation, if it be granted that law that is sufficient for Buffalo is also sufficient for New York; all that is lacking is a city administration imbued with a desire to carry out the provisions of the law with due regard to the experience which has been acquired, and in a proper spirit of economy, that the health and well-being of the tenement population may be safeguarded at the least possible cost to the taxpayers.

A PLAN FOR TENEMENTS IN CONNECTION WITH A MUNICIPAL PARK

BY I. N. PHELPS STOKES

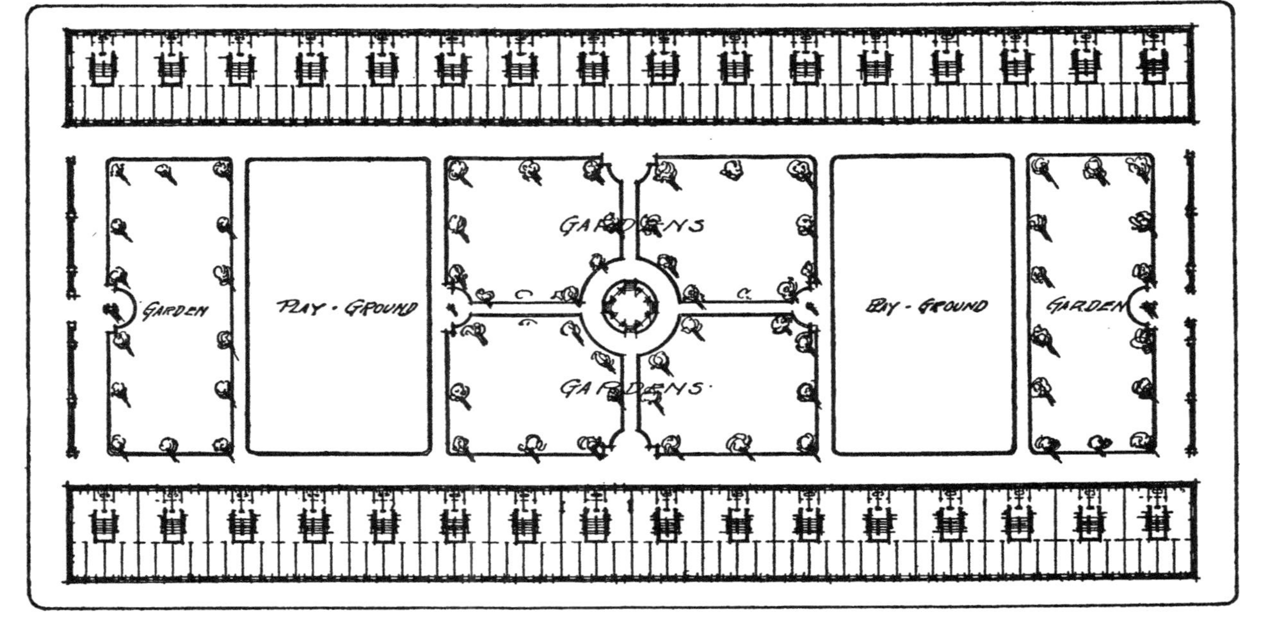

·SUGGESTIVE·PLAN·FOR·BLOCK
OF·PARK-TENEMENTS·

AREA OCCUPIED BY BUILDINGS ($33\frac{1}{3}$% OF BLOCK) = 27,000 SQ. FT.
AREA OCCUPIED BY PARK ($66\frac{2}{3}$%) — 53,000 " "
TOTAL AREA OCCUPIED BY BLOCK — 80,00 " "

NUMBER OF ROOMS PER BLOCK 1152
· BUILDINGS SIX STORIES HIGH ·

A PLAN FOR TENEMENTS IN CONNECTION WITH A MUNICIPAL PARK

The 25-foot lot has been accused of responsibility for much of the evil that exists in the condition of New York tenement houses. While this to a certain extent is true, it must be borne in mind that it is not the width of the lot, but the proportion, or rather disproportion, between its width and depth that is to blame. A lot 25 feet wide by 100 feet deep presents conditions almost exactly the reverse of the ideal, making necessary a more or less complicated type of plan in which recourse must be had to courts or shafts to light those rooms which do not open directly upon the street or yard. With these dimensions reversed, we have an area which in shape and dimensions is adapted to the simplest and best form of plan — a building only two rooms deep with apartments running through from front to rear. Unfortunately, from a commercial standpoint, the high cost of land in the crowded districts of New York practically prohibits a distribution, no matter how desirable, which would leave a large fraction of the block vacant and unproductive. To overcome this difficulty it is suggested that the city acquire, through condemnation proceedings, some of the most overcrowded and unsanitary blocks of old tenements in districts where there is the greatest need of small parks or playgrounds; that the old buildings be removed, the central portions converted into small public parks or playgrounds, and the narrow strips between the parks and side streets sold, under proper restrictions, for the erection of tenement houses. Or if it be found that the city has not the constitutional right to acquire more than it intends itself actually to use — then the central portion only might be taken, and in all probability the owners of the remaining property would be willing, either themselves to erect tenements, or to sell their land for this purpose to individuals or corporations. As every square foot of these outer strips could be used productively, without any loss from courts, shafts, or yards, their value in proportion to their area would be much higher than that of the middle portion of the block. (See Tenement House Economics, Table VI.)

From the following brief calculations it will be seen that in sections of the city where land can be bought at an average price of $9 per square foot, or $22,500 per 25 × 100 foot lot, if these strips were sold at

$11.14 per square foot, the cost per room, for land and improvements, would be the same as the cost per room (equivalent in size, but in other respects far inferior) in the ordinary type of double-decker.

I. Ordinary type of double-decker (14 rooms to a floor).

Cost of construction of 6-story double-decker tenement house containing 84 rooms and covering 75% of a lot 25′ × 100′ at 16¢ per cubic foot	$22,500.00
Cost of land (2500 square feet) at $9 per square foot	22,500.00
Total cost of land and improvements for 25′ × 100′ lot	$45,000.00
Cost per room	$535.71

II. Proposed park plan (2 rooms deep).

Cost of construction of 6-story park tenement containing 36 rooms and covering 33% of lot 25′ × 100′ at 16¢ per cubic foot	$10,000.00
Assuming the city to buy the entire lot (in connection with the rest of the block) at a cost of $9 per square foot, to retain for a park ⅔, or 1666.66 square feet, at $7.93 per square foot or $13,216.61, and to sell the remaining ⅓, or 833.33 square feet, at $11.14 per square foot	9285.56
Total cost of land and improvements	$19,285.56
Cost per room (same as in I)	$535.71

The following comparison of the housing capacity of various blocks of tenements of a uniform size of 200 × 400 feet is interesting. The calculations are based upon buildings 6 stories in height and an assumed population of 1½ persons per room.

I. Block composed entirely of typical double-decker tenements.

No. rooms	2688
No. persons	4032

II. Block built upon plans such as those recently drawn by architects in conformity with the provisions of the proposed new Tenement House Code (average number rooms to a floor per 25-foot unit equals 12).

No. rooms	2304
No. persons	3456

III. Actual block bounded by Chrystie, Forsythe, Canal, and Bayard Streets — model and statistics concerning which were exhibited at the late Tenement House Exhibition and given on page 112 of Vol. I.

No. rooms	1588
No. persons	2781

(No allowance has been made for the stores which occupy the front portions of the ground floor of most of the buildings. If these stores were replaced by rooms, the total number of the latter would be increased to about 1700 and the number of persons to about 3000.)

IV. Block of park tenements.

No. rooms	1152
No. persons	1728

From this comparison it appears that 62.13 per cent, or about two-thirds, of the population of an average block in one of the most densely populated sections of the city could be rehoused under almost ideal conditions on one-third of the same block, leaving the other two-thirds — open to the street at both ends — available for a public park or playground. And this could be accomplished without raising rents and at a saving to the city of over $1 per square foot in the cost of the land.

TENEMENT HOUSE ECONOMICS

TABLES AND EQUATIONS SHOWING RELATION OF GROSS REVENUES AND RENTS, WITH VARYING LIGHT AND AIR SPACES, TO THE COST OF LAND AND THE NUMBER AND HEIGHT OF STORIES

* TABLE I

Ratio of Light and Air Space to Area of Lot to give Various Revenues, at Different Prices of Land, when Number of Stories is Six, Height of Each 11½ Feet. Cost of Building, 16 Cents per Cubic Foot. At an Annual Rent of 2 Cents per Cubic Foot

Cost of Land per Square Foot	Gross Revenues to Investment					
	11%	10.5%	10%	9%	8%	7%
Dollars	Ratio	Ratio	Ratio	Ratio	Ratio	Ratio
3.75	—	—	—	$\frac{9}{100}$	$\frac{40}{100}$	$\frac{57}{100}$
3.25	—	—	—	$\frac{22}{100}$	$\frac{49}{100}$	$\frac{62}{100}$
2.75	—	—	$\frac{1}{100}$	$\frac{36}{100}$	$\frac{56}{100}$	$\frac{68}{100}$
2.25	—	—	$\frac{18}{100}$	$\frac{48}{100}$	$\frac{68}{100}$	$\frac{74}{100}$
2.00	—	$\frac{5}{100}$	$\frac{28}{100}$	$\frac{53}{100}$	$\frac{68}{100}$	$\frac{76}{100}$
1.75	—	$\frac{17}{100}$	$\frac{37}{100}$	$\frac{59}{100}$	$\frac{72}{100}$	$\frac{80}{100}$

Note.—Land valued at from $4375 to $9375 per lot, 25 × 100 feet.

† TABLE II

Number of Stories of Building at an Annual Rental of 2 Cents per Cubic Foot, to give Various Revenues, with Varying Light and Air Spaces. Cost of Land, $3.00 per Square Foot. Cost of Building, 16 Cents per Cubic Foot. Height of Stories, 11½ Feet.

Gross Revenue	RATIO OF LIGHT AND AIR SPACE TO AREA OF LOT					
	20%	30%	35%	40%	45%	50%
Per Cent	Stories	Stories	Stories	Stories	Stories	Stories
11	15	17	19	20	22	24
10½	11	12	14	15	16	17
10	8	9	10	11	12	13
9	6	6	7	7	8	9
8	4	4	5	5	6	6
7	3	3	4	4	4	5

* See "Equations." † See "Equations."

‡TABLE III

Rents per Annum per Cubic Foot of Building to give Various Revenues with Varying Light and Air Spaces. Cost of Land, $3.00 per Square Foot. Cost of Building, 16 Cents per Cubic Foot. Number of Stories, 6. Height of Each Story, 11½ Feet.

Gross Revenue	Ratio of Light and Air Space to Area of Lot					
	20%	30%	35%	40%	45%	50%
Per Cent	Cents	Cents	Cents	Cents	Cents	Cents
11	2.36	2.44	2.50	2.56	2.63	2.72
10½	2.25	2.33	2.38	2.44	2.51	2.59
10	2.14	2.22	2.26	2.32	2.39	2.47
9	1.93	1.99	2.04	2.09	2.15	2.22
8	1.71	1.77	1.81	1.86	1.91	1.98
7	1.50	1.55	1.59	1.63	1.67	1.73

Note.—Rents, $1.50 to $2.75 per cubic foot, will give 75 cents to $1.00 per room.

‡TABLE IV

Rents per Annum per Cubic Foot of Building at Various Prices for Land, with Varying Light and Air Spaces. Gross Revenue, 9% of Investments. Cost of Building, 16 Cents per Cubic Foot. Number of Stories, 6. Height of Each Story, 11½ Feet.

Cost of Land per Square Foot	Ratio of Light and Air Space to Area of Lot					
	20%	30%	35%	40%	45%	50%
Dollars	Cents	Cents	Cents	Cents	Cents	Cents
4.75	2.21	2.32	2.39	2.47	2.57	2.68
4.25	2.13	2.23	2.29	2.36	2.45	2.55
3.75	2.05	2.13	2.19	2.25	2.33	2.42
3.25	1.97	2.04	2.09	2.15	2.21	2.29
2.75	1.89	1.95	1.99	2.04	2.09	2.16
2.25	1.81	1.86	1.89	1.93	1.97	2.03

Note.—Land valued at from $5,625 to $11,850 per lot, 25 × 100 feet.

‡ See "Equations."

‡TABLE V

RENTS PER ANNUM PER CUBIC FOOT OF BUILDING AT VARIOUS PRICES FOR LAND, WITH VARYING HEIGHTS OF STORIES. GROSS REVENUES, 9% OF INVESTMENT. RATIO OF LIGHT AND AIR SPACE TO AREA OF LOT, $\frac{35}{100}$. COST OF BUILDING, 16 CENTS PER CUBIC FOOT. NUMBER OF STORIES, 7.

COST OF LAND PER SQUARE FOOT	HEIGHTS OF STORIES OF BUILDING					
	9.5	10.0	10.5	11.0	11.5	12.0
Dollars	Cents	Cents	Cents	Cents	Cents	Cents
4.75	1.549	1.544	1.539	1.535	1.530	1.526
4.25	1.538	1.533	1.529	1.525	1.521	1.517
3.75	1.526	1.522	1.517	1.515	1.512	1.508
3.25	1.515	1.511	1.507	1.505	1.502	1.499
2.75	1.503	1.500	1.496	1.495	1.492	1.490
2.25	1.492	1.489	1.486	1.485	1.483	1.481

TABLE VI

RELATION OF ORIGINAL COST OF LOT PER SQUARE FOOT TO THE PRICE OF GROUND AREA OF PARK TENEMENT, AND TO COST OF TENEMENT PARK AREA, WHEN COST OF ROOM AND WEEKLY RENTALS ARE THE SAME.

ORIGINAL COST OF LOT	COST PER ROOM	WEEKLY RENTALS	PRICE PER SQUARE FOOT	PRICE PER SQUARE FOOT
Per Square Foot	Construction and Land	Per Room	Park-Tenement Ground	Tenement Park Area
$5.00	$416.66	$0.7211	$6.00	$4.50
6.00	446.43	.7726	7.29	5.36
8.00	505.95	.8757	9.86	7.07
9.00	535.71	.9272	11.14	7.93
10.00	565.47	.9787	12.43	8.78
12.00	625.00	1.0817	15.00	10.50

Basis of old tenements, limited to 75% of lot area, six stories, each 12.5 feet, at 16 cents per cubic foot, 84 rooms.

Basis of new park tenements, limited to 33⅓% of lot area, leaving 66⅔% for tenement park. Tenement, six stories, each 12.5 feet, at 16 cents per cubic foot, 36 rooms.

Gross revenue, 9% on investment.

Weekly rentals, varying from 72 cents to $1.08.

Price of lots, 100 × 25 feet, varying from $12,500 to $30,000.

‡ See "Equations."

EQUATIONS

$$\left[\left(A - a\frac{nhQ}{100} + AC\right)\right]\frac{k}{100} = (A - a)nh\frac{r}{100}. \qquad 1$$

$$\left(1 - \frac{a}{A}\right)nhQ + 100\,ck = \left(1 - \frac{a}{A}\right)100\,nhr. \qquad 2$$

$$* \therefore \left(1 - \frac{a}{A}\right) = \frac{100\,ck}{(100\,r - kQ)nh}\ (3);\ \text{and} \therefore n = \frac{100\,ck}{b\left(1 - \frac{a}{A}\right)(100\,r - kQ)}. \qquad 4\,\dagger$$

$$\ddagger \therefore r = \frac{k}{100}\left[Q + \frac{100\,c}{\left(1 - \frac{a}{A}\right)nh}\right]\ (5);\ \text{and} \therefore k = \frac{100\,r}{Q + \frac{100\,c}{\left(1 - \frac{a}{A}\right)nh}}. \qquad 6$$

$$\therefore Q = 100\left[\frac{r}{k} - \frac{c}{\left(1 - \frac{a}{A}\right)nh}\right]. \qquad 7$$

EXPLANATION

A — Is area of building lot in square feet.
a — Is area of light and air space in square feet.
n — Is number of stories to building, counting basement.
h — Is height of stories, or distance between floors in feet.
c — Is cost of land — dollars per square foot.
k — Is gross revenue on investment — rents per 100 cents.
Q — Is cost price of building — cents per cubic foot, including roof and foundation.
r — Is annual rent — cents per cubic foot.

FOREIGN IMMIGRATION AND THE TENEMENT HOUSE IN NEW YORK CITY

BY KATE HOLLADAY CLAGHORN

FOREIGN IMMIGRATION AND THE TENEMENT HOUSE IN NEW YORK CITY

THAT foreign immigration should have had a distinct and decided effect on housing conditions in New York City is obvious, when it is remembered that two-thirds in earlier years and four-fifths in later years, of the great flood of immigration pouring into the United States since 1820, has come by way of the port of New York, leaving behind it, in its passage, no inconsiderable proportion of its volume in the city itself.

Just what this proportion is from year to year cannot be told with certainty. For the period before 1850 there are no definite statistics showing even the numbers of the foreign-born in the city, at different times. And for the period before 1834 it is difficult to adduce any direct evidence as to the effect of immigration upon housing, for the question of housing itself had not then begun to attract general attention. In that period immigration was absolutely light, but in comparison with the city's population from year to year, relatively heavy.

In 1794, at the close of a ten-year period, in which it was estimated there had been an average of 4000 arrivals from foreign countries each year, there seems to have been a suddenly heavy influx of foreigners, as many as 10,000 arrivals, it is supposed.

The city by this time was growing rapidly toward the north; streets were being raised and paved; and the dock frontage extended farther out into the water.

These docks, in process of construction, became gathering places of all sorts of filth, making a belt of offensiveness along the river front from which, it may be supposed, prosperous residents of the quarter were glad to draw back. In describing the circumstances connected with the outbreak of yellow fever in New York in 1796, Dr. John H. Griscom ("History . . . of the Visitations of Yellow Fever at New York," pp. 7 and 8) speaks of the new dock at Whitehall, of which the piles only had been put down, making a crib with an area nine feet deep, which had been filling in for a year "with the accidental accumulations of all manner of filth, street dirt, dead animals, etc.," and speaks of a similar condition at Exchange

Slip, which was "the receptacle of an extensive common sewer." In the neighborhood of the docks were a large number of old wooden houses, many of which, built before the raising and paving of the streets, had their lower floors two or three feet below the surface of the pavements. This was especially the case at the extreme southern end of the island — in the first, second, and fourth wards, but well around on the East Side, near the water front, other offensive neighborhoods had grown up.

In such undesirable quarters, it would be natural to suppose, the immigrant population, owing to their poverty, if for no other reason, had to find their first homes. And there is direct testimony to show that they did so. Dr. Griscom, in describing the outbreak of yellow fever in 1795, says that "it prevailed on the borders of the East River, in the low streets, and what was formerly the swamp, and in the narrow alleys. A small part only of the citizens fled; most of them remained and pursued their occupations in the greater part of the city, with perfect safety." He then notes that of the 730 persons carried off by the epidemic, "at least 500 . . . were foreigners (452 belonged to one Catholic congregation), most of whom had been so short a time in the country that the pastor, Rev. Mr. O'Brien, did not know them."

Immigration from 1806 to 1816 was unusually light, owing to disturbances caused by the wars of that period. In 1817, however, arrivals from foreign countries reached an unprecedented number, 22,240 immigrants being recorded at the various ports of entry. In this year also the Erie Canal was begun, and that era of internal improvements inaugurated which called so many able-bodied laborers from abroad and spread them all over the country by the middle of the forties.

Besides the able-bodied laborers, however, many of whom indeed remained to find work in the city instead of going to the country, came a considerable proportion of out-and-out paupers, who, almost to a man — and woman — stayed in the city to become a burden upon charity.

Mayor Colden, of New York, taking office in 1818, found it one of his earliest duties to aid in the establishment of a "Society for the Prevention of Pauperism," and stated in November, 1819, that, during the preceding twenty months, 18,930 foreign "emigrants" (as they were then called) had arrived in the city and been reported at his office.

Immigration at this time was mainly from Great Britain and Ireland. In 1820 immigrants from those countries made up 72 per cent of the total immigration, and of these by far the greater proportion was Irish.

It is difficult to get definite information as to tenement conditions at this period. It is known, however, that a "cellar population" was in existence by 1822, as is shown by accounts of the "Bancker Street fever"; but in this quarter the cellar inhabitants were mainly colored people.

By 1827 immigration was increasing rapidly, and continued to increase, with some slight fluctuations, until 1834, when the total of arrivals at all ports was 67,948—about three times the number recorded for 1817. By this time a considerable German immigration had begun. It is a significant coincidence that in this year of especially high immigration perhaps the first distinct complaint as to housing conditions in the city was made.

Gerritt Forbes, City Inspector of the Board of Health, in his report for the year, assigns as especial causes of the high death-rate, "intemperance, and the crowded and filthy state in which a great proportion of our population live," and speaks of "so many mercenary landlords who only contrive in what manner they can stow the greatest number of human beings in the smallest space."

By 1835 the sixth ward had evidently become the centre of the Irish immigrant population, and had entered upon its notorious history of violence, as is shown by the "Five Points Riot" of June 21, —"an Irish brawl," one historian calls it, arising out of an attempt to form a separate Irish regiment.

In an account of an epidemic of continued fever that broke out in 1837 in parts of the sixth, tenth, and fourteenth wards, it is noted that the cases occurred in the midst of a poor population, "principally Irish and German, whose habits . . . are more or less filthy, and who live crowded together, with a family in every room in the house, and sometimes more." All cases occurred west of the Bowery, and it is noted that there was far greater crowding here than to the east of that street. All cases reported were in basements, or in first floors beneath which were neither basements nor cellars.

Another year of especially heavy immigration saw another complaint against bad housing. In 1842 there were over 100,000 foreign arrivals at all ports, and in that year was made the first detailed and comprehensive report upon housing conditions in the city. This report was made by Dr. John H. Griscom, then City Inspector of the Board of Health, at the close of his annual report of interments for the year, and in it he notes the high death-rate of the foreign-born, especially of the Irish, and attributes a large part of the evil to their crowded condition.

By this time the main outlines of a housing system developed in connection with foreign immigration had come into view, which remained practically the same until the close of the Civil War — indeed, until the close of the decade following the war.

These are best seen, perhaps, in a concrete example given by Dr. Griscom in his "Sanitary Condition of the Laboring Population of New York" in 1845. Dr. B. W. McCready, reporting, at Dr. Griscom's request, certain cases of typhus that had broken out, a year or so previously, in the rear of 49 Elizabeth Street, says: —

"The front building, a small, two-story frame house, was partly occupied by the proprietor or lessee of the building as a liquor store, and partly sublet to several Irish families. A covered alleyway led to the rear building. This was a double frame house, three stories in height. It stood in the centre of the yard. Ranged next the fence were a number of pigsties and stables, which surrounded the yard on three sides. From the quantity of filth, liquid and otherwise, thus caused, the ground, I suppose, had been rendered almost impassable, and to remedy this, the yard had been completely boarded over, so that the earth could nowhere be seen. These boards were partially decayed, and by a little pressure, even in dry weather, a thick greenish fluid could be forced up through their crevices. The central building was inhabited wholly by negroes. In this building there occurred, in the course of six weeks, nine cases of typhus fever."

At the solicitation of the doctor the alderman of the ward visited the houses. As a result "the number of pigs about the establishment was reduced to that allowed by law" (!), and some other improvements were made.

In this example it is seen how the old-fashioned frame house, once occupied, perhaps, by prosperous owners, had been turned over to tenement uses; how a "tenement house," especially built for the purpose of containing several poor families, had been erected at the rear of the older building in the original yard; how the inferior rear building had been given up to the inferior — that is, less prosperous — race; how filth, disease, and disorder (the last not shown, indeed, in this case, but in many others) result from such conditions.

The two principal types of tenement houses thus indicated each developed evils all its own. The use of the old, one-family dwelling as a tenement was mainly responsible for the growth of that great "cellar population" which was the constant object of anxious attention on the part of philanthropists and sanitary reformers for many years.

The barrack, run up expressly for tenement purposes, and planted in every possible patch or corner of unoccupied space in the poorer neighborhoods, in the back yards of old dwellings, as in the example above, or in sets or rows, one behind the other, or side by side, along narrow "courts" and "alleys," brought darkness and dampness, with all their attendant evils, above ground, thus practically making a new "cellar population" not confined to the cellars, but placed in layers, one above the other, up to six stories in height.

That the development of a tenement house system as thus described was due to the demands for housing created by immigration, was stated again and again by contemporary observers.

An especially interesting feature in the tenement system of the time was the practice of subletting, an important phase both in the life of the immigrant and in the housing problem.

Dr. Griscom, in his report on the "Sanitary Condition of the Laboring Population of New York" in 1845, says:—

"The system of tenantage to which large numbers of the poor are subjected, I think must be regarded as one of the principal causes of the helpless and noisome manner in which they live. The basis of these evils is the subjection of the tenantry to the merciless inflictions and extortions of the sub-landlord. . . . The owner is relieved of trouble; the lessee tries to make and save as much as possible, sufficient sometimes to enable him to purchase the property in a short time.

"The tenements, in order to admit a greater number of families, are divided into small apartments, as numerous as decency will admit. Regard to comfort, convenience, and health is the last motive; indeed, the great ignorance of this class of speculators (who are very frequently foreigners and keep a grog-shop on the premises) would prevent a proper observance of these had they the desire. These closets, for they deserve no other name, are then rented to the poor, from week to week, or month to month, the rent being almost invariably required in advance, at least for the first few terms. The families moving in first after the house is built find it clean, but the lessee has no supervision over their habits, and however filthy the tenement may become, he cares not so that he receives his rent. He and his family are often steeped as low in depravity and discomforts as any of his tenants, being above them only in the possession of money, and doubtless often beneath them in moral worth and sensibility."

In the Report of the Association for Improving the Condition of the Poor, for 1853, it is stated that "the evils the laboring classes suffer from the enumerated causes are greatly aggravated by a species of subletting which extensively prevails in most parts of the city, often subjecting them to the merciless exactions of capricious and unprincipled landlords, and also to the influence of circumstances which cannot fail to degrade them."

Sometimes a second "sub-owner," or agent, is in evidence. An investigating committee in 1857 talked with one of these men and learned some facts which led them to state in their minutes, after reporting the talk: —

"The foregoing colloquy satisfied the committee of the evils of the 'middleman' system. The buildings under consideration (Folsom's Barracks) are first built as a speculation in the cheapest manner, and then the owner delegates his brother to oversee them; the brother again gives them in charge to a third party, who, he says, can 'do better with them than he can.' Here we have two agents between landlord and tenant, both, of course, drawing substance from the miserable people inhabiting these filthy houses."

This system of course raised rents very materially, as each "middleman" had to have his profit. The increase was stated to be anywhere from 12 to 25 per cent, upon a total rental value already enormous.

That the sub-landlord was, more often than not, originally an immigrant himself, is an interesting feature in the situation. It is one of the difficulties the sympathizer with struggling humanity is baffled with, that the man who has just succeeded in climbing one round of the ladder is the first to kick down, if he can, the man just below him. And so these Irish and German sub-landlords were among the hardest and most unprincipled of those who dealt with the newly arriving immigrant. They were, usually, keepers of groggeries or "groceries" (which latter seem to have been almost the equivalent of the former at that period), and so added the enticements of vice to the other evils they pressed upon the poor tenants.

From 1842 on immigration increased and the tenement house system grew. Immigration rose rapidly after 1844, and this rise was again followed by complaints about housing. The Association for Improving the Condition of the Poor began a movement for the bettering of housing conditions in 1846, and in 1853, in which year immigration amounted to nearly 400,000 arrivals, presented its First Report of a Committee on the Sanitary Condition of the Laboring Classes.

Immigration fell off during the early years of the Civil War, but rose rapidly again in 1863 and 1864. In the latter year the Council of Hygiene presented its classical report on sanitary conditions in New York, showing most objectionable housing conditions in the city.

All descriptions and statistics of the period show that a large proportion of our foreign immigrants found their homes in tenement houses; and that practically all the tenement house population was made up of foreigners, of either the first or second generation.

No account of housing conditions in New York as affected by immigration would be complete without some mention of the "squatter" or "shanty" population. These people, pressing through the thickly settled prosperous districts of the city to the unused land beyond, covered large tracts with their little cabins, made of waste lumber, etc., and planted upon land for which no rent was paid. Such squatters were found in the twentieth ward at a very early date. Many were Germans, of the rag-picking fraternity; but many Irish also lived in this way.

The results of this combination — the immigrant and the tenement house — were notoriously bad; the question naturally arises, Did the immigrant cause the evils of the tenement house, or did the tenement house corrupt the immigrant?

Contemporary observers laid a good share of the blame for the evil conditions that had arisen upon the landlords, and upon the city government which allowed these landlords to work their will unchecked. It is obvious that the newly arrived immigrant had no way of expressing his own ideas as to what was proper and decent in the way of housing accommodations; he had to take what was provided for him. Needing a habitation at once, and without capital to build it, he was obliged to look for one already built; and being new to the country, he could not go far in that search; he was practically forced into accepting whatever was offered him. A candid consideration of the facts seems to show plainly that the desire of excessive profit on the part of landlords was the primary cause of the tenement house evil.

The original character of the tenants, however, has to be taken somewhat into account. Immigration until after the war, at least as far as it affected the tenement house population, was predominantly Irish and German — before 1827 it was predominantly Irish. All of these people were poor; but the Irish showed decided traits of out-and-out pauperism. Reports of the Association for Improving the Condition of the Poor year after year speak of the special call upon their resources by the pauper class of "emigrants," whom they do not always distinguish racially, but whom we know to have been largely Irish. It is not to be supposed that all Irish were paupers; but, as the Association for Improving the Condition of the Poor reports point out, a special winnowing process was all the time going on to draw off the enterprising and industrious from the cities to the railroads and farms of the West, leaving behind the paupers and vagrants, who were, even before the elements were thus separated, an unduly large proportion of the Irish population. Intemperance and violence were other noteworthy Irish characteristics. The German immigrant, like the Irishman, was poor, was dirty in his personal habits; but he was not criminal, not violent, not notably intemperate, not so great a pauper.

The Annual Report of the Association for Improving the Condition of the Poor, 1860, shows the following average percentage of relief at the almshouse for the years 1854–1860: —

Natives of the United States	14.2 %
Natives of Ireland	69 %
Natives of England and Scotland	4.5 %
Natives of Germany	10.8 %
Natives of all other countries	1.5 %
	100.0 %

That is, nearly 7 Irish were relieved to 1 German. The Irish population at this time, however, being nearly twice that of the German, the actual ratio is about 3½ Irish to 1 German, and 5 Irish to 1 American.

But although so many of the laboring population were drawn out of the city, it was not simply the paupers who remained behind. The city itself called for and kept within its limits a considerable working population; and down to the close of the war it was found that, except temporarily, in times of special commercial depression, there was work enough for every able-bodied man who chose to take it. Some such conditions may be said, with certain reservations and modifications, to exist to this day. The commercial importance of the city has to some extent overshadowed its importance as one of the great manufacturing centres of the country; but such it has grown to be, and as such it needs an army of workers within its own immediate limits to carry on its industries. Add to this the constant call for unskilled labor in the never ending course of city improvement, — in road making and mending, laying and relaying of tracks, cutting tunnels and so forth, — and it is easily seen why the immigrant remains so persistently in the busy city that he knows, rather than strike out for a remote agricultural district, the opportunities of which he does not know.

As to the industrious classes, the report of the Association for Improving the Condition of the Poor for 1852 states, "A considerable part of our bakers, carpenters, cabinetmakers, shoemakers, tailors, etc., are Germans; many of the stonecutters, masons, pavers, cartmen, hackmen, etc., are Irish." But the largest class of workers among the Irish were unskilled day laborers; among the Germans what is regarded as a curious new industry was carried on. This was "rag-picking," and Dr. Griscom speaks of this new class of "chiffonniers" as "most filthy and degraded" in person and habits. He seems to think that they were direct importations from Paris, London, and other cities, but there is no evidence to support this. These "chiffonniers" were largely German by race, presumably from country districts at home, taking to this occupation through their frugal habit of saving everything savable, and finding occasion for carrying it on in the general prodigality of dumping all sorts of refuse in all parts of the city. The investigating committee of the New York State Assembly, reporting in 1857, gives a vivid picture of a colony of such workers on the East Side. This was at No. 88 Sheriff Street, a rambling row of wooden tenements which was known as "Rag-picker's Paradise," and was "inhabited by Germans, who dwell in small rooms, in almost fabulous gregariousness, surrounded by scores of dogs, and canopied by myriads of rags fluttering from lines crossing their filthy yards, where bones of dead animals and noisome collections of every kind were reeking with pestiferous smells. One establishment . . . contains more than fifty families."

The report notes, however, with regard to these apparently so degraded beings, that they were really on the upward road.

"It is said that habits of economy and constant application to their wretched business enable nearly all, sooner or later, to accumulate sufficient funds to enable them to migrate to the West. We were told of a colony of three hundred of these people, who occupied a single basement,[1] living on offal and scraps, and who saved money enough to purchase a township on one of the Western prairies." However, the report adds, this means of livelihood is precarious, and in dull seasons the children are sent out to sweep crossings or beg.

Without doubt, people of dirty habits would be likely to have dirty habitations; and a pauperized, intemperate, and violent people would not only destroy the property they lived in, but would make it the centre of all sorts of vice and crime. But it is easy to see that the tenement house was admirably calculated to foster the most undesirable characteristics of these immigrant people, and to choke out to a very decided degree the good characteristics they might develop. It was not merely easy to be dirty in the wretched, crazy, crowded dwellings; it was almost impossible to be anything else.

Croton water was not introduced until 1842, sewerage not until later. In 1844 sewers were laid in a few streets, but no lateral drains had been made from houses, and people were gravely discussing whether a sewer was a proper means of carrying off house drainage of various kinds. The great number of tenement houses constructed during this period were, of course, without the sanitary conveniences now thought essential for decency in living; and many of these tenements exist to this day, without sewer connections, running water, or gas. There was a general negligence as to filth in the city at large, throughout all of this earlier period of growth, which added to

[1] This seems incredible.

the evil effect of the tenement house. Especially prominent in sanitary reports between 1840 and 1865 are the undrained, uneven, and filthy streets, the pigsties and stables everywhere allowed, the manure heaps piled up for sale in many quarters of the city, the bone-boiling, fat-rendering, and soap-making establishments, the match factories, glue and varnish works, etc., and above all, the slaughter-houses, found in every part of the city. It was the general filthiness of the streets, the careless disposal of all sorts of refuse in gutters, ash-barrels, and vacant lots, that enabled the "chiffonnier" to pursue his filthy calling. Dr. Griscom, as early as 1842, says that the remedy for the evils brought about by the dirty ways of "these wretched, unwashed exotics," the "chiffonniers," is clean streets; a remedy which, simple as it was, had to wait half a century for its trial, to the complete success of the prediction.

The slaughter-houses were notorious evils. The terrible stench they generated, the droves of swine, which, allowed to run in the slaughter-house yards as scavengers, were also allowed freely to roam the streets, made them centres of filth and offence; and the cruelty, brutality, and roughness, — for the men employed in them were of the most hardened and intemperate class, — exposed freely to the view of all who chose to come and look on, as it was a favorite neighborhood amusement of the children to do, made them "no ordinary schools of vice."

As late as 1864 there were six of these establishments in the fourteenth ward alone, a quarter that had been for a long time thickly built up, and was in the central part of the city.

In the eleventh ward, also thickly populated, the inspector reporting to the Council of Hygiene found nineteen slaughter-houses. He says: "In most instances the condition of these places is excessively filthy, and utterly reckless of any regard to sanitary regulations or the laws of decency. The worst class of these slaughter-pens is found in rear buildings amidst the most densely packed tenant houses. A written description can convey no adequate idea of the shameless and brutal scenes that are daily witnessed in and about these butcheries."

The tenement house bred, not only filth, but disease. We cannot ascribe altogether to constitutions enfeebled in their native land, to poverty, to natural uncleanliness, the high death-rate of the foreign-born in New York before 1864. Dr. Griscom gave it as his opinion in 1842 that the first cause of bad health in New York was "the crowded condition with insufficient ventilation of a great number of dwellings in this city."

And as to morals, it is plain that the uncomfortable, crowded barracks, with their unwholesome conditions, increased the inducements to intemperance, and the opportunities for violence and immorality.

It was felt during this early period, by those especially interested in the question, that the bad housing provided for the immigrants was the main cause of the greatest evils arising from their coming; and that improved housing would work a most satisfactory change in the immigrant's character. An instance given of improved housing in Boston at this early time shows the soundness of this expectation:—

"The tenants were chiefly Irish, taken as they offered themselves, rejecting only those of known bad habits. Many of them at the time were out of employment, and with very slender resources. But the rents were paid with great punctuality, . . . and no repairs were found necessary, excepting a few lights in the cellar windows."

And Dr. Griscom says, confidently: "Examples almost without number might be adduced of the happy influence upon the appearance, actual comforts, and health of poor tenants, of kindness and judicious indulgence on the part of the landlord."

But what had been done was, in general, exactly the reverse. Instead of providing properly for the accommodation of the hosts of foreigners who were seen to be coming in ever increasing numbers, year after year, we had, as the Assembly Committee of 1857 reproves us with doing, placed at their disposal "districts, localities, neighborhoods, and dwellings, specially, as it were, adapted to the habits and associations of the most degraded of foreign paupers, enabling them at once to renew their familiarity with squalor, misery, and vicious practices." "Is it thus," the committee pertinently asks, "and with such incentives to the continuance and perpetuation of their customary filthiness and improvidence that we are to render these immigrants good and useful citizens?"

After the war, the tide of immigration rose rapidly until 1873, when there were 459,803 arrivals, after which, owing to disturbed industrial conditions, it suddenly fell, and continued to fall until 1878, there being less than 150,000 arrivals, when it began to rise again, with unexampled rapidity, reaching in 1882 a height never attained before or since, with a total of 788,992 arrivals. Again the tide fell, owing to industrial depression. It rose again to a high point in 1888, with 546,889 arrivals, and in 1892, with 579,663 arrivals, and the year ending June 30, 1900, has given us the highest number since 1892, 448,572 arrivals, an increase of over a hundred thousand from the preceding year.

And again, as in the earlier period, protests against housing conditions are seen to follow closely upon times of heavy immigration. In 1867 the first special law in reference to tenement houses in New York was passed. There were at that time about 15,000 tenement houses in the city. In 1877 there were said to be about 25,000 tenement houses, probably an overestimate. The tenement house law of 1879 is an exception to the generally observed order of things, as it was agitated and passed in a period of light immigration. By 1881 there were said (by a more accurate calculation, probably, than that of 1877) to be 22,000 tenement houses in the city, containing a population of about half a million. The State Tenement House Commission of 1884 followed the enormous influx of immigrants in 1882. In 1887 there were 30,055 tenement houses, and 39,128 in 1893.

In 1894 another Tenement House Commission followed at a short interval another period of heavy immigration; and the past two years, during which the tide has been rising again, have seen still another agitation, taking shape in a commission against tenement house evils.

The features of especial interest to be noted in the period since the war, especially the period since 1880, with regard to the relation between the foreign element and the tenement house are, the results of their life in the tenement houses as seen in the second generation, the change in relative numerical proportion of different race elements coming in, the change in the social character of immigration thus indicated, and the effects of the mingling of these different elements one with another, and with immigrants of a former generation.

As to the first point, the actual deterioration of immigrants in the second generation, through the influence of the tenement house, it is difficult to adduce direct statistical evidence, such as increase in crime-rate, death-rate, or rate of pauperism, since so many other elements besides that of race have to be taken into account.

But common observation gives a moral certainty of the broad fact that in tenement house life the immigrant has degenerated to a greater or less degree.

A sort of selective process, always going on, forces out or kills off those of the immigrant population who are not satisfied with or not able to endure tenement conditions, leaving behind a peculiar "type," that is the despair of those who are working for social betterment to-day.

This is especially noticeable among the Irish of the second or third generation, this people having lingered the most persistently in the tenement house.

Take the children, for instance. One who visits the public schools in poor neighborhoods will notice in almost every class room certain pupils too old and too large for the grade they are in, anæmic looking, lethargic in manner. On inquiry about one case after another, one is apt to hear each time that the child is American-born of Irish parentage.

At a little later age this type is found as a corner loafer, a member of a "gang," a recruit for the criminal population in which the "native-born of foreign parentage" hold so high a proportion.

Example after example might be given of tenement house families in which the parents — industrious peasant laborers — have found themselves disgraced by idle and vicious grown sons and daughters. Cases taken from the records of charitable societies almost at random show these facts again and again. This case, for instance, chosen quite at haphazard, is highly typical: —

A decent, industrious Irishwoman, now a widow, who came over in the sixties or early seventies, has three sons. One of these is to-day an absolutely worthless drunkard; one works intermittently; one is consumptive. She is now obliged to depend on charitable aid. Here in this one case are shown the various ways in which degradation can work — toward actual vice, toward relaxation of moral fibre, and toward physical disease.

An old-age "type" of the Irish tenement neighborhood to-day is the ancient harpy — half beggar, half rowdy — who infests the free-and-easy "furnished room houses" — the last stage of degeneracy to which the old family residence has come. Half of her time is spent on "the Island"; the other half in the streets and lodging houses, begging, drinking, cursing, reviling passers-by, until she is again borne away in the patrol wagon.

Such types are seen especially in the upper West Side, in the sixteenth, twentieth, and twenty-second wards, where the Irish element was pushed in the second generation by the incoming of other races at the lower end of the city. Of especially evil association are the names of "Battle Row," "The Devil's Kitchen," and "Bull-Dog Alley."

"Battle Row" was a notable locality. The houses were out of repair and very dirty; the walls trickled with moisture; the stairs and halls were dark. A woman living there was asked why she could not keep her rooms and her children a little cleaner; "Oh!" said she, "what's the use; my old man is drunk now, and my boy and girl that should be supporting me are gone away to the bad; 'tis the dirty thieving loafers around here did it all. What's the use?"

In the older parts of the city similar effects were seen. In the fourth ward conditions were notorious. The following are scenes in a typical rookery in Catherine Street described in 1879: —

"Here, in one room is a lodger, evidently a saloon girl, asleep on a lounge, her features bloated and her temples gashed; the three children in the room evidently do not regard the sight as a novelty.

Across the yard, another woman, elderly and comfortably dressed, apparently a lodger also, has a frightful black eye, which she tries to hide; there are young children here also. . . . Behind a cart in the yard four sturdy young fellows were stretched playing cards at 2 P.M." Basements, cellars, and hallways of tenement houses were infested by the criminal and vicious of both sexes, — products of the tenements, — who made these their common carousing ground and means of escape from the police; and, incidentally, carried on the influences of corruption by their enforced contact with decent families living upstairs in the same dwellings.

While this second generation of an earlier population has been growing up, the racial composition of the foreign element in the city has been undergoing important changes which are of interest in connection with the housing problem.

Immigration before the war was almost exclusively Irish, British, and German. Scandinavians began to come after the war in noticeable numbers, reaching their largest proportion in the decade 1881–1890, when they made up 10 per cent of the total immigration.

Since the war the proportion of Irish to the total immigration has steadily decreased in each decade, while the proportion of Germans, 37 per cent in the decade 1851–1860, has remained large until the past decade, when it dropped from 28 per cent in 1881–1890 (containing the record year, 1882, of German arrivals) to 14 per cent in 1891.

Between 1871 and 1880, for the first time, immigrants from Italy, Austria-Hungary, Russia, and Poland appeared as a noticeable element in immigration, all three groups together, however, making up only 6½ per cent of the whole. From 1881 to 1890 they were 18 per cent of all arrivals — nearly one-fifth; and between 1890 and 1900 were almost one-half — 48 per cent to be exact — while Irish, British, Germans, and Scandinavians together made up 42 per cent.

PERCENTAGE OF IMMIGRATION OF CERTAIN NATIONALITIES TO TOTAL IMMIGRATION FOR SUCCESSIVE PERIODS

	1831-40	1841-50	1851-60	1861-70	1871-80	1881-90	1891-99
Irish	35	46	35	19	16	12.5	10.1
British	13	15	17	26	19	14.5	9.7
German	25	25	37	34	26	28	15.5
French	8						
Scandinavian				5	8	11	8.8
Russian and Polish						5	14.8
Hungarian						7	15.2
Italian						6	16.4

This change in the racial character of immigration is seen even more strikingly when the last two years of the decade are taken singly.

In 1898–1899 immigrants from Italy, Austria-Hungary, and Russia (including Finland), were 65 per cent of all immigrants; in 1899–1900 68½ per cent; while British, Irish, Germans, and Scandinavians together were only 27 per cent in the former year and 22 per cent in the latter year.

The three newer elements just named, Italians, Austro-Hungarians, and Russians, not only made their first noticeable appearance together in approximately equal numbers, but have maintained a tolerably equal proportion ever since, with a tendency on the part of the Italians to outstrip the others.

The real race composition of the newer immigrants, however, is more or less concealed under the nomenclature formerly used in the statistics of immigration, and still used in the United States Census, which shows country of birth only. The terms "Russian" and "Pole," for example, cover Hebrews and Slavs indiscriminately. "Austrian" and "Hungarian" may indicate any one of many races of the most diverse social affinities — Slavs, Magyars, Hebrews, and Germans. The classification now used in statistics of immigration shows distinctions of race as well as country of birth, and thus gives a clearer idea of the actual changes that have taken place in the character of immigration in these later years, and the social effects to be looked for.

According to these figures, in the year ending June 30, 1900, the Irish made up only 8 per cent of all arrivals, Germans (including a considerable proportion from Austria and Russia) and Scandinavians together, 14 per cent, while 13½ per cent of the arrivals were Hebrews, 22½ per cent Italians, and 25 per cent of the various Slavic races.

These newer races have been affecting housing conditions each in its own manner. As has already been pointed out, a large proportion of all of our immigrants enter the country through the port of New York. The table on page 82 shows how high a proportion now come in that way as compared with earlier years, when immigration was more largely Irish, British, and German.

IMMIGRATION TO THE UNITED STATES AND TO THE PORT OF NEW YORK

Year	To United States	To Port of New York	Percentage of Total Immigrants landing at Port of New York
1878	138,469	72,163	52
1879	177,826	99,224	50
1880	457,257	263,726	56
1881	669,431	400,871	60
1882	788,992	502,171	64
1883	603,322	406,697	67
1884	518,592	354,702	68
1885	395,346	287,223	73
1886	334,203	266,370	80
1887	490,109	376,005	77
1888	546,889	418,423	77
1889	444,427	338,784	76
1890	455,302	364,086	80
1891	560,319	448,403	80
1892	623,084	489,810	78
1893	502,917	404,337	80
1894	314,467	253,586	81
1895	279,948	219,006	78
1896	343,267	263,709	80
1897	230,832	180,556	78
1898	229,299	178,748	78
1899	311,715	242,573	78
1900	448,572	341,712	78

Immigration statistics for the year ending June 30, 1900, give some indication of the respective tendencies of the newer peoples to remain in the city. These show that of the Austro-Hungarian group, and the Slavonic peoples comprised in the Russian group, about 75 per cent land at New York, while only 17 per cent gave New York State as their destination. These people go in large proportion to the mining regions of the interior, and do not at present greatly affect housing conditions in the city; although at one time there was a sufficient influx of Bohemians to create a crowded tenement quarter in the East Side of the city, uptown.

As to the Hebrews, 73 per cent of all Hebrew arrivals landed at the port of New York, and 72 per cent of all Hebrew arrivals gave New York State as their destination. This means that an especially large number of Hebrew immigrants settle in New York City. Of the Italians not less than 97 per cent of all arrivals in 1900 landed at New York, while only 55 per cent gave New York State as their destination.

The Italians are regarded as more or less a floating population in the city, both because of their supposed habit of going home to Italy when employment is hard to find here, and because they migrate into and out of the city in bands, as there is call for their work there or elsewhere. But large numbers of them are in New York at all times, in transit or permanently. Census statistics for the past three decades show just how far this changing volume of immigration has been affecting the racial composition of the city's population.

FOREIGN-BORN POPULATION, NEW YORK CITY

Number of Persons born in	Census of 1880		Census of 1890		Census of 1900[2]	
England, Scotland and Wales	39,276		48,114		47,796	
Ireland	198,595		190,418		178,886	
Germany	163,482		210,723		189,720	
Denmark, Norway, and Sweden	5,183		10,139		17,024	
Total, Group I.		406,536		459,394		433,426
Italy	12,223		39,951		103,795	
Austria-Hungary[1]	16,937		47,514		107,616	
Russia and Poland	13,571		55,549		145,805	
Total, Group II.		42,731		143,014		357,216
All other foreign countries		29,403		37,535		60,240
Total foreign-born		478,670		639,943		850,882

It is here seen that the English, Scotch, and Welsh have decreased slightly in the past decade, following a fairly noticeable increase in the previous decade; that the Irish have steadily and considerably decreased throughout the period; that the Germans, after a great increase between 1880 and 1890, dropped greatly between 1890 and 1900; and that the Scandinavians are the only members of this general group of older immigrants that have increased throughout.

Taking this group as a whole, while there are to-day more of them in New York than there were in 1880, there are some thousands fewer than there were in 1890.

The newer peoples, on the contrary, show large increases in each decade, which are made sufficiently plain in the table. The group as a whole, in fact, increased more than threefold between 1880 and 1890, and much more than doubled between 1890 and 1900, showing a population in that year equal to more than four-fifths of the total of the older group.

[1] Includes Bohemia and Austrian Poland.

[2] New York County only; equivalent territory to "New York City" in censuses of 1880 and 1890.

As has already been pointed out, the classification of the census does not indicate race. Thus, of the Austro-Hungarians in the table, it cannot be told how many are Magyars, Slavs, Germans, or Hebrews. From the immigration statistics and general observation, however, it is certain that a considerable proportion are Hebrews, and in like manner that practically all of the "Russians" in the city are of the Hebrew race.

It will be seen, then, that the main factors in immigration of to-day, as affecting the housing problem in New York City, are the Italians and the Hebrews.

Italians were noticeable elements of population in the sixth ward, the quarter of the Five Points, as far back as 1864. The early comers were largely rag-pickers and organ-grinders, and many children were brought here under padroni to beg, to shine boots and shoes, and sell newspapers, or to go about with the hand-organ in the streets.

Between 1879 and 1885 frequent mention is made of Italian neighborhoods in the northern part of the fourteenth ward, just below Houston Street. A colony in Jersey Street, running from Crosby Street to Mulberry, just south of Houston, and now completely occupied by business blocks, was especially noticed. It is thus described in 1884: —

"In Jersey Street exist two courtyards, one of which we illustrate. Six three-story houses are in each. These houses are old, and long ago worn out. They are packed with tenants, rotten with age and decay, and so constructed as to have made them very undesirable for dwelling purposes in their earliest infancy. The Italians who chiefly inhabit them are the scum of New York chiffonniers, and as such, saturated with the filth inseparable from their business. . . . The courtyard swarms with, in daytime, females in the picturesque attires of Genoa and Piedmont, moving between the dirty children. The abundant rags, paper, sacks, barrows, barrels, wash-tubs, dogs, and cats, are all festooned overhead by clothes-lines weighted with such garments as are only known in Italy. Sorting is chiefly done indoors, but at times a rag-picker may be seen at his work in any convenient spot to be had. . . . In each yard live twenty-four families (nominally only, because lodgers here as elsewhere are always welcome), paying rents of from $6 to $9 monthly for two rooms, the inner one being subdivided by a partition consisting perhaps of a simple curtain, and measuring, when so arranged, about 5 × 6 feet each."

An earlier report of the same society, made in 1879, gives the following additional touches of description: —

"Here in the yard of No. 5 Jersey Street, on lines strung across, were thousands of rags hung up to dry; on the ground, piled against the board fences, rags mixed with bones, bottles, and papers; the middle of the yard covered with every imaginable variety of dirt. . . . We then turned to go into the cellars, in which was a large and a small room (containing a cook-stove and sleeping-bunks). There was scarcely standing room for the heaps of bags and rags, and right opposite to them stood a large pile of bones, mostly having meat on them in various stages of decomposition. . . . Notwithstanding the dense tobacco smoke, the smell could be likened only to that of an exhumed body."

As to the character of the people living there, this earlier report says: —

"Jersey Street at first sight looks like a pestilence-breeding, law-breaking colony. A more intimate acquaintance with it, and a few words with one or two white and colored inhabitants, confirmed the first but not the second impression; no more peaceable, thrifty, orderly neighbors could be found than these Italians. They do not beg, are seldom or never arrested for theft, are quiet; though quick to quarrel among themselves, are equally ready to forgive. The officer on duty mentioned that this colony, numbering, perhaps, two hundred Italian families, cannot be matched by any similar number, of corresponding social condition, in New York City, for their law-abiding qualities. He seemed quite proud of them."

The description of a house in Crosby Street in 1879 shows again, as was already shown in 1842, how the economically inferior race — in this case the newer immigrant — is pushed into the rear tenement; and shows also, incidentally, how the Irish family of the second generation rivalled — we should judge by the description, surpassed — the Italian family of new arrival in filth, certainly in disorder: —

"No. — Crosby Street, a very low class of tenement house, bearing a bad reputation. The visitor for the section stated that it was the worst house and inhabited by the worst people he had ever met with, and that having refused relief to some of the tenants, he was afraid to enter it. . . . Four buildings, two front and two rear, each six stories high, stood separated by a yard about twenty feet in width. . . . The rear buildings are occupied exclusively by Italians, all rag-pickers, the front by Irish and a few Germans. An investigation of the front house revealed a shocking amount of dirt; in some instances the floors were invisible under the refuse and garbage. One family represented the mother as out at work, though I afterwards learned she was in her bedroom drunk, while the youngest daughter, half nude, was sitting on the floor fairly surrounded by dirt, and the eldest, as she answered my questions, held her hand over her nose, which I could see was bruised and bleeding."

It hardly needs to be pointed out how closely these descriptions of the early type of Italian immigrants parallel what was told us of the German "chiffonnier" population of the forties and fifties; and yet to-day the German is looked upon as so many degrees higher in the scale than the Italian that any likeness in original condition between the two is usually overlooked.

In the Italian immigration, following the advance guard of rag-pickers and organ-grinders, came a vast army of unskilled day laborers — practically the same class that the early Irish immigration afforded.

It is, probably, due somewhat to remembrances of the organ-grinding period, that our impression of the Italian is of an idle, roving vagabond. But to-day the laboring class makes up the great majority of the Italian immigrant population, and on the streets and railroads, and in construction work of all kinds, is taking the place occupied by the Irish forty years ago. The Italian laborer and his family may be said, indeed, to be more steady and sober, more provident, more generally reliable than their Irish predecessors. Untidy in their habits they undoubtedly are, although not so much so as the rag-pickers who preceded them. But landlords bear testimony to their promptness in paying rent, and to their general good care of the premises they occupy — that is, to the absence of the special gift of destructiveness that seemed to incite the Irish tenant to break everything breakable about a place.

There are not wanting indications to show that the Italian immigrant population will not be the dead weight in our tenement districts that they have been thought likely to be. While the newly arrived immigrant is a day laborer, or a peddler, his son is likely to want to be something else. Italians are found keeping small shops in every quarter of the city, — for fruit, wine, groceries, candy, ice-cream, etc. They keep cafés and restaurants and dry-goods stores; are shoemakers, watchmakers, and barbers. The Italian boot-black has distinctly elevated his occupation, bringing to it better appointments, a higher standard of work, and a certain pride in keeping up to standards that makes this almost an artistic profession. Even the fruit peddlers "compose" their wares in harmonies of color and arrangement that show an instinct of order and beauty which must certainly come to something under favoring circumstances.

The young Italians, boys and girls, are going into factories like the boys and girls of any other race; the boys are found in business offices in increasing numbers; the girls are going into department stores, dressmaking and tailoring establishments, and so on. Many Italian families have moved out of the city altogether, to suburban places, where they buy property and become prosperous in much the fashion of the Germans before them. Many such families are to be found in many Long Island and Westchester villages.

The Hebrew immigrant, like the Italian, is poor, is unclean in his personal habits, will submit to excessive overcrowding when he first comes over; but, like the Italian, he is industrious, saving, careful of property. He may in general be counted on to pay rent, but not so certainly, perhaps, as the Italian.

The Italian immigrants are, when they come here, little given to drink or violence; the Hebrews even less so. And the Hebrew, like the Italian, is distinctly on the upward road. It is a common saying among those who are familiar with them that in ten years the Hester Street family has moved up on Lexington Avenue.

Owing partly to accident, partly to differences in racial character, the Italian and Hebrew demands for housing have been met in a somewhat different way. Italians have found their way largely into the parts of the city previously occupied by the Irish — the fourth, sixth, eighth, and fourteenth wards, and have established themselves in the old "front and rear" tenement already abandoned by their Irish occupants, or about to be abandoned in consequence of the incoming of this new people. The Hebrews, on the other hand, are especially associated with the big "double-decker" or "dumb-bell" tenement. These houses were erected in great numbers on the East Side, which was not so fully taken up with the old type of tenement as the wards entered by the Italians; and here the Hebrews made their way, pushing out the Germans as the Italians were pushing out the Irish. In 1892 vast numbers of Hebrews landed here, in consequence of the persecutions in Russia; and the stream has continued in great volume ever since. And since 1892 great numbers of the big "dumb-bells" have been erected, replacing the smaller dwellings, which simply could not, by any degree of crowding, be made to hold the incoming thousands. Colonies both of Italians and Hebrews have been started in Harlem, and there the "dumb-bells" have been erected for both races.

There is a noticeable demand on the part of both Hebrews and Italians, however, for a better class of housing, as is shown by the erection of more expensive tenements — almost "apartment houses" in appearance — in the fourth ward and elsewhere. The standard of life of both races seems to rise duly, when opportunity permits. An investigator into economic conditions in tenement families testified before the Tenement House Commission of 1894 that, among the results of a statistical canvass of 600 families on the East Side, appeared the fact that an increase in wage marked a decrease in density of overcrowding in every case.

One drawback to improving conditions in tenement house life for the Hebrews has been their peculiar devotion to the occupation of tailoring — to the "sweat-shop system." This is also growing among the Italians — more among deserted or widowed women, as a stop-gap occupation, however, than among the men as a regular trade, as it is seen among the Hebrews. But it is noticeable how few of the younger generation are going into this occupation. In time, then, it may be supposed that this particular form of occupation, with the evil conditions depending on it, will be outgrown — a process which may be materially hastened by proper sanitary laws and the proper enforcement of them.

Both Hebrews and Italians show their growing share in the general prosperity by the rise of many of them to the rank of sub-landlords and landlords. Many if not most of the large tenement houses now going up for the accommodation of Jewish immigrants are erected by Jewish speculators who, in many cases, themselves began life in this country in the tenements. And Italian tenement house property is largely owned by Italians of a similar class.

There can be no possible doubt that the tenement house exerts a positively harmful effect upon these newly arriving peoples, who are, in the main, honest, industrious, and temperate.

In the first place, it works to break down the fairly vigorous health that they bring with them. Dr. Griscom, in his "Report on the Sanitary Condition of the Laboring People" in 1845, set forth very strongly the loss to a state involved in the debilitation of vigor in its laboring classes. As he found it, so now, it is impossible to show, in a brief report, anything conclusive as to this loss based upon death-rates. It seems fairly well agreed upon, however, that the Hebrews who come here have a remarkable tenacity of life, but are rapidly becoming tubercular from their occupations, and life in the tenement house combined; that of the Italians, the few coming here from city slums appear to stand the conditions well enough, but the vast majority, who are from the country, feel the effects of the change very greatly. The adult laborer, with his outdoor occupation, gets along fairly well; but the children show a decided tendency to anæmia and rickets.

The most serious evil is wrought by bringing sober, decent, orderly people, as most of the new immigrants are, in contact, in the tenement house, with the corrupted remnant of an earlier generation. Not until very lately have the Jews and Italians been street-walkers and rowdies. With everything arranged to favor their becoming so, it is no wonder that some fall into the traps laid for them. In the "Big Flat" of notoriously evil memory was to be seen this mixture of races, this mingling of good and bad.

In this house, six stories high, on the first floor, as described in

1886, were "rooms for fourteen families, and they are mostly occupied by low women and street-walkers. . . . The hallways are hang-outs for all the hoodlums of the neighborhood. . . . You will never see any of the tenants living above the second floor standing around the lower floor or doors." The quiet, respectable people referred to as living on the upper floors were largely Polish Jews. The anything but respectable inhabitants of the lower floors were of native birth, if a record of arrests made in that building is any indication.

A better housing system — some little forethought in providing properly for the needs of new immigrants — would do away with many of these evils; it would prevent the positive dragging down of peoples that have much of promise in them when they come. It is probably impossible to do away with the tenement house altogether. Large numbers of people must live within a comparatively short distance of the heart of the city, on account of their occupations. The new races coming in are, besides, distinctly gregarious in their habits, as it is the normal tendency of mankind to be. The Anglo-Saxon race is perhaps the only one that has shown any decided taste for personal isolation. The Scandinavian shows some traces of it. The German can put up with an isolated life for a time, to gain a special end, but he does not enjoy it especially.

Many efforts have been made to induce immigration from the city, and colonization in country places; but these have never succeeded, and probably never will succeed on a large scale.

There is no doubt, however, that the tenement house could be vastly improved — could be made, perhaps, fairly wholesome; and that the foreign immigrant could be made a satisfactory tenant in it. And there is every reason to suppose, further, that with proper surroundings within and without the tenement, he may be trained up rapidly to be a good citizen, as he is now struggling to be through the hindrances laid in his way by the greed of landlords and the neglect of municipal governments.

SOURCES OF INFORMATION RELATING TO FOREIGN IMMIGRATION AND TENEMENT CONDITIONS

Annual Report of the City Inspector of the Board of Health, New York, 1834. By Gerritt Forbes. (Library of Academy of Medicine, 17 West 43d Street.)

Annual Report of the Interments in the City and County of New York for the Year 1842, with Remarks thereon, and a Brief View of the Sanitary Condition of the City. Presented to the Common Council by John H. Griscom, M.D., City Inspector. New York, James Van Norden, Printer to the Board of Assistant Aldermen, 1843. Document No. 59. (Library of Academy of Medicine, 17 West 43d Street.)

Annual Report of the City Inspector of the Board of Health, New York, 1844. (Library of Academy of Medicine, 17 West 43d Street.)

Annual Reports of the Association for Improving the Condition of the Poor for 1852, 1853, 1854, 1857, 1858, 1859, 1860, 1873, 1879, 1880, 1881, 1884, 1886. (Library of Charity Organization Society, 105 East 22d Street.)

First Report of a Committee on the Sanitary Condition of the Laboring Classes in the City of New York, with Remedial Suggestions. New York, John F. Trow, Printer, 1853. Pamphlet, 32 pages. (Published in Annual Report of the Association for Improving the Condition of the Poor for 1853.)

History of Immigration. By Bromwell.

History of the Visitations of Yellow Fever at New York. By John H. Griscom, M.D.

Report of the Council of Hygiene and Public Health of the Citizens' Association of New York upon the Sanitary Condition of the City. D. Appleton & Co., 360 pages. A number of maps, diagrams, and illustrations. (Library of Charity Organization Society, 105 East 22d Street.)

Report of the Select Committee appointed to examine into the Condition of Tenant Houses in New York and Brooklyn, March 9, 1857. Assembly Document No. 205. 54 pages. (State Library, Albany, N.Y.)

Report of the Tenement House Commission of the State of New York, February 17, 1885. Senate Document No. 36. 235 pages. (State Library, Albany, N.Y.)

Report of the Tenement House Committee of 1894. Albany, James B. Lyon, State Printer, 1895. 649 pages. (Library of Charity Organization Society, 105 East 22d Street.)

Sanitary Condition of the Laboring Population of New York, 1845. By John H. Griscom, M.D.

The Tenement House Problem in New York, January 16, 1888. Senate Document No. 16. 52 pages. (Library of Charity Organization Society, 105 East 22d Street.)

U. S. Census Reports.

APPENDIX I

THE PROCEEDINGS OF THE COMMISSION

THE PROCEEDINGS OF THE COMMISSION

THE Tenement House Commission, appointed under the authority of Chapter 279 of the Laws of 1900, submits herewith the following summarized account of its proceedings.

The law under which it was appointed is as follows: —

"CHAPTER 279 OF THE LAWS OF 1900

"AN ACT appointing a committee to examine into the tenement house question in cities of the first class, and to report to the next legislature a code of tenement house laws.

"Became a law April 4, 1900, with the approval of the governor.

"Passed, three-fifths being present.

"*The People of the State of New York, represented in Senate and Assembly, do enact as follows:* —

"SECTION 1. The governor of the state of New York is herewith authorized and empowered to appoint a commission to be known as the tenement house commission. Said commission shall elect a chairman and appoint a secretary; it may employ such counsel, assistants and experts from time to time as it may deem necessary. The total expense of the committee shall not exceed the sums hereinafter appropriated. It may fix the number of commissioners necessary for a quorum, make rules for its government and direction of its work, and fill the vacancies in the commission caused by death or otherwise.

"SEC. 2. The duties of said commission shall be to make a careful examination into the tenement houses in cities of the first class; their condition as to the construction, healthfulness, safety, rentals and the effect of tenement house life on the health, education, savings and morals of those who live in tenement houses, and all other phases of the so-called tenement house question in these cities that can affect the public welfare.

"SEC. 3. The commission shall have power to subpœna witnesses before it, with or without papers, by a subpœna signed by the chairman, to administer them oaths and to compel their attendance by attachment to be issued on the order of the commission and served by any policeman of said cities; witnesses shall be paid the fee paid witnesses in courts of record.

"SEC. 4. The members of the commission shall receive no compensation for their services, but the expenses and disbursements incurred by them in the discharge of their duties as said commissioners shall be paid. The commission shall have power to fix the compensation of its counsel and other employees.

"SEC. 5. Said commission shall make a full report of its work to the next legislature at its opening or as soon thereafter as practicable, with such recommendations as it deems wise to enable the best and highest possible condition for tenement house life in said cities to be attained, and the commission shall cease to exist when such report is made.

"SEC. 6. The sum of ten thousand dollars is hereby appropriated out of any moneys in the treasury not otherwise appropriated for the purpose of carrying out the provisions of this act. The expenses, disbursements, payment of counsel fees and compensation of other employees of the commission shall be made on the approval of the chairman of the commission and the audit of the comptroller.

"SEC. 7. This act shall take effect immediately."

The Commission was appointed on April 16 by the governor, the following persons being named as members: Raymond F. Almirall, Hugh Bonner, Paul D. Cravath, Robert W. de Forest, William A. Douglas, Otto M. Eidlitz, George B. Fowler, F. Norton Goddard, E. R. L. Gould, Williams Lansing, William J. O'Brien, James B. Reynolds, I. N. Phelps Stokes, Myles Tierney, and Alfred T. White. Dr. Gould being unable to accept the appointment, Mr. Charles S. Brown was appointed in his place. The Commission held its first meeting on April 20. At this meeting a permanent organization was effected by the election of Mr. Robert W. de Forest as Chairman of the Commission. On April 26 Mr. Lawrence Veiller was appointed Secretary, and at a later date Mr. Edward B. Whitney was appointed Counsel and Mr. Winthrop E. Dwight, Associate Counsel. At an early date members of the Commission personally visited different types of tenement houses, both in this city and in Buffalo, so as to acquaint themselves with the evils sought to be remedied.

The Commission at once familiarized itself with the work done by previous Commissions, and to this end had prepared a history of the entire movement for tenement house reform from 1834 until the present time. It was also important for the Commission to know precisely what laws had been enacted at different times in regard to this subject, and what changes had taken place in these laws. Accordingly, a history of all tenement house legislation in this State from 1852 to the present time was prepared, showing the development of tenement house regulation, including all the changes that had taken place within that period either by State law or municipal ordinance. The Commission also had collected the laws of all the leading American cities bearing upon this subject, and had prepared a special report on housing conditions in twenty-seven of the largest cities, as well as a comparative study of the different tenement house regulations in each of them. It has also had prepared a similar report on housing conditions and tenement house regulations in leading European cities. All of these matters have been embodied in special reports forming part of the report of the Commission.

Early in its work the Commission conferred with members of previous Tenement House Commissions, and with others who had given special attention to this subject.

On May 14, 1900, the following subcommittees were appointed: 1st. On Tenement House Construction — I. N. Phelps Stokes, Chairman, and Messrs. Almirall, Bonner, Eidlitz, Fowler, Tierney, and Brown. 2d. On Moral and Social Influence of Tenement House Life — James B. Reynolds,

Chairman, and Messrs. Goddard, Almirall, and Fowler. 3d. On Tenement House Labor—James B. Reynolds, Chairman, and Messrs. Goddard, O'Brien, and Stokes. 4th. On Housing Conditions in Buffalo—Messrs. William A. Douglas and Williams Lansing. 5th. Executive Committee—The Chairman and Vice-Chairman, also Messrs. Bonner, Reynolds, Tierney, White, and Stokes.

At an early date the Commission sought and obtained from the different city officials charged with the enforcement of the tenement house laws a frank expression of their views upon this important subject, and on June 20 a conference was had with the heads of these departments. There were present at this conference Messrs. Thomas J. Brady, John Guilfoyle, and Daniel Campbell, Commissioners of Buildings for the Boroughs of Manhattan and the Bronx, Brooklyn, Queens and Richmond respectively; also, Dr. Charles F. Roberts, Sanitary Superintendent of the Department of Health, Fire Chief Edward F. Croker, and Mr. Augustus Docharty, Secretary of the Fire Department.

The Commission came to the conclusion at an early period that it was out of the question to investigate all the tenement houses in the city, as there were over 82,000 of such buildings. It was deemed, however, very desirable to ascertain to what extent tenement house evils were due to defect of law, and to what extent to its non-enforcement. It was therefore decided to inspect practically all the new tenement houses in course of construction in the city. Such an inspection was made, and the results of this inspection have been embodied in a special report appended to the report of the Commission; 1046 buildings were thus inspected.

In regard to the existing tenement houses, the evils were so generally well known that it was not deemed advisable or necessary to enter into a very detailed examination of these buildings. Accordingly, therefore, the Commission decided that with the means and time at their disposal it would be wise to confine such an investigation to a few typical blocks in different quarters of the city, and to ascertain whether the laws in reference to existing buildings were being enforced in the more important particulars. Eight blocks, comprising 327 buildings, located in distinctively tenement districts, and in different quarters of the city, were selected. In selecting these blocks, attention was given to the fact that they contained nearly all the different types of tenement houses erected at different times in this city. Similar investigations of 155 typical tenement houses were made in different parts of Brooklyn, Queens, and Richmond.

It was also decided to have a special examination made of the rear tenement houses, especially the so-called "back to back" rear tenements. These buildings had been given special attention by the Committee of 1894, and had been severely condemned. As a result of this condemnation, the Board of Health, in 1896, condemned or had permanently vacated about a hundred of such buildings. The Commission therefore decided to ascertain whether there were any more buildings of this kind in the city, and with this end in view, all such buildings were examined; 438 inspections of such houses were made, involving 644 tenement houses.

It was also deemed desirable to have an inspection made of the tenement houses in the Boroughs of Manhattan and Brooklyn, and also in Queens and Richmond, in regard to the question of fire-escapes, so as to determine whether such buildings were properly equipped, and whether the fire-escapes were badly encumbered or not.

In Manhattan the entire seventeenth ward was examined, and a portion of the seventeenth ward in Brooklyn was similarly examined, as well as parts of Queens and Richmond. In all, 1726 houses were thus inspected. The results of these examinations have been presented in the form of a special report.

A sanitary inspection of typical tenement houses in the Boroughs of Manhattan and the Bronx, as well as Brooklyn, was also made, and these results have been set forth in a special paper. Over 100 actual inspections of tenement houses were thus made, affecting 337 buildings.

In order to determine how tenement houses should be constructed in regard to safety from fire, it became necessary to ascertain how fires ordinarily spread through tenement houses, and also to know a number of other facts having a bearing upon this subject. To determine these facts it was found necessary to examine over 60,000 records of the Fire Department.

The Commission has also had tabulated very complete and full statistics in reference to the 42,700 tenement houses in the Borough of Manhattan, which has involved the counting and tabulation of 427,000 records.

The Commission also, in addition to its investigation of tenement house fires, has caused an investigation to be made to ascertain the number of wooden air shafts in the tenement houses in the city. This investigation has affected about 2600 tenement houses.

Early in June a printed list of forty-seven different questions was prepared by the Commission. These questions dealt with practically all of the more important points of tenement house construction in regard to which change in the law might be desirable.

About 1600 circulars were sent out to every person known to have any special interest in the subject of tenement house reform, and also to architects, builders, owners of tenements, and especially to the owners of every tenement house for which plans had been filed in the Department of Buildings since January 1, 1900; also to real estate agents, insurance agents, physicians, dwellers in tenements, settlement workers living in tenement districts, and charitable societies, as well as to the different labor organizations. Accompanying these circulars was a letter requesting an expression of opinion, not only upon the special points involved in the list of questions, but also requesting general recommendations to the Commission. A copy of this circular will be found in Appendix X. This circular was made public in the press, and was given widespread attention throughout the country. Over a hundred different persons sent written replies, involving over 4700 definite answers. The suggestions made in this manner to the Commission were of great value in helping them to determine what was the public sentiment in regard to the different questions involved, and also were of great assistance in enabling them to make definite recommendations. All these suggestions have been carefully considered.

Foremost among these was a suggestion made at the very beginning of the Commission's work by Mr. R. Fulton Cutting, in reference to encouraging the building of better tenements by exempting from taxation buildings properly constructed.

A suggestion along very similar lines was also made to the Commission by Dr. E. R. L. Gould, the President of the City and Suburban Homes Company, in his testimony to the effect that the present tax laws unjustly discriminated against corporations whose capital was invested in improved tenements, taxes being levied both on the real estate of the corporation as well as on its capital stock, while individuals owning tenement houses were taxed only on their real estate.

The attention of the Commission has been called to the apparent injustice of the present charges for marshals' fees in connection with the eviction of tenants for non-payment of rent and other causes.

Among other suggestions made to the Commission were the following:

That the making or finishing of clothes, artificial flowers, or similar forms of labor in tenement houses be prohibited.

That some scheme be devised to drive the factories out of New York City, and thus remove a very large part of the tenement population, who probably would follow their place of employment.

That in all new tenement houses, it should be compulsory to carry up the walls above the roof, or provide fences, so as to provide roof playgrounds and prevent the children from falling into the street.

Another proposition made from similar motives was that all back yard fences in tenement districts be taken down and removed, and the spaces be thrown together into single large areas to be utilized as playgrounds.

A tenant living in a district where there are many stables, urged that stables should not be allowed in a block where two-thirds of the buildings are tenement houses.

Representatives of the Master Plumbers' Association urged upon the Commission the passage of a law prohibiting janitors in tenement houses from making repairs to the plumbing work, and also urged the passage of a law requiring an annual test of the plumbing in all tenement houses.

Another recommendation was to prohibit absolutely the drying of clothes in air shafts. Other persons wished the Tenement House Commission to recommend that no inside stairways should be permitted in tenement houses; that all tenement houses should be provided with window guards so as to prevent accidents from persons falling out of windows; that in new tenement houses over four stories in height elevators should be required; that the roofs of tenement houses should be arranged for baths and for wash rooms; that a law should be passed forbidding as many as four families on a floor on a 25-foot lot; that the erection of a tenement house on a 25-foot lot should be absolutely prohibited; that a greater percentage of the lot should be permitted to be occupied where the building is on a wider lot than 25 feet; that it should be compulsory to furnish hot water in all new tenement houses; that no liquor store should be allowed in a tenement house; that ash chutes should be provided in all new tenement houses; that the windows in the walls of tenement buildings should not be placed opposite each other, but that they should be "staggered," so that a person in one room could not look into another room directly opposite. The Commission was also urged to recommend a law requiring the licensing of all builders, also the licensing of architects. Another recommendation was that all future tenement houses should be fireproof throughout; another that all partitions in tenement houses should be solid and fireproof; that there should be a separate seat provided for children in water-closets; that basement dwellings in tenement houses should be absolutely prohibited; that wooden furring should not be permitted to be used in lining walls, but that all walls should be lined with hollow brick; that it be compulsory to provide a dumb-waiter in all new tenement houses. In regard to bathing facilities, there was a great variety of recommendations, varying from requiring a private bath for each family to requiring a series of common baths in the basement. Other suggestions along these lines were: Making it compulsory to have a movable partition between the wash-tubs; that the wash-tubs should be made at least four feet long, so that they could be used as a bath, and that no water tax should be placed upon such tub, or tubs with movable partitions. Another person urged that it should be compulsory for the landlord to furnish hot water for bathing purposes. Other recommendations of equally wide range and varying degrees of usefulness have been made to the Commission.

The Commission has held eight public hearings, the testimony taken at these hearings amounting to about 1000 pages. One of these hearings was held in Buffalo and the other seven in New York.

The hearing in Buffalo was held at the Hotel Iroquois on October 27, at 11 A.M., and the following persons were present, most of whom testified before the Commission: Dr. D. J. Constantine, the Tenement House Inspector of the Board of Health; Dr. Ernest Wende, President of the Board of Health; Captain John W. Ryan, of the eighth precinct of police; Fire Chief McConnell; Miss Mary E. Remington, manager of an improved tenement house; Mrs. Bernard Bartow and Miss Viola Bryant, of the State Charities Aid Association; Mr. T. Guilford Smith, President of the Buffalo Charity Organization Society; Mr. Frederick Almy, Secretary, and Miss Marion I. Moore, Assistant Secretary of the Buffalo Charity Organization Society; Mrs. James B. Parke, of the Women's Union; Miss Emily S. Holmes, head-worker of the Westminster House Settlement; Inspectors Edward G. Burns and Adam Meister, of the Buffalo Charity Organization Society; Miss Louise Montgomery and Miss Florence L. Pease, of Welcome Hall Settlement; Dr. John H. Pryor, Mr. Martin F. Murphy, President of the State Federation of Labor; Mr. V. Altman, business agent of the Garment Workers; and a number of other representatives of labor organizations, and many other citizens.

Many of those testifying urged that a number of old buildings in the lower part of the city should be condemned as not fit for habitation, and that others should be provided with adequate fire-escapes. Several witnesses testified that in the Polish section of the city there was overcrowding in certain cases, but that, as a rule, the great majority of the Poles lived in small one story and one and one-half story wooden cottages containing but one family, and that, in many cases, the houses were owned by the occupants.

A number of witnesses expressed the opinion that a tenement house system was not necessary in the city of Buffalo, and that such a system should be discouraged; that it was essential to a right state of civilization that people should live in separate houses and have their own homes, and that the great majority of people in Buffalo did so.

The first hearing in New York was held on November 16, and was devoted entirely to the subject of the Tenements and Tuberculosis, and upon that occasion the following witnesses testified: Dr. John H. Pryor, of Buffalo; Dr. Herman M. Biggs, of the Department of Health; Dr. Alfred Meyer; Mr. Lee K. Frankel, Manager of the United Hebrew Charities; Dr. S. A. Knopf; Dr. Alfred R. Guerard; and Mr. Frank Tucker, General Manager of the Association for Improving the Condition of the Poor.

The second hearing was held on November 24, and was devoted to the subject of the General Evils of the Tenement House System. Among the witnesses who testified before the Commission at this hearing were the following: Dr. Elgin R. L. Gould, President of the City and Suburban Homes Company; Mr. Jacob A. Riis, author of "How the Other Half Lives," and other books on this subject; Miss Lillian D. Wald, head-worker of the Nurses' Settlement; Mr. Ernest Flagg, Architect, and author of "The Tenement House Evil and Its Cure"; Mrs. V. G. Simkhowitch, head-worker of Friendly Aid Settlement; Rev. W. T. Elsing, of the De Witt Memorial Church; Miss M. M. Brown, of the Nurses' Settlement; Miss Elizabeth S. Williams, head-worker of the College Settlement; Dr. L. Neuhof, physician of the Good Samaritan Dispensary.

At the third hearing, held on November 26, the subject of the General Evils of the Tenement House System was continued. Among the persons who testified were the following; Miss Agnes Daley, formerly of the College Settlement and a resident in a new tenement house for nine months; Mr. Henry Moscowitz, a tenement house dweller; Rev. Gaylord S. White, pastor of a church in one of the tenement house districts in Brooklyn; Mr. Frank Tucker, of the Association for Improving the Condition of the Poor; Mrs. J. A. Miller, a tenement house dweller for twelve years; Mr. A. A. Hill, head-worker of a settlement on the West Side of the city; Mr. Edward T. Devine, General Secretary of the Charity Organization Society; Mrs. Florence Kelly, Secretary of the National Consumers' League, and formerly chief factory inspector of the State of Illinois.

The fourth public hearing of the Tenement House Commission was held on November 29, and was devoted to the special subject of Vice in Tenement Districts. Among the persons who testified at this hearing were the following: Mr. Emil Fuchs, a tenement house dweller; Dr. Pierre Siegelstein, a physician living in tenement house districts; Rev. Robert L. Paddock, of the Pro-Cathedral Church; Miss Ruth Price, of the Rescue Army; Professor Felix Adler; Mrs. Charles R. Lowell; Mr. Henry Moscowitz, a tenement house dweller; Mr. Orrin B. Booth, of the Rescue Army; Rev. Francis J. Clay Moran of the Church Association for the Advancement of the Interests of Labor; Mr. George W. Morgan, Secretary of the Committee on Public Morality.

The fifth public hearing of the Tenement House Commission was held on November 30, and was devoted to the special subject of Tenement House Labor. Among the persons who testified were the following: Mrs. Frederick Nathan, President of the Consumers' League; Mr. Henry White, Secretary of the National Garment Workers of America; Rev. Francis J. Moran; Mr. Meyer Schoenfeld, formerly of the Garment Makers' Union; Mr. H. Grossman, Business Agent of the Cloak Makers' Union; Mr. Moses de Costa, of the Cigar Makers' Union; Mr. Daniel S. Jacobs, of the Cigar Makers'.

The sixth public hearing of the Tenement House Commission was held on December 10. The hearing was devoted to the subject of the Enforcement of the Law in Regard to the Construction of New Buildings. Among the persons who testified were the following: Mr. Thomas J. Brady, Commissioner of Buildings for Manhattan and the Bronx; Mr. John A. Dooner, Superintendent of Buildings for the Boroughs of Manhattan and the Bronx; Mr. John Guilfoyle, Commissioner of Buildings for the Borough of Brooklyn; Mr. Daniel Campbell, Commissioner of Buildings for the Boroughs of Queens and Richmond.

The seventh public hearing of the Tenement House Commission was held on December 11, and the hearing was devoted to the question of the Enforcement of the Tenement House Laws by the Building and Health Departments. Among the witnesses who testified were the following: Mr. Michael C. Murphy, President of the Department of Health; Mr. Eugene Otterbourg, Assistant Corporation Counsel, assigned to the Department of Buildings; Dr. Charles F. Roberts, Sanitary Superintendent of the Department of Health; Dr. Frederick H. Dillingham, Assistant Sanitary Superintendent of the Department of Health for the Borough of Manhattan; Dr. Robert A. Black, Assistant Sanitary Superintendent of the Department of Health for the Borough of Brooklyn; Dr. J. L. Feeny, Assistant Sanitary Superintendent of the Department of Health for the Borough of Richmond.

The Commission has at all times sought to place itself in an attitude of coöperation with all societies and individuals and has had frequent conferences with different bodies as to matters affected by the tenement house question.

The Commission is under great obligation to the following-named persons, who have conducted special examinations at its request, viz.: Dr. Hermann M. Biggs, Mr. H. L. Cargill, Miss Kate Holladay Claghorn, Dr. Elgin R. L. Gould, Dr. Arthur B. Guerard, Mr. John Todd, Mr. Frank Tucker, and Mr. Albert L. Webster.

The Secretary, as well as the Counsel and Associate Counsel, have taken part in almost all its deliberations, and have had quite as much part in making and framing its conclusions as if each of them had been entitled to a personal vote. It would belittle their services to make them the subject of any special commendation.

The Commission also wishes to express its indebtedness to those employees who, by their faithful, careful, efficient, and conscientious work, have helped to make the labors of the Commission successful, and to this end desires to mention for special commendation the following persons: Miss M. L. Acton, Mr. William J. Crawford, Miss Helen Herold, Mr. George E. Jennings, Jr., Miss L. J. Moulton, Mr. Charles Mohr, and Mr. W. A. Robertson.

APPENDIX II

THE PROPOSED CODE OF TENEMENT HOUSE LAWS (WITH EXPLANATORY NOTES)

THE PROPOSED CODE OF TENEMENT HOUSE LAWS[1]

In preparing this Code the Commission has sought to arrange and classify it in such way as to make it perfectly clear to every person who may have occasion to use it, and to this end has divided the Code into chapters, grouping the different parts in such divisions as fire provisions, light and ventilation provisions, sanitary provisions, remedies, etc. Under each chapter it has been sought to separate the provisions relating entirely to new buildings from those which relate to existing tenement houses. Following each section in which important changes have been made will be found a statement calling attention to these changes and pointing out some of the chief reasons for them.

"An Act in relation to Tenement Houses in the City of New York.

"*The People of the State of New York represented in Senate and Assembly do enact as follows:*

"CHAPTER I. DEFINITIONS

"Section 1. *Application.* All the provisions of this act have reference only to the city of New York.[2]

"Sec. 2. *Definitions.* Certain words used in this act are defined for the purposes thereof as follows:

"(1.) A tenement house is any house or building, or portion thereof, which is rented, leased, let or hired out, to be occupied, or is occupied as the home or residence of three families or more living independently of each other, and doing their cooking upon the premises, or by more than two families upon any floor, so living and cooking, but having a common right in the halls, stairways, yards, water-closets or privies, or some of them."

> This is the definition in the Charter. This is also, in principle, the definition in Chicago, Philadelphia, St. Louis, Boston, Baltimore, Buffalo, San Francisco, Milwaukee, Washington, Minneapolis, Providence, Kansas City, Mo., Denver, and Syracuse, with slight differences in some of the cities as to the number of families, which varies between three and five.

"(2.) A yard is an open unoccupied space on the same lot with a tenement house, between the extreme rear line of the house and the rear line of the lot.

[1] This code as adopted by the Legislature is to be found in Chapter 334 of the laws of 1901 of the State of New York. Further amendments to it are to be found in Chapter 555 of the laws of 1901, Chapter 352 of the laws of 1902, and Chapter 179 of the laws of 1903.

[2] As finally submitted by the Commission and enacted, it applied to cities of the first class, and not to New York alone.

"(3.) A court is an open unoccupied space, other than a yard, on the same lot with a tenement house. A court not extending to the street or yard is an inner court. A court extending to the street or yard is an outer court. If it extends to the street it is a street court. If it extends to the yard it is a yard court.

"(4.) A shaft includes exterior and interior shafts, whether for air, light, elevator, dumbwaiter, or any other purpose. A vent shaft is one used solely to ventilate or light a water-closet compartment or bathroom.

"(5.) A public hall is a hall, corridor or passageway not within an apartment.

"(6.) A stair hall includes the stairs, stair landings and those portions of the public halls through which it is necessary to pass in going between the entrance floor and the roof.

"(7.) A basement is a story partly but not more than one-half below the level of the curb.

"(8.) A cellar is a story more than one-half below the level of the curb.

"(9.) A fireproof tenement house is one the walls of which are constructed of brick, stone, iron or other hard incombustible material, and in which there are no wood beams or lintels, and in which the floors, roofs, stair halls and public halls are built entirely of brick, stone, iron or other hard incombustible material, and in which no woodwork or other inflammable material is used in any of the partitions, furrings or ceilings. But this definition shall not be construed as prohibiting, elsewhere than in the stair halls or entrance halls, the use of wooden flooring on top of the fireproof floors or the use of wooden sleepers, nor as prohibiting wooden handrails and hardwood treads such as described in Section 18 of this act.

"(10.) The word shall is always mandatory, and not directory, and denotes that the house shall be maintained in all respects according to the mandate, as long as it continues to be a tenement house.

"Sec. 3. *Buildings converted or altered.* A building not erected for use as a tenement house, if hereafter converted or altered to such use, shall thereupon become subject to all the provisions of this act affecting tenement houses hereafter erected.

"Sec. 4. *Buildings in process of erection.* A tenement house not now completed, but upon which work has been actually commenced, after approval of the plans therefor by the Department of Buildings, shall be subject only to the provisions of this act affecting now existing tenement houses.

"Sec. 5. *Corner lots.* When a lot is situated at a corner of two streets, if it has more frontage upon one street than the other, the lesser frontage shall be deemed the width and the greater frontage the depth of the lot within the meaning of this act; and when the width is greater than twenty-five feet, the excess over said twenty-five feet shall not be deemed part of a corner lot, but shall be subject to the provisions of this act in relation to lots other than corner lots.

"CHAPTER II. PROTECTION FROM FIRE

"Title 1. *Provisions applicable only to tenement houses hereafter erected*

"Sec. 11. *Fireproof tenements, when required.* Every tenement house hereafter erected exceeding fifty-seven feet, or exceeding five stories or part of stories, in height above the curb level, shall be a fireproof tenement house, nor shall any tenement house be altered so as to exceed such height without being made a fireproof tenement house; provided, that this section shall not apply to a building of a height not exceeding sixty-seven feet, and not exceeding six stories or parts of stories in height above the curb level if such building shall have a frontage exceeding forty feet. A cellar is not a story within the meaning of this section."

The law in 1885 limited the height of all tenement houses, whether fireproof or non-fireproof, to 70 feet on streets of 60 feet or less in width and to 80 feet on broader streets, and this remained the law until 1897. The law in Philadelphia requires all tenement houses over four stories high to be fireproof; and the Boston law limits the height of non-fireproof tenements to 65 feet; in Washington the height of such buildings must not exceed five stories.

"SEC. 12. *Fire escapes.* Every non-fireproof tenement house hereafter erected, unless provided with fireproof outside stairways directly accessible to each apartment, shall have fire escapes located and constructed as in this section required.

"(1.) The fire escapes shall be located both on the front and rear of the building at each story above the ground floor, and where there is an apartment not containing any room fronting on either the street or yard, an additional fire escape shall be provided for such apartment. Where, however, there are not more than four rooms in a line comprising part of one apartment, and the apartment extends from the street to the yard, the rear fire escape may be omitted. Fire escapes may project into the public highway to a distance not greater than four feet beyond the building line.

"(2.) The fire escapes shall consist of outside open iron balconies and stairways. The stairways shall be placed at an angle of not more than sixty degrees, with steps not less than six inches in width and twenty inches in length, and with a rise of not more than nine inches. The balcony on the top floor, except in the case of a front fire escape, shall be provided with a goose-neck ladder leading from said balcony to and above the roof.

"(3.) *Balconies.* The balconies shall not be less than three feet in width, taking in at least one window of each apartment at each story above the ground floor. They shall be below and not more than one foot below the window sills and extend in front of and not less than nine inches beyond each window. There shall be a landing not less than twenty-four inches square at the head and foot of each stairway. The stairway opening on each platform shall be of a size sufficient to provide clear headway.

"(4.) *Floors of balconies.* The floors of balconies shall be of wrought iron or steel slats not less than one and a half inches by three-eighths of an inch, placed not more than one and one-quarter inches apart, and well secured and riveted to iron battens one and a half inches by three-eighths of an inch, not over three feet apart and riveted at the intersection. The openings for stairways in all buildings shall not be less than twenty-one inches wide and thirty-six inches long, and such openings shall have no covers of any kind. The platforms or balconies shall be constructed and erected to safely sustain in all their parts a safe load at a ratio of four to one, of not less than eighty pounds per square foot of surface.

"(5.) *Railings.* The outside top rail shall extend around the entire length of the platform and in all cases shall go through the wall at each end, and be properly secured by nuts and four-inch square washers at least three-eighths of an inch thick, and no top rail shall be connected at angles by cast iron. The top rail of balconies shall be one and three-quarter inches by one-half inch of wrought iron, or one and a half inch angle iron one-quarter inch thick. The bottom rails shall be one and one-half inches by three-eighths of an inch wrought iron, or one and a half inch angle iron, one-quarter inch thick, well leaded into the wall. The standards or filling-in bars shall not be less than one-half inch round or square wrought iron, well riveted to the top and bottom rails and platform frame. Such standards or filling-in bars shall be securely braced by outside brackets at suitable intervals, and shall be placed not more than six inches from centres; the height of railings shall in no case be less than two feet nine inches.

"(6.) *Stairways.* The stairways shall be constructed and erected to fully sustain in all their parts a safe load at a ratio of four to one of not less than one hundred pounds per step, with the exception of the tread which must safely sustain at said ratio a load of two hundred pounds. The treads shall be flat open treads not less than six inches wide and with a rise of not more than nine inches. The stairs shall be not less than twenty inches wide. The strings shall be not less than three inch channels of iron or steel, or other shape equally strong, and shall rest upon and be fastened to a bracket, which shall be fastened through the wall as hereinafter provided. The strings shall be securely fastened to the balcony at the top, and the steps in all cases shall be double-riveted or bolted to the strings. The stairs shall have three-quarter inch handrails of wrought iron, well braced.

"(7.) *Brackets.* The brackets shall not be less than one-half inch by one and three-quarters inches wrought iron placed edge-wise, or one and three-quarters inch angle iron, one-quarter inch thick, well braced; they shall not be more than four feet apart, and shall be braced by means of not less than three-quarters of an inch square wrought iron, and shall extend two-thirds of the width of the respective balconies or brackets. The brackets shall go through the wall and be turned down three inches, or be properly secured by nuts and four inch square washers at least three-eighths of an inch thick. On new buildings the brackets shall be set as the walls are being built. When brackets are put on tenement houses already erected the part going through the wall shall not be less than one inch in diameter with screw nuts and washers not less than five inches square and one-half an inch thick.

"(8.) *Drop-ladders.* No drop-ladder shall be required from the lower balcony when the floor of such balcony is not more than fourteen feet above the sidewalk or ground.

"(9.) *Painting.* All the parts of such fire escapes shall receive not less than two coats of paint, one in the shop, and one after erection. All fire escape balconies shall contain a plate firmly fastened to the standards or filling-in bars near the top railing in front of each window, such plate to contain in plain, large, prominent, raised letters, each letter to be not less than one-half an inch in length, the following words: 'Any one placing any encumbrance on this balcony will be fined $10.'"

The present law[1] leaves the location and manner of construction of all fire escapes entirely in the discretion of the Commissioner of Buildings. The Commissioner has adopted printed regulations on this subject prescribing the method of construction. So important a subject as this should be embodied in the statute, and should not be subject to change at the pleasure of any official. In Chicago, Philadelphia, San Francisco, Jersey City, Minneapolis, Rochester, and in other cities, these details are specified in the statute. The above provisions of Section 12 are the present regulations of the Department of Buildings, with such changes as have been deemed necessary. Where the present regulations have been departed from the provisions of the Philadelphia law have generally been followed. It will be noted that these fire escape provisions apply only to non-fireproof buildings. Under the provisions of this section, vertical ladders will no longer be permitted upon new fire escapes, but iron stairs, with a hand-rail, such as are now being placed on many of the more substantial buildings, must be provided. The present regulations of the Building Department require this, but the requirement is frequently "waived." The Special Report on this subject shows that vertical ladders are almost never used by the tenants, and that in nearly every case the tenants have to be *rescued from the fire escapes* by firemen and policemen. It is obvious that women, children, and aged people cannot without risk use such ladders. At the request of the Fire Department a provision has been added that the top fire escape shall have a ladder leading to the roof, so as to assist the firemen in their work. In regard to the location of fire escapes, the general practice at present is to place the balconies on the rear of the building only, and not on the front. The value of a fire escape is not only as a place of refuge for the tenants, but also as a means of enabling the firemen to quickly reach the fire within the building, and to rescue any persons in danger. It is apparent, therefore, that such escapes should be located on the front of the building as well as on the rear. Moreover, it is the natural impulse of persons in a fire to rush to the *front* windows where the street is located, where the fire engines are to be found, and where help may be expected. Furthermore, the kitchens of flats and apartments are generally at the rear, and it is in the kitchens that most of the fires originate, so that escape by the rear fire escapes is generally cut off. The stairs and halls of the buildings are seldom of much value as a means of escape, because they immediately become filled with smoke. From every consideration, therefore, it seems desirable that the fire escapes shall be on the front of the building, when it is not fireproof. The Commission strongly condemns the present practice of placing gratings without ladders or stairs, in the air shafts between the windows of adjoining houses, to serve in lieu of fire escapes on the front of the buildings. The special report on tenement house fires shows that over one-fourth of the fires spread through the air shafts. This practice seems to have arisen only within the last two or three years. It saves only a few dollars to the builder. The Commis-

[1] Wherever the words "the present law" occur in this report it means the laws in force in 1900.

sion has recommended that the present drop-ladder, now required at the first balcony, be no longer required, for the reason that these ladders are seldom used; because of their weight and size, they are usually hung to the balcony above and in case of fire are more of a hindrance than a help.

"SEC. 13. *Bulkheads.* Every tenement house hereafter erected shall have in the roof a fireproof bulkhead with a fireproof door to the same, and shall have fireproof stairs with a guide or handrail leading to the roof, and such stairs shall be kept free from encumbrance at all times. No bulkhead door shall at any time be locked with a key, but it may be fastened on the inside by movable bolts or hooks."

This has practically been the law in Brooklyn since 1852 and in Manhattan since 1862.

"SEC. 14. *Stairs and public halls.* Every tenement house hereafter erected shall have at least one flight of stairs extending from the entrance floor to the roof, and the stairs and public halls therein shall each be at least three feet wide in the clear."

The present law does not specify a minimum width for public halls and stairs. It has become necessary, however, to prescribe such a width, as the present halls are so narrow that it is difficult for people to pass each other in them. The narrow halls also greatly increase the danger in case of fire.

In Chicago the law requires that the halls shall be at least 3 feet wide for every 2000 square feet of ground covered by the building, and shall increase 6 inches in width for every 500 additional square feet. In Philadelphia the halls must be at least 3 feet wide in houses containing less than fifteen rooms; where there are more than fifteen rooms, they must be 3 feet 6 inches wide, and in houses where there are over twenty-five rooms the halls must be 4 feet wide. There are similar requirements in the laws of other cities.

"SEC. 15. *Stairways in non-fireproof buildings.* Every non-fireproof tenement house hereafter erected containing over eighty rooms shall also have an additional flight of stairs for every additional eighty rooms or fraction thereof; if said house contains not more than one hundred and twenty rooms, in lieu of an additional stairway, the stairs and public halls throughout the entire building may each be at least one-half wider than is specified in sections fourteen and twenty of this act."

The Building Code in relation to certain classes of buildings provides that there shall be an increased number of stairs proportionate to the width of the building. It is apparent that this method of determining the number of stairs is not so logical as making it depend on the number of persons using the stairs, which is best measured by the number of rooms.

"SEC. 16. *Stairways in fireproof buildings.* Every fireproof tenement house hereafter erected containing over one hundred and twenty rooms shall also have an additional flight of stairs for every additional one hundred and twenty rooms or fraction thereof; but if said house contains not more than one hundred and eighty rooms, in lieu of an additional stairway the stairs and public halls throughout the entire building may each be at least one-half wider than is specified in Sections fourteen and twenty of this act; and a power passenger elevator, enclosed in a separate shaft from the stairs, and distant not less than thirty-five feet from the main flight of stairs, shall be deemed the equivalent of an additional flight."

In fireproof buildings, much greater latitude may safely be given than in non-fireproof buildings, and where there are elevators, still further concessions may be granted, as the stairs in such cases are seldom used.

"SEC. 17. *Stairways, continued.* Each flight of stairs mentioned in the last three sections shall have an entrance on the entrance floor from the street or street court, or from an inner court which connects directly with the street. All stairs shall be constructed with a rise of not more than seven and one-half inches and with treads not less than ten inches wide and not less than three feet long in the clear. Where winders are used, all treads at a point eighteen inches from the strings on the well side shall be at least ten inches wide."

The present law does not specify what the amount of rise or the width of treads shall be. It seems desirable to specify a maximum height of stair and a minimum width, not only on account of the danger of steep stairs, but for other reasons as well. The testimony taken before the Commission disclosed the fact that the steep stairs in the tenement houses were very injurious to women. The present law prohibits "winders"; it appears, however, that they are often used. Under the conditions here prescribed, it would seem that they might safely be allowed.

"SEC. 18. *Stair halls.* The stair halls in all non-fireproof as well as fireproof tenement houses hereafter erected shall be constructed of fireproof material throughout, except as in this section specified. The risers, strings and banisters shall be of metal or stone. The treads shall be of metal, slate or stone, or of hard wood not less than two inches thick. Wooden hand rails to stairs will be permitted if constructed of hard wood. The floors of all stair halls shall be constructed of iron or steel beams and fireproof filling and no wooden flooring or sleepers shall be permitted. All windows on stair halls opening on courts shall be of good quality wire-glass in frames of fireproof material."

The present law requires that in tenement houses over three stories in height above the cellar, the entrance hall and the entire stair well and stairs shall be built of slow-burning construction or fireproof material. Prior to the Charter, the law read "of *such* slow-burning or fireproof construction, *as the Superintendent of Buildings shall decide.*" The Charter, however, took away this discretionary power. Notwithstanding this fact, the Commission finds that the Department of Buildings permits under this section of the law the stairs and public halls to be constructed entirely of wood. In the Borough of Manhattan, the Commission found 113 new tenement houses, or 97 per cent of all, being thus constructed with wooden stairs, and in 82 cases these stairs were enclosed with ordinary wooden stud partitions instead of fireproof material.

The Commission therefore has framed a provision, setting forth clearly how such halls and stairs shall be constructed in accordance with the manifest intent of present law.

"SEC. 19. *Stair halls, continued.* In every non-fireproof tenement house hereafter erected all stair halls shall be enclosed on all sides with brick walls. The doors opening from stair halls shall be fireproof and self-closing, and if provided with glass such glass shall be good quality wire-glass. There shall be no transom or movable sash opening from a stair hall to any other part of the house. Except on the entrance floor, each stair hall shall be shut off from all non-fireproof portions of the public halls and from all other non-fireproof parts of the building, on each story, by self-closing fireproof doors, and if glass is used in such doors it shall be of good quality wire-glass."

In framing all these provisions regarding halls and stairs, the Commission has proceeded upon the theory that in tenement houses which are not fireproof, the stairs and all those portions of the building through which the tenants must pass in escaping from the building should be absolutely fireproof, and that such portions should be completely shut off from all non-fireproof parts of the building. The results of the two fires instanced in the Special Report on Tenement House Fires indicate clearly that this is essential. The present law requires this only for tenement houses over five stories in height, and where also there are as many as four families on a floor. We believe that it should apply to all tenement houses hereafter erected, whatever their height.

This was required by the law of this State as early as 1867, and it would seem that the law now, thirty-four years later, might at least give equal protection to human life.

"SEC. 20. *Entrance halls.* Every entrance hall in a tenement house hereafter erected shall be at least three feet six inches wide in the clear, from the entrance up to and including the stair enclosure, and beyond this point at least three feet wide in the clear. It shall be enclosed with brick walls, and shall comply with all the conditions of the preceding sections of this act as to the construction of stair halls. If such entrance hall is the only entrance to more than one flight of stairs, said hall shall be increased one foot in width in every part for each such additional flight of stairs. In every such house access shall be had from the street to the yard, either in a direct line or through a court."

The present law does not prescribe any minimum width for such halls; it is apparent, however, that this should be done. That this hall should be fireproof is required by the present law. The Commission is of opinion also that access should be had from street to yard so as to enable the firemen to have quick access to the rear of the building, and also to afford the tenants better means of egress in case of fire, as well as to secure more adequate ventilation.

"SEC. 21. *First tier of beams.* In all non-fireproof as well as fireproof tenement houses hereafter erected five stories or more in height, exclusive of the cellar, the first floor above the cellar, or, if there be no cellar, above the lowest story, shall be constructed fireproof with iron or steel beams and fireproof flooring; and the bottom flanges and all exposed portions of such iron or steel beams below the abutments of the floor arches or filling shall be entirely encased with hard-burnt clay or porous terra cotta or with metal lath properly secured and plastered on the under side. In all non-fireproof tenement houses hereafter erected less than five stories in height, where the first floor above the cellar, or, if there be no cellar, above the lowest story, is not constructed fireproof with iron or steel beams and fireproof flooring, the cellar ceiling of said tenement house shall be lathed with wire or metal lath, and plastered thereon with two coats of brown mortar of good materials."

This is the present law.

"SEC. 22. *Partitions, Construction of.* In all non-fireproof tenement houses hereafter erected, fore and aft stud partitions which rest directly over each other shall run through the wooden floor beams and rest upon the plate of the partition below, and shall have the studding filled in solid between the uprights to the depth of the floor beams with suitable incombustible materials. In all fireproof tenement houses hereafter erected, all partitions shall rest directly upon the fireproof floor construction, and extend to the fireproof beam filling above."

This is the present law. The Commission would have liked to have required that all partitions in new tenement houses should be solid and also fireproof. The advantages of such a form of construction are very great; it takes away one of the places where vermin may lodge, and also greatly reduces the danger from spread of fire. The Commission, however, in view of the additional expense that this would entail, have not seen their way clear to making such recommendation at the present time.

"SEC. 23. *Cellar stairs in non-fireproof buildings.* In non-fireproof tenement houses hereafter erected there shall be no inside stairs communicating between the cellar or other lowest story and the floor next above, but such stairs shall in every case be located outside the building, and if enclosed shall be constructed entirely fireproof and be enclosed in a fireproof enclosure with fireproof self-closing doors at all openings."

As one-quarter of all the fires originate in the cellars, and most of these at night, it is desirable that the cellars shall be completely shut off from the other parts of the building. The present law requires the cellar stairs to be located to the rear of the stairs leading to the upper stories, *when practicable.* This, however, has proved too indefinite a provision to accomplish the desired result. The Fire Department has for years urged the adoption of this provision, and its adoption was also recommended by the Tenement House Commission of 1894. The Commission believes that this requirement is desirable, as otherwise there would be a continuous shaft throughout the building for the spread of fire originating in the cellar. Moreover, they find that this is the present practice in the great majority of cases, so that it would work no hardship.

"SEC. 24. *Cellar stairs in fireproof buildings.* In every fireproof tenement house hereafter erected the stairs communicating between the cellar or other lowest story and the floor next above, if not located underneath the stairs leading to the upper stories, may be placed inside of the said building; provided, that the portion of the cellar or other lowest story into which said stairs lead is entirely shut off by fireproof walls from those portions thereof which are used for the storage of fuel, or in which heating appliances, boilers or machinery are located. All openings in such walls shall be provided with self-closing fireproof doors."

In fireproof buildings where the portions of the cellar containing inflammable material are completely shut off from the other portions of the building, cellar stairs inside the building, in the opinion of the Commission, may safely be permitted.

"SEC. 25. *Closet under first story stairs.* In non-fireproof tenement houses hereafter erected no closet of any kind shall be constructed under any staircase leading from the first story, exclusive of the cellar, to the upper stories, but such space shall be left entirely open and kept clear and free from encumbrance."

This has been the law of this State since 1892. The Commission believes, however, that it need not apply to buildings which are fireproof throughout.

"SEC. 26. *Cellar entrance.* In every tenement house hereafter erected there shall be an entrance to the cellar or other lowest story from the outside of the said building. In such tenement houses, unless the entire ceiling and floor above the cellar or other lowest story is constructed fireproof, all receptacles for fuel or storage in the cellar or other lowest story shall be constructed entirely of fireproof materials."

The object of this requirement is to assist firemen in fighting cellar fires, not only giving them quick access to the cellar, but also permitting the fire to be vented. Where the first floor above the cellar is not constructed fireproof the Commission is of opinion that all receptacles for fuel in the cellar should be constructed of fireproof material. So many cellar fires start in the wood-bins that it seems essential that this safeguard should be had. The law in 1867, thirty-four years ago, required this. The Board of Fire Underwriters have urged that this law be reënacted.

"SEC. 27. *Fire stops.* In tenement houses hereafter erected, in all walls all the courses of brick from the under side of the floor beams to the top of the same shall project a distance of at least two inches beyond the inside face of the wall so as to provide an effective fire stop; and wherever floor beams run parallel to a wall such beams shall always be kept at least two and one-half inches away from the inside line of the wall, and the space between the beams and the wall shall be built up solidly with brickwork from the under side of the floor beams to the top of the same so as to form an effective fire stop."

> The present law in this respect does not entirely meet the situation, not providing for cases where the beams are parallel to the wall. This requirement is necessary to prevent fire spreading quickly through the building, through air spaces, and feeding upon furring strips and other wooden material.

"SEC. 28. *Wooden tenement houses.* Within the fire limits of the city of New York no wooden tenement house shall hereafter be erected, and no wooden building not now used as a tenement house shall hereafter be altered or converted to such use. Outside of the fire limits, wooden tenement houses not exceeding two stories in height, exclusive of the cellar, may be erected, but shall not provide accommodations for, or be occupied by, more than four families in all, or more than two families on any floor; and such houses need not comply with the foregoing provisions of this act in reference to protection from fire nor with the provisions of Sections twenty-nine, thirty, thirty-one, thirty-two, thirty-six, thirty-seven and thirty-eight of this act."

> Since 1887 the law of this State has prohibited the erection of wooden buildings to be occupied by more than two families. This, however, applied only to the old city of New York before consolidation. The Commission is of opinion that this requirement should not apply to the outlying sections of the boroughs of Queens, Richmond, and even parts of Brooklyn and the Bronx, and has therefore recommended that tenement houses outside of the fire limits may be constructed of wood, provided that they do not exceed two stories in height, and are not occupied by more than four families in all, or by more than two families on any floor. In such cases, of course, none of the provisions of the law in regard to fireproof stairs, etc., should apply.

"TITLE 2. *Provisions applicable only to now existing tenement houses.*

"SEC. 29. *Fire escapes.* Every now existing non-fireproof tenement house, unless provided with fireproof outside stairways directly accessible to each apartment, shall have fire escapes located and constructed as described in Section twelve of this act. But a fire escape now erected upon such house shall be deemed sufficient except as provided in the next two sections.

"SEC. 30. *Fire escapes, continued.* In every now existing non-fireproof tenement house there shall be a separate fire escape directly accessible to each apartment, exclusive of fire escapes in air shafts and courts; and a party-wall fire escape balcony on the rear of the building connecting with the window of an adjoining building shall be deemed a sufficient fire escape only when the two buildings are completely separated by an unpierced fire wall throughout their entire height and length. All wooden floor slats and floors in fire escape balconies shall be replaced by proper iron slats or floors. No wooden balcony or wooden outside stairs shall be deemed part of a lawful fire escape.

"SEC. 31. *Fire escapes, continued.* Whenever a now existing non-fireproof tenement house is not provided with sufficient means of egress in case of fire the Department of Buildings may order such additional fire escapes or other means of egress as in its judgment may be necessary."

The views of the Commission in reference to this subject have been fully set forth under Section 12.

"SEC. 32. *Scuttles, bulkheads and ladders.* Every now existing tenement house shall have in the roof a bulkhead or scuttle constructed as in this section required. No scuttle shall be less in size than two feet by three feet, and all scuttles shall be covered on the outside with metal and shall be provided with stationary iron ladders or stairs leading thereto and easily accessible to all tenants of the building and kept free from encumbrance, and all scuttles and ladders shall be kept so as to be ready for use at all times. Every bulkhead shall be fireproof with a fireproof door to the same and shall have fireproof stairs with a guide or handrail leading to the roof, and such stairs shall be kept free from encumbrance at all times. No scuttle and no bulkhead door shall at any time be locked with a key, but either may be fastened on the inside by movable bolts or hooks."

This has practically been the law since 1852 in Brooklyn, and since 1862 in Manhattan.

"SEC. 33. *Stair halls, public halls and entrance halls.* If any now existing tenement house shall be so altered as to increase the number of rooms therein by twenty per centum or more, or if such building is increased in height, the entire stair halls, entrance halls and other public halls of the whole building shall be made to conform to the requirements of sections fourteen to twenty, inclusive, of this act."

It is of course proper that if an existing tenement house is enlarged or materially altered, it should comply in all essential particulars with the laws for new tenement houses. The law, however, should not apply to minor alterations, as this might prevent the owner of such a building from improving it. The Commission has, therefore, sought to draw the line at the point where the number of rooms in the building has been materially increased.

"SEC. 34. *Tenements damaged by fire.* If any now existing tenement house shall hereafter be damaged by fire or otherwise to an amount greater than one-half of the value thereof, exclusive of the value of the foundation, such building shall not be repaired or rebuilt except in conformity with the foregoing provisions of this act for the construction of tenement houses hereafter erected. If the stairs in any now existing tenement house shall be damaged by fire or otherwise to an amount greater than one-half of the value thereof, the entire stairs in the said tenement house shall be reconstructed in accordance with the provisions of this act for stairs in tenement houses hereafter erected."

Where a tenement house is only slightly damaged by fire, it is proper that the owner should be allowed to restore it to its original condition; where, however, the building is so damaged that the greater part of it has to be rebuilt, it should be rebuilt in accordance with the present laws. This method of determining the amount of damage is employed in the present building laws, and has been employed in former legislation upon this subject (Consol. Act, Sec. 497).

"TITLE 3. *Provisions applicable to all tenement houses hereafter erected or now existing.*

"SEC. 35. *Fire escapes.* All fire escapes hereafter constructed upon tenement houses shall be located and constructed as described in Section twelve of this act. The owner of every tenement house shall keep all the fire escapes thereon in good order and repair, and whenever rusty shall have them properly painted with two coats of paint. No person shall at any time place any encumbrance of any kind before or upon any such fire escape."

This is practically the present law with slight changes. The provision in reference to the encumbrance of fire escapes has been simplified.

"SEC. 36. *Stairways.* In every tenement house all stairways shall be provided with proper banisters and railings and kept in good repair."

This is the present law.

"SEC. 37. *Shafts.* All shafts hereafter constructed in tenement houses shall be constructed fireproof throughout, with fireproof self-closing doors at all openings, at each story, except window openings in vent shafts; and, if they extend to the cellar, shall also be enclosed in the cellar with fireproof walls and fireproof self-closing doors at all openings. In no case shall any shaft be constructed of materials in which any inflammable material or substance enters into any of the component parts. But nothing in this section contained shall be so construed as to require such enclosures about elevators or dumb-waiters in the well-hole of stairs where the stairs themselves are enclosed in brick or stone walls, and are entirely constructed of fireproof materials as hereinbefore provided."

This, with one exception, is the present law, and has been the law of this State since 1887. The exception is that the present law does not require dumb-waiter shafts to be fireproof if they extend only through three stories of a building. Every person who made recommendations to the Commission on this subject urged that all dumb-waiter shafts should be fireproof throughout. The necessity of such a requirement cannot be doubted.

"Sec. 38. *Plastering behind wainscoting.* When wainscoting is hereafter placed in any tenement house, or any building in process of alteration into a tenement house, the surface of the wall or partition behind such wainscoting shall be plastered down to the floor line, and any intervening space between said plastering and said wainscot shall be filled in solid with incombustible material."

This has been the law since 1892.

"Sec. 39. *Wooden buildings on same lot with a tenement house.* No wooden building of any kind whatsoever shall hereafter be placed or built upon the same lot with a tenement house within the fire limits of the City of New York."

The present law permits wooden sheds of a certain size and wooden outhouses to be constructed even within the fire limits. Where the danger from fire affects so many lives, no reasonable precaution should be omitted that will reduce this danger.

"Sec. 40. *Combustible materials.* No tenement house, nor any part thereof, shall be used as a place of storage for any combustible article except under such conditions as may be prescribed by the Fire Department of the City of New York, under authority of a written permit issued by said department. No tenement house, nor any part thereof, shall be used as a place of storage for any article dangerous to life or health, nor for the storage of feed, hay, straw, excelsior or cotton, nor for the storage or handling of rags."

This is with certain changes the present law, and also what has been the law of this State since 1862. The changes are as follows: The Charter permits the storage of feed, hay, and straw in a tenement house, under conditions laid down by the Fire Department. The Commission believes that this should be absolutely prohibited. The Commission has, however, not forbidden the storage of combustible articles in tenement houses under appropriate rules of the Fire Department, as it would obviously be unfair to prohibit the sale of kerosene oil in a grocery store which might be in a tenement house.

"Sec. 41. *Bakeries and fat boiling.* No bakery and no place of business in which fat is boiled shall be maintained in any tenement house which is not fireproof throughout, unless the ceiling and side walls of said bakery or of the said place where fat boiling is done are made safe by fireproof materials around the same, and there shall be no openings either by door or window, dumb-waiter shafts or otherwise, between said bakery or said place where fat is boiled in any tenement house and the other parts of the said building."

This is the present law slightly changed, as the verbiage of the latter was somewhat ambiguous.

"Sec. 42. *Other dangerous businesses.* All transoms and windows opening into halls from any portion of a tenement house where paint, oil, spirituous liquors or drugs are stored for the purpose of sale or otherwise, shall be glazed with wire-glass or they shall be removed and closed up as solidly as the rest of the wall; and all doors leading into any such hall from such portion of said house shall be made fireproof."

This is the present law, except that the present law limits this requirement to stores on the first floor. It is apparent that the danger is even greater where there are such stores in the basement.

"CHAPTER III. LIGHT AND VENTILATION

"TITLE 1. *Provisions applicable only to tenement houses hereafter erected.*

"SEC. 51. *Percentage of lot occupied.* No tenement house hereafter erected shall occupy more than ninety per centum of a corner lot, or more than seventy per centum of any other lot, the measurements in all cases to be taken at the ground level; provided, that the space occupied by fire escapes of the size hereinbefore prescribed shall not be deemed a part of the lot occupied."

The law since 1879 has limited the percentage of lot permitted to be occupied on an interior lot to 65 per cent, but discretionary power has been given to different officials to modify this requirement in special cases, except for about a year in 1891–1892, when such discretionary power was withdrawn. In 1895 the amount of space to be occupied was limited to 65 per cent, but discretionary power was given to the Superintendent of Buildings to permit 75 per cent to be occupied "where the light and ventilation of the building was materially improved." The result has been that in ninety-nine cases out of a hundred, this discretion has been exercised, and the exception has become the rule. The Commission finds that the practice at the present time is to build on 75 per cent of the lot. The Commission therefore renews the recommendation made by the Tenement House Committee of 1894 that no more than 70 per cent of the lot be permitted to be occupied in the case of an interior lot, and no more than 90 per cent in the case of a corner lot. The Commission believes that this will be adequate in view of the other provisions made elsewhere in this Code for courts and other open spaces.

"SEC. 52. *Height.* The height of no tenement house hereafter erected shall by more than one-third exceed the width of the widest street upon which it stands. Such height shall be the perpendicular distance measured in a straight line from the curb level to the highest point of the building exclusive of cornices and bulkheads, provided such bulkheads are not more than eight feet high and do not exceed in area ten per centum of the area of the roof; the measurements in all cases shall be taken through the centre of the façade of the house."

The laws of this State have recognized since 1885 that the height of buildings of this kind should be regulated by the width of the street on which they face. The law of 1885, Chapter 454, limited the height of such buildings to 70 feet where the streets were 60 feet or less in width, and to 80 feet on streets over 60 feet in width. This remained the law of this State for twelve years, and should, in the opinion of this Commission, be the law to-day. By the law of 1897, however, buildings were allowed to be erected to a height of 150 feet upon streets 80 feet or over in width and to a height of 100 feet on streets less than 80 feet in width.

While the Commission would like to limit the height of tenement houses, including apartment houses, to the limits prescribed by the law of 1885, it appreciates that this is rather a part of the general problem of high buildings than of the tenement house problem in particular, and that it would be manifestly illogical to limit an apartment house to 80 feet, while a hotel or an apartment hotel would still be permitted to be erected to a height of 150 feet. The Commission believes, however, that high buildings, particularly in residential quarters, are a serious detriment to the welfare of the city from every point of view, and that their height should be further restricted. It would call attention to the fact that the law in Washington requires that no building shall exceed in height the width of the street in front, and that residence buildings shall never be over 90 feet high. In Europe the requirements upon this subject are much more stringent than in this country. In Manchester, England, where the street is not over 30 feet in width the buildings are not allowed to exceed two stories in height, while on streets between 30 and 36 feet in width dwelling houses may be three stories high.

In Liverpool the height of no dwelling house may exceed the width of the street upon which it faces; and it is further provided that no house built on a court shall be of a greater height than 30 feet nor contain more than two stories above the ground floor.

In Edinburgh no house may exceed one and one-fourth times the width of the street or court upon which it faces, and no house shall in any case exceed 60 feet in height without the consent of the local authorities.

In Glasgow the law requires that the height of dwelling houses shall not be greater than the width of the street on which they face. In the laws of Berlin there is a similar requirement.

In Paris the height of dwelling houses is determined by the width of the street. For houses on streets of 24 feet or less in width the building shall not exceed a height of 39 feet. Where the street is not over 32 feet in width the height of the building is limited to 50 feet; where the street is 65 feet in width the height of the building is limited to 65 feet. The Paris law also prohibits any building from containing more than seven stories above the ground floor.

"Sec. 53. *Yards.* Behind every tenement house hereafter erected there shall be a yard extending across the entire width of the lot and at every point open from the ground to the sky unobstructed, except that fire escapes or unenclosed outside stairs may project not over three feet from the rear line of the house. The depth of said yard, measured from the extreme rear wall of the house to the rear line of the lot, shall be as set forth in the two following sections.

"SEC. 54. *Yards of interior lots.* Except upon a corner lot the depth of the yard behind every tenement house hereafter erected sixty feet in height shall be not less than twelve feet in every part. Said yard shall be increased in depth one foot for every additional twelve feet of height of the building, or fraction thereof; and may be decreased in depth one foot for every twelve feet of height of the building less than sixty feet; but it shall never be less than ten feet in depth in any part."

Since the passage of the first tenement house law in 1867, the law has required that there shall be a yard space of 10 feet at the rear of the building. This law was framed at a time when the majority of the tenement houses in the city were three stories high, only a few as much as four stories in height, and practically none higher. Such houses then accommodated about eight families in each. It is obvious, therefore, that a yard space which was sufficient for a building three stories high is not sufficient for a building six stories in height, and that such yard space should increase proportionately with the increase in the height of the building. The Commission therefore recommends that the depth of the yard for a building six stories high shall be not less than 12 feet, and that this space shall be increased in proportion as the building increases in height, and shall be decreased to a minimum of 10 feet in proportion as the building is lower. The Commission would have preferred to recommend that such yards should be at least 15 feet in depth, but refrains from so doing from practical and commercial considerations.

In connection with this subject of yard space, it is important to note what the laws are in European cities upon this subject.

In Manchester the law requires that the yard shall have a minimum depth of 10 feet, and that for buildings 35 feet in height this yard space shall be 25 feet in depth. The law in Liverpool requires that where houses are between 20 and 30 feet in height the depth of the yard must be 10 feet, and that where houses exceed 30 feet in height the yard space must be 15 feet. In Edinburgh the law requires that the yard space at the rear must be equal to three-fourths of the area to be occupied by the building in cases where the building is not more than four stories in height, and where the building is more than four stories in height then the yard space must be equal in area to the area of the house. In other leading European cities there are similar provisions.

"SEC. 55. *Yards of corner lots.* The depth of the yard behind every tenement house hereafter erected upon a corner lot shall be not less than ten feet in every part."

Since 1867 the law has made no distinction between corner lots and other lots in regard to the amount of yard space, requiring a minimum space of 10 feet, but giving to the officials charged with the enforcement of the law the right to lessen or modify this distance in special cases. In 1880 the law for the first time limited this discretion to corner lots, but not until 1895 was any other difference made between interior and corner lots. The law of 1895 provided that the yard space on corner lots should not be less than 5 feet in depth, and that such yard space might start at the second story. It is to be borne in mind that the open space on corner lots is the only means of securing through ventilation in the interior of the block, and that unless such open spaces are left there will simply be a stagnant well of vitiated air inside of the block, which has very little opportunity of being renewed. The law in Edinburgh requires that a clear opening 15 feet wide shall be left at two opposite points of the block to furnish through ventilation, and the law in Glasgow is similar. The Commission, therefore, has recommended that the yard space should start at the ground or curb level, and not be permitted to start at the second story. The present law so provides. The law of 1895 permitted the yard space for a corner lot to start at the second story; the Charter, however, changed this so as to require the yard space to start at the ground level.

"SEC. 56. *Yard spaces of lots running through from street to street.* Wherever a tenement house hereafter erected is upon a lot which runs through from one street to another street, and said lot is not less than seventy feet nor more than one hundred feet in depth, there shall be a yard space through the centre of the lot midway between the two streets, which space shall extend across the full width of the lot and shall never be less than twelve feet in depth from wall to wall; but where the ground floor of such building is used or intended to be used as a store, such yard space may start at the second tier of beams. Where such lot is over one hundred feet in depth such yard space shall conform to the provisions of section sixty-two of this act for inner courts, and shall be left through the centre of the lot midway between the two streets."

There is no provision in the present law upon this subject, and the Commission finds that in some cases the Department of Buildings has permitted buildings of this kind to cover the entire lot, making allowance for air shafts, but leaving no yard space of any kind. It is apparent that under certain conditions this may be permitted. In other cases, however, an open space should certainly be left. The Commission, therefore, has framed a provision to meet such cases.

"SEC. 57. *Courts.* No court of a tenement house hereafter erected shall be covered by a roof or skylight, but every such court shall be at every point open from the ground to the sky unobstructed, and shall conform to the requirements of the following sections: provided, that an apartment not containing any room fronting upon the street or yard may have a fire escape in a court, projecting not more than three feet from the wall of the house."

Prior to 1895 the law did not prohibit the covering over of a court. The law of 1895 forbade this in the case of a court less than ten square feet in area, and such a space was deemed not to be part of the free air space, but was considered part of the building. This is the present law upon this subject. The Commission recommends that no court shall be allowed to be roofed over under any circumstances.

"SEC. 58. *Outer courts.* Where one side of an outer court is situated on the lot line, the width of the said court, measured from the lot line to the opposite wall of the building, for tenement houses sixty feet in height shall not be less than six feet in any part; and for every twelve feet of increase or fraction thereof in the height of the said building, such width shall be increased six inches throughout the entire height of said court; and for every twelve feet of decrease in the height of the said building below sixty feet, such width may be decreased six inches, but no such court shall be less than four feet six inches wide in any part."

The Commission recommends that the present air shafts be prohibited in all future tenement houses, as they are of no value in supplying either light or air, but, on the contrary, are a serious detriment to the building. The evidence upon this point is overwhelming. In place of air shafts the Commission would recommend that the provisions of the laws in Buffalo and Philadelphia be followed, and that courts sufficiently large to secure adequate light and ventilation to all rooms be provided. The Commission has therefore sought to establish a principle regulating the size of such courts, and in doing so has based its conclusions largely upon a law already found in existence in the cities of Buffalo and Philadelphia, which has worked in practice admirably. The Commission, therefore, at the start has distinguished between open courts or outer courts and closed courts or inner courts; that is, between courts open on one entire side, and thus permitting the circulation of air and the admission of sunlight from street or yard, and courts that are entirely enclosed on all four sides by the building. It is apparent that the size of all courts should bear a definite relation to the height of the building, just as the height of the building should be regulated by the width of the street. The Commission has provided that such width shall be increased in proportion as the building increases in height, and may be similarly decreased as the building is less in height. The Commission also believes it desirable to distinguish between outer courts which may be situated on the lot line and outer courts between wings of the same building. Where such a court is situated on the lot line, it is not only possible but very probable that the owner of the adjoining property will leave a similar court so as to secure the advantage of a larger space. The Commission, therefore, has recommended that the minimum width of such courts shall be 6 feet for a building 60 feet in height, and that the court shall be increased 6 inches in width for every additional 12 feet of height. Such a method of increase is already recognized in principle by the present regulations of the Department of Buildings, which require air shafts to be increased 4 inches in width for each story above the fifth story.

"SEC. 59. *Outer courts, continued.* Where an outer court is situated between wings or parts of the same building, or between different buildings on the same lot, the width of the said court, measured from wall to wall, for tenement houses sixty feet in height shall not be less than twelve feet in any part; and for every twelve feet of increase or fraction thereof in the height of the said building, such width shall be increased one foot throughout the entire height of the said court; and for every twelve feet of decrease in the height of the said building below sixty feet, such width of the said court may be decreased 1 foot, but no such court shall ever be less than nine feet in width in any part."

Where an outer court is located between wings of a building it is apparent that the court should be twice as wide as in the case where it is situated on the lot line. In such cases the Commission has provided that the minimum width of such court shall be 12 feet for buildings 60 feet in height, with a provision that the width shall increase 1 foot for every additional 12 feet in height of the building.

This provision is almost identical with the provision of the Philadelphia law, which requires that an outer court on the lot line shall be 8 feet as a minimum width, and where such court is between wings of a building shall be not less than 12 feet in width. The Buffalo law requires that outer courts shall be at least 8 feet wide for a building four stories in height and 1 foot wider for each additional story above four stories.

The law in Berlin requires that the width of such a court shall be at least 8 feet, and that where there are windows opening upon a court (the equivalent of our court between wings) such court shall be 20 feet in width.

"SEC. 60. *Outer courts, continued.* Wherever an outer court changes its initial horizontal direction, or wherever any part of such court extends in a direction so as not to receive direct light from the street or yard, the length of such portion of said court shall never exceed the width of said portion; such length to be measured from the point at which the change of direction commences. Wherever an outer court is less in depth than the minimum width prescribed by this section, then its width may be equal to, but not less than its depth, provided that such width is never less than four feet in the clear. This exception shall also apply to each offset or recess in outer courts. And no window except windows of water-closet compartments, bathrooms or halls shall open upon any offset or recess less than six feet in its least dimension."

This section has been framed to provide for cases where an outer court might suddenly change its direction and extend in a direction parallel to the street for a considerable length, being almost in such cases the equivalent of an inner court, and not receiving direct light from the street. It is apparent that in such cases such portions of the court should be materially increased in width. An attempt has also been made in this section to provide for cases in which it might be desired to have a very shallow street court or yard court simply to light one or more rooms, and which might not be greater than 8 feet in depth. It would obviously be unfair to require such a court to be 12 feet wide, and the Commission has therefore provided in this section for such contingencies.

"SEC. 61. *Inner courts.* Where one side of an inner court is situated on the lot line, the width of the said court measured from the lot line to the opposite wall of the building, for tenement houses sixty feet in height shall not be less than twelve feet in any part, and its other horizontal dimension shall not be less than twenty-four feet in any part; and for every twelve feet of increase or fraction thereof in the height of the said building, such width shall be increased six inches throughout the entire height of said court, and the other horizontal dimension shall be increased one foot throughout the entire height of said court; and for every twelve feet of decrease in the height of the said building below sixty feet, such width may be decreased six inches and the other horizontal dimension may be decreased one foot, but no such court shall be less than ten and a half feet in width in any part, nor less than twenty-one feet in its other horizontal dimension."

In regard to inner courts, or courts enclosed on all four sides, the Commission has sought to provide that such courts shall be of a size sufficient to provide adequate light and ventilation. There has been a decided sentiment in the community against these courts, and the Commission has been urged to prohibit them entirely. This, however, would not be expedient, as such courts when of a sufficient size are adequate for purposes of light and ventilation. Where such a court is situated on the lot line the Commission has recommended that the minimum width of the court from the lot line to the building shall be 12 feet and its other least dimension shall be 24 feet, these minima being prescribed for a building 60 feet in height. If the owner of the adjoining property repeats an inner court of similar dimensions on his lot, as he is likely to do, it would give a large court 24 feet by 24 feet. In determining the other minimum dimension of this court the Commission has adopted the principle of the law passed in 1867, which prescribed the distance between front and rear tenement houses, requiring a distance of 25 feet where the buildings were over three stories in height. It is apparent that the inner court should be treated in exactly the same way as the space between a front and rear tenement house, and that the distance between the two wings of a building should not be appreciably less than that provided in the case of front and rear tenements. The Commission has provided that all inner courts shall increase in both dimensions as the building increases in height beyond 60 feet, and may similarly be decreased in both dimensions for a corresponding decrease in height.

"SEC. 62. *Inner courts, continued.* Where an inner court is not situated upon the lot line, but is enclosed on all four sides, the least horizontal dimension of the said court for tenement houses sixty feet in height, shall not be less than twenty-four feet; and for every twelve feet of increase or fraction thereof in the height of the said building, the said court shall be increased one foot in each horizontal dimension, throughout the entire height of said court; and for every twelve feet of decrease in the height of the said building below sixty feet, the horizontal dimensions of the said court may be decreased one foot in each direction, but no such court shall ever be less than twenty-one feet in its least horizontal dimension. Offsets or recesses in inner courts will be permitted, but where the depth of such offset or recess is less than the minimum width prescribed, then the width of said offset or recess may be equal to but not less than its depth, provided that such width is never less than four feet in the clear. And no window except windows of water-closet compartments, bath rooms or halls shall open upon any offset or recess less than six feet in its least dimension."

Where an inner court is enclosed on four sides, it is apparent that its width should be equal to twice the width of such a court where it is situated on the lot line. The Commission has, therefore, provided for minimum dimensions, with a requirement that both dimensions of such court shall increase in proportion to the height of the building.

"Sec. 63. *Inner courts, continued.* Every inner court shall be provided with one or more horizontal intakes or ducts at the bottom. Said intakes or ducts shall be not less in total area than four per centum of the area of said inner court. Each such intake or duct shall be at least five square feet in area, and shall always communicate directly with the street or yard. Wherever the said intakes or ducts consist of a passageway or passageways, such passageway shall be left open, or if not open there shall always be provided in said passageway or passageways open grilles or transoms of a size not less than five square feet each, and such open grilles or transoms shall never be covered over by glass or in any other way. There shall be at least two such grilles or transoms in each such passageway, one at the inner court and the other at the street or yard, as the case may be."

Where large inner courts have been used in tenement houses, it has been found that, while they may adequately light the rooms, they do not provide adequate ventilation unless there is some means of creating a draught; that otherwise the air simply remains stagnant within the four walls. The Commission has, therefore, required that there shall always be at the bottom of such court a horizontal intake or duct to provide a circulation of air.

"Sec. 64. *Outer and inner courts.* Nothing contained in the foregoing sections concerning outer and inner courts shall be construed as preventing windows at the angles of said courts, provided that the running length of the wall containing such windows does not exceed six feet. In construing said sections the height of the building is to be measured from the curb level to the top of the highest wall enclosing or forming such court."

The present law does not provide for the turning of a corner in a court making an angle. According to the present practice, this is permitted. It is important that the law should state clearly what may be done in such cases.

"SEC. 65. *Rear tenements.* No separate tenement house shall hereafter be erected upon the rear of a lot fifty feet or less in width where there is a tenement house on the front of the said lot, nor upon the front of any such lot upon the rear of which there is such a tenement house."

While the tenement house law has never hitherto forbidden in terms the erection of a rear tenement house, it has practically prohibited it by prescribing the distance that shall be maintained between the front and rear buildings.

"SEC. 66. *Buildings on same lot with tenement houses.* If any building is hereafter placed on the same lot with a tenement house the space between the said buildings shall always be of such size and arranged in such manner as is prescribed in Section sixty-two of this act for inner courts; and no building of any kind shall be hereafter placed upon the same lot with a tenement house so as to decrease the minimum size of courts or yards as hereinbefore prescribed. And if any tenement house is hereafter erected upon any lot upon which there is already another building, it shall comply with all of the provisions of this act, and in addition the space between the said building and the said tenement house shall be of such size and arranged in such manner as is prescribed in Section sixty-two of this act for inner courts, the height of the highest building on the lot to regulate the dimensions."

It is, of course, essential that if proper open spaces and courts are provided for new tenement houses, they shall be kept open, and shall not at some future date be encroached upon. It is also important to provide for the case of two buildings being erected on the same lot. It is apparent that in such cases the space between the buildings is exactly the same as an inner court, and should be so treated in the law. The provisions in this section as to the distance between such buildings are in this regard practically the provisions of the first Tenement House Act of 1867, which have been continued in all subsequent legislation.

"SEC. 67. *Rooms, lighting and ventilating of.* In every tenement house hereafter erected every room, except water-closet compartments and bathrooms, shall have at least one window opening directly upon the street or upon a yard or court."

The law since 1879 has required that every living room or room used for sleeping purposes shall have at least one window admitting light and air directly from the public street or yard, and this provision has been reënacted in all subsequent legislation. It is the present law upon this subject, the Charter requiring that in all new tenement houses each room must have a separate window opening into the outer air. In the case of water-closet compartments and bathrooms, while it is desirable, the Commission does not feel that it is essential that such rooms should in every case open upon courts of a size prescribed in this act, and has therefore made an exception in these cases.

"Sec. 68. *Windows in rooms.* In every tenement house hereafter erected the total window area in each room, except water-closet compartments and bathrooms, shall be at least one-tenth of the superficial area of the room, and the top at least of one window shall not be less than seven feet six inches above the floor, and the upper half of it shall be made so as to open the full width. No such window shall be less than twelve square feet in area between the stop beads."

This is the present law and what has been the law in this State since 1867.

"Sec. 69. *Windows in water-closet compartments and bathrooms.* In every tenement house hereafter erected the total window area in a water-closet compartment or bathroom shall not be less than three square feet in area for each, and no such window shall be less than one foot in width, measured between stop beads."

This is the present requirement of the Building Department.

"Sec. 70. *Rooms, size of.* In every tenement house hereafter erected all rooms, except water-closet compartments and bathrooms, shall be of the following minimum sizes: In each apartment there shall be at least one room containing not less than one hundred and twenty square feet of floor area, and each other room shall contain at least seventy square feet of floor area. Each room shall be in every part not less than nine feet high from the finished floor to the finished ceiling; provided that an attic room need be nine feet high in but one-half its area."

The law has never prescribed a minimum size for rooms; it has, however, prescribed a minimum height and a minimum cubic air space for the persons occupying them, which should practically have the same effect. The Commission finds that the more practical method of enforcing a requirement as to the amount of cubic air space is by prescribing a minimum size of room. Moreover, the rooms in new tenement houses have become so small that it is now necessary to lay down minimum dimensions. The Commission has, therefore, recommended that such minimum dimensions be established, and that no room used for sleeping purposes be less than 70 square feet in floor area. In regard to the height of rooms, the Commission finds that the present law provides in one place for a minimum height of 7 feet, in another place for a minimum height of 8 feet, and the regulations of the Building Department provide for a minimum height of 9 feet 4 inches, the present practice being to construct rooms of the height of 9 feet and 4 inches. The Commission thinks that it is unnecessary to make so great a height as 9 feet and 4 inches compulsory, and therefore recommends that not more than 9 feet be required.

"Sec. 71. *Alcoves.* In every tenement house hereafter erected where any room adjoins another room, and has eighty per centum or more of one entire side open to the other room, and there is no door between, it shall be considered as part of the said room. Under other circumstances every alcove shall be deemed a separate room for all purposes within the meaning of this act."

The present law makes no provision for alcove rooms, although the Building Department requires that alcove rooms must comply with all the requirements of other rooms. As an alcove room is not defined, it becomes a nice question at times where to draw the line. The Commission has therefore sought to establish such a point of division.

"SEC. 72. *Public halls.* In every tenement house hereafter erected every public hall shall have at least one window opening directly upon the street or upon a yard or court. Either such window shall be at the end of said hall, with the plane of the window at right angles to the axis of the said hall, or there shall be at least one window opening directly upon the street or upon a yard or court for every twenty feet in length or fraction thereof of said hall. In such halls recesses or returns the length of which does not exceed twice the width of the hall will be permitted without an additional window. But wherever the length of such recess or return exceeds twice the width of the hall the above provisions in reference to one window for every twenty feet of hallway shall be applied. Any part of a hall which is shut off from any other part of said hall by a door or doors shall be deemed a separate hall within the meaning of this section."

Since the very beginning of tenement house legislation the evils of the dark, unventilated hallways have been thoroughly recognized, and efforts have been made to correct these evils. The very first law, that of 1867, provides: "That the halls on each floor shall open directly to the external air with suitable windows and shall have no room or other obstruction at the end unless sufficient light or ventilation is otherwise provided for in a manner approved by the Board of Health." This provision has been reënacted in all subsequent legislation upon this subject and is part of the present law. A further provision was added in 1887, that if the halls of such a house did not open directly to the external air with suitable windows at the ends of the halls, the building should not be used or occupied unless sufficient light and ventilation is otherwise provided. The Commission finds that these two important provisions of the law have practically never been enforced, and that most serious evils have resulted from the lack of their enforcement. The Commission also finds that in new tenement houses constructed during the past few years a great number of the buildings have been erected with totally dark halls. It has therefore provided in its recommendations that every *public* hall shall have at least one window opening either on the street or a yard or upon an adequate court, and that the window shall be located in such part of the hall as to secure sufficient light and ventilation.

"SEC. 73. *Windows for public halls, size of.* In every tenement house hereafter erected one at least of the windows provided to light each public hall or part thereof shall be at least two feet six inches wide and five feet high, measured between stop beads."

The tenement house law has never provided a minimum size of window for halls, although it has provided a minimum size for windows in rooms. It is obvious that what is necessary in the case of rooms is necessary in the case of halls.

"SEC. 74. *Windows for stair halls, size of.* In every tenement house hereafter erected the aggregate area of windows to light or ventilate stair halls shall be at least twenty-one square feet for each floor. There shall be provided for each story at least one of said windows, which shall be at least three feet wide and five feet high, measured between the stop beads."

A similar requirement is necessary for the windows which light and ventilate the public stairs of buildings.

"SEC. 75. *Privacy.* In every apartment of three or more rooms in a tenement house hereafter erected, access to every room including bathrooms and water-closet compartments, shall be had without passing through any bedroom."

The law has never required any provision for privacy in a tenement house. The Building Department regulations, however, have provided for some years that access to all rooms must be direct without passing through a bedroom. The Commission recommends that this requirement be embodied in the law, as it is obvious that it is not conducive to morality or decency to make it necessary for people to pass through a bedroom in order to reach the water-closet.

"TITLE 2. *Provisions applicable only to now existing tenement houses.*

"SEC. 76. *Percentage of lot occupied.* No now existing tenement house shall hereafter be enlarged, or its lot be diminished, so that the house occupy more than ninety per centum of a corner lot, or more than seventy per centum of any other lot, the measurements in all cases to be taken at the ground level; provided that the space occupied by fire escapes of the size hereinbefore prescribed shall not be deemed a part of the lot occupied."

It is, of course, desirable that existing tenement houses shall not be allowed to be altered so as to cover a greater percentage of the lot than would be permitted in the case of new tenement houses.

"SEC. 77. *Yards.* No now existing tenement house shall hereafter be enlarged or its lot be diminished, so that the yard shall be less than five feet in depth when the building is on a corner lot or less than twelve feet in depth in other cases, the measurements in all cases to be taken from the extreme rear wall of the building to the rear lot line, and across the full width of the lot, and such yard shall be at every point open from the ground to the sky, except as provided in Section fifty-three of this act."

It is apparent that in existing tenement houses the present yard space should not be allowed to be encroached upon by extending the buildings beyond the limits provided in the case of new tenement houses.

"SEC. 78. *Additional rooms and halls.* Any additional room or hall that is hereafter constructed or created in a now existing tenement house shall comply in all respects with the provisions of the foregoing sections of this chapter as to the size, arrangement, light and ventilation of rooms and halls in tenement houses hereafter erected."

Previous tenement house laws have in a great majority of their provisions applied to buildings that might be altered, as well as to buildings that might be thereafter erected. It is manifestly unjust to require that if the owner of a tenement house wishes to make some slight alteration in his building, which will materially improve it, he must comply with all the provisions of the law relating to the construction of new tenement houses. If, on the other hand, however, the owner of an existing tenement house desires to add any rooms or halls to his building, it is, of course, proper that the different halls and rooms thus added should comply with the provisions of the law in reference to halls and rooms in new tenement houses, otherwise the owner of a building might extend his building to almost any distance and evade the provisions of the law in regard to light and ventilation in new tenement houses.

"SEC. 79. *Rooms, lighting and ventilation of, continued.* No room in a now existing tenement house shall hereafter be occupied for living purposes unless it shall have a window upon the street, or upon a yard not less than five feet deep, or upon a court or shaft of not less than twenty-five square feet in area, open to the sky without roof or skylight, or unless such room has a sash window opening into an adjoining room in the same apartment which itself has a window opening on the street, or on a yard not less than five feet deep, said sash window having at least fifteen square feet of glazed surface, being at least three feet high and five feet wide between stop beads, and at least one-half thereof being made to open readily. Furthermore, no room in a now existing tenement house which does not have a window opening directly upon the street or upon a yard not less than five feet deep or upon a court or shaft of not less than twenty-five square feet in area open to the sky without roof or skylight shall hereafter be occupied for living purposes unless such room contains at least sixty square feet of floor area, and also at least six hundred cubic feet of air space; and no such room shall be so occupied unless there is six hundred cubic feet of air to each individual occupying the same. No such room shall be so occupied unless it be in every part not less than eight feet high from the finished floor to the finished ceiling; provided, that an attic room need be eight feet high in but half its area."

There are in this city a number of old, insanitary tenement houses containing small, dark rooms without any means of light or ventilation to the outer air. In some cases these rooms communicate with an adjoining room which opens to the street or to the yard, and in other cases there are even as many as three or four rooms in a line, only one of which communicates with the outer air. As the law since 1879 has required that every living room in a tenement house thereafter erected should have a window opening directly to the outer air, it is apparent that these buildings have for more than twenty years been violating fundamental sanitary rules. The public health demands that these rooms shall either be made fit for human habitation or shall not be used for living purposes. The Commission, therefore, has recommended that no room in an existing tenement house shall be occupied for living purposes unless it has proper means of ventilation. Where such a room has no window to the outer air, but adjoins a room which has such communication, then if a glass partition with a movable sash of sufficient size is provided between the two rooms the Commission believes that the inner room may be permitted to be occupied, but such inner room then must contain at least 60 square feet of floor area, and also at least 600 cubic feet of air space for each occupant.

"SEC. 80. *Public halls, lighting of.* In every now existing tenement house four stories or over in height, whenever a public hall on any floor is not light enough in the daytime to permit a person to read in every part thereof without the aid of artificial light, the wooden panels in the doors located at the ends of the public halls and opening into rooms shall be removed, and ground glass or wire glass panels of an aggregate area of not less than four square feet for each door shall be substituted; or in lieu of removing the panels in the doors a fixed sash window of wire glass of an area of not less than five square feet may be cut into the partitions separating the said hall from a room which opens directly upon the street or upon a yard, court, or shaft of the dimensions specified in the last section; or said public hall may be lighted by a window or windows at the end thereof with the plane of the window at right angles to the axis of the said hall, said window opening upon the street or upon a yard, court, or shaft of said dimensions."

Allusion has already been made to the very serious evils of dark halls, and the grave moral evils as well as the evils from the point of view of sanitation and health. The Tenement House Commission appointed by the Legislature in 1894 sought to remedy these evils by recommending that in dark hallways a light should be kept burning in each hall from sunrise until ten o'clock at night. The Commission finds that this law is a dead letter; that the hallways in most of the tenement houses in this city are pitch-black, and that in hardly any case is a light kept burning in the daytime. It is apparent that such a law must be very difficult of enforcement even if the Department of Health had a large force of inspectors, as it is very simple for the owner or janitor to turn out the light after the inspector's back is turned, so that really to enforce the law an army of inspectors would be needed. The Commission has therefore sought to substitute a provision which, when once enforced, will stay enforced. It recommends that the wooden panels in the doors leading from the public halls to the rooms shall be taken out, and that ground glass or wire glass panels shall be substituted; or, in lieu of this, a proper window shall be cut into the hall at the end communicating with the outer air. This will involve only a comparatively slight expense, and will accomplish great improvement in the condition of the hallways. It is a method that has been often adopted, and has worked admirably in the construction of new tenement houses, and in many of the old tenements.

"SEC. 81. *Light and vent shafts in existing buildings.* Any shaft used or intended to be used to light or ventilate rooms used or intended to be used for living purposes, and which may be hereafter placed in a now existing tenement house, shall not be less in area than twenty-five square feet, nor less than four feet in width in any part, and such shaft shall under no circumstances be roofed or covered over at the top with a roof or skylight; but if such shaft is provided at the bottom with a horizontal intake or duct, of a size not less than two square feet, and communicating directly with the street or yard, such shaft may be of a size not less than three feet by five feet, provided that not more than two rooms on any floor open thereon, and that if it be used to light or ventilate any living room no water-closet open upon it."

The Commission realizes that the owners of existing tenement houses may desire to put in an air shaft in order to light and ventilate rooms which may now be totally without light or ventilation. If such shafts are hereafter placed in an existing building, it is entirely proper that they should conform to the minimum size laid down in the present law, and the Commission has prepared this section so as to encourage such improvements in old tenement houses.

"TITLE 3. *Provisions applicable to all tenement houses hereafter erected or now existing.*

"SEC. 82. *Public Halls.* In every tenement house a proper light shall be kept burning by the owner in the public hallways, near the stairs, upon the entrance floor, and upon the second floor above the entrance floor of said house, every night from sunset to sunrise throughout the year, and upon all other floors of the said house from sunset until ten o'clock in the evening."

The present law requires that a light shall be kept burning in all hallways from sunset until ten P.M. The Fire Department has requested that this law be changed so as to require a light to be kept burning on every floor all night, claiming that many tenement house fires are caused by persons coming home late at night, lighting matches in the halls and throwing them down half-extinguished. For reasons of morality, as well as for the ordinary comfort of tenement dwellers, it is essential that halls in the tenement houses be kept lighted a reasonable time. The Commission has not followed the entire recommendation of the Fire Department because of the expense involved, but has recommended that the hall on the entrance floor and the hall two flights above shall be kept lighted all night, and that in the other hallways lights shall be kept burning until ten P.M.

"SEC. 83. *Skylights.* In every tenement house there shall be in the roof, directly over each stair well, a ventilating skylight with both ridge ventilators and fixed louvres, the glazed surface thereof to be not less than twenty-five square feet in area."

The law since 1867 has required that in every tenement house there shall be an adequate and proper ventilating skylight. It has not, however, specified the size of such skylight, but left it to the discretion of the Commissioner of Buildings. The Commission believes that it is proper that a minimum size be specified in the statute.

"SEC. 84. *Chimneys or fire places.* In every tenement house there shall be adequate chimneys running through every floor with an open fire place or grate, or place for a stove, properly connected with one of said chimneys for every apartment."

This is the present law and has been the law since 1867.

"SEC. 85. *Vent shafts.* Every vent shaft hereafter constructed in a tenement house shall be at least twenty square feet in area, and the least dimension of such shaft shall not be less than four feet; and if the building be above sixty feet in height such shaft shall throughout its entire height be increased in area three square feet for each additional twelve feet of height or fraction thereof; and for each twelve feet of height less than sixty feet such shaft may be decreased in area three square feet. A vent shaft may be enclosed on all four sides but shall not be roofed or covered over in any way. Every such shaft shall be provided with a horizontal intake or duct at the bottom, communicating with the street or yard or with a court; such duct or intake to be not less than one and one-half square feet in total area."

The Commission has recommended that water-closet compartments and bath-rooms shall be allowed to ventilate on a smaller open space than that prescribed for bedrooms and living rooms. The present law provides that all water-closet compartments shall have a window opening to the outer air, but in special cases such water-closets are permitted to be ventilated by means of a small metal flue or duct.

"CHAPTER IV. SANITARY PROVISIONS

"TITLE 1. *Provisions applicable only to tenement houses hereafter erected.*

"SEC. 91. *Basements and Cellars.* In tenement houses hereafter erected no room in the cellar shall be constructed, altered, converted or occupied for living purposes. And no room in the basement shall be constructed, altered, converted or occupied for living purposes, unless all of the following conditions are complied with:

"1. Such room shall be at least nine feet high in every part from the floor to the ceiling.

"2. The ceiling of such room shall be at least four feet and six inches above the surface of the street or ground outside of or adjoining the same.

"3. There shall be appurtenant to such room the use of a separate water-closet, constructed and arranged as required by Section ninety-five of this act.

"4. Such room shall have a window or windows opening upon the street, or upon a yard or court. The total area of windows in such room shall be at least one-eighth of the superficial area of the room, and one-half of the sash shall be made to open the full width, and the top of each window shall be within six inches of the ceiling.

"5. All walls surrounding such room shall be made dampproof in the manner specified in the next section.

"6. The floor of such room shall be made dampproof and water proof in the manner specified in the next section."

The Commission has recommended certain changes in the present law in regard to living rooms to be occupied in basements of future tenement houses. There has been a very strong demand to prohibit entirely the occupation of basement rooms. The Commission, however, has not seen its way clear to making so drastic a recommendation. It therefore recommends that in all tenement houses hereafter erected the height of such rooms must be at least 9 feet, and that at least one-half of the height of the room shall be above the curb level; also that the rooms shall be properly ventilated and that the walls and floors shall be water-proof. This is a change from the present law. The present law requires such rooms to be 8 feet high instead of 9 feet, and that the ceiling shall be 2 feet above the curb instead of 4 feet 6 inches, and further requires that in front of the rooms and extending across the full width of the house there shall be an open area at least 2 feet 6 inches wide and constructed in a certain manner. The Commission believes that such area is not necessary, provided the ceiling is high enough above the ground and the walls and floors are made damp-proof.

"SEC. 92. *Basements and Cellars, continued.* Every tenement house hereafter erected shall have all walls below the ground level and all cellar or lowest floors made dampproof and waterproof. Such dampproofing and waterproofing shall run through the walls and up the same as high as the ground level and shall be continued throughout the floor, and the said cellar or lowest floor shall be properly constructed so as to prevent dampness or water from entering."

The Commission believes it to be desirable that all walls below the ground level shall be made damp-proof whether the basement is occupied for living purposes or not, and that cellar floors shall be water-tight and similarly damp-proof. The law since 1867 has provided that cellar floors shall be properly cemented and water-tight.

"SEC. 93. *Shafts, courts, areas and yards.* In every tenement house hereafter erected the bottom of all shafts, courts, areas and yards which extend to the basement for light or ventilation of living rooms, must be six inches below the floor level of the part occupied or intended to be occupied. All shafts, courts, areas and yards shall be properly concreted, graded and drained, and shall be properly connected with the street sewer so that all water may pass freely into it."

This is the present requirement of the Building Department.

"SEC. 94. *Water supply.* In every tenement house hereafter erected there shall be in each apartment a proper sink with running water."

This is the present requirement of the Building Department.

"SEC. 95. *Water-closet accommodations.* In every tenement house hereafter erected there shall be a separate water-closet in a separate compartment within each apartment, provided that where there are apartments consisting of but one or two rooms there shall be at least one water-closet for every three rooms. All water-closet compartments must have a window opening upon the street or yard or upon a court or vent shaft. Every water-closet compartment shall be provided with proper means of lighting the same at night. If fixtures for gas or electricity are not provided in said compartment, then the door of said compartment shall be provided with ground glass or wire glass panels, or with a ground glass or wire glass transom, not less in area than four square feet. The floor of every water-closet compartment shall be made waterproof with asphalt, cement, tile, stone, metal or some other waterproof material; and such waterproofing shall extend at least six inches above the floor so that the said floor can be washed or flushed out without leaking. No drip trays shall be permitted. No water-closet fixtures shall be enclosed with any woodwork."

The present law requires at least one water-closet for every two families in a new tenement house and permits the location of such water-closets in the public hallway of the building. The Commission recommends that in every tenement house hereafter erected there shall be a separate water-closet for each family and that this water-closet shall be located within the apartment. No one who has made any recommendation to the Commission on this subject has not agreed with this view. As a matter of fact the Commission finds that it is becoming the practice for builders to provide such water-closet accommodations in the new tenement houses. In 61 per cent of the houses erected during 1900 and examined by the Commission it was found that a private water-closet for each family was thus provided. The present law requires that all water-closet compartments shall have a window opening upon the outer air. The Commission recommends in effect the continuance of this provision. It further recommends that every water-closet compartment shall be provided with proper means of lighting the same at night, as it finds that where such closets cannot be lighted at night they are apt to be kept in an unclean condition. The present law requires that the floor of every water-closet compartment shall be made waterproof. The Commission recommends that this be continued.

"SEC. 96. *Plumbing.* In every tenement house hereafter erected all plumbing pipes shall wherever possible be exposed, or if such pipes are covered there shall be at each floor access to all rising lines through removable panels; said panels shall always be as wide as the whole stack of pipes, and at least two feet and six inches in height."

It is important that plumbing pipes should in all cases be exposed so that if there is any leak they may be readily reached, and for the more important reason that if the pipes are covered up the work is apt to be slighted. The Commission has not thought it best to make this compulsory in all cases, but would recommend that the pipes be exposed wherever possible.

"TITLE 2. *Provisions applicable only to now existing tenement houses.*

"SEC. 97. *Basements and Cellars.* Hereafter in any now existing tenement house no room in the basement or cellar shall be occupied for living purposes without a written permit from the Department of Health, and such permit shall be kept readily accessible in said room. And no such room shall hereafter be occupied unless all the following conditions are complied with:

"1. Such room shall be at least eight feet high in every part from the floor to the ceiling.

"2. The ceiling of such room shall be in every part at least two feet above the surface of the street or ground outside of or adjoining the same.

"3. There shall be appurtenant to such room the use of a separate water-closet.

"4. There shall be outside of and adjoining such room, and extending along the entire frontage thereof, an open space of at least two feet six inches wide in every part. The bottom of said space shall be at least six inches below the level of the floor of the room, and such space shall be well and effectually drained by a drain the bottom of which shall be at least one foot below the level of the floor of the room.

"5. Such room shall have a window or windows opening to the outer air of at least nine square feet in size clear of the sash frame, and at least four and one-half square feet of which shall have been made to readily open for purposes of ventilation.

"6. If the house is situated over marshy ground, or ground on which water lies, or ground on which there is water pressure from below, the lowest floor shall have been made waterproof and dampproof."

This is the present law upon this subject, with the omission of some unnecessary portions and with slight changes in the language, intended to make its meaning more clear.

"SEC. 98. *Water-closets.* In all now existing tenement houses the woodwork enclosing all water-closets shall be removed from the front of said closet, and the space underneath the seat shall be left open. The floor or other surface beneath and around the closet shall be maintained in good order and repair and shall be kept well painted with white paint."

The investigations of the sanitary inspectors of the Commission show that in old tenement houses where the water-closets are enclosed with wood-work the closets are apt to get in a very filthy condition, and that it is desirable that such woodwork be removed and the floor underneath the closet be properly painted with a light-colored paint, so that all dirt may be readily seen. The plumbing regulations of the Building Department have for many years forbidden the enclosing of water-closets in new work. From estimates which have been made the Commission finds that this change will be comparatively inexpensive.

"SEC. 99. *Public sinks.* In all now existing tenement houses the woodwork enclosing sinks located in the public halls or stairs shall be removed, and the space underneath said sinks shall be left open. The floors and wall surfaces beneath and around the sink shall be maintained in good order and repair, and shall be kept well painted with white paint."

The present plumbing rules forbid the enclosing of a sink with woodwork in new plumbing. The same objection that pertains to the enclosing of water-closets pertains with equal effect to the enclosing of sinks, and the Commission recommends that woodwork around old sinks be removed.

"SEC. 100. *Privy Vaults and School Sinks.* In all now existing tenement houses, all school-sinks, privy vaults or other similar receptacles now used to receive fecal matter, urine or sewage, shall before January 1, 1903, be completely removed and the place where they were located properly disinfected under the direction of the Department of Health. Such appliances shall be replaced by individual water-closets of durable non-absorbent material, properly sewer-connected, and with individual traps, and properly connected flush-tanks providing an ample flush of water to thoroughly cleanse the bowl. The seats of the water-closets shall be hinged and attached to the bowl of the closet. Each water-closet shall be located in a compartment completely separated from every other water-closet. The floors of the water-closet compartment shall be waterproof as provided in section ninety-five of this act. Such water-closets may be located in the yard if necessary, and, if so, long hopper closets may be used; all traps, flush tanks and pipes shall be protected against the action of frost. There shall be provided at least one such water-closet for every two families in said tenement house. Except as in this section otherwise provided such water-closets and all plumbing in connection therewith shall be in accordance with the Building Code of the City of New York."

The use of privy vaults in connection with tenement houses has for a number of years been prohibited, the first law upon this subject having been enacted in 1887, and the Board of Health has gradually condemned the great majority of these vaults. There are, however, still in the city a number of school sinks located in the yards, which are the only privy accommodations for the occupants of the tenement house. These school sinks were in nearly every case found by the Commission's sanitary inspectors to be in a horrible condition and a serious menace to the health of the occupants of such houses and the neighboring houses. From their construction it is very difficult to flush them, and the inspectors found many cases where they had not been flushed for weeks. In summer the stench is intolerable, and unquestionably causes a good deal of sickness. Moreover, the school sinks found in nearly all the buildings were in a horrible condition, in some cases simply indescribable. The Commission therefore recommends that within two years all existing school sinks now used in connection with tenement houses be removed and proper water-closet accommodations be substituted. The Commission has not attempted to specify whether such water-closets shall be placed in the yard or within the tenement house; it has left this to the option of the owner. The Commissioners realize that in some cases it might be difficult to protect such water-closets from the action of frost if they are located in the yard, but know that in any case they can be located in the house simply by giving up one room to such purpose. Every consideration of the public health demands that this action be taken, and the Commission finds, after having estimates made, that the cost will not be so great as to make this measure an undue hardship upon the owners of tenement houses.

"TITLE 3. *Provisions applicable to all tenement houses, whether hereafter erected or now existing.*

"SEC. 101. *Basements and Cellars.* The floor of the cellar or lowest floor of every tenement house shall be water tight, and the cellar ceiling shall be plastered."

This is the present law and has been the law since 1867.

"SEC. 102. *Cellar Walls and Ceilings.* The cellar walls and ceilings of every tenement house shall be thoroughly whitewashed or painted a light color by the owner at least once a year; and no tenement house hereafter erected, whether or not it has now been actually commenced, shall be occupied until this has been done for the first time."

The present law requires the walls and ceilings of all tenement houses to be whitewashed once a year. If this law were applied to the better grade of flats and apartment houses, or even to the better tenement houses, it would undoubtedly work great hardship and be resented by the entire community. The Commission therefore recommends that only the cellar walls and ceilings be whitewashed once a year, leaving to the Department of Health the power and duty of requiring the walls of tenement houses to be cleaned when necessity requires it.

"Sec. 103. *Roofs.* The roof of every tenement house shall be kept in good repair and so as not to leak, and all rain water shall be so drained and conveyed therefrom as to prevent its dripping on to the ground or causing dampness in the walls, ceilings, yards or areas."

This is the present law and has been the law since 1867.

"Sec. 104. *Water supply.* Every tenement house shall have water furnished in sufficient quantity at one or more places on each floor occupied by or intended to be occupied by one or more families. The owner shall provide proper and suitable tanks, pumps or other appliances to receive and to distribute an adequate and sufficient supply of such water at each floor in the said house, at all times of the year, during all hours of the day and night. But a failure in the general supply of water by the city authorities shall not be construed to be a failure on the part of such owner, provided that proper and suitable appliances to receive and distribute such water have been provided in said house."

This is the present law, although slight changes have been made in the form of expression.

"Sec. 105. *Cleanliness of buildings.* Every tenement house and every part thereof shall be kept clean and free from any accumulation of dirt, filth or garbage or other matter in or on the same, or in the yards, courts, passages, areas or alleys connected with or belonging to the same. The owner of every tenement house or part thereof shall thoroughly cleanse all the rooms, passages, stairs, floors, windows, doors, walls, ceilings, privies, water-closets, cesspools, drains, halls, cellars, roofs and all other parts of the said tenement house, or part of the house of which he is the owner, to the satisfaction of the Department of Health, and shall keep the said parts of the said tenement house in a cleanly condition at all times. No person shall place filth, urine or fecal matter in any place in a tenement house other than that provided for the same, or keep filth, urine or fecal matter in his apartment or upon his premises such length of time as to create a nuisance."

This is the present law, with the exception that the words "Water-closets, cellars and roofs" have been added, and that a requirement has been added that the owner shall *keep* all the parts of the tenement house in a cleanly condition.

"Sec. 106. *Shafts and courts.* In every tenement house there shall be, at the bottom of every shaft and inner court, a self-closing fireproof door giving sufficient access to such shaft or court to enable it to be properly cleaned out."

This is a new provision, necessitated by the fact that it is very difficult to clean out the rubbish at the bottom of an ordinary air shaft, because a door has not been provided in the cellar so that people may get into the shaft.

"Sec. 107. *Walls of courts and shafts.* The walls of all yard-courts, inner-courts and shafts unless built of a light color brick or stone shall be thoroughly whitewashed by the owner at least once in three years, or shall be thoroughly painted a light color by him at least once in five years; and no tenement house hereafter erected, whether or not it has now been actually commenced, shall be occupied until this has been done for the first time."

This is a new provision and is urged for two reasons, first, chiefly to furnish a little more light by means of the present air shaft, and, second, as a sanitary measure.

"SEC. 108. *Wall Paper.* No wall paper shall be placed upon a wall or ceiling of any tenement house unless all wall paper shall be first removed therefrom and said wall and ceiling thoroughly cleaned."

This is the present law.

"SEC. 109. *Receptacles for ashes, garbage and refuse.* The owner of every tenement house shall provide for said building proper and suitable conveniences or receptacles for ashes, rubbish, garbage, refuse and other matter."

This is the present law and has been the law since 1867. It has been slightly changed in verbiage in order to simplify it and make it clearer.

"SEC. 110. *Prohibited uses.* No horse, cow, calf, swine, sheep or goat shall be kept in a tenement house, or on the premises thereof, and no tenement house shall be used for a lodging house or stable, or for the storage or handling of rags."

The keeping of animals mentioned in this section has been prohibited by the laws of this State since 1867, and the prohibition of the use of tenement houses for the purpose of lodging houses or for the storage and handling of rags has existed since 1891 and is the present law.

"SEC. 111. *Janitor or housekeeper.* Whenever there shall be more than eight families living in any tenement house, in which the owner thereof does not reside, there shall be a janitor, housekeeper or some other responsible person who shall reside in said house and have charge of the same, if the Department of Health shall so require."

This is the present law and has been the law since 1887.

"SEC. 112. *Overcrowding.* No room in any tenement house shall be so overcrowded that there shall be afforded less than four hundred cubic feet of air to each adult, and two hundred cubic feet of air to each child under twelve years of age occupying such room, and no apartment in any tenement house shall be so overcrowded that there shall be afforded in the living rooms and bedrooms of said apartment less than six hundred cubic feet of air to each individual occupying such apartment. Nothing in this section shall be construed as conflicting with the provisions of Section seventy-nine of this act."

The present law requires that there shall be 400 cubic feet of air space to each adult, and 200 cubic feet of air space to each child under twelve years of age in every room in a tenement house. This change in the law was made in 1895; the law prior to that time having required 600 cubic feet of air space to each individual. The present law limits the space only to rooms where there is insufficient ventilation in the opinion of the sanitary superintendent of the Department of Health. It is apparent that a distinction should be made between rooms in new tenement houses which will be adequately supplied with light and air, and rooms in existing tenement houses which are inadequately supplied with light and air. The Commission therefore recommends that in every room in every tenement house there shall be at least 400 cubic feet of air to each adult and 200 cubic feet of air to each child under twelve years of age, and that in every apartment or suite of rooms there shall be at least 600 cubic feet of air for each individual in the combined living and bed rooms, and further requires that no interior room in an existing tenement house which has not direct light and air shall be occupied unless there is at least 600 cubic feet of air to each individual in such a room. There is further provision as to overcrowding in Section 79.

"SEC. 113. *Space around pipes.* In all tenement houses, where plumbing or other pipes pass through floors or partitions, the openings around such pipes shall be sealed or made air-tight with plaster, or other incombustible materials, so as to prevent the passage of air or the spread of fire from one floor to another or from room to room."

This is a new provision. It is urged for two reasons, because the space left around pipes now serves to conduct foul air from one room to another, and also is very dangerous in case of contagious disease in a tenement house. This space around plumbing pipes is also a frequent means of permitting the spread of fire from one part of a building to another.

"CHAPTER V. REMEDIES.

"TITLE 1. *General Powers and Duties.*

"SEC. 121. *Permit to Commence Building.* No tenement house shall be hereafter constructed until a written permit to commence the construction thereof shall have been granted by the Commissioner of Buildings for the borough in which said building is situated. No such permit shall be issued until after examination and approval of the plans for such building."

This and the next section are new. The Commission believes that they furnish the simplest and most efficient means by which the Building Department may prevent violations of this act. The system is in force in several foreign cities with good practical effect.

"SEC. 122. *Certificate of Compliance.* No building hereafter constructed as or altered into a tenement house shall be occupied in whole or in part for human habitation, until the issuance of a certificate signed by the Commissioner of Buildings for the borough in which said building is situated, that said building conforms in all respects to the requirements of this Act. Such certificate shall be issued within ten days after written application therefor, if said building at the date of such application shall be entitled thereto.

"SEC. 123. *Unlawful Occupation.* If any building hereafter constructed as or altered into a tenement house be occupied in whole or in part for human habitation in violation of the last section, during such unlawful occupation any bond or note secured by a mortgage upon said building, or the lot upon which it stands, may be declared due at the option of the mortgagee. No rent shall be recoverable by the owner or lessee of such premises for said period, and no action or special proceeding shall be maintained therefor, or for possession of said premises for non-payment of such rent. The Department of Water Supply shall not permit water to be furnished in any such tenement house, and said premises shall be deemed unfit for human habitation, and the Department of Health shall cause them to be vacated accordingly."

This is new.

"SEC. 124. *Enforcement of the Act.* It shall be the duty of the Department of Health to enforce the provisions of this Act as to all tenement houses which are occupied for human habitation; and it shall be the duty of the Department of Buildings to enforce the provisions of this Act as to all tenement houses in course of construction or alteration.

"SEC. 125. *Violations.* Nothing in this Act shall be construed to abrogate or impair the powers of the Department of Health, the Department of Buildings, or of the Courts, to enforce the provisions of the Charter or Building Code of the City of New York, or to prevent or punish violations thereof.

"SEC. 126. *Penalties for Violations.* Every person who shall violate or assist in the violation of any provision of this Act shall be guilty of a misdemeanor punishable by imprisonment for ten days for each and every day that such violation shall continue, or by a fine of not less than ten dollars nor more than one hundred dollars if the offence be not wilful, or of two hundred and fifty dollars if the offence be wilful, and in every case of ten dollars for each day after the first that such violation shall continue, or by both such fine and imprisonment in the discretion of the Court; provided, that the punishment for a violation of Section one hundred and thirty-one of this act shall be a fine of fifty dollars; and provided further, that the penalty for encumbrance of a fire escape by an occupant of the tenement house shall be a fine of ten dollars, which the nearest police magistrate shall have jurisdiction to impose."

A simplification of the present system (see Charter, Sections **1262, 1313, 1322**; Building Code, Section **103**).

"SEC. 127. *Violation of Building Code.* Any owner, agent, architect, builder, contractor, sub-contractor, or foreman who shall, in the construction or alteration of any building intended to be used as a tenement house, knowingly violate any of the provisions of the Building Code of the City of New York, shall be guilty of a misdemeanor.

"SEC. 128. *Procedure.* Except as herein otherwise specified, the procedure for the prevention of violations of this Act, or for the vacation of premises unlawfully occupied, or for other abatement of nuisance in connection with a tenement house, shall be as set forth in Titles I., IV., V. and VI. of Chapter XIX. of the Greater New York Charter.

"SEC. 129. *Liens.* Every fine imposed by judgment under Section one hundred and twenty-six of this act upon a tenement house owner shall be a lien upon the house in relation to which the fine is imposed from the time of the filing of a certified copy of said judgment in the office of the clerk of the county in which said tenement house is situated, subject only to taxes, assessments and water rates and to such mortgage and mechanics' liens as may exist thereon prior to such filing; and it shall be the duty of the Department of Health upon the entry of said judgment, to forthwith file the copy as aforesaid, and such copy, upon such filing, shall be forthwith indexed by the clerk in the index of mechanics' liens."

New in its general application, but in analogy to certain present provisions — such as Charter, Sections 1278, 1290; Building Code, Section 150.

"TITLE 2. *Registry of names and service of papers.*

"SEC. 131. *Registry of Owner's Names.* Every owner of a tenement house and every lessee of the whole house, or other person having control of a tenement house, shall file in the Department of Health a notice containing his name and address, and also a description of the property, by street number or otherwise, as the case may be, in such manner as will enable the Department of Health easily to find the same; and also the number of apartments in each house, the number of rooms in each apartment, the number of families occupying the apartments, and the trades or occupations carried on therein. In case of a transfer of any tenement house, it shall be the duty of the grantor or grantee of said tenement house to file in the Department of Health a notice of such transfer, stating the name of the new owner, within thirty days after such transfer. In case of the devolution of said property by will, it shall be the duty of the executor and the devisee, if more than twenty-one years of age, and in case of the devolution of such property by inheritance without a will, it shall be the duty of the heirs, or in case all of the heirs are under age, it shall be the duty of the guardians of such heirs, and in case said heirs have no guardians, it shall be the duty of the administrator of the deceased owner of said property to file in said Department a notice, stating the death of the deceased owner, and the names of those who have succeeded to his interest in said property, within thirty days after the death of the decedent, in case he died intestate, and within thirty days after the probate of his will, if he died testate."

Charter, Section 1313.

"Sec. 132. *Registry of Agent's Name.* Every owner, agent, or lessee of a tenement house may file in the Department of Health a notice containing the name and address of an agent of such house for the purpose of receiving service of process, and also a description of the property by street number or otherwise, as the case may be, in such manner as will enable the Department of Health easily to find the same. The name of the owner or lessee may be filed as agent for this purpose."

New. Compare Sections 134, 144.

"Sec. 133. *Service of Notices and Orders.* Every notice or order of the Department of Health in relation to a tenement house shall be served five days before the time for doing the thing in relation to which it shall have been issued. The posting of a copy of such notice or order in a conspicuous place in the tenement house, together with the mailing of a copy thereof, on the same day that it is posted, to each person, if any, whose name has been filed with the Department of Health in accordance with the provisions of Sections one hundred and thirty-one and one hundred and thirty-two of this act, at his address as therewith filed, shall be sufficient service thereof."

Charter, Section 1313, slightly amended.

"Sec. 134. *Service of Summons.* In any action brought by the Department of Health in relation to a tenement house for injunction, vacation of the premises, or other abatement of nuisance, or to establish a lien thereon, it shall be sufficient service of the summons to serve the same as notices and orders are served under the provisions of the last section; provided, that if the address of any agent whose name and address have been filed in accordance with the provisions of Section one hundred and thirty-two of this act is in the city of New York, then a copy of the summons shall also be delivered at such address to a person of proper age, if upon reasonable application admittance can be obtained and such person found; and provided also, that personal service of the summons upon the owner of such tenement house shall be sufficient service thereof upon him."

New. An owner, to be assured notice of an action *quasi in rem*, must file his name or that of his agent, and there can be no delay on account of inability to procure personal service in such an action.

"Sec. 135. *Indexing Names.* The names and addresses filed in accordance with Sections one hundred and thirty-one and one hundred and thirty-two shall be indexed under direction of the Registrar of Records of the Department of Health, in such manner that all of those filed in relation to each tenement house shall be together, and readily ascertainable. The Board of Health shall provide the Registrar with the necessary books and clerical assistance for that purpose, and the expense thereof shall be paid by the city. Said indexes shall be public records, open to public inspection during business hours."

New.

"Title 3. *Prostitution in Tenement Houses.*

"Sec. 141. *Vagrancy.* A woman who knowingly resides in or commits prostitution in a house of prostitution or assignation of any description in a tenement house or solicits any man or boy to enter therein for purposes of prostitution shall be deemed a vagrant, and upon conviction thereof shall be committed to a county jail for a term not exceeding six months from the date of commitment. The procedure in such case shall be the same as that provided for other cases of vagrancy in Chapter XIV. of the Greater New York Charter."

All the provisions of this title are new. They are intended to make it worth while for all houses of prostitution to remove from where they are so dangerous to the morals of young children. This section is recommended by several judges of courts accustomed to deal with such offenders.

"Sec. 142. *Lien.* A tenement house shall be subject to a penalty of one thousand dollars, if it or any part of it shall be used for the purpose of a house of prostitution or assignation of any description, with the permission of the owner thereof, or his agent, and said penalty shall be a lien upon the house and the lot upon which the house is situated.

"Sec. 143. *Permission of Lessee.* If a tenement house, or any part thereof, shall be used for the purpose of a house of prostitution or assignation of any description with the permission of the lessee of the whole of said tenement house, or his agent, the lease shall be terminable at the election of the lessor.

"Sec. 144. *Permission of Owner.* A tenement house shall be deemed to have been used for the purpose specified in the last two sections with the permission of the owner and lessee thereof, if summary proceedings for the removal of the tenants of said tenement house, or of so much thereof as is unlawfully used, shall not have been commenced within five days after notice of such unlawful use, served by the Department of Health in the manner prescribed by Section one hundred and thirty-three of this act.

"Sec. 145. *Rules of Evidence.* In a prosecution against an owner or agent of a tenement house under Section three hundred and twenty-two of the Penal Code, or in an action to establish a lien under Section one hundred and forty-two of this act, the general reputation of the premises in the neighborhood shall be competent evidence, but shall not be sufficient to support a judgment without corroborative evidence, and it shall be presumed that their use was with the permission of the owner and lessee; provided, that such presumption may be rebutted by evidence.

"Sec. 146. *Title of Action and Parties.* Said action shall be brought against the tenement house as defendant. Said house may be described in the title of the action by its street number, or in any other method sufficiently precise to secure identification. The property shall be described in the complaint. The plaintiff shall be the Department of Health.

"Sec. 147. *Jurisdiction and Procedure.* Said action shall be brought in the Supreme Court in the county in which the property is situated.

At or before the commencement of the action the complaint shall be filed in the office of the clerk of the county, together with a notice of the pendency of the action, containing the names of the parties, the object of the action and a brief description of the property affected thereby. Said notice shall be immediately recorded by the clerk in accordance with the provisions of Section sixteen hundred and seventy-two of the Code of Civil Procedure. The owner or lessee of said building, or both, may appear in said action and answer or demur to the complaint within twenty days after its service. The issues so raised, if any, shall be tried at the Special Term, and the action shall be preferred like other actions in which the Department of Health is a party.

"SEC. 148. *Judgment.* The judgment in such action, if in favor of the plaintiff, shall establish the penalty sued for as a lien upon said premises, subject only to taxes, assessments and water rates, and to such mortgage and mechanics' liens as may exist thereon prior to the filing of the notice of pendency of the action.

"SEC. 149. *Sale of Property.* At any time after the entry of any judgment establishing a lien upon tenement property the Department of Health, if there be no stay pending appeal, may apply to the Court for leave to sell such property. Upon such application the Court, if it deem advisable, may order such property to be sold at public auction, subject to taxes, assessments and water rates, and to such mortgage and mechanics' liens as aforesaid. The deed to the purchaser shall be made by the Department of Health. The Justices of the Appellate Division of the Supreme Court of the First and Second Departments may establish rules of practice, which shall be followed by the Department of Health in the conduct of said sales in said Departments respectively."

A sale of the property will only be proper when it is unencumbered, or so little encumbered as to assure a bid high enough to cover the city's lien.

"SEC. 150. *Receivership.* Whenever the lien or liens upon a tenement property, established by judgment, shall amount to one thousand dollars or over, if there be no stay pending appeal, the Department of Health shall appoint a receiver of the rents and profits of said property. Said receiver shall give security for the performance of his duties in the manner and form fixed by said Department. He shall have the powers and duties of a receiver of rents and profits of real estate appointed by the Supreme Court; provided, that the Corporation Counsel shall act as his counsel and that he shall not be allowed any expenditure for counsel fees, and provided, that his commissions shall be ten per cent. of his collections, which sum shall be full compensation for his services and those of any agent or agents whom he may employ. Said receivership shall continue until the amount of said liens, with interest thereon at the rate of six per cent., and of said commissions, have been fully paid; provided, that nothing in this section shall be construed to prevent any prior lienor from applying to the Court in a proper case for a receiver of the property."

The plan of enforcing a lien upon rents is not new (Charter, Sections 1176, 1276, 1297). This section provides a more efficient method of practical enforcement.

"Sec. 151. *Cancellation of notice of pendency of the action.* If an action to establish a lien upon tenement property terminate otherwise than in a judgment establishing such a lien, or if said judgment be fully paid, said notice may be cancelled in the manner prescribed by Section one thousand six hundred and seventy-four of the Code of Civil Procedure.

"CHAPTER VI. GENERAL PROVISIONS.

"Sec. 161. *Repeal.* Sections one thousand three hundred and four, one thousand three hundred and five, one thousand three hundred and six, one thousand three hundred and seven, one thousand three hundred and eight, one thousand three hundred and nine, one thousand three hundred and ten, one thousand three hundred and eleven, one thousand three hundred and twelve, one thousand three hundred and thirteeen, one thousand three hundred and seventeen, one thousand three hundred and eighteen, one thousand three hundred and nineteen, one thousand three hundred and twenty, one thousand three hundred and twenty-one, one thousand three hundred and twenty-two and one thousand three hundred and twenty-three of the Greater New York Charter, in so far as they relate to tenement houses, are hereby repealed.

"Sec. 162. *Building Regulations.* Except as herein otherwise specified, every tenement house shall be constructed and maintained in conformity with the existing law, but no ordinance, regulation or ruling of any municipal authority shall modify or dispense with any provision of this act.

"Sec. 163. *Penalties.* All penalties collected under this act shall be paid into the treasury of the City of New York.

"Sec. 164. *Time for Compliance.* All alterations hereby required upon now existing tenement houses shall be made within one year hereafter, or at such earlier period as may be fixed by the Department of Buildings, as to the requirements of Chapter II., or by the Department of Health, as to the other requirements of this act.

"Sec. 165. *When to take effect.* This act shall take effect immediately; provided, that Sections one hundred and thirty-four and one hundred and forty-four shall not take effect until three months after the passage thereof."

APPENDIX III

THE ACT FOR THE CREATION OF A SEPARATE TENEMENT HOUSE DEPARTMENT IN THE CITY OF NEW YORK

THE ACT FOR THE CREATION OF A SEPARATE TENEMENT HOUSE DEPARTMENT

AN ACT to amend Chapter three hundred and seventy-eight of the laws of eighteen hundred and ninety-seven, entitled "An act to unite into one municipality, under the corporate name of The City of New York, the various communities lying in and about New York harbor, including the city and county of New York, the city of Brooklyn, and the county of Kings, the county of Richmond and part of the county of Queens, and to provide for the government thereof," by creating a tenement house department, and defining its powers and duties.[1]

The People of the State of New York, represented in Senate and Assembly, do enact as follows:

SECTION 1. Chapter three hundred and seventy-eight of the laws of eighteen hundred and ninety-seven is hereby amended by inserting therein a new chapter, to be known as Chapter XIXa, and to read as follows:

CHAPTER XIXA. TENEMENT HOUSE DEPARTMENT

TITLE 1. *Organization of department; officers and employees.*
2. *Powers and duties of department.*
3. *Records and reports; miscellaneous provisions.*

TITLE 1

ORGANIZATION OF DEPARTMENT; BUREAUS; OFFICERS AND EMPLOYEES

SEC. 1340. Department created; tenement house commissioner.
1341. Deputy commissioner.
1342. Bureaus; division of department for Brooklyn, Queens and Richmond.
1343. Officers and employees.
1344. Duties of Bureaus.
1344a. Offices and expenses.
1344b. Seal.
1344c. Annual report.
1344d. Publication of statistics and other data.
1344e. Uniforms and badges.
1344f. Reports of inspectors.
1344g. Proofs, affidavits and oaths.
1344h. Complaint book.
1344i. Attorneys.

[1] This proposed legislation was enacted with a few slight changes and is to be found in chapter 19-A of the Greater New York Charter, known as Chapter 466 of the laws of 1901, as amended by Chapter 439 of the laws of 1903.

Department created; tenement house commissioners

§ 1340. In addition to the departments enumerated in section ninety-six of this charter, there is hereby created a tenement house department. The head of such department shall be called the tenement house commissioner. He shall be appointed by the mayor, and shall hold office subject to removal by the mayor, as provided in chapter four of this charter. He shall receive an annual salary of seven thousand and five hundred dollars, and shall execute an official bond in the sum of twenty thousand dollars, conditioned on the faithful performance of his duties and a faithful and accurate disbursement and accounting of all moneys received by him in his official capacity.

Deputy Commissioner

1341. The tenement house commissioner shall appoint, and may remove, one or more deputy tenement house commissioners, who shall receive annual salaries of not more than five thousand dollars each. During the disability, or absence from the city, of the commissioner, such deputy shall perform the duties and possess the powers of such commissioner.

Bureaus; division of department for Brooklyn, Queens and Richmond

1342. There shall be in the tenement house department, (1) A new building bureau; (2) An inspection bureau; (3) A bureau of records; and such other bureaus as the commissioner may deem necessary.

A separate division of the department may be established in the borough of Brooklyn, with jurisdiction over tenement houses in the borough of Brooklyn, and also in the discretion of the commissioner, in the boroughs of Queens or Richmond, or both. The commissioner may designate the deputy commissioner or some other officer of the department as the executive head of such division, who shall perform such duties and possess such powers as may be delegated to him by the commissioner. A branch of each of the bureaus above specified may be established in such division.

Officers and employees

1343. The tenement house commissioner shall appoint, and may remove, all registrars, examiners, inspectors, clerks and employees employed in the tenement house department, and fix the salaries of such officers and employees.

In the new building bureau there shall be not less than three plan examiners and not less than sixteen inspectors of light and ventilation. In the inspection bureau there shall be not less than one hundred and ninety inspectors, including such persons as may be detailed by the police board for service in the tenement house department. The commissioner shall appoint a chief inspector and deputy chief inspector over such bureau. In the other bureaus there shall be such registrars, clerks and employees as are necessary to perform the duties thereof.

All such officers and employees shall be subject to the supervision and control of the commissioner, and shall perform such duties as are assigned by him. Such commissioner may make regulations governing each such bureau, and branch thereof, not inconsistent with law.

Duties of bureaus

1344. The new building bureau shall file, record and examine plans and specifications for the light and ventilation of tenement houses hereafter altered or erected, and of buildings to be altered or reconstructed for use as tenement houses. It shall inspect all such houses and buildings in the course of construction or alteration and record all violations of the New York Tenement House Act, in respect thereto.

The inspection bureau shall inspect all completed tenement houses, and record all violations of the tenement house laws and ordinances. The commissioner shall prescribe the duties of the inspectors connected with such bureau, and may assign them to such part of the city as he may deem best.

The bureau of records shall contain records of every tenement house in the city to be kept in the manner and form prescribed by the commissioner.

Such other bureaus as may be organized by the commissioner shall perform the duties prescribed by him, and he may assign thereto such inspectors and officers as may be necessary.

Offices and expenses

1344a. The commissioner may provide offices for the use of the department, its bureaus and the branches thereof. Such commissioner may, subject to the other provisions of this charter, make such incidental and additional expenditures, having due regard to economy, as the purposes and provisions of this chapter may require. He may provide that the failure of an inspector, officer or employee of the department to properly perform his duty shall cause a forfeiture of the whole or any part of the salary or compensation of such inspector, officer or employee.

Seal

1344b. The commissioner may design and adopt a seal for the department and cause the same to be used in the authentication of the orders and proceedings of the department, and for such other purposes as he may prescribe. The courts shall take judicial notice of such seal, and of the signature of the commissioner and deputy commissioner of such department.

Annual report

1344c. The commissioner shall make an annual report at some time prior to the first day of March of each year to the Mayor of the city of New York of all the operations of his department for the year ending on the preceeding 31st day of December. Such report shall, if ordered by the Mayor, be published in the city record, and shall also be published in book form for public information. The Mayor may, at any time, call for a fuller report, or for a report upon any portion of the work of said department, whenever he deems it for the public good so to do.

Publication of statistics and other data

1344d. The commissioner may provide for the publicity of the papers, files, reports, records and the proceedings of his department, whenever he deems it necessary for the public good and public service. There shall be kept in such department statistics of all tenement houses, which shall be contained in the annual report of such department.

Uniforms and badges

1344e. The commissioner may provide or designate a suitable uniform to be worn by inspectors. He may also provide a badge of metal, with a suitable inscription thereon, and require it to be worn by the inspectors and officers of the department.

Reports of inspectors

1344f. Each of such inspectors shall report in writing, at least once in each week, to the commissioner. The form, manner and scope of such reports shall be prescribed by the commissioner. Such reports shall be filed in the department.

Proofs, affidavits and oaths

1344g. Proofs, affidavits and examinations as to any matter arising in connection with the performance of any of the duties of the tenement house department may be taken by or before the tenement house commissioner, or his deputy, or such other person as he may designate; and such commissioner, deputy or other person may administer oaths in connection therewith.

Complaint book

1344h. The commissioner shall cause to be kept in his department a general complaint book, or several such books, in which may be entered by any person any complaint in reference to tenement houses, with the name and residence of the complainant, the name of the person complained of, the date of the entry of the complaint and suggestions of any proper remedy. Such book shall be open to public examination during the office hours of the department, subject to such regulations as the commissioner may prescribe. The tenement house commissioner shall cause the facts in regard to all complaints to be investigated.

Attorneys

1344i. The corporation counsel shall assign to such department such assistant counsel as may be needful, in the manner provided by chapter seven of this charter.

TITLE 2

POWERS AND DUTIES OF DEPARTMENT

General powers and duties

1344j. All the rights and powers possessed by the health department of the city of New York with respect to the sanitary inspection of tenement houses are hereby conferred upon the tenement house department; and the tenement house department is hereby charged with the duty of enforcing the New York Tenement House Act. Nothing herein contained shall abrogate or impair the existing powers of the department of health of the city of New York. The tenement house department shall have the powers and shall perform the duties specified in this chapter.

Transfer of powers of other departments

1334k. Such rights, powers and duties as are now possessed by the fire department and police department of the city of New York with respect to the prevention of incumbrance or obstruction of fire escapes on tenement houses, are hereby transferred to and conferred upon the tenement house department. All rights, powers and duties now possessed by the department of buildings in the city of New York with respect to the light and ventilation of tenement houses and with respect to the equipment of completed tenement houses with fire escapes, are transferred to and conferred upon the tenement house department.

Approval of plans and specifications for light and ventilation

1344l. Before the construction or alteration of a tenement house, or the alteration or conversion of a building for use as a tenement house, is commenced, the owner, or his agent or architect, shall submit to the tenement house department a detailed statement in writing, verified by the person making the same, of the specifications for the light and ventilation of such tenement house or building, upon a blank or form to be furnished by such department, and also a full and complete copy of the plans of such work. Such statement shall give in full the name and residence, by street and number, of the owner or owners of such tenement house or building. If such construction, alteration, or conversion, is proposed to be made by any other person than the owner of the land in fee, such statement shall contain the full name and residence, by street and number, not only of the owner of the land, but of every person interested in such tenement house, either as owner, lessee or in any representative capacity. The statements herein provided for may be made by the owner, or the person who proposes to make the construction, alteration or conversion, or by his agent or architect. No person, however, shall be recognized as the agent of the owner, unless he shall file with the tenement house department a written instrument, signed by such owner, designating him as such agent. Such specifications, plans and statements shall be filed in the office of the tenement house department and shall be deemed public records, but no such specifications, plans or statements shall be removed from said department, or copied.

The commissioner shall cause all such plans and specifications to be examined. If such plans and specifications conform to the provisions of the New York Tenement House Act, they shall be approved by such commissioner, and a written certificate to that effect shall be issued to the person submitting the same. The Commissioner may, from time to time, approve changes in any plans and specifications previously approved by him, provided the plans and specifications when so changed shall be in conformity with law.

The construction, alteration or conversion of such tenement house or building, or any part thereof, shall not be commenced until the filing of such specifications, plans and statements, and the approval thereof by the tenement house commissioner, as above provided.

No permit shall be granted and no plan approved by the department of buildings of the city of New York for the construction or alteration of a tenement house, or for the alteration or conversion of any building for use as a tenement house, until there has been filed in such department a certificate of the tenement house commissioner, issued as above provided.

Inspection of tenement houses in course of construction

1344m. The commissioner shall cause an inspection and examination to be made of all tenement houses in the course of construction or alteration, and also of all buildings in course of alteration or conversion for use as tenement houses, for the purpose of ascertaining whether such tenement houses or buildings are being constructed, altered or converted in conformity with the law, and the plans and specifications on file in the office of the department, and approved by the commissioner.

Certificate to owner of tenement house hereafter erected or altered

1344n. Within ten days after notice from the owner of a tenement house or building constructed, altered or converted, the tenement house commissioner shall cause an inspection thereof to be made, and, if it is found that said tenement house or building has been constructed, altered or converted in conformity with law in respect to the light and ventilation of tenement houses, and with the plans and specifications approved by the tenement house commissioner, such commissioner shall in such case, and in no other, cause a written certificate to be issued to the owner of such tenement house or building to the effect that such tenement house or building has been so constructed, altered or converted. No such tenement house or building shall be used or occupied as a tenement house until such certificate has been issued by such commissioner. No permit shall be granted by the department of water supply to turn on the water in any such tenement house, unless such certificate of the tenement house commissioner has been issued.

Inspection of completed tenement houses

1344o. Except as hereinafter otherwise provided, the tenement house commissioner shall cause an inspection of every completed tenement house in the city to be made at least once in each month. Such inspection shall include examination of cellars, halls, rooms, water-closets, privies, plumbing, yards, areas, fire escapes, roof, shafts, courts, tanks and all other parts of such tenement houses and the premises connected therewith. In tenement houses where the average rental of the apartments therein is twenty-five dollars a month or more, such inspection may be made less often than once a month as above provided, in the discretion of the tenement house commissioner. The tenement house commissioner shall prescribe the manner in which such inspections shall be made.

The inspectors shall immediately report to the tenement house department all violations of the New York Tenement House Act, and the tenement house commissioner shall issue such orders as he may deem necessary requiring the removal of the defect or a cessation of the act which is in violation of such law.

Injunctions, when to be granted against the department

1344p. No preliminary injunction shall be granted against the tenement house department or its officers except by the supreme court, at a special term thereof, after service of at least five days' notice of the motion for such injunction, together with copies of the papers upon which the motion for such injunction is to be made. Whenever such department shall seek any provisional remedy or shall prosecute an appeal, it shall not be necessary, before obtaining or prosecuting the same, to give an undertaking.

Power of attorney for the department

1344q. The counsel assigned by the corporation counsel to the tenement house department shall sue for and collect all penalties, and take charge of and conduct all legal proceedings imposed or provided by this chapter, or by the New York Tenement House Act, and all other tenement house laws, regulations and ordinances. All suits or proceedings instituted for the enforcement of the several provisions of this chapter, or for the recovery of penalties imposed by the New York Tenement House Act, shall be brought in the name of the tenement house department of the city of New York, by such counsel. The commissioner shall cause all notices of violations to be submitted to such counsel and it shall be his duty to prosecute the same. The penalties recovered shall be paid to such counsel. He shall on the first of each month render to the commissioner an itemized statement of all moneys collected by him and pay over the same to the tenement house commissioner. He shall at the same time render a statement of the necessary disbursements incurred or paid in the prosecution of the actions and proceedings instituted by him. The tenement house commissioner shall pay monthly the amount of such moneys so collected to the comptroller of the city of New York.

No personal liability

1344r. An officer or employee of the tenement house department shall not be liable for acts done by him, in good faith, in the performance of his official duties, pursuant to the direction of the commissioner or the rules and regulations of the department. Any person whose property has been unjustly or illegally destroyed or injured pursuant to the order, regulation or ordinance of such tenement house department, or its officers or employees, for which no personal liability exists as aforesaid, may maintain a proper action against the city for the recovery of the proper compensation or damage. Every such suit shall be brought within six months after the cause of action arose, and the recovery shall be limited to the damages suffered.

Right of entry of officers of department

1344s. The tenement house commissioner and his deputy and all inspectors of the tenement house department and such other persons as are authorized by the commissioner, may without fee or hindrance enter, examine and survey all premises, grounds, erections, structures, apartments, buildings and every part thereof in the city, and all cellars and passages of every sort and inspect the safety and sanitary condition, and make plans, drawings and descriptions thereof, according to the regulations of the department. The owner or his agent or representative and the lessee or occupant of every tenement house or part thereof, and every person having the care and management thereof, shall at all times when required by any of such officers or persons give them free access to such house and every part thereof.

Punishment for false returns and deceptive reports

1344t. Any inspector, officer or employee of such tenement house department who shall knowingly make thereto a false or deceptive report or statement in connection with his duties, or shall accept or receive any bribe or other compensation as a condition of or an inducement for not faithfully discovering or fully reporting or otherwise acting in accordance with his duty in any respect, shall be guilty of a misdemeanor and punishable by imprisonment for not more than one year and by a fine of not more than five hundred dollars. If such officer, inspector or employee be convicted of such offense, he shall forfeit his office, and in addition all compensation due or to become due from such department.

Falsely personating an officer

1344u. If any person, not an officer, inspector or employee of such department or acting under the authority thereof, falsely represents himself as such, or if any such person shall use, wear or display, without authority, any shield or other insignia or emblem such as is worn by such an officer, inspector or employee, he shall be guilty of a misdemeanor.

Application of provisions of chapter nineteen

1344v. The provisions of chapter nineteen of this charter, relative to the department of health, which provide:

1. For the repair of buildings, as contained in Section 1171 of such chapter.
2. For proceedings relative to dangerous and improperly constructed buildings, as contained in Section 1176 thereof.
3. For assistance and co-operation of the police department, as contained in Section 1202 thereof.
4. Punishment for violations of orders and the service of such orders, as contained in Sections 1222 and 1224 thereof.
5. For legal proceedings and punishment for disobedience of orders and ordinances, as contained in title four thereof.
6. For reimbursements and lien of expenses incurred by such department in the execution of its orders as contained in title five thereof.

7. For suits for the abatement or removal of nuisances, and for proceedings, and the powers and duties of such department in respect to such nuisances, as contained in title six thereof; and the definition of the word "nuisance" and other matters in respect thereto, as contained in section 1229 thereof, shall apply to the supervision and regulation of tenement houses by the tenement house department, its officers, agents and employes, unless otherwise specified in, or inconsistent with, the provisions of this chapter. All the provisions of the sections and titles above specified shall be so applicable to such tenement house department, its officers, agents and employees.

Title 3

RECORDS AND REPORTS; MISCELLANEOUS PROVISIONS

Records in Department

1344w. The tenement house commissioner shall provide a system for keeping the records of tenement houses by card catalogue and street number, or otherwise. Such records shall include:

(1.) A diagram of each tenement house showing the shape of the building, its width and depth, also the measurements of the unoccupied area, showing shafts, courts, yards and other open spaces. Such diagram shall include a diagram of the second or typical floor of the building, showing the sizes and arrangement of the rooms, and all doors, stairs, windows, halls and partitions.

(2.) A statement of the date or the approximate date when the building was erected.

(3.) The deaths occurring in the tenement house during each year and the annual death rate therein. Such statement shall show whether such deaths were of adults or children, and, if occasioned by tuberculosis, typhoid fever, diphtheria, scarlet fever, smallpox, measles, or by any other contagious or infectious disease, it shall state the disease causing death.

(4.) The cases of sickness occurring in the tenement house and the nature of the disease. Such records shall also show whether such cases of sickness were of children or adults.

(5.) The arrests of persons residing in the tenement house.

Reports from different institutions and departments

1344x. All dispensaries and hospitals in the city of New York shall make weekly statements to the tenement house department as to the cases of sickness received in such hospital or treated in such dispensary from each tenement house. Such statement shall show the location of the tenement house, by street and number, from which the case was received, and the nature of the sickness treated, whether the patient was an adult or child and the date of the treatment.

The police department of the city of New York shall furnish to the tenement house department a weekly statement of the number of arrests of persons living in tenement houses, which shall show the location of the tenement house, by street and number, the offense with which the person is charged, the age and name of the offender, and such other information as the tenement house department may require. The tenement house commissioner shall prescribe and furnish blank forms for making such statements.

Other reports to the department

1344y. Such department may require reports and information of such facts relative to the condition of persons residing in tenement houses, as the commissioner may deem to be useful in carrying out the purposes of this chapter and the tenement house laws, regulations and ordinances, from all dispensaries, hospitals, charitable or benevolent societies, infirmaries, prisons and schools, and from the managers, principals and officers thereof; the managers, principals and officers of such institutions shall promptly give such information and make such reports, verbal or in writing, as may be required by the commissioner.

Transfer of property, etc., from other departments

1344z. Upon the organization of the tenement house department hereby created, and upon notice thereof from the tenement house commissioner to the department of health and department of buildings, such books, papers, records, and other matters belonging to, or in the custody of, such departments of health or buildings, and used in such departments in connection with tenement houses, as the tenement house commissioner may require for carrying out the provisions of this chapter and the enforcement of the tenement house laws, regulations and ordinances, shall be transferred by such department of health and department of buildings to the tenement house department hereby created.

Co-operation of other departments

1344aa. It shall be the duty of all city departments at all times, when requested so to do, to co-operate with the tenement house department and to furnish such department with such information, reports and assistance as may be required.

Details of men to assist tenement house department

1344bb. The police board, upon the requisition of the tenement house commissioner, shall detail to the service of said tenement house department for the purpose of the enforcement of the acts relating to tenement and lodging houses not more than one hundred suitable officers and men of experience of at least five years' service in the police force, provided that the tenement house department shall pay monthly to the police department a sum equal to the pay of all officers and men so detailed. These officers and men shall belong to the sanitary company of police, shall report to the tenement house commissioner. The tenement house commissioner may report back to the police department for punishment any member of said company guilty of any breach of order or discipline, or of neglecting his duty, and thereupon the police board shall detail another officer or man in his place, and the discipline of the said members of the sanitary company shall be in the jurisdiction of the police department, but at any time the tenement house commissioner may object to any member of said sanitary company on the ground of inefficiency, and thereupon another officer or man shall be detailed in his place.

Definitions

1344cc. The term "department," when used in this chapter, shall mean the tenement house department. The term "commissioner," when used in this chapter, shall mean the tenement house commissioner. The term "tenement house," when used in this chapter, shall be deemed to refer to a tenement house, which is subject to the provisions of the New York Tenement House Act, and defined therein.

Saving Clause

1344dd. Nothing in this chapter shall affect or in any way impair any act done or right accruing, accrued or acquired, or liability, penalty, forfeiture or punishment incurred prior to the time this chapter takes effect, but the same may be asserted, enforced, prosecuted or inflicted, as fully and to the same extent as if the tenement house department had not been created and the powers and duties of the department of health, the department of buildings, and the police department, in respect to tenement houses and the laws, rules and ordinances relating thereto had not been transferred to such tenement house department, as provided in this chapter. All actions and proceedings, civil or criminal, commenced under or by virtue of statutes creating and conferring powers and imposing duties on such department of health, department of buildings, and police department, in respect to tenement houses and for the enforcement of laws, rules and ordinances relative thereto, and pending immediately prior to the taking effect of this chapter, may be prosecuted and defended to final effect by the tenement house department in the same manner as they might by such department of health, department of buildings or police department, if this chapter had not been passed. All such actions and proceedings shall be prosecuted and defended in the name of the tenement house department.

1344ee. This act shall take effect on the first day of January, 1902.

APPENDIX IV

OTHER PROPOSED LEGISLATION

OTHER PROPOSED LEGISLATION

An Act to amend chapter three hundred and seventy-eight of the laws of eighteen hundred and ninety-seven, entitled "An Act to unite into one municipality under the corporate name of The City of New York, the various communities lying in and about New York harbor, including the city and county of New York, the city of Brooklyn and the county of Kings, the county of Richmond and part of the county of Queens, and to provide for the government thereof."[1]

The People of the State of New York, represented in Senate and Assembly, do enact as follows:

Section 1. Section thirteen hundred and fourteen of chapter three hundred and seventy-eight of the laws of eighteen hundred and ninety-seven, is hereby amended to read as follows:

Inspection; Officers to have access

§ 1314. It shall be the duty of the board of health to cause a careful inspection to be made of every tenement and lodging at least twice in each year until the first of January, nineteen hundred and two. And whenever the board of health has made any order concerning a tenement or lodging house it shall cause a reinspection to be made of the same within six days after it has been informed that the order has been served. The keeper of any lodging house and the owner, agent of the owner, lessee or occupant of any tenement-house, and every other person having the care and management thereof, shall, at all times, when required by any officer of the department of health, or by any officer upon whom any duty is conferred by this title, give him free access to such house, and to every part thereof. The owner or keeper of any lodging-house, and the owner, agent of the owner and the lessee of any tenement-house or part thereof, shall, whenever any person in such house is sick of fever, or of any infectious, pestilential or contagious disease, and information thereof has been given to such owner, keeper, agent or lessee, give immediate notice thereof to the board of health, or to some officer of the same, and thereupon said board shall cause the same to be immediately cleansed or disinfected, at the expense of the owner, in such manner as it may deem necessary and effectual, and it may also cause the blankets, bedding and bed-clothes used by any such sick person to be thoroughly cleansed, scoured and fumigated, or, in extreme cases, to be destroyed.

[1] This proposed amendment was incorporated in the general amendment to the Greater New York Charter, which is to be found in Chapter 466 of the laws of 1901.

SECTION 2. Section thirteen hundred and twenty-four of said act is hereby amended to read as follows:

Sanitary company of police

§ 1324. The board of health shall make requisitions upon the police board for the detail of at least twenty-five [fifty] and not more than fifty [one hundred] suitable officers and men of at least five years' service in the police force, who shall be selected for their peculiar fitness for the enforcement of the provisions of the sanitary code [and the acts relating to tenement and lodging houses]. These officers and men shall be detailed to such service by the police board, and the department of health shall pay to the police department monthly, the amount of the pay of the officers and men so detailed, who shall belong to the sanitary company of the police and shall report to the board of health. [At least thirty of the officers and men so detailed shall be employed exclusively in the enforcement of the laws relating to tenement and lodging houses.] The board of health may report back to the police board for punishment, any member of said company guilty of any breach of orders or discipline, or of neglecting his duty, and thereupon the police board shall detail another officer or man in his place, and the discipline of the said members of the sanitary company shall be in the jurisdiction of the police department; but at any time the board of health may object to the efficiency of any member of said sanitary company and thereupon another officer or man shall be detailed in his place.

SECTION 3. Section two hundred and thirty of said act is hereby amended by omitting subdivision ninth thereof. [Ninth — The sum of ten thousand dollars to the credit of the department of health, to be known as the tenement house fund, to be expended by the board of health.]

SECTION 4. This act shall go into effect on January first, nineteen hundred and two.

AN ACT to amend the Public Health Law in relation to tenement houses.[1]

The People of the State of New York represented in Senate and Assembly, do enact as follows:

SEC. 1. Article one of the Public Health Law is hereby amended by adding thereto an additional section to be known as Sec. 13, and to read as follows:

SEC. 13. The board shall have power to examine into the enforcement of the laws relating to tenement houses in any city of the first class. Whenever required by the governor, it shall make such an examination and shall report the results thereof to the governor within the time prescribed by him therefor.

SEC. 2. This act shall take effect immediately.

[1] This legislation is to be found in Chapter 283 of the laws of 1901.

APPENDIX V

THE TENEMENT HOUSE ACT AS AMENDED IN 1901, 1902, AND 1903

(Chapters 334 and 555, Laws of 1901; Chapter 352, Laws of 1902; Chapter 179, Laws of 1903)

THE TENEMENT HOUSE ACT

An Act in Relation to Tenement Houses in Cities of the First Class.
Became a Law April 12, 1901

CHAPTER I. DEFINITIONS

Section 1. *Short Title and Application.* — This act may be cited as the Tenement House Act, and its provisions shall apply to cities of the first class.

§ 2. *Definitions.* — Certain words used in this act are defined for the purposes thereof as follows:

(1) A tenement house is any house or building, or portion thereof, which is rented, leased, let or hired out, to be occupied, or is occupied as the home or residence of three families or more living independently of each other, and doing their cooking upon the premises, or by more than two families upon any floor, so living and cooking, but having a common right in the halls, stairways, yards, water-closets or privies, or some of them.

(2) A yard is an open unoccupied space on the same lot with a tenement house, between the extreme rear line of the house and the rear line of the lot.

(3) A court is an open unoccupied space, other than a yard, on the same lot with a tenement house. A court not extending to the street or yard is an inner court. A court extending to the street or yard is an outer court. If it extends to the street it is a street court. If it extends to the yard it is a yard court.

(4) A shaft includes exterior and interior shafts, whether for air, light, elevator, dumbwaiter, or any other purpose. A vent shaft is one used solely to ventilate or light a water-closet compartment or bathroom.

(5) A public hall is a hall, corridor or passageway not within an apartment.

(6) A stair hall includes the stairs, stair landings and those portions of the public halls through which it is necessary to pass in going between the entrance floor and the roof.

(7) A basement is a story partly but not more than one-half below the level of the curb.

(8) A cellar is a story more than one-half below the level of the curb.

(9) A fireproof tenement house is one the walls of which are constructed of brick, stone, iron or other hard incombustible material, and in which there are no wood beams or lintels, and in which the floors, roofs, stair halls and public halls are built entirely of brick, stone, iron or other

hard incombustible material, and in which no woodwork or other inflammable material is used in any of the partitions, furrings or ceilings. But this definition shall not be construed as prohibiting, elsewhere than in the stair halls or entrance halls, the use of wooden flooring on top of the fireproof floors or the use of wooden sleepers, nor as prohibiting wooden handrails and hard-wood treads such as described in section eighteen of this act.

(10) The word shall is always mandatory, and not directory, and denotes that the house shall be maintained in all respects according to the mandate, as long as it continues to be a tenement house.

(11) Wherever the words, charter, ordinances, regulations, department of buildings, department of health, department of water supply, fire department, department charged with the enforcement of this act, corporation counsel, city treasury or fire limits occur in this act they shall be construed as if followed by the words "of the city in which the tenement house is situated." Wherever the words "is occupied" are used in this act applying to any building, such words shall be construed as if followed by the words "or is intended, arranged or designed to be occupied."

(12) The height of a tenement house is the perpendicular distance measured in a straight line from the curb level to the highest point of the roof beams, the measurements in all cases to be taken through the centre of the facade of the house. Where a building is on a corner lot and there is more than one grade or level, the measurements shall be taken through the centre of the facade on the street having the greatest grade.

§ 3. *Buildings Converted or Altered.* — A building not erected for use as a tenement house, if hereafter converted or altered to such use, shall thereupon become subject to all the provisions of this act affecting tenement houses hereafter erected.

§ 4. *Buildings in Process of Erection.* — A tenement house not now completed, but the excavation for which shall have been commenced in good faith on or before the first day of June, nineteen hundred and one, after approval of the plans therefor by the department of buildings, and the first tier of beams of which shall have been set on or before the first day of August, nineteen hundred and one, shall be subject only to the provisions of this act affecting now existing tenement houses; provided that the plans for said house were filed in said department on or before the tenth day of April, nineteen hundred and one, and were in accordance with the laws in force at the time of filing, and that the building is built in accordance with such laws.

§ 5. *Alterations and Change in Occupancy.* — No tenement house shall at any time be altered so as to be in violation of any provision of this act. If any tenement house or any part thereof is occupied by more families than provided in this act, or is erected, altered or occupied contrary to law, such tenement house shall be deemed an unlawful structure, and the department charged with the enforcement of this act[1] may cause such building to be vacated. And such building shall not again be occupied until it or its occupation, as the case may be, has been made to conform to the law.

[1] Tenement House Department.

CHAPTER II. PROTECTION FROM FIRE

Title I

Section 11. *Fireproof Tenements, When Required.* — Every tenement house hereafter erected exceeding six stories or parts of stories, in height above the curb level, shall be a fireproof tenement house, nor shall any tenement house be altered so as to exceed such height without being made a fireproof tenement house. A cellar the ceiling of which does not extend more than two feet above the curb level is not a story within the meaning of this section.

§ 12. *Fire Escapes.*— Every non-fireproof tenement house hereafter erected, unless provided with fireproof outside stairways directly accessible to each apartment, shall have fire escapes located and constructed as in this section required, except that tenement houses that are less than four stories in height and which also do not contain accommodations for more than four families in all, may be equipped with such other iron, steel, or wire cable fire escapes as may be approved by the department charged with the enforcement of this act,[1] such escapes must be capable of sustaining two thousand pounds, and be of sufficient length to reach from the top floor to the ground, and with rungs not more than twelve inches apart and not less than fifteen inches in length.

(1) The fire escapes shall open directly from at least one room in each apartment at each story above the ground floor, other than a bath room or water closet compartment, and shall not include the window of a stair hall, and no fire escape shall be placed in a court except as provided in section fifty-seven of this act. Fire escapes may project into the public highway to a distance not greater than four feet beyond the building line.

(2) The fire escapes shall consist of outside open iron balconies and stairways. The balcony on the top floor, except in case of a front fire escape, shall be provided with a goose-neck ladder leading from said balcony to and above the roof. Such goose-neck ladder shall be securely fastened to the wall of the building and to the roof, and there shall be a space of not less than eighteen inches between the outside line of such ladder and the outer rail of the top fire-escape balcony. Such ladder shall be constructed as provided for drop ladders in subdivision eight of this section; the strings shall be in one piece and shall not be connected in parts by rivets and bolts; such ladders shall be arranged to rest at the bottom on brackets, and not on the slats forming the floor of the balcony.

(3) *Balconies.* — The balconies shall not be less than three feet in width, taking in at least one window of each apartment at each story above the ground floor. They shall be below and not more than one foot below the window sills and extend in front of and not less than nine inches beyond each window. There shall be a landing not less than twenty-four inches square at the head and foot of each stairway. In every case there shall be a passageway between the string of the stairway and the wall of the building or the outer rail of the balcony, as the case may be, such passageway to be not less than fourteen inches wide in every part. The stairway opening on each platform shall be of a size sufficient to provide clear headway.

(4) *Floor of Balconies.* — The floors of balconies shall be of wrought

[1] Tenement House Department.

iron or steel slats not less than one and a half inches by three-eighths of an inch, placed not more than one and one-quarter inches apart, and well secured and riveted to iron battens one and a half inches by three-eighths of an inch, not over three feet apart and riveted at the intersection. The ends of such floor slats shall project beyond the platform frame, but shall not rest on the bottom rail. The openings for stairways in all balconies shall not be less than twenty-one inches wide and thirty-two inches long, and such openings shall have no covers of any kind. The platforms or balconies shall be constructed and erected to safely sustain in all their parts a safe load at a ratio of four to one, of not less than eighty pounds per square foot of surface.

(5) *Railings.* — The outside top rail shall extend around the entire length of the platform and in all cases shall go through the wall at each end, and be properly secured by nuts and four-inch square washers at least three-eighths of an inch thick, and no top rail shall be connected at angles by cast iron. The top rail of balconies shall be one and three-quarter inches by one-half inch of wrought iron, or one and a half inch angle iron one-quarter inch thick. The bottom rails shall be one and one-half inches by three-eighths of an inch wrought iron, or one and a half inch angle iron, one-quarter inch thick, well leaded or cemented into the wall. The ends of all rails which go through the walls shall be worked out to not less than three-quarter inch bolt size for top rails, or one-half inch bolt size for bottom rails, and if constructed as separate pieces shall be properly secured to the rails with not less than two one-half inch rivets. The standards or filling-in bars shall be not less than one-half inch round or square wrought iron, well riveted to the top and bottom rails and platform frame. Such standards or filling-in bars shall be securely braced by outside brackets at suitable intervals, and shall be placed not more than six inches from centres; the height of railings shall in no case be less than two feet nine inches.

(6) *Stairways.* — The stairways shall be placed at an angle of not more than sixty degrees, with steps not less than six inches in width and twenty inches in length, and with a rise of not more than nine inches; and shall be constructed and erected to fully sustain in all their parts a safe load at a ratio of four to one of not less than one hundred pounds per step, with the exception of the tread which must safely sustain at said ratio a load of two hundred pounds. The treads shall be flat open treads or may be constructed of flat bars, not over one and one-half inches wide, riveted to angle irons of a size not less than one and one-half inch, with the open spaces between such bars not over three-quarters of an inch wide. The strings shall be not less than three-inch channels of iron or steel, or three-eighths by four-inch bars, or two three-eighths by one and one-half inch bars properly latticed, or two one-quarter by one and one-half inch angles properly latticed, or other shape equally strong. Unless of channel or angle iron they shall be stiffened by the use of braces properly leaded into or bolted through the wall, and also bolted through the string at a height of not less than seven feet above the floor of the balcony. They shall rest upon and be bolted to a bracket, which shall be fastened through the wall as hereinafter provided. The strings shall be securely bolted to a bracket at the top, and the steps in all cases shall be double-riveted or bolted to the strings. The stairs shall have three-quarter inch handrails of wrought iron, well braced.

(7) *Brackets.* — The brackets shall not be less than one-half inch by one and three-quarter inches wrought iron, placed edgewise, or one and three-quarter inch angle iron, one-quarter inch thick, well braced; they shall not be more than four feet apart, and shall be braced by means of not less than three-quarters of an inch square wrought iron, and shall extend two-thirds of the width of the respective balconies or brackets, The brackets shall go through the wall and be turned down three inches. or be properly secured by nuts and four-inch square washers at least three-eighths of an inch thick. On new buildings the brackets shall be set as the walls are being built. When brackets are put on tenement houses already erected the part going through the wall shall not be less than one inch in diameter with screw nuts and washers not less than five inches square and one-half an inch thick. If the end going through the wall is separately constructed it shall be properly connected to the bracket with not less than two five-eighths inch rivets staggered.

(8) *Drop-ladders.* — A drop-ladder shall be required from the lowest balcony. Such drop ladder shall be of sufficient length to reach from the lowest balcony or platform to a safe landing place beneath. It shall be not less than fifteen inches in width, with strings not less than one-half inch by two inches and rungs not less than five-eighths of an inch in diameter placed not over twelve inches apart and properly riveted through the strings. Where the lowest balcony is more than fourteen feet above the ground beneath the same, a suitable landing platform shall be provided. Such platform shall be located not more than ten feet above the ground and shall be connected with the fire escapes above by a stairway constructed as in this section required. Such platform shall be not less than four feet in length by three feet in width, and shall be provided at each end with proper railings and a drop ladder to reach the ground. Except as above specified, it shall be constructed in conformity with the other provisions of this section.

(9) *Painting.* — All the parts of such fire escapes shall receive not less than two coats of paint, one in the shop and one after erection. All fire escape balconies shall contain a plate firmly fastened to the standards or filling-in bars near the top railing in front of and facing at least one window in each apartment using such balcony, such plate to contain in plain, large, prominent, raised letters, each letter to be not less than one-half an inch in length, the following words: "Any one placing any encumbrance on this balcony will be fined ten dollars." The lettering on such plates shall be painted with a paint of a color different from that used on the body of the plate so that the letters will be prominent and distinct.

(10) *Fire Escapes on Wooden Tenement Houses.* — All fire escapes hereafter constructed on wooden tenement houses shall conform in all particulars to the provisions of section twelve of this act except as hereinafter mentioned: The rise of the steps of the stairways shall be not more than eleven inches; the strings shall be not less than one-quarter inch by four inch bars properly braced to the wall as described in subdivision six of this section; the brackets and top rails shall be secured by bolts through the wall. In no case shall said bolts pass through the studs of said wall, but shall be properly fastened with washers and screw nuts through a wrought iron or steel plate, such plate to be not less than three inches by one-quarter inch, and to pass across and bear upon the entire inner faces of at least two studs. The said plate shall be backed and re-enforced by

solid blocking as thick as the studding, firmly secured to the studs across which the plate passes. The bottom rails shall be secured in a similar manner, or by means of lag screws not less than five-eighths of an inch in diameter and four inches long, properly screwed into bored holes in the studs, said holes to be not more than seven-sixteenths of an inch in diameter and the centre of such holes not to be within one and one-quarter inches of the sides of the studs.

§ 13. *Bulkheads.* — Every tenement house hereafter erected shall have in the roof a fireproof bulkhead with a fireproof door to the same, and shall have fireproof stairs with a guide or handrail leading to the roof, except that in tenement houses hereafter erected, which do not exceed four stories and cellar in height, and which also are not occupied or arranged to be occupied by more than two families on any floor, such bulkheads may be of wood covered with metal on both sides. The stairs leading to such bulkheads shall be constructed as specified in sections fourteen to twenty of this act.

§ 14. *Stairs and Public Halls.* — Every tenement house hereafter erected shall have at least one flight of stairs extending from the entrance floor to the roof, and the stairs and public halls therein shall each be at least three feet wide in the clear.

§ 15. *Stairways in Non-fireproof Buildings.* — Every non-fireproof tenement house hereafter erected containing over twenty-six apartments or suites of rooms above the entrance story shall also have an additional flight of stairs for every additional twenty-six apartments or fraction thereof; if said house contains not more than thirty-six apartments above the entrance story, in lieu of an additional stairway, the stairs, stair halls and entrance halls throughout the entire building may each be at least one-half wider than is specified in sections fourteen and twenty of this act.

§ 16. *Stairways in Fireproof Buildings.* — Every fireproof tenement house hereafter erected containing over thirty-six apartments or suites of rooms above the entrance story shall also have an additional flight of stairs for every additional thirty-six apartments or fraction thereof; but if said house contains not more than forty-eight apartments above the entrance story, in lieu of an additional stairway the stairs, stair halls and entrance halls throughout the entire building may each be at least one-half wider than is specified in sections fourteen and twenty of this act. And if said house contains not more than eighty-four apartments above the entrance story in lieu of three stairways there may be but two stairways, provided that one of such stairways and the stair halls and entrance halls connected therewith are at least one-half wider than is specified in sections fourteen and twenty of this act.

§ 17. *Stairways, Continued.* — Each flight of stairs mentioned in the last three sections shall have an entrance on the entrance floor from the street or street court, or from an inner court which connects directly with the street. All stairs shall be constructed with a rise of not more than eight inches and with treads not less than ten inches wide and not less than three feet long in the clear. Winders will not be permitted except in a tenement house provided with a power passenger elevator. Where winders are used, all treads at a point eighteen inches from the strings on the well side shall be at least ten inches wide.

§ 18. *Stair Halls.* — The stair halls in all non-fireproof as well as fireproof tenement houses hereafter erected shall be constructed as in this section and the two following sections specified. In tenement houses hereafter erected which either are occupied or are arranged to be occupied by more than two families on any floor, or which exceed four stories and cellar in height, the stair halls shall be constructed of fireproof material throughout. The risers, strings and banisters shall be of metal or stone. The treads shall be of metal, slate or stone, or of hard wood not less than two inches thick. Wooden hand rails to stairs will be permitted if constructed of hard wood. The floors of all such stair halls shall be constructed of iron or steel beams and fireproof filling and no wooden flooring or sleepers shall be permitted. In tenement houses hereafter erected which do not exceed four stories and cellar in height and which also are not occupied or arranged to be occupied by more than two families on any floor, the stair halls shall either be constructed of iron beams and fireproof filling, or shall be filled in between the floor beams with at least five inches of cement deafening. In such houses the stairs shall be iron or stone, or may be of wood, provided the soffits are covered with metal lath and plastered with two coats of mortar, or with good quality plasterboards not less than one-half inch in thickness, made of plaster and strong fibre and all joints made true and well-pointed.

§ 19. *Stair Halls, Continued.* — In every non-fireproof tenement house hereafter erected which either is occupied or is arranged to be occupied by more than two families on any floor, or which exceeds four stories and cellar in height, all stair halls shall be enclosed on all sides with brick walls. The doors opening from such stair halls shall be fireproof and self-closing, and if provided with glass such glass shall be good quality wire-glass. There shall be no transom or movable sash opening from such stair hall to any other part of the house. Each stair hall shall be shut off from all non-fireproof portions of the public halls and from all other non-fireproof parts of the building, on each story, by self-closing fireproof doors, and if glass is used in such doors it shall be of good quality wire-glass. In tenement houses hereafter erected which do not exceed four stories and cellar in height and which also are not occupied or arranged to be occupied by more than two families on any floor, the stair halls shall be enclosed on all sides with brick walls or with partitions of angle iron and fireproof blocks not less than four inches thick; in tenement houses hereafter erected which do not exceed three stories and cellar in height, and which also are not occupied or arranged to be occupied by more than two families on any floor, the stair halls may be enclosed with wooden stud partitions, provided such partitions are covered on both sides with metal lath, or with good quality plaster boards not less than one-half inch in thickness, made of plaster and strong fibre and all joints made true and well-pointed, and provided that the space between the studs is filled in with brick to the height of the floor beams.

§ 20. *Entrance Halls.* — Every entrance hall in a tenement house hereafter erected shall be at least three feet six inches wide in the clear, from the entrance up to and including the stair enclosure, and beyond this point at least three feet wide in the clear, and shall comply with all the conditions of the preceding sections of this act as to the construction of stair halls, except that in a fireproof tenement house hereafter erected it may be enclosed with terra cotta blocks not less than four inches thick and angle iron construction, instead of brick walls. If such entrance hall is the only entrance to more than one flight of stairs, that portion of said hall between the entrance and the first flight of stairs shall be increased one-half in width in every part for each such additional flight of stairs. In every tenement house hereafter erected, access shall be had from the street to the yard, either in a direct line or through a court.

§ 21. *First Tier of Beams.*—In all non-fireproof as well as fireproof tenement houses hereafter erected five stories or more in height, exclusive of the cellar, the first floor above the lowest cellar, or, if there be no cellar, above the lowest story, shall be constructed fireproof with iron or steel beams and fireproof flooring; and the bottom flanges and all exposed portions of such iron or steel beams below the abutments of the floor arches or filling shall be entirely encased with hard-burnt clay or porous terra cotta or with metal lath properly secured and plastered on the under side. In all non-fireproof tenement houses hereafter erected less than five stories in height, where the first floor above the lowest cellar, or, if there be no cellar, above the lowest story, is not constructed fireproof with iron or steel beams and fireproof flooring, the cellar ceiling of said tenement house shall be lathed with metal lath and plastered thereon with two coats of brown mortar of good materials, or shall be covered with plaster boards not less than one-half inch in thickness, made of plaster and strong fibre and all joints made true and well pointed.

§ 22. *Partitions, Construction of.*—In all non-fireproof tenement houses hereafter erected, fore and aft stud partitions which rest directly over each other shall run through the wooden floor beams and rest upon the plate of the partition below, and shall have the studding filled in solid between the uprights to the depth of the floor beams with suitable incombustible materials. In all fireproof tenement houses hereafter erected, all partitions shall rest directly upon the fireproof floor construction, and extend to the fireproof beam filling above.

§ 23. *Cellar Stairs in Non-fireproof Buildings.*—In non-fireproof tenement houses hereafter erected which either are occupied or are arranged to be occupied by more than two families on any floor, or which exceed four stories and cellar in height, there shall be no inside stairs communicating between the lowest cellar or other lowest story and the floor next above, but such stairs shall in every case be located outside the building, and if enclosed shall be constructed entirely fireproof and be enclosed in a fireproof enclosure with fireproof self-closing doors at all openings. This provision however shall not apply to the stairs leading from the entrance story to the upper stories in tenement houses hereafter erected where there is no cellar or other story below the said entrance story. In tenement houses hereafter erected which do not exceed four stories and cellar in height and which also are not occupied or arranged to be occupied by more than two families on any floor, the stairs leading to the cellar may be located inside the building, provided they are entirely enclosed with brick walls and are provided with fireproof self-closing doors at both the top and bottom.

§ 24. *Cellar Stairs in Fireproof Buildings.*—In every fireproof tenement house hereafter erected the stairs communicating between the lowest cellar or other lowest story and the floor next above, if not located underneath the stairs leading to the upper stories, may be placed inside of the said building; provided, that the portion of the cellar or other lowest story into which said stairs lead is entirely shut off by fireproof walls from those portions thereof which are used for the storage of fuel, or in which heating appliances, boilers or machinery are located. All openings in such walls shall be provided with self-closing fireproof doors.

§ 25. *Closet under First Story Stairs.*—In non-fireproof tenement houses hereafter erected no closet of any kind shall be constructed under any staircase leading from the first story, exclusive of the cellar, to the upper stories, but such space shall be left entirely open and kept clear and free from encumbrance.

§ 26. *Cellar Entrance.* — In every tenement house hereafter erected there shall be an entrance to the cellar or other lowest story from the outside of the said building.

§ 27. *Fire Stops.* — In tenement houses hereafter erected, in all walls where wooden furring is used all the courses of brick from the under side of the floor beams to the top of the same shall project a distance of at least two inches beyond the inside face of the wall so as to provide an effective fire stop; and wherever floor beams run parallel to a wall and wooden furring is used such beams shall always be kept at least two and one-half inches away from the inside line of the wall, and the space between the beams and the wall shall be built up solidly with brickwork from the under side of the floor beams to the top of the same, so as to form an effective fire stop.

§ 28. *Wooden Tenement Houses.* — Within the fire limits no wooden tenement house shall hereafter be erected, and no wooden building not now used as a tenement house shall hereafter be altered or converted to such use. But outside of the fire limits, tenement houses not exceeding three stories in height, exclusive of the cellar, may be erected of wood, but shall not provide accommodations for, or be occupied, if two stories in height, by more than four families in all, or more than two families on any floor; nor if three stories in height by more than three families in all, nor by more than one family on any floor. No such building shall exceed forty feet in height, and the side walls of all such buildings shall be brick filled. And such houses, whether of wood or other material, need not comply with the provisions of the following named sections of this act; thirteen, fifteen, sixteen, eighteen, nineteen, twenty, twenty-one, twenty-two, twenty-three, twenty-four, twenty-seven, thirty-seven and thirty-eight, and such houses which do not exceed two stories in height need not have either fire escapes or stairs extending to the roof.

Title II

§ 29. *Fire Escapes.* — Every non-fireproof tenement house, unless provided with fireproof outside stairways directly accessible to each apartment, shall have fire escapes located and constructed as described in section twelve of this act. But a fire escape now erected upon such house shall be deemed sufficient except as provided in the next two sections.

§ 30. *Fire Escapes, Continued.* — In every non-fireproof tenement house there shall be a separate fire escape directly accessible to each apartment, exclusive of fire escapes in air shafts and courts; and a party-wall fire escape balcony on the building connecting with the window of an adjoining building shall be deemed a sufficient fire escape only when the two buildings are completely separated by an unpierced fire wall throughout their entire height and length. All wooden floor slats and floors in fire escape balconies shall be replaced by proper iron slats or floors. No wooden balcony or wooden outside stairs shall be deemed part of a lawful fire escape.

§ 31. *Fire Escapes, Continued.* — Whenever a non-fireproof tenement house is not provided with sufficient means of egress in case of fire the department charged with the enforcement of this act[1] may order such additional fire escapes or other means of egress as in its judgment may be necessary.

§ 32. *Scuttles, Bulkheads, Ladders and Stairs.* — Every tenement house shall have in the roof a bulkhead or scuttle. No scuttle shall be less in size than two feet by three feet, and all scuttles shall be covered on the outside with metal and shall be provided with stairs or stationary ladders leading thereto and easily accessible to all tenants of the building and kept free from encumbrance, and all scuttles and ladders shall be kept so as to be ready for use at all times. No scuttle shall be located in a closet or room, but all scuttles shall be located in the ceiling of the public hall on the top floor, and access through the scuttle to the roof must be direct and uninterrupted. When deemed necessary by the department charged with the enforcement of this act,[1] scuttles shall be hinged so as to readily open. Every bulkhead hereafter constructed in a tenement house shall be constructed as provided in section thirteen of this act, and shall have stairs with a guide or handrail leading to the roof, and such stairs shall be kept free from encumbrance at all times. No scuttle and no bulkhead door shall at any time be locked with a key, but either may be fastened on the inside by movable bolts or hooks. All key-locks on scuttles and on bulkhead doors shall be removed. No stairs leading to the roof in any tenement house shall be removed and replaced with a ladder.

§ 33. *Stair Halls, Public Halls and Entrance Halls.* — If any now existing tenement house shall be so altered as to increase the number of rooms therein by thirty-three and one-third per centum or more, or if such building is increased in height so that the said building is more than four stories or parts of stories above the curb level, and also the number of rooms is increased therein, the entire stair halls, entrance halls and other public halls of the whole building shall be made to conform to the requirements of sections fourteen to twenty, inclusive, of this act.

§ 34. *Alteration of Wooden Tenement Houses.* — No wooden tenement house shall be increased in height so as to exceed three stories, exclusive of the cellar, nor shall it be altered so as to be occupied, if less than three stories, by more than two families on any floor nor by more than four families in all; nor, if three stories, by more than one family an any floor, nor by more than three families in all.

Title III

§ 35. *Fire Escapes.* — All fire escapes hereafter constructed upon tenement houses shall be located and constructed as described in section twelve of this act. The owner of every tenement house shall keep all the fire escapes thereon in good order and repair, and whenever rusty shall have them properly painted with two coats of paint. No person shall at any time place any encumbrance of any kind before or upon any such fire escape.

[1] Tenement House Department.

§ 36. *Stairways.* — In every tenement house all stairways shall be provided with proper banisters and railings and kept in good repair. In any tenement house any new stairs that may be hereafter constructed leading from the first story to the cellar or basement, shall be entirely enclosed with brick walls, and be provided with fireproof self-closing doors at both the top and the bottom. No public hall or stairs in a tenement house shall be reduced in width so as to be less than the minimum width prescribed in sections fourteen to twenty inclusive of this act.

§ 37. *Shafts.* — All shafts hereafter constructed in tenement houses shall be constructed fireproof throughout, with fireproof self-closing doors at all openings, at each story, except window openings in vent shafts; and, if they extend to the cellar, shall also be enclosed in the cellar with fireproof walls and fireproof self-closing doors at all openings. In no case shall any shaft be constructed of materials in which any inflammable material or substance enters into any of the component parts. But nothing in this section contained shall be so construed as to require such enclosures about elevators or dumb-waiters in the well-hole of stairs where the stairs themselves are enclosed in brick or stone walls, and are entirely constructed of fireproof materials as hereinbefore provided.

§ 38. *Plastering behind Wainscoting.* — When wainscoting is hereafter placed in any tenement house, or any building in process of alteration into a tenement house, the surface of the wall or partition behind such wainscoting shall be plastered down to the floor line, and any intervening space between said plastering and said wainscot shall be filled in solid with incombustible material.

§ 39. *Wooden Buildings on Same Lot with a Tenement House.* — No wooden building of any kind whatsoever shall hereafter be placed or built upon the same lot with a tenement house within the fire limits. And, within the fire limits, no wooden tenement house, and no wooden structure or other building on the same lot with a tenement house, shall hereafter be enlarged, extended or raised; except that a wooden extension not exceeding in total area seventy square feet may be added to an existing wooden tenement house, provided such extension is used solely for bath rooms or water-closets.

§ 40. *Combustible Materials.* — No tenement house, nor any part thereof, nor of the lot upon which it is situated, shall be used as a place of storage, keeping or handling of any combustible article except under such conditions as may be prescribed by the fire department, under authority of a written permit issued by said department. No tenement house, nor any part thereof, nor of the lot upon which it is situated, shall be used as a place of storage, keeping or handling of any article dangerous or detrimental to life or health, nor for the storage, keeping or handling of feed, hay, straw, excelsior, cotton, paper stock, feathers or rags.

§ 41. *Bakeries and Fat Boiling.* — No bakery and no place of business in which fat is boiled shall be maintained in any tenement house which is not fireproof throughout, unless the ceiling and sidewalls of said bakery or of the said place where fat boiling is done are made safe by fireproof materials around the same, and there shall be no openings either by door or window, dumb-waiter shafts or otherwise, between said bakery or said place where fat is boiled in any tenement house and the other parts of the said building.

§ 42. *Other Dangerous Businesses.* — All transoms and windows opening into halls from any portion of a tenement house where paint, oil, spirituous liquors or drugs are stored for the purpose of sale or otherwise, shall be glazed with wire-glass or they shall be removed and closed up as solidly as the rest of the wall; and all doors leading into any such hall from such portion of said house shall be made fireproof.

CHAPTER III. LIGHT AND VENTILATION

Title I

§ 51. *Percentage of Lot Occupied.* — No tenement house hereafter erected shall occupy more than ninety per centum of a corner lot, or more than seventy per centum of any other lot, except as otherwise provided in sections sixty-one and sixty-two of this act; provided, that the space occupied by fire escapes of the size hereinbefore prescribed shall not be deemed a part of the lot occupied. For the purposes of this section the measurements shall be taken at the ground level, except that where such a building has no basement, and the cellar ceiling is not more than two feet above the curb level, the measurements as to percentage of lot occupied may be taken at the level of the second tier of beams. The provisions of this section shall not apply to a tenement house hereafter erected running through from one street to another street, provided, that the lot on which it is situated does not exceed one hundred feet in depth.

§ 52. *Height.* — The height of no tenement house hereafter erected shall by more than one-half exceed the width of the widest street upon which it stands. Such height shall be the perpendicular distance measured in a straight line from the curb level to the highest point of the roof beams; provided that where there are bulkheads exceeding ten feet in height or exceeding in area ten per centum of the area of the roof, the measurements shall be taken to the top of the bulkhead; but this shall not apply to elevator enclosures not exceeding fifteen feet in height. The measurements in all cases shall be taken through the centre of the facade of the house.

§ 53. *Yards.* — Behind every tenement house hereafter erected there shall be a yard extending across the entire width of the lot, and except upon a corner lot, at every point open from the ground to the sky unobstructed, except that fire escapes or unenclosed outside stairs may project not over four feet from the rear line of the house. The depth of said yard, measured from the extreme rear wall of the house to the rear line of the lot, shall be as set forth in the two following sections.

§ 54. *Yards of Interior Lots.* — Except upon a corner lot the depth of the yard behind every tenement house hereafter erected sixty feet in height shall be not less than twelve feet in every part. Said yard shall be increased in depth one foot for every additional twelve feet of height of the building, or fraction thereof; and may be decreased in depth one foot for every twelve feet of height of the building less than sixty feet; but it shall never be less than ten feet in depth in any part.

§ 55. *Yards of Corner Lots.* — The depth of the yard behind every tenement house hereafter erected upon a corner lot shall be not less than ten feet in every part, provided that where such lot is less than one hundred feet in depth, the depth of the yard may be not less than ten per centum of the depth of such lot, but shall never be less than five feet in every part, nor less than the minimum width of an outer court on the lot line as prescribed by section fifty-eight of this act. Where a tenement house hereafter erected on a corner lot has no basement and the cellar ceiling is not more than two feet above the curb level, said yard may start at the level of the second tier of beams. Where a corner lot is more than fifty feet in width, the yard for that portion in excess of fifty feet shall conform to the provisions of section fifty-four of this act.

§ 56. *Yard Spaces of Lots running through from Street to Street.* — Wherever a tenement house hereafter erected is upon a lot which runs through from one street to another street, and said lot is not less than seventy feet nor more than one hundred feet in depth, there shall be a yard space through the centre of the lot midway between the two streets, which space shall extend across the full width of the lot and shall never be less than twelve feet in depth from wall to wall, and shall be increased in depth as prescribed in section fifty-four of this act. But where such building has no basement and the cellar ceiling is not more than two feet above the curb level, such yard space may start at the level of the second tier of beams. Where such lot is over one hundred feet in depth such yard space shall be left through the centre of the lot midway between the two streets, and shall extend across the entire width of the lot, and shall not be less than twenty-four feet in depth from wall to wall, and shall be increased in depth as prescribed in section fifty-four of this act. Where a single tenement house hereafter erected runs through from one street to another street and also occupies the entire block, no yard need be provided. Where a single tenement house hereafter erected is situated on a lot formed by the intersection of two streets at an acute angle, the yard of the said house need not extend across the entire width of the lot, provided that it extends to a point in line with the middle line of the block.

§ 57. *Courts.* — No court of a tenement house hereafter erected shall be covered by a roof or skylight, but every such court shall be at every point open from the ground to the sky unobstructed, except as hereinafter otherwise provided, and shall conform to the requirements of the following sections; provided, that an apartment not containing any room fronting upon the street or yard shall have a fire escape in a court, projecting not more than four feet from the wall of the house. Such fire escape shall directly connect at the bottom of such court with a fireproof passageway, not less than three feet wide and seven feet high, leading in a straight and direct line to the street.

§ 58. *Outer Courts.* — Where one side of an outer court is situated on the lot line, the width of the said court, measured from the lot line to the opposite wall of the building, for tenement houses sixty feet in height shall not be less than six feet in any part; and for every twelve feet of increase or fraction thereof in height of the said building, such width shall be increased six inches throughout the entire height of said court; and for every twelve feet of decrease in the height of the said building below sixty feet, such width may be decreased six inches. Wherever an outer court exceeds sixty-five feet in length and does not extend from the street to the yard, the entire court shall be increased in width one foot for every additional thirty feet or fraction thereof in excess of sixty-five feet. Except that in tenement houses hereafter erected not exceeding four stories and cellar in height and which also are not occupied or arranged to be occupied by more than eight families in all, or by more than two families on any floor, and in which also each apartment extends through from the street to the yard, the width of an outer court situated on the lot line shall not be less than four feet in any part provided that the length of such outer court does not exceed thirty-six feet.

§ 59. *Outer Courts, Continued.* — Where an outer court is situated between wings or parts of the same building, or between different buildings on the same lot, the width of the said court, measured from wall to wall, for tenement houses sixty feet in height shall not be less than twelve feet in any part; and for every twelve feet of increase or fraction thereof in the height of the said building, such width shall be increased one foot throughout the entire height of the said court; and for every twelve feet of decrease in the height of the said building below sixty feet, such width of the said court may be decreased one foot. Wherever an outer court exceeds sixty-five feet in length, the entire court shall be increased in width two feet for every additional thirty feet or fraction thereof in excess of sixty-five feet. Except that in tenement houses hereafter erected not exceeding four stories and cellar in height and which also are not occupied or arranged to be occupied by more than eight families in all, or by more than two families on any floor, and in which also each apartment extends through from the street to the yard, the width of an outer court situated between wings or parts of the same building, or between different buildings on the same lot, measured from wall to wall, shall be not less than eight feet in any part provided that the length of said outer court does not exceed thirty-six feet.

§ 60. *Outer Courts, Continued.* — Wherever an outer court changes its initial horizontal direction, or wherever any part of such court extends in a direction so as not to receive direct light from the street or yard, the length of such portion of said court shall never exceed the width of said portion; such length to be measured from the point at which the change of direction commences. Wherever an outer court is less in depth than the minimum width prescribed by this title then its width may be equal to, but not less than its depth, provided that such width is never less than four feet in the clear. This exception shall also apply to each offset or recess in outer courts. And no window except windows of water-closet compartments, bath-rooms or halls shall open upon any offset or recess less than six feet in width.

§ 61. *Inner Courts.* — Where one side of an inner court is situated on the lot line, the width of the said court measured from the lot line to the opposite wall of the building, for tenement houses sixty feet in height shall not be less than twelve feet in any part, and its other horizontal dimension shall not be less than twenty-four feet in any part; and for every twelve feet of increase or fraction thereof in the height of the said building, such width shall be increased six inches throughout the entire height of said court, and the other horizontal dimension shall be increased one foot throughout the entire height of said court; and for every twelve feet of decrease in the height of the said building below sixty feet, such width may be decreased six inches and the other horizontal dimension may be decreased one foot. Except that in tenement houses hereafter erected not exceeding four stories and cellar in height and which also are not occupied or arranged to be occupied by more than eight families in all, or by more than two families on any floor, and in which also each apartment extends through from the street to the yard, and which also do not occupy more than seventy-two per centum of the lot, in the case of an interior lot, the width of an inner court situated on the lot line measured from the lot line to the opposite wall of the building shall not be less than eight feet in any part, and its other horizontal dimension shall not be less than fourteen feet in any part. Except also that in such tenement houses which do not exceed three stories and cellar in height, and which also are not occupied, or arranged to be occupied, by more than six families in all, or by more than two families on any floor, a portion of such inner court may be occupied by a bath room extension, provided that such extension has no window facing an opposite building, and that it does not occupy a portion of such court greater than four and one-half feet in width, or seven feet in length, and that between such extension and the lot line the court is never less than three and one-half feet in width. In such last named tenement houses which do not occupy more than sixty-five per centum of the lot, in the case of an interior lot, where an inner court for its entire length immediately adjoins an existing inner court of equal or greater size in an adjoining building or adjoins such a court in an adjoining building actually in course of construction at the same time, the width of such inner court measured from the lot line to the opposite wall of the building shall be not less than four feet in any part, and not less than eight feet from wall to wall, and its other horizontal dimension shall be not less than twelve and one-half feet.

§ 62. *Inner Courts, Continued.*—Where an inner court is not situated upon the lot line, but is enclosed on all four sides, the least horizontal dimension of the said court for tenement houses sixty feet in height, shall not be less than twenty-four feet; and for every twelve feet of increase or fraction thereof in the height of the said building, the said court shall be increased one foot in each horizontal dimension, throughout the entire height of said court; and for every twelve feet of decrease in the height of the said building below sixty feet, the horizontal dimensions of the said court may be decreased one foot in each direction. Except that in tenement houses hereafter erected not exceeding four stories and cellar in height and which also are not occupied or arranged to be occupied by more than eight families in all, or by more than two families on any floor, and in which also each apartment extends through from the street to the yard, and which also do not occupy more than seventy-two per centum of the lot, in the case of an interior lot, the least horizontal dimension of an inner court not situated on the lot line, but enclosed on all four sides, shall not be less than fourteen feet. Except also that in such tenement houses which do not exceed three stories and cellar in height and which also are not occupied, or arranged to be occupied, by more than six families in all, or by more than two families on any floor, and which do not occupy more than sixty-five per centum of the lot, in the case of an interior lot, the width of such inner court shall not be less than eight feet in any part, and its other horizontal dimension shall not be less than twelve and one-half feet. In inner courts which are not less than ten feet wide in any part, offsets and recesses will be permitted, but where the depth of such offset or recess is less than the minimum width prescribed, then the width of said offset or recess may be equal to but not less than its depth, provided that such width is never less than four feet in the clear. And no window except windows of water-closet compartments, bath-rooms or halls shall open upon any offset or recess less than six feet in width.

§ 63. *Inner Courts, Continued.* — Every inner court shall be provided with one or more horizontal intakes at the bottom. Such intakes shall always communicate directly with the street or yard, and shall consist of a passageway not less than three feet wide and seven feet high which shall be left open, or if not open there shall always be provided in said passageway open grilles or transoms of a size not less than five square feet each, and such open grilles or transoms shall never be covered over by glass or in any other way. There shall be at least two such grilles or transoms in each such passageway, one at the inner court and the other at the street or yard, as the case may be.

§ 64. *Outer and Inner Courts.* — Nothing contained in the foregoing sections concerning outer and inner courts shall be construed as preventing windows at the angles of said courts, provided that the running length of the wall containing such windows does not exceed six feet. Except that in outer or inner courts of a less size than the minimum prescribed for tenement houses sixty feet in height, the running length of the wall containing windows in the angles of said courts, shall not exceed four feet. Nothing in this section contained shall be construed so as to permit the reduction of any inner court by cutting off the corners thereof when such court is less than eight feet in width, measured from the lot line to the opposite wall of the building. In construing said sections the height of the building is to be measured from the curb level to the top of the highest wall enclosing or forming such court. When a tenement house hereafter erected exceeding three stories in height has no basement and the cellar ceiling is not more than two feet above the curb level, the courts mentioned in the seven preceding sections may start at the level of the second tier of beams. Where an inner court starts at the second tier of beams, a portion of such court having a least horizontal dimension equal to the minimum width of the court as prescribed by sections sixty-one and sixty-two of this act, shall be left unbuilt upon, and shall communicate directly with the intake required by section sixty-three of this act. Nothing in this section contained shall be construed so as to permit any room without a window opening on the street or yard or on a court in every part the dimensions prescribed in the foregoing sections. Where a court starts at the level of the second tier of beams in whole or in part, and the bottom of said court is a skylight over a store or hall, proper access to the top of said skylight shall be provided, and said skylight shall be so arranged as to be easily cleaned.

§ 65. *Rear Tenements.* — No separate tenement house shall hereafter be erected upon the rear of a lot fifty feet or less in width where there is a tenement house on the front of the said lot, nor upon the front of any such lot upon the rear of which there is such a tenement house.

§ 66. *Buildings on Same Lot with Tenement Houses.* — If any building is hereafter placed on the same lot with a tenement house there shall always be maintained between the said buildings an open unoccupied space extending upwards from the ground and extending across the entire width of the lot; where either building is sixty feet in height such open space shall be twenty-four feet from wall to wall; and for every twelve feet of increase or fraction thereof in the height of such building, such open space shall be increased one foot in depth throughout its entire width, and for every twelve feet of decrease in the height of such building below sixty feet, the depth of such open space may be decreased one foot. And no building of any kind shall be hereafter placed upon the same lot with a tenement house so as to decrease the minimum size of courts or yards as hereinbefore prescribed. And if any tenement house is hereafter erected upon any lot upon which there is already another building, it shall comply with all of the provisions of this act, and in addition the space between the said building and the said tenement house shall be of such size and arranged in such manner as is prescribed in this section, the height of the highest building on the lot to regulate the dimensions.

§ 67. *Rooms, Lighting and Ventilation of.* — In every tenement house hereafter erected every room, except water-closet compartments and bathrooms, shall have at least one window opening directly upon the street or upon a yard or court of the dimensions specified in sections fifty-three to sixty-five of this act, and such window shall be so located as to properly light all portions of such rooms. Wherever a room in such tenement house opens upon an inner court less than ten feet wide, measured from the lot line to the opposite wall of the building, such room shall be provided with a sash window, communicating with another room in the same apartment, such window to contain not less than ten square feet of glazed surface, and to be made so as to readily open. No tenement house shall be so altered that any room or public hall or stairs shall have its light or ventilation diminished in any way not approved by the department charged with the enforcement of this act.[1]

§ 68. *Windows in Rooms.* — In every tenement house hereafter erected the total window area in each room, except water-closet compartments and bathrooms, shall be at least one-tenth of the superficial area of the room, and the top at least of one window shall not be less than seven feet six inches above the floor, and the upper half of it shall be made so as to open the full width. No such window shall be less than twelve square feet in area between the stop beads.

§ 70. *Rooms, Size of.* — In every tenement house hereafter erected all rooms, except water-closet compartments and bathrooms, shall be of the following minimum sizes: In each apartment there shall be at least one room containing not less than one hundred and twenty square feet of floor area, and each other room shall contain at least seventy square feet of floor area. Each room shall be in every part not less than nine feet high from the finished floor to the finished ceiling; provided that an attic room need be nine feet high in but one-half its area.

§ 71. *Alcoves.* — Alcove rooms must conform to all the requirements of other rooms.

§ 72. *Public Halls.* — In every tenement house hereafter erected, which is occupied or arranged to be occupied by more than two families on any floor or which exceeds four stories and cellar in height, every public hall shall have at least one window opening directly upon the street or upon a yard or court. Either such window shall be at the end of said hall, with the plane of the window at right angles to the axis of said hall or there shall be at least one window opening directly upon the street or upon a yard or court in every twenty feet in length or fraction thereof of said hall; but this provision for one window in every twenty feet of hallway shall not apply to that portion of the entrance hall between the

[1] Tenement House Department.

entrance and the first flight of stairs, provided that the entrance door contains not less than five square feet of glazed surface. In every public hall in such tenement house recesses or returns the length of which does not exceed twice their width will be permitted without an additional window. But wherever the length of such recess or return exceeds twice its width the above provisions in reference to one window in every twenty feet of hallway shall be applied. Any part of a hall which is shut off from any other part of said hall by a door or doors shall be deemed a separate hall within the meaning of this section. In every tenement house hereafter erected where the public hall is not provided with a window opening directly to the outer air as above provided, there shall be a stair-well not less than twelve inches wide extending from the entrance floor to the roof, and all doors leading from such public halls shall be provided with translucent glass panels of an area of not less than five square feet for each door, and also with fixed transoms of translucent glass over each door.

§ 73. *Windows and Skylights for Public Halls, Size of.* — In every tenement house hereafter erected one at least of the windows provided to light each public hall or part thereof shall be at least two feet six inches wide and five feet high, measured between stop beads. In every such house there shall be in the roofs, directly over each stair-well, a ventilating skylight provided with ridge ventilators having a minimum opening of forty square inches, or such skylight shall be provided with fixed or movable louvres; the glazed roof of such skylight shall be not less than twenty square feet in area. In tenement houses hereafter erected where the stairs and public halls are not provided with windows on each floor opening directly to the outer air, the skylights shall be provided with both such ridge ventilators, and also with fixed or movable louvres or movable sashes.

§ 74. *Windows for Stair Halls, Size of.* — In every tenement house hereafter erected the aggregate area of windows to light or ventilate stair halls shall be at least eighteen square feet for each floor. There shall be provided for each story at least one of said windows, which shall be at least two and a half feet wide and five feet high, measured between the stop beads. A sash door shall be deemed the equivalent of a window in sections seventy-two, seventy-three, and seventy-four of this act, provided that such door contains the amount of glazed surface prescribed for such windows.

§ 75. *Privacy.* — In every apartment of three or more rooms in a tenement house hereafter erected, access to every living room and bedroom and to at least one water-closet compartment shall be had without passing through any bedroom.

Title II

§ 76. *Percentage of Lot Occupied.* — No tenement house shall hereafter be enlarged, or its lot be diminished, so that a greater percentage of the lot shall be occupied by buildings or structures than provided in section fifty-one of this act, the measurements may be taken at the level of the second tier of beams; provided that the space occupied by fire escapes of the size hereinbefore prescribed, and by chimneys or flues located in yards and attached to the houses which do not exceed five square feet in area and do not obstruct light or ventilation, shall not be deemed a part of the lot occupied.

§ 77. *Yards.*—No tenement house shall hereafter be enlarged or its lot be diminished, so that the yard shall be less in depth than the minimum depths prescribed in sections fifty-three, fifty-four, fifty-five and fifty-six of this act for tenement houses hereafter erected. The measurements in all cases to be taken from the extreme rear wall of the building to the rear lot line, and across the full width of the lot, and such yard shall be at every point open from the ground to the sky, except as provided in sections fifty-three and seventy-six of this act.

§ 77*a*. *Height.*—No tenement house shall be increased in height so that the building shall exceed by more than one-half the width of the widest street on which it stands.

§ 78. *Additional Rooms and Halls.*—Any additional room or hall that is hereafter constructed or created in a tenement house shall comply in all respects with the provisions of chapter three of this act, except that such rooms may be of the same height as the other rooms on the same story of the house.

§ 79. *Rooms, Lighting and Ventilation of, Continued.*—No room in a now existing tenement house shall hereafter be occupied for living purposes unless it shall have a window upon the street, or upon a yard not less than four feet deep, or upon a court or shaft of not less than twenty-five square feet in area, open to the sky without roof or skylight. Provided, however, that such room may be occupied for living purposes if it has a sash window opening into an adjoining room in the same apartment which latter room either opens directly on the street or on a yard of the above dimensions, or itself connects directly by a similar sash window with such an outer room. Said sash windows shall be at least three feet by five feet between stop beads, and both halves shall be made so as to readily open. Where it is not possible to construct a window of this width, then such window may be of such size as may be prescribed by the department charged with the enforcement of this act,[1] but such window shall never contain less than fifteen square feet of glazed surface. An alcove opening of no less dimension than said sash window, in addition to the usual door opening, shall be deemed its equivalent.

§ 80. *Public Halls, Lighting of.*—In every tenement house four stories or over in height, whenever a public hall on any floor is not light enough in the daytime to permit a person to read in every part thereof without the aid of artificial light, the wooden panels in the doors located at the ends of the public halls and opening into rooms shall be removed, and ground glass, or other translucent glass or wire glass panels of an aggregate area of not less than four square feet for each door shall be substituted; or in lieu of removing the panels in the doors a fixed sash window of wire glass of an area of not less than five square feet may be cut into the partitions separating the said hall from a room which opens directly upon the street or upon a yard, court, or shaft of the dimensions specified in the last section; or said public hall may be lighted by a window or windows at the end thereof with the plane of the window at right angles to the axis of the said hall, said window opening upon the street or upon a yard, court, or shaft of said dimensions. In every such house where the public halls and stairs are not provided with windows opening directly to the

[1] Tenement House Department.

street or yard, and such halls and stairs are, in the opinion of the department charged with the enforcement of this act,[1] not sufficiently lighted, the owner of such house shall keep a proper light burning in the hallway, near the stairs, upon each floor, as may be necessary, from sunrise to sunset.

§ 81. *Light and Vent Shafts in Existing Buildings.* — Any shaft used or intended to be used to light or ventilate rooms used or intended to be used for living purposes, and which may be hereafter placed in a tenement house, erected prior to April tenth, nineteen hundred and one, shall not be less in area than twenty-five square feet, nor less than four feet in width in any part, and such shaft shall under no circumstances be roofed or covered over at the top with a roof or skylight; every such shaft shall be provided at the bottom with a horizontal intake or duct, of a size not less than four square feet, and communicating directly with the street or yard, and such duct shall be so arranged as to be easily cleaned out.

Title III

§ 82. *Public Halls.* — In every tenement house a proper light shall be kept burning by the owner in the public hallways, near the stairs, upon the entrance floor, and upon the second floor, above the entrance floor of said house, every night from sunset to sunrise throughout the year, and upon all other floors of the said house from sunset until ten o'clock in the evening.

§ 83. *Skylights.* — In every tenement house there shall be in the roof, directly over each stair well, a ventilating skylight. Provided, that this section shall not apply to a tenement house now having a bulkhead in the roof over the main stairs, which bulkhead is provided with windows made so as to readily open, and with not less than twelve square feet of glass in the top of said bulkhead. In tenement houses erected prior to April tenth, nineteen hundred and one, the roofs of such skylights shall contain the following amounts of glazed surface; not less than twelve square feet in any tenement house; in four story buildings not less than fifteen square feet; in five story buildings not less than eighteen square feet; in buildings over five stories three square feet for each additional story. In tenement houses erected prior to April tenth, nineteen hundred and one, where the public halls and stairs are heated by steam heat or other artificial heat, such skylights shall be provided with ridge ventilators having a minimum opening of forty square inches, and also with either fixed louvres or movable louvres, or movable sashes, as the owner may elect. In tenement houses erected prior to April tenth, nineteen hundred and one, in which the halls are not heated by artificial heat, and which exceed three stories in height, or which are occupied or arranged to be occupied by more than four families in all, such skylights shall be provided with ridge ventilators having a minimum opening of forty square inches, and also with fixed louvres. In such houses which do not exceed four stories in height, and which are not occupied or arranged to be occupied by more than four families in all, such skylights shall be provided with ridge ventilators having a minimum opening of forty square inches. All skylights hereafter placed in any tenement house shall conform to the provisions of section seventy-three of this act. All existing dome lights or other obstructions to skylight ventilation shall be removed.

[1] Tenement House Department.

§ 84. *Chimneys or Fireplaces.* — In every tenement house there shall be adequate chimneys running through every floor with an open fireplace or grate, or place for a stove, properly connected with one of said chimneys for every apartment.

§ 85. *Vent Shafts.* — Every vent shaft hereafter constructed in a tenement house shall be at least twenty square feet in area, and the least dimension of such shaft shall not be less than four feet; and if the building be above sixty feet in height such shaft shall throughout its entire height be increased in area three square feet for each additional twelve feet of height or fraction thereof; and for each twelve feet of height less than sixty feet such shaft may be decreased in area three square feet. A vent shaft may be enclosed on all four sides but shall not be roofed or covered over in any way. Every such shaft shall be provided with a horizontal intake or duct at the bottom, communicating with the street or yard or with a court; such duct or intake to be not less than four square feet in total area, and to be so arranged as to be easily cleaned out.

CHAPTER IV. SANITARY PROVISIONS

Title I

§ 91. *Basements and Cellars.* — In tenement houses hereafter erected no room in the cellar or in the basement shall be constructed, altered, converted or occupied for living purposes, unless all of the following conditions are complied with:

1. Such room shall be at least nine feet high in every part from the floor to the ceiling. Provided, that in buildings already erected and not now used as tenement houses but hereafter altered or converted to such use, such room shall be not less than seven feet high in every part.
2. The ceiling of such room shall be at least four feet and six inches above the surface of the street or ground outside of or adjoining the same.
3. There shall be appurtenant to such room the use of a separate water-closet, constructed and arranged as required by section ninety-five of this act.
4. Such room shall have a window or windows opening upon the street, or upon a yard or court. The total area of windows in such room shall be at least one-eighth of the superficial area of the room, and one-half of the sash shall be made to open the full width, and the top of each window shall be within six inches of the ceiling.
5. All walls surrounding such room shall be damp-proof.
6. The floor of such room shall be damp-proof and water-proof.

§ 92. *Basements and Cellars, Continued.* — Every tenement house hereafter erected shall have all walls below the ground level and all cellar or lower floors damp-proof and water-proof. When necessary to make such walls and floors damp-proof and water-proof, the damp-proofing and water-proofing shall run through the walls and up the same as high as the ground level and shall be continued throughout the floor, and the said cellar or lowest floor shall be properly constructed so as to prevent dampness or water from entering. All cellars and basements in such tenement houses shall be properly lighted and ventilated to the satisfaction of the department charged with the enforcement of this act.[1]

[1] Tenement House Department.

§ 93. *Shafts, Courts, Areas and Yards.* — In every tenement house hereafter erected the bottom of all shafts, courts, areas and yards which extend to the basement for light or ventilation of living rooms, must be six inches below the floor level of the part occupied or intended to be occupied. In every tenement house all shafts, courts, areas and yards shall be properly graded and drained, and connected with the street sewer so that all water may pass freely into it. And when required by the department charged with the enforcement of this act[1] shall be properly concreted.

§ 94. *Water Supply.* — In every tenement house hereafter erected there shall be in each apartment a proper sink with running water.

§ 95. *Water-closet Accommodations.* — In every tenement house hereafter erected there shall be a separate water-closet in a separate compartment within each apartment, provided that where there are apartments consisting of but one or two rooms, there shall be at least one water-closet for every three rooms. Every water-closet and bath hereafter placed in any tenement house shall be placed in a compartment completely separated from every other water-closet and bath; such compartment shall be not less than two feet and four inches wide, and shall be enclosed with plastered partitions, which shall extend to the ceiling. In tenement houses erected after April tenth, nineteen hundred and one, such compartments shall have a window opening directly upon the street or yard, or upon a court or vent shaft. In tenement houses erected prior to April tenth, nineteen hundred and one, such compartments shall have a window opening directly upon the street, or upon a yard not less than four feet deep, or upon a court or shaft of not less than twenty-five square feet in area, open to the sky without roof or skylight. Every such window shall be at least one foot by three feet between stop beads, and the entire window shall be made so as to readily open. When, however, such water-closet compartment is located on the top floor and is lighted and ventilated by a skylight over it, or is located at the bottom of a shaft or court of lawful size, and is lighted and ventilated by a skylight over it at the bottom of such shaft or court, no window shall be necessary, provided the roof of such skylight contains at least three square feet of glazed surface and is arranged so as to readily open. Nothing in this section in regard to the separation of water-closet compartments from each other shall apply to a general toilet room containing several water-closets hereafter placed in a tenement house, provided such water-closets are supplemental to the water-closet accommodations required by law for the use of the tenants of the said house. Nothing in this section in regard to the ventilation of water-closet compartments shall apply to a water-closet hereafter placed in a tenement house, where it is provided to replace a defective fixture in the same position and location. No water-closet shall be maintained in the cellar of any tenement house without a special permit in writing from the department charged with the enforcement of this act,[1] which shall have power to make rules and regulations governing the maintenance of such closets. Every water-closet compartment hereafter placed in any tenement house shall be provided with proper means of lighting the same at night. If fixtures for gas or electricity are not provided in said compartment, then the door of said compartment shall be provided with translucent glass panels, or with a translucent glass transom, not less in area

[1] Tenement House Department.

than four square feet. The floor of every such water-closet compartment shall be made water-proof with asphalt, tile, stone, or some other water-proof material; and such water-proofing shall extend at least six inches above the floor so that the said floor can be washed or flushed out without leaking. No drip trays shall be permitted. No water-closet fixtures shall be enclosed with any woodwork.

§ 96. *Plumbing.* — In every tenement house hereafter erected all plumbing pipes shall be exposed, when so required by the department charged with the enforcement of this act.[1] In all tenement houses hereafter erected where plumbing or other pipes pass through floors or partitions, the openings around such pipes shall be sealed or made air tight with plaster, or other incombustible materials, so as to prevent the passage of air or the spread of fire from one floor to another or from room to room.

Title II

§ 97. *Basements and Cellars.* — Hereafter in any tenement house no room in the basement or cellar shall be occupied for living purposes without a written permit from the department charged with the enforcement of this act,[1] and such permit shall be kept readily accessible in the main living room of the apartment containing such room. And no such room in a tenement house erected prior to April tenth, nineteen hundred and one, shall hereafter be occupied unless all the following conditions are complied with. The said written permit shall be issued when all of the said conditions are complied with. If refused, the reason for such refusal shall be stated by said department, in writing, and a copy thereof shall be kept in a proper book in the office of said department, and be accessible to the public.

1. Such room shall be at least seven feet high in every part from the floor to the ceiling.

2. The ceiling of such room shall be in every part at least two feet above the surface of the street or ground outside of or adjoining the same.

3. There shall be appurtenant to such rooms the use of a water-closet.

4. There shall be outside of and adjoining such room, and extending along the entire frontage of at least one of the rooms of the apartment, an open space of at least two feet six inches wide in every part, unless such room extends for more than one-half of its height above the curb level. Such space shall be well and effectually drained.

5. Such room shall have a window or windows opening to the outer air of at least nine square feet in size clear of the sash frame, and which shall have been made to readily open for purposes of ventilation.

6. If the house is situated over marshy ground, or ground on which water lies, or ground on which there is water pressure from below, the lowest floor shall have been made water-proof and damp-proof.

7. Such room shall have sufficient light, shall be well drained and dry, and shall be fit for human habitation.

§ 98. *Water-closets.* — In all now existing tenement houses the woodwork enclosing all water-closets shall be removed from the front of said closets, and the space underneath the seat shall be left open. The floor or other surface beneath and around the closet shall be maintained in good

[1] Tenement House Department.

order and repair and if of wood shall be kept well painted with light-colored paint.

§ 99. *Public Sinks.* — In all now existing tenement houses the woodwork enclosing sinks located in the public halls or stairs shall be removed, and the space underneath said sinks shall be left open. The floors and wall surfaces beneath and around the sink shall be maintained in good order and repair, and if of wood shall be kept well painted with light-colored paint.

§ 100. *Privy Vaults, School Sinks and Water-closets.* — In all now existing tenement houses, where a connection with a sewer is possible, all school sinks, privy vaults or other similar receptacles used to receive fecal matter, urine or sewage, shall before January first, nineteen hundred and three, be completely removed and the place where they were located properly disinfected under the direction of the department charged with the enforcement of this act. Such appliances shall be replaced by individual water-closets of durable non-absorbent material, properly sewer connected, and with individual traps, and properly connected flush tanks providing an ample flush of water to thoroughly cleanse the bowl. Each water-closet shall be located in a compartment completely separated from every other water-closet, and such compartment shall contain a window of not less than three square feet in area opening directly to the outer air. The floors of the water-closet compartments shall be water-proof as provided in section ninety-five of this act. Where water-closets are placed in the yard to replace school sinks or privy vaults long hopper closets may be used; but all traps, flush tanks and pipes shall be protected against the action of frost. In such cases, the structure containing the water-closets shall not exceed ten feet in height; and shall not be considered as increasing the percentage of the lot occupied nor shall it be subject to the provisions of section sixty-six of this act, provided that it does not occupy more than fifty per centum of the open space or yard in which it is placed, and provided further that the use of said structure is limited solely to water-closet purposes. Such structure shall be provided with a ventilating skylight in the roof, of an adequate size, and each water-closet shall be located in a compartment completely separated from every other water-closet. Proper and adequate means for lighting the structure at night shall be provided. There shall be provided at least one water-closet for every two families in every now existing tenement house. Except as in this section otherwise provided such water-closets and all plumbing in connection therewith shall be in accordance with the ordinances and regulations in relation to plumbing and drainage.

Title III

§ 101. *Basements and Cellars.* — The floor of the cellar or lowest floor of every tenement house shall be water-tight. And the cellar ceiling shall be plastered, when so required by the department charged with the enforcement of this act,[1] except where the first floor above the cellar is constructed of iron beams and fireproof filling.

§ 102. *Cellar Walls and Ceilings.* — The cellar walls and ceilings of every tenement house shall be thoroughly whitewashed or painted a light color by the owner and shall be so maintained. Such whitewash or paint

[1] Tenement House Department.

shall be renewed whenever necessary, as may be required by the department charged with the enforcement of this act.[1]

§ 103. *Repairs.* — Every tenement house and all the parts thereof shall be kept in good repair and the roof shall be kept so as not to leak, and all rain water shall be so drained and conveyed therefrom as to prevent its dripping on to the ground or causing dampness in the walls, ceilings, yards or areas.

§ 104. *Water Supply.* — Every tenement house shall have water furnished in sufficient quantity at one or more places on each floor occupied by or intended to be occupied by one or more families. The owner shall provide proper and suitable tanks, pumps or other appliances to receive and to distribute an adequate and sufficient supply of such water at each floor in the said house, at all times of the year, during all hours of the day and night. But a failure in the general supply of water by the city authorities shall not be construed to be a failure on the part of such owner, provided that proper and suitable appliances to receive and distribute such water have been provided in said house.

§ 105. *Cleanliness of Buildings.* — Every tenement house and every part thereof shall be kept clean and free from any accumulation of dirt, filth or garbage or other matter in or on the same, or in the yards, courts, passages, areas or alleys connected with or belonging to the same. The owner of every tenement house or part thereof shall thoroughly cleanse all the rooms, passages, stairs, floors, windows, doors, walls, ceilings, privies, water-closets, cesspools, drains, halls, cellars, roofs and all other parts of the said tenement house, or part of the house of which he is the owner, to the satisfaction of the tenement house department,[2] and shall keep the said parts of the said tenement house in a cleanly condition at all times. No person shall place filth, urine or fecal matter in any place in a tenement house other than that provided for the same, or keep filth, urine or fecal matter in his apartment or upon his premises such length of time as to create a nuisance.

§ 106. *Shafts and Courts.* — In every tenement house there shall be, at the bottom of every shaft and inner court, a door giving sufficient access to such shaft or court to enable it to be properly cleaned out. In shafts or courts of a less size than prescribed in sections sixty-one and sixty-two of this act, such door shall be fireproof and self-closing. Provided, that where there is already a window or door in a tenement house, giving proper access to such shaft or court, such window or door shall be deemed sufficient.

§ 107. *Walls of Courts and Shafts.* — The walls of all yard-courts, inner-courts and shafts unless built of a light color brick or stone shall be thoroughly whitewashed by the owner or shall be painted a light color by him, and shall be so maintained. Such whitewash or paint shall be renewed whenever necessary, as may be required by the department charged with the enforcement of this act.[1]

§ 108. *Wall Paper.* — No wall paper shall be placed upon a wall or ceiling of any tenement house unless all wall paper shall be first removed therefrom and said wall and ceiling thoroughly cleaned.

§ 109. *Receptacles for Ashes, Garbage and Refuse.* — The owner of every tenement house shall provide for said building proper and suitable

[1] Tenement House Department.

[2] "Department of health" in original act. Changed by Greater New York Charter to "tenement house department."

conveniences or receptacles for ashes, rubbish, garbage, refuse and other matter.

§ 110. *Prohibited Uses.* — No horse, cow, calf, swine, sheep or goat shall be kept in a tenement house, or on the same lot or premises thereof, and no tenement house, or the lot or premises thereof shall be used for a lodging house or stable, or for the storage or handling of rags. Except that, outside of the fire limits, not more than two horses may be kept on such lot or premises, provided they are stabled at least twenty feet distant from any building used for living purposes, and that such stabling is not detrimental to health in the opinion of the department charged with the enforcement of this act.[1]

§ 111. *Janitor or Housekeeper.* — Whenever there shall be more than eight families living in any tenement house, in which the owner thereof does not reside, there shall be a janitor, housekeeper or some other responsible person who shall reside in said house and have charge of the same, if the department charged with the enforcement of this act[1] shall so require.

§ 112. *Overcrowding.* — No room in any tenement house shall be so overcrowded that there shall be afforded less than four hundred cubic feet of air to each adult, and two hundred cubic feet of air to each child under twelve years of age occupying such room.

CHAPTER V. REMEDIES

Title I

GENERAL POWERS AND DUTIES

§ 121. *Permit to commence Building.* — Before the construction or alteration of a tenement house, or the alteration or conversion of a building for use as a tenement house is commenced, and before the construction or alteration of any building or structure on the same lot with a tenement house, the owner, or his agent or architect, shall submit to the department charged with the enforcement of this act[1] a detailed statement in writing, verified by the affidavit of the person making the same, of the specifications for the construction and for the light and ventilation of such tenement house or building, upon a blank or form to be furnished by such department, and also a full and complete copy of the plans of such work. Such statement shall give in full the name and residence, by street and number, of the owner or owners of such tenement house or building. If such construction, alteration, or conversion, is proposed to be made by any other person than the owner of the land in fee, such statement shall contain the full name and residence, by street and number, not only of the owner of the land, but of every person interested in such tenement house, either as owner, lessee or in any representative capacity. Said affidavit shall allege that said specifications and plans are true and contain a correct description of such tenement house, building, structure, lot and proposed work. The statements and affidavits herein provided for may be made by the owner, or the person who proposes to make the construction, alteration or conversion, or by his agent or architect. No person, however, shall be recognized as the agent of the owner, unless he shall file with the said department a written instrument, signed by such owner, designating

[1] Tenement House Department.

him as such agent. Any false swearing in a material point in any such affidavit shall be deemed perjury. Such specifications, plans and statements shall be filed in the said department and shall be deemed public records, but no such specifications, plans or statements shall be removed from said department. The said department shall cause all such plans and specifications to be examined. If such plans and specifications conform to the provisions of this act and to the building ordinances and regulations they shall be approved by such department, and a written certificate to that effect shall be issued to the person submitting the same. The department may, from time to time, approve changes in any plans and specifications previously approved by it, provided the plans and specifications when so changed shall be in conformity with law. The construction, alteration or conversion of such tenement house, building, or structure or any part thereof, shall not be commenced until the filing of such specifications, plans and statements, and the approval thereof, as above provided. The construction, alteration or conversion of such house, building or structure, shall be in accordance with such approved specifications and plans. Any permit or approval which may be issued by the department charged with the enforcement of this act[1] but under which no work has been done above the foundation walls within one year from the time of issuance of such permit or approval, shall expire by limitation. Said department shall have power to revoke or cancel any permit or approval in case of any failure or neglect to comply with any of the provisions of this act, or in case any false statement or representation is made in any specifications, plans or statement submitted or filed for such permit or approval.

§ 122. *Certificate of Compliance.* — No building hereafter constructed as or altered into a tenement house shall be occupied in whole or in part for human habitation until the issuance of a certificate by the department aforesaid that said building conforms in all respects to the requirements of this act. Such certificate shall be issued within ten days after written application therefor, if said building at the date of such application shall be entitled thereto.

§ 123. *Unlawful Occupation.* — If any building hereafter constructed as or altered into a tenement house be occupied in whole or in part for human habitation in violation of the last section, during such unlawful occupation any bond or note secured by a mortgage upon said building, or the lot upon which it stands, may be declared due at the option of the mortgagee. No rent shall be recoverable by the owner or lessee of such premises for said period, and no action or special proceeding shall be maintained therefor, or for possession of said premises for non-payment of such rent. The department of water supply shall not permit water to be furnished in any such tenement house, and said premises shall be deemed unfit for human habitation, and the tenement house department[2] shall cause them to be vacated accordingly.

§ 124. *Enforcement.* — Except as herein otherwise provided, the provisions of this act shall be enforced by the department of any city to which this act applies, which is now charged with the enforcement of laws, ordinances and regulations relating to similar subject matter in tenement houses.

§ 125. *Violations.* — Nothing in this act shall be construed to abrogate

[1] Tenement House Department. [2] See Note 2, p. 191.

or impair the powers of the department of health, the department of buildings, or of the courts, to enforce any provisions of the charter or building ordinances and regulations, not inconsistent with this act, or to prevent or punish violations thereof.

§ 126. *Penalties for Violations.* — Every person who shall violate or assist in the violation of any provision of this act shall be guilty of a misdemeanor punishable by imprisonment for ten days for each and every day that such violation shall continue, or by a fine of not less than ten dollars nor more than one hundred dollars if the offence be not wilful, or of two hundred and fifty dollars if the offence be wilful, and in every case of ten dollars for each day after the first that such violation shall continue, or by both such fine and imprisonment in the discretion of the court; provided, that the punishment for a violation of section one hundred and thirty-one of this act shall be a fine of fifty dollars; and provided further, that the penalty for encumbrance of a fire escape by an occupant of the tenement house shall be a fine of ten dollars, which the nearest police magistrate shall have jurisdiction to impose. The owner of any tenement house or part thereof, or of any building or structure upon the same lot with a tenement house, or of the said lot, where any violation of this act or a nuisance exists, and any person who shall violate or assist in violating any provision of this act, or any notice or order of the department charged with its enforcement,[1] shall also jointly and severally for each such violation and each such nuisance be subject to a civil penalty of fifty dollars. Such persons shall also be liable for all costs, expenses and disbursements paid or incurred by said department, by any of the officers thereof or by any agent, employe or contractor of the same, in the removal of any such nuisance or violation. Any person who having been served with a notice or order to remove any such nuisance or violation, shall fail to comply with said notice or order within five days after such service, or shall continue to violate any provision or requirement of this act in the respect named in said notice or order, shall also be subject to a civil penalty of two hundred and fifty dollars. For the recovery of any such penalties, costs, expenses or disbursements, an action may be brought in any court of civil jurisdiction in said cities. In case the notice required by section one hundred and thirty-one of this act is not filed, or in case the owner, lessee or other person having control of such tenement house does not reside within the state, or cannot after diligent effort be served with process therein, the existence of a nuisance or of any violation of this act, or of any violation of an order or a notice made by said department, in said tenement house or on the lot on which it is situated, shall subject said tenement house and lot to a penalty of two hundred and fifty dollars. Said penalty shall be a lien upon said house and lot.

§ 127. *Violation of Building Laws, Ordinances and Regulations.* — Any owner, agent, architect, builder, contractor, sub-contractor, or foreman who shall, in the construction or alteration of any building intended to be used as a tenement house, knowingly violate any of the provisions of the building laws, ordinances or regulations shall be guilty of a misdemeanor.

§ 128. *Procedure.* — Except as herein otherwise specified, the procedure for the prevention of violations of this act, or for the vacation of premises unlawfully occupied, or for other abatement of nuisance in connection with a tenement house, shall be as set forth in charter and ordi-

[1] Tenement House Department.

nances. In case any tenement house, building or structure or any part thereof is constructed, altered, converted or maintained in violation of any provision of this act or of any order or notice of the department charged with its enforcement,[1] or in case a nuisance exists in any such tenement house, building or structure or upon the lot on which it is situated, said department may institute any appropriate action or proceeding to prevent such unlawful construction, alteration, conversion or maintenance, to restrain, correct or abate such violation or nuisance, to prevent the occupation of said tenement house, building or structure, or to prevent any illegal act, conduct or business in or about such tenement house or lot. In any such action or proceeding said department may, by affidavit setting forth the facts, apply to the supreme court, or to any justice thereof, for an order granting the relief for which said action or proceeding is brought, or for an order enjoining all persons from doing or permitting to be done any work in or about such tenement house, building, structure or lot, or from occupying or using the same for any purpose, until the entry of final judgment or order. In case any notice or order issued by said department is not complied with, said department may apply to the supreme court, or to any justice thereof, for an order authorizing said department to execute and carry out the provisions of said notice or order, to remove any violation specified in said notice or order, or to abate any nuisance in or about such tenement house, building or structure, or the lot upon which it is situated. The court, or any justice thereof, is hereby authorized to make any order specified in this section. In no case shall the said department or any officer thereof or the city be liable for costs in any action or proceeding that may be commenced in pursuance of this act. In an action to establish a lien under this act, the procedure shall be as set forth in sections one hundred and thirty-four and one hundred and forty-six to one hundred and fifty-one of this act. The judgment in any such action may provide for the sale of said property, and for such other remedies to secure the enforcement thereof as the court may deem proper.

§ 129. *Liens.* — Every fine imposed by judgment under section one hundred and twenty-six of this act upon a tenement house owner shall be a lien upon the house in relation to which the fine is imposed from the time of the filing of a certified copy of said judgment in the office of the clerk of the county in which said tenement house is situated, subject only to taxes, assessments and water rates and to such mortgage and mechanics' liens as may exist thereon prior to such filing; and it shall be the duty of the tenement house department,[2] upon the entry of said judgment, to forthwith file the copy as aforesaid, and such copy, upon such filing, shall be forthwith indexed by the clerk in the index of mechanics' liens.

§ 130. *Lis Pendens.* — In any action or proceeding instituted by the department charged with the enforcement of this act,[2] the plaintiff or petitioner may file in the county clerk's office of the county where the property affected by such action or proceeding is situated, a notice of the pendency of such action or proceeding. Said notice may be filed at the time of the commencement of the action or proceeding, or at any time afterwards before final judgment or order, or at any time after the service of any notice or order issued by said department. Such notice shall have the same force and effect as the notice of pendency of action provided for

[1] Tenement House Department. [2] See Note 2, p. 191.

in the code of civil procedure. Each county clerk with whom such notice is filed shall record it, and shall index it to the name of each person specified in a direction subscribed by the corporation counsel. Any such notice may be vacated upon the order of a judge or justice of the court in which such action or proceeding was instituted or is pending, or upon the consent in writing of the corporation counsel. The clerk of the county where such notice is filed is hereby directed to mark such notice and any record or docket thereof as canceled of record, upon the presentation and filing of such consent or of a certified copy of such order.

Title II

REGISTRY OF NAMES AND SERVICE OF PAPERS

§ 131. *Registry of Owners' Names.* — Every owner of a tenement house and every lessee of the whole house, or other person having control of a tenement house, shall file in the department charged with the enforcement of this act,[1] a notice containing his name and address, and also a description of the property, by street number or otherwise, as the case may be, in such manner as will enable the department charged with the enforcement of this act[1] easily to find the same; and also the number of apartments in each house, the number of rooms in each apartment, and the number of families occupying the apartments. In case of a transfer of any tenement house, it shall be the duty of the grantor or grantee of said tenement house to file in the department charged with the enforcement of this act[1] a notice of such transfer, stating the name of the new owner, within thirty days after such transfer. In case of the devolution of said property by will, it shall be the duty of the executor and the devisee, if more than twenty-one years of age, and in case of the devolution of such property by inheritance without a will, it shall be the duty of the heirs, or in case all of the heirs are under age, it shall be the duty of the guardians of such heirs, and in case said heirs have no guardians, it shall be the duty of the administrator of the deceased owner of said property to file in said department a notice, stating the death of the deceased owner, and the names of those who have succeeded to his interest in said property, within thirty days after the death of the decedent, in case he died intestate, and within thirty days after the probate of his will, if he died testate.

§ 132. *Registry of Agent's Name.* — Every owner, agent, or lessee of a tenement house may file in the tenement house department[2] a notice containing the name and address of an agent of such house, for the purpose of receiving service of process, and also a description of the property by street number or otherwise, as the case may be, in such manner as will enable the department of health easily to find the same. The name of the owner or lessee may be filed as agent for this purpose.

§ 133. *Service of Notices and Orders.* — Every notice or order in relation to a tenement house shall be served five days before the time for doing the thing in relation to which it shall have been issued. The posting of a copy of such notice or order in a conspicuous place in the tenement house, together with the mailing of a copy thereof, on the same day that it is posted, to each person, if any, whose name has been filed with the tenement house department[2] in accordance with the provisions of sections

[1] Tenement House Department. [2] See Note 2, p. 191.

one hundred and thirty-one and one hundred and thirty-two of this act, at his address as therewith filed, shall be sufficient service thereof.

§ 134. *Service of Summons.*—In any action brought by any city department in relation to a tenement house for injunction, vacation of the premises, or other abatement of nuisance, or to establish a lien thereon, it shall be sufficient service of the summons to serve the same as notices and orders are served under the provisions of the last section; provided, that if the address of any agent whose name and address have been filed in accordance with the provisions of section one hundred and thirty-two of this act is in the city in which the tenement house is situated, then a copy of the summons shall also be delivered at such address to a person of proper age, if upon reasonable application admittance can be obtained and such person found; and provided also, that personal service of the summons upon the owner of such tenement house shall be sufficient service thereof upon him.

§ 135. *Indexing Names.*—The names and addresses filed in accordance with sections one hundred and thirty-one and one hundred and thirty-two shall be indexed under direction of the registrar of records of the tenement house department,[1] in such a manner that all of those filed in relation to each tenement house shall be together, and readily ascertainable. The tenement house department[1] shall provide the registrar with the necessary books and clerical assistance for that purpose, and the expense thereof shall be paid by the city. Said indexes shall be public records, open to public inspection during business hours.

Title III

PROSTITUTION IN TENEMENT HOUSES

§ 141. *Vagrancy.*—A woman who knowingly resides in or commits prostitution in a house of prostitution or assignation of any description in a tenement house or solicits any man or boy to enter therein for purposes of prostitution shall be deemed a vagrant, and upon conviction thereof shall be committed to a county jail for a term not exceeding six months from the date of commitment. The procedure in such case shall be the same as that provided by law for other cases of vagrancy.

§ 142. *Lien.*—A tenement house shall be subject to a penalty of one thousand dollars, if it or any part of it shall be used for the purpose of a house of prostitution or assignation of any description, with the permission of the owner thereof, or his agent, and said penalty shall be a lien upon the house and the lot upon which the house is situated.

§ 143. *Permission of Lessee.*—If a tenement house, or any part thereof, shall be used for the purpose of a house of prostitution or assignation of any description with the permission of the lessee of the whole of said tenement house, or his agent, the lease shall be terminable at the election of the lessor. And the owner shall be entitled to recover possession of said tenement house by summary proceedings in the manner provided by title two of chapter seventeen of the code of civil procedure.

§ 144. *Permission of Owner.*—A tenement house shall be deemed to have been used for the purpose specified in the last two sections with the permission of the owner and lessee thereof, if summary proceedings for the removal of the tenants of said tenement house, or of so much thereof

[1] Tenement House Department.

as is unlawfully used, shall not have been commenced within five days after notice of such unlawful use, served by the tenement house department[1] in the manner prescribed by law for the service of notices and orders in relation to tenement houses.

§ 145. *Rules of Evidence.* — In a prosecution against an owner or agent of a tenement house under section three hundred and twenty-two of the penal code, or in an action to establish a lien under section one hundred and forty-two of this act, the general reputation of the premises in the neighborhood shall be competent evidence, but shall not be sufficient to support a judgment without corroborative evidence, and it shall be presumed that their use was with the permission of the owner and lessee; provided, that such presumption may be rebutted by evidence.

§ 146. *Title of Action and Parties.* — Said action shall be brought against the tenement house as defendant. Said house may be described in the title of the action by its street number, or in any other method sufficiently precise to secure identification. The property shall be described in the complaint. The plaintiff, except as hereinafter provided, shall be the tenement house department.[1] In case any taxpayer of any city to which this act applies, shall request such department in writing to institute an action under this title against any tenement house specified in such request, and such department shall not institute such action within ten days after receiving such request, then any taxpayer of said city may institute and maintain such action against such tenement house in his own name, and in such case the court may in its discretion require security for costs.

§ 147. *Jurisdiction and Procedure.* — Said action shall be brought in the supreme court in the county in which the property is situated. At or before the commencement of the action the complaint shall be filed in the office of the clerk of the county, together with a notice of the pendency of the action, containing the names of the parties, the object of the action and a brief description of the property affected thereby. Said notice shall be immediately recorded by the clerk in accordance with the provisions of section sixteen hundred and seventy-two of the code of civil procedure. The owner or lessee of said building, or both, may appear in said action and answer or demur to the complaint and the subsequent proceedings in the action shall be the same as in other actions brought to establish a lien or encumbrance upon real property, and the action shall be entitled to a preference in the trial or hearing thereof.

§ 148. *Judgment.* — The judgment in such action, if in favor of the plaintiff, shall establish the penalty sued for as a lien upon said premises, subject only to taxes, assessments and water rates, and to such mortgage and mechanics' liens as may exist thereon prior to the filing of the notice of pendency of the action.

§ 149. *Sale of Property.* — At any time after the entry of any judgment establishing a lien upon tenement property the tenement house department,[1] if there be no stay pending appeal, may apply to the court for leave to sell such property. Upon such application the court, if it deem advisable, may order such property to be sold at public auction, subject to taxes, assessments and water rates and to such mortgage and mechanics' liens as aforesaid. The deed to the purchaser shall be made by the tenement house department.[1] The justices of the appellate division of the supreme court of any judicial department may establish rules of practice, which

[1] See Note 2, p. 191.

shall be followed by such department in the conduct of said sales in said department.

§ 150. *Receivership.* — Whenever the lien or liens upon a tenement property, established by judgment, shall amount to one thousand dollars or over, if there be no stay pending appeal, the tenement house department[1] shall appoint a receiver of the rents and profits of said property. Said receiver shall give security for the performance of his duties in the manner and form fixed by said department. He shall have the powers and duties of a receiver of rents and profits of real estate appointed by the supreme court; provided, that the corporation counsel shall act as his counsel and that he shall not be allowed any expenditure for counsel fees, and provided, that his commissions shall be ten per centum of his collections, which sum shall be full compensation for his services and those of any agent or agents whom he may employ. Said receivership shall continue until the amount of said liens, with interest thereon at the rate of six per centum, and of said commissions, have been fully paid; provided, that nothing in this section shall be construed to prevent any prior lienor from applying to the court in a proper case for a receiver of the property.

§ 151. *Cancellation of Notice of Pendency of the Action.* — If an action to establish a lien upon tenement property terminate otherwise than in a judgment establishing such a lien, or if said judgment be fully paid, said notice may be cancelled in the manner prescribed by section one thousand six hundred and seventy-four of the code of civil procedure.

CHAPTER VI. GENERAL PROVISIONS

§ 161. *Repeal.* — All statutes of the state and ordinances of the city so far as inconsistent with the provisions of this act are hereby repealed; provided, that nothing in this act contained shall be construed as repealing or abrogating any present law or ordinance in any city of the first class, further restricting or prohibiting the occupation of cellars, or increasing the amount of air space to each individual occupying a room, or as prohibiting any future ordinance in respect thereto.

§ 162. *Building Regulations.* — Except as herein otherwise specified, every tenement house shall be constructed and maintained in conformity with the existing law, but no ordinance, regulation or ruling of any municipal authority shall modify or dispense with any provision of this act.

§ 163. *Penalties.* — All penalties collected under this act shall be paid into the city treasury.

§ 164. *Time for Compliance.* — All alterations hereby required upon now existing tenement houses shall be made within one year from the time when this act shall take effect, or at such earlier period as may be fixed by the departments charged with the enforcement of this act.

§ 165. *When to take Effect.* — This act shall take effect immediately; provided, that sections one hundred and thirty-four and one hundred and forty-four shall not take effect until three months after the passage thereof.

[1] See Note 2, p. 191.

APPENDIX VI

A HISTORY OF TENEMENT HOUSE LEGISLATION IN NEW YORK, 1852–1900

BY LAWRENCE VEILLER

PREFACE

THIS history embraces all legislation in New York State in relation to tenement houses up to 1900. It purposely does not include those provisions of law which relate to general powers of city departments in regard to tenement houses in common with other buildings, nor such general questions of building construction as thickness of walls, quality of building materials, etc. It also does not include the laws in relation to tenement house labor, as these are more properly labor laws than tenement house laws, nor does it include certain minor provisions of the New York Charter which do not directly affect this inquiry.

Most of this legislation is to be found in the different tenement house acts, in the general building laws of New York and Brooklyn, in the health laws of these cities, and also in the charters and local ordinances.

In preparing this history, the different provisions of law have been classified with reference to their purpose, as "Fire Provisions," "Health Provisions," "Light and Ventilation Provisions," etc.

Following the general description of the changes that have taken place in reference to these different subjects, will be found in small type, in each case, the text of the different enactments upon this subject, arranged chronologically.

The present law (in 1900) upon each point will also be found in the enactments of 1897 and 1899, indicated by an asterisk placed before these sections.

At the end of this history will be found a list of all laws with their exact titles and the dates of their enactment, for purposes of reference.

A HISTORY OF TENEMENT HOUSE LEGISLATION IN NEW YORK, 1852–1900

SINCE 1647 there have been laws relating to buildings in New York City. In that year, an ordinance was enacted, appointing surveyors of buildings to regulate the erection of new houses within or around the city of New Amsterdam. This ordinance dealt chiefly with chimney fires, seeking to minimize the dangers arising from improperly constructed chimneys.

From this time up to the year 1849, numerous ordinances of different kinds were adopted, relating to the construction of buildings, nearly all of them for the purpose of reducing the danger from fire. The first important piece of legislation, however, in reference to buildings, was not enacted until 1849, when an act was passed, entitled "An Act for the more effectual prevention of fires in the city of New York." This law provided for, in a very detailed manner, the way in which new buildings should be constructed, and is, practically, the basis of all building laws enacted since that time.

In 1852 the first building law in reference to the city of Brooklyn was passed, forming the basis of the Brooklyn building law. In this law are to be found the first provisions in reference to furnishing means of egress in case of fire in buildings, applying to tenement houses as well as to buildings of other kinds. The word "tenement house," however, does not occur in the statutes until the year 1862, when it is found for the first time in Chapter 356 of the laws of that year, although there had been numerous provisions before that time, between 1852 and 1862, in reference to houses occupied by more than three families, as will be seen from a study of the different provisions contained in this report. The first tenement law was passed in 1867.

ADMINISTRATION OF THE LAW

THE BUILDING LAWS. — The enforcement of the building laws and ordinances was originally vested in the fire wardens of the city, a number of men appointed in each ward for the purpose of preventing fires and performing in certain respects functions analogous to those now performed by the building inspectors and the fire marshals.

In 1844 the fire wardens were abolished, and their duties and powers were transferred to the Police Department. In 1849 they were conferred on the assistant engineers of the Fire Department, where the responsibility for enforcing the building laws remained until 1862, when these powers and duties were transferred to the newly created "department for the survey and inspection of buildings." The duty of enforcing the building laws remained in this department until 1880, at which time the department was abolished and once more made a bureau of the Fire Department. The Fire Department retained these powers and duties until 1892, when the Bureau of the Fire Department was abolished and a new Department of Buildings was created. This is the department at the present time vested with the responsibility and duty of enforcing the building laws.

THE TENEMENT HOUSE LAWS. — The first tenement house act, which was the Act of 1867, placed the responsibility for its enforcement upon the newly created Metropolitan Board of Health, and the Board of Health since that time until 1892 has had almost entirely the sole responsibility for enforcing these laws. Such provisions of the general building laws as affect the construction of buildings, especially with a view to the prevention of dangers from fire, have always been enforced by the Building Department or its equivalent — the Bureau of Buildings of the Fire Department.

The second tenement house act, in 1879, amended the Act of 1867 and still left the responsibility for its enforcement with the Board of Health. In 1892, however, when the Building Department was created, besides transferring the powers and duties of the Bureau of Buildings of the Fire Department to the newly created Department of Buildings, the powers and duties of the Board of Health in relation to the plumbing and drainage, and the light and ventilation of new buildings were also transferred to the Building Department, simply leaving with the Board of Health jurisdiction over these subjects as they affected old buildings already constructed. The new tenement house act of 1895 placed the responsibility for its enforcement, so far as it affected existing buildings, upon the Board of Health, and in relation to new tenement houses upon the Department of Buildings, and this division of responsibility remains at the present time, having been continued in the Greater New York Charter. Certain laws in relation to tenement houses, however, also place the responsibility for their enforcement upon the Fire Department — as for example, the provision that fire-escapes shall not be encumbered; here there is a divided responsibility for the enforcement of the statute, both the Police Department and the Fire Department being directed to enforce this provision.

THE HEALTH LAWS. — From 1804 to 1850 the duty of enforcing the health provisions in reference to all buildings in the city of New York was lodged with the "City Inspector" and the health wardens of the city. The health wardens were men appointed in each ward, charged with the duties of general sanitary inspection, and in the early years, the Board of Health, as it was then constituted, was also charged with the responsibility for cleaning the streets, and had several other powers, which it does not now possess. In 1850 an act was passed transferring all the powers then vested in the local Board of Health to the Mayor and Common Council of the city. In 1866, as a result of the terrible disclosures of the sanitary condition of the city, made by the Council of Hygiene, the first health law of the city was enacted. This law took away from the local authorities all jurisdiction over the health of the city and vested all powers and responsibilities of this nature in a newly created state board, known as the Metropolitan Board of Health. This law is one of the most important laws that has ever been enacted in this State and is the basis of all subsequent health and sanitary laws, not only in New York, but in most of the other American cities. Under the provisions of this act, the Governor was directed within fifteen days after its passage to appoint, with the concurrence of the Senate, four persons, who should be residents of the metropolitan district, three of whom were to be physicians and one who was to be a resident of Brooklyn. These four, with the Health Officer of the Port of New York, were constituted, for the time being, the Sanitary Commissioners of the metropolitan district, and with the Commissioners of the Metropolitan Police, who should never exceed four in number, they constituted the Metropolitan Board of Health. The Sanitary Commissioners were to hold office for the following terms: One for one year, one for two years, one for three years and one for four years, and until their successors were appointed. After the expiration of these terms the term of office of future sanitary commissioners was to be four years, and they were to be appointed always by the Governor, with the concurrence of the Senate. Any vacancies in their number that might occur were to be filled in a similar manner. Each Sanitary Commissioner was to receive a salary of $2500 a year, and each police commissioner was to receive, in addition to his regular salary, the sum of $500 a year for his service as a member of the Board of Health. In order to insure a full attendance at all of the meetings of the Board, it was provided that for every regular meeting that any commissioner should fail to attend, the sum of $10 was to be deducted from his salary.

The President of the Board was vested with all the powers previously given to the City Inspector in reference to the cleaning of the streets, and the Board was authorized to appoint a chief executive officer, who was to be an experienced and skilful physician, to be known as the Sanitary Superintendent. The Board was also authorized to appoint two assistant superintendents, one of whom should be a resident of the city of Brooklyn, and who was to perform his duties in that city; also, it was provided that not more than fifteen sanitary inspectors might be appointed by the Board, and the Board was authorized to prescribe their duties and the salary of each. At least ten of these inspectors were required to be physicians of skill and of practical professional experience, and the rest were to be selected in reference to their practical knowledge of scientific or sanitary matters. Each inspector was required to make a written report of his work to the Board twice a week and was also required to call the attention of the Board to such facts as came within his personal knowledge that he deemed worthy of their special consideration. The Board was also authorized to employ clerks and other subordinates as well as retain attorneys and rent and equip offices, etc.

It is interesting to find that in this act the Board of Health was authorized to condemn buildings that were unfit for habitation if they were likely to prove injurious to the public health, whether they were so unfit from the drainage or ventilation thereof, or from lack of repair, or any other cause; and the Board was given very large powers to order any building or part of a building to be cleaned or altered or improved as might be necessary. It was also distinctly specified that it should be the duty of every owner or part owner, and also of every lessee, tenant and occupant of any room or apartment or building to keep the same thoroughly clean. Any person violating any of the provisions of this act or the provisions of any law or ordinance adopted by the Board of Health was liable to arrest, and such violation was constituted a misdemeanor.

In the presence of great and imminent peril to the public health, by reason of impending pestilence, the Board was granted very unusual and extraordinary powers; but such powers were not to be exercised except with the written assent of at least six members of the Board, and only after a public proclamation by the Governor as to the existence of such danger. The Board was also authorized to establish a code of health ordinances for the protection of the public health in the district. These ordinances were to be published for three weeks, at least, in the public press before they should take effect. The law also provided for the duties and rights of the employees of the Department, and other powers of the Board not especially concerned with the regulation of tenement houses.

In 1870 the powers vested in the Metropolitan Board of Health by the Act of 1866 were transferred to a local Board of Health created by the new charter adopted in that year. This local Board of Health succeeded to all the powers and duties of the State Board, and the enforcement of the health laws has been vested in this local body without change since that time.

ADDITIONAL POWERS OF THE BOARD OF HEALTH AND DEPARTMENT OF BUILDINGS TO MAKE REGULATIONS.—The Tenement House Act of 1867, in addition to the specific powers which were given to the Board of Health, also vested that body with certain discretionary powers to make rules and regulations as to cellars and as to ventilation, when the Board was satisfied that such regulations would secure equally well the health of the occupants, and provided that such regulations should not be inconsistent with the provisions of the existing laws. These powers were somewhat added to in 1892, when it was provided that, in addition to the power to make regulations as to cellars and ventilation, the Board should also have power to make regulations as to the proportion of any lot to be covered by a tenement or lodging house, as to light and ventilation, the supply of water above the first story, and the use of such buildings for a stable or for the storage of rags. In 1895, in addition to these powers given to the Board of Health, the new tenement house act also gave to the Superintendent of Buildings the power to make rules and regulations not inconsistent with the other provisions of the act, these regulations to govern the arrangement and distribution of the uncovered area, the size, lighting, location and arrangement of air shafts, rooms, cellars and halls; and the Superintendent of Buildings was also empowered to modify or change these regulations from time to time. These powers of both the Board of Health and the Building Department were continued in the Greater New York Charter, and exist at the present day, excepting that the Department of Buildings no longer has the power to modify or change the regulations.

(1867) — Chapter 908, Section 18.

"The Metropolitan Board of Health shall have authority to make other regulations as to cellars and as to ventilation, consistent with the foregoing, where it shall be satisfied that such regulations will secure equally well the health of the occupants."

(1882) — Chapter 410, Section 667. — Continued.

(1888) — Brooklyn — Chapter 583, Section 39. (Brooklyn Consol. Act.) Provisions of Law of 1867, reënacted.

(1892) — Chapter 329, Section 1. (Section 667, Consol. Act, amended as follows):

"The Board of Health shall have authority *within present provisions of the law*, to make other regulations than the foregoing in special cases as to the proportion of any lot to be covered by any tenement or lodging house, as to cellars, supply of water above the first floor in any house, and the providing of fixtures therefor, light and ventilation, and the use of buildings or premises for a tenement house, for a school or stable, or for the storage of rags, when it shall be satisfied that such regulations will secure equally well the health of the occupants and the public health, provided however, that in all such cases any modifications made by such regulations shall be in accordance with the conditions of a permit in writing, issued by the said board of health."

(1895) — Chapter 567, Section 8. (Amends Section 661, Consol. Act.)

"The superintendent of buildings is hereby empowered and directed to make rules and regulations not inconsistent with the requirements of this title, and which in addition to the requirements of this title shall be the conditions of approval for the plans and permits; these rules and regulations shall govern the arrangement and distribution of the uncovered area, size, lighting, location and arrangement of shafts, rooms, cellars and halls, and may be modified or changed from time to time by the superintendent of buildings."

(1895) — Chapter 567, Section 12. (Amends Section 667, Consol. Act.)

"The superintendent of buildings shall have authority to make other regulations as to light and ventilation of all new tenement or lodging-houses consistent with the foregoing; when he shall be satisfied that such regulations will secure equally well the health and safety of the occupants; likewise the board of health shall have authority to make other regulations as to cellars and as to ventilation of completed buildings, consistent with the foregoing, where it shall be satisfied that such regulations will secure equally well the health of the occupants."

***(1897) — Chapter 378, Greater New York Charter, Section 1304.**

"Every house, building or portion thereof in the city of New York, used, occupied, leased or rented for a tenement or lodging-house must conform in its construction, appurtenances and premises to the requirements of this title, and its use and occupation shall be regulated subject to the ordinances of the Sanitary Code, applicable thereto, and the orders of the board of health duly made, pursuant to its authority, duty and powers conferred and enjoined upon it in this chapter."

***(1897) — Chapter 378, Greater New York Charter, Section 1323.**

Provisions of Section 12, Chapter 567 of the laws of 1895, continued with the exception that the words "superintendent of buildings" are changed to "department of buildings."

SANITARY INSPECTORS. — The first health law in New York State, viz.: that enacted in 1866, authorized the newly created Board of Health to appoint as many as fifteen sanitary inspectors, and to prescribe their duties and regulate their salaries; ten of these inspectors were required to be physicians of skill and of practical professional experience in the cities embraced by the metropolitan district, and the remaining inspectors were to be selected with reference to their practical knowledge of scientific or sanitary matters; each inspector was required to make a written report twice a week to the Board of Health, stating what work he had done, and also calling the attention of the Board to any matters which he thought might be of interest to them and to the public health. In 1887 this provision of the health law was amended by increasing the number of sanitary inspectors from fifteen to twenty-five, and the number of those who were required to be physicians of experience, from ten to twenty. In the same year another act was passed, at a later date, amending this law, which provided that the number of sanitary inspectors should be increased from fifteen to a number not exceeding forty; and of these, twenty were to be physicians of skill and practical experience. In 1895, in the amended tenement house law, it was provided that the number of sanitary inspectors should be at least thirty-five, and that the Board of Health should have the power to appoint at least five additional inspectors if the Board deemed it needful. In the Greater New York Charter, with the consolidation of the work of the Health Departments of Brooklyn and of New York and the other boroughs, it became necessary to increase the number of these

* Indicates the existing law in 1900.

sanitary inspectors; the Charter accordingly increased this number from thirty-five to fifty, and authorized the Board of Health to appoint twenty additional sanitary inspectors whenever they deemed it needful; also the number of inspectors required to be physicians of skill and practice was increased from twenty to thirty, and the sanitary inspectors were no longer required to make a written report twice a week, once a week being deemed sufficient.

(1866) — Chapter 74, Section 11.

"The Metropolitan board of health may appoint and commission such number of 'sanitary inspectors' as the board may deem needful, not exceeding 15, and, from time to time, prescribe the duties and salaries of each of said inspectors, and the place of their performance (and of all other persons exercising any authority under said board except as herein especially provided); but at least 10 of such inspectors shall be physicians of skill and of practical professional experience in said district, and the residue thereof shall be selected with reference to their practical knowledge of scientific or sanitary matters, which may especially qualify them for such inspectors. Each of such inspectors shall, twice in each week, make a written report to the said board, stating what duties he has performed, and where he has performed them, and also such facts as have come to his knowledge connected with the purposes of this act, as are by him deemed worthy the attention of said board."

(1882) — Chapter 410, Section 588. — Continued.

(1887) — Chapter 84, Section 4. (Amends Section 588, Consol. Act.)

Continued, but number of sanitary inspectors increased from 15 to 25; number of same to be physicians increased from 10 to 20.

(1887) — Chapter 489, Section 1.

Above provision amended as follows: Number of sanitary inspectors increased from 15 to "not exceeding 40," number of same to be physicians increased from 10 to 20, also the following additional clause inserted: "The additional sanitary inspectors heretofore duly appointed and commissioned may be included among the sanitary inspectors mentioned in this section, and may continue to act as such without re-appointment. All of the said inspectors shall have such practical knowledge of scientific or sanitary matters as qualify them for the duties of their office."

(1895) — Chapter 567, Section 3. (Amends Section 588, Consol. Act.)

"The board of health shall appoint and commission at least 35 sanitary inspectors, and shall have power to appoint five additional sanitary inspectors, if it deems that number needful, and from time to time prescribe the duties and salaries of each of said inspectors, and the place of their performance and of all other persons exercising any authority under said board, except as herein especially provided; but twenty of such inspectors shall be physicians of skill and of practical professional experience in said city; the additional sanitary inspectors heretofore duly appointed and commissioned may be included among the sanitary inspectors mentioned in this section, and may continue to act as such without re-appointment, but nothing herein contained shall curtail any of the powers vested in the health department by section 580 of this act, and the number of sanitary inspectors for whom provision is made in this section shall be exclusive of the special inspectors for whom provision is made in section 580. All of the said inspectors shall have such practical knowledge of scientific or sanitary matters as qualify them for the duties of their office. Each of said inspectors shall twice in each week, make a written report to said board stating what duties he has performed, and where he has performed them, and also such facts as have come to his knowledge connected with the purposes of this chapter, as are by him deemed worthy of the attention of said board, or such as its regulations may require of him; which reports with the other reports herein elsewhere mentioned shall be filed among the records of the said board."

*** (1897) — Chapter 378, Greater New York Charter, Chapter 19, Title 1, Section 1185.**

Provisions of the law of 1895 continued with the following changes: Number of sanitary inspectors increased from at least 35 to at least 50; number of additional inspectors authorized to be appointed increased from 5 to 20; number of inspectors to be physicians of skill and practice increased from 20 to 30; also inspectors only required to make a report once a week instead of twice a week.

SANITARY POLICE. — In 1879, in the amendment to the tenement house law, provision was made for the appointment of a corps of sanitary police for the purpose of enforcing the provisions of the different tenement house acts, it being found that very often a uniformed officer was much more successful in such work than the ordinary sanitary inspector; accordingly, the new law provided that the Board of Police might, upon requisition of the Board of Health, detail to the service of the Health Department a squad of not more than thirty men who should all be men of at least five years' experience on the police force; and the Board of Health was required to pay the salaries of such policemen, although the discipline of these men was left entirely with the police commissioners; if any member of this company was not satisfactory, the Board of Health was authorized to request the detailing of another man in his place. This provision of the law was amended in the following year, a new clause being added authorizing the Police Department to appoint additional policemen to fill the vacancies caused in the force by the detailing of these men to the Board of Health. In 1887, the number of sanitary police detailed to the Board of Health was increased from thirty to forty-five, and it was especially provided that at least fifteen of these men should be employed exclusively in the enforcement of the laws relating to tenement and lodging houses. In 1895 the number of sanitary police was increased to fifty, and the number of men to be employed exclusively in inspecting tenement and lodging houses was increased from fifteen to twenty. A clause was also added empowering the Police Department to appoint twenty-five additional men to fill the vacancies created in the police force by this detail. It was also provided that the sanitary policemen who should be detailed to the service of the Board of Health should be selected for their peculiar fitness from amongst those who should pass a civil service examination, conducted by the Municipal Civil Service Board. With the consolidation of the different communities into Greater New York, in 1897, it became

* Indicates the existing law in 1900.

necessary to increase the number of sanitary police, owing to the increased territory to be inspected. The Charter provided, therefore, that there should be at least fifty and not more than one hundred sanitary police detailed to the Board of Health by the Police Department, and that these men should be selected for their peculiar fitness, and that at least thirty of them should be employed exclusively in the enforcement of the laws relating to tenement and lodging houses. All the other provisions of this law in reference to the payment and discipline of the men were reënacted. These provisions of the Charter constitute the present law (in 1900) upon the subject.

(1879) — Chapter 504, Section 5.

"The board of police of the city of New York, upon requisition of the board of health of the city of New York, shall detail to the service of the said board of health, for the purpose of the enforcement of the provisions of this act, and of Chapter 908 of the laws of 1867, in said city, not exceeding thirty suitable officers and men of experience, of at least five years' service in the police force; provided that the board of health shall pay monthly to the board of police a sum equal to the pay of all officers and men so detailed. These officers and men shall belong to the sanitary company of police, and shall report to the president of the board of health. The board of health may report back to the board of police, for punishment, any member of said company guilty of any breach of orders or discipline or of neglecting his duty, and thereupon the board of police may detail another officer or man in his place; and the discipline of said members of the sanitary company shall be in the jurisdiction of the board of police; but at any time the board of health may object to the efficiency of any member of said company, and thereupon another officer or man may be detailed in his place."

(1880) — Chapter 399, Section 2. (Section 5, Chapter 504, of the Laws of 1879, amended by adding to the end the following provision.)

"The board of police shall have the power, and it shall be their duty to fill all vacancies in the police force of the city caused by the detailing of said officers and men upon the requisition of the board of health, and to make new appointments to said force equal in number to the officers and men now, or who may hereafter be detailed to the service of the board of health under and by virtue of the provisions of this act."

(1887) — Chapter 84, Section 1. (Amends Section 296, Consol. Act.)

"The board of police upon the requisition of the board of health, shall detail to the service of the said board of health, for the purpose of the enforcement of the provisions of the sanitary code, and of the acts relating to tenement and lodging-houses, not exceeding forty-five suitable officers and men of experience of at least five years' service in the police force, provided that the board of health shall pay monthly to the board of police a sum equal to the pay of all officers and men so detailed. At least fifteen of the officers and men so detailed shall be employed exclusively in the enforcement of the laws relating to tenement and lodging-houses. These officers and men shall belong to the sanitary company of police and shall report to the president of the board of health. The board of health may report back to the board of police for punishment any member of said company guilty of any breach of orders or discipline, or of neglecting his duty, and thereupon the board of police may detail another officer or man in his place, and the discipline of said members of the sanitary company shall be in the jurisdiction of the board of police, but at any time the board of health may object to the efficiency of any member of said sanitary company, and thereupon another officer or man may be detailed in his place. The board of police shall have the power, and it shall be their duty to fill all vacancies in the police force in the city caused by the detailing of said officers and men upon the requisition of the board of health. And the board of police are hereby authorized and empowered to appoint fifteen additional men to the police force subject to all the rules and regulations relating to and governing the appointment of patrolmen in said city."

(1895) — Chapter 567, Section 1. (Amends Section 296, Consol. Act.)

Provisions of Chapter 504 of the laws of 1879 as amended by Chapter 399 of the laws of 1880, as amended by Chapter 84 of the laws of 1887, reënacted with the following changes: The number of men to be at least fifty; with a further provision that at least twenty shall be employed exclusively on tenement and lodging-houses, and also, by adding at the end of the section the following new clause: "and the board of police are hereby authorized and empowered to appoint twenty-five additional men to the police force subject to all the law, rules and regulations relating to and governing the appointment of patrolmen in said city; and the officers thus detailed to the service of the said board of health shall be selected for their peculiar fitness from amongst those who shall pass a civil service examination conducted by the supervisory board of commissioners of the New York municipal civil service."

*** (1897) — Chapter 378, Greater New York Charter, Section 1324.**

"The board of health shall make requisition upon the police board for the detail of at least 50 and not more than 100 suitable officers and men of at least five years' service in the police force, who shall be selected for their peculiar fitness, for the enforcement of the provisions of the sanitary code and the acts relating to tenement and lodging-houses. These officers and men shall be detailed to such service by the police board, and the department of health shall pay to the police department monthly, the amount of the pay of the officers and men so detailed, who shall belong to the sanitary company of the police and shall report to the board of health. At least thirty of the officers and men so detailed shall be employed exclusively in the enforcement of the laws relating to tenement and lodging-houses. The board of health may report back to the police board for punishment, any member of said company guilty of any breach of orders or discipline, or of neglecting his duty, and thereupon the police board shall detail another officer or man in his place, and the discipline of the said members of the sanitary company shall be in the jurisdiction of the police department; but at any time the board of health may object to the efficiency of any member of said sanitary company and thereupon another officer or man shall be detailed in his place."

ENTRY TO TENEMENT OR LODGING HOUSES — RIGHTS OF PUBLIC OFFICIALS. — The first tenement house act provides very specifi-

* Indicates the existing law in 1900.

cally that all public officials, sanitary inspectors and others, charged with the duty of enforcing the health laws or the tenement house laws, shall have the right of entry to all buildings in the performance of their duties, and the owner, lessee and occupant of every tenement house is especially charged to give such officials free access to their house and to every part of it. This has remained the law unchanged since it was originally enacted.

(1867) — Chapter 908, Section 10.

"The keeper of any lodging house, and the owner, agent of the owner, lessee, and occupant of any tenement-house, and every other person having the care or management thereof shall at all times, when required by any officer of the Metropolitan board of health or by any officer upon whom any duty or authority is conferred by this act, give him free access to such house and to every part thereof."

(1882) — Chapter 410, Section 658. — Continued.

(1887) — Chapter 84, Section 8. — Continued.

(1888) — Brooklyn — Chapter 583, Section 32. (Brooklyn Consol. Act.) Provisions of the Law of 1867, reënacted.

*** (1897) — Chapter 378, Greater New York Charter, Section 1314.**

"The keeper of any lodging-house, and the owner, agent of the owner, lessees or occupant of any tenement-house, and every other person having the care and management thereof, shall, at all times, when required by any officer of the department of health, or by any officer upon whom any duty is conferred by this title, give him free access to such house, and to every part thereof."

INSPECTION OF TENEMENT HOUSES AT REGULAR INTERVALS. — In 1887, in the amended tenement house act, it was provided that the Board of Health should make a regular semi-annual inspection of every tenement and lodging house in the city; and also that whenever any order had been made by the Board of Health concerning a tenement or lodging house, a reinspection of the building should be made within six days after the Board of Health was informed that the order had been complied with. This is the present law upon the subject with the exception that the Charter requires that such reinspection shall be made within six days after the order is served, instead of waiting for notice that it has been complied with.

(1887) — Chapter 84, Section 8.

"It shall be the duty of the board of health to cause a careful inspection to be made of every tenement or lodging-house at least twice in each year. And whenever the board of health has made any order concerning a tenement or lodging-house, it shall cause a re-inspection to be made of the same within six days after it has been informed that the order has been obeyed."

*** (1897) — Chapter 378, Greater New York Charter, Section 1314.**

Continued with the following change: Last word "obeyed" changed to "served."

*** Indicates the existing law in 1900.**

POSTING OF OWNER'S NAME. — The first tenement house law required, among other things, that the name of the owner and also of the agent of every tenement house should be posted in a conspicuous place in the public hall or on the entrance door of every tenement house. This requirement was enacted so as to facilitate the work of the Health Department in the service of papers upon the responsible persons. It was also felt that the publicity thus given would have the effect of making owners of tenement houses more careful in their management, and would prevent them from allowing the buildings to get out of repair and prevent the buildings from being kept in an improper condition. The law in 1887 was considerably changed and very much strengthened, the new law requiring that, instead of posting the owner's name on the door of the house, every owner of a tenement house or lodging-house or any person having control of it, should file in the Department of Health a statement containing his name and address, also a description of the property by street number, or in such other way as would readily identify it; also the number of apartments in each building, the number of rooms in each apartment, the number of families occupying each apartment and the trades or occupations carried on in them; and it was further provided, in the same law, that all notices and orders of the Board of Health in reference to tenement or lodging-houses should be deemed sufficiently served if a copy of the notice or order was posted in a conspicuous place in the house, and also if an additional copy was mailed to the owner of the building at the address given in his statement filed at the Board of Health. This law was amended in 1895 by a further provision, requiring that in case of a transfer of any tenement or lodging house, the name of the new owner should be filed with the Board of Health within thirty days, and imposing a penalty of from $10 to $50 for a failure to file such notice. These provisions of the laws of 1895 and of 1887 have been reënacted in the Charter and are the present law (in 1900) upon the subject.

(1867) — Chapter 908, Section 9.

"Every tenement or lodging-house shall have legibly posted or painted on the wall or door in the entry, or some public accessible place, the name and address of the owner or owners, and of the agent or agents, or any one having charge of the renting and collecting of the rents for the same; and service of any papers required by this act or by any proceedings to enforce any of its provisions, or of the acts relating to the Metropolitan board of health, or the department for the survey and inspection of buildings shall be sufficient if made upon the person or persons so designated as owner or owners, agent or agents."

(1882) — Chapter 410, Section 657. — Continued.

(1887) — Chapter 84, Section 7. (Previous provision repealed, and the following new section enacted.)

"Every owner of a tenement or lodging-house, and every person having control of a tenement or lodging-house, shall file in the board of health a notice containing his name and address, and also a description of the property by street number, or otherwise as the case may be, in such manner as will enable the board of health easily to find the same; and also the number of apartments in each house, the number of rooms in each apartment, the number of families occupying each apartment and the trades or occupations carried on therein. Every person claiming to have an interest in any tenement or lodging-house may file his name and address in the department of health. All notices and orders of the board of health required by law to be served in relation to a tenement or lodging-house shall be served by posting in some conspicuous place in the house, a copy of the notice or order, five days before the time for doing the thing in relation to which said notice or order was issued. The posting of a copy of an order or notice, in accordance with this section, shall be sufficient service upon the owner of the property affected. It shall be the duty of the board of health to cause a copy of every such notice or order to be mailed, on the same day that it is posted in the house, addressed to the name and address of each person who has filed with the department of health, the notice provided for in this section."

(1888) — Brooklyn — Chapter 583, Section 31. (Brooklyn Consol. Act.) Provisions of Law of 1867, reënacted.

(1895) — Chapter 567, Section 6. (Provisions of Chapter 84, Section 7, of the Laws of 1887, continued with the following new clause added.)

"In case of a transfer of any tenement-house, or lodging-house, it shall be the duty of the grantor and grantee of said tenement or lodging-house to file in the department of health a notice of such transfer stating the name of the new owner within thirty days after such transfer. In case of the devolution of said property by will, it shall be the duty of the executor and of the devisee, if more than twenty-one years of age, and in case of the devolution of such property by inheritance without a will, it shall be the duty of the heirs, or in case all of the heirs are under age, it shall be the duty of the guardians of such heirs, and in case said heirs have no guardians, it shall be the duty of the administrator of the deceased owner of said property to file in said department a notice stating the death of the deceased owner and the names of those who have succeeded to his interest in said property, within thirty days after the death of said decedent in case he died intestate, and within thirty days after the probate of his will, if he died testate. A failure to file such notice shall make said property and the owners thereof liable to a penalty of not less than $10 nor more than $50. Said penalty may be collected in the manner prescribed in section 665 of this act."

*** (1897) — Chapter 378, Greater New York Charter, Section 1313. — Continued.**

OWNER'S RESPONSIBILITY. — The main responsibility for compliance with the different provisions of the tenement house acts has been in all cases placed upon the owner of the tenement house primarily, and after him on the lessee of the whole house rather than upon the occupant of the individual apartment or set of rooms. The first tenement house act contained a provision to this effect, and such provision has been continued in all succeeding acts. It was also provided in this tenement house law that if the date of the erection of a tenement house should become a material fact in any proceeding on the part of the Health Department to enforce

* Indicates the existing law in 1900.

the law, it should be the duty of the owner to prove the date of the erection of the building and not the duty of the Board of Health.

(1867) — Chapter 908, Section 16.

"In every proceeding for a violation of this act, and in every such action for a penalty, it shall be the duty of the owner of the house to prove the date of its erection or conversion to its existing use, if that fact shall become material, and the owner shall be prima facie, the person liable to pay such penalty, and after him the person who is the lessee of the whole house, in preference to the tenant or lessee of a part thereof. In any such action the owner, lessee and occupant or any two of them, may be made defendants, and judgment may be given against the one or more shown to be liable, as if he or they were sole defendant or defendants."

(1879) — Chapter 504, Section 6.

"In every proceeding for a violation of this act, and in every such action for a penalty, the owner shall be prima facie, the person liable to pay such a penalty, and after him the person who is the lessee of the whole house, in preference to the tenant or lessee of a part thereof. In any such action the owner, lessee and occupant or any two of them may be made defendants, and judgment may be given against the one or more shown to be liable as if he or they were sole defendant or defendants."

(1882) — Chapter 410, Section 665. Provisions of Law of 1867, continued.

(1888) — Brooklyn — Chapter 583, Section 37. Provisions of Laws of 1867, continued.

(1895) — Chapter 567, Section 11. (Amends Section 665, Consol. Act.) — Continued.

***(1897) — Chapter 378, Greater New York Charter, Section 1322. — Continued.**

PUNISHMENT FOR VIOLATION OF THE TENEMENT HOUSE LAW. — The Act of 1867 made a violation of this provision a misdemeanor, punishable by a fine of not less than $10 or more than $100, or by imprisonment for not more than ten days for each and every day the violation might continue, or by both the fine and imprisonment in the discretion of the court. Any person violating the law was also made liable to a further penalty of $10 a day for each and every day that the offence should continue, and the Board of Health was authorized to sue for and collect such penalties, which were to be paid over to the treasurer of the Board. The Act of 1879 amended this slightly, requiring that the penalties when recovered should be paid over to the City Chamberlain and become part of the tenement house fund; and the Act of 1895 provided that the penalty should be paid to the Comptroller instead of to the Chamberlain. This is the present law upon this subject.

(1867) — Chapter 908, Section 16.

"Every owner or other person violating any provision of this act after the same shall take effect, shall be guilty of a misdemeanor punish-

*** Indicates the existing law in 1900.**

able by a fine of not less than ten dollars nor more than one hundred dollars, or by imprisonment for not more than ten days for each and every day that such violation shall continue, or by both such fine and imprisonment in the discretion of the court. He shall also be liable to pay a penalty of ten dollars for each and every day that such offense shall continue. Such penalty may be sued for and recovered by the Metropolitan board of health and when rècovered shall be paid over to the treasurer of said board."

(1879) — Chapter 504, Section 6.

"Every owner or other person violating any provisions of this act shall be liable to pay a penalty of ten dollars for each and every day that such offense shall continue. Such penalty may be sued for and recovered by the board of health, and when recovered shall be paid over to the city chamberlain, and become part of the tenement-house fund."

(1882) — Chapter 410, Section 665. — Continued.

(1888) — Brooklyn — Chapter 583, Section 37.

"Every owner or other person violating any provisions of Sections 24 to 36 both inclusive (tenement-house law) of this title shall be guilty of a misdemeanor punishable by a fine of not less than ten dollars nor more than one hundred dollars, or by imprisonment for not more than ten days for each and every day that such violation shall continue, or by both such fine and imprisonment in the discretion of the court. He shall also be liable to pay a penalty of ten dollars for each and every day that such offense shall continue. Such penalty may be sued for and recovered by the health commissioner and when recovered shall be paid over to the treasurer of the city of Brooklyn."

(1895) — Chapter 567, Section 11. (Amends Section 665, Consol. Act.)

"Every owner or other person violating any provision of this title shall be guilty of a misdemeanor, punishable by a fine of not less than $10 nor more than $100, or by imprisonment for not more than ten days for each and every day that such violation shall continue, or by both such fine and imprisonment, in the discretion of the court. He shall also be liable to pay a penalty of $10 for each and every day that such offense shall continue. Such penalty may be sued for and recovered by the board of health in any civil tribunal of said city, and when recovered shall be paid over to the city chamberlain[1] and become part of the tenement-house fund, directed by section 194, subdivision 9 of this act, to be annually appropriated to the credit of the health department and to be expended by the board of health. . . . No part[2] of Chapter 275 of the laws of 1892, or of any other act shall be so construed as to abrogate or impair the power of the board of health to sue for and recover such a penalty whether the liability to pay said penalty shall arise from a violation of the laws, ordinances or sections of the sanitary code, in regard to light, ventilation, plumbing and drainage, so far as the same affects the sanitary condition of the premises; and except that the department of buildings of the city of New York shall have jurisdiction and cognizance over all matters and things in this title contained which relate to the construction[3] of buildings or structures or any part thereof, and as to light, ventilation, drainage and plumbing.[4] Any penalty[5] for a violation of the provisions of this title in respect to the matters aforesaid[6] shall be sued for and recovered in the same manner as the violations of the building laws of the city of New York are now sued for and recovered by the department of buildings in the city of New York; and said penalty so collected shall be paid to the comptroller[7] of the city of New York to be applied as other penalties collected by said department are applied."

*** (1897) — Chapter 378, Greater New York Charter, Section 1322.**

Provisions of the law of 1895 continued with the following slight changes: Beginning with the word "and" after the word "chamberlain"[1] omit all the matter from there down to the beginning of the words "No part"; [2] also, after the word "construction"[3] insert the words "or alteration;" also after the word "plumbing"[4] insert the words "of such buildings when in process of construction or alteration." After the word "penalty"[5] insert the words "hereinabove mentioned." After the word "aforesaid"[6] insert the words "within the jurisdiction and cognizance of the department of buildings." For the word "comptroller,"[7] substitute the word "chamberlain."

INJUNCTION TO RESTRAIN PERSONS VIOLATING PROVISIONS OF THE TENEMENT HOUSE LAW. — In addition to the other remedies of civil and criminal actions given to the Board of Health by previous statutes, the Board of Health in 1887 was given the remedy of injunction in certain cases, *i.e.* where there was any violation of the terms and conditions of the plan for any tenement or lodging house approved by the Board of Health, or of the conditions of the permit granted by the Board for the light and ventilation of the buildings, or where there was any violation of the provisions of the tenement house laws in reference to the percentage of the lot occupied, the amount of space left vacant at the rear of the building, the amount of space left vacant between front and rear tenement houses, and other similar provisions, any court of record or any judge or justice of a court of record was authorized to restrain, by an injunction order, the further progress of the building, but only after an action had been brought by the Health Department and only upon proof by affidavit of such violation, and that a service of the notice of the violation or non-compliance of the law had been made upon the owner or builder of the house, or other person superintending the building operations. These powers of the Health Department were, in 1892, transferred to the Department of Buildings, all of their powers, in relation to light and ventilation in new buildings being vested in the new Building Department. Since 1892 there has been no change in the law, and it is the present law upon this subject.

(1887) — Chapter 84, Section 10.

"In case of any violation of the provisions of this section, or of any failure to comply with, or of any violation of the terms and conditions of the plan for such tenement or lodging-house approved by the said board of health, or of the conditions of the permit granted by the board of health for such house, or for the air, light and ventilation of the same, any court of record or any judge or justice thereof, shall have power at any time after service of notice of violation, or of non-compliance of the owner,

* Indicates the existing law in 1900.

builder, or other person superintending the building or converting of any said house, upon proof by affidavit of any violation or non-compliance as aforesaid, or that a plan for the light and ventilation of said house has not been approved by the board of health, to restrain by injunction order in an action by the health department of the further progress of any violation as aforesaid. No undertaking shall be required as a condition of granting an injunction, or by reason thereof."

(1887) — Chapter 288, Section 1. — Continued.

(1891) — Chapter 204, Section 1. — Continued.

(1892) — Chapter 238, Section 1. — Continued.

(1895) — Brooklyn — Chapter 539, Section 1. (Amends Section 55, Consol. Act.) — Continued.

(1895) — Chapter 567, Section 8. (Amends Section 661, Consol. Act.) — Continued.

(1896) — Brooklyn — Chapter 355, Section 1. (Amends Section 55, Brooklyn Consol. Act.) — Continued.

***(1897) — Chapter 378, Greater New York Charter, Section 1318.**

Continued with the following addition: After the word "by" and before the words "board of health" insert the words "department of buildings or by."

BOARD OF APPEAL. — Since the creation of the Department of Buildings, in 1862, there has always been some body vested with the power of modifying or setting aside the law in special cases. The act of 1862 gave to the "department for the survey and inspection of buildings" full power in reference to the manner of construction, kind or quality of materials to be used in the erection of any building in the city, where the law did not specifically provide for it, and the Department was also authorized to make all materials and methods of construction conform to the true intent, meaning and spirit of the building laws. In addition, the Department was given discretionary power to modify or vary any of the provisions of the act in special cases, but *only where it did not conflict with public safety or the public good*, in order that substantial justice might be done and the *spirit of the law conserved*, but such modification could only be granted *upon an order being obtained from the Supreme Court*, after a sworn petition had been made to the court setting forth the reasons why the provisions of the law should be modified in each special case. This provision of the law of 1862 was reënacted in the building law of 1866 and again in 1871, but was in 1874 very materially changed. The new act took away from the Supreme Court the power to modify the law and vested this power in a newly created "board of examiners." This Board of Examiners was constituted in the following manner: Its members consisted of the Superintendent of Buildings, a representative of the examining committee of the New York Chapter of the American Institute of Architects, one of the ex-presidents of the New York Board of Underwriters and two members of the Mechanics and Traders' Exchange, one of whom was required to be a master carpenter and one a

* Indicates the existing law in 1900.

master mason, and all of these persons were to be selected by their respective organizations, excepting, of course, the Superintendent of Buildings. The law provided in no way for the removal of the members of this Board, but allowed the Board to perpetuate itself from year to year. The same law also required that no application to modify the law should be passed unless it received at least three affirmative votes of the Board; also that no member of the Board should pass upon any question in which he was pecuniarily interested. The Board was to meet upon the call of the Superintendent of Buildings, and each member, excepting the Superintendent, was to receive ten dollars for each meeting that he attended, but in no case were they to receive compensation for more than two meetings in any month. In 1882 this law was slightly changed, the chief clerk of the Bureau of Buildings of the Fire Department acting as clerk of the Board, instead of the Superintendent of Buildings. In 1885, however, the law was very much modified, the powers of the Superintendent of Buildings to vary or modify the provisions of the laws being very much restricted. This power was to be exercised only in case of alterations to old buildings, in the use of party walls belonging to different owners where the party walls could not be taken down; and generally, only where there were *practical difficulties* in the way of carrying out the *strict letter of the law*, the purpose of the modifications being to see that the spirit of the law was observed and public safety secured and substantial justice done. It was further provided that no modification of the law should be permitted unless a record of it was kept by the Superintendent of Buildings and a certificate issued to the person applying for the modification, and such certificate was not to be issued until it had first been passed upon by the Board of Examiners appointed under the Act of 1874; the composition of this Board was in this year somewhat changed. The two members of the Mechanics and Traders' Exchange were no longer required to be carpenters and masons, and a member of the Society of Architectural Iron Manufacturers, and a member of the Real Estate Owners and Builders' Association were added to the members of the Board. In the new Board, four affirmative votes were necessary to pass an application instead of three. In addition to the reasons above set forth for modifying the law, it was further provided that in cases where it was claimed by the owner of the building or his representative, that the provisions of the building law did not directly apply to the form of construction he desired to use, or that an equally good and more desirable form of construction could be employed than that required by the law, then the owner was given the right to present a petition to the Board of Examiners, asking to be authorized to use such a form of construction, and the Board was empowered to grant or reject his petition, and it was also added that their decision should be final. In 1892 this part of the law was again changed, and the law materially weakened; the previous act had permitted modifications of the law only in cases of alterations to old buildings in the use of party walls belonging to different owners, where the party walls could not be taken down; this provision was stricken from the new law. The chief of the Fire Department was added to the Board, and five affirmative votes were considered necessary instead of four to the granting of any application, and the Superintendent of Buildings and the Chief Clerk of the Building Department were authorized to receive compensation at the rate of ten dollars a day in addition to their other salaries for each meeting that they might attend. The Greater New York Charter reënacted most of the provisions of the law of 1892 in reference to this subject, though in a slightly modified form; it gave to each Commissioner of Buildings the power to pass upon any question relating to the manner of construction or the kind of materials to be used in the erection of any building, and to require that such materials and manner of construction should conform to the true intent of the building laws, and in case the commissioner should reject or refuse to approve any special form of construction, then the owner of the building was authorized to appeal from his decision to the Board of Buildings (which was composed of the three commissioners); but no such appeal could be made except where the amount of money involved by the decision exceeded the sum of $1000. This provision of the law, however, applied only to the boroughs of Brooklyn, Queens and Richmond, but not to the boroughs of Manhattan and the Bronx; in the latter boroughs any appeal from the decision of the commissioner is required to be taken to the Board of Examiners, created by the Act of 1874, and added to by subsequent acts. The law sets forth in considerable detail the conditions under which such appeals may be taken, and provides that the decision of the Board of Buildings in the boroughs of Brooklyn, Queens and Richmond and the decision of the Board of Examiners in the boroughs of Manhattan and the Bronx shall be final, and that no other appeal may be made. Another section of the Charter also gives to each Commissioner of Buildings, with the approval of the other two commissioners, the power to vary or modify any rule or regulation of the Board of Buildings, and also the power to vary or modify any existing law or ordinance relating to the construction of buildings, where there are practical difficulties in the way of carrying out the strict letter of the law, so that the spirit of the law may be observed and public safety secured and substantial justice done, but no such variation of the statute is to be allowed except by a vote of a majority of the Board of Buildings.

The Building Code, a local ordinance adopted in 1899 by the Municipal Assembly (under authority vested in it by Section 647 of the Greater New York Charter), provides also that each Commissioner of Buildings shall have power, with the approval of the Board of Buildings, to vary, not only any existing law or ordinance, but also any of the provisions of Chapter 12 of the Greater New York Charter, in relation to the erection of buildings, pursuant to the provisions of Section 650 of the Charter above quoted. The act also provides that the Board of Examiners for the boroughs of Manhattan and the Bronx shall be continued as provided for in the Charter and in the previous acts.

(1862) — Chapter 356, Section 36.

"The department created under this act (the department for the survey and inspection of buildings) shall have full power in passing upon any question relative to the mode, manner of construction or materials to be used in the erection, alteration, or repair of any building in the city of New York, where the same is not specially provided for herein to make the same conform to the true intent, meaning and spirit of the several provisions thereof; and shall also have discretionary power upon application therefor to modify or vary any of the several provisions of this act to meet the requirements of special cases, where the same do not conflict with public safety and the public good, so that substantial justice may be done; but no such deviation shall be permitted except a record of the same shall be kept by said department, and a certificate be first issued to the party applying for the same, such certificate shall be issued only upon an order first being obtained therefor upon a sworn petition setting forth the facts upon application to a special term of the supreme court in the city of New York, said supreme court hereby being authorized to grant such order in its discretion."

(1866) — Chapter 873, Section 33. — Continued.

(1871) — Chapter 625, Section 31. — Continued.

(1874) — Chapter 547, Section 8.

Provisions of previous laws amended as follows: The provision giving to the Department of Buildings the power to modify the law reënacted, down to the words "applying for the same,"[1] the rest of this section is very materially changed, the supreme court no longer being the body to grant such changes in the law. The following section is all new matter: —

"Such certificates shall be issued only upon an application setting forth the facts sworn to by the applicant, and after said application shall have been passed upon favorably by a board of examiners consisting of the superintendent of buildings, a member of the examining committee of the New York Chapter of American Institute of Architects, one of the ex-presidents of the New York Board of Underwriters, and two members of the Mechanics & Traders' Exchange of said city, one of the latter of whom shall be a master carpenter and one a master mason; all of whom, except said superintendent shall be selected by their respective organizations, and so certified by the proper officers to the said superintendent; no application shall be considered as passed by said board unless the same receive three affirmative votes; no member of said board shall pass upon any question in which he is pecuniarily interested. The said board shall meet upon notice from the said superintendent who shall be chairman of the board, and shall keep the record of its proceedings, which shall be filed in the office of the said department. The members of said board, excepting the said superintendent, shall each be entitled to and shall receive $10 for each attendance at a meeting of said board to be paid by the comptroller of the city of New York from the contingent fund of said department upon the voucher of said superintendent, but in no case shall they be entitled to receive compensation for more than two meetings in any one month."

(1882) — Chapter 410, Section 504.

Provisions of the law of 1874 continued with the following slight changes: Wherever the word "superintendent" occurs, substitute the word "inspector," and wherever the words "building department" occur substitute the words "bureau of buildings of the fire department;" also, instead of the Superintendent of Buildings being required to act as clerk of the Board of Examiners it is provided that the Chief Clerk of the Bureau of Buildings shall act as clerk of the said Board and keep the record of its proceedings.

(1885) — Chapter 456, Section 31.

"The superintendent of buildings shall have full power (except as herein otherwise provided for) in passing upon any question relative to the mode, manner of construction, or materials to be used in the erection or alteration of any building or other structure provided for in this title, in any part of the city of New York, to make the same to conform to the true intent and meaning of the several provisions thereof. He shall also have power to vary or modify the provisions of this title, upon application therefor in writing, only in case of alteration of old buildings, or the use of party walls belonging to different owners, where the same cannot be taken down, and where there are practical difficulties in the way of carrying out the strict letter of this law, so that the spirit of the law is observed, the public safety secured, and substantial justice done; but no such deviation shall be permitted except a record of the same shall be kept by the said superintendent of buildings, and a certificate be first issued to the party applying for the same; such certificate shall not be issued until a board of examiners consisting of a member of the New York chapter of American Institute of Architects, one member of the New York Board of Underwriters, two members of the Mechanics and Traders' Exchange of said city, one member of the Society of Architectural Iron Manufacturers of said city, and one member of the Real Estate Owners and Builders' Association of said city, who shall be an architect or builder, all of whom shall be appointed by their respective organizations (and so certified to annually to said superintendent of buildings) shall also approve the proposed modifications of the law. The said examiners shall each take the usual oath of office before entering upon the performance of their duties. The superintendent shall be ex-officio a member of said board and be chairman thereof. No vote of concurrence shall be passed by said board unless the same shall receive four affirmative votes. In cases in which it is claimed by an owner, in person or by his representative, that the provisions of this title do not directly apply, or that an equally good and more desirable form of construction can be employed in any specific case than that required by this title, then such person shall have the right to present a petition to the board of examiners, and may appear before said board and be heard; and said board shall consider such petition in its regular order of business, and as soon as practicable render a decision thereon. The said board of examiners are hereby authorized and empowered to grant or reject such petition, and their decision shall be final. If such decision is favorable to said petitioner a certificate shall be issued by the superintendent of buildings in accordance therewith. No member of said board shall pass upon any question in which he is pecuniarily interested. The said board shall meet once in each week upon notice from the superintendent of buildings. The chief clerk in the office of the superintendent of buildings shall be clerk of said board, and shall keep a record of its proceedings, which shall be kept in the office of the superintendent of buildings. The members of said board, excepting the superintendent, shall each be entitled to and shall receive ten dollars for each attendance of a meeting of said board, to be paid by the comptroller from the contingent fund upon the voucher of the superintendent of buildings, certified to by the board of fire commissioners."

(1892) — Chapter 275, Section 40.

Provisions of the law of 1885 amended as follows: After the words "he shall also have power to vary or modify the provisions of this title upon application therefor in writing," the following clause in the law of

1885 has been omitted, "only in case of alteration of old buildings, or the use of party walls belonging to different owners, where the same cannot be taken down";. also, the new law requires that such application shall be made by an owner of the building or structure or his representative. The law of 1892 also provides that of the two members of the Mechanics and Traders' Exchange on the Board of Examiners one shall be a master mason and one a master carpenter, and also the Chief of the Fire Department is added to the members of the board. Five affirmative votes in the new law are considered necessary to the granting of an application instead of four; also in the new law the Superintendent of Buildings is to receive compensation at the rate of ten dollars a day for each meeting that he may attend, as is also the chief clerk of the Building Department. The other provisions of the law are continued without change.

***(1897) — Chapter 378, Greater New York Charter, Chapter 12, Sections 649–650.**

"Each commissioner shall have power and it shall be his duty, subject to the provisions of law and the ordinances of the municipal assembly and the general rules and regulations established by the board, to pass upon any question relative to the mode, manner of construction or materials to be used in the erection or alteration of any building or other structure erected or to be erected within the borough or boroughs under his jurisdiction which is included within the provisions of this chapter or of any existing law applicable to such borough or boroughs relating to the construction, alteration or removal of buildings or other structures, and to require that such mode, manner of construction, or materials shall conform to the true intent and meaning of the several provisions of this chapter and of the laws and ordinances aforesaid and the rules and regulations established by the board. Whenever a commissioner to whom such question has been submitted shall reject or refuse to approve the mode, manner of construction or materials proposed to be followed or used in the erection or alteration of any such building or structure, or when it is claimed that the rules and regulations of the board or the provisions of law or of said ordinances do not apply or that an equally good and more desirable form of construction can be employed in any specific case, the owner of such building or structure, or his duly authorized agent, may appeal from the decision of such commissioner to the board in any case where the amount involved by such decision shall exceed the sum of one thousand dollars; provided, however, that in the boroughs of Manhattan and the Bronx such appeal shall be taken to the board of examiners, established by chapter 456 of the laws of 1885 and the several acts amendatory thereof or supplemental thereto. The commissioner for the boroughs of Manhattan and the Bronx shall be ex-officio a member and the chairman of said board of examiners. The other members of said board of examiners shall be the persons mentioned and described in section 31 of said chapter 456 of the laws of 1885 and the several acts amendatory thereof or supplemental thereto. The appeal authorized by this section may be taken within ten days from the entry of a decision upon the records of the commissioner by filing with the commissioner rendering such decision and with the secretary of the board established by this act or with the clerk of the board of examiners, as the case may be, a notice of appeal stating specifically

* Indicates the existing law in 1900.

the questions which the appellant desires to have passed upon by the board of buildings or by the board of examiners, as the case may be, and by filing with the secretary of the board of buildings or the clerk of the board of examiners, as the case may be, copies of all papers required by law or by the rules and regulations of the board of buildings to be submitted to the commissioner upon an application for a building permit, and the board of buildings or the board of examiners, as the case may be, shall thereafter fix a day within a reasonable time for the hearing of such appeal, and upon such hearing the appellant may be represented either in person or by his agent or attorney. The decision of the board of buildings or the board of examiners, as the case may be, upon such appeal, shall be rendered without unnecessary delay and such decision shall be final."

Section 650.

"Each commissioner shall have power with the approval of the board, to vary or modify any rule or regulation of the board or the provisions of this chapter or of any existing law or ordinance relating to the construction, alteration or removal of any building. or structure erected or to be erected within his jurisdiction upon an application to him therefor in writing by the owner of such building or structure or his duly authorized agent, where there are practical difficulties in the way of carrying out the strict letter of the law, so that the spirit of the law shall be observed and public safety secured and substantial justice done; but no such variation or modification shall be granted or allowed except by a vote of a majority of the board. Where such application has been filed with a commissioner the owner of such building or structure or his duly authorized agent shall have the right to present a petition to such commissioner and the board, setting forth the grounds for the desired variation or modification, and may appear before said board and be heard. The board shall fix a date within a reasonable time for a hearing upon such application and shall as soon as practicable render a decision thereon, which decision shall be final. The particulars of each such application and of the decision of the board thereon shall be entered upon the records of the board, and if the application is granted a certificate therefor shall be issued by the commissioner to whom the application is made and shall be countersigned by the secretary of the board."

***(1899) — The Building Code — (An ordinance adopted December 20, 1899). Section 148.**

"Each commissioner of buildings shall have power, with the approval of the board, to vary or modify any rule or regulation of the board, or the provisions of chapter 12, of the Greater New York charter, or of any existing law or ordinance relating to the construction, alteration or removal of any building or structure erected or to be erected within his jurisdiction, pursuant to the provisions of section 650 of the Greater New York charter."

*** Section 149.**

"The board of examiners for the boroughs of Manhattan and The Bronx shall be constituted as prescribed by section 649 of the Greater New York charter. Each of said examiners shall take the usual oath of

*** Indicates the existing law in 1900.**

office before entering upon his duties. No members of said board shall pass upon any question in which he is pecuniarily interested. The said board shall meet as often as once in each week upon notice from the commissioner of buildings.

"The members of said board of examiners, and the clerk of said board, shall each be entitled to and shall receive ten dollars for each attendance at a meeting of said board, to be paid by the comptroller from the annual appropriation to be made therefor upon the voucher of the commissioner of buildings for the boroughs of Manhattan and The Bronx."

TENEMENT HOUSE FUND.—In 1879 a special fund, known as the tenement house fund, amounting to $10,000, was required to be appropriated annually for the use of the Board of Health in connection with tenement house work. This provision of the law was reënacted in the Consolidation Act and is a part of the Greater New York Charter, being the present law upon this subject.

(1879)—Chapter 504, Section 4.

"The board of estimate and apportionment of the city of New York shall, within twenty days after the passage of this act, transfer from any unexpended balances standing to the credit of any department of said city, or shall otherwise provide, and shall annually hereafter appropriate to the credit of the health department, the sum of $10,000, to be known as the 'tenement-house fund,' to be expended by the board of health."

(1882)—Chapter 410, Section 194, Part 9.

"The board of estimate and apportionment shall annually include in its final estimate the following sums, which shall be annually raised and appropriated.

"The sum of $10,000 to the credit of the health department to be known as the tenement-house fund, to be expended by the board of health."

*** (1897)—Chapter 378, Greater New York Charter, Section 230, Part 9—Continued.**

PERMANENT TENEMENT HOUSE COMMISSION.—The tenement house law of 1887 was enacted as a result of the investigations of the Tenement House Commission appointed by the legislature in 1884. This Commission was very much impressed with the fact that a large part of the evils of the tenement house system was due to the fact that there was no permanent body interested in securing tenement house reform, and the Commission felt that if there were such a permanent body, matters would be very much remedied. They accordingly enacted a requirement that the Mayor of the city of New York, with certain of his officials, should constitute a Tenement House Commission to consider the subject of tenement house reform. These public officials consisted of the following: The Mayor, the Commissioner of the Department of Public Works, a delegate from the Bureau of Buildings of the Fire Department, and the Commissioner of Street Cleaning. This body was required to meet annually between the fifteenth day of No-

* Indicates the existing law in 1900.

vember and the thirtieth day of December, for the purpose of considering the subject of tenement and lodging houses in the city, and to make such recommendations for improvement of the laws affecting them, as they might deem to be for the public welfare; their recommendations were to be sent to the Governor of the State and also to the Senate and Assembly on or before the fifteenth day of January in each year, and this body was, in addition, empowered to consider also the way in which such laws were being enforced in the city. This provision of the law, however, was repealed in 1895, as it was found that the different city officials were so fully occupied with their regular duties, that it was impossible for them to give any time or thought to this very large and important question.

(1887) — Chapter 84, Section 2. (Amends Section 533, Consol. Act.)

"The mayor and one commissioner from the department of health, a commissioner of the department of public works, one delegate from the bureau of inspection of buildings, and the commissioner of the department of street cleaning, shall meet annually, between the 15th day of November and the 30th day of December, for the purpose of considering the subject of tenement and lodging-houses in the city, and shall make such recommendations of improvement in the laws affecting tenement and lodging-houses as they may deem for the good of the people of the city; they shall cause such recommendations to be sent to the governor of the state, and to the senate and assembly annually on or before the 15th day of January; they shall also consider the subject of the execution of said laws, and shall recommend to the board of health such changes in the same as they may deem to be for the good of the people of the city."

(1895) — Chapter 567. — Repealed.

FIRE PROVISIONS

EGRESS OR ESCAPE IN CASE OF FIRE, MEANS OF. — The first provision in reference to this subject was enacted in the year 1852 in the Brooklyn law, when it was provided that all buildings should have scuttles in the roof made of or covered with metal. In 1860 a further provision was added, that there should be a ladder or stairs leading to such scuttles, and in the same year the New York law was amended, requiring, in addition to scuttles and ladders, a system of fire-escapes upon all dwelling houses occupied by more than eight families. This law provided that, outside of the building in question, but connected with it, in such a way as to afford a place of refuge for the tenants, there should be a set of stairs in a fireproof building. This was practically a plan for a separate tower fire-escape, and has been advocated by many persons at different times. The law further provided that if such a system of tower fire-escapes was not adopted, there should be, on the outside of the building, fire-escape balconies of metal connected by fireproof stairs, and that, in addition, the rooms on each floor should communicate by doors. If neither the tower escape nor the fire-escape balconies were furnished, then the building was required to be constructed fireproof throughout; there was a further provision that all scuttle ladders should be iron, if movable, and that the size of the scuttle should not be less than two feet by three feet. In 1862 the law was again amended, the tower fire-escape no longer being required; nor was it required that where buildings were not built as provided in the previous law, they should be fireproof throughout. The new law applied to all dwelling houses containing six families above the first floor, and which were also more than forty feet high, and also to all dwelling houses containing more than eight families above the first floor, irrespective of their height. A scuttle in the roof was still required to be provided; all rooms on each floor were to connect by doors from front to rear; and every building of this kind was to have on the outside a practical fireproof fire-escape of a form to be approved by the Department of Buildings. There was also a further provision for means of egress, where front and rear tenement houses were built on the same lot; in such cases, the front and rear buildings were to be connected by an iron bridge over the roof, but where such buildings were built fireproof, and where there were two or three of such buildings adjoining each other, of equal height and with flat roofs, the bridge was not required.

The next change in the law was in 1866. The law of that year provided that all buildings of any kind should have scuttles or bulkheads in the roof, constructed fireproof, with stairways or iron ladders leading to them; with the further provision that the ladders should be kept so as to be ready for use at all times, and the scuttles were not to be less in size than two feet by three feet. The other provisions of the law of 1862, in reference to placing fire-escapes on such building, and having the different rooms connect by doors, etc., were reënacted. In 1867 the first tenement house law was passed; this provided that every building used as a tenement or lodging house should be provided with a proper fire-escape of a form to be approved by the Inspector of Buildings.

In the same year an amendment was passed to the general building laws; this required that every dwelling house occupied by four or more families above the first floor should have a proper scuttle in the roof, with a stairway leading thereto; also, that all the rooms on each floor should connect by doors from front to rear; that all such buildings should have on the outside a practical fire-escape of a form to be approved by the Superintendent of Buildings; and with the further important provision that no front and rear tenement houses should thereafter be erected upon the same lot, unless each of the said houses was built fireproof. In addition, the Superintendent of Buildings was given very large powers to order alterations made in existing dwelling houses occupied by four or more families above the first floor, to secure a safe and secure means of escape in case of fire, and was authorized to make such alterations himself, upon application to the Supreme Court for an order so to do, in case the owner should fail to make them within a reasonable time, the expense of such alterations to become a lien upon the property. The next year this law was again amended, the new law providing that all dwelling houses occupied by two or more families on any floor above the first, and also that all dwelling houses more than three stories in height, containing more than four families, should have a proper bulkhead in the roof, with a stairway leading thereto; that all rooms should connect by doors from front to rear, and that the building should have on the outside a proper fire-escape. The powers granted to the Superintendent of Buildings, under the law of the previous year, in reference to making alterations in buildings already erected. were reënacted.

This law was repealed in 1871, and considerably modified. The new law required that any dwelling house more than two stories in height, occupied by two or more families above the first floor, and also all dwelling houses, either thereafter erected or already built, more than three stories in height, and occupied by three or more families above the first story, should be provided with such fire-escapes, alarms, doors and ventilators, as might be directed by the Superintendent of Buildings. In 1874 a new amendment to the law was passed, continuing the provisions of the previous act with a slight change, the ventilators not being required. This law was reënacted in the Consolidation Act of 1882, except that the powers previously vested in the Superintendent of Buildings were transferred to the Fire Department. In the same year, the provision of the Tenement House Act of 1867, requiring all tenement houses to have proper fire-escapes, approved by the Superintendent of Buildings, was reënacted. In 1885 the law was again amended, and a similar provision was enacted, requiring that all dwelling houses already erected, or that thereafter were to be erected, over two stories in height and occupied by two or more families on any floor above the first, should be provided with such good and sufficient fire-escapes or other means of egress in case of fire, as might be directed by the Superintendent of Buildings, and the Superintendent of Buildings was expressly authorized to direct that such means of egress be provided in all cases. In 1887 the law was again changed, the provisions of the previous year being reënacted, with the following additional provision: That similar fire-escapes should be provided for every building already erected, or that might thereafter be erected, more than four stories in height, occupied, or built to be occupied, by three or more families above the first story. In the same law it was also provided that in every tenement house over five stories in height thereafter erected, to be occupied by two or more families on any floor above the first, at least one flight of stairs should extend to the roof and be enclosed in a fireproof bulkhead.

In 1888 the Brooklyn Consolidation Act was passed, grouping together all previous enactments, and the provisions of the previous laws requiring a scuttle in the roof, with proper ladders or stairs leading thereto, were reënacted. It was also provided that any dwelling house already erected, over two stories in height and occupied by two or more families on any floor above the first, or by three or more families above the first story, should be provided with such fire-escapes and doors as might be directed by the Commissioner of Buildings; and a special penalty of $500 was imposed for the violation of this provision, it being deemed a misdemeanor. In 1892 the New York Building Law was again amended, and the provisions of previous statutes were reënacted, with a further provision that the Superintendent of Buildings should have full and exclusive power within the city to direct fire-escapes and other means of egress to be provided upon buildings of this kind. In 1894 the Brooklyn Consolidation Act was amended, giving the Brooklyn Commissioner the same full and exclusive power as was given to the New York Commissioner in 1892.

In 1897, in the Greater New York Charter, the provisions of the Tenement House Act of 1867 were reënacted, requiring that every tenement house should be provided with a proper fire-escape or such means of egress as might be approved by the Department of Buildings; and in 1899, a local ordinance was adopted, known as "The Building Code," which, among other things, contained provisions upon this subject. Where fireproof apartment or tenement houses had a frontage of over forty feet, and where such buildings were over eighty-five feet in height, then they were required to have at least two separate fireproof stairways, accessible from each apartment, leading from the ground floor to the roof, and one of such stairways was required to be remote from elevator shafts. The Building Code also reënacted the provisions of the law of 1892, requiring that all tenement houses should be provided with good and sufficient fire-escapes and stairways, or other means of egress, as the Department of Buildings might direct, giving to this Department full and exclusive power and authority to direct such means of egress upon any building of this class. The present law is found in the provisions of the Charter and of the Building Code above quoted.

(1852) — Brooklyn — Chapter 355, Section 7.

"Every building hereafter erected or built within the fire limits as aforesaid, shall have a scuttle or place of egress in the roof thereof. All scuttle frames and scuttle doors on every brick or stone dwelling-house or other building hereafter to be erected or built within the fire limits as aforesaid, shall be made of or covered with copper, zinc, tin or iron."

(1860) — Brooklyn — Chapter 474, Section 7. (Repeals Chapter 355, of the Laws of 1852.)

"Every building having scuttles now built or hereafter erected or built, shall have a scuttle or place of egress in the roof thereof, with a ladder or stairs placed on the inside. All scuttle frames and scuttle doors on every brick or stone dwelling or other building hereafter to be erected or built within the fire limits shall be made of or covered with copper, tin, zinc or iron."

(1860) — Chapter 470, Section 25.

"In all dwelling-houses which are built for the residence of more than eight families there shall be a fireproof stairs in a brick or stone or fireproof building attached to the exterior walls, and all the rooms on every story must communicate by doors; or if the fireproof stairs are not built as above then there must be fireproof balconies on each story on the outside of the building, connected by fireproof stairs, and all the rooms on every story must communicate by doors. If the buildings are not built with either the stairs or balconies as above specified then they must be built fireproof throughout. All ladders or stairs from upper stories to scuttles or roofs of any building shall, if movable, be of iron; and if not movable may be of wood; and all scuttles shall not be less than three feet by two feet."

(1862) — Chapter 356, Section 27. (Repeals Section 25, Chapter 470, of the Laws of 1860.)

"All dwelling-houses, in any part of the city of New York, already erected, or that may hereafter be built, that now are, or may be more than forty feet high, that shall be occupied by or built to contain six or more families above the first story, and all dwelling-houses that shall be occupied by or built to contain eight or more families above the first story, shall have the stairway connected with a proper scuttle or other opening, leading to the roof, and all the rooms on each floor shall connect by doors from front to rear, and every said dwelling-house shall have placed thereon a practical fireproof fire escape that shall be approved of by the department for the survey and inspection of buildings in the city of New York, and all front and rear tenement houses on the same lot shall be connected by an iron bridge; provided, that where any such building shall be built fireproof throughout, or where there are two or more dwelling-houses adjoining, and of equal height and with flat roofs, the same may be exempt from the requirements of this section."

(1866) — Chapter 873, Section 23.

"All buildings in the city of New York whether already erected or hereafter to be built shall have scuttle frames and doors or bulkheads leading to the roof, made of or covered with some fireproof material, and shall have stairways or stationary iron ladders leading to the same, and all such scuttles or stairways or ladders leading to the roof shall be kept so as to be ready for use at all times, and all scuttles shall not be less in size than two feet by three feet."

(1866) — Chapter 873, Section 32.

"All dwelling-houses in any part of the city of New York already erected, or that may hereafter be built, that now are or may be forty feet high that shall be built to contain or be occupied by six or more families above the first story, and all dwelling-houses that shall be built to contain or be occupied by eight or more families above the first story, shall have a stairway connected with a proper scuttle or other opening, leading to the roof, and all the rooms on each floor shall connect by doors from front to rear; and every such dwelling-house shall have placed thereon a practical fireproof fire escape that shall be approved of by the department for the survey and inspection of buildings in the city of New York, and all front and rear tenement-houses on the same lot shall be connected by an iron bridge; provided, that where any such building shall be built fireproof throughout, or where there are two or more dwelling-houses adjoining and of equal height and with flat roofs, the same may be exempt from the requirements of placing thereon fireproof fire escapes."

(1866) — Brooklyn — Chapter 858, Section 7.

"Every building hereafter erected or built within the fire limits shall have a scuttle or place of egress in the roof thereof of proper size, and shall have ladders or stairways leading to the same, and all such scuttles and stairways or ladders leading to the roof shall be kept in readiness for use at all times. All scuttle frames and scuttle doors shall be made of or covered with copper, zinc, tin or iron."

(1867) — Chapter 908, Section 3.

"Every house, building, or portion thereof in the cities of New York and Brooklyn, designed to be used, occupied, leased or rented, or which is used, occupied, leased or rented for a tenement or lodging-house, shall be provided with a proper fire escape or means of escape in case of fire, to be approved in New York by the inspector of buildings, and in Brooklyn by the assistant sanitary superintendent of the Metropolitan board of health."

(1867) — Chapter 939, Section 10. (Amends Section 32, Chapter 873, of the Laws of 1866.)

"All dwelling-houses that now are or may hereafter be erected in the city of New York, to contain or be occupied by four or more families above the first story, shall have a stairway connected with a proper opening, leading to the roof, and all the rooms on each floor shall connect by doors from front to rear; and every such dwelling-house shall have placed thereon a practical fireproof fire escape, that shall be approved of by the superintendent of buildings, and in no case hereafter shall a front and rear tenement house be erected on the same lot unless the said houses, and each of them, shall be built fireproof."

(1867) — Chapter 939, Section 10.

"In all dwelling-houses *already erected* in the city of New York intended to be occupied by four or more families above the first story, the superintendent of buildings shall have power to determine what alterations are necessary to be made in such buildings in order to afford a safe and secure means of escape in case of fire, and shall proceed therein as follows, to wit: He shall cause a notice to be served on the owner of said building (or where the owner cannot be found after diligent search for twenty-four hours, the notice shall be posted on the premises, and shall have all the effect of a personal service,) directing him to make the alterations set forth in said notice within the time specified therein, and in case the said owner refuses or neglects to comply with said order, the said superintendent shall thereupon apply to the supreme court for an order to proceed to make the alterations specified in said notice, and all costs and expenses and disbursements in the carrying out of said order shall become a lien upon the said building, and the supreme court, in the discretion of the judge to whom application shall be made, is hereby authorized to grant such order and take such proceedings as shall be necessary to make the same effectual, and to enforce said lien in accordance with the mechanic's lien law in the city of New York."

(1868) — Chapter 634, Section 2. (Amends Section 10, Chapter 939, of the Laws of 1867.)

"All dwelling-houses now erected, occupied by or built to contain two or more families on any of the floors above the first story, and all dwelling-houses now erected, more than three stories in height occupied by or built to contain four or more families, shall have a stairway connected with a proper bulkhead leading to the roof, and all rooms shall connect by doors from front to rear, and every such dwelling-house shall have placed thereon a practical fireproof fire escape that shall be approved of by the superintendent of buildings."

(1868) — Chapter 634, Section 2. (Amends Section 10, Chapter 939, of the Laws of 1867.)

Alterations to Existing Buildings. — "In all cases where any of the provisions of this section are not fully complied with either in buildings already erected or hereafter to be built, the superintendent of buildings shall have full power to make the same conform to the requirements of this section, and he shall proceed therein as follows, to wit: He shall cause a personal notice to be served on the owners, lessee, agent or any other person having a contingent interest therein, or in case no such person shall be found, then on any person in possession of said buildings, directing him or them to make the alterations set forth in said notice, within the time specified therein; and in case said owner or any of the persons thus notified refuses or neglects to comply with said order, the said superintendent shall thereupon apply to the supreme court at special term, for an order to proceed to make the alterations specified in said notice, and all costs, expenses and disbursements incurred in carrying out of said order, shall become a lien upon said building, and the supreme court at special term in the discretion of the judge to whom application shall be made, is hereby authorized to grant such order, and take such proceedings as shall be necessary to make the same effectual, and to enforce said lien in accordance with the mechanic's lien law of the city of New York, and in case the notice hereinbefore mentioned shall be served on any lessee or party in possession it shall be the duty of the person upon whom such service is made to give immediate notice thereof to the owner or agent of said building, personally, if such person shall be within the limits of the city of New York, and his residence shall be known, and if not within said city, then by depositing a copy of said notice in the post office in New York, properly enclosed and addressed to such owner or agent at his then place of residence, if known, and by paying the postage thereon. And in case any lessee or party in possession shall neglect and refuse to give said notice as herein provided, he shall be personally liable to the owner or owners of said buildings for all damages he or they shall sustain by reason thereof."

(1868) — Brooklyn — Chapter 632, Section 17. (Provisions of Section 7, Chapter 858, of the Laws of 1866, continued.)

(1871) — Chapter 625, Section 28. (Repeals all previous acts.)

"Any dwelling-house now erected or that may hereafter be erected in said city, more than two stories in height, occupied by or built to be occupied by two or three families on any one of the floors above the first story, and all dwelling-houses now erected or that may hereafter be erected more than three stories in height, occupied by or built to be occupied by three or more families above the first story, and any building already erected or that may be hereafter erected more than two stories in height occupied as or built to be occupied as a lodging-house, shall be provided with such fire escapes, alarms, doors and ventilators as shall be directed and approved of by the superintendent of buildings."

(1874) — Chapter 547, Section 7. (Amends Section 28, Chapter 625, of the Laws of 1871.)

"Any dwelling-house now erected, or that may hereafter be erected, more than two stories in height, occupied by, or built to be occupied by, two or three families, on any floor above the first, and all buildings now erected, or that may be hereafter erected, more than four stories in height, occupied by, or built to be occupied by, three or more families, above the first story, and any building already erected, or that may hereafter be erected, more than three stories in height, occupied or used, or built to be occupied or used, as a lodging-house, and all buildings in an isolated position already erected or that may hereafter be erected, more than three stories in height built to contain or that does contain, or is occupied by, three or more families above the first story, shall be provided with such fire escapes, alarms and doors as shall be directed by the superintendent of buildings."

(1882) — Chapter 410, Section 499 (Consol. Act). Continued, with the exception that the words "fire department" are substituted for the words "superintendent of buildings" at the end.

(1882) — Chapter 410, Section 651. (Provisions of Section 3, Chapter 908, Laws of 1867, continued.)

(1885) — Chapter 456, Section 28. (Section 499, Consol. Act, amended.)

"All dwelling-houses now erected, or that may hereafter be erected more than two stories in height, occupied or built to be occupied by two or more families on any floor above the first, and all buildings already erected more than three stories in height, occupied or used as a lodging-house, shall be provided with such good and sufficient fire escapes or other means of egress in case of fire as shall be directed by the superintendent of buildings, and said superintendent shall direct such means of egress to be provided in all cases."

(1887) — Chapter 566, Section 26. (Amends Section 499, Consol. Act.)

"All dwelling-houses now erected, or that may hereafter be erected, more than two stories in height, occupied by or built to be occupied by two or more families on any floor above the first, and all buildings now erected, or that may hereafter be erected, more than four stories in height, occupied by or built to be occupied by three or more families above the first story, and every building already erected or that may hereafter be erected, more than three stories in height, occupied and used as a lodging-house, shall be provided with such good and sufficient fire escapes or other means of egress in case of fire as shall be directed by the superintendent of buildings, and said superintendent shall direct such means of egress to be provided in all cases where he shall deem the same necessary."

(1887) — Chapter 566, Section 26. (Amends Section 499, of the Consol. Act.)

"At least one flight of stairs in each of said buildings (every dwelling-house exceeding five stories in height hereafter erected or altered to be occupied by two or more families on any floor above the first, and every dwelling-house over sixty feet in height, hereafter erected or altered to be occupied by two or more families on any floor above the first, and every dwelling-house over sixty feet in height hereafter erected or altered to be occupied by more than one family) shall extend to the roof and be enclosed in a bulkhead of fireproof materials."

(1888) — Brooklyn — Chapter 583, Consol. Act, Section 16.

"Every building that is now or may be hereafter erected shall have a scuttle or place of egress in the roof thereof of proper size, to be approved by the said commissioner, and shall have ladders or stairways leading to the same; and all said scuttles and stairways or ladders leading to the roof shall be kept in readiness for use at all times. And all scuttle frames or scuttle doors shall be made of or covered with copper, zinc, tin or iron."

(1888) — Brooklyn — Chapter 583, Consol. Act, Section 16.

"Any dwelling-house now erected or that may hereafter be erected in the city more than two stories in height, occupied or built to be occupied by two or more families on any one of the floors above the first story, and all dwelling-houses now erected or that may hereafter be erected more than two stories in height, occupied by or built to be occupied by three or more families above the first story, and any building already erected or that may hereafter be erected more than two stories in height, occupied as or built to be occupied as a lodging-house, shall be provided with such fire escapes and doors as shall be directed and approved by the commissioner. Any person after being notified by said commissioner who shall neglect to place upon any such building the fire escape herein provided for, shall forfeit the sum of five hundred dollars, and shall be deemed guilty of a misdemeanor."

(1892) — Chapter 275, Section 34. (Amends Section 498, Consol. Act.)

"Every dwelling-house occupied by or built to be occupied by three or more families above the first story, and every building already erected, or that may hereafter be erected, more than three stories in height, occupied and used as a lodging-house, shall be provided with such good and sufficient fire escapes, stairways, or other means of egress in case of fire as shall be directed by the superintendent of buildings, and said superintendent shall have full and exclusive power and authority within said city to direct fire escapes and other means of egress to be provided upon and within said buildings or any of them. All buildings requiring fire escapes shall have stationary iron ladders leading to the scuttle opening in the roof thereof, and all scuttles and ladders shall be kept so as to be ready for use at all times."

(1894) — Brooklyn — Chapter 481, Section 28. (Amends Consol. Act.)

"Every dwelling-house occupied by or built to be occupied by three or more families above the first story, and every building already erected, or that may hereafter be erected more than three stories in height, occupied and used as a lodging-house, shall be provided with such good and sufficient fire escapes, stairways or other means of egress in case of fire as shall be directed by the commissioner of buildings. Said commissioner shall have full and exclusive power and authority within said city to direct fire escapes and other means of egress to be provided upon and within said buildings or any of them, and to direct the same to be repaired, renewed or replaced where they are or become out of repair, unsafe or inadequate."

(1894) — Brooklyn — Chapter 481, Section 28. (Amends Consol. Act.)

"All buildings requiring fire escapes shall have stationary iron ladders leading to the scuttle opening in the roof thereof, and all scuttles and ladders shall be kept so as to be ready for use at all times and easily accessible to all tenants. If a bulkhead is used in place of a scuttle it shall have stairs; the door in the bulkhead or any scuttle shall, at no time, be locked, but may be fastened on the inside by movable bolts or hooks; and, if a bulkhead, shall have stairs, with hand rail leading to the roof."

*** (1897) — Chapter 378, Greater New York Charter, Section 1306.**

"Every such house (tenement and lodging-house) shall be provided with a proper fire escape or means of egress in case of fire, to be approved by the department of buildings."

*** (1899) — The Building Code — (An ordinance adopted December 20, 1899). Section 53.**

"Fireproof apartment-houses or tenement-houses, if constructed entirely in accordance with the requirements of section 105 of this Code for fireproof

* Indicates the existing law in 1900.

construction, may be erected to a height not to exceed 150 feet but not more than twelve stories in height upon all streets and avenues exceeding 79 feet in width, and 125 feet but not more than ten stories in height upon all streets and avenues not exceeding 79 feet in width, but any such building when exceeding 100 feet in height shall not be less than 40 feet in width. If any such building shall have a frontage exceeding 40 feet and exceeds 85 feet in height, it shall have at least two separate fireproof stairways, accessible from each apartment, leading from the ground floor to the roof, one of which shall be remote from elevator shafts."

***(1899) — The Building Code — (An ordinance adopted December 20, 1899). Section 103.**

"Every dwelling-house occupied or built to be occupied by three or more families, shall be provided with such good and sufficient fire escapes, stairways or other means of egress in case of fire as shall be directed by the department of buildings; and said department shall have full and exclusive power and authority within said city to direct fire escapes and other means of egress to be provided upon and within said buildings or any of them."

SCUTTLES AND LADDERS. — A provision that there should be a scuttle in the roof as a means of egress in case of fire was the very first provision enacted in reference to tenement houses, occurring for the first time in the Brooklyn Building Law of 1852. Every law that has been enacted since then has contained a provision upon this subject, the law being slightly changed from time to time, each time being strengthened. The main changes have been one defining the minimum size of the scuttle, and another providing that such scuttle shall be equipped with iron ladders or stairs leading to it, and still other provisions providing that the scuttles in tenement houses shall never be kept locked, so as to be sure that persons would have a quick means of escape to the roof.

(1852) — Brooklyn — Chapter 355, Section 7.

"Every building hereafter erected or built within the fire limits as aforesaid, shall have a scuttle or place of egress in the roof thereof. All scuttle frames and scuttle doors on every brick or stone dwelling-house or other building hereafter to be erected or built within the fire limits as aforesaid, shall be made of or covered with copper, zinc, tin or iron."

(1860) — Brooklyn — Chapter 474, Section 7. (Repeals Chapter 355 of the Laws of 1852.)

"Every building having scuttles now built or hereafter erected or built, shall have a scuttle or place of egress in the roof thereof with a ladder or stairs placed on the inside. All scuttle frames and scuttle doors on every brick or stone dwelling or other building hereafter to be erected or built within the fire limits shall be made of or covered with copper, tin, zinc or iron."

(1860) — Chapter 470, Section 25.

"In all dwelling-houses which are built for the residence of more than eight families all ladders or stairs from upper stories to scuttles or roofs of

*** Indicates the existing law in 1900.**

any building shall, if movable, be of iron, and if not movable may be of wood; and all scuttles shall not be less than three feet by two feet."

(1862) — Chapter 356, Section 27.

"All dwelling-houses in any part of the city of New York already erected or that may hereafter be built, that now are or may be more than forty feet high, that shall be occupied by or built to contain six or more families above the first story, and all dwelling-houses that shall be occupied by or built to contain eight or more families above the first story, shall have a stairway connected with a proper scuttle or other opening leading to the roof."

(1866) — Chapter 873, Section 23.

"All buildings in the city of New York whether already erected or hereafter to be built shall have scuttle frames and doors or bulkheads leading to the roof, made of or covered with some fireproof material, and shall have stairways or stationary iron ladders leading to the same, and all such scuttles or stairways or ladders leading to the roof shall be kept so as to be ready for use at all times, and all scuttles shall not be less in size than two feet by three feet."

(1866) — Chapter 873, Section 32.

"All dwelling-houses in any part of the city of New York already erected, or that may hereafter be built, that now are or may be forty feet high that shall be built to contain or be occupied by six or more families above the first story, and all dwelling-houses that shall be built to contain or occupied by eight or more families above the first story, shall have a stairway connected with a proper scuttle or other opening, leading to the roof."

(1866) — Brooklyn. Chapter 858, Section 7.

"Every building hereafter erected or built within the fire limits shall have a scuttle or place of egress in the roof thereof of proper size, and shall have ladders or stairways leading to the same, and all such scuttles and stairways or ladders leading to the roof shall be kept in readiness for use at all times. All scuttle frames and scuttle doors shall be made of or covered with copper, zinc, tin or iron.

(1867) — Chapter 939, Section 10. (Amends Section 32, Chapter 873, of the Laws of 1866.)

"All dwelling-houses that now are or may hereafter be erected in the city of New York to contain or be occupied by four or more families above the first story, shall have a stairway connected with a proper opening, leading to the roof, and all the rooms on each floor shall connect by doors from front to rear; and every such dwelling-house shall have placed thereon a practical fireproof fire escape, that shall be approved of by the superintendent of buildings, and in no case hereafter shall a front and rear tenement house be erected on the same lot, unless the said houses, and each of them, shall be built fireproof."

(1868) — Chapter 634, Section 2. (Amends Section 10, Chapter 939, of the Laws of 1867.)

"All dwelling-houses now erected, occupied by or built to contain two or more families on any of the floors above the first story, and all dwelling-houses now erected, more than three stories in height occupied by or built to contain four or more families, shall have a stairway connected with a proper bulkhead leading to the roof."

(1868) — Brooklyn — Chapter 632, Section 17. (Provisions of Section 7, Chapter 858, of the Laws of 1866, continued.)

(1871) — Chapter 625, Section 23.

"All buildings to have scuttle frames and covers or bulkheads and doors, made of, or covered with some fireproof material; and all scuttles shall have stationary iron ladders leading to the same; and all such scuttles or ladders shall be kept so as to be ready for use at all times; and all scuttles shall not be less in size than 2 feet by 3 feet; and if a bulkhead is used or substituted in any building in place of a scuttle, it shall have stairs with a sufficient guard or hand-rail leading to the roof; and in case the building shall be a tenement-house the door in the bulkhead, or any scuttle shall at no time be locked but may be fastened on the inside by movable bolts or hooks."

(1874) — Chapter 547, Section 7. — Continued.

(1882) — Chapter 410, Section 494. (Consol. Act.)

"All buildings in the city of New York, whether already erected or hereafter to be built, shall have scuttle frames and covers, or bulkheads and doors, made of or covered with some fireproof material, and all scuttles shall have stationary iron ladders leading to the same, and all such scuttles or ladders shall be connected so as to be ready for use at all times, and all scuttles shall not be less in size than two feet by three feet; and if a bulkhead is used or substituted in any building in place of a scuttle, it shall have stairs with a sufficient guard or hand-rail leading to the roof; and in case the building shall be a tenement-house, the door in the bulkhead or any scuttle, shall at no time be locked, but may be fastened on the inside by movable bolts or hooks."

(1885) — Chapter 456, Section 23. — Continued.

(1887) — Chapter 566, Section 22. (Amends Chapter 494, Consol. Act.)

"All buildings in the city of New York now built, or hereafter to be built, shall have scuttles or bulkheads covered with some fireproof materials, with ladders or stairs leading thereto. The scuttles in all tenement-houses shall have stationary iron ladders leading to the same, and all scuttles and ladders shall be kept so as to be ready for use at all times, and no scuttle shall be less in size than two by three feet. If a bulkhead is used in place of a scuttle, it shall have stairs with sufficient guard or hand-rail leading to the roof; and in case the building shall be a tenement-house the door in the bulkhead or any scuttle, shall at no time be locked but may be fastened on the inside by movable bolts or hooks."

(1887) — Chapter 566, Section 26. (Amends Section 499, Consol. Act.)

"At least one flight of stairs in each of said buildings (every dwelling-house exceeding five stories in height hereafter erected or altered to be occupied by two or more families on any floor above the first, and every dwelling-house over sixty feet in height, hereafter erected or altered to be occupied by two or more families on any floor above the first, and every dwelling-house over sixty feet in height hereafter erected or altered to be occupied by more than one family) shall extend to the roof and be inclosed in a bulkhead of fireproof materials."

(1888) — Brooklyn — Chapter 583, Consol. Act, Section 16.

"Every building that is now or may be hereafter erected shall have a scuttle or place of egress in the roof thereof of proper size to be approved by the said commissioner, and shall have ladders or stairways leading to the same; and all said scuttles and stairways or ladders leading to the roof shall be kept in readiness for use at all times. And all scuttle frames or scuttle doors shall be made of or covered with copper, zinc, tin or iron."

(1892) — Chapter 275, Section 30. (Amends Section 494, Consol. Act.)

"All buildings shall have scuttles or bulkheads covered with some fireproof materials with ladders or stairs leading thereto. No scuttle shall be less in size than two by three feet."

(1892) — Chapter 275, Section 34. (Amends Section 498, Consol. Act.)

"All buildings requiring fire escapes shall have stationary iron ladders leading to the scuttle opening in the roof thereof, and all scuttles and ladders shall be kept so as to be ready for use at all times. If a bulkhead is used in place of a scuttle, it shall have stairs with sufficient guard or hand-rail leading to the roof. In case the building shall be a tenement-house, the door in the bulkhead or any scuttle shall at no time be locked but may be fastened on the inside by movable bolts or hooks."

(1894) — Chapter 481, Section 23. (Amends Consol. Act.)

"All buildings shall have scuttles or bulkheads, covered with some fireproof material, with ladders or stairs leading thereto, and easily accessible to all tenants. No scuttle shall be less in size than two by three feet."

(1894) — Brooklyn — Chapter 481, Section 28. (Amends Consol. Act.)

"All buildings requiring fire escapes shall have stationary iron ladders leading to the scuttle opening in the roof thereof, and all scuttles and ladders shall be kept so as to be ready for use at all times and easily accessible to all tenants. If a bulkhead is used in place of a scuttle it shall have stairs; the door in the bulkhead or any scuttle shall, at no time, be locked, but may be fastened on the inside by movable bolts or hooks; and, if a bulkhead, shall have stairs, with hand-rail leading to the roof."

(1895) — Brooklyn — Chapter 292, Section 22.

"All buildings shall have scuttles or bulkheads covered with some fireproof material, with ladders or stairs leading thereto and easily accessible to all tenants. No scuttle shall be less in size than two by three feet."

***(1899) — The Building Code — (An ordinance adopted December 20, 1899). Section 92.**

"All dwelling-houses more than four stories in height hereafter erected or altered shall have scuttles or bulkheads covered with some fireproof materials with ladders or stairs leading thereto, and easily accessible to all occupants. No scuttle shall be less in size than 2 by 3 feet."

* Indicates the existing law in 1900.

***(1899) — The Building Code — (An ordinance adopted December 20, 1899.) Section 103.**

"All buildings requiring fire escapes shall have stationary iron ladders leading to the scuttle opening in the roof thereof, and all scuttles and ladders shall be kept so as to be ready for use at all times. If a bulkhead is used instead of a scuttle, it shall have stairs with sufficient guard or hand-rail leading to the roof. In case the building shall be a tenement-house, the door in the bulkhead or any scuttle shall at no time be locked, but may be fastened on the inside by movable bolts or hooks."

FIRE-ESCAPES, REPAIR OF. — Although fire-escapes were required on buildings as early as 1860, it was not until 1871 that any provision was enacted requiring fire-escapes to be kept in repair and painted so that rust would not destroy their usefulness. This law, enacted in 1871, requiring the owners to keep the escapes in good repair and properly painted, has been reënacted in every piece of legislation upon this subject and is practically the law at the present time.

(1871) — Chapter 625, Section 28.

"The owner or owners of any buildings upon which any fire escapes may now be or may hereafter be erected, shall keep the same in good order and repair, and well painted."

(1874) — Chapter 547, Section 7. — Continued.

(1882) — Chapter 410, Section 499. — Continued.

(1885) — Chapter 456, Section 28. — Continued.

(1887) — Chapter 566, Section 26. — Continued.

(1888) — Brooklyn — Chapter 583, Section 16. (Brooklyn Consol. Act.) — Continued.

(1892) — Chapter 275, Section 34. (Amends Section 498, Consol. Act.)

"The owner or owners of any building upon which a fire escape is erected shall keep the same in good repair and properly painted."

(1894) — Brooklyn — Chapter 481, Section 28. (Amends Brooklyn Consol. Act.) — Continued.

*** (1899) — The Building Code — (An ordinance adopted December 20, 1899.) Section 103.**

"The owner or owners of any building upon which a fire escape is erected shall keep the same in good repair and properly painted."

FIRE-ESCAPES, ENCUMBRANCE OF. — Prior to 1871, there was no law prohibiting the encumbering of fire-escapes. In this year, however, a provision was enacted prohibiting any person from placing an encumbrance of any kind upon any fire-escape. No penalty, however, was provided for the violation of this statute, nor was the responsibility for its enforcement placed upon any special official. The law was reënacted in 1874, and again in 1882, but not until 1885 were the above defects remedied. In

* Indicates the existing law in 1900.

that year the provisions of the previous law were reënacted, but an additional clause was passed placing the responsibility upon the occupants of tenement houses for any encumbrance of fire-escapes and placing the duty of enforcing the law upon firemen, policemen and members of the Building Department, who, upon finding any fire-escape balcony encumbered, were to notify the occupant to remove such encumbrances and to keep the balcony clear. Upon the failure of the occupant to do so, the officer charged with the enforcement of the law was directed to apply to the nearest police magistrate for a warrant for the arrest of the occupant of the premises, and upon proving that the fire-escape had been obstructed, the occupant was to be fined not more than $10 for each offence, or to be imprisoned for not more than ten days in the discretion of the court. At the same time there was a further provision enacted requiring the manufacturer of fire-escapes to fasten to all new balconies a plate containing a notice to the effect that any person placing any encumbrance on such balcony was liable to a penalty of $10 and to imprisonment for ten days. In 1887 this law was again enacted with slight changes, not affecting its substance.

In 1888 the Brooklyn building law was amended, and the provisions of the law of 1871 simply prohibiting the encumbrance of fire-escapes were reënacted, no provision being made for its enforcement. In 1892 the New York building law was again changed, and the provisions of the acts of 1885 and 1887 were again reënacted with slight verbal changes, the responsibility being still placed upon the occupant of the premises, and the remedy still being arrest and a fine of $10. In 1894 a new law was passed for the city of Brooklyn; this placed the responsibility for the obstruction of fire-escapes upon the owner of the building, requiring him to keep all fire-escapes free from obstructions. It also placed the responsibility upon the occupant as well as the owner, and reënacted the provisions of the New York law of 1892, making a violation of this section a misdemeanor, and the remedy the arrest of the offender and the imposing of a fine of not more than $25 for each offence, or imprisonment for ten days, in the discretion of the court. The Building Code, enacted in 1899, a local ordinance, continued the main provisions of the New York law of 1892 and the Brooklyn law of 1894, placing the responsibility upon the occupant of the premises, the enforcement of the law being lodged with the Fire and Police Departments and no longer with the Department of Buildings. The penalty for a violation of the law was still arrest and a fine of $10 or imprisonment for ten days.

(1871) — Chapter 625, Section 28.

"No person shall at any time place any encumbrance of any kind whatsoever upon any fire escapes now erected or that may hereafter be erected in said city."

(1874) — Chapter 547, Section 7. — Continued.

(1882) — Chapter 410, Section 499. — Continued.

(1885) — Chapter 456, Section 28. (Amends Section 499, Consol. Act.)

Previous provisions continued with additional provision that the occupants of all dwelling houses, etc., to which outside fire-escapes are attached, shall keep the same clear and free of all encumbrances, and it shall be the duty of all firemen, policemen, and every officer of the bureau of inspection of buildings who shall discover any fire-escape, balcony or ladder of any fire-escape encumbered in any way, after a notice to remove (any encumbrance) and to keep the same clear shall be given, and a failure to comply (therewith, to) apply to the nearest police magistrate for a warrant to arrest the occupant or occupants of said premises of which the fire-escape forms a part, and the party shall be brought before said magistrate, and if the case of obstruction be proved, the parties whose duty it is to keep them free shall be fined not more than $10 for each offence, or may be imprisoned not to exceed ten days in the city prison, or both, in the discretion of said magistrate.

In constructing all balcony fire-escapes, the manufacturer thereof shall securely fasten thereto, in a conspicuous place, a cast-iron plate having suitable raised letters on same to read as follows — "Notice ! ! Any person placing any encumbrance on this balcony is liable to a penalty of $10 and imprisonment for 10 days."

(1887) — Chapter 566, Section 26. (**Amends Section 499, Consol. Act.**)

"No person shall at any time place any encumbrance of any kind whatsoever before or upon any fire escape on any building in said city. It shall be the duty of all firemen, policemen and every officer of the bureau of inspection of buildings, who shall discover any fire escape, balcony or ladder of any fire escape encumbered in any way to forthwith verbally notify and require the occupant of the premises or apartment to which said fire escape, balcony or ladder is attached, or for whose use the same is provided, to remove such encumbrance and keep the same clear. If said notice shall not be complied with by the removal of such encumbrance, and keeping said fire escape, balcony, or ladder free from encumbrance then it shall be the duty of said policeman, fireman, or officer of the bureau of inspection of buildings to apply to the nearest police magistrate for a warrant for the arrest of the occupant or occupants of the premises or apartment of which the fire escape forms a part, and the said parties shall be brought before the said magistrate, as for a misdemeanor, and upon conviction the occupant or occupants of said premises or apartment shall be fined not more than ten dollars for each offense or may be imprisoned not to exceed ten days, or both in the discretion of the court."

(1888) — Brooklyn — Chapter 583, Section 16. (**Brooklyn Consol. Act.**) **Provisions of Act of 1871 reënacted.**

(1892) — Chapter 275, Section 34. (**Amends Section 498, Consol. Act.**)

"No person shall at any time, place any encumbrance of any kind whatsoever before or upon any fire escape. It shall be the duty of every fireman and policeman who shall discover any fire escape, balcony or ladder of any fire escape encumbered in any way, to forthwith report the same to the commanding officer of his company or precinct, and such commanding officer shall forthwith cause the occupant of the premises or apartment to which said fire escape, balcony or ladder is attached, or for whose use the same is provided, to be notified, either verbally or in writing, to remove such encumbrance, and keep the same clear. If said notice shall not be complied with by the removal forthwith of such encumbrance, and keeping said fire escape, balcony or ladder free from encumbrance, then it shall be the duty of said commanding officer, to apply to the nearest police magistrate for a warrant for the arrest of the occupant or occupants of the said premises or apartment of which the fire escape forms a part, and the said parties shall be brought before the said magistrate, as for a misdemeanor; and, on conviction, the occupant or occupants of said premises or apartment shall be fined not more than $10 for each offense, or may be imprisoned not to exceed ten days, or both, in the discretion of the court. In constructing all balcony fire escapes, the manufacturer thereof shall securely fasten thereto, in a conspicuous place, a cast iron plate having suitable raised letters on the same, to read as follows: 'Notice! Any Person Placing Any Encumbrance On This Balcony Is Liable To A Penalty of $10 & Imprisonment for Ten Days.'"

(1894) — Brooklyn — Chapter 481, Section 28. (Amends Consol. Act.)

"The owner or owners of any building upon which a fire escape is erected shall keep the same free from obstructions. No person shall at any time place any encumbrances of any kind whatsoever before or upon any fire escape. It shall be the duty of every fireman and policeman who shall discover any fire escape balcony or ladder of any fire escape encumbered in any way, to forthwith report the same to the commanding officer of his company or precinct, and the occupant of the premises or apartment to which said fire escape balcony or ladder is attached, or for whose use the same is provided, shall be notified, either verbally or in writing, to remove such encumbrance and keep the same clear. If said notice shall not be complied with by the removal forthwith of such encumbrances, and keeping said fire escape balcony or ladder free from encumbrances, then it shall be the duty of said commanding officer to apply to the nearest police magistrate for a warrant for the arrest of the occupant or occupants of the said premises or apartment of which the fire escape forms a part, and the said parties shall be brought before the said magistrate as for a misdemeanor; and, on conviction the occupant or occupants of said premises or apartment shall be fined not more than twenty-five dollars for each offense, or may be imprisoned not to exceed ten days, or both, in the discretion of the court. In construction of all balcony fire escapes the manufacturer thereof shall securely fasten thereto in a conspicuous place, a cast iron plate, having suitable raised letters on the same to read as follows: 'Notice ! Any person placing encumbrances on this balcony is liable to a penalty of twenty-five dollars and imprisonment for ten days."

*** (1899) — The Building Code — (An ordinance adopted December 20, 1899.) Section 103.**

"No person shall at any time place any encumbrance of any kind whatsoever before or upon any fire escape, balcony or ladder. It shall be the duty of every fireman and policeman who shall discover any fire escape balcony or ladder of any fire escape encumbered in any way, to forthwith report the same to the commanding officer of his company or precinct, and such commanding officer shall forthwith cause the occupant of the premises or apartment to which said fire escape, balcony or ladder is attached or for whose use the same is provided, to be notified, either verbally or in writing, to remove such encumbrance and keep the same clear. If said notice shall not be complied with by the removal, forthwith, of such encumbrance, and keeping said fire escape, balcony or ladder free

* Indicates the existing law in 1900.

from encumbrance, then it shall be the duty of said commanding officers to apply to the nearest police magistrate for a warrant for the arrest of the occupant or occupants of the said premises or apartment of which the fire escape forms a part, and the said parties shall be brought before the said magistrate, as for a misdemeanor; and, on conviction, the occupant or occupants of said premises or apartment shall be fined not more than $10 for each offense, or may be imprisoned not to exceed ten days, or both, in the discretion of the court. In constructing all balcony fire escapes, the manufacturer thereof shall securely fasten thereto, in a conspicuous place, a cast iron plate having suitable raised letters on the same, to read as follows: Notice: 'Any person placing any encumbrance on this balcony is liable to a penalty of ten dollars and imprisonment for ten days.'"

STAIRWAYS AND PUBLIC HALLS, CONSTRUCTION OF. — After the providing of means of egress for persons in case of fire, the next important provision to be enacted is naturally one requiring those portions of the buildings through which persons would pass in the course of such egress to be made safe.

The first law in reference to the construction of public stairways and public halls was enacted in 1867, by an amendment to the general building laws passed in that year. This law required that in all dwelling houses intended to be occupied by four families or more, thereafter to be erected, all stairs should be constructed of stone or iron, and the floor beams of the halls were to be of iron with brick arches turned between them.

In the following year this requirement was considerably modified, fireproof stairs or halls not being required in new buildings, provided that such buildings did not contain more than two families on any floor, and provided, further, that they did not exceed four stories in height and that the stairs in them continued to the roof and had proper bulkheads, and that the rooms on each floor connected by doors from front to rear, and that the buildings were equipped with proper fire-escapes; otherwise, the halls and stairs and hall partitions from the cellar to the roof were to be constructed fireproof. In 1871 this section was again amended to the effect that no building should thereafter be erected or altered to be occupied by more than six families, unless the halls, stairs, and hall partitions were constructed fireproof. These provisions were repealed in 1874.

In 1885, in an amendment to the general building laws, the requirements in reference to this subject were again changed, the new law requiring that in all dwelling and apartment houses over 60 feet in height thereafter erected or altered, and which were arranged to be occupied by two or more families on any floor above the first, the halls and stairs should be enclosed with brick walls, and the floors, stairs and ceilings of the halls should be made entirely fireproof; and the stairs should extend to the roof and end in a bulkhead of fireproof material. This provision was reënacted in 1887 with very slight change, it simply being extended to all dwelling houses over five stories in height erected or altered after July 5, 1887, and which were arranged to be occupied by two or more families on any floor above the first. In 1892 the building laws were materially amended, and the provisions of the law of 1887 were changed so as to apply to all tenement houses thereafter erected, arranged for one or more families on any floor instead of two or more families, and which also were over five stories in height. The law, however, permitted the flooring and the sleepers underneath the flooring, in the halls, to be made of wood, and the treads and hand-rails of the stairs also to be made of hard wood. An additional clause, however, was further added to this section, requiring that when the hallways and stairs were placed centrally in or back from the front line of the building, a hallway enclosed in brick walls should be provided on the first story, connecting the public halls with the street. In 1895 the tenement house law was again modified; this law, among other things, provided that in new tenement houses or buildings thereafter altered for the purposes of a tenement house, where such buildings were over five stories high above the cellar, and where they also contained as many as four suites of rooms on a floor, then all staircases should be fireproof throughout. In all other tenement houses thereafter erected or altered over three stories in height above the cellar, the entrance hall and the entire stair well and the stairs were required to be built of semi-fireproof or slow-burning construction, it being left discretionary with the Superintendent of Buildings what the form of such construction should be. In such buildings it was also provided that no wainscoting should be allowed in the hallways, except of cement or other fireproof material, but it permitted the hand-rails and banisters of the stairs to be of hard wood.

There was a further provision that on the second floor of all tenement houses, that were not fireproof throughout, the stairs and public halls should be shut off from the private halls and other parts of the house by double-swinging fireproof doors, and that such doors should be locked every night not later than ten o'clock. Presumably the object of this section was to confine the spread of fire to the public hallway and stairs and keep it from the other parts of the building. The law, however, was so framed that it was impossible of enforcement, and, as a result, was repealed in the Greater New York Charter, enacted two years later. The Charter also made some other slight changes of no great importance. The provisions of the Charter, which are practically the provisions of the law of 1895, are the present law upon this subject, with also the provisions of section 53 of the Building Code, a local ordinance. The Building Code provides that in all new tenement houses over five stories in height, or having five stories and a basement above the cellar, the halls and stairs shall be enclosed in brick walls, and that the floors, stairs and ceilings in these halls and stairways shall be made of iron, steel, brick, stone, tile, cement or other hard incombustible material. The law, however, permits the flooring and the sleepers underneath the flooring to be of wood, and the hand-rails of the stairs to be of hard wood, and the treads of the stairs to be oak not less than $1\frac{5}{8}$ inches thick. There is a further provision that in such buildings there shall be a hallway in the first story enclosed in fireproof walls leading to the street.

(1867) — Chapter 939, Section 10.

"In all dwelling houses intended to be occupied by four families or more, that shall hereafter be erected in the said city, all stairs shall be of stone or iron, and the floor beams of halls shall be of iron with brick arches turned between them."

(1868) — Chapter 634, Section 2. (Amends Section 10, Chapter 939, Laws of 1867.)

"All buildings that shall be hereafter erected or built to contain not more than two families on any of the floors above the first story, and which does not exceed four stories in height, may be built without fireproof stairs or halls, provided the stairs continue to the roof and have proper bulkheads and ventilators, and all the rooms connect by doors from front to rear, and also provided that a practical fireproof escape is attached to said buildings that shall be approved of by the Superintendent of Buildings. In all dwelling houses built to contain more families than are provided for in this section the halls, stairs and hall partition walls, from the cellar to the roof, shall be constructed fireproof, and the stairs shall continue to the roof with proper bulkhead and ventilators."

(1871) — Chapter 625, Section 28.

"And no building shall be erected or altered to be occupied by more families than as hereinbefore provided for in this section (six families) unless the partitions and stairs shall be constructed fireproof."

(1874) — Chapter 547, Section 7. — Repealed.

(1885) — Chapter 456, Section 21. (Amends Section 492, Consol. Act.)

"All dwelling houses which are known as tenement or apartment houses, which are arranged for or occupied by two or more families on any floor above the first exceeding 60 feet in height, which may be hereafter built, or buildings which may be hereafter altered to be occupied as above stated, shall have the halls and stairs enclosed with 12 inch brick walls, and the floors, stairs and ceilings of the halls shall be made wholly of iron, brick, stone, slate or marble. The stairs of said houses shall extend to the roof and be enclosed with a bulkhead built entirely of fireproof materials, as hereinbefore provided."

(1887) — Chapter 566, Section 26. (Amends Section 499, Consol. Act.)

"Every dwelling-house exceeding 5 stories in height hereafter erected or altered (July 5th, 1887) to be occupied by 2 or more families on any floor above the first, and every dwelling house over 60 feet in height hereafter erected or altered to be occupied by more than 1 family, shall have the halls and stairs enclosed with 12 inch brick walls. The floors, stairs and ceilings in said halls and stairways shall be made wholly of iron, brick, stone or other hard incombustible materials, and at least one flight of such stairs in each of said buildings shall extend to the roof and be enclosed in a bulkhead built of fireproof materials."

(1892) — Chapter 275, Section 16. (Amends Section 480, Consol. Act.)

"Every tenement house, apartment house and dwelling house hereafter erected or altered to be occupied by one or more families on any floor above the first, exceeding five stories in height, or having a basement and five stories in height above the cellar, shall have the halls and stairs enclosed with twelve inch brick walls. The floors, stairs and ceilings in said halls and stairways shall be made of iron, brick, stone, or other hard incombustible materials, excepting that the flooring and sleepers underneath the same may be of wood, and the treads and hand rails of the stairs may be of hard wood, provided that where wooden treads are used the underside of the stairs shall be entirely lathed with iron or wire lath and plastered thereon, or covered with metal. At least one flight of such stairs in each of said buildings shall extend to the roof, and be enclosed in a bulkhead built of fireproof materials. When the said hallways and stairways are placed centrally in, or back from the front line of the building, a connecting fireproof hallway enclosed with brick walls shall be provided on the first story and extend to the street."

(1895) — **Chapter 567, Section 8. (Amends Section 661, Consol. Act.)**

"In all tenement houses hereafter constructed, or buildings hereafter converted to the purposes of a tenement house, all staircases shall be fireproof; but this provision as to staircases shall not apply to buildings which are not over 5 stories high above the cellar, and which contain not more than three suites of rooms on a floor. Every tenement house hereafter constructed, or buildings hereafter converted to the purposes of a tenement house, which building exceeds three stories in height or has basement with three stories above the cellar, shall have the entrance hall and entire stairwell and stairs built of [such] slow burning construction of fireproof material [as the superintendent of buildings shall decide]; also no wainscoting shall be allowed in the main halls except of cement, or other fireproof material; [excepting that the hand-rails and balusters can be of hard wood]; at least one flight of such stairs shall extend to the roof and be inclosed in a bulkhead building of fireproof material; [on second floor of all tenement-houses not fireproof throughout all entrances from stairs to halls shall be closed off with fireproof double swing doors; it shall be the duty of the owner or lessee of such tenement-house to have said door on second floor closed every night at not later than 10 o'clock]."

* (1897) — **Chapter 378, Greater New York Charter, Section 1318.**

Matter in brackets above, omitted.

* (1899) — **The Building Code — (An ordinance adopted December 20, 1899.) Section 53.**

"All non-fireproof apartment-houses and tenement-houses exceeding five stories in height, or having a basement and five stories in height above a cellar, shall be constructed as in this section before described, and shall also have the halls and stairs enclosed with 12 inch brick walls. Eight inch brick walls not exceeding 50 feet in their vertical measurement, may enclose said halls and stairs, and be used as bearing walls where the distance between the outside bearing walls does not exceed 33 feet, and the area between the said brick enclosure walls does not exceed 180 superficial feet. The floors, stairs and ceilings in said halls and stairways shall be made of iron, steel, brick, stone, tile, cement, or other hard incombustible materials, excepting that the flooring and sleepers underneath the same may be of wood and the hand-rails of the stairs may be of hard wood, and the treads may be of oak not less than 1 and 5-8 of an inch in thickness, provided that where such wooden treads are used the under side of the stairs shall be entirely lathed with iron or wire lath and plastered thereon, or covered with metal. At least one flight

* Indicates the existing law in 1900.

of such stairs in each of said buildings shall extend to the roof, and be enclosed in a bulkhead built of fireproof materials. The said halls and stairways shall have a connecting fireproof hallway enclosed with suitable walls of brick, or such other fireproof materials including the ceiling in all cases as may be approved by the Commissioner of Buildings having jurisdiction, in the first story and extend to the street."

HALLWAYS AND STAIRWAYS, REGULATIONS FOR CONSTRUCTION OF. — Since 1867 the Superintendent of Buildings has had discretionary power to make regulations to determine the method of constructing halls and stairways. This power was without limitation until in 1885, when it was added that such regulations should not be inconsistent with the provisions of the existing statutes upon the subject.

(1867) — Chapter 939, Section 10.

"In all tenement-houses that shall hereafter be erected in said city, the superintendent of buildings shall have power in determining the method of constructing halls and stairways."

(1868) — Chapter 634, Section 2. (Amends Section 10, Chapter 939, Laws of 1867.) — Continued.

(1871) — Chapter 625, Section 28. — Continued.

(1874) — Chapter 547, Section 7. — Continued.

(1882) — Chapter 410, Section 499. (Consol. Act.) — Continued.

Power to make regulations transferred from the Superintendent of Buildings to the Fire Department.

(1892) — Chapter 275, Section 35. — Section 499 repealed.

(1895) — Chapter 567, Section 8. (Amends Section 661, Consol. Act.)

"The superintendent of buildings is hereby empowered and directed to make rules and regulations not inconsistent with the requirements of this title, and which in addition to the requirements of this title shall be the conditions of approval for the plans and permits; these rules and regulations shall govern the arrangement and distribution of the uncovered area, size, lighting, location and arrangement of shafts, rooms, cellars and halls, and may be modified or changed from time to time by the superintendent of buildings."

HALL PARTITIONS, CONSTRUCTION OF. — It is, of course, useless to make provisions requiring hallways to be fireproof unless the partitions separating such hallways from the other parts of the house are similarly made safe. This has been recognized since 1867, when the first law in reference to safe egress was enacted. In that year it was provided that in all dwelling houses intended to be occupied by four families or more thereafter erected, the hall partitions from the foundation to the roof should be constructed of brick not less than 12 inches thick. This important provision of the law was very much weakened by an amendment passed in the following year, which permitted tenement houses that were not over four stories in height, and which were arranged for not more than two families on a floor, to be erected without such fireproof stairs or walls. This, however, was only permitted upon condition that the building should have stairs leading to the roof; that the rooms on each floor should connect by doors from front to rear, and that the building should be provided with proper fire-escapes. In all new tenement houses built to contain more than eight families, the partition walls from the cellar to the roof were required to be constructed fireproof. In 1871 this provision was again amended; in new tenements, which were over three stories in height and which were arranged for from three to six families, the hall partitions from front to rear, from the cellar to the bottom of the second story floor beams, were required to be built of brick, and in all tenement houses erected to contain more than six families above the first story, these partitions were required to be constructed fireproof. In 1874 these most important provisions were entirely repealed, and there was no law whatsoever upon this subject until 1885. The law of 1885 provided that in all new tenements, over 60 feet in height and arranged for more than two families on any floor above the first, the halls and stairs should be enclosed in 12-inch brick walls. Two years later this law was changed so as to make it apply to any new tenement house over 60 feet in height, arranged for more than one family on a floor instead of two. In 1892 this provision was substantially reënacted. In 1895 the tenement house law was again changed; among other things, it was provided that in new tenement houses over three stories in height, or three stories and basement in height, the entire stair well and stairs and entrance hall should be built of slow-burning construction or fireproof material, it being left discretionary with the Commissioner of Buildings what such material should be. It was also provided that there should be no fanlight or window placed in the partition or interior wall between the public hall and private hall of any tenement house which was not fireproof, or in the partition between the public hallway and rooms, so as to prevent the spread of fire from the hall to the rooms, and, also, from the rooms to the hall.

The Charter reënacted that part of the law of 1895 requiring the hallway to be built semi-fireproof or of slow-burning construction, but repealed the provisions of the previous law prohibiting the placing of transoms and windows in the partitions between the public hallways and upper halls and rooms. In the Building Code, an ordinance adopted in 1899, it is provided that in all non-fireproof tenement houses thereafter erected which are over five stories in height, the halls and stairs shall be enclosed in 12-inch brick walls. This, with the provisions of the Charter, constitutes the present law upon the subject.

(1867) — Chapter 939, Section 10.

"In all dwelling-houses intended to be occupied by four families or more that shall hereafter be erected in said city, the hall partitions from foundation to roof, shall be of brick, not less than 12 inches thick, with sufficient ventilating flues; the floor beams shall be of iron with brick arches turned between them."

(1868) — Chapter 634, Section 2. (Amends Section 10, Chapter 939, Laws of 1867.)

"All buildings that shall be hereafter erected or built to contain not more than two families on any of the floors above the first story, and which does not exceed four stories in height, may be built without fireproof stairs or halls, provided the stairs continue to the roof and have proper bulkheads and ventilators, and all the rooms connect by doors from front to rear, and also provided that a practical fireproof fire escape is attached to said buildings that shall be approved of by the Superintendent of Buildings. In all dwelling-houses built to contain more families than are provided for in this section, the halls, stairs and hall partition walls, from the cellar to the roof, shall be constructed fireproof, and the stairs shall continue to the roof with proper bulkhead and ventilators."

(1871) — Chapter 625, Section 28.

"In any building hereafter erected more than three stories in height, occupied by, or built to be occupied by three and not more than six families above the first story, the hall partition and partitions from front to rear from the cellar to the top of the second story beams, shall be built of brick."

(1871) — Chapter 625, Section 28.

"And no building shall be erected or altered to be occupied by more families than as hereinbefore provided for in this section, (six families) unless the partitions and stairs shall be constructed fireproof."

(1874) — Chapter 547, Section 7. — Repealed.

(1885) — Chapter 456, Section 21. (Amends Section 492, Consol. Act.)

"All dwelling-houses which are known as tenements or apartment-houses, which are arranged for or occupied by two or more families on any floor above the first, exceeding 60 feet in height, which may be hereafter built, or buildings which may be hereafter altered to be occupied as above stated, shall have the halls and stairs enclosed with 12 inch brick walls."

(1887) — Chapter 566, Section 26. (Amends Section 499, Consol. Act.)

"Every dwelling-house exceeding 5 stories in height hereafter erected or altered (July 5th, 1887) to be occupied by 2 or more families on any floor above the first, and every dwelling-house over 60 feet in height hereafter erected or altered to be occupied by more than 1 family, shall have the halls and stairs enclosed with 12 inch brick walls."

(1892) — Chapter 275, Section 16. (Amends Section 480, Consol. Act.)

"Every tenement-house, apartment-house and dwelling-house hereafter erected or altered to be occupied by one or more families on any floor above the first, exceeding five stories in height, or having a basement and five stories in height above the cellar, shall have the halls and stairs enclosed with 12 inch brick walls. The floors, stairs and ceilings in said halls and stairways shall be made of iron, brick, stone or other hard incombustible materials, excepting that the flooring and sleepers underneath the same may be of wood. When the said halls and stairways are placed centrally in, or back from the front line of the building, a connecting fireproof hallway enclosed with brick walls shall be provided on the first story, and extend to the street."

(1895) — Chapter 567, Section 8. (Amends Section 661, Consol. Act.)

"Every tenement-house hereafter constructed or buildings hereafter converted to the purposes of a tenement-house, which building exceeds three stories in height or has basement with three stories above the cellar, shall have the entrance hall and entire stairwell and stairs built of such slow burning construction or fireproof material as the superintendent of buildings shall decide. No fan light or window shall be hereafter placed in the partition or interior wall between the main and private halls of any tenement-house which is not fireproof, and any room in the same."

*** (1897) — Chapter 378, Greater New York Charter, Section 1318.**

"Every tenement-house hereafter constructed, or buildings hereafter converted to the purpose of a tenement-house, exceeding three stories in height, or having a basement with three stories above the cellar, shall have the entrance hall and entire stairwell and stairs built of slow burning construction or fireproof material."

*** (1899) — The Building Code — (An ordinance adopted December 20, 1899). Section 53.**

"All non-fireproof apartment-houses and tenement-houses exceeding five stories in height, or having a basement and five stories in height above a cellar, shall be constructed as in this section before described, and shall also have the halls and stairs enclosed with twelve inch brick walls. Eight inch brick walls not exceeding fifty feet in their vertical measurement, may enclose said halls and stairs, and be used as bearing walls where the distance between the outside bearing walls does not exceed thirty-three feet, and the area between the said brick enclosure walls does not exceed one hundred and eighty superficial feet."

PARTITIONS. — Not until 1882 was any attempt made to lessen the danger from the spread of fire in a building between the partitions. In that year it was required that the space between the studding of such partitions should be filled in solidly with suitable incombustible material, so as to prevent the quick spread of fire from floor to floor. This has been the law since that time until 1899, when the Building Code repealed the law of 1892 and limited this requirement to residence buildings only.

(1892) — Chapter 275, Section 16. (Amends Section 480, Consol. Act.)

"Fore and aft stud partitions that rest directly over each other shall run through the wooden floor beams and rest on the plate of the partition below, and shall have the studding filled in solid between the uprights to the depth of the floor beams with suitable incombustible materials."

(1894) — Brooklyn — Chapter 481, Section 13. (Amends Chapter 583 of the Laws of 1888.) Above provisions continued.

(1895) — Brooklyn — Chapter 292, Section 21. — Continued.

*** (1899) — The Building Code — (An ordinance approved December 20, 1899). Section 51.**

"In *residence* buildings where fore and aft stud partitions rest directly over each other, they shall run down between the wood floor beams and rest on the top plate of the partition below, and shall have the studding filled in solid between the uprights to the depth of the floor beams with suitable incombustible materials."

* Indicates the existing law in 1900.

SHAFTS — CONSTRUCTION OF ELEVATOR SHAFTS. — In view of the many provisions for the construction of halls and stairways in tenement houses enacted for so many years, it would seem that a provision in reference to the construction of all shafts would be among the first that would be enacted. Not until 1887, however, was there any law upon this subject. In that year the building law was amended and it was provided that all elevator shafts in all buildings thereafter erected should be constructed fireproof, with fireproof doors to all openings. This has practically been the law unchanged until the present time. It was slightly amended in 1895, when a supplementary provision was enacted, requiring that the elevator shafts in cellars of tenement houses should be entirely fireproof, and that if there were any openings in the cellars, such openings should be provided with self-closing fireproof doors.

(1887) — Chapter 566, Section 15. (Amends Section 487, Consol. Act.)

"All elevators hereafter placed in any building in said city, except such fireproof buildings as have been or may be erected in accordance with section 492 of this act, shall be enclosed in suitable walls of brick, or with a suitable frame work of iron and burnt clay filling, or of such other fireproof material and form of construction as may be approved by the superintendent of buildings. Said walls or construction shall extend through and at least three feet above the roof, and shall have suitable openings in the same to be provided with fireproof doors. But elevators may be put in the wellhole of stairs, in buildings without such brick or fireproof enclosures, where the stairs are enclosed in brick or stone walls, and the stairs are themselves entirely constructed of stone, brick, iron or slate."

(1892) — Chapter 275, Section 28. (Amends Section 492, Consol. Act.)

"All elevators hereafter placed in any building, except such fireproof buildings as shall be or may be erected in accordance with Section 484 of this title, shall be enclosed in suitable walls of brick, or with a suitable frame work of iron and burnt clay filling, or of such other fireproof material and form of construction as may be approved by the superintendent of buildings. Said walls or construction shall extend through and at least three feet above the roof, and all openings in the same shall be provided with fireproof doors and made solid for three feet above the floor level and with grill openings above. Elevators may be put in the wellhole of stairs in buildings, without such brick or fireproof enclosures, where the stairs are enclosed in brick or stone walls, and the stairs are constructed as specified in section 480 of this title."

(1894) — Brooklyn — Chapter 481, Section 21. (Amends Brooklyn Consol. Act.)

Same provisions continued.

(1895) — Chapter 567, Section 8. (Amends Section 661, Consol. Act.)

"In all tenement-houses hereafter constructed or buildings hereafter converted to the purposes of a tenement-house, the openings to the elevators or lifts in the cellar and at every opening, on every story, shall be provided with self-closing fireproof doors. This provision however shall not apply to such elevators in tenement-houses which are operated by a conductor stationed within the car; but if such elevators run to the cellar they must be enclosed in the cellar with fireproof walls, and the door to the cellar, if any, must be fireproof and self closing."

*** (1897) — Chapter 378, Greater New York Charter, Section 1318. — Continued.**

*** (1899) — The Building Code — (An ordinance adopted December 20, 1899.) Section 86.**

"All elevators hereafter placed in any building, except such fireproof buildings as have been or may be hereafter erected, shall be enclosed in suitable walls of brick, or with a suitable frame work of iron and burnt clay filling, or of such other fireproof material and form of construction as may be approved by the department of buildings. All openings in said walls shall be provided with fireproof shutters or fireproof doors, made solid for three feet above the floor level, except that the doors used for openings in buildings intended for the occupancy of one family may be of wood covered on the inner surfaces and edges with metal, not including the openings in the cellar, nor above the roof in any such shaft walls. When the shaft does not extend to the ground, the lower end shall be enclosed in fireproof materials."

SHAFTS — CONSTRUCTION OF DUMB-WAITER SHAFTS. — Prior to 1887, there was no law upon this subject. In that year the building law was amended so as to require all dumb-waiter shafts thereafter erected extending through more than three stories in any building to be constructed fireproof with fireproof doors to all openings, and this has practically been the law until the present day, *i.e.* in 1900. In 1899, in the Building Code, a local ordinance, it was provided, in addition to the above requirements, that where such a shaft did not extend to the floor level of the lowest story, the bottom of the shaft should also be constructed of fireproof material.

(1887) — Chapter 566, Section 15. (Amends Section 487, Consol. Act.)

"All dumb-waiter shafts hereafter placed in any dwelling-houses which extend through more than three stories, except such fireproof buildings as have been or may be erected in accordance with Section 492 of this act, shall be enclosed in suitable walls of brick, or with a suitable frame work of iron and burnt clay filling, or of such other fireproof material and form of construction as may be approved by the superintendent of buildings. Said walls or construction shall extend through and at least three feet above the roof, and shall have suitable openings in the same to be provided with fireproof doors, but elevators may be put in the wellhole of stairs, in buildings without such brick or fireproof enclosures, where the stairs are enclosed in brick or stone walls, and the stairs are themselves entirely constructed of stone, brick, iron or slate."

(1892) — Chapter 275, Section 28. (Amends Section 492, Consol. Act.)

"All dumb-waiter shafts hereafter placed in any building, except such as do not extend through more than three stories in dwelling-houses, shall be enclosed in suitable walls of brick, or with a suitable framework of iron and burnt clay filling, or of such other fireproof material and form of construction as may be approved by the superintendent of buildings."

* Indicates the existing law in 1900.

(1894) — Brooklyn — Chapter 481, Section 21. (Amends Brooklyn Consol. Act.) Above provisions continued.

*** (1899) — The Building Code — (An ordinance adopted December 20, 1899.) Section 97.**

"All dumb-waiter shafts, except such as do not extend more than three stories above the cellar or basement in dwelling-houses, shall be enclosed in suitable walls of brick or with burnt clay blocks, set in iron frames of proper strength or fireproof blocks strengthened with metal dowels, or such other fireproof material and form of construction as may be approved by the commissioner of buildings having jurisdiction. Said walls or construction shall extend at least 3 feet above the roof and be covered with a skylight at least three-fourths the area of the shaft, made with metal frames and glazed. All openings in the enclosure walls or construction shall be provided with self-closing fireproof doors. When the shaft does not extend to the floor level of the lowest story, the bottom of the shaft shall be constructed of fireproof material."

SHAFTS — CONSTRUCTION OF LIGHT AND VENT SHAFTS. — Before 1887, interior light shafts and vent shafts were permitted to be constructed of inflammable material, and a large number of such shafts were constructed in many tenement houses in New York City, being formed merely of wooden studs with lath and plaster. The 1887 law, however, required that all walls or partitions forming interior light shafts should be built fireproof, and that they should be carried up 3½ feet above the level of the roof. This has been the law upon this subject until the present time (in 1900).

(1887) — Chapter 566, Section 16. (Amends Section 487, Consol. Act.)

"In all buildings hereafter erected all walls or partitions forming interior light shafts shall be built of brick or such other fireproof material as may be approved by the superintendent of buildings. All light shafts whether exterior or interior, hereafter erected shall be carried up not less than three and one-half feet above the level of the roof."

(1892) — Chapter 275, Section 16. (Amends Section 480, Consol. Act.)

"In every building hereafter erected all the walls or partitions forming interior light or vent shafts shall be built of brick or such other fireproof materials as may be approved by the superintendent of buildings. The walls of all light or vent shafts whether exterior or interior, hereafter erected, shall be carried up not less than three and one-half feet above the level of the roof."

(1894) — Brooklyn — Chapter 481, Section 11. (Amends Chapter 583 of the Laws of 1888.)

"In every building more than three stories in height hereafter erected, all the walls or partitions forming interior light or vent shafts, shall be built of brick or such other fireproof materials as may be approved by the Commissioner of Buildings."

* Indicates the existing law in 1900.

*** (1899) — The Building Code — (An ordinance adopted December 20, 1899.) Section 48.**

"In every building hereafter erected or altered, all the walls or partitions forming interior light or vent shafts shall be built of brick, or such other fireproof materials as may be approved by the Commissioner of Buildings having jurisdiction. The walls of all light or vent shafts, whether exterior or interior, hereafter erected, shall be carried up not less than 3 feet above the level of the roof, and the brick walls coped as other parapet walls."

BEAMS, FIRST TIER TO BE FIREPROOF. — As early as 1871 there were laws requiring the beams over the cellar floor or lowest story to be fireproof, it being recognized that a large number of tenement house fires originated in the cellars, which were usually filled with inflammable materials, coal and wood bins, etc. The law of 1871 provided that in all buildings thereafter erected more than three stories high and arranged for as many as three families and not more than six families above the first story, where the cellar was to be used for storing coal or wood or other articles, the first floor over the cellar was to be constructed fireproof. This excellent provision was repealed in 1874 and was not reënacted until 1892, when the general building laws were amended. The law of that year required that in every new tenement house five stories high, arranged for one or more families, on any floor above the first, the floor over the cellar or lowest story should be constructed fireproof. This law was reënacted in the Building Code and is the present law (in 1900) upon the subject.

(1871) — Chapter 625, Section 28.

"In any building hereafter erected more than three stories in height, occupied by or built to be occupied by three and not more than six families above the first story, in which the cellar is to be used for the purpose of storing coal, wood, or other articles, the floor above the cellar, with the stairs leading thereto, if the stairs lead from the inside of the building, shall be constructed fireproof."

(1874) — Chapter 547, Section 7. — Repealed.

(1892) — Chapter 275, Section 16. (Section 480, Consol. Act, amended as follows:)

"Every building hereafter erected or altered to be occupied as a lodging-house, and every tenement-house, apartment-house and dwelling-house five stories in height, or having a basement and four stories in height above the cellar, hereafter erected or altered to be occupied by one or more families on any floor above the first, shall have the first floor above the cellar or lowest story constructed fireproof with iron or steel beams and brick arches."

*** (1899) — The Building Code — (An ordinance adopted December 20, 1899.) Section 53.**

"Every non-fireproof building hereafter erected or altered for an apartment or tenement-house, five stories in height, or having a basement and four stories in height above a cellar, to be occupied by one or more families

* Indicates the existing law in 1900.

on any floor above the first shall have the first floor above the cellar or lowest story constructed fireproof in such manner as required in section 106 of this code."

BEAMS, SECOND TIER TO BE FIREPROOF. — As tenement house fires often originate in stores upon the ground floor of such buildings, it has been thought to be desirable for the beams over the store floor and the flooring between them to be of fireproof material. This was recognized as far back as 1867, the building laws of that year requiring that in all dwelling houses intended to be occupied by four families or more, thereafter erected, where the lower part of the building was to be used for business purposes of any kind, the first tier of beams above the store floor should be of iron with brick arches. In the following year the law was changed, but this provision was practically reënacted. In 1871 the building law was again amended, requiring that in all buildings thereafter erected more than three stories high, and occupied by three families, and not more than six families, where the first story was used for business purposes of any kind, the first floor and the ceiling above the store floor should be constructed fireproof. This provision was, in 1874, repealed, and was not reënacted until 1899. The Building Code, adopted in that year, provided that wherever there was a store on the first floor in a new tenement house or any tenement house thereafter altered where the building was over five stories high, the second tier of beams, as well as the first tier of beams, should be entirely fireproof.

(1867) — Chapter 939, Section 10.

"In all dwelling-houses intended to be occupied by four families or more, that shall hereafter be erected in said city, in cases where the lower part of the building is used for business purposes of any kind, the first tier of beams above the store floor shall be of iron, with brick arches."

(1868) — Chapter 634, Section 2. (Amends Section 10, Chapter 939, of the Laws of 1867.)

"In all cases (in all dwelling-houses now erected, occupied by or built to contain two or more families on any of the floors above the first story, and all dwelling-houses now erected, more than three stories in height, occupied by or built to contain four or more families) where the lower part of the building is used for business purposes of any kind, the first floor and ceiling above the store floor shall be constructed fireproof."

(1871) — Chapter 625, Section 28.

"And where the lower part of any building hereafter erected more than three stories in height occupied by, or built to be occupied by three and not more than six families above the first story, is to be used for business purposes of any kind, the first floor, if there is a cellar below, and the ceiling above the store floor, shall be constructed fireproof."

(1874) — Chapter 547, Section 7. — Repealed.

*** (1899) — The Building Code — (An ordinance adopted December 20, 1899.) Section 53.**

"When any such non-fireproof building (hereafter erected or altered

* Indicates the existing law in 1900.

for an apartment-house or tenement-house) exceeding five stories in height or having a basement and five stories in height above a cellar has a store on the first story, the entire second story floor shall also be constructed fireproof."

CELLAR STAIRS.— The first provision of any kind relating to this subject was enacted in 1871, when it was provided that in any building thereafter erected over three stories in height and arranged for more than three and not more than six families, where the cellar was to be used for the purpose of storing coal or wood or other articles, the stairs leading to the upper story, if they were inside of the building, should be constructed fireproof. This important and necessary provision of law was, unfortunately, repealed in 1874, and no further legislation was had upon this subject until 1892. In that year the general building laws were amended so that every new tenement house five stories or more in height, or having a basement and four stories above a cellar, arranged for one or more families on any floor above the first, should have the cellar stairs leading to the floor above, if they were on the inside of the building, located to the rear of the staircase leading from the first story to the upper stories, and entirely enclosed in brick walls and furnished with self-closing fireproof doors at the top and bottom of such flight of stairs, thus endeavoring to do away with making the stairs a continuous flue from cellar to roof, so that if a fire should start in the cellar it would not so quickly communicate to the other parts of the house. It was provided also that no closet should be constructed underneath the first story staircase, and that the space under it should be left entirely open and kept free from encumbrances; this provision of law was deemed necessary because so many fires had started from janitors keeping oily, greasy rags in little closets of this kind located under the stairs, and the result has been that, under such circumstances, the fire has spread through the entire building before there was time to check it. This provision of the laws of 1892 was reënacted in the amendment to the tenement house laws in 1895. The Charter, however, made a very decided change in this provision, repealing the requirement that the cellar stairs should be located to the rear of the staircase leading from the first story to the upper stories, and the Building Code, adopted in 1899, continued the change of the Charter, stating that the cellar stairs should be located, *when practicable,* to the rear of the staircase leading from the first story to the upper stories. The other provisions, however, of the law of 1892, with the exception of forbidding the construction of a closet under the stairs, were reënacted in the Code.

(1871) — Chapter 625, Section 28.

"In any building hereafter erected more than three stories in height, occupied by, or built to be occupied by three and not more than six families above the first story, in which the cellar is to be used for the purpose of storing coal, wood or other articles, the floor above the cellar, with the stairs leading thereto, if the stairs lead from the inside of the building, shall be constructed fireproof."

(1874) — Chapter 547, Section 7. — Repealed.

(1892) — Chapter 275, Section 16. (Section 480, Consol. Act, amended as follows):

"In every tenement-house, apartment-house and dwelling-house five stories in height, or having a basement and four stories in height above the cellar, hereafter erected or altered to be occupied by one or more families on any floor above the first, the stairs from the cellar or lowest story to the fireproof floor next above, when placed within any such building, shall be located to the rear of the staircase leading from the first story to the upper stories and be enclosed with brick walls. The opening through the brick wall of such enclosure into the lowest story shall have an iron door, or a tin covered wooden door (constructed as hereinafter described in Section 491 of this title) and shall be self-closing. When the stairs from the first story to the cellar or lowest story are located in an open side court the door opening leading thereto from the first story may be placed underneath the staircase in the first story, and the strings and railings of such outside stairs shall be of iron, and if the stairs be enclosed from the weather incombustible material only shall be used for that purpose. No closet shall be constructed underneath the first story staircase but the space thereunder shall be left entirely open and kept free from encumbrance. Every tenement-house, apartment-house and dwelling-house exceeding 5 stories in height, or having a basement and 5 stories in height above the cellar shall be constructed as in this section before described."

(1895) — Chapter 567, Section 8. (Amends Section 661, Consol. Act.)

"In all tenement-houses hereafter constructed or buildings hereafter converted to the purposes of a tenement-house, the stairway communicating between said cellar or basement and the floor next above when placed within any such building [shall be located to the rear of the staircase leading from the first story to the upper stories and] be inclosed with brick walls, and such stairway shall be provided with fireproof doors at the top and bottom of said flight of stairs."

*** (1897) — Chapter 378, Greater New York Charter, Section 1318. (Provisions of the laws of 1895 continued with the following amendment:)**

The words in brackets "shall be located to the rear of the staircase leading from the first story to the upper stories and," omitted.

*** (1899) — The Building Code — (An ordinance adopted December 20, 1899.) Section 53.**

"The stairs from the cellar or lowest story to the fireproof floor next above, when placed within any such building, shall be located, *when practicable*, to the rear of the staircase leading from the first story to the upper stories and be enclosed with brick or stone walls, and such stairway shall be provided with self-closing fireproof doors at the top and bottom of said flight of stairs. When such stairway is placed underneath the first story staircase, it shall be constructed fireproof and be roofed over with fireproof material, and be also enclosed with brick walls, with self-closing fireproof doors at the top and bottom of said flight of stairs. When the stairs from the first story to the cellar or lowest story are located in an open side court the door leading

* Indicates the existing law in 1900.

thereto from the first story may be placed underneath the staircase in the first story, and the strings and railings of such outside stairs shall be of iron, and if the stairs be enclosed from the weather incombustible material only shall be used for that purpose. No closet shall be constructed underneath the first story staircase, but the space thereunder shall be left entirely open and kept free from incumbrance, but this shall not prohibit the enclosing without openings the under portions of the staircase from the foot of the same to a point where the height from the floor line to the soffit of the staircase shall not exceed five feet."

CELLAR ENTRANCE.—In 1887 a law was passed requiring that in every dwelling house arranged for two or more families above the first story there should be a separate entrance to the cellar from the outside of the building. This provision was enacted so as to enable the firemen to have access to cellars to fight cellar fires. This has practically been the law until the present time (in 1900), with the exception of the fact that in 1892 the law was made to apply to basements instead of cellars.

(1887)—Chapter 566, Section 26. (Amends Section 499, Consol. Act.)

"Every dwelling-house arranged for or occupied by 2 or more families above the first story, hereafter erected, (July 5th, 1887) shall be provided with an entrance to the cellar thereof from the outside of such building."

(1892)—Chapter 275, Section 34. (Amends Section 498, Consol. Act.)

Amended by substituting the word "basement" for the word "cellar."

(1894)—Brooklyn—Chapter 481, Section 28. (Amends Brooklyn Consol. Act.) Above provisions reënacted.

(1895)—Chapter 567, Section 8. (Amends Section 661, Consol. Act.)

"An open area shall be constructed from the level of the cellar to the sidewalk in front of and extending the full width of such houses (all tenement-houses hereafter constructed or buildings hereafter converted to the purposes of a tenement-house) which shall contain a staircase to give access to the cellar from the street. Where stores are located on the first floor the area may be covered with suitable vault lights or gratings."

***(1897)—Chapter 378, Greater New York Charter, Section 1318.—Continued. (Slight verbal changes of no importance.)**

***(1899)—The Building Code—(An ordinance adopted December 20, 1899.) Section 74.**

"Every dwelling-house arranged for or occupied by two or more families above the first story, hereafter erected, shall be provided with an entrance to the basement thereof from the outside of such building."

CELLAR CEILINGS.—In 1891 the first law upon this subject was passed requiring that cellar ceilings should be plastered or filled in with deafening between the beams. In the following year the law was amended so as to require the ceiling over every cellar or lowest floor in *all* dwelling houses when the beams were made of wood to be protected with iron or wire lath, and also plastered with brown mortar. This has been the law

* Indicates the existing law in 1900.

until 1899, when these requirements were limited to residence buildings more than four stories in height.

(1891) — Chapter 39, Section 1.

"Every tenement-house shall have the cellar ceiling plastered or filled in with deafening between the beams or ceiled with tongued and grooved boards not less than three-quarters of an inch in thickness, lined with builders' paper."

(1892) — Chapter 275, Section 16. (Amends Section 480, Consol. Act.)

"The ceiling over every cellar or lowest story in dwelling-houses when the beams are of wood shall be lathed with iron or wire lath, and plastered thereon with two coats of brown mortar of good materials."

(1894) — Brooklyn — Chapter 481, Section 11. (Amends Chapter 583 of the Laws of 1888.)

"The ceiling over every cellar or lowest floor in dwelling-houses more than four stories in height, when the beams are of wood shall be lathed with wire or metal lath and plastered thereon with two coats of brown mortar of good materials."

*** (1899) — The Building Code — (An ordinance adopted December 20, 1899.) Section 58.**

"The ceiling over every cellar or lowest floor in every residence building more than four stories in height, hereafter erected, when the beams are of wood, shall be lathed with iron or wire lath and plastered thereon with two coats of brown mortar of good materials, or such other fireproof covering as may be approved by the commissioner of buildings having jurisdiction."

CELLAR WOOD-BINS. — In order to minimize the dangers from fire, it was felt that it was necessary to do away with as much inflammable material as possible in the cellars of tenement houses. In 1867, therefore, the law required that in all dwellings arranged for four families or more, the receptacles for fuel in the cellar should be constructed wholly of fireproof materials. This provision was repealed in 1871.

(1867) — Chapter 939, Section 10.

"In all dwelling-houses occupied or intended to be occupied by four families or more, now erected, or that shall hereafter be built all receptacles for fuel when placed in the cellar of said houses shall be constructed wholly of fireproof materials."

(1868) — Chapter 634, Section 2. (Amends Section 10, Chapter 939 of the Laws of 1867.)

"In all dwelling-houses now erected, occupied by or built to contain two or more families on any of the floors above the first story, and all dwelling-houses now erected more than three stories in height, occupied by or built to contain four or more families, no receptacles for fuel shall be placed in the cellars of said houses unless wholly constructed of fireproof materials."

(1871) — Chapter 625. — Repealed.

* Indicates the existing law in 1900.

WOODEN TENEMENTS, WHEN PROHIBITED. — The chances for escape in case of fire in wooden buildings are so slight that it has been recognized for some time that buildings of this class should not be occupied by large numbers of persons. In 1885 the law prohibited any wooden tenement house or any frame house, intended to be occupied by more than two families, to be built north of 149th Street; and in 1887 the law prohibited the erection of any wooden building to be occupied by more than two families, and also forbade the alteration of any existing wooden building to be occupied by more than the above number of persons.

In 1892 the law was again amended prohibiting the erection of any wooden building to be occupied by more than one family on a floor, and forbidding the alteration of any existing building to be occupied by more than three families. These provisions of the law were, however, all done away with in the Building Code, a local ordinance adopted in 1899. This Code, in Section 146, permits a wooden tenement house to be built to be occupied by as many as six families, and in such buildings allows the cellar stairs to be located under the main stairs and states specifically that the cellar stairs need not be enclosed in brick walls.

(1885) — Chapter 456, Section 24. (Amends Section 495, Consol. Act.)

"No frame tenement-house or frame house for more than two families shall be built north of 149th Street."

(1887) — Chapter 566, Section 23. (Amends Section 495, Consol. Act.)

"No frame dwelling-house hereafter erected (July 5th, 1887) shall be occupied by more than 2 families, nor shall any frame building already erected be altered to be occupied by more than two families."

(1892) — Chapter 275, Section 31. (Amends Section 495, Consol. Act.)

"No frame dwelling-house, hereafter erected shall be occupied by more than one family on each floor, nor shall any frame building already erected be altered to be occupied by more than three families."

(1894) — Brooklyn — Chapter 481, Section 25. (Amends Brooklyn Consol. Act.)

"No frame dwelling-house hereafter erected shall be occupied by more than two families on each floor, nor shall any frame building already erected be altered to be occupied by more than two families on each floor."

(1894) — Brooklyn — Chapter 481, Section 26. (Amends Brooklyn Consol. Act.)

"No frame building that may hereafter be erected shall be built to a height exceeding forty feet and divided into more than three stories to be used as a dwelling or a tenement-house."

***(1899) — The Building Code — (An ordinance adopted December 20, 1899). Section 146.**

"No frame building exceeding 3 stories in height shall hereafter be erected to be occupied by more than six families, nor shall any frame

* Indicates the existing law in 1900.

building already erected, be altered to be occupied by more than six families, nor more than three stories in height. The cellar stairs in frame buildings may be placed directly under the main stairs and no brick wall shall be necessary to enclose the same; nor shall areas be required to be built across the front of frame buildings, except where the cellar or basement is used for living purposes."

*** (1899) — The Building Code — (An ordinance adopted December 20, 1899.) Section 147.**

"Within portions of the City of New York where streets have not been or are not legally established and are outside of the prescribed fire limits, tenement-houses for occupancy by not more than six families may be built of wood, but shall in all other respects comply with the several provisions of this Code relating to such structures; but for all other buildings or structures only so much of the requirements, regulations and restrictions of this Code shall apply as in the opinion of the commissioner of buildings having jurisdiction may be necessary for safety and health."

FIREPROOF TENEMENTS, WHEN REQUIRED. — It is interesting to find that as early as 1860 any tenement house erected to be occupied by more than eight families had to be built fireproof, unless the buildings were provided with fireproof stairs in a brick or stone fireproof building attached to the exterior walls, and unless the rooms on every story communicated directly by doors from front to rear, or unless there were practicable fire-escapes in place of fireproof stairs. This law, however, was repealed in 1862. In 1867 there was a provision requiring that all new front and rear buildings, built on the same lot, should be fireproof throughout; the year 1871 saw the repeal of this clause of the law. The height to which non-fireproof tenements may be erected has varied considerably in many different amendments that have been made to the building law. The first provision enacted was in 1885, when it was required that every building thereafter erected over 70 feet high should be built fireproof. In 1887 the limit was made 80 feet instead of 70, and in 1892 it was increased to 85 feet. In 1896, however, it was changed back to 70 feet and in the following year it was again made 75 feet. In the same year a provision was passed limiting the height of fireproof dwelling houses containing one or more power passenger elevators used as dwellings by more than one family. In this law the height was regulated in proportion to the widest street or avenue on which the building stood, and was limited to 150 feet upon all streets and avenues over 79 feet in width, and to 100 feet on all streets and avenues less than 79 feet in width. The Building Code in 1899 (the present law upon this subject in 1900) limits the height of non-fireproof tenements to 85 feet, provided that the first and second stories are fireproof, and to 75 feet when the first floor only is fireproof. Fireproof tenements under this section of the Code may be erected to a height of 150 feet, but must not exceed twelve stories, when such buildings front on streets or avenues over 79 feet in width; when the buildings front upon streets or avenues less than 79 feet in width, then the height shall not exceed 125 feet or ten stories,

* Indicates the existing law in 1900.

(1860) — Chapter 470, Section 25.

"All dwelling-houses which are built for the residence of more than eight families must be built fireproof throughout if the buildings are not built with either stairs or balconies as specified as follows: 'There shall be a fireproof stairs in a brick or stone or fireproof building, attached to the exterior walls and all the rooms on every story must communicate by doors; or if fireproof stairs are not built as above, then there must be fireproof balconies on each story on the outside of the building connected by fireproof stairs, and all rooms on every story must communicate by doors.'"

(1867) — Chapter 939, Section 10. (Amends Section 32, Chapter 873, of the Laws of 1866.)

"In no case hereafter shall a front and rear tenement-house be erected on the same lot, unless said houses, and each of them, shall be built fireproof."

(1868) — Chapter 634, Section 2. (Amends Section 10, Chapter 939 of the Laws of 1867.) — Continued.

(1871) — Chapter 625. — Repealed.

(1885) — Chapter 456, Section 21. (Amends Section 492, Consol. Act.)

"Every building hereafter erected the height of which exceeds 70 feet shall be built fireproof."

(1887) — Chapter 566, Section 20. (Amends Section 492, Consol. Act.)

Amended by changing "70" to "80."

(1889) — Chapter 297, Section 1. (Amends Section 492, Consol. Act.) — Continued.

(1892) — Chapter 275, Section 20. (Amends Section 484, Consol. Act.)

The law amended to apply to buildings over 85 feet high.

(1894) — Brooklyn — Chapter 481, Section 15.

"Every building hereafter erected the height of which exceeds 85 feet shall be built fireproof."

(1896) — Chapter 723, Section 1. (Amends Section 484, Consol. Act.)

"Every building hereafter erected the height of which exceeds 70 feet shall be built fireproof."

(1897) — Chapter 557, Section 1. (Amends Section 484, Consol. Act.)

"Every building the height of which exceeds 75 feet shall be built fireproof."

(1897) — Chapter 321.

"The height of all fireproof dwelling-houses and all fireproof houses containing one or more power passenger elevators used or intended to be used as dwellings for more than one family now or hereafter constructed or completed, shall be regulated in proportion to the width of the widest street and avenue upon which they abut, and such height measured from the sidewalk line and taken in all cases through the centre of the façade of the house to be erected, including attics, cornices and mansards, shall not exceed one hundred and fifty feet upon all streets and avenues exceeding seventy-nine feet in width, and one hundred feet upon all streets and avenues not exceeding seventy-nine feet in width. All buildings mentioned in the first section of this act provided the same have a frontage exceeding forty-five feet and exceed one hundred and thirty-seven feet in height, shall have two separate fireproof stairways leading from the ground floor to the roof, one of which shall be remote from the elevator shaft."

*** (1899) — The Building Code — (An ordinance adopted December 20, 1899.) Section 53.**

"No non-fireproof apartment-house, tenement-house or dwelling-house shall be hereafter erected more than six stories in height, nor exceed a height of 75 feet, unless such building has both the first and second story floors constructed fireproof, and then the height shall be not more than seven stories nor exceed 85 feet in height. Fireproof apartment-houses or tenement-houses, if constructed entirely in accordance with the requirements of section 105 of this Code, for fireproof construction may be erected to a height not to exceed 150 feet but not more than 12 stories in height upon all streets and avenues exceeding 79 feet in width, and 125 feet but not more than 10 stories in height upon all streets and avenues not exceeding 79 feet in width, but any such building when exceeding 100 feet in height shall be not less than 40 feet in width. If any such building shall have a frontage exceeding 40 feet and exceeds 85 feet in height, it shall have at least two separate fireproof stairways accessible from each apartment, leading from the ground floor to the roof, one of which shall be remote from elevator shafts."

COMBUSTIBLE MATERIALS, STORAGE OF, PROHIBITED. — Since 1862 there have been different provisions of the law prohibiting the storage of combustible materials in tenement houses. These provisions have been reënacted in different years with very slight changes.

(1862) — Chapter 356, Section 27.

" No dwelling-houses already erected or that may hereafter be built, that now are or may be more than forty feet high, that shall be occupied or built to contain six or more families above the first story and no dwelling-house that shall be occupied by or built to contain eight or more families above the first story shall have any hay, straw, hemp, flax, wood, shavings, burning fluid, turpentine, camphene or any other combustible material, stored therein, or kept for sale, except in such quantities as shall be provided for by ordinances of the common council of said city."

(1866) — Chapter 873, Section 32.

"No dwelling-houses in any part of the city of New York already erected or that may hereafter be built, that now are or may be more than forty feet high, that shall be built to contain or be occupied by six or more families, above the first story, and no dwelling-houses that shall be built to contain or occupied by eight or more families above the first story shall have any hay, straw, hemp, flax, wood, shavings, burning fluid, turpentine, camphene or any other combustible material stored therein, or

* Indicates the existing law in 1900.

kept on sale, except in such quantities as shall be provided for by law or by ordinances of the common council in the said city."

(1867) — Chapter 908, Section 8.

"No tenement or lodging-house nor any portion thereof, shall be used as a place of storage for any combustible article, or any article dangerous to life or detrimental to health."

(1867) — Chapter 939, Section 10.

"No dwelling-houses intended to be occupied by four families or more, now built or which may hereafter be built shall have any hay, straw, hemp, flax, wood, shavings, burning fluid, turpentine, camphene or any other combustible material stored therein, or kept on sale, except in such quantities as shall be provided for by law."

(1868) — Chapter 634, Section 2. — Continued with the following change: The word "stored" is changed to "stand."

(1871) — Chapter 625, Section 28.

"No dwelling-house now built, or which may be hereafter erected, shall have any hay, straw, hemp, flax, shavings, burning fluid, turpentine, camphene or any other combustible material stored therein or kept on sale, except in such quantities as shall be provided by law."

(1874) — Chapter 547, Section 7. — Repealed.

(1882) — Chapter 410, Section 656. (Provisions of Chapter 908, Laws of 1867, continued.)

(1888) — Brooklyn — Chapter 583, Section 30. (Provisions of Chapter 908, Laws of 1867, continued.)

(1888) — Brooklyn — Chapter 583, Section 47. (Brooklyn Consol. Act.)

"No building situated or hereafter erected in the city, occupied in whole or in part as a dwelling, or occupied by any family or families, shall have any hay, straw, hemp, flax, shavings, burning fluid, camphene, or any other combustible material stored therein, or in any part thereof, or kept on sale except in such quantities as shall be provided for by law, or by ordinance of the common council of said city."

(1895) — Chapter 567, Section 5. (Amends Section 656, Consol. Act.)

"No tenement or lodging-house nor any portion thereof shall be used as a place of storage for any combustible article or any article dangerous to life or detrimental to health."

(1895) — Chapter 567, Section 5.

"After the first day of September, 1895, no part of any tenement-house shall be used for the storage of feed, hay or straw, except by a permit of and under such conditions as may be prescribed by the fire department."

*** (1897) — Chapter 378, Greater New York Charter, Section 1312.**

The first provisions of section 5, law of 1895, continued with the following change: After the word "lodging-house" insert the words "or premises, nor any portion thereof."

* Indicates the existing law in 1900.

*** (1897) — Chapter 378, Greater New York Charter, Section 1312.**

Second provision of the law of 1895 continued, excepting the words "after the first day of September, 1895," are omitted.

DANGEROUS BUSINESSES IN TENEMENTS. — It was found in 1894 by the Tenement House Commission, in the course of their investigations, that many tenement house fires were caused by boiling fat in cellars of tenement houses, in making crullers. As a result, the amended tenement house law, passed in 1895, prohibited the boiling of fat in the cellars of tenements, unless the tenement house was fireproof throughout, or unless the place where the fat boiling was done was made safe by fireproof material on the walls and ceilings, and in such other way as the Fire Department might direct. In order to give every safeguard to the people in the tenements, it was further provided that there should be no openings between the place where the fat was boiled and the other parts of the tenement house, and if such openings existed they were to be closed up solidly with fireproof materials. This law was reënacted in the Charter and is the law at the present time (in 1900).

PAINTS, OILS, DRUGS, ETC. — The Tenement House Law of 1895 also provided that where paint, oil, spirituous liquors or drugs were stored or kept for the purposes of sale on the first floor of any tenement house, there should be no opening leading from such place into the public hall of the tenement house, and any openings that might exist in such buildings were required to be closed up solidly. This is practically the present law (in 1900), except that a slight amendment was made to the law in the Charter, there being a provision that the transoms and windows opening into the halls, instead of being closed up solidly, might be glazed with wire glass.

(1895) — Chapter 567, Section 5. (Amends Section 656, Consol. Act.)

"After the first day of September, 1895, no bakery or place of business in which fat is boiled shall be maintained in any tenement-house which is not fireproof, or where the ceiling and sidewalls of the place, where said fat boiling is done, are not made safe by fireproof material around the same, except by permit of and under such conditions as may be prescribed by the fire department. After the first day of September, 1895, all transoms, windows, doors and other openings leading into halls, or into rooms opening into halls, from bakeries or places of business, in which fat is boiled in the basements, cellars or on the first floors, of all tenement-houses in the city of New York, shall be solidly closed with the same material as the walls or partitions in which the openings exist, so that there shall be no opening between said bakeries, or other places of business of said floor in which fat is boiled, and the other parts of the tenement-house in which the same shall be situated."

*** (1897) — Chapter 378, Greater New York Charter, Section 1311.**

Last provisions of the law of 1895 continued, with the following change: The words at the beginning "After the first day of September, 1895," omitted; also in the fourth line the word "other" omitted.

* Indicates the existing law in 1900.

*** (1897) — Chapter 378, Greater New York Charter, Section 1312.**

The first provision of the law of 1895 in reference to bakeries continued, except that the first words, "After the first day of September, 1895," are omitted.

(1895) — Chapter 567, Section 5. (Amends Section 656, Consol. Act.)

"After the first day of September, 1895, all transoms and windows opening into halls from any portion of the first floor of any tenement-house where paint, oil, spirituous liquors or drugs are stored or kept for the purpose of sale, or otherwise, shall be removed and closed up as solidly as the rest of the wall; and all doors leading into any such hall or room from such portion of said floor, of said tenement-house used as aforesaid, shall be made fireproof."

*** (1897) — Chapter 378, Greater New York Charter, Section 1311.**

Continued, with the following change: After the words "or otherwise" insert the words "shall be glazed with wire glass, or they."

PRECAUTIONS AGAINST FIRE. — In addition to the many provisions for securing safe egress in case of fire a law was passed in 1892, requiring the owners of all tenement houses to provide such means of communicating alarms of fire as the Fire Commissioners might direct, and also to provide such fire hose, extinguishers, buckets and hooks as might be required by the Fire Department. This provision was reënacted in the Charter and is the law at the present day (in 1900).

(1892) — Chapter 703, Section 1. (Amends Section 454, Consol. Act.)

"The owners or proprietors of all tenement-houses and apartment-houses and lodging-houses shall provide such means of communicating alarms of fire, accident or danger to the police and fire departments respectively as the board of fire commissioners or the board of police commissioners may direct, and shall also provide such fire hose, fire extinguisher, buckets, firehooks, firedoors, and other means of preventing and extinguishing fires as said board of fire commissioners may direct."

*** (1897) — Chapter 378, Greater New York Charter, Section 762. — Continued.**

PLASTERING BEHIND WAINSCOTING. — Many fires have spread throughout a house by a person throwing a match upon the floor near the baseboard at the wall, and there being an air space at this point, the fire has spread rapidly through the floors and partitions. In order to prevent such occurrences, a special provision of the law was enacted in 1892, requiring that the surface of the wall or partition behind any wainscoting should be plastered down to the floor line and the intervening space between the plastering and the wainscoting filled in solid with incombustible material. This provision was reënacted in the Building Code and is the law at the present day.

(1892) — Chapter 275, Section 16. (Amends Section 480, Consol. Act.)

"When wood wainscoting is used in any building hereafter erected

* Indicates the existing law in 1900.

the surface of the wall or partition behind such wainscoting shall be plastered down to the floor line, and any intervening space between the said plastering and wainscot shall be filled in solid with incombustible material."

(1894) — Brooklyn — Chapter 481, Section 11. (Amends Chapter 583 of the Law of 1888.)

"When wood wainscoting is used in any building hereafter erected, the surface of the wall or partition behind such wainscoting and on all furred walls or stud partitions, shall be plastered down to the floor line."

***(1899) — The Building Code — (An ordinance adopted December 20, 1899). Section 72.**

"When wainscoting is used, in any building hereafter erected, the surface of the wall or partition behind such wainscoting shall be plastered flush with the grounds and down to the floor line."

FIREPROOF SHUTTERS. — In 1871 it appears there was a provision of law requiring fireproof shutters upon tenement-houses. This was obviously a mistake, as such shutters could be of no use upon a building of this kind and must necessarily be a detriment. The law was repealed in 1874.

(1871) — Chapter 625, Section 28.

"All the window openings of all rear buildings, and all the rear window openings of all buildings mentioned in this section (any building hereafter erected more than three stories in height, occupied by or built to be occupied by three and not more than six families above the first story), shall be provided with fireproof blinds."

(1874) — Chapter 547, Section 7. — Repealed.

LIGHT AND VENTILATION PROVISIONS

SPACE BETWEEN FRONT AND REAR TENEMENT HOUSES. — When the first tenement house law was enacted, in 1867, the evils of rear tenement houses were very great, in many cases front and rear buildings being built on the same lot with a very small space intervening. The first provision of a tenement house law in reference to light and ventilation would naturally, therefore, be one defining the minimum space that should be left between front and rear buildings.

The law in 1867 provided that in the future when any tenement or lodging house was built on the *front* of a lot where there was another building on the rear of the lot, there should be at least 10 feet between the buildings from the ground up, provided the buildings were one story high; when they were two stories high, the distance was to be not less than 15 feet; when three stories high, the distance was to be 20 feet, and when more than three stories high, the distance was required to be 25 feet. A clause was added, however, giving discretionary power to the Board of

* Indicates the existing law in 1900.

Health to modify these distances in special cases. This law was defective in that it only provided for buildings erected on the *front* of a lot and did not prohibit the erection of a tenement house on the rear of a lot where there was already another building on the front, or prescribe the distances that should be between such buildings under such circumstances. This defect was not remedied until twelve years afterward, when the Tenement House Act was amended in 1879, although in 1871, in an amendment to the general building laws, an effort was made to do so. The law of 1871 provided that thereafter no front and rear tenement houses should be erected on the same lot, unless there was an open space of at least 28 feet between them, extending for the whole width of the lot. This provision, however, was repealed three years later. In 1879, however, the Tenement House Act was amended, and the defect of the law of 1867 was remedied, the new law providing that there should be sufficient open spaces between front and rear tenement houses, without regard as to whether the front or the rear building was erected first, and the discretionary power given to the Board of Health to modify these spaces in special cases was still continued. This has remained the law until 1895, when this discretionary power was taken away. There was also another change in the law of 1895, it being deemed unlawful to erect such front and rear tenement houses without a permit from the Superintendent of Buildings, unless there were such open spaces as provided for in previous statutes. In the following year, the Brooklyn Building Law was amended and this part of the tenement house requirements was reënacted, and the discretionary power to modify and lessen the distance between front and rear tenement houses was again added to the law, this time being vested in the Commissioner of Buildings instead of the Board of Health. In 1897, with the adoption of the Greater New York Charter, the provisions in relation to Brooklyn and New York were brought again under one law, as they had been in 1867, the previous provisions being reënacted and the Department of Buildings being again given discretionary power to lessen or modify the spaces between front and rear houses in special cases. This is the present law upon the subject (in 1900).

(1867) — Chapter 908, Section 13.

"It shall not be lawful hereafter to erect for or convert to the purposes of a tenement or lodging-house, a building on the front of any lot where there is another building on the rear of the same lot, unless there is a clear open space exclusively belonging thereto and extending upwards from the ground of at least ten feet between said buildings, if they are one story high above the level of the ground; if they are two stories high, the distance between them shall not be less than fifteen feet; if they are three stories high, the distance between them shall be twenty feet; and if they are more than three stories high, the distance between them shall be twenty-five feet. But when thorough ventilation of such open spaces can be otherwise secured, said distances may be lessened or modified in special cases by a permit from the Metropolitan board of health."

(1871) — Chapter 625, Section 28.

"And in no case shall a front and rear tenement-house be erected on the same lot, unless there shall be an open space of at least 28 feet, the whole width of the lot, between the same."

(1874) — Chapter 547, Section 7. — Repeals above, Section 28, Chapter 625.

(1879) — Chapter 504, Section 1. (Amends Section 13, Chapter 908, Laws of 1867.)

"It shall not be lawful hereafter to erect for, or convert to the purposes of a tenement or lodging-house, a building on any lot where there is another building on the same lot, unless there is a clear open space exclusively belonging thereto and extending upward from the ground of at least ten feet between said buildings if they are one story high, above the level of the ground; if they are two stories high, the distance between them shall not be less than fifteen feet; if they are three stories high, the distance between them shall be not less than twenty feet; and if they are more than three stories high the distance between them shall be not less than twenty-five feet. But when thorough ventilation of such open spaces can be otherwise secured, said distances may be lessened or modified in special cases by a permit from the board of health."

(1880) — Chapter 399, Section 1. (Amends Section 13, Chapter 908, Laws of 1867.)

Provisions of the law of 1879 continued, but the word "spaces" changed to "space" in reference to the discretionary powers of the Board of Health to modify distances between front and rear buildings and at back of rear buildings.

(1882) — Chapter 410, Section 661. Provisions of Section 13, Chapter 908 of the Laws of 1867, as amended by Section 1, Chapter 504, Laws of 1879, and by Section 1, Chapter 399 of the Laws of 1880, continued.

(1887) — Chapter 84, Section 10. (Amends Section 661, Consol. Act.)

"It shall not be lawful hereafter to erect or convert to the purposes of a tenement or lodging-house, a building on any lot where there is another building on the same lot, or to build, or to erect any building on any lot whereon there is already a tenement or lodging-house, unless there is a clear open space exclusively belonging thereto, and extending upward from the ground of at least 10 feet between said buildings if they are one story high above the level of the ground; if they are two stories high, the distance between them shall not be less than 15; if they are three stories high the distance between them shall not be less than 20 feet; and if they are more than three stories high the distance between them shall not be less than 25 feet; but when thorough ventilation of such open spaces can be otherwise secured, such distances may be lessened or modified in special cases by a permit from the board of health."

(1887) — Chapter 288, Section 1. (Amends Section 661, Consol. Act.) — Continued.

(1888) — Brooklyn — Chapter 583, Section 34. (Brooklyn Consol. Act.) (Provisions of law of 1867, Section 13, as amended by Chapter 504 of the law of 1879, reënacted.)

(1891) — Chapter 204, Section 1. (Provisions of Section 10, Chapter 84 of the Laws of 1887, continued.)

(1892) — Chapter 238, Section 1. (Provisions of Chapter 204 of the Laws of 1891, continued.)

(1895) — Brooklyn — Chapter 539, Section 1. (Amends Section 55 of the Brooklyn Consol. Act.)

Provisions of Section 10, Chapter 84 of the Laws of 1887, as amended by Chapter 204 of the Laws of 1891, continued with the following amendment: The phrase "But when thorough ventilation of such open spaces can be otherwise secured such distances may be lessened or modified in special cases by a permit from the board of health," has been stricken out.

(1895) — Chapter 567, Section 8. (Amends Section 661, Consol. Act.)

Provisions of Section 10, Chapter 84 of the Laws of 1887, continued, with the following changes: At the beginning after the words "It shall not be lawful" insert "without a permit from the superintendent of buildings." Also wherever the words "board of health" occur, the words "department of buildings" have been substituted.

(1896) — Brooklyn — Chapter 355, Section 1. (Amends Section 55, Brooklyn Consol. Act.)

"It shall not be lawful without a permit from the commissioner of buildings, to alter, erect or convert to the purposes of a tenement or lodging-house, a building on any lot where there is another building on the same lot, or to build or erect any building on any lot whereon there is already a tenement or a lodging-house, unless there is a clear open space exclusively belonging thereto, and extending upwards from the ground of at least ten feet between said buildings, if they are one story high above the level of the ground; if they are two stories high, the distance between them shall not be less than fifteen feet; if they are three stories high, the distance between them shall not be less than twenty feet; if they are more than three stories high, the distance between them shall not be less than twenty-five feet, but when thorough ventilation can be otherwise secured, such distances may be lessened or modified in special cases by a permit from the department of buildings."

*** (1897) — Chapter 378, Greater New York Charter, Section 1318. (Provisions of Section 8, Chapter 567, of the Laws of 1895, continued.)**

"It shall not be lawful without a permit from the department of buildings to alter, erect or convert to the purpose of a tenement or lodging-house, a building on any lot where there is another building on the same lot; nor shall it be lawful to build or to erect any building on any lot whereon there is already a tenement or lodging-house, unless there is a clear open space belonging exclusively thereto, and extending upward from the ground of at least ten feet between said buildings if they are one story high above the level of the ground; if they are two stories high the distance between them shall not be less than 15 feet; if they are three stories high the distance then shall not be less than 20 feet; if they are more than three stories high the distance between them shall not be less than 25 feet, but when thorough ventilation of such open spaces can be otherwise secured, such distances may be lessened or modified in special cases by a permit from the department of buildings."

* Indicates the existing law in 1900.

YARDS OF TENEMENT HOUSES. — As in a number of cases, new tenement houses were being built covering almost the entire lot, running back to the lot limit, thus backing up against buildings on adjoining lots, it was necessary at an early date to provide that a certain portion of every lot should be left vacant at the rear for a back yard, so as to bring light and air to the rear rooms of the building. The first tenement law, the Act of 1867, provided that in all buildings erected after that time, there should be a clear open space of 10 feet between the back of the tenement house and *any other building*, but discretionary power was given to the Board of Health to modify this distance in special cases. As can be readily seen, this law was singularly defective, in that it only provided that there should be a space of 10 feet between the back of a rear tenement house and *any other building*, the result of which was that where there did not happen at the time to be a building erected on the lot directly behind the one in question, the building in question might be built up to the very lot line and no space left. This defect of the law was not remedied until 1879, when the law was changed so as to require a clear open space of 10 feet between the back of any new tenement house and the *rear line* of the same lot. Discretionary power, in special cases, was still given to the Board of Health, and this has remained the law until 1887, when the discretionary power was taken away. It is singular that no exception was made of corner lots until 1887. Chapter 288 of the laws enacted in the same year, but at a later date than the amendment to the Tenement House Act, provided that this space, as to corner lots, might be modified in special cases by the Board of Health. This has practically remained the present law until 1895, when the Tenement House Act was changed. In that year it was enacted that no new corner tenement house should come within 5 feet of the rear of the lot line above the first story, the entire lot being permitted to be covered on the first floor. On interior lots, a space of 10 feet between the back of the building and the rear of the lot was required, and all discretionary power as to this point was taken away from the Board of Health and the Department of Buildings. This provision was reënacted in the Greater New York Charter, but with an important change. It was felt to be inadvisable to permit a corner building to cover the entire lot upon the first story, as it did not permit sufficient ventilation through the block; consequently the new law prohibited any corner tenement house from coming within 5 feet of the rear line of the lot. This is the present law (in 1900) upon this subject. In addition to this provision, however, the Department of Buildings has adopted certain regulations in reference to this subject, to the effect that where corner tenements are over 80 feet high, the space at the rear shall be 5 feet 4 inches; where they are over 85 feet high, the space shall be 5 feet 8 inches, and so on, through a varying schedule of distances, up to a height of 150 feet. Under the provisions of the Charter, the Department of Buildings is given power to make certain regulations in relation to tenement houses not inconsistent with the Charter. It is questionable whether any of the regulations above quoted have any legal value, as they seem to be at variance with the provisions of the Charter, which states that the distance shall not be less than 5 feet.

(1867) — Chapter 908, Section 13.

"At the rear of every building hereafter erected for, or converted to the purposes of a tenement or lodging-house on the back part of any lot, there shall be a clear open space of 10 feet between it and any other building; but when thorough ventilation of such open spaces can be otherwise secured said distances may be modified in special cases by a permit from the Metropolitan board of health."

(1879) — Chapter 504, Section 1. (Amends Section 13, Chapter 908, Laws of 1867.)

"At the rear of every building hereafter erected for or converted to the purposes of a tenement or lodging-house on any lot, there shall be a clear, open space of not less than 10 feet between it and the rear line of the lot. But when thorough ventilation of such open spaces can be otherwise secured, such distances may be lessened or modified in special cases by a permit from the board of health."

(1880) — Chapter 399, Section 1. (Amends Section 13, Chapter 908, of the Laws of 1867.)

"At the rear of every building hereafter erected for or converted to the purposes of a tenement or lodging-house on any lot, there shall be a clear open space of not less than ten feet between it and the rear line of the lot. But when thorough ventilation of such open space can be otherwise secured such distances may be lessened or modified in special cases, or the open spaces may be dispensed with on corner lots by a permit from the board of health."

(1882) — Chapter 410, Section 661. (Provisions of Chapter 504 of the Law of 1879, reënacted.)

"At the rear of every building hereafter erected for or converted to the purpose of a tenement or lodging-house on any lot, there shall be a clear, open space of not less than 10 feet between it and the rear line of the lot. But when thorough ventilation of such open space can be otherwise secured, said distances may be lessened or modified in special cases by a permit from the board of health."

(1887) — Chapter 84, Section 10. (Amends Section 661, Consol. Act.)

"At the rear of every building hereafter erected for or converted to the purposes of a tenement or lodging-house on any lot, there shall be and remain a clear open space of not less than 10 feet between it and the rear line of the lot."

(1887) — Chapter 288, Section 1.

Provisions of Chapter 84 of the Laws of 1887 amended by adding at the end "But this provision may be modified as to corner lots in special cases by a permit from the board of health."

(1888) — Brooklyn — Chapter 583, Section 34. (Brooklyn Consol. Act.) Provisions of Laws of 1867 as amended by Laws of 1879 and 1880, re-enacted.

(1891) — Chapter 204, Section 1.

Provisions of the law in reference to space at rear of new tenements as contained in Section 10, Chapter 84 of the Laws of 1887; and also in Section 1, Chapter 288 of the Laws of 1887, amended as follows: "But this provision may be modified as to corner lots, and may be changed or modified *as to lodging-houses* in special cases by a permit from the board of health."

(1892) — Chapter 238, Section 1. (Provisions of Chapter 204 of the Laws of 1891.) — Continued.

(1895) — Brooklyn — Chapter 539, Section 1. (Amends Section 55, Brooklyn Consol. Act.)

"There shall be and remain a clear, open space of not less than ten feet between the rear end of said lot and any building thereon."

(1895) — Chapter 567, Section 8. (Amends Section 661, Consol. Act.)

"At the rear of every building hereafter erected for or converted to the purposes of a tenement or lodging-house on any lot, there shall be and remain a clear, open space of not less than 10 feet between it and the rear end of the lot. But this provision shall not apply to corner lots in which, however, no such building shall come within 5 feet of the rear of said lot above the first story."

(1896) — Brooklyn — Chapter 355, Section 1. (Amends Section 55, Brooklyn Consol. Act.)

"At the rear of every building hereafter erected for or converted for the purposes of a tenement or lodging-house on any lot, there shall be and remain a clear, open space of not less than ten feet between it and the rear end of the lot."

*** (1897) — Chapter 378, Greater New York Charter, Section 1318.**

Provisions of Chapter 567, Laws of 1895, continued, with the following amendment: The words "above the first story" at the end, stricken out.

*** (1900) — Regulations of the Department of Buildings.**

"At the rear of every tenement or lodging-house on any corner lot there shall be and remain above the first story a clear space of not less than five feet between it and the rear end of the lot, up to eighty feet in height and

Over 80 feet, five feet four inches.
Over 85 feet, five feet eight inches.
Over 90 feet, six feet.
Over 95 feet, six feet four inches.
Over 100 feet, six feet eight inches.
Over 105 feet, seven feet.
Over 110 feet, seven feet four inches.
Over 115 feet, seven feet eight inches.
Over 120 feet, eight feet.
Over 125 feet, eight feet four inches.
Over 130 feet, eight feet eight inches.
Over 135 feet, nine feet.
Over 140 feet, nine feet four inches.
Over 145 feet, nine feet eight inches.
Over 150 feet, ten feet.

"Where the width of a corner lot is greater than an ordinary city lot it must have a clear space of not less than ten feet in the rear of that portion in excess of an ordinary city lot, or, in lieu thereof, an open court not less than one of the same widths as above, and beginning at

* Indicates the existing law in 1900.

the street or avenue, which must extend the full width of the lot and continue to the first interior room. And such interior portion of a corner tenement or lodging-house must conform to all the requirements of a tenement or lodging-house situated on an inside lot."

PERCENTAGE OF LOT OCCUPIED. — Although the first and most important tenement house law was enacted in 1867, yet not until twelve years later was there any provision in the law limiting the percentage of the lot permitted to be occupied by a new tenement house. It is exceedingly strange that a provision should not have been contained in the first legislation upon this subject, and it is only accounted for by the fact that the great majority of new tenement houses in 1867 were only four stories high, and seldom covered more than 60 per cent of the lot. In the Act of 1879, however, the percentage of lot permitted to be occupied by a new tenement house was limited to 65 per cent. This, however, was not to apply to corner lots, and in addition the Board of Health was given discretionary power to permit it to be modified in special cases. This provision as to the percentage of the lot applied only to New York, and not till 1895 was this defect in the Brooklyn law remedied. The 1879 law also contained a singular defect, in that it made no provision for existing tenement houses that might be altered or enlarged, so that under this law one might take an old tenement house and alter it so as to cover 100 per cent of the lot, and yet any one building a new tenement house and a better building was limited to 65 per cent. This defect of the law was remedied in 1887, when the law was made to apply to old buildings altered or enlarged to be used as tenement houses, as well as to new buildings; and the other provisions of the previous statutes were all reënacted. In 1891 an important amendment to the New York laws was passed; prior to that time, the Board of Health had discretionary power to permit more than 65 per cent of the lot to be occupied in special cases. The Act of 1891, however, limited this provision strictly to corner tenements and to lodging houses, thus taking away all such discretionary powers in relation to tenement houses built on ordinary interior lots. This important provision was reënacted in 1892, but, also, in the same year a law, passed at a later date, gave the Board of Health the power to make regulations in addition to those provided for by the statute, in special cases, as to the proportion of any lot to be covered by any tenement or lodging house. In 1895 the Brooklyn Building Law was amended and the defects of the law in this respect were remedied, the new law limiting the percentage of lot to be occupied to 70 per cent; but this was not to apply to corner buildings, which were permitted to occupy as much as 90 per cent of the lot, and no discretionary power was given to the Commissioner of Buildings or the Board of Health to modify this provision of the law. In the same year the New York Tenement House Law was also changed; the provisions of previous statutes were reënacted prohibiting any new tenement house from covering more than 65 per cent of the lot, and also prohibiting any existing tenement or lodging house from being enlarged or altered to cover a greater area. A new clause was added, however, to the effect that "where the light and ventilation of such tenement or lodging houses were, in the opinion of the Superintendent of Buildings materially improved, he might permit such tenement or lodging house to occupy an area not exceeding 75 per centum of the lot." In addition to limiting the percentage of lot to be occupied to 65 per cent, the law of this year also provided that if any shaft or court should be of a less area than 25 square feet, it should not be considered as part of the free air space in computing the amount of the lot covered by the building, but should be considered as part of the building itself. In the same act are to be found additional provisions giving increased discretionary powers to the Superintendent of Buildings to make rules and regulations not inconsistent with the requirements of the existing law. These rules and regulations were limited, however, to the arrangement and distribution of the uncovered area, the size, lighting, ventilation, and arrangement of shafts, rooms, cellars, and halls, and the Superintendent of Buildings was authorized to modify or change such regulations from time to time. In 1896 the Brooklyn Building Law was amended so as to make the Brooklyn law conform to the law of 1895 for New York, and the power given to the Commissioner of Buildings to permit 75 per cent of the lot to be covered in certain cases is very clearly stated. The Greater New York Charter continued the provisions of the laws of 1895 without change. This is the present law upon the subject with the following supplementary regulations adopted by the Department of Buildings under the authority given them in Section 1318 of the Charter. These regulations provide that in any tenement house 80 feet high, on an interior lot, 75 per cent of the lot may be covered; in tenement houses 90 feet high, 73 per cent may be covered; in tenement houses 100 feet high, 71 per cent; in tenement houses 110 feet high, 69 per cent; in tenement houses 120 feet high, 67 per cent, and in tenement houses over 120 feet high, 65 per cent, and a similar schedule of decreasing percentages with increasing heights is adopted for tenement houses on corner lots. As no ordinary tenement house is permitted to be erected more than 85 feet high, this scale of decreased percentages has very little bearing upon the tenement house problem and would only apply to fireproof apartment houses, where these percentages of the lots would naturally be voluntarily left unbuilt upon by the architect of the building.

(1879) — Chapter 504, Section 1. (Amends Section 13, Chapter 908, Laws of 1867.)

"No one continuous building shall be built or converted to the purposes of a tenement or lodging-house in the city of New York, upon an ordinary city lot, to occupy more than 65 per centum of the said lot, and in the same proportion if the lot be greater or less in size than 25 feet by 100 feet; but this provision shall not apply to corner lots and may be modified in other special cases by a permit from the board of health."

(1880) — Chapter 399, Section 1. (Amends Section 13, Chapter 908, Laws of 1867.) — Continued.

(1882) — Chapter 410, Section 661. — Continued.

(1887) — Chapter 84, Section 10. (Amends Section 661, Consol. Act.)

"No one continuous building shall be built for or converted to the purposes of a tenement or lodging-house in the city of New York, upon an ordinary city lot, and no existing tenement or lodging-house shall be enlarged or altered or its lot be diminished so that it shall occupy more than sixty-five per centum of the said lot, and in the same proportion if the lot be greater or less in size than twenty-five feet by one hundred feet; but this provision shall not apply to corner lots, and may be modified in other special cases by a permit from the board of health."

(1887) — Chapter 288, Section 1. — Continued.

(1891) — Chapter 204, Section 1.

Provisions of Section 10, Chapter 84 of the Laws of 1887, in reference to percentage of lot, continued, but with the following important change: The laws of 1887, after limiting the percentage to 65 per cent, had this clause: "But this provision shall not apply to corner lots and may be modified in other special cases by a permit from the board of health." In the amendment of 1891 this clause reads as follows: "But this provision shall not apply to corner lots, and may be modified or changed in special cases *as to lodging-houses* by a permit from the board of health."

(1892) — Chapter 238, Section 1. (Provisions of Chapter 204 of the Laws of 1891.) Continued.

(1892) — Chapter 329, Section 1.

"The board of health shall have authority within present provisions of law to make other regulations than the foregoing in special cases as to the proportion of any lot to be covered by any tenement or lodging-house when it shall be satisfied that such regulations will secure equally well the health of the occupants and the public health, provided, however, that in all such cases any modifications made by such regulations shall be in accordance with the conditions of a permit in writing issued by the said board of health." (Became a law April 19, 1892.)

(1895) — Brooklyn — Chapter 539, Section 1. (Amends Section 55, Brooklyn Consol. Act.)

"No one continuous building shall be built for or converted to the purposes of a tenement or lodging-house in the city of Brooklyn, upon an ordinary city lot, and no existing tenement or lodging-house shall be enlarged or altered or its lot be diminished so that it shall occupy more than seventy per centum of the said lot, and in the same proportion if the lot be greater or less in size than 25 × 100 feet; but in the case of corner lots the building or buildings may, by special permit from the commissioner of buildings, be made to occupy not more than ninety per centum of the lot."

(1895) — Chapter 567, Section 8. (Amends Section 661, Consol. Act.)

"No one continuous building hereafter constructed shall be built or converted to the purposes of a tenement or lodging-house in the city of New York, upon an ordinary city lot, and no existing tenement or lodging-house shall be enlarged or altered, or its lot be diminished so that it shall occupy more than 65 per centum of the area of said lot, but where the light and ventilation of such tenement or lodging-house are, in the opinion of the superintendent of buildings, materially improved, he may permit such tenement or lodging-house to occupy an area not exceeding 75 per centum of the said lot, and in the same proportion if the lot be greater or less in size than 25 × 100 feet; but this provision shall not apply to corner lots, in which, however, no such building hereafter constructed, above the first story shall occupy more than 92 per centum of the area of a lot. In computing the amount of the lot covered by a building, any shaft or court of less than 25 square feet in area shall be considered as part of the building and not as part of the free air space."

(1895) — Chapter 567, Section 8. (Amends Section 661, Consol. Act.)

"The superintendent of buildings is hereby empowered and directed to make rules and regulations not inconsistent with the requirements of this title, and which in addition to the requirements of this title shall be the conditions of approval for the plans and permits; these rules and regulations shall govern the arrangement and distribution of the uncovered area, size, lighting, location and arrangement of shafts, rooms, cellars and halls, and may be modified or changed from time to time by the superintendent of buildings."

(1896) — Brooklyn — Chapter 355, Section 1. (Amends Section 55, Brooklyn Consol. Act.)

"No one continuous building shall be built for or converted to the purposes of a tenement or lodging-house in the city of Brooklyn, upon an ordinary city lot, and no existing tenement or lodging-house shall be enlarged or altered, or its lot be diminished so that it shall occupy more than 65 per centum of the area of said lot, but when the interior light and ventilation of such tenement or lodging-house are, in the opinion of the commissioner of buildings, adequately provided for, he may permit such tenement or lodging-house to occupy an area not exceeding 75 per centum of the said lot, and in the same proportion if the lot be greater or less in size than 25 by 100 feet. But this provision shall not apply to corner lots, in which, however, no such building hereafter constructed, above the first story, shall occupy more than 92 per centum of the area of said lot above the first story. In computing the amount of the lot covered by a building, any shaft or court of less than 25 square feet in area shall be considered as part of the building and not as part of the free air space."

*** (1897) — Chapter 378, Greater New York Charter, Section 1318. (Provisions of Chapter 567, Laws of 1895.) — Continued.**

*** (1899) — Regulations of the Department of Buildings.**

"Section 1318, Greater New York Charter, restricts the occupancy of any tenement or lodging-house on any ordinary city lot to 65 per centum of the area of said lot, when such lot is not a corner lot, and empowers the commissioner of buildings to extend such occupancy to 75 per centum of the area of the aforesaid lot provided the light and ventilation of such tenement or lodging-house are, in the opinion of the commissioner of buildings, materially improved. The same section also provides that no tenement or lodging-house shall occupy more than 92 per centum of the area of a corner lot above the first story. Percentages of lot area allowed in this provision of the law are as follows: —

Up to 80 feet in height	75 per cent.
Up to 90 feet in height	73 per cent.
Up to 100 feet in height	71 per cent.
Up to 110 feet in height	69 per cent.
Up to 120 feet in height	67 per cent.
Above 120 feet in height	65 per cent.

* Indicates the existing law in 1900.

"Percentages of area of corner lots allowed under this provision of law as follows:—

Up to 80 feet in height	92 per cent.
Up to 90 feet in height	90 per cent.
Up to 100 feet in height	88 per cent.
Up to 110 feet in height	86 per cent.
Up to 120 feet in height	84 per cent.
Up to 130 feet in height	82 per cent.
Up to 140 feet in height	80 per cent.
Up to 150 feet in height	78 per cent.
Above 150 feet in height	75 per cent.

"For buildings greater than 50 feet frontage, the former tables of percentages will apply to that part which is in excess of 50 feet, and the latter scale for that which is under 50 feet.

"While the uncovered area cannot be less than the above, it must be greater where required by the further regulations for shafts and fixing distance required at rear."

AIR AND LIGHT SHAFTS. — Before 1879 few tenement houses were constructed containing an air shaft, most of them being buildings four stories high and about 54 to 60 feet in depth. Not being any deeper than this on the lot, the buildings were only four rooms deep, thus permitting a large front room, getting its light and air from the street, and a large rear room, getting its light and air from the yard, which, in most cases, was 40 feet deep by 25 feet wide; the two inner rooms of these four rooms getting their light and air from the front and rear rooms, which, under such circumstances, were able to furnish an ample supply. In a few cases, however, tenement houses were erected much deeper on the lot, some of them having six and seven rooms in a line instead of four. The first tenement house law, therefore, contained a provision that in every habitable room of a less size than 100 square feet in area, unless the room communicated directly with the outer air or unless it was provided with an open fireplace, there should be a separate means of ventilating the room; this means to be by a separate air shaft extending to the roof, or in some other way as the Board of Health might direct. This provision applied to old tenement houses as well as to new ones, and quite a number of small ventilating flues of the size of a chimney flue, about 4 inches by 6 inches, were put in many buildings of this kind. This is the only provision in the tenement house law in reference to air shafts until 1895, no previous law having required air shafts, nor any minimum size or width of such shaft having been prescribed. In this year, however, it was provided that any air shaft or court less than 25 square feet in area should not count as part of the unoccupied space of the lot. And it was further provided that no air shaft in the future should be covered over with a roof or skylight, unless it happened to be less than 10 square feet in size. Similar provisions were adopted in an amendment to the general building laws of the City of Brooklyn, enacted in the year following. In addition to these requirements of the law of 1895, the Superintendent of Buildings was given discretionary power to make rules and regulations and to modify the same from time to time as to the size, lighting, location, and arrangement of all shafts for light and air. All of these provisions of the law of 1895 were reënacted in the Greater New York Charter, with the exception that the Superintendent of Buildings, although empowered to make such regulations, was no longer given the authority to modify or change them. In this year, for the first time, was a minimum width prescribed for light and air shafts, the width determined on being 28 inches. This is the present law (in 1900) upon this subject with the following supplementary requirements adopted by the Department of Buildings in their regulations. These regulations require that every light and air shaft or court, for habitable rooms, must not be less than 25 square feet in area, up to and including the fifth story of such buildings, and above the fifth story, must be increased in area 5 square feet for every additional story. Also that the width of such shafts above the fifth story must be increased 4 inches for every additional story. It is also provided that where a common shaft or court is located between two tenement houses on different lots, the shafts must be double the width and area that they would be on a single lot and that such shafts shall, of course, be similarly increased in height above the fifth story. It is further provided that where there are five in erior rooms in a line on any floor, the area of the shaft or court lighting and ventilating such rooms must be 50 per cent greater than above described, and where there are six interior rooms in a line on any floor, the area of such shaft or court must be at least 100 per cent greater than the area required above. The following minimum area for light shafts is also established. Where there are twelve rooms on any floor of a tenement house erected on an ordinary interior lot, the shafts and courts lighting and ventilating the interior rooms must have an area equal to 215 square feet, and where there are fourteen rooms on a floor, the area of the shafts and courts must not be less than 265 square feet; and it is further required that these shafts or courts in such cases shall be enlarged at their central portions, so as to provide windows at the ends of each set of rooms, where there are front and rear sets of apartments on a floor. In corner buildings, the requirements are, of course, different. In such houses, where there are four families on a floor, and six rooms on the inside portion, the shaft to light and ventilate the interior rooms must have an area equal to 107½ square feet; and where there are seven rooms instead of six the area of such shaft must be 132½ square feet, and the shafts must also be enlarged at their central portions to provide end windows for the rooms.

(1867) — Chapter 908, Section 14.

"Every habitable room of a less area than one hundred superficial feet if it does not communicate directly with the external air, and is without an open fireplace, shall be provided with special means of ventilation, by a separate air shaft extending to the roof, or otherwise, as the board of health may prescribe."

(1879) — Chapter 504, Section 2. — Continued.

(1882) — Chapter 410, Section 662. — Continued.

(1888) — Brooklyn — Chapter 583, Section 35. (Brooklyn Consol. Act.) Provisions of the Law of 1867, reënacted.

(1895) — Brooklyn — Chapter 539, Section 1. Provisions of Brooklyn Consol. Act, continued.

(1895) — Chapter 567, Section 8. (Amends Section 661, Consol. Act.)

"The superintendent of buildings is hereby empowered and directed to make rules and regulations not inconsistent with the requirements of this title, and which in addition to the requirements of this title shall be the conditions of approval for the plans and permits; these rules and regulations shall govern the arrangement and distribution of the uncovered area, size, lighting, location and arrangement of shafts, rooms, cellars and halls, and may be modified or changed from time to time by the superintendent of buildings."

(1895) — Chapter 567, Section 8. (Amends Section 661, Consol. Act.)

"In computing the amount of the lot covered by a building, any shaft or court less than twenty-five square feet in area shall be considered as part of the building and not as part of the free air space. No shaft or court hereafter constructed in a tenement-house, except elevator shafts or staircase wells, except any shaft the area of which does not exceed ten square feet shall be covered with a roof, skylight or otherwise."

(1896) — Brooklyn — Chapter 355, Section 1. (Amends Section 55, Brooklyn Consol. Act.)

"In computing the amount of the lot covered by a building, any shaft or court of less than twenty-five square feet in area shall be considered as part of the building and not as part of the free air space."

*** (1897) — Chapter 378, Greater New York Charter, Section 1318.**

Provisions of Section 8, Chapter 567, Laws of 1895, continued, with the exception that the superintendent of buildings no longer is given power to modify or change the regulations, from time to time.

*** (1897) — Chapter 378, Greater New York Charter, Section 1318.**

"In all cases, both for corner and interior lots, the interior courts or shafts shall not be less than 2 feet 4 inches wide at their narrowest parts. In computing the amount of the lot covered by a building, any shaft or court of less than 25 square feet in area shall be considered as part of the building and not as part of the free air space."

*** (1891) — Chapter 378, Greater New York Charter, Section 1319. Provisions of Section 14, Chapter 908, of the Laws of 1867, continued.**

*** (1900) — Regulations of the Department of Buildings.**

AREA OF SHAFTS AND COURTS. — "Except as hereinafter otherwise stated, every light and air shaft or court for habitable rooms must be at least twenty-five square feet in area up to and including five stories in height, and be increased five square feet in area for each additional story beyond the fifth, and not less than two feet four inches wide in the clear at every point up to and including five stories in height, and be increased four inches in width for each additional story beyond the fifth. Light or ventilating shafts or courts between two houses, and common to both, must be double this area and not less than four feet eight inches wide up to and including five stories in height and be increased eight inches in width for each additional story beyond the fifth. Where there are five interior rooms

* Indicates the existing law in 1900.

in a line on a floor the area of each shaft or court must be fifty per cent. greater than above described, and where there are six interior rooms in a line on a floor the area of such shaft or court must be at least one hundred per cent. greater than the minimum above stated."

INCREASED AREAS OF SHAFTS AND COURTS.—"Where there are twelve rooms on a floor of a tenement-house erected on an ordinary city lot, except a corner lot, the shafts and courts to light and ventilate the interior rooms must have an area equal to two hundred and fifteen square feet, and where there are fourteen rooms on a floor of a similar tenement house the area of such shafts and courts must not be less than two hundred and sixty-five square feet, and these shafts or courts must be enlarged at their central portion so as to provide windows at the ends of each set of rooms where there are front and rear sets of apartments on a floor."

SHAFTS IN CORNER HOUSES.—"In every corner house on an ordinary city lot having four families on a floor, and six rooms on the inside portion thereof, the shaft to light and ventilate interior rooms must have an area equal to one hundred and seven and one-half square feet; and where there are seven rooms the area of such shaft must be one hundred and thirty-two and one-half square feet, and these shafts must be enlarged at their central portions to provide end windows as above described."

SHAFTS TO BE FREE FROM OBSTRUCTIONS.—"All shafts over ten square feet in area must be free and clear from skylights or any other covering or obstruction at the top, and must be of the same area throughout.

"Tenement-houses not over four stories in height, which cover less than sixty-five per cent. of lot area, must have exterior light shafts of not less than fifteen square feet area in each shaft, but not more than two rooms in each apartment may open thereon.

"Tenement-houses three stories or less in height, and which cover less than sixty-five per cent. of lot area, may have shafts not less than ten square feet in area, but not more than two rooms in each apartment may open thereon."

VENTILATION, REGULATIONS FOR—POWERS OF BOARD OF HEALTH AND DEPARTMENT OF BUILDINGS.—Since 1867 the Board of Health has had authority to make additional regulations as to ventilation of tenement houses not inconsistent with the existing laws. This, prior to 1892, applied to new tenement houses as well as to old ones. As in 1892, jurisdiction over the light and ventilation of new tenements was taken from the Board of Health and given solely to the Department of Buildings, the Building Department has since that time had the power to make such regulations, while the Board of Health has retained its powers to make these regulations in reference to existing tenement houses.

(1867) — Chapter 908, Section 18.

"The Metropolitan board of health shall have authority to make other regulations as to ventilation consistent with the foregoing where it shall be satisfied that such regulations will secure equally well the health of the occupants."

(1882) — Chapter 410, Section 667. — Continued.

(1888) — Brooklyn — Chapter 583, Section 39. (Brooklyn Consol. Act.) Provisions of law of 1867 reënacted.

(1892) — Chapter 329, Section 1. (Amends Section 667, Consol. Act.)

"The board of health shall have authority, within present provisions of law, to make other regulations than the foregoing in special cases as to light and ventilation in any tenement or lodging-house, when it shall be satisfied that such regulations will secure equally well the health of the occupants and the public health, provided, however, that in all such cases any modifications made by such regulations, shall be in accordance with the conditions of a permit in writing issued by the said board of health."

(1895) — Chapter 567, Section 8. (Amends Section 661, Consol. Act.)

"The light and ventilation, for all buildings hereafter erected for or converted to the purposes of tenement or lodging-houses, must be provided in accordance with the requirements of this title and the conditions of a plan and permit previously approved in writing by the superintendent of buildings, and no existing tenement or lodging-house shall be enlarged or altered or its lot diminished without a similar permit. The superintendent of buildings is hereby empowered and directed to make rules and regulations not inconsistent with the requirements of this title, and which in addition to the requirements of this title shall be the conditions of approval for the plans and permits; these rules and regulations shall govern the arrangement and distribution of the uncovered area, size, lighting, location and arrangement of shafts, rooms, cellars and halls, and may be modified or changed from time to time by the superintendent of buildings."

(1895) — Chapter 567, Section 12. (Amends Section 667, Consol. Act.)

"The superintendent of buildings shall have authority to make other regulations as to light and ventilation of all new tenement or lodging-houses consistent with the foregoing; when he shall be satisfied that such regulations will secure equally well the health and safety of the occupants; likewise the board of health shall have authority to make other regulations as to cellars and as to ventilation of completed buildings consistent with the foregoing, where it shall be satisfied that such regulations will secure equally well the health of the occupants."

***(1897) — Chapter 378, Greater New York Charter, Section 1318.**

Provisions of Section 8, Chapter 567, of the Laws of 1895, continued, with the following changes: Wherever the words "superintendent of buildings" occur, substitute "department of buildings"; also the following sentence at the end has been omitted, "and may be modified or changed from time to time by the superintendent of buildings."

***(1897) — Chapter 378, Greater New York Charter, Section 1323. Provisions of Section 12, Chapter 567, of the Laws of 1895, continued.**

***(1900) — Sanitary Code of the Department of Health, Section 21.**

"No person shall hereafter erect, or cause to be erected, or converted

* Indicates the existing law in 1900.

to a new purpose by alteration any building or structure, or change the construction of any part of any building by addition or otherwise, so that it, or any part thereof, shall be inadequate or defective in respect to strength, ventilation, light, sewerage, or of any other usual, proper or necessary provision or precaution for the security of life and health; nor shall the builder, lessee, tenant, or occupant of any such, or of any other building or structure, cause or allow any matter or thing to be or to be done in or about any such building or structure dangerous or prejudicial to life or health."

***(1900) — Sanitary Code of the Department of Health, Section 22.**

"That no owner or lessee of any building or any part thereof, shall lease or let, or hire out the same or any portion thereof, to be occupied by any person, or allow the same to be occupied, as a place in which or for any one, to dwell or lodge, except when said buildings or such parts thereof are sufficiently lighted, ventilated, provided and accommodated, and are in all respects in that condition of cleanliness and wholesomeness for which this code or any law of this State provides, or in which they or either of them require any such premises to be kept."

ROOMS, VENTILATION AND LIGHTING OF. — The first provisions of any kind upon this subject are to be found in the Tenement House Act of 1867. Here it is provided that in every building used as a tenement house, every room which is used as a sleeping room and which does not communicate directly with the external air, shall have a window or transom not less in size than 3 square feet, over the door which connects with an adjoining room; provided, that the adjoining room itself communicates with the external air; and, in addition, this inner room shall also have a transom or window not less than 3 square feet in size, leading into an entry or hall of the house; or where this was not practicable from the situation of the rooms, then there was to be a window or transom leading from this inner room in question into some adjoining room, which communicated with the hall of the house. This applied, of course, to all tenement houses, to those already existing as well as to those newly erected. In the same year it was provided that in every new tenement house or in every building thereafter altered to be used as a tenement house, every habitable room should have at least one window connecting with the external air, or if this were not done, then the room should have over the door a ventilator of perfect construction connecting it with another room, or with the hall, which should have a connection with the external air, and this ventilator was to be so arranged as to produce a cross current of air.

In 1879, twelve years later, these provisions of the first tenement house law were reënacted with the following additional requirement, that in all tenement houses, every room used for sleeping should have at least one window with a movable sash, not less in size than 12 square feet, admitting light and air from the public street or the yard of the said house. This was a most important improvement and would have been of unquestionable value, were it not for the fact that a clause was added giving discretionary power to the Board of Health to permit other means of lighting and

* Indicates the existing law in 1900.

ventilating such rooms. No change in any of these provisions was made until 1895, when this discretionary power was taken away from the Board of Health, the amended tenement house law of that year requiring that in all tenement houses thereafter constructed or in any way converted to the purposes of a tenement house, each room should have a window opening into the outer air. This law, however, did not define what constituted the "outer air"; it is questionable whether an air shaft enclosed on all four sides and only 28 inches wide and 60 feet high can be considered really to be "outer air." In the same year the Superintendent of Buildings was given additional powers to make rules and regulations governing the size, lighting, location and arrangement of rooms, and was authorized to modify or change such regulations from time to time. The Greater New York Charter continued all the provisions of the law of 1895, requiring that every habitable room in all new tenement houses should have a separate window opening into the outer air, and also contained a provision of the old law that was directly in conflict with this requirement, stating that every habitable room should have at least one window connecting with the external air, *or*, if it did not have this, a ventilator connecting the room with another room or hall which should be connected with the outer air. These provisions of the Charter are the present law upon this subject. In addition there is a regulation of the Department of Buildings to the effect that every habitable room, except those opening on the main halls, must have a transom so arranged as to produce cross ventilation.

(1867) — Chapter 908, Section 2.

"Every house, building, or portion thereof, in the cities of New York and Brooklyn, designed to be used, occupied, leased, or rented, or which is used, occupied, leased, or rented for a tenement or lodging-house, shall have in every room which is occupied as a sleeping-room, and which does not communicate directly with the external air, a ventilating or transom window, having an opening or area of three square feet, over the door leading into and connected with the adjoining room, if such adjoining room communicates directly with the external air, and also a ventilating or transom window of the same opening or area, communicating with the entry or hall of the house, or where this is, from the relative situation of the rooms, impracticable, such last-mentioned ventilating or transom window shall communicate with an adjoining room that itself communicates with the entry or hall."

(1867) — Chapter 908, Section 14.

"Every habitable room in every tenement and lodging-house hereafter erected or converted shall have at least one window connecting with the external air or over the door a ventilator of perfect construction connecting it with a room or hall which has a connection with the external air, and so arranged as to produce a cross current of air."

(1879) — Chapter 504, Section 2. (Amends Section 14, Chapter 908, Laws of 1867.)

"In every tenement or lodging-house hereafter erected or converted every habitable room shall have at least one window connecting with the external air, or over the door a ventilator of perfect construction connecting it with a room or hall which has a connection with the external air, and so arranged as to produce a cross current of air. The full area of window or windows in every room communicating with the external air shall be at least one-tenth of the superficial area of every such room; and the top of one, at least, of such windows shall not be less than seven feet and six inches above the floor, and the upper half at least shall be made so as to open the full width. Every habitable room of a less area than one hundred superficial feet, if it does not communicate directly with the external air, and is without an open fireplace, shall be provided with special means of ventilation, by a separate air shaft extending to the roof, or otherwise as the board of health may prescribe. But in all houses hereafter erected or converted in the city of New York, which shall be used, occupied, leased or rented for a tenement or lodging-house, every room used, let or occupied by any person or persons for sleeping shall have at least one window with a movable sash having an opening of not less than twelve square feet, admitting light and air directly from the public street or the yard of the said house, unless sufficient light and ventilation shall be otherwise provided, in a manner and upon a plan approved by the board of health."

(1882) — Chapter 410, Section 650. Provisions of Section 2, Chapter 908, Laws of 1867, continued.

(1882) — Chapter 410, Section 662. Section 2 of Chapter 908 of the Laws of 1867, as amended by Section 2, Chapter 504 of the Laws of 1879, continued.

(1888) — Brooklyn — Chapter 583, Sections 25 and 35. (Brooklyn Consol. Act.) Provisions of law of 1867, reënacted.

(1895) — Brooklyn — Chapter 539, Section 1. (Amends Section 46, Brooklyn Consol. Act.) Provisions of Section 2, Chapter 908, Laws of 1867, reënacted as follows:

"Every house, building or portion thereof, in the city of Brooklyn, designed to be used, occupied, leased or rented, or which is used, occupied, leased or rented for a tenement or lodging-house, shall have in every room which is occupied as a sleeping-room, and which does not communicate directly with the external air, a ventilating or transom window, having an opening or area of 3 square feet, over the door leading into and connected with the adjoining room, if such adjoining room communicates with the external air, and also a ventilating or transom window of the same opening or area, communicating with the entry or hall of the house; or where this is, from the relative situation of the rooms, impracticable, such last-mentioned ventilating or transom window shall communicate with an adjoining room that itself communicates with the entry or hall."

(1895) — Brooklyn — Chapter 539, Section 1. (Amends Section 56, Brooklyn Consol. Act.)

"In all houses erected or converted after June first, 1895, which shall be used, occupied, leased or rented for a tenement or lodging-house, every room used, let or occupied by any person or persons for sleeping shall have at least one window, with a movable sash having an opening of not less than twelve square feet, admitting light and air directly from the public street or the yard of the said house, unless sufficient light and ventilation shall be otherwise provided, in a manner and upon a plan approved by the department of buildings."

(1895) — Brooklyn — Chapter 539, Section 1. (Amends Section 56, Brooklyn Consol. Act.) Provisions of Section 14, Chapter 908, Laws of 1867, continued.

(1895) — Chapter 567, Section 8. (Amends Section 661, Consol. Act.)

"In all tenement-houses hereafter constructed and buildings hereafter converted to the purposes of a tenement-house each room must have a separate window opening into the outer air."

(1895) — Chapter 567, Section 8. (Amends Section 661, Consol. Act.)

"The superintendent of buildings is hereby empowered and directed to make rules and regulations not inconsistent with the requirements of this title, and which in addition to the requirements of this title shall be the conditions of approval for the plans and permits; these rules and regulations shall govern the arrangement and distribution of the uncovered area, size, lighting, location and arrangement of shafts, rooms, cellars and halls, and may be modified or changed from time to time by the superintendent of buildings."

*** (1897) — Chapter 378, Greater New York Charter, Section 1307.**

"Every house, building, or portion thereof in the city designed to be used, occupied, leased or rented, or which is used, occupied, leased or rented for a tenement or lodging-house, shall have in every room which is occupied as a sleeping-room and which does not communicate directly with the external air, a ventilating or transom window having an opening or area of three square feet, over the door leading into and connecting with the adjoining room, if such adjoining room communicates with the external air, and also a ventilating or transom window of the same opening or area communicating with the entry or hall of the house, or where this is, from the relative situation of the rooms, impracticable, such last-mentioned ventilating or transom window shall communicate with an adjoining room that itself communicates with the entry or hall."

*** (1897) — Chapter 378, Greater New York Charter, Section 1318. Provisions of Section 8, Chapter 567 of the Laws of 1895, continued.**

*** (1897) — Chapter 378, Greater New York Charter, Section 1319.**

"Every habitable room shall have at least one window connecting with the external air, or over the door a ventilator of perfect construction, connecting it with a room or hall which has a connection with the external air and so arranged as to produce a cross current of air. The total area of window or windows in every room communicating with the external air shall be at least one-tenth of the superficial area of every such room; and the top of one, at least, of such windows shall not be less than 7 feet 6 inches above the floor, and the upper half, at least, shall be made so as to open the full width."

*** (1900) — Regulations of the Department of Buildings.**

"Every habitable room except those opening on the main halls must have a ventilating or transom window so arranged as to produce a cross current of air."

*** Indicates the existing law in 1900.**

*** (1900) — Sanitary Code of the Department of Health, Section 23.**

"No person having the right and power to prevent the same shall knowingly cause or permit any person to sleep or remain in any cellar, or in any bathroom or in any room where there is a water-closet, or in any place dangerous or prejudicial to life or health, by reason of a want of ventilation or drainage, or by reason of the presence of any poisonous, noxious, or offensive substance, or otherwise."

WINDOWS IN HABITABLE ROOMS, SIZE OF. — The law of 1867, in addition to providing in detail the way in which living rooms should be ventilated, also prescribed what should be the mininum size of all windows, and what should be the minimum area of windows in every habitable room. This minimum area was to be at least one-tenth of the superficial area of the whole room, and the windows were to be so constructed that the top of one of them at least should not be less than 7½ feet above the floor, and the upper half of the window was to be so arranged that it would readily open the full width. This has been the law upon the subject, without change, from 1867 to 1897, and is the present law. There is, however, a supplementary requirement of the Building Department to the effect that no window in any living room in any new tenement house shall be less than 12 square feet in area, the measurements to be taken between the stop beads.

(1867) — Chapter 908, Section 14.

"The total area of window or windows in every room communicating with the external air shall be at least one-tenth of the superficial area of every such room; and the top of one at least, of such windows shall not be less than 7 feet and 6 inches above the floor, and the upper half, at least, shall be made so as to open the full width."

(1879) — Chapter 504, Section 2. — Continued.

(1882) — Chapter 410, Section 662. — Continued.

(1888) — Brooklyn — Chapter 583, Section 35. (Brooklyn Consol. Act.) Provisions of Law of 1867, reënacted.

(1895) — Brooklyn — Chapter 539, Section 1. (Amends Section 56, Brooklyn Consol. Act.) — Continued.

***(1897) — Chapter 378, Greater New York Charter, Section 1319. — Continued.**

*** (1900) — Regulations of the Department of Buildings.**

"The windows in every habitable room of every tenement house hereafter erected or altered must be at least 12 square feet area for living rooms, measured between the stop-beads. Said windows must be so constructed so as to be readily opened."

ROOMS, SIZE OF. — It is singular that there has been no provision of any kind upon this subject in any of the tenement laws adopted in this state. The only requirement is the regulation of the Department of Buildings

* Indicates the existing law in 1900.

that no habitable room shall have an air space of less than 600 cubic feet, although the Sanitary Code of the Board of Health has for a number of years required that there should be 400 cubic feet of air space for every adult.

*** (1900) — Regulations of Department of Buildings.**

"No habitable room shall have a smaller air space than 600 cubic feet."

ROOMS, ALCOVE ROOMS. — It has not been thought necessary in the law to distinguish alcove rooms from other rooms. A regulation of the Building Department, however, requires that alcove rooms must conform to the requirements of other rooms.

*** (1900) — Regulations of Department of Buildings.**

"Alcove rooms must conform to all the requirements of ordinary rooms."

ROOMS, HEIGHT OF. — The very first tenement house law prescribed a minimum of 8 feet for all habitable rooms, excepting rooms in the attic, which were required to be 8 feet in height throughout not less than one-half their area. These requirements have been the law upon this subject from 1867 to the present time. In addition to the provisions of the Charter to this effect, there is a supplementary provision contained in the regulations of the Building Department, to the effect that the finished height of all rooms must be 9 feet 4 inches, and that the height of ceilings for living rooms in cellars and basements must be at least 8 feet. From 1867 to 1874 the Superintendent of Buildings was given the power to determine the height of ceilings. In 1874, however, this power was taken away.

(1867) — Chapter 908, Section 14.

"In every tenement and lodging-house hereafter erected or converted every habitable room, except rooms in the attic, shall be in every part not less than eight feet in height from the floor to the ceiling."

(1879) — Chapter 504, Section 2. (Amends Section 14, Chapter 908, Laws of 1867.) — Continued.

(1882) — Chapter 410, Section 662. — Continued.

(1888) — Brooklyn — Chapter 583, Section 35. (Brooklyn Consol. Act.) Provisions of law of 1867, reënacted.

(1895) — Brooklyn — Chapter 539, Section 1. (Amends Section 56, Brooklyn Consol. Act.) — Continued.

*** (1897) — Chapter 378, Greater New York Charter, Section 1319.**

"In every such house hereafter erected or converted every habitable room, except rooms in the attic, shall be in every part not less than 8 feet in height from the floor to the ceiling."

*** (1900) — Regulations of the Department of Buildings.**

"The height of ceilings when finished for living rooms in cellars or basements must be eight feet; on all other floors 9 feet 4 inches."

*** Indicates the existing law in 1900.**

ROOMS IN ATTIC.

(1867) — Chapter 908, Section 14.

"Every habitable room in the attic of any tenement and lodging-house hereafter erected or converted shall be at least eight feet in height from the floor to the ceiling, throughout not less than one-half the area of such room."

(1879) — Chapter 504, Section 2. (Amends Section 14, Chapter 908, Laws of 1867.) — Continued.

(1882) — Chapter 410, Section 662. — Continued.

(1888) — Brooklyn — Chapter 583, Section 35. (Brooklyn Consol. Act.) Provisions of Law of 1867, reënacted.

(1895) — Brooklyn — Chapter 539, Section 1. (Provisions of Section 56 of Brooklyn Consol. Act, continued.)

*** (1897) — Chapter 378, Greater New York Charter, Section 1319.**

"Every habitable room in the attic of any such building shall be at least 8 feet in height from the floor to the ceiling, throughout not less than one-half the area of such room."

(1867) — Chapter 939, Section 10.

"In all tenement houses that shall hereafter be erected in said city the Superintendent of Buildings shall have power in determining the height of ceilings, which shall not be less than 8 feet."

(1868) — Chapter 634, Section 2. — Continued.

(1871) — Chapter 625, Section 28. — Continued; clause "which shall not be less than 8 feet" stricken out.

(1874) — Chapter 547, Section 7. — Repealed.

ROOMS, VENTILATION OF — CHIMNEYS TO BE PROVIDED. — The first Tenement Act, passed in 1867, required that in every new tenement house there should be adequate chimneys running through every floor, with an open fireplace or grate or place for a stove, properly connected with the chimney, for each set of apartments. This has remained the law since that time and is the law at the present day.

(1867) — Chapter 908, Section 15.

"Every tenement and lodging-house hereafter erected or converted, shall have adequate chimneys running through every floor, with an open fireplace or grate, or place for a stove, properly connected with one of said chimneys, for every family and set of apartments."

(1882) — Chapter 410, Section 663. — Continued.

(1887) — Chapter 84, Section 11. — Continued.

(1888) — Brooklyn — Chapter 583, Section 36. (Brooklyn Consol. Act.) Provisions of law of 1867, reënacted.

* Indicates the existing law in 1900.

(1890) — Chapter 486, Section 1. — Continued.

(1891) — Chapter 39, Section 1. — Continued.

(1895) — Brooklyn — Chapter 539, Section 1. (Amends Section 57, Brooklyn Consol. Act.)

Provisions of law of 1867 continued, with the exception that these provisions only apply to houses erected or converted after June 1, 1895, instead of to tenement-houses erected or converted after 1867.

(1895) — Chapter 567, Section 9. (Amends Section 663, Consol. Act.) — Continued.

*** (1897) — Chapter 378, Greater New York Charter, Section 1320.**

"Every such house erected after May 14th, 1867, or converted, shall have an adequate chimney for a stove, properly connected with one of said chimneys for every family set of apartments."

HALLS, LIGHTING AND VENTILATION OF. — The evils of the dark, unventilated hallways have been recognized very clearly for over thirty years, and the first law enacted in reference to tenement houses sought to remedy these evils. The law provided that the halls on each floor of every tenement house thereafter erected should open directly to the external air with suitable windows, and should have no room or other obstruction *at the end.* A clause, however, was added at the end of the law to the effect that this must be done "unless sufficient light or ventilation was otherwise provided for in said halls in a manner approved by the Board of Health." This has remained the law from 1867 to the present time and is the law at the present day. In addition to this requirement, a further provision was added in 1887 to the effect that if a tenement house was occupied by more than two families on a floor, and the halls did not open directly to the external air with suitable windows, without a room or other obstruction at the end, it should not be used, occupied, leased, or rented. This law has been continued since 1887 and is the present law upon this subject, and is to be found in the Greater New York Charter, in Section 1304. In addition to these provisions, in 1895, the Superintendent of Buildings was given power to make further rules and regulations not inconsistent with existing laws, these rules and regulations to govern the size, lighting, location, and arrangement of halls; and he was authorized to change or modify such regulations from time to time. In the same year an important amendment was added to the law upon this subject, requiring that in all tenement houses, whether old or new, where there was no window in the hallway opening on the outer air, a light should be kept burning by the owner or lessee of the house, in the hallway of every floor, between the hours of 8 A.M. and 10 P.M., unless the hallway should be otherwise sufficiently lighted. It was also added that in every tenement house in the city, the owner or lessee should keep a light burning in the hallway upon every floor at night, from sunset until 10 P.M. These additional provisions of the law of 1895 have been reënacted in the Charter and are the present law upon the subject, with the further supplementary regulations of the Department of Buildings, providing that the main hallway in all

*** Indicates the existing law in 1900.**

new tenement houses must be lighted and ventilated by a skylight provided with louvres or with a ridge ventilator; and that, where there are no windows to the outer air, or fan-lights or partition windows to afford sufficient light to the halls, the stair-well (the open space between the stairs and the corridor or hall) shall be 9 inches wide, in buildings not over three stories high, and 12 inches wide in buildings over three stories; also private halls were to be lighted by fan-lights or partition windows. In addition to these provisions as to the lighting and ventilation of halls, there has been a provision since 1867 requiring that in every building used as a tenement house there shall be in the roof at the top of the hall an adequate and proper ventilator of a form to be approved by the city officials charged with the enforcement of the building and health laws.

(1867) — Chapter 908, Section 15.

"The halls on each floor shall open directly to the external air with suitable windows, and shall have no room or other obstruction at the end, unless sufficient light or ventilation is otherwise provided for said halls, in a manner approved by the Metropolitan Board of Health."

(1882) — Chapter 410, Section 663. — Continued.

(1887) — Chapter 84, Section 5. (Amends Section 649, Consol. Act.)

"No house, building, or portion thereof in the city of New York, shall be used, occupied, leased or rented for a tenement or lodging-house unless the same conforms in its construction and appurtenances to the requirements of this title; and if occupied by more than one family on a floor, and if the halls do not open directly to the external air, with suitable windows, without a room or other obstruction at the end, it shall not be used, occupied, leased or rented, unless sufficient light and ventilation is otherwise provided for in said halls."

(1887) — Chapter 84, Section 11. (Amends Section 663, Consol. Act.)

"Every tenement house erected after May 7th, 1887, or converted shall have the halls on each floor open directly to the external air, with suitable windows, and shall have no room or other obstruction at the end, unless sufficient light or ventilation is otherwise provided for in said halls in a manner approved by the board of health."

(1888) — Brooklyn — Chapter 583, Section 36. (Brooklyn Consol. Act.) Provisions of Law of 1867, reënacted.

(1890) — Chapter 486, Section 1. (Provisions of Chapter 84, Section 11, of the Laws of 1887, continued.)

(1891) — Chapter 39, Section 1. — Continued.

(1895) — Brooklyn — Chapter 539, Section 1. (Provisions of Consol. Act, continued.)

(1895) — Chapter 567, Section 8. (Amends Section 661, Consol. Act.)

"The superintendent of buildings is hereby empowered and directed to make rules and regulations not inconsistent with the requirements of this title, and which in addition to the requirements of this title shall be the conditions of approval for the plans and permits; these rules and regulations shall govern the arrangement and distribution of the uncovered area, size, lighting, location and arrangement of shafts, rooms, cellars and halls, and may be modified or changed from time to time by the superintendent of buildings."

(1895) — Chapter 567, Section 9. (Amends Section 663, Consol. Act.)

Provisions of Section 11, Chapter 84 of the Laws of 1887, continued, with the change: Substitute for the words "board of health" at the end, the words "superintendent of buildings." Also, the following additional section is added: "The owner or lessee of every tenement or lodging-house in the city of New York shall keep a light burning in the hallway upon each floor of said house from sunset until 10 P.M. throughout the year. In every tenement-house in the said city in which there is a hallway or hallways with no window opening from such hallway outside of said house, a light shall be maintained by said owner or lessee in each such hallway between the hours of 8 A.M. and 10 P.M. of each day unless said hallways shall be otherwise sufficiently lighted. The fire department of the city of New York is hereby vested with authority to prescribe reasonable regulations concerning such precautions as may be necessary to prevent danger from fire arising from such lights."

*** (1897) — Chapter 378, Greater New York Charter, Section 1304.**

Provisions of Section 5, Chapter 84 of the Laws of 1887, continued, but somewhat changed in form, amended as follows: "If occupied by more than one family on a floor; and if the halls do not open directly to the external air, with suitable windows, without a room or other obstruction at the end, it shall not be used, occupied, leased or rented, unless sufficient light and ventilation is otherwise provided for in said halls, approved so far as relates to construction by the department of buildings, and if the building be completed, approved so far as relates to health and sanitary conditions, by the board of health."

*** (1897) — Chapter 378, Greater New York Charter, Section 1320. (Provisions of Section 9, Chapter 567, of the Laws of 1895, continued.)**

*** (1897) — Chapter 378, Greater New York Charter, Section 1318.**

Provisions of Section 8, Chapter 567 of the Laws of 1895, continued, except that the words "department of buildings" are substituted for the words "superintendent of buildings"; and that the Superintendent of Buildings is no longer empowered to modify such regulations from time to time.

*** (1900) — Regulations of the Department of Buildings.**

"The main hall must be lighted and ventilated by a skylight provided with louvres or ridge ventilator. Where there are no windows to the outer air, fanlights or partition windows to afford sufficient light to the halls, the stairwell must be 9 inches wide for buildings three stories or less, and 12 inches for buildings more than three stories in height. Private halls must be lighted by fanlights, sash doors or partition windows."

(1867) — Chapter 908, Section 2.

"Every house, building, or portion thereof in the cities of New York

* Indicates the existing law in 1900.

and Brooklyn, designed to be used, occupied, leased or rented, or which is used, occupied, leased or rented for a tenement or lodging-house, shall have in the roof at the top of the hall, an adequate and proper ventilator, of a form approved in New York by the inspector of buildings, and in Brooklyn by the assistant sanitary superintendent of the Metropolitan board of health."

(1882) — Chapter 410, Section 650. — Continued.

(1888) — Brooklyn — Chapter 583, Section 25. — Continued.

(1895) — Brooklyn — Chapter 539, Section 1. Above Provisions continued.

(1895) — Chapter 567, Section 8. (Amends Section 661, Consol. Act.)

"The superintendent of buildings is hereby empowered and directed to make rules and regulations not inconsistent with the requirements of this title, and which in addition to the requirements of this title shall be the conditions of approval for the plans and permits; these rules and regulations shall govern the arrangement and distribution of the uncovered area, size, lighting, location and arrangement of shafts, rooms, cellars and halls, and may be modified or changed from time to time by the superintendent of buildings."

*** (1897) — Chapter 378, Greater New York Charter, Section 1307.**

"Every such house or building shall have in the roof, at the top of the hall, an adequate and proper ventilator of a form approved by the department of buildings."

HEIGHT OF TENEMENT HOUSES, LIMITATION OF. — The increasing number of tall tenement houses that have been erected in recent years have shut off a very large portion of the light and air available for the rooms. No attempt, however, was made to limit the height of tenement houses from this point of view until 1885, when it was required that the height of all dwelling houses for more than one family thereafter erected should be regulated in proportion to the width of the streets and avenues upon which they fronted. This height was not to exceed 70 feet, where the streets and avenues were not more than 60 feet wide, and was limited to 80 feet where the streets and avenues were over 60 feet in width. In 1897 a further requirement upon this subject was enacted, applying only to fireproof apartment houses, and also only where there were one or more power passenger elevators used in the building. The height of buildings of this kind was by this act regulated in proportion to the width of the widest street or avenue upon which they fronted; where the street or avenue was over 79 feet wide, then the buildings could be erected to a height as great as 150 feet; where the streets or avenues were less than 80 feet, such buildings were limited to 100 feet in height. The only other provision upon this subject is to be found in the Building Code, a local ordinance, adopted in 1899. This provides that tenement houses may be erected to a height of 150 feet if fireproof and if situated upon a street over 79 feet wide, and where such buildings are situated on streets 80 feet or less in width, then the height is limited to 125 feet.

* Indicates the existing law in 1900.

(1885) — Chapter 454.

"The height of all dwelling-houses used or intended to be used as dwellings for more than one family, and hereafter to be erected in the city of New York, shall be regulated in proportion to the width of the streets and avenues upon which they front. Such height measured from the sidewalk line and taken in all cases through the centre of the facade of the house to be erected, including attics, cornices and mansards shall not exceed 70 feet upon all streets and avenues not exceeding 60 feet in width, and 80 feet upon all streets and avenues exceeding 60 feet in width."

(1897) — Chapter 321.

"The height of all fireproof dwelling-houses and of all fireproof houses containing one or more power passenger elevators used or intended to be used as dwellings for more than one family now or hereafter constructed or completed, shall be regulated in proportion to the width of the widest street and avenue upon which they abut, and such height measured from the sidewalk line and taken in all cases through the centre of the facade of the house to be erected, including attics, cornices and mansards, shall not exceed 150 feet upon all streets and avenues exceeding 79 feet in width, and 100 feet upon all streets and avenues not exceeding 79 feet in width. All buildings mentioned in the first section of this act, provided the same have a frontage exceeding 45 feet and exceeding 137 feet in height, shall have two separate fireproof stairways leading from the ground floor to the roof, one of which shall be remote from elevator shafts."

* **(1899) — The Building Code — (An ordinance adopted December 20, 1899.) Section 53.**

"Fireproof apartment-houses, or tenement-houses, if constructed entirely in accordance with the requirements of section 105 of this Code, for fireproof construction may be erected to a height not to exceed 150 feet, but not more than 12 stories in height upon all streets and avenues exceeding 79 feet in width, and 125 feet, but not more than 10 stories in height upon all streets and avenues not exceeding 79 feet in width, but any such building when exceeding 100 feet in height shall be not less than 40 feet in width. If any such building shall have a frontage exceeding 40 feet, and exceeds 85 feet in height, it shall have at least two separate fireproof stairways accessible from each apartment, leading from the ground floor to the roof, one of which shall be remote from elevator shafts."

SANITARY OR HEALTH PROVISIONS

CELLARS AND BASEMENTS — CONDITIONS OF OCCUPANCY. — The greatest evil existing in tenement houses when the first tenement house law was enacted, in 1867, was the occupancy of cellars for living purposes. Most of these cellars were totally unfit for habitation, they were dark, located beneath the sidewalk in many cases, were generally damp and often flooded with water. The first tenement house law, therefore, naturally set down in very great detail the conditions under which cellars or basement rooms might be occupied for living purposes.

* Indicates the existing law in 1900.

In the first place, it was provided that no cellar not previously occupied as a dwelling should be thereafter occupied for such purpose without a permit from the Board of Health; and also no cellar of any kind was to be occupied as a dwelling without a permit from the Health Department, unless all of the following conditions were complied with: —

1. All rooms had to be at least 7 feet high in every part.

2. The ceiling of every such room had to be at least 1 foot higher than the surface of the street or ground adjoining.

3. There was required to be outside of and adjoining the room an open space extending along its entire front; such space was to be not less than 2 feet 6 inches wide in every part; the bottom of it was to be 6 inches below the level of the floor of the room; and the space was to be well and effectually drained by a drain, the top of which should be at least 1 foot below the level of the floor of the room.

4. There was required to be a clear air space of at least 1 foot below the floor of the room except where the floor was cemented.

5. There was required to be appurtenant to this room the use of a water-closet or privy kept and provided as required in other sections of the act.

6. The room was required to have a window opening on the outer air of at least 9 square feet in size, clear of the sash frame; this window was to have a glazed sash, at least $4\frac{1}{2}$ square feet of which was to be made so as to open for purposes of ventilation. But where there was an inner room which was part of the set of apartments containing the front room, it was deemed a sufficient compliance with the provisions of the statute, if the back or inner room was connected with the front room by a door, and also by a proper ventilating or transom window; and also, where it was practicable, connected by a proper ventilating or transom window with some hall or passage communicating with the outer air.

7. It was also required that in the area adjoining the room, there should be steps necessary for access to the cellar; but these steps were not to be so placed as to be across or opposite the windows, and there was to be between every part of the steps and the external wall of the room a clear space of at least 6 inches; also the rise of the steps was to be open; it was also permitted to place other steps over the area in front of the room, if these steps were not so placed as to be across or opposite the windows.

It was further provided in this law that after July 1, 1868, no cellar or underground room should be used as a place of sleeping without a *written* permit from the Board of Health. This has remained the law upon this subject until 1897, and it is practically the law at the present time. An important change, however, was made in this law in 1895, when the cellar ceilings of living rooms were required to be 2 feet above the level of the adjoining ground instead of 1 foot. This is also one of the provisions of the Sanitary Code of the Health Department. The present law upon this subject is the law of 1867, with this change, and with a further supplementary regulation of the Building Department that the height of ceilings in cellars or basement living rooms shall be at least 8 feet.

(1867) — Chapter 908, Section 6.

"From and after the 1st day of July, 1867, it shall not be lawful, without a permit from the Metropolitan Board of Health, to let, or occupy, or suffer to be occupied separately as a dwelling, any vault, cellar, or underground room built or rebuilt after said date or which shall not have been so let or occupied before said date. And from and after July 1, 1867, it shall not be lawful without such permit to let or continue to be let, or to occupy, or to suffer to be occupied separately as a dwelling any vault, cellar, or underground room whatsoever, unless the same be in every part thereof at least seven feet in height, measured from the floor to the ceiling thereof, nor unless the same be for at least one foot of its height above the surface of the street or ground adjoining or nearest to the same, nor unless there be outside of and adjoining the said vault, cellar, or room, and extending along the entire frontage thereof, and upwards from six inches below the level of the floor thereof, up to the surface of the said street or ground an open space of at least two feet and six inches wide in every part, nor unless the same be well and effectually drained by means of a drain, the uppermost part of which is one foot, at least, below the level of the floor of such vault, cellar, or room, nor unless there is a clear space of not less than one foot below the level of the floor, except where the same is cemented, nor unless there be appurtenant to such vault, cellar or room, the use of a water-closet or privy kept and provided as in this act required; nor unless the same have an external window opening of at least nine superficial feet clear of the sash frame, in which window opening there shall be fitted a frame filled in with glazed sashes, at least four and a half superficial feet of which shall be made so as to open for the purpose of ventilation. Provided, however, that in the case of an inner or back vault, cellar, or room, let or occupied along with a front vault, cellar, or room, as part of the same letting or occupation, it shall be a sufficient compliance with the provisions of this act if the front room is provided with a window as hereinbefore provided, and if the said back vault, cellar, or room, is connected with the said front vault, cellar, or room by a door, and also by a proper ventilating or transom window, and, where practicable, also connected by a proper ventilating or transom window, or by some hall or passage communicating with the external air. Provided always that in any area adjoining a vault, cellar, or underground room there may be steps necessary for access to such vault, cellar, or room, if the same be so placed as not to be over, across or opposite to the said external window, and so as to allow between every part of such steps and the external wall of such vault, cellar, or room, a clear space of six inches at least, and if the rise of said steps is open; and provided further that over or across any such area there may be steps necessary for access to any building above the vault, cellar, or room to which such area adjoins if the same be so placed as not to be over, across or opposite to any such external window."

(1867) — Chapter 908, Section 7.

"From and after the 1st day of July, 1868, no vault, cellar, or underground room shall be so occupied as a place of lodging or sleeping, except the same shall be approved in writing, and a permit given therefor by the Metropolitan board of health."

(1882) — Chapter 410, Sections 654, 655. — Continued.

(1888) — Brooklyn — Chapter 583, Sections 28 and 29. (Brooklyn Consol. Act.) Provisions of law of 1867, reënacted.

(1895) — Chapter 567, Section 4. (Amends Section 654, Consol. Act.)

"It shall not be lawful without a permit from the superintendent of buildings to construct, during the erection of a tenement or lodging-house, nor after the completion of such tenement or lodging-house, any room or rooms in any basement or cellar to be occupied wholly or in part as a dwelling, nor shall it be lawful without a permit from the board of health to let or occupy, or suffer to be occupied separately as a dwelling, any vault, cellar or underground room built or rebuilt after July 1, 1867, or which shall not have been so let or occupied before said date. It shall not be lawful, without such permit, to let or continue to be let, or to occupy or suffer to be occupied separately as a dwelling, any vault, cellar, basement, or room wholly or in part underground, unless the same be in every part thereof at least seven feet in height, measured from the floor to the ceiling thereof, nor unless the same be for at least two feet of its height above the surface of the street or ground adjoining or nearest to the same, nor unless there be outside of and adjoining the said vault, cellar, room, or basement, and extending along the entire frontage thereof, and upwards from six inches below the level of the floor thereof, up to the surface of the said street or ground an open space of at least two feet and six inches wide in every part, nor unless the same be well and effectually drained by means of a drain, the uppermost part of which is one foot at least below the level of the floor of such vault, cellar, or room, nor unless there is a clear space of not less than one foot below the level of the floor, except where the same is cemented, nor unless there be appurtenant to such vault, cellar, or room, the use of a water-closet or privy kept and provided as in this title required; nor unless the same have an external window opening of at least nine superficial feet clear of the sash frame, in which window opening there shall be fitted a frame filled in with glazed sashes, at least 4½ superficial feet of which shall be made so as to open for the purpose of ventilation. Provided, however, that in the case of an inner or back vault, cellar, or room, let or occupied along with a front vault, cellar or room, as part of the same letting or occupation, it shall be a sufficient compliance with the provisions of this section if the front room is provided with a window as hereinbefore provided, and if the said back vault, cellar or room is connected with the front vault, cellar or room, by a door, and also by a proper ventilating or transom window, and, where practicable, also connected by a proper ventilating or transom window, or by some hall or passage communicating with the external air. Provided always that in any area adjoining a vault, cellar or underground room or basement, there may be steps necessary for access to such vault, cellar or room, if the same be so placed as not to be over, across or opposite to the said external window, and so as to allow between every part of such steps and the external wall of such vault, cellar or room, a clear space of six inches at least, and if the rise of said steps is open; and provided further that over or across any such area there may be steps necessary for access to any building above the vault, cellar or room to which such area adjoins, if the same be so placed as not to be over, across or opposite to any such external window."

*** (1897) — Chapter 378, Greater New York Charter, Section 1309. — Continued.**

* Indicates the existing law in 1900.

*** (1900) — Regulations of the Department of Buildings.**

"The height of ceilings when finished for living rooms in cellars or basements, must be 8 feet; on all other floors 9 feet 4 inches."

*** (1900) — Sanitary Code of the Department of Health, Section 22.**

"Nor shall any such person rent, let, hire out, or allow, having power to prevent the same, to be used as or for a place of sleeping or residence, any portion or apartment of any building, which apartment or portion has not at least 2 feet of its height and space above the level of every part of the sidewalk and curbstone of any adjacent street, nor of which the floor is damp by reason of water from the ground, or which is impregnated or penetrated by any offensive gas, smell or exhalation prejudicial to health. But this section shall not prevent the leasing, renting, or occupancy of cellars or rooms less elevated than aforesaid, and as a part of any building rented or let, when they are not let or intended to be occupied or used by any person as a sleeping apartment, or as a principal or sole dwelling apartment."

Section 23. "No person having the right and power to prevent the same shall knowingly cause or permit any person to sleep or remain in any cellar, or in any bathroom, or in any room where there is a water-closet, or in any place dangerous or prejudicial to life or health, by reason of a want of ventilation or drainage, or by reason of the presence of any poisonous, noxious or offensive substance, or otherwise."

*** (1897) — Chapter 378, Greater New York Charter, Section 1310.**

"No vault, cellar or underground room shall be occupied as a place of lodging or sleeping except the same shall be approved in writing, and a permit given therefor by the board of health."

CELLARS — REGULATIONS FOR. — The Board of Health since 1867 has been given power to make regulations in reference to cellars which should not conflict with the existing laws upon the subject, and similar powers were granted to the Commissioner of Buildings in reference to new tenement houses in the Act of 1895.

(1867) — Chapter 908, Section 18.

"The Metropolitan Board of Health shall have authority to make other regulations as to cellars consistent with the foregoing where it shall be satisfied that such regulations will secure equally well the health of the occupants."

(1882) — Chapter 410, Section 667. — Continued.

(1888) — Brooklyn — Chapter 583, Section 39. (Brooklyn Consol. Act.) Provisions of Law of 1867, reënacted.

(1892) — Chapter 329, Section 1. (Amends Section 667, Consol. Act.)

"The board of health shall have authority, within present provisions of law to make other regulations than the foregoing in special cases as to cellars when it shall be satisfied that such regulations will secure equally well the health of the occupants and the public health, provided, however,

* Indicates the existing law in 1900.

that in all such cases any modifications made by such regulations, shall be in accordance with the conditions of a permit in writing issued by the said board of health."

(1895) — Chapter 567, Section 8. (Amends Section 661, Consol. Act.)

"The superintendent of buildings is hereby empowered and directed to make rules and regulations not inconsistent with the requirements of this title and which, in addition to the requirements of this title, shall be the conditions of approval for the plans and permits; these rules and regulations shall govern the arrangement and distribution of the uncovered area, size, lighting, location and arrangement of shafts, rooms, cellars and halls, and may be modified or changed from time to time by the superintendent of buildings."

(1895) — Chapter 567, Section 12. (Amends Section 667, Consol. Act.)

"The board of health shall have authority to make other regulations as to cellars and as to ventilation in completed buildings, consistent with the foregoing, where it shall be satisfied that such regulations will secure equally well the health of the occupants."

*** (1897) — Chapter 378, Greater New York Charter, Section 1323. — Continued.**

CELLAR FLOORS. — From the very first enactment of any legislation upon the subject of tenement houses, there has been a provision in reference to preventing dampness in cellars, the law of 1867 requiring that every tenement house thereafter erected or converted should have the cellar floor properly cemented so as to be water-tight. This remained the law upon this subject until 1887, when the law was somewhat amplified and considerably strengthened, the new law requiring that every tenement house, whether old or new, should have the floor of the cellar made water-tight, and when the house was located over filled-in ground or ground on which water lies, the cellar floor was to be effectually covered so as to prevent evaporation or dampness. In addition, there was a further provision that the Board of Health should see to it that the cellars of all existing houses should be made to conform to all of these requirements before June 1, 1890. This has been the law upon this subject since that date until the present time, with the exception that, in 1890, the time, before which the Board of Health was required to have all such cellar floors made water-tight was extended from 1890 to 1892.

(1867) — Chapter 908, Section 15.

"Every tenement-house hereafter erected or converted shall have the floor of the cellar properly cemented so as to be water-tight."

(1882) — Chapter 410, Section 663. — Continued.

(1887) — Chapter 84, Section 11. (Amends Section 663, Consol. Act.)

"Every tenement house shall have the floor of the cellar made water-tight; and when the house is located over filled-in ground, or over marshy ground, or ground on which water lies, the cellar floor shall be covered so

* Indicates the existing law in 1900.

as to effectually prevent evaporation or dampness. It shall be the duty of the board of health (to see) that the cellars of all tenement houses are so made or altered as to comply with this section before January 1, 1890."

(1888) — Brooklyn — Chapter 583, Section 36. (Brooklyn Consol. Act.) Provisions of Law of 1867, reënacted.

(1890) — Chapter 486, Section 1. (Provisions of Chapter 84, of the laws of 1887, continued with the following amendment: Instead of the last word "1890" insert the word "1892.")

(1891) — Chapter 39, Section 1. (Provisions of Chapter 486, of the Laws of 1890, continued.)

(1892) — Chapter 275, Section 16. (Amends Section 480, Consol. Act.)

"The floor of the cellar or lowest story in every tenement-house, apartment-house and lodging-house hereafter erected shall be concreted with suitable materials not less than three inches thick."

(1895) — Brooklyn — Chapter 539, Section 1. (Amends Section 57, Brooklyn Consol. Act.)

Provisions of law of 1867 reënacted, but made only to apply to tenement houses erected or converted after June 1, 1895.

(1895) — Chapter 567, Section 9. (Amends Section 663, Consol. Act.)

Provisions of Section 11, Chapter 84 of the Laws of 1887, continued.

* **(1897) — Chapter 378, Greater New York Charter, Section 1320.**

Continued with the following change: The words at the end, "before January 1, 1890," have been omitted.

* **(1899) — The Building Code — (An ordinance adopted December 20, 1899.) Section 57.**

"The floor of the cellar or lowest story in every dwelling-house, apartment-house, tenement-house and lodging-house hereafter erected, shall be concreted not less than four inches thick."

CELLAR CEILINGS, PLASTERING OF. — Before 1887 there was no requirement whatsoever upon this subject. In that year it was provided that every tenement house should have the cellar ceiling plastered. This has practically been the law since 1887, and is the present law upon this subject.

(1887) — Chapter 84, Section 11. (Amends Section 663, Consol. Act.)

"Every tenement-house shall have the cellar ceiling plastered."

(1890) — Chapter 486, Section 1. (Amends Section 663, Consol. Act.)

"Every tenement-house shall have the cellar ceiling plastered, or sealed with tongued and grooved boards not less than three-quarters of an inch in thickness, lined with builders' lining paper."

* Indicates the existing law in 1900.

(1891) — Chapter 39, Section 1. (Amends Section 663, Consol. Act.)

"Every tenement-house shall have the cellar ceiling plastered, or filled in with deafening between the beams, or sealed with tongued and grooved boards not less than three-quarters of an inch in thickness, lined with builders' lining paper."

(1895) — Chapter 567, Section 9. (Amends Section 665, Consol. Act.)

"Every tenement-house shall have the cellar ceiling plastered."

***(1897) — Chapter 378, Greater New York Charter, Section 1320. — Continued.**

WATER SUPPLY. — Since the earliest days it has been recognized that where a large number of persons live in one building it is of paramount importance to have a proper supply of water for their use. The first Tenement House Act, that of 1867, provided that every tenement house thereafter erected should have water furnished at one or more places either in the house or in the yard, so that the same might be adequate and reasonably convenient for the use of the occupants. In 1887 an important amendment was made in this law, requiring that instead of water being furnished in the yard, it should be supplied at one or more places *on each floor* of every tenement house erected or converted after May 14, 1867; and placed the responsibility of furnishing such water upon the owner of the building, and required that *all* tenement houses, whether old or new, should be provided with a similar supply of water by the owners, whenever the Board of Health should so direct. A clause was added to the effect that a failure in the general supply of city water should not be construed as being a failure to comply with the law, on the part of the owner where he had provided suitable appliances to receive and distribute such water. The Board of Health was also directed to see to it that all tenement houses in the city should be supplied with water in this manner before January 1, 1889. In 1892 the Board of Health was given additional powers authorizing them to make other regulations in special cases as to the supply of water above the first floor in any tenement house. The law of 1887 is practically the law of the present day, having been reënacted in the Greater New York Charter, with the exception that the Charter has removed the time limit within which the Board of Health is required to see that all tenement houses are supplied with water and with proper fixtures. In addition to these provisions of the Charter there is a regulation of the Department of Buildings which requires, that in every new tenement house connected with a public sewer, running water must be provided over a sink in each set of apartments.

(1867) — Chapter 908, Section 15.

"Every tenement and lodging-house hereafter erected or converted shall have Croton, Ridgewood, or other water furnished at one or more places in such house, or in the yard thereof, so that the same may be adequate and reasonably convenient for the use of the occupants thereof."

* Indicates the existing law in 1900.

(1882) — Chapter 410, Section 663. — Continued; the word "Ridgewood" stricken out.

(1887) — Chapter 84, Section 11. (Amends Section 663, Consol. Act.)

"Every tenement-house erected or converted after May 14, 1867, shall have Croton or other water furnished in sufficient quantity at one or more places on *each floor*, occupied, or intended to be occupied by one or more families; and all tenement-houses shall be provided with a like supply of water by the owners thereof, whenever they shall be directed so to do by the board of health. But a failure in the general supply of water by the city authorities shall not be construed to be a failure on the part of such owner, provided that proper and suitable appliances to receive and distribute such water are placed in said house. Provided that the board of health shall see to it that all tenement-houses are so supplied before January 1, 1889."

(1888) — Brooklyn — Chapter 583, Section 36. (Brooklyn Consol. Act.) Provisions of Law of 1867, reënacted.

(1890) — Chapter 486, Section 1. — Continued.

(1891) — Chapter 39, Section 1. — Continued.

(1892) — Chapter 329, Section 1.

"The board of health shall have authority, within present provisions of law to make other regulations than the foregoing in special cases as to the supply of water above the first floor in any house, and the providing of fixtures therefor, when it shall be satisfied that such regulations will secure equally well the health of the occupants and the public health, provided, however, that in all such cases any modifications made by such regulations shall be in accordance with the conditions of a permit in writing issued by the said board of health."

(1895) — Brooklyn — Chapter 539, Section 1. (Amends Section 57, Brooklyn Consol. Act.)

"Every tenement and lodging-house erected or converted after June 1, 1895, shall have Ridgewood or other water furnished at one or more places in such house, or in the yard thereof, as the health commissioner may designate, so that the same may be adequate and reasonably convenient for the use of the occupants thereof."

(1895) — Chapter 567, Section 9. (Amends Section 663, Consol. Act.) Provisions of Section 11, Chapter 84 of the Laws of 1837, continued.

*** (1897) — Chapter 378, Greater New York Charter, Section 1320.**

Provisions of the law of 1887, as amended by the law of 1895, continued with slight verbal changes, and at the end instead of the last sentence beginning with "provided that," insert the following, "The board of health shall require all tenement-houses to be so supplied."

*** (1900) — Regulations of the Department of Buildings.**

"In every tenement-house, connected with any public sewer running water must be provided over a sink in each set of apartments."

* Indicates the existing law in 1900.

ROOFS TO BE KEPT IN REPAIR. — It was provided in 1867 that the roofs of all tenement houses should be kept in good repair so as not to leak, and all rain water was required to be drained or conveyed from roofs in such a way as to prevent its dripping on the ground or causing dampness in the walls, yard, or area. This has been the law since that time and is the present law upon this subject.

(1867) — Chapter 908, Section 4.

"The roof of every tenement and lodging-house in the cities of New York and Brooklyn, shall be kept in good repair, and so as not to leak, and all rain water shall be so drained or conveyed therefrom as to prevent its dripping on to the ground, or causing dampness in the walls, yard or areas."

(1882) — Chapter 410, Section 652. — Continued.

(1888) — Brooklyn — Chapter 583, Section 26. (Brooklyn Consol. Act.) — Continued.

*** (1897) — Chapter 378, Greater New York Charter, Section 1306. — Continued.**

CLEANLINESS OF BUILDINGS. — Before the passage of any tenement house law, it was required by the Health Act of 1866 that every owner and person interested in any building should keep the same and all parts of it in a clean condition, so that it should not be dangerous or prejudicial to life or health. The Tenement House Act of 1867 reënacted these provisions, but more specifically in their relation to tenement houses. This act provides that every tenement or lodging house and every part of the same shall be kept clean and free from any accumulation of dirt or filth or garbage, or other matter, in the building, or in the yard, or alley leading to it. The owner of a tenement house was further required to thoroughly cleanse all the rooms and halls, stairs, floors, and windows, as well as the doors, walls, ceilings, privies, cesspools, and drains of the house as often as the Board of Health might require. This is the law at the present day, having been reënacted in the Greater New York Charter.

(1866) — Chapter 74, Section 14.

"And it is hereby declared to be the duty of every owner and part owner and person interested, and of every lessee, tenant and occupant of, or in any place, water, ground, room, stall, apartment, building, erection, vessel, vehicle, matter and thing in said district, and of every person conducting or interested in business therein or thereat, and of every person who has undertaken to clean any place, ground or street therein, and of every person, public officer and board having charge of any ground, place, building or erection therein, to keep, place, and preserve the same and every part, and the sewerage, drainage and ventilation thereof, in such condition, and to conduct the same in such manner that it shall not be dangerous or prejudicial to life or health."

* Indicates the existing law in 1900.

(1867) — Chapter 908, Section 9.

"Every tenement or lodging-house, and every part thereof, shall be kept clean and free from any accumulation of dirt, filth, garbage or other matter in or on the same, or in the yard, court, passage, area or alley connected with or belonging to the same. The owner or keeper of any lodging-house, and the owner or lessee of any tenement-house or part thereof, shall thoroughly cleanse all the rooms, passages, stairs, floors, windows, doors, walls, ceilings, privies, cesspools and drains thereof of the house or part of the house of which he is the owner or lessee, to the satisfaction of the Metropolitan board of health, so often as shall be required by or in accordance with any regulation or ordinance of said board."

(1882) — Chapter 410, Section 657. — Continued.

(1887) — Chapter 84, Section 7. — Continued.

(1888) — Brooklyn — Chapter 583, Section 31. (Brooklyn Consol. Act.) Provisions of Law of 1867, reënacted.

(1895) — Chapter 567, Section 6. — Continued.

*** (1897) — Chapter 378, Greater New York Charter, Section 1310. — Continued.**

And the following additional clause inserted after the word "any" (in the last line), "Order of the board of health and any."

WHITEWASHING OF WALLS AND CEILINGS. — Since 1867 the law has required that the owner of every tenement house shall whitewash the walls and ceilings twice a year. The earlier laws stated that this work should be done in the months of April and October, but the later enactments have left the time to the discretion of the Board of Health, and also require that it be done once a year instead of twice.

(1867) — Chapter 908, Section 9.

"The owner shall well and sufficiently to the satisfaction of the board of health whitewash the walls and ceilings of every tenement-house twice at least in every year, and in the months of April and October, unless the said board shall otherwise direct."

(1882) — Chapter 410, Section 657. — Continued.

(1887) — Chapter 84, Section 7. — Continued.

(1888) — Brooklyn — Chapter 583, Section 31. (Brooklyn Consol. Act.) Provisions of Law of 1867, reënacted.

(1895) — Chapter 567, Section 6. — Continued.

*** (1897) — Chapter 378, Greater New York Charter, Section 1310.**

"The owner or lessee of any tenement-house or part thereof, shall well and sufficiently to the satisfaction of the health department, whitewash the walls and ceilings thereof once at least in every year."

* Indicates the existing law in 1900.

*** (1900) — Sanitary Code of the Department of Health, Section 29.**

"The walls and ceilings throughout any tenement or lodging-house shall be thoroughly whitewashed as required by the board of health, and not less than once in each year."

WALL PAPER. — In 1895 the tenement house law was amended so as to require that before any new wall paper was placed upon any wall or ceiling of any tenement or lodging house, all the old paper should be first removed and the walls and ceiling thoroughly cleaned. This is the present law upon this subject.

(1895) — Chapter 567, Section 6. (Amends Section 657, Consol. Act.)

"No wall paper shall be placed upon a wall or ceiling of any tenement or lodging-house, unless all wall paper shall be first removed therefrom and said wall and ceiling thoroughly cleaned."

*** (1897) — Chapter 378, Greater New York Charter, Section 1310. — Continued.**

YARDS AND AREAS TO BE SEWER CONNECTED. — Where there is a sewer in the street upon which a tenement house stands, the law has required since as early as 1867 that the yard or area shall be connected with the sewer, so that all water from the roof and all liquid filth shall pass freely into it; if there is no sewer in the street, then the yard or area is to be so graded that the water will flow into the street gutter by a passageway beneath the sidewalk, this passageway to be covered by a permanent cover, but so arranged as to allow obstructions to be removed. This has been the law practically without change since that date until the present time, and is the present law upon this subject, with an additional requirement of the Building Department, that yards, areas, light shafts, and courts shall be properly graded and drained, and also flagged and concreted.

(1867) — Chapter 908, Section 5.

"In all cases where a sewer exists in the street upon which the house or building stands, the yard or area shall be so connected with the same that all water from the roof or otherwise, and all liquid filth shall pass freely into it. Where no sewer exists in the street, the yard or area shall be so graded that all water, from the roof or otherwise, and all filth shall flow freely from it and all parts of it into the street gutter by a passage beneath the sidewalk, which shall be covered by a permanent cover, but so arranged as to permit access to remove obstructions or impurities."

(1882) — Chapter 410, Section 653. — Continued.

(1887) — Chapter 84, Section 6. (Amends Section 653, Consol. Act.)

"In all cases where a sewer exists in the street or avenue upon which a house or building stands, the yard or area shall be connected with the sewer, that all water from the roof or otherwise, and all liquid filth shall

* Indicates the existing law in 1900.

pass freely into the sewer. Where there is no sewer in the street or avenue or adjacent thereto, to which connection can be made, the yard and area shall be so graded that all water from the roof or otherwise, and all filth shall flow freely therefrom into the street gutter, by a passage beneath the sidewalk, which passage shall be covered by a permanent cover, but so arranged as to permit access to remove obstruction or impurities."

(1888) — Chapter 422, Section 1. — Continued.

(1888) — Brooklyn — Chapter 583, Section 27. (Brooklyn Consol. Act.) Provisions of Law of 1867, reënacted.

(1889) — Chapter 211, Section 1. — Continued.

*** (1897) — Chapter 378, Greater New York Charter, Section 1308. — Continued.**

*** (1900) — Regulations of the Department of Buildings.**

"Yards, areas, light shafts, and courts shall be properly graded, flagged or concreted and drained."

GARBAGE AND REFUSE. — Since 1867 the law has required the owner of every tenement house to have proper and suitable conveniences or receptacles for receiving garbage and other refuse matters.

(1867) — Chapter 908, Section 8.

"Every tenement or lodging-house shall have the proper and suitable conveniences or receptacles for receiving garbage and other refuse matters."

(1882) — Chapter 410, Section 656. — Continued.

(1888) — Brooklyn — Chapter 583, Section 30. (Brooklyn Consol. Act.) Provisions of Law of 1867, reënacted.

(1895) — Chapter 567, Section 5. (Amends Section 656, Consol. Act.) — Continued.

*** (1897) — Chapter 378, Greater New York Charter, Section 1312. — Continued.**

ASHES AND RUBBISH. — The first tenement house law also provided that every tenement-house erected after May 14, 1867, should have proper conveniences or receptacles for ashes and rubbish. This has been the law since that time without change, and is the present law.

(1867) — Chapter 908, Section 15.

"Every tenement-house hereafter erected or converted shall have proper conveniences and receptacles for ashes and rubbish."

(1882) — Chapter 410, Section 663. — Continued.

(1887) — Chapter 84, Section 11. — Continued.

* Indicates the existing law in 1900.

(1888) Brooklyn — Chapter 583, Section 36. (Brooklyn Consol. Act.) Provisions of Law of 1867, reënacted.

(1890) — Chapter 486, Section 1. — Continued.

(1891) — Chapter 39, Section 1. — Continued.

(1895) — Brooklyn — Chapter 539, Section 1. — Continued.

(1895) — Chapter 567, Section 9. (Amends Section 663, Consol. Act.)— Continued.

***(1897) — Chapter 378, Greater New York Charter, Section 1320. Provisions of the Law of 1867, continued.**

ANIMALS, KEEPING OF, PROHIBITED. — The Act of 1867 forbade the keeping of a horse, cow or calf, swine or pig, or sheep or goat in a tenement or lodging house. This provision of the law has continued to the present time, the Charter adding a further requirement that no such animal should be kept in any part of a tenement house.

(1867) — Chapter 908, Section 8.

"Nor shall any horse, cow, calf, swine, pig, sheep or goat be kept in a tenement or lodging-house."

(1882) — Chapter 410, Section 656. — Continued.

(1888) — Brooklyn — Chapter 583, Section 30. (Brooklyn Consol. Act.) Provisions of Law of 1867, reënacted.

(1895) — Chapter 567, Section 5. — Continued.

***(1897) — Chapter 378, Greater New York Charter, Section 1312.**

"Nor shall any horse, cow, calf, swine, pig, sheep or goat be kept in said house or on the premises thereof."

STABLES IN TENEMENT HOUSES PROHIBITED — TENEMENTS NOT TO BE USED FOR LODGING HOUSES, PRIVATE SCHOOLS, OR STORAGE OF RAGS. — In the amendment to the tenement house laws of 1891 it was provided that no building or premises that were occupied for a tenement house should be used for a lodging house or as a private school or as a stable, and the storage and handling of rags was forbidden upon the premises. This law was slightly changed in the following year, a clause being added that this should not be done except with a permit from the Board of Health, and a further clause to the effect that this part of the law should not apply to buildings or premises used as stables prior to January 1, 1892. In the same year, in another act passed at a later date, the Board of Health was given authority to make other regulations in reference to these subjects, when they were satisfied that such regulations would secure equally well the health of the occupants and the public health, but only upon condition that any modification made by the Board of Health in these requirements,

* Indicates the existing law in 1900.

should be in accordance with a written permit issued by the Board. In the amendment to the Tenement House Act in 1895 this law was somewhat changed, the use of a tenement house as a lodging house or stable or for the storage and handling of rags was absolutely forbidden; such a building was, however, allowed to be used as a private school upon obtaining a special permit from the Board of Health. This is the present law upon this subject, except that a slight change was made in the Charter, limiting the conditions under which the Board of Health might grant a permit for the use of a tenement house or part of a tenement house as a private school. The regulations of the Building Department also provide that no stable or coal-yard may be maintained on any lot on which it is proposed to erect a tenement or lodging house.

(1891) — Chapter 204, Section 1. (Amends Section 661, Consol. Act.)

"No building or premises while occupied for a tenement-house shall be used for a lodging-house, private school, stable or for the storage and handling of rags."

(1892) — Chapter 238, Section 1.

"No building or premises occupied for a tenement-house, shall be used for a lodging-house, private school, stable or for the storage and handling of rags unless with a permit in writing from the board of health; but nothing herein contained shall be construed to apply to a building or premises so used for a stable prior to January 1, 1892."

(1892) — Chapter 329, Section 1.

"The board of health shall have authority, within present provisions of law, to make other regulations than the foregoing in special cases as to the use of building or premises occupied for a tenement house, for a school or stable, or for storage of rags, when it shall be satisfied that such regulations will secure equally well the health of the occupants and the public health, provided, however, that in all such cases any modifications made by such regulations, shall be in accordance with the conditions of a permit in writing issued by the said board of health."

(1895) — Brooklyn — Chapter 539, Section 1. (Amends Section 55, Brooklyn Consol. Act.) Provisions of Section 1, Chapter 238, of the Laws of 1892, reënacted with the following change: The date of January 1, 1892, changed to June 1, 1895.

(1895) — Chapter 567, Section 8. (Amends Section 661, Consol. Act.)

"No building or premises occupied for a tenement-house shall be used for a lodging-house, private school, stable or for the storage and handling of rags, but the board of health may, by a special permit, allow the maintenance of a private school in such a house."

(1896) — Brooklyn — Chapter 355, Section 1. (Amends Section 55, Brooklyn Consol. Act.) Provisions of Chapter 539, of the Laws of 1895, continued.

*** (1897) — Chapter 378, Greater New York Charter, Section 1318.**

Provisions of Section 8, Chapter 567 of the Laws of 1895, continued with the following amendment: After the words "by a special permit"

*** Indicates the existing law in 1900.**

insert the following; "fixing the conditions thereof in writing, and providing there be the necessary cubic air space and ventilation."

*** (1900) — Regulations of the Department of Buildings.**

"Where the premises are occupied as a tenement-house no part thereof may be used for a lodging-house or private school, nor may they be used for the storage and handling of rags. No stable or coal-yard may be maintained on any lot whereon it is proposed to erect a tenement or lodging-house, or convert any building to the purposes of a tenement or lodging-house."

SMOKE-HOUSES IN TENEMENTS PROHIBITED. — The sanitary code of the Department of Health prohibits any person from making or using a smoke-house, or room or any apparatus for smoking meat, without a written permit from the Board of Health, and subject to the conditions that may be imposed by the board.

*** (1900) — Sanitary Code of the Department of Health, Section 21.**

"No person shall make or use a smokehouse or room or apparatus for smoking meat, in any tenement or lodging-house, without a permit in writing from the board of health, and subject to the conditions thereof."

JANITOR REQUIRED FOR TENEMENT HOUSES. — In 1879 it was felt that a large part of the evils of the tenement house system was due to the fact that in many cases there was no person living in the house whose duty it was to take care of it, and keep it clean and in good repair. Accordingly the Tenement House Act of that year required that whenever there should be more than ten families living in any tenement house in which the owner himself did not reside, there should be a janitor or housekeeper, or other responsible person, living in the house, and having charge of the same, and it was left to the discretion of the Board of Health to decide when such janitor or housekeeper should be required. Eight years later this law was amended by changing this provision so as to apply to buildings having more than eight families instead of more than ten families. The law in this amended form is the present law on this subject.

(1879) — Chapter 504, Section 3.

"Whenever there shall be more than ten families living in any tenement-house, in which the owner thereof does not reside, there shall be a janitor, housekeeper, or some other responsible person, who shall reside in the said house, and have charge of the same, if the board of health shall so require."

(1882) — Chapter 410, Section 664. — Continued.

(1887) — Chapter 84, Section 12.

This provision amended so as to apply to buildings having more than eight families, instead of more than ten.

* Indicates the existing law in 1900.

(1895) — Chapter 567, Section 10. (Amends Section 664, Consol. Act.) Provisions of Section 12, Chapter 84 of the Laws of 1887, continued.

*** (1897) — Chapter 378, Greater New York Charter, Section 1321. — Continued.**

OVERCROWDING IN TENEMENT HOUSES. — The Tenement House Act of 1879, among other things, provided that, whenever the Sanitary Superintendent of the Board of Health should certify to the Board that in any tenement house there was less than 600 cubic feet of air to each occupant, the Board of Health might, if it deemed it wise or necessary, issue an order requiring the number of occupants of the building or of a room in the same to be reduced so that the number of inmates should not exceed one person for every 600 cubic feet of air space; and such excess in the number of occupants was required to be reduced within ten days' time. This latter provision, however, as to the period of time in which this change was to be made was repealed in 1887. In 1895 this provision of the statute was somewhat modified, the Board of Health having the power to reduce the overcrowding, only when a tenement house or room was without sufficient ventilation and air, and also when so overcrowded that there was less than 400 cubic feet of air for each adult, and less than 200 cubic feet of air for each child under twelve years of age. Under these circumstances the Board was authorized to issue an order requiring the number of occupants to be reduced. This is the law at the present day. There is, however, a further provision of the sanitary code to the effect that no owner of a tenement house shall allow the same to be overcrowded or allow so great a number of persons to live or sleep in such a house as to cause any danger or detriment to life or health.

(1879) — Chapter 504, Section 3.

"Whenever it shall be certified to the board of health of the city of New York, by the sanitary superintendent that any tenement-house or room therein is so overcrowded that there shall be afforded less than 600 cubic feet of air to each occupant of such building or room, the said board may, if it deem the same to be wise or necessary, issue an order requiring the number of occupants of such building or room to be reduced, so that the inmates thereof shall not exceed one person to each 600 cubic feet of air space in such building or room. Such excess in the number of occupants shall be reduced to the standard hereby designated within ten days after the service of an order therefor upon the owner, lessee, occupant, or agent of such building or room."

(1882) — Chapter 410, Section 664. — Continued.

(1887) — Chapter 84, Section 12. Provisions of this section, reënacted, last clause from "such excess" down to "room," repealed.

(1895) — Chapter 567, Section 10. (Amends Section 664, Consol. Act.)

"Whenever it shall be certified to the board of health by the sanitary superintendent that any tenement-house or room therein being without sufficient ventilation is so overcrowded that there shall be afforded less

* Indicates the existing law in 1900.

than 400 cubic feet of air to each adult and 200 cubic feet of air to each child under 12 years of age occupying such building or room, the said board shall issue an order requiring the number of occupants of such building or room to be reduced in accordance with this provision."

*** (1897) — Chapter 378, Greater New York Charter, Section 1321. — Continued with the following slight change: after the word "superintendent" insert the words "or an assistant sanitary superintendent."**

*** (1900) — Sanitary Code of the Department of Health, Section 24.**

"No owner, lessee or keeper of any tenement-house or lodging-house shall cause or allow the same to be overcrowded or cause or allow so great a number of persons to dwell, be, or sleep in any such house or any portion thereof, as thereby to cause any danger or detriment to life or health."

CONTAGIOUS DISEASES TO BE REPORTED. — The Tenement House Act of 1867 was enacted a few years after New York City had been visited by cholera, and at a time when there had been throughout the city many epidemics of typhoid and typhus fevers and other contagious diseases. It was to be expected, therefore, that the new law would contain a provision upon this subject. This act required that whenever any person in a tenement or lodging house is sick of fever or of any infectious, pestilential, or contagious disease, and such sickness is known to the owner or agent of the house, then the owner or agent must at once notify the Board of Health, and the Board of Health was required to cause the building to be inspected, and, if found necessary, to be immediately cleaned or disinfected at the expense of the owner, and the board was also authorized to fumigate and clean the blankets, bedding, and bedclothes used by any such sick person, or in extreme cases to destroy them. This is the present law upon this subject.

(1867) — Chapter 908, Section 10.

"The owner or keeper of any lodging-house, and the owner, agent of the owner, and the lessee of any tenement-house, or part thereof, shall, whenever any person in such house is sick of fever, or of any infectious, pestilential, or contagious disease, and such sickness is known to such owner, keeper, agent, or lessee, give immediate notice thereof to the Metropolitan board of health, or to some officer of the same, and thereupon said board shall cause the same to be inspected, and may, if found necessary, cause the same to be immediately cleansed or disinfected at the expense of the owner, in such manner as they may deem necessary and effectual; they may also cause the blankets, bedding and bedclothes used by any such sick person to be thoroughly cleansed, scoured and fumigated, or in extreme cases, to be destroyed."

(1882) — Chapter 410, Section 658. — Continued.

(1887) — Chapter 84, Section 8. — Continued.

(1888) — Brooklyn — Chapter 583, Section 32. (Brooklyn Consol. Act.) Provisions of the Law of 1867, reënacted.

* Indicates the existing law in 1900.

*** (1897) — Chapter 378, Greater New York Charter, Section 1314.**

"The owner or keeper of any lodging-house, and the owner, agent of the owner, and the lessee of any tenement-house or part thereof, shall, whenever any person in such house is sick of fever, or of any infectious, pestilential or contagious disease, and information thereof has been given to such owner, keeper, agent or lessee, give immediate notice thereof to the board of health, or to some officer of the same, and thereupon said board shall cause the same to be immediately cleansed or disinfected at the expense of the owner, in such manner as it may deem necessary and effectual, and it may also cause the blankets, bedding and bedclothes used by any such sick person to be thoroughly cleansed, scoured and fumigated, or, in extreme cases, to be destroyed."

VACATION OF TENEMENTS UNFIT FOR HABITATION. — The first tenement house law provided that, whenever the Sanitary Superintendent of the Board of Health should certify to the board that any building or part of a building was unfit for human habitation because it was so infected with disease as to be likely to cause sickness among the occupants, or because it was dangerous to life from want of repair, the Board of Health might issue an order requiring all persons to vacate the building, and the building or part of it was to be vacated within ten days, and in special cases within a shorter period, but this period should never be less than twenty-four hours. It was further provided that the Board of Health when issuing an order should have the same affixed conspicuously on the building, and also have a copy served personally upon the owner or his representative, and this order should set forth the reasons why the building was to be vacated. If the Board was satisfied that the danger from the house had ceased to exist, then it was authorized to revoke the order. This provision of the law was somewhat amended some years later in the Act of 1887, the new act setting forth further conditions under which the Board of Health might be authorized to order a tenement house to be vacated. The previous law had granted this power only when a building was so infected with disease as to be likely to cause sickness among the occupants, or when it was dangerous to life from want of repair. The new law added also that such a building should be vacated when it was unfit for human habitation because of defects in drainage, plumbing, or ventilation, or because of the construction of the building; and also, when there existed a nuisance on the premises which was likely to cause sickness among the occupants. This has been the law since 1887 up to the present time, and is the present law upon this subject.

(1867) — Chapter 908, Section 11.

"Whenever it shall be certified to the board of health by the sanitary superintendent, that any building or part thereof is unfit for human habitation, by reason of its being so infected with disease as to be likely to cause sickness among the occupants, or by reason of its want of repair has become dangerous to life, said board may issue an order, and cause the same to be affixed conspicuously on the building or part thereof, and to be personally served upon the owner, agent, or lessee, if the same can be found in this State, requiring all persons therein to vacate such build-

* Indicates the existing law in 1900.

ing for the reasons to be stated therein as aforesaid. Such building, or part thereof, shall, within ten days thereafter, be vacated; or within such shorter time, not less than twenty-four hours, as in said notice may be specified; but said board, if it shall become satisfied that the danger from said house, or part thereof, has ceased to exist, may revoke said order, and it shall thenceforward become inoperative."

(1882) — Chapter 410, Section 659. — Continued.

(1887) — Chapter 84, Section 9.

"Whenever it shall be certified to the board of health of the health department of the city of New York by the sanitary superintendent, that any building or part thereof in the city of New York is infected with contagious disease, or by reason of want of repair has become dangerous to life, or is unfit for human habitation because of defects in drainage, plumbing, ventilation, or the construction of the same, or because of the existence of a nuisance on the premises, and which is likely to cause sickness among its occupants, the said board of health may issue an order requiring all persons therein to vacate such building or part thereof, for the reasons to be stated therein as aforesaid.

"Said board shall cause said order to be affixed conspicuously in the building or part thereof and to be personally served on the owner, lessee, agent, occupant or any person having the charge or care thereof; if the owner, lessee or agent cannot be found in the city of New York or do not reside therein or evade or resist service then said order may be served by depositing a copy thereof in the post-office in the city of New York, properly inclosed and addressed to such owner, lessee or agent at his last known place of business or residence, and prepaying the postage thereon; such building or part thereof shall within ten days after said order shall have been posted and mailed as aforesaid, or within such shorter time not less than twenty-four hours, as in said order may be specified, be vacated, but said board whenever it shall become satisfied that the danger from said building or part thereof has ceased to exist, or that said building has been repaired so as to be habitable, may revoke said order."

(1888) — Brooklyn — Chapter 583, Section 33. (Brooklyn Consol. Act.) Provisions of the Law of 1867, reënacted.

(1895) — Chapter 567, Section 7. Provisions of Section 9, Chapter 84, of the Laws of 1887, continued.

***(1897) — Chapter 378, Greater New York Charter, Section 1315. — Continued.**

CONDEMNATION OF TENEMENTS UNFIT FOR HABITATION. — Among the different powers given to the newly created Metropolitan Board of Health by the Act of 1866 was the power, whenever any building or part of a building was, in the opinion of the Board, in a condition dangerous to life or health, to declare the building a public nuisance and order the building removed or altered in such manner as the Board might specify. It was further provided that, upon the nuisance being abated, the Board might modify their order or revoke it. These powers of the Board have been

* Indicates the existing law in 1900.

continued in succeeding acts relating to the organization of the Health Department, and were not materially changed until 1895, when the new tenement house law, passed as a result of the investigations of the Tenement House Commission appointed by the Legislature in 1894, materially modified the powers of the Board, in reference to the condemnation of buildings unfit for human habitation. The new act provided that the Board of Health might condemn and order removed any building or part of a building, under certain circumstances set forth in detail in the law. These circumstances were the following: When the building, in the opinion of the Board, was unfit for human habitation because of age or defects in the drainage or in the plumbing, or because of infection with contagious disease, or because of lack of ventilation, or because of the existence of a nuisance on the premises which was likely to cause sickness among the occupants of the building, or among the occupants of other buildings in the city, or because the building stopped ventilation in other buildings, or in other ways made or helped to make other buildings adjacent to be unfit for habitation, or dangerous or injurious to health, or because it prevented proper measures from being carried into effect for removing any nuisance injurious to health, or for removing other sanitary evils in such other buildings, then, the power to condemn or destroy a building, under these circumstances, was granted; but only when it was shown that the building was so unfit for habitation that the evils in the building, or the evils caused by the building, could not be remedied by repairs or in any other way, except by its destruction or by the destruction of a part of it. The law also provided very carefully for the legal proceedings to be taken in condemning buildings under such circumstances, giving the owner of the building the right to demand a survey of it, in a manner similar to the surveys carried on by the Building Department in the case of unsafe buildings. (In such cases a representative of the Department and a representative of the owner of the building, and a third person, an architect representing the American Institute of Architects, meet and examine the building to see whether the order to make it safe is just or not, and the decision of a majority of this Board of Survey is considered to be final, except, of course, that the courts can pass upon the subject.) The Board of Health was also authorized to institute proceedings in the supreme court for the condemnation of buildings in question; and upon the institution of these proceedings the owner of the building or any person interested in it, was permitted in his answer to dispute the necessity of its destruction, and by the terms of the act, the supreme court is prohibited from appointing commissioners until proof has been made of the necessity of the building's destruction. The law also sets forth in very minute detail what evidence may be presented in such proceedings.

First, it is required to be proved that the rental of the building was enhanced because the building was used for illegal purposes, or because it was so overcrowded as to be dangerous to the health of the inmates.

Second, that the building was in a state of defective sanitation, or not in reasonably good repair.

And third, that the building was unfit for human habitation and not reasonably capable of being made fit for such habitation. The law further provides that if the Commissioners appointed by the court are satisfied, from the evidence presented, that the building should be destroyed, then the method of determining the amount of compensation to the owner of the property was to be in accordance with the following provisions of the statute. First, where it was proved that the rental of the building had been enhanced because the building had been *used for illegal purposes*, or because it was *overcrowded or dangerous to health*, then the compensation was to be based on the rental of the *building* as distinguished from the ground rent which might have been obtained if the building was occupied for legal purposes and only by the proper number of persons. In the second case, where a building was proved to be in a state of *defective sanitation* and not in reasonably good repair, then the amount of compensation to be paid the owner was to be the amount estimated as the *value of the building after having been put in a sanitary condition* or into reasonably good repair, but with the deduction of the estimated expense of such repairs or alterations. In the third case, where it was proved that a building was *unfit for human habitation* and not reasonably capable of being made fit for habitation, then the amount of compensation to the owner of the property was to be merely the *value of the materials of the building*. This law, modelled largely after the English law on this subject, has been re-enacted in the Greater New York Charter, and is the law of the present day, with one or two slight changes as to the form of legal proceedings, somewhat strengthening the provisions of the Act.

(1866) — Chapter 74, Section 14.

"Whenever any building, erection, excavation, premises, business pursuit, matter or thing, or the sewerage, drainage or ventilation thereof, in said district (Metropolitan district) shall, in the opinion of said board (Metropolitan board of health) whether as a whole or in any particular, be in a condition or in effect dangerous to life or health, said board may take and file among its records what it shall regard as sufficient proof to authorize its declaration that the same, to the extent it may specify, is a public nuisance, or dangerous to life or health; and said board may thereupon enter in its records the same as a nuisance, and order the same to be removed, abated, suspended, altered or otherwise improved or purified, as said order shall specify, and shall cause said order before its execution to be served on the owner, occupant or tenant thereof, or some of them, which to said board, may appear most directly interested in its execution, provided said parties, or any of them, are in said district and can be found, and such service can be conveniently made, and if any party so served (or intended to be according to this law) shall, before its execution is commenced, or within three days after such service or attempted service, apply to said board, or the president thereof, to have said order or its execution stayed or modified, it shall then be the duty of said board to temporarily suspend or modify said order, or the execution thereof (save in cases of imminent danger from impending pestilence, when said board may exercise extraordinary powers as *herein elsewhere specified*), and to give such parties or party together, as the case in the opinion of the board may require, a reasonable and fair opportunity to be heard before said board; and to present facts and proofs (according to the rules or directions of said board) against said declaration and the execution of said order, or in favor of its modification, according to the regulations of the board; and the board shall enter in its minutes such facts and proof as it may receive, and its proceedings on such hearing, and any other proof it may take; and thereafter may rescind, modify or reaffirm its said declaration and order, and require execution of said original, or of a new or modified order to be made, in such form and effect as it may finally determine."

(1866) — Chapter 74, Section 14.

"The Metropolitan board of health may order or cause any excavation, erection, vehicle, vessel, water-craft, room, building, place, sewer, pipe, passage, premises, ground, matter or thing (in said district or adjacent waters) regarded by said board as in a condition dangerous or detrimental to life or health, to be purified, cleaned, disinfected, altered or improved."

(1882) — Chapter 410, Consol. Act, Chapter 12, Section 535. Provisions of Law of 1866, continued.

(1895) — Chapter 567, Section 7.

"Whenever in the opinion of the board of health of the health department of the city of New York, any building or part thereof in the city of New York, an order to vacate which has been made by said board, is, by reason of age, defects in drainage, plumbing, infection with contagious disease, or ventilation, or because of the existence of a nuisance on the premises, which is likely to cause sickness among its occupants or among the occupants of other property in the city of New York, or because it stops ventilation in other buildings, or otherwise makes or conduces to make other buildings adjacent to the same unfit for human habitation, or dangerous or injurious to health; or because it prevents proper measures from being carried into effect for remedying any nuisance injurious to health or other sanitary evils in respect of such other buildings; so unfit for human habitation that the evils in or caused by said building cannot be remedied by repairs or in any other way except by the destruction of said building, or of a portion of the same, said board of health may [1] condemn the same and order it removed, provided the owner or owners of said building can demand a survey of said building in the manner provided for in case of unsafe buildings, and may institute proceedings in the supreme court in the county of New York for the condemnation of said building.[2] Said proceedings shall be instituted and carried on in the manner prescribed by the code of civil procedure, except as modified by this act. Upon the institution of said proceedings the owner of said building or any person interested therein may in his answer dispute the necessity of the destruction of said building or part thereof as the case may be. In such case, the court shall not appoint commissioners unless proof is made of the necessity of said destruction. In such proceeding evidence shall be receivable by the commissioners to prove:

"1. That the rental of the building was enhanced by reason of the same being used for illegal purposes or being so overcrowded as to be dangerous or injurious to the health of the inmates; or

"2. That the building is in a state of defective sanitation, or is not in reasonably good repair; or

"3. That the building is unfit, and not reasonably capable of being made fit, for human habitation; and if the commissioners are satisfied by such evidence, then the compensation —

"(a) Shall in the first case, so far as it is based on rental, be based on the rental of the building, as distinct from the ground rent, which would have been obtainable if the building was occupied for legal purposes and only by the number of persons whom the building was under all the circumstances of the case fitted to accommodate without such overcrowding as is dangerous or injurious to the health of the inmates, and

"(b) Shall in the second case be the amount estimated as the value of the building if it had been put into a sanitary condition, or into reasonably good repair, after deducting the estimated expense of putting it into such condition or repair; and

"(c) Shall in the third case be the value of the materials of the buildings.

"Nothing in this section contained shall repeal any part of section 535 of this act or impair any of the powers thereby vested in the board of health."

*** (1897) — Chapter 378, Greater New York Charter, Section 1316.**

Provisions of the law of 1895 continued with the following changes, not affecting the meaning of the statute: After the word "may"[1] insert the following words: "If it deem such course just and proper," and after the word "building"[2] insert the following in place of the present *sentence:* "Said proceeding shall be instituted through a petition addressed to said court containing a brief statement of the reasons therefor, and shall not be required to contain further allegations of facts than those which have actuated the board of health in this proceeding, which shall then be carried on in the manner prescribed by chapter 21 of this act." Also at the end of the section add the following: "For the payment of all awards and the expenses of all such proceedings, the comptroller shall issue and sell from time to time as may be necessary, and in the manner hereinbefore provided, corporate stock of the city of New York." (This takes the place of the last sentence in the provisions of the law of 1895.)

SANITARY ARRANGEMENTS

WATER-CLOSET ACCOMMODATIONS. — Prior to the passage of the first Tenement House Act in 1867, there was no law requiring water-closet accommodations to be provided for the use of occupants of tenement houses. This law provided that every tenement and lodging house in the cities of New York and Brooklyn should be provided with good and sufficient water-closets or privies of a form and construction to be approved by the Board of Health, and that such water-closets and privies should not be less in number than one for every twenty occupants of a tenement house. There was a further clause added, however, to the effect that such water-closets or privies might be used in common by the occupants of any two or more houses, provided the access to the water-closets was convenient and direct, and provided that the number of occupants using them did not exceed the proportion required for every privy or water-closet. This law was changed in 1887 so as to require either water-closets or improved privy sinks, and the number of occupants for each water-closet was limited to one water-closet for every fifteen persons in lodging houses, and there was to be not less than one closet or sink for every two families in tenement houses. The law was again amended in the following year, so as to require not less than one closet for every fifteen occupants of tenement

* Indicates the existing law in 1900.

houses, and also not less than one closet or sink for every floor or story of such a house. The year after an amendment to the law was passed repealing the provisions of the previous year. This new act simply required that there should be not less than one closet for every fifteen occupants. This is the present law upon this subject, to be found in the Greater New York Charter. In addition to the provisions of the Charter there are a number of regulations of the Building Department bearing upon the subject. These require that the general water-closet accommodations shall not be placed in the cellar of a tenement house, and that no permanent water-closet shall be placed in the yard, also that there must be at least one water-closet on every floor, and that where there is more than one family on a floor there must be one additional water-closet on that floor for every additional fifteen persons or fraction thereof. The sanitary code of the Health Department also requires that the owner or lessee of every tenement house shall provide for the use of the tenants adequate privies or water-closets which shall be properly constructed as required by the rules of the Health Department and the Department of Buildings.

(1867) — Chapter 908, Section 5.

"Every tenement and lodging-house in the cities of New York and Brooklyn, shall be provided with good and sufficient water-closets or privies, of a construction approved by the Metropolitan board of health. Such water-closets or privies shall not be less in number than one to every twenty occupants of said house; but water-closets or privies may be used in common by the occupants of any two or more houses, provided the access is convenient and direct, and provided the number of occupants in the houses for which they are provided, shall not exceed the proportion above required for every privy or water-closet."

(1882) — Chapter 410, Section 653. — Continued.

(1887) — Chapter 84, Section 6. (Amends Section 655, Consol. Act.)

"Every tenement and lodging-house or building shall be provided with as many good and sufficient water-closets, improved privy sinks or other similar receptacles as the board of health shall require, but in no case shall there be less than one for every fifteen occupants in lodging-houses, and not less than one for every two families in dwelling-houses."

(1888) — Chapter 422, Section 1.

"Every tenement and lodging-house or building, shall be provided with as many good and sufficient water-closets, improved privy sinks or other similar receptacles, as the board of health shall require, but in no case shall there be less than 1 for every 15 occupants, and not less than 1 for every floor or story of such tenement or lodging-house."

(1888) — Brooklyn — Chapter 583, Section 27. (Brooklyn Consol. Act.) Provisions of the Law of 1867, reënacted.

(1889) — Chapter 211, Section 1. (Section 653, Consol. Act, amended as follows:)

"Every tenement and lodging-house or building shall be provided with as many good and sufficient water-closets, improved privy sinks or other similar receptacles as the board of health shall require, but in no case shall there be less than one for every fifteen occupants."

*** (1897) — Chapter 378, Greater New York Charter, Section 1308. (Provisions of Section 1, Chapter 211 of the Laws of 1889, continued.)**

*** (1900) — Regulations of the Department of Buildings.**

"The general water-closet accommodations must not be placed in the cellar and no permanent water-closet may be placed in the yard. In tenement-houses there must be one water-closet on each floor, and where there is more than one family on a floor there must be one additional water-closet on that floor for every additional fifteen persons or fraction thereof."

*** (1900) — Regulations for plumbing and drainage adopted by the Department of Buildings, Section 121.**

"The general water-closet accommodations for a tenement or lodging-house cannot be placed in the cellar. No water-closet can be placed outside of the building."

*** (1900) — Regulations for plumbing and drainage adopted by the Department of Buildings, Section 130.**

"In all sewer-connected occupied buildings there must be at least one water-closet, and there must be additional water-closets so that there will never be more than 15 persons per closet."

*** (1900) — Sanitary Code of the Department of Health, Section 25.**

"Every person who shall be the owner, lessee, or keeper or manager of any tenement-house, or lodging-house, shall provide or cause to be provided, for the accommodation thereof and for the use of the tenants, lodgers and boarders thereat, adequate privies or water-closets, and the same shall be so adequately ventilated, and shall at all times be kept in such cleanly and wholesome condition, as not to be offensive, or be dangerous or detrimental to life or health. And no offensive smell or gases from or through any outlet or sewer, or through any such privy or water-closet, shall be allowed by any person aforesaid to pass into such house or any part thereof, or into any other house or building."

WATER-CLOSET CONSTRUCTION. — The First Tenement House Act required that every tenement and lodging house should be provided with good and sufficient water-closets or privies of a form and construction to be approved by the Board of Health, and also that such water-closets and privies should have proper doors, traps, soil pans, and such other suitable works and arrangements as might be necessary to insure their efficient operation. It was also required that wherever there was a sewer in the street adjoining the lot upon which the building stood, the water-closets or privies should be properly connected with the street sewer; also, that all water-closets and vaults should be provided with proper traps, and that all connections should be properly made and tight, and that they should have a sufficient water supply so as to properly flush them. The owner, lessee and occupant of any tenement house was also made responsible for keeping such closets or privies free from improper substances, and was required to remove any obstructions in them and to prevent any exhalations from the closets that might be dangerous or prejudicial to life or health. In 1887 this law was amended slightly, all of the provisions of the previous act

* Indicates the existing law in 1900.

being reënacted, with a further requirement that all the water-closets and privy sinks and pipes and parts of the same should be properly ventilated to prevent the escape of deleterious gas and odors. It was also added that all the drainage and plumbing work, all the water-closets, sinks, and other receptacles in and for every tenement house, should be of such form, construction, arrangement, location, materials, workmanship, and description as might be required by the Board of Health. In 1895, in the new tenement house law, it was provided that every water-closet thereafter constructed in a tenement house should have a window opening to the outer air, and also that the floor of the water-closet compartment should be made waterproof, and that such waterproofing should extend at least 6 inches above the floor so that the floor might be flushed out without leaking. This is practically the present law, having been reënacted in the Greater New York Charter. There is a further provision added, however, in reference to the ventilation of water-closet compartments, to the effect that, if provided with a ventilating flue or duct, the water-closet may have the window opening on a court or shaft containing 25 square feet in area. The Charter also requires that the waterproof base around the floor of the compartment shall be 16 inches high instead of 6 inches; this is undoubtedly due to an error in printing, as there is no reason for this requirement. There are also a few supplementary rules of the Department of Buildings upon this subject. One requires that where tenement houses and lodging houses are not over three stories in height, the water-closet compartment may have its window open on a ventilating shaft as small as 10 square feet in area; another, that the partition enclosing the water-closet rooms must extend to the ceiling.

(1867) — Chapter 908, Section 5.

"Every tenement and lodging-house in the cities of New York and Brooklyn, shall be provided with good and sufficient water-closets or privies, of a construction approved by the Metropolitan board of health, and shall have proper doors, traps, soil pans, and other suitable works and arrangements, so far as may be necessary to insure the efficient operation thereof. Every such house situated upon a lot on a street, in which there is a sewer, shall have the water-closets or privies furnished with a proper connection with the sewer, which connection shall be in all parts adequate for the purpose, so as to permit entirely and freely to pass whatever enters the same. Such connection with the sewer shall be of a form approved in New York by the Croton Aqueduct Board, and in Brooklyn by the Board of Water Commissioners. All such water-closets and vaults shall be provided with the proper traps and connected with the house sewer by a proper tight pipe, and shall be provided with sufficient water and other proper means of flushing the same; and every owner, lessee, and occupant shall take adequate measures to prevent improper substances from entering such water-closets or privies, or their connections, and to secure the prompt removal of any improper substances that may enter them, so that no accumulation shall take place, and so as to prevent any exhalations therefrom, offensive, dangerous, or prejudicial to life or health, and so as to prevent the same from being or becoming obstructed."

(1882) — Chapter 410, Section 653. — Continued.

(1887) — Chapter 84, Section 6. (Amends Section 653, Consol. Act.)

"Every tenement and lodging-house or building shall be provided with as many good and sufficient water-closets, improved privy sinks or other similar receptacles as the board of health shall require, but in no case shall there be less than one for every fifteen occupants in lodging-houses, and not less than one for every two families in dwelling-houses. The water-closets, sinks and receptacles shall have proper doors, soil pipes and traps, all of which shall be properly ventilated to prevent the escape of deleterious gas and odors, soil pans, cisterns, pumps and other suitable works and fixtures necessary to insure the efficient operation, cleansing and flushing thereof. Every tenement and lodging-house situated upon a lot on a street or avenue in which there is a sewer, shall have a separate and proper connection with the sewer; and the water-closets, sinks, and other receptacles shall be properly connected with the sewer by proper pipes made thoroughly air-tight. Such sewer connection and all the drainage and plumbing work, water-closets, sinks and other receptacles, in and for every tenement and lodging-house shall be of the form, construction, arrangements, location, materials, workmanship and description, to be approved, or such as may be required by the board of health of the health department of the city of New York. Every owner, lessee and occupant shall take adequate measures to prevent improper substances from entering such water-closets or sinks or their connections, and to secure the prompt removal of any improper substances that may enter them, so that no accumulation shall take place, and so as to prevent any exhalations therefrom, offensive, dangerous and prejudicial to life or health, and so as to prevent the same from being or becoming obstructed."

(1888) — Chapter 422, Section 1. (Amends Section 653, Consol. Act.) — Continued.

(1888) — Brooklyn — Chapter 583, Section 27. (Brooklyn Consol. Act.) Provisions of the Law of 1867, reënacted.

(1889) — Chapter 211, Section 1. (Amends Section 653, Consol. Act.) — Continued.

(1895) — Chapter 567, Section 8. (Amends Section 661, Consol. Act.)
"Each water-closet must have a window opening into the outer air; the floor of each water-closet must be made waterproof with asphalt, cement, tile, metal or some other waterproof material; and such waterproofing must extend at least six inches above the floor so that said floor can be washed or flushed out without leaking."

*** (1897) — Chapter 378, Greater New York Charter, Section 1308.**
Provisions of Section 1, Chapter 422 of the Laws of 1888, continued, with the following change only: Substitute for the words "board of health of the health department of the city of New York," the words "as may be required by the rules and regulations of the department of buildings of the city of New York."

*** (1897) — Chapter 378, Greater New York Charter, Section 1308.**
Remaining part of this section (Sect. 6, Chap. 84, Laws of 1887), as amended by Section 1, Chapter 211 of the Laws of 1889 continued with the following change: the words "department of buildings" substituted for the words "board of health."

* Indicates the existing law in 1900.

*** (1897) — Chapter 378, Greater New York Charter, Section 1318.**

Provisions of Section 8, Chapter 567 of the Laws of 1895 continued, with the following changes: After the first sentence insert the following, "and such water-closet inclosure if provided with a ventilating flue or duct, may have the window opening on any court or shaft containing at least 25 square feet in area." Also, the waterproof base above floor to be 16 inches instead of 6 inches; and also after the words "above the floor" insert the words "except at the door opening."

*** (1900) — Regulations of the Department of Buildings.**

"No privy vaults or cesspool will be maintained on the premises where a connection can be made with a public sewer."

*** (1900) — Regulations of the Department of Buildings.**

"The floor and a base 16 inches high of each water-closet apartment in every tenement and lodging-house must be made waterproof."

*** (1900) — Rules for Plumbing and Drainage adopted by the Department of Buildings, Sections 119 and 120.**

"In tenement-houses and lodging-houses the water-closet and urinal apartments must have a window opening to the outer air except that tenement or lodging-houses three stories or less in height may have such window opening on a ventilating shaft not less than 10 square feet in area. In all buildings the outside partition of such apartment must extend to the ceiling or be independently ceiled over and these partitions must be air-tight; the outside partitions must include a window opening to outer air on the lot whereon the building is situated, or some other approved means of ventilation must be provided."

CERTAIN NUISANCES PROHIBITED. — In 1887 it was found that many persons in tenement houses, instead of making use of the proper sanitary conveniences, were apt to create nuisances in different parts of the building. It was accordingly provided, in the law, that any person who should place filth, urine, or fœcal matter in any place in a tenement house, other than that provided for the same, and any person who should keep filth, urine, or fœcal matter in his apartment or upon his premises, such length of time as to create a nuisance, was guilty of a misdemeanor. This is the present law upon this subject.

(1887) — Chapter 84, Section 6.

"Every person who shall place filth, urine or foecal matter in any place in a tenement-house other than that provided for the same, and every person who shall keep filth, urine or fœcal matter in his apartment or upon his premises such length of time as to create a nuisance shall be guilty of a misdemeanor."

(1888) — Chapter 422, Section 1. — Continued.

(1889) — Chapter 211, Section 1. — Continued.

*** (1897) — Chapter 378, Greater New York Charter, Section 1308. — Continued.**

* Indicates the existing law in 1900.

CESSPOOLS AND PRIVIES PROHIBITED. — Since the time of the first tenement house law, in 1867, the use of a cesspool in connection with a tenement house has been rigorously prohibited, except where, from the nature of the case, when there was no sewer in the street to which connection could be made, it was unavoidable. Where cesspools were built, they were required to be constructed water-tight and arched or securely covered over, and no offensive smell or gases were to be allowed to escape from them. This provision of the law, twenty years later, was made also to apply to privy vaults as well as to cesspools, and it was further provided that no privy vault or cesspool should be allowed in connection with a tenement house without a permit from the Board of Health, and constructed in such manner as the Board of Health might prescribe. A further clause was added to this act, requiring the Board of Health to see to it that no privy vault should remain connected with a tenement house in the city later than January 1, 1887. As this law was not enacted until May, 1887, January, 1888, was probably meant. This was the law upon this subject without change until the enactment of the Greater New York Charter, when the last clause stating that the Board of Health should see to it that no privy vault remained connected with a tenement house in the city was dropped.

(1867) — Chapter 908, Section 5.

"No cesspool shall be allowed in or under or connected with any such house, except when it is unavoidable, and in such case it shall be constructed in such situation and in such manner as the Metropolitan board of health may direct. It shall in all cases be water-tight, and arched or securely covered over, and no offensive smell or gases shall be allowed to escape therefrom, or from any privy or privy vault."

(1882) — Chapter 410, Section 653. — Continued.

(1887) — Chapter 84, Section 6. (Amends Section 653, Consol. Act.)

"No privy, vault or cess-pool shall be allowed in or under or connected with any such house except when it is unavoidable, and a permit therefor shall have been granted by the board of health, and in such case it shall be constructed in such situation and in such manner as the board of health may direct. It shall in all cases be watertight, and arched or securely covered over, and no offensive smell or gases shall be allowed to escape therefrom or from any closet, sink or privy. It shall be the duty of the board of health to enforce the provisions of this section in regard to privy vaults as soon as practicable, but said board shall permit no privy vault to remain connected with a tenement-house later than January 1, 1887 (so in the original, 1888 meant), except in the cases especially named in this section."

(1888) — Chapter 422, Section 1. — Continued.

(1888) — Brooklyn — Chapter 583, Section 27. (Brooklyn Consol. Act.) Provisions of the Law of 1867, reënacted.

(1889) — Chapter 211, Section 1. — Continued.

*** (1897) — Chapter 378, Greater New York Charter, Section 1308. Continued down to "It shall be the duty, etc.," which last clause is dropped.**

* Indicates the existing law in 1900.

PLUMBING, RULES AND REGULATIONS FOR. — Before 1881 there were no laws in reference to this subject in New York. In that year an act was passed requiring that the drainage and plumbing of all buildings thereafter erected in New York and Brooklyn should be executed in accordance with plans previously approved in writing by the Board of Health, and that suitable drawings and descriptions of the plumbing and drainage of all new buildings should in every case be submitted to the Health Department and there kept on file. The Board of Health was also authorized to receive and place on file drawings and descriptions of the plumbing and drainage of buildings erected prior to the passage of the act, and any violation of this law was constituted a misdemeanor, and the Board of Health was given the power to restrain the progress of any plumbing work by injunction proceedings, where, in their opinion, such action was necessary. The same law also provided for a system of registration of all plumbers carrying on plumbing business, requiring every master or journeyman plumber carrying on his trade in the cities of New York and Brooklyn, to register his name and address at the Health Department, under such rules and regulations as might be prescribed by the Board of Health. And after March 1, 1882, it was not lawful for any person to carry on the trade of plumbing in these cities, unless he had registered as provided; and a list of the registered plumbers of the city was required to be published once a year in the *City Record.* The amendment to the tenement house law of 1887 also required that the drainage and plumbing work of every tenement and lodging house should be of a form, construction, arrangement, materials, and workmanship as might be required by the Board of Health. In 1892 the powers of the Board of Health in reference to plumbing in *new* buildings were transferred to the Department of Buildings created under the act of that year. In the same year a special law was passed appointing an Examining Board of Plumbers throughout the different cities of the state; this act required that every person desiring or intending to carry on the trade of a plumber in any city of the State, as employing or master plumber, should first submit to an examination before an Examining Board, as to his experience and qualifications in such trade or calling, and after the first day of March, 1893, it was not lawful for any person in any city of the State to carry on the business of plumbing unless he had first obtained a certificate of competency from the Examining Board. The same law further provided that, on or before the first day of March in the year 1893, every employing or master plumber in any of the cities of the State, should register his name and address at the office of the local Board of Health, under such rules and regulations as the Board might prescribe, and that, if such plumber should hold at the time a certificate of competency from the Examining Board of Plumbers, then he should also receive from the local Board of Health a certificate of registration. The Board of Health was also given the power to cancel or revoke any certificate of registration for a violation of any of the rules and regulations for plumbing and drainage of the city, provided that, first, the plumber violating such rules should have had a notice of not less than ten days stating the grounds of the complaint made against him, and such notice to be served upon him, and also provided that he should have a hearing before the Board of Health upon this subject. But the cancellation of such certificate was not to be deemed legal unless concurred in by a majority of the local Board of Examiners. This act also provided for the appointment of inspectors of plumbing throughout the different cities of the State. In the following year, the law was amended, a fee of $5 being required to be paid by each candidate for a certificate, upon his examination. This act was materially amended in 1896, when a totally new plumbing law was enacted dealing with very much the same subjects and making very slight changes in the previous requirements. This new law applied to the city of New York only. It provided, among other things, that every employing or master plumber should register his name and address once a year in the Department of Buildings, and that he should thereupon receive a certificate of registration from the Department of Buildings, if he had previously held a certificate of competency from the Examining Board of Plumbers; and the Superintendent of Buildings was authorized to cancel any certificate of registration for a violation of the plumbing rules and regulations of the city after a hearing had before him. It was also made unlawful for any person to expose the sign of "Plumber" or "Plumbing" unless he had complied with all the provisions of the law relating to registration and examination. The Department of Buildings was charged with the enforcement of the new act, and the Superintendent of Buildings was authorized to appoint Inspectors of Plumbing to secure its enforcement. The duties of these inspectors are described in detail in the act. A violation of the act was made a misdemeanor, and the Department of Buildings was authorized to institute criminal proceedings against any plumber violating it, and the Superintendent of Buildings was also authorized to adopt rules and regulations for the plumbing and drainage of all buildings in the city of New York; such rules and regulations to be published in the *City Record* for eight successive weeks before they should become operative.

(1881) — Chapter 450 — Plumbing — Registration of Plumbers.

Under the provisions of this act every master or journeyman plumber carrying on his trade in the cities of New York and Brooklyn is required to register his name and address at the Health Department, under such rules and regulations as might be prescribed by the Board of Health. After this date (March 1, 1882) it was not lawful for any person to carry on the trade of plumbing in said cities unless registered as provided. It was further provided that a list of registered plumbers of the city of New York should be published in the *City Record* at least once every year.

(1881) — Chapter 410, Section 536. — Continued.

(1896) — Chapter 803, Section 1.

"Once in every year, every employing or master plumber carrying on his trade, business or calling, in the city of New York, shall register his name and address at the office of the department of buildings in said city under such rules and regulations as said department shall prescribe, and thereupon he shall be entitled to receive a certificate of such registration from said department, provided, however, that such employing or master plumber shall, at the time of applying for such registration, hold a certificate of competency from the examining board of plumbers of said city. The time for making such registration shall be during the month of March in each year. Where, however, a person obtains a certificate of competency at a time other than in the month of March in any year, he may register within thirty days after obtaining such certificate of competency, but he must also register in the month of March in each year as above provided. Such registration may be cancelled by the superintendent of buildings for a violation of the rules and regulations for the plumbing and drainage of such city, duly adopted and in force pursuant to the provisions of this act, or whenever the person so registered ceases to be a master or employing plumber, after a hearing had before said superintendent, and upon a prior notice of not less than ten days, stating the grounds of complaint and served upon the person charged with the violation of the aforesaid rules and regulations. After the passage of this act it shall not be lawful for any person or copartnership to engage in, or carry on the trade, business or calling of employing or master plumber in the city of New York, unless the name and address of such person and of each and every member of such copartnership shall have been registered as above provided.

"In the city of New York it shall be unlawful for any person or persons to expose the sign of 'Plumber' or 'Plumbing,' or a sign containing words of similar import and meaning, unless said person or persons shall have obtained a certificate of competency from the examining board of plumbers of said city, and shall have registered as herein provided.

"The department of buildings is hereby charged with the enforcement of the provisions of this act, through the superintendent of buildings, and in addition to such officers or employees as are now provided by law to be appointed by him, he shall appoint inspectors of plumbing. It shall not be lawful for any inspector of plumbing of said department to engage in conducting or carrying on business as a plumber while holding office therein. Any inspector of plumbing for any neglect of duty or omission to properly perform his duty, or violation of rules, or neglect or disobedience of orders, or incapacity, or absence without leave, may be punished by the superintendent of buildings, by forfeiting and withholding pay for a specified time, or by suspension from duty with or without pay; but this provision shall not be deemed to abridge the right of said superintendent to remove or dismiss any inspector of plumbing from the service of said department at any time in his discretion.

"The duties of inspectors of plumbing appointed under the provisions of this act, in addition to those which may be required by the superintendent of buildings, shall be to inspect the construction and alteration of all plumbing work performed in said city, and to report in writing the results of such inspection to the said superintendent. The said inspectors shall also ascertain whether the employing or master plumber having charge of the construction, repairing or alteration of any plumbing work performed in the city of New York is registered as herein provided, and if such person is not so registered then such inspectors shall forthwith report to said department the name of such plumber. The department of buildings may present a petition to a justice of the supreme court or to a special term thereof for an order restraining the person so reported from acting as an employing or master plumber until he registers pursuant to the provisions of this act. Said petition shall state that the said person is engaged in plumbing work as an employing or master plumber without having so registered, and shall be verified by the inspector making the said report. Upon the presentation of the petition the justice or court shall grant an order requiring such plumber to appear before him or before the said term of the supreme court on a date therein specified, not less than two, nor more than six days after the granting thereof, to show cause why he should not be permanently enjoined until he has obtained a certificate of registration as herein required. A copy of such petition and order shall be served upon such person not less than twenty-four hours before the return thereof. On the date specified in such order the justice or court before whom the same is returnable shall hear the proofs of the parties, and may, if he deems necessary, take testimony in relation to the allegations of the petition. If the justice or court is satisfied that such plumber is practicing without having registered as provided in this act, an order shall be granted enjoining him from acting as an employing or master plumber until he has so registered. No undertaking shall be required as a condition to the granting or issuing of such injunction order, or by reason thereof. If after the entry of such order in the county clerk's office of the city and county of New York such person shall, in violation of such order, practice as an employing or master plumber, he shall be deemed guilty of criminal contempt of court, and be punished as for a criminal contempt in the manner provided by the code of civil procedure, but in no case shall the department of buildings be liable for costs in any such proceeding, but they may be allowed against the defendant or defendants in the discretion of the justice or court."

(1892) — Chapter 602 — Plumbing — Examination of Plumbers. (An act appointing an examining board of plumbers in cities of the State of New York, Section 5.)

"Any person desiring or intending to conduct the trade, business or calling of a plumber or of plumbing, in any of the cities in this state as employing or master plumber shall be required to submit to an examination before such board of examiners as to his experience and qualifications in such trade, business or calling; and after the first day of March, 1893, it shall not be lawful in any city of this state for any person to conduct such trade, business or calling unless he shall have first obtained a certificate of competency from such board."

Section 6 provides that "On or before the first day of March, 1893, every employing or master plumber carrying on his trade, business or calling in any of the cities of this state, shall register his name and address at the office of the board of health, under such rules and regulations as the respective board of health of each of the cities shall prescribe, and thereupon he shall receive a certificate of such registration, provided, however, that such employing or master plumber shall, at the time of applying for registration hold a certificate of competency from an examining board; but such registration may be canceled by such board of health for a violation of the rules and regulations for the plumbing and drainage of said city duly adopted and in force therein, after a hearing had before said board of health, and upon a prior notice of not less than ten days, stating the grounds of complaint and served upon the person charged with the violation of the aforesaid rules and regulations, but such revocation shall not be operative unless concurred in by a majority of the local board of examiners. And after the first day of March, 1893, it shall not be lawful for any person to engage in or carry on the trade, business or calling of an employing or master plumber in any of the cities of the state unless his name and address shall have been registered as above provided." (This act further provides for the appointment of inspectors of plumbing, their compensation and method of procedure in case of violations of the law.)

(1893) — Chapter 262.

Amends provisions of law of 1892 in reference to charging a fee of 5 dollars for the examination of plumbers, and provides how such money shall be paid, and also authorizes the examining board to hire suitable quarters and to incur certain expenses, etc.

PLUMBING, RULES AND REGULATIONS FOR.

(1881) — Chapter 450, Section 3.

"The drainage and plumbing of all buildings hereafter erected in New York and Brooklyn shall be executed in accordance with plans previously approved in writing by the board of health of the said health departments of said cities, suitable drawings and descriptions of the said plumbing and drainage shall in each case be submitted and placed on file in the health department. The said boards of health are also authorized to receive and place on file drawings and descriptions of the plumbing and drainage of buildings erected prior to the passage of this act." Any violation of the act was constituted a misdemeanor, and the commissioner of health was authorized to restrain by injunction proceedings in violations.

(1882) — Chapter 410, Section 501. — Continued.

(1882) — Chapter 410, Section 537. — Continued.

(1887) — Chapter 84, Section 6.

"All the drainage, plumbing work, water-closets, sinks and other receptacles in and for every tenement and lodging-house shall be of a form, construction, arrangement, location, materials, workmanship and description to be approved, or such as may be required by the board of health of the health department of the city of New York."

(1892) — Chapter 275, Section 37. (Provisions of Section 501, Consol. Act, amended as follows:)

"The superintendent of buildings and department of buildings" substituted for "board of health" wherever it occurs in this section; also last sentence of this section amended so as to read as follows: "Any person violating any provisions of this section shall be deemed guilty of a misdemeanor."

(1896) — Chapter 803, Section 5.

"Hereafter the plumbing and drainage of all buildings, both public and private, in the city of New York, shall be executed in accordance with the rules and regulations adopted by the superintendent of buildings. Said rules and regulations and any change thereof shall be published in the 'City Record' on eight successive Mondays before the same shall become operative. Suitable drawings and descriptions of the said plumbing and drainage shall in each case be submitted and placed on file in the department of buildings, and the same shall not be commenced or proceeded with until the said drawings and descriptions shall have been so filed and approved by the superintendent of buildings. Repairs or alterations of such plumbing or drainage may be made without the filing and approval of drawings and descriptions in the department of buildings, but such repairs or alterations shall not be construed to include cases where new vertical and horizontal lines of soil, waste, vent or leader pipes are proposed to be used. Notice of such repairs or alterations shall be given to the said department before the same are commenced in such cases as shall be prescribed by the rules and regulations of the said department, and the work shall be done in accordance with the said rules and regulations.

"§ 6. Whenever any inspector or any person reports a violation of any of said rules and regulations, or a deviation from any said drawings and descriptions filed with and approved by the superintendent of buildings, said department shall first serve a notice of such violation upon the plumber doing the work. Such notice may be served personally or by mail, and if by mail it may be addressed to such plumber at the address registered by him at the department of buildings, but the failure of an employing or master plumber to register pursuant to the provisions of this act will relieve the said department from the requirement of giving such notice. Unless such violation is removed or in process of removal within three days after the date of the serving or mailing of such notice, exclusive of the day of serving or mailing, the said department may proceed as hereinafter provided. A master or employing plumber within the meaning of this act is any person who hires or employs a person or persons to do plumbing work.

"§ 7. Any person violating any of the provisions of sections one, two and five of this act shall be deemed guilty of a misdemeanor, and upon conviction shall be fined for each offense in a sum not exceeding $250, or by imprisonment for a term not exceeding three months, or by both, and in addition shall forfeit any certificate of competency or registration which he may hold under the provisions thereof.

"§ 8. The attorney to the said department of buildings shall prosecute all actions for injunction authorized under the provisions of this act, and shall also take charge of the prosecution of all persons under section 7 thereof.

"§ 9. Nothing herein contained shall be so construed as to abrogate or impair any of the powers of the health department of the city of New York."

GENERAL PROVISIONS

DEFINITION OF A TENEMENT HOUSE.—The first Tenement House Act defined a tenement house as any building or portion of a building which was occupied as the home or residence of more than three families living independently of each other and doing their cooking upon the premises; or a building occupied by two families or more upon one floor, so living and cooking and having a common right in the public parts of the building, that is, the halls, stairways, yards, etc. This definition remained unchanged until 1887, when it was modified so as to apply to buildings occupied by three families or more instead of four families or more. This has remained the definition of a tenement house without change until the present time and is the present law.

(1867) — Chapter 908, Section 17.

"A tenement-house within the meaning of this act shall be taken to mean and include every house, building, or portion thereof which is rented, leased, let or hired out to be occupied, or is occupied as the home or residence of more than three families, living independently of another, and doing their cooking upon the premises, or by more than two families upon a floor, so living and cooking, but having a common right in the halls, stairways, yards, water-closets, or privies, or some of them."

(1882) — Chapter 410, Section 666. — Continued.

(1887) — Chapter 84, Section 13.

This definition amended so as to apply to buildings containing three families or more instead of "more than three families."

(1888) — Brooklyn — Chapter 583, Section 38. (Brooklyn Consol. Act.) Provisions of Law of 1867, reënacted.

(1891) — Brooklyn — Chapter 270, Section 1. (Brooklyn Tenement House Law.)

Definition of a tenement house as given in Section 38, Chapter 583 of the Laws of 1888, amended so as to conform with the definition of a tenement house contained in the New York law, *i.e.* Section 13, Chapter 84 of the Laws of 1887.

(1897) — Chapter 378, Greater New York Charter, Section 1305.

"A tenement-house within the meaning of this title shall be taken to mean and include any house or building or portion thereof, which is rented, leased, let, or hired out to be occupied, or is occupied as the home or residence of three families or more living independently of each other, and doing their cooking upon the premises, or by more than two families upon any floor, so living and cooking, but having a common right in the halls, stairways, yards, water-closets or privies, or some of them."

*** (1900) — Sanitary Code, Department of Health, Section 3.**

Continued with the following slight changes: for the word "any" (line 2), substitute the word "every"; before the word "home" (fourth line), insert the word "house"; instead of the word "any" before the word "floor" (sixth line), insert the word "a."

DEFINITION OF A LODGING HOUSE. — The first Tenement House Act also defined a lodging house as any building or portion of a building in which persons were lodged for a period less than a week. This definition is the present one and has been continued through all the different acts without change.

(1867) — Chapter 908, Section 17.

"A lodging-house shall be taken to mean and include any house or building or portion thereof, in which persons are harbored, or received, or lodged for hire, for a single night, or for less than a week at one time, or any part of which is let for any person to sleep in for any term less than a week."

(1882) — Chapter 410, Section 666. — Continued.

(1887) — Chapter 84, Section 13. — Continued.

* Indicates the existing law in 1900.

(1888) — Brooklyn — Chapter 583, Section 38. (Brooklyn Consol. Act.) Provisions of Law of 1867, reënacted.

(1891) — Brooklyn — Chapter 270, Section 1. (Brooklyn Law.) Previous provision continued.

*** (1897) — Chapter 378, Greater New York Charter, Section 1305. — Continued.**

*** (1900) — Sanitary Code of the Department of Health, Section 3. — Continued.**

DEFINITION OF A CELLAR. — In the Tenement House Act of 1867, a cellar was defined as every basement or lower story of any building one-half or more of the height of which was below the level of the adjoining street. This is the present law upon this subject, there having been no change in the definition since it was originally enacted.

(1867) — Chapter 908, Section 17.

"A cellar shall be taken to mean and include every basement or lower story of any building or house of which one-half or more of the height from the floor to the ceiling is below the level of the street adjoining."

(1882) — Chapter 410, Section 666. — Continued.

(1887) — Chapter 84, Section 13. — Continued.

(1888) — Brooklyn — Chapter 583, Section 38. (Brooklyn Consol. Act.) Provisions of Law of 1867, reënacted.

(1891) — Brooklyn — Chapter 270, Section 1. Previous provisions continued.

*** (1897) — Chapter 378, Greater New York Charter, Section 1305. — Continued.**

*** (1900) — Sanitary Code of the Department of Health, Section 3.**

Continued with the following slight change. Between the words "basement" and "lower story" (line 1) insert the word "and" instead of the word "or."

STAIRS. — The first Tenement House Act required that all stairs should be provided with proper banisters or proper railings and that these should be kept in good repair. This provision of the law has been reënacted through all the different years and is the present law upon this subject.

(1867) — Chapter 908, Section 4.

"All stairs shall be provided with proper banisters or railings, and shall be kept in good repair."

(1882) — Chapter 410, Section 652. — Continued.

(1888) — Brooklyn — Chapter 583, Section 26. (Brooklyn Consol. Act.) — Continued.

* Indicates the existing law in 1900.

*** (1897) — Chapter 378, Greater New York Charter, Section 1306.**

"All stairs shall be provided with proper banisters and railings and shall be kept in good repair."

WINDOW GUARDS. — In 1897 an amendment was made to the tenement house laws, requiring that in all new tenement houses every window above the ground floor which did not lead directly to a fire-escape balcony, and where the window-sills were not more than three feet above the floor, iron or steel guards, at least 10 inches high, should be placed outside of the windows. This law was passed because of the many accidents which had occurred through children falling out of windows. It was the purpose of the framers of the law to have it apply to all tenement houses, it being especially needed in the old buildings. The law was, however, so amended in its passage through the legislature as to apply only to new tenement houses, thus practically destroying its effect. As a consequence, the framers of the law secured its repeal in 1899.

(1897) — Chapter 672, Section 661. (Consol. Act amended by adding to the said section the following:)

"In all buildings hereafter to be constructed and coming under the classification of tenement-houses, and in all buildings hereafter converted into tenement-houses, all windows opening above the first or ground floor not leading directly to fire-escape balconies, and which have the window sills less than 36 inches over the floor of the rooms in which situated, shall be provided with iron or steel guards, or guards of such other hard metal and pattern as the superintendent of buildings approves of, such guards to be at least 10 inches high, and the top railings of the same provided with pike heads not over 6 inches apart, and be firmly secured to the mason work in all new buildings, and to the window frames in old buildings, if so approved by the superintendent of buildings."

(1899) — Chapter 161, repealed.

PRIVACY.—None of the different tenement house laws has contained any provision as to the privacy of persons in such buildings. The regulations of the Building Department, however, provide that the rooms shall be so arranged that persons in order to get to any room need not pass through a bedroom.

*** (1900) — Regulations of the Department of Buildings.**

"Access to all rooms must be had without passing through a bedroom."

COMMISSIONS OF INQUIRY. — The first legislative commission to investigate the tenement house problem was appointed in 1856 by a resolution of the Assembly. This Commission consisted of five members of the Legislature.

In 1884 an act was passed providing for a Commission to inquire into the character and condition of tenement houses in the city of New York; eleven men were named in the act as members of this Commission who

* Indicates the existing law in 1900.

were to serve without compensation, although their expenses were to be paid and the sum of $5000 was appropriated for such expenses. The Commission was required to report their recommendations and findings to the next Legislature, on or before January 15, and was empowered to subpœna witnesses and compel their attendance; and they were also given authority to require the production of any books, papers, or documents they might need. In 1894 another Commission of Inquiry was appointed, the Governor being directed to appoint seven persons, who should be citizens of New York, to examine into the tenement houses of the city, their condition as to construction, healthfulness, safety, rentals and the effect of tenement house life upon the education, savings, and morals of those who lived in such buildings, and all other phases of the tenement house question that could affect the public welfare. The Commission was authorized to employ a secretary and counsel and such assistants and experts as might be necessary, and the sum of $10,000 was appropriated for their expenses. The members of the committee were to serve without compensation, although the expenses incurred by them in the performance of their duties were to be paid. Power to subpœna witnesses with or without papers was given to them, such subpœnas to be served by any policeman of the city, and all witnesses were to be paid the regular fee paid to witnesses in courts of record. The committee was also required to make a full report to the next Legislature of its work, with such recommendations as it might deem wise to enable the best and highest possible conditions for tenement house life to be attained. The Commission ceased to exist upon the making of this report.

In 1900 a law was passed authorizing the Governor to appoint another Commission to investigate the tenement house question.

This act was almost identical with the act of 1894, except that the number of persons serving on the Commission was not specified, and that the law applied to cities of the first class instead of solely to the city of New York.

(1884) — Chapter 488.

"Alexander Shaler, Joseph W. Drexel, S. O. Vanderpoel, Felix Adler, Oswald Ottendorfer, Moreau Morris, Anthony Reichardt, Joseph J. O'Donohue, Abbott Hodgeman, Charles F. Wingate and William P. Esterbrook are hereby appointed a commission to investigate and inquire into the condition of tenement-houses, lodging-houses and cellars in the city of New York. The thus constituted commission shall have power and are hereby authorized to subpoena witnesses and compel their attendance, and to require the production of any books, papers or documents in the possession or under the control of any person subpoenaed to appear before them. And the chairman shall have power to administer oaths to the witnesses before said commission. A refusal to obey a subpoena of the commission is hereby made a misdemeanor. The commission shall have power to employ a stenographer. No member of the commission shall receive any compensation for his services. Any vacancy or vacancies occurring in such commission shall be filled by election by the balance of the commission. The commission shall report the evidence, together with their recommendation, to the legislature on or before January 15, 1885. The sum of $5,000 is hereby appropriated to pay the expenses of the commission hereby created."

(1894) — Chapter 479.

"Section 1. The governor shall appoint seven persons, citizens and residents of New York, a committee to be known as the Tenement-House Committee. Said committee shall meet within ten days after the passage of this act for organization. It shall elect a chairman and appoint a secretary, it may employ such counsel, assistants and experts from time to time as it may deem necessary. The total expense of the committee shall not exceed the sums hereinafter appropriated. It may fix the number of commissioners necessary for a quorum, make rules for its government and the direction of its work, and fill all vacancies in the committee by death or otherwise.

"§ 2. The duties of said committee shall be to make a careful examination into the tenement-houses of the city of New York, their condition as to construction, healthfulness, safety, rentals and the effect of tenement-house life on the health, education, savings and morals of those who live in such habitations and all other phases of the so-called tenement-house question in the city that can affect the public welfare.

"§ 3. The committee shall have power to subpoena witnesses before it with or without papers by a subpoena signed by the chairman, to administer them oaths and to compel their attendance by attachment to be issued on the order of the committee and served by any policeman of said city; witnesses shall be paid the fee paid witnesses in courts of record.

"§ 4. The members of the committee shall receive no compensation for their services, but the expenses and disbursements incurred by them in the discharge of their duties as said commissioners shall be paid. The commission shall have power to fix the compensation of its counsel and other employes.

"§ 5. Said committee shall make a full report to the next legislature at its opening of its work with such recommendations as it deems wise to enable the best and highest possible condition for tenement-house life in said city to be attained and the committee shall cease to exist when such report is made.

"§ 6. The sum of ten thousand dollars is hereby appropriated out of any moneys in the treasury not otherwise appropriated for the purposes of carrying out the provisions of this act. The expenses, disbursements, payment of counsel fees and compensation of other employes of the committee shall be made on the approval of the chairman of the committee and the audit of the comptroller."

(1900) — Chapter 279.

"Section 1. The governor of the state of New York is herewith authorized and empowered to appoint a commission to be known as the tenement-house commission. Said commission shall elect a chairman and appoint a secretary; it may employ such counsel, assistants and experts from time to time as it may deem necessary. The total expense of the committee shall not exceed the sums hereinafter appropriated. It may fix the number of commissioners necessary for a quorum, make rules for its government and direction of its work, and fill the vacancies in the commission caused by death or otherwise.

"§ 2. The duties of said commission shall be to make a careful examination into the tenement-houses in cities of the first class; their condition as to the construction, healthfulness, safety, rentals and the effect of tenement-house life on the health, education, savings and morals of those who live in tenement-houses, and all other phases of the so-called tenement-house question in these cities that can affect the public welfare.

§ 3. The commission shall have power to subpoena witnesses before it, with or without papers, by a subpoena signed by the chairman, to administer them oaths and to compel their attendance by attachment to be issued on the order of the commission and served by any policeman of said cities; witnesses shall be paid the fee paid witnesses in courts of record.

"§ 4. The members of the commission shall receive no compensation for their services, but the expenses and disbursements incurred by them in the discharge of their duties as said commissioners shall be paid. The commission shall have power to fix the compensation of its counsel and other employes.

"§ 5. Said commission shall make a full report of its work to the next legislature at its opening or as soon thereafter as practicable, with such recommendations as it deems wise to enable the best and highest possible condition for tenement-house life in said cities to be attained, and the commission shall cease to exist when such report is made.

"§ 6. The sum of ten thousand dollars is hereby appropriated out of any moneys in the treasury not otherwise appropriated for the purpose of carrying out the provisions of this act. The expenses, disbursements, payment of counsel fees and compensation of other employes of the commission shall be made on the approval of the chairman of the commission and the audit of the comptroller."

A LIST OF ALL LAWS ENACTED IN THE STATE OF NEW YORK IN REFERENCE TO TENEMENT HOUSES, AND ALSO ALL GENERAL BUILDING LAWS

1849. Chapter 84, p. 118. — An act for the more effectual prevention of fires in the city of New York, and to amend the acts heretofore passed for that purpose.
Passed March 7, 1849. Took effect June 1, 1849.
(General Building Law.)

1849. Chapter 195, p. 296. — An act to amend an act "For the more effectual prevention of fires in the city of New York (chapter 84, Laws of 1849), and to amend the acts heretofore passed for that purpose."
Passed April 4, 1849.

1851. Chapter 66, p. 72. — An act to repeal an act entitled "An act to amend an act for the more effectual prevention of fires in the city of New York, and to amend the acts heretofore passed for that purpose" passed April 4, 1849 (chapter 195, Laws of 1849), and to amend an act entitled "An act for the more effectual prevention of fires in the city of New York, and to amend the acts heretofore passed for that purpose" passed March 7, 1849 (chapter 84, Laws of 1849).
Passed March 28, 1851.

1852. * Chapter 355, p. 552. — An act to establish fire limits, and for the more effectual prevention of fires in the city of Brooklyn.
Passed April 16, 1852. Took effect May 1, 1852.
(General Building Law. The first Brooklyn law.)

1855. Chapter 6, p. 11. — An act respecting excavations in the cities of New York and Brooklyn.
Passed January 24, 1855.
(A new act.)

1856. Chapter 18, p. 21. — An act further to amend "An act for the more effectual prevention of fires in the city of New York" passed March 7, 1849 (chapter 84, Laws of 1849).
Passed February 19, 1856.

1857. * Chapter 225, p. 485. — An act in reference to party walls in the city of New York.
Passed April 1, 1857.
(A new act.)

1860. * Chapter 470, p. 905. — An act to provide against unsafe dwellings in the city of New York.
Passed April 17, 1860. Took effect June 1, 1860.
(A new act, repeals, all previous laws inconsistent. General Building Law.)

1860. * Chapter 472, p. 937. — An act to establish fire limits and for the more effectual prevention of fires in the eastern district of the city of Brooklyn.
Passed April 17, 1860.

* **Laws marked thus contain provisions in reference to tenement houses.**

(Repeals all previous laws inconsistent.
General Building Law.)

1862. * Chapter 356, p. 574. — An act to provide for the regulation and inspection of buildings, the more effectual prevention of fires, and the better preservation of life and property in the city of New York.

Passed April 19, 1862. Took effect May 1, 1862. (Repeals chapter 470, Laws of 1860, and all other previous acts inconsistent. A General Building Law.)

"Tenement-house" occurs for the first time in this law.

1863. Chapter 273, p. 483. — An act to amend an act entitled "An act to provide for the regulation and inspection of buildings, the more effectual prevention of fires, and the better preservation of life and property in the city of New York," passed April 19, 1862 (chapter 356, Laws of 1862).

Passed April 29, 1863.

1864. Chapter 466, p. 1110. — An act to amend an act entitled "An act to provide for the regulation and inspection of buildings, the more effectual prevention of fires and the better preservation of life and property in the city of New York," passed April 19, 1862 (chapter 356, Laws of 1862).

Passed April 30, 1864.

1866. * Chapter 74, p. 114, Vol. 1. — An act to create a Metropolitan sanitary district and board of health therein, for the preservation of life and health, and to prevent the spread of disease.

Passed February 26, 1866. Took effect March 1, 1866.

(First General Health Law for the cities of New York and Brooklyn.)

1866. * Chapter 858, p. 1970, Vol. 2. — An act to establish fire limits, and for the more effectual prevention of fires in the city of Brooklyn.

Passed April 30, 1866. Took effect May 1, 1866.

(General Building Law. Repeals all previous acts inconsistent.)

1866. * Chapter 873, p. 2009, Vol. 2. — An act to amend and reduce to one act, the several acts relating to buildings, and the keeping and storage of combustible materials in the city of New York.

Passed May 4, 1866. Took effect June 1, 1866.

(Repeals all previous laws inconsistent. A General Building Law.)

1867. * Chapter 908, p. 2265, Vol. 2. — An act for the regulation of tenement and lodging-houses in the cities of New York and Brooklyn.

Passed May 14, 1867. Took effect May 1, 1867.

(The first tenement house act.)

1867. Chapter 939, p. 2324, Vol. 2. — An act to amend "An act to amend and reduce to one act, the several acts relating to buildings, and the keeping and storage of combustible materials in the city of New York," passed May 4, 1866 (chapter 873, Laws of 1866).

Passed May 17, 1867.

(Amends General Building Law.)

1868. * Chapter 634, p. 1352, Vol. 2. — An act to amend section 31, of chapter 873, of the laws of 1866, passed May 4, 1866, and section

* Laws marked thus contain provisions in reference to tenement houses.

10, chapter 939, passed May 17, 1867, relating to buildings and the keeping and storage of combustible material in the city of New York.
Passed May 6, 1868.
(Amends General Building Law.)

1868. Chapter 632, p. 1329, Vol. 2. — An act to amend an act, entitled "An act to establish fire limits and for the further prevention of fires in the city of Brooklyn," passed April 30, 1866.
Passed May 6, 1868. Took effect May 1, 1868.
(General Building Law. Repeals all previous acts inconsistent.)

1870. Chapter 383, p. 881, Vol. 1. — An act to make further provision for the government of the city of New York.
(Section 26 takes from the Metropolitan board of health all powers vested in said board by Chapter 74, Laws of 1866, and confers them on a local board of health.)
Passed April 26, 1870.

1871. * Chapter 625, p. 1334, Vol. 2. — An act to amend and reduce to one act the several acts relating to buildings in the city of New York, passed May 4, 1866, May 17, 1867, and May 6, 1868.
Passed April 20, 1871.
(General Building Law. Repeals all previous acts inconsistent.)

1873. Chapter 355, p. 505. — An act to reorganize the local government of the city of New York.
Passed April 30, 1873.
(Article XI provides for the organization and duties of the local health department.)

1874. * Chapter 547, p. 734. — An act to amend an act entitled, "An act to amend and reduce to one act, the several acts relating to buildings in the city of New York, passed May 4, 1866, May 17, 1867, and May 6, 1868," passed April 20, 1871.
Passed May 22, 1874.
(Amends General Building Law.)

1879. * Chapter 504, p. 554. — An act to amend chapter 908, of the Laws of 1867, entitled "An act for the regulation of tenement and lodging-houses in the cities of New York and Brooklyn."
Passed June 16, 1879.
(Amends Tenement House Act.)

1880. Chapter 399, p. 575, Vol. 1. — An act to further amend chapter 908, of the Laws of 1867, entitled "An act for the regulation of tenement and lodging-houses in the cities of New York and Brooklyn," as amended by chapter 504, of the Laws of 1879.
Passed May 26, 1880.
(Amends Tenement House Act.)

1880. * Chapter 521, p. 729, Vol. 1. — An act to amend chapter 335 of the Laws of 1873, entitled "An act to reorganize the local government of the city of New York," and to reduce the burden of taxes to be levied in said city.
Passed May 29, 1880.
(Department of buildings abolished, and powers and duties transferred to the Bureau of Buildings of the Fire Department.)

1881. Chapter 424, p. 584, Vol. 1. — An act to limit the operation of chap-

*** Laws marked thus contain provisions in reference to tenement houses.**

ter 625 of the Laws of 1871, entitled "An act to amend and reduce to one act, the several acts relating to buildings in the city of New York, passed May 4, 1866, May 17, 1867, May 6, 1868," in the twelfth, twenty-third and twenty-fourth wards of the city of New York, north of One Hundred and Fortieth street.

Passed May 28, 1881.

(Amends General Building Law.)

1881. Chapter 450, p. 614, Vol. 1.—An act to secure the registration of plumbers and the supervision of plumbing and drainage, in the cities of New York and Brooklyn.

Passed June 4, 1881.

(First Plumbing Law.)

1882. * Chapter 410, Consolidation Act, title 5, p. 125, sections 471–517.

(A General Building Law. Repeals all previous acts inconsistent.)

Title 7, p. 181, sections 649–667, tenement houses.

(Repeals all previous acts inconsistent.)

1884. * Chapter 448, p. 523.—An act to provide for a commission to inquire into the character and condition of tenement-houses in the city of New York.

Passed June 2, 1884.

1885. * Chapter 454, p. 763.—An act to regulate the height of dwelling-houses in the city of New York.

Passed June 9, 1885.

(A new act.)

1885. * Chapter 456, p. 764.—An act to amend chapter 410 of the Laws of 1882, entitled "An act to consolidate into one act and to declare the special and local laws affecting public interests in the city of New York," so far as the same relates to the bureau of buildings and the erection of buildings in said city.

Passed June 9, 1885.

(General Building Law. Repeals all previous building laws inconsistent.)

1887. Chapter 84, p. 94.—An act to amend chapter 410, of the Laws of 1882, entitled "An act to consolidate into one act and to declare the special and local laws affecting public interests in the city of New York," in relation to the powers and duties of the health fund and the board of health, and the health department of the city of New York, and for the preservation of the public health.

Passed March 25, 1887.

(Amends Tenement House Laws.)

1887. * Chapter 288, p. 362.—An act to amend section 661, of chapter 410, of the Laws of 1882, entitled "An act to consolidate into one act and to declare the special and local laws affecting public interests in the city of New York," as amended by chapter 84, of the Laws of 1887.

Passed May 6, 1887.

(Amends Tenement House Act.)

1887. * Chapter 489, p. 619.—An act to amend chapter 410, of the Laws of 1882, entitled "An act to consolidate into one act and to declare the special and local laws affecting public interests in the

*** Laws marked thus contain provisions in reference to tenement houses.**

city of New York," in relation to the powers and duties of the board of health and the officers of the health department of the city of New York.
Passed June 1, 1887.
(Relates to appointment of sanitary inspectors.)

1887. * Chapter 566, p. 738. — An act to amend chapter 410, of the Laws of 1882, entitled "An act to consolidate into one act and to declare the special and local laws affecting public interests in the city of New York," in so far as the same regulates the construction of buildings in said city.
Passed June 15, 1887. Took effect twenty days later.
(A General Building Act amending the General Building Laws.)

1888. * Chapter 422, p. 696. — An act to amend chapter 410, of the Laws of 1882, entitled "An act to consolidate into one act and to declare the special and local laws affecting public interests in the city of New York," the board of health, and of the health department of the city of New York, and for the preservation of the public health.
Passed May 28, 1888.
(Amends Tenement House Laws in relation to water-closets.)

1888. * Chapter 583, p. 949, Brooklyn Consolidation Act. — An act to revise and combine in a single act all existing special and local laws affecting public interests in the city of Brooklyn.
Title 14, p. 1023, sections 1–59.
(General Building Law. Repeals all previous acts inconsistent. Also contains General Tenement House Law, repealing all previous acts inconsistent.)
Passed June 9, 1888. Took effect June 2, 1888.

1889. * Chapter 211, p. 259. — An act to amend chapter 410, of the Laws of 1882, entitled "An act to consolidate into one act and to declare the special and local laws affecting public interests in the city of New York," as amended by chapter 422, of the Laws of 1888, in relation to the powers and duties of the health fund and the board of health, and of the health department of the city of New York, and for the preservation of the public health.
Passed May 2, 1889.
(Amends Tenement House Laws in relation to water-closets.)

1889. * Chapter 297, p. 371. — An act to amend chapter 410, of the Laws of 1882, entitled "An act to consolidate into one act and to declare the special and local laws affecting public interests in the city of New York," in so far as the same regulates the construction of buildings in said city.
Passed May 23, 1889.
(Amends General Building Laws in reference to fireproof buildings.)

1890. * Chapter 486, p. 883. — An act to amend section 663 of chapter 410, of the Laws of 1882, entitled "An act to consolidate into one act and to declare the special and local laws affecting public interests in the city of New York," as amended by chapter 84 of the Laws of 1887, in relation to the powers, duties and health fund of the board of health, and of the health department of the city of New York, and for the preservation of the public health.

* Laws marked thus contain provisions in reference to tenement houses.

Passed June 4, 1890.
(Amends Tenement House Acts.)

1891. * Chapter 39, p. 53. — An act to amend chapter 486, of the Laws of 1890, entitled "An act to amend section 663 of chapter 410, of the Laws of 1882, entitled 'An act to consolidate into one act and to declare the special and local laws affecting public interests in the city of New York,' as amended by chapter 84, of the Laws of 1887, in relation to the powers, duties and health fund of the board of health, and of the health department of the city of New York, and for the preservation of the public health."
Passed March 2, 1891.
(Repeals previous law and amends Tenement House Act.)

1891. * Chapter 204, p. 397. — An act to amend section 661, of chapter 410, of the Laws of 1882, entitled "An act to consolidate into one act and to declare the special and local laws affecting public interests in the city of New York," as amended by chapter 84 and chapter 288, of the Laws of 1887, in relation to tenement and lodging-houses and the erection thereof.
Passed April 16, 1891.
(Important law. Amends Tenement House Act.)

1891. * Chapter 270, p. 498. — An act to amend chapter 583, of the Laws of 1888, entitled "An act to revise and combine in a single act all existing special and local laws affecting public interests in the city of Brooklyn," in relation to the department of health.
Passed April 28, 1891.
(Amends Tenement House Act by defining a tenement house.)

1892. * Chapter 238, p. 490. — An act to amend section 661, of chapter 410, of the Laws of 1882, entitled "An act to consolidate into one act and to declare the special and local laws affecting public interests in the city of New York," as amended by chapter 84 and chapter 288, of the Laws of 1887, and as further amended by chapter 204, of the Laws of 1891, in relation to tenement and lodging-houses.
Passed April 7, 1892.
(Important. Amends Tenement House Act.)

1892. * Chapter 275, p. 543. — An act to create a department of buildings in the city of New York and to amend chapter 410, of the Laws of 1882, entitled "An act to consolidate into one act and to declare the special and local laws affecting public interests in the city of New York," in so far as the same relates to the fire and building departments of said city, and by adding a new section thereto, creating a bureau to be known as "the Bureau of Fire Alarms, Telegraph and Electrical Appliances."
Passed April 9, 1892.
(A General Building Law, repeals all previous acts inconsistent, creates a new Department of Buildings and transfers powers previously vested in Fire Department to said new Department, also transfers powers of Board of Health in reference to plumbing and drainage, and light and ventilation of new buildings to Building Department.)

1892. * Chapter 329, p. 685. — An act to amend section 667, of chapter 410, of the Laws of 1882, entitled "An act to consolidate into one act

* Laws marked thus contain provisions in reference to tenement houses.

and to declare the special and local laws affecting public interests in the city of New York," relating to occupation of tenement-houses, etc.
Passed April 19, 1892.
(Amends Tenement House Act.)

1892. Chapter 602, p. 1148. — An act to secure the registration of plumbers and the supervision of plumbing and drainage in the cities of the state of New York.
Passed May 16, 1892.
(A new General Act appointing Examining Boards of Plumbers, etc.)

1892. * Chapter 703, p. 1451. — An act to amend sections 454 and 465, of chapter 410, of the Laws of 1882, entitled "An act to consolidate into one act and to declare the special and local laws affecting public interests in the city of New York," and also to amend such chapters by inserting a new section, to be known as section 454½, relating to the fire department of the said city.
Passed May 19, 1892. Took effect June 1, 1892.
(Provides for a system of fire alarms in tenement houses.)

1893. Chapter 162, p. 277. — An act to amend chapter 602, of the Laws of 1892, entitled "An act to secure the registration of plumbers and the supervision of plumbing and drainage in the cities of the state of New York."
Passed March 21, 1893.
(Amends General State Plumbing Law.)

1894. * Chapter 479, p. 963. — An act appointing a commission to examine into the tenement-house question in the city of New York, and to report to the next legislature.
Passed May 4, 1894.

1894. Chapter 481, p. 1008. — An act to amend chapter 583, of the Laws of 1888, entitled "An act to revise and combine in a single act all existing special and local laws affecting public interests in the city of Brooklyn," in relation to the department of buildings.
Passed May 4, 1894. Took effect June 3, 1894.
(A General Building Law, repeals all previous acts inconsistent.)

1895. Chapter 292, p. 380, Vol. 2, part 1. — An act to amend sections 1, 6, 7, 10, 13, 22, 23 and 61 of title 14, chapter 583, of Laws of 1888, entitled "An act to revise and combine in a single act, all existing special and local laws affecting public interests in the city of Brooklyn," as said title is amended by chapter 481, of the Laws of 1894, relating to the building department of the city of Brooklyn.
Passed April 11, 1895.
(Amends General Building Law.)

1895. * Chapter 539, p. 955, Vol. 2, part 1. — An act to amend sections 24, 46, 55, 56 and 57 of title 14, chapter 583, of Laws of 1888, entitled "An act to revise and combine in a single act all existing special and local laws affecting public interests in the city of Brooklyn," as said title is amended by chapter 481, of the Laws of 1894, relating to the building department of the city of Brooklyn.
Passed May 3, 1895.
(Amends Tenement House Act.)

* Laws marked thus contain provisions in reference to tenement houses.

1895. * Chapter 567, p. 1099, Vol. 2, part 1. — An act to amend chapter 410, of the Laws of 1882, entitled "An act to consolidate into one act and to declare the special and local laws affecting public interests in the city of New York," as subsequently amended by chapter 84, of the Laws of 1887, and chapter 288, of the Laws of 1887, and chapter 275, of the Laws of 1892, and otherwise so as to provide for the improvement of tenement and lodging-houses in the city of New York.
Took effect May 9, 1895.
(Important. Amends Tenement House Act.)

1896. * Chapter 355, p. 390, Vol. 2. — An act to amend chapter 583, of the Laws of 1888, entitled "An act to revise and combine in a single act all existing special and local laws affecting the public interests in the city of Brooklyn," as amended by chapter 539, of the Laws of 1895, in relation to the department of buildings.
Took effect April 21, 1896.
(Amends Tenement House Act.)

1896. Chapter 610, p. 730, Vol. 2. — An act to amend chapter 410 of the Laws of 1882, entitled "An act to consolidate into one act and to declare the special and local laws affecting public interests in the city of New York," in relation to buildings in said city.
Took effect May 13, 1896.
(Amends building laws in reference to bay windows.)

1896. Chapter 643, p. 767, Vol. 2. — An act to amend chapter 583, of the Laws of 1888, entitled "An act to revise and combine in a single act all existing special and local laws affecting public interests in the city of Brooklyn."
Took effect May 13, 1896.
(Amends General Building Law.)

1896. Chapter 723, p. 880, Vol. 2. — An act to amend section 484, chapter 410, of the Laws of 1882, entitled "An act to consolidate into one act and to declare the special and local laws affecting the public interests in the city of New York."
Took effect May 19, 1896.
(Amends General Building Law in relation to fireproof dwellings.)

1896. Chapter 803, p. 1052, Vol. 2. — An act in relation to plumbing in the city of New York.
Took effect May 21, 1896.
(A new act regulating plumbing.)

1897. Chapter 321, p. 293, Vol. 2. — An act to regulate the height of fireproof dwelling-houses in the city of New York.
(A new act.)

1897. * Chapter 378, Greater New York Charter. — An act to unite into one Municipality under the corporate name of the city of New York the various communities lying in and about New York harbor, including the city and county of New York, the city of Brooklyn, county of Kings, the county of Richmond, and a part of the county of Queens, and to provide for the government thereof.
Took effect May 4, 1897.
Title 7, p. 462, sections 1304–1325.

* Laws marked thus contain provisions in reference to tenement houses.

(Important. Amends Tenement House Act, and repeals all previous acts.)

1897. Chapter 557, p. 835. — An act to amend section 484, of chapter 410, of the Laws of 1882, entitled "An act to consolidate into one act and to declare the special and local laws affecting the public interests in the city of New York," as amended by chapter 723 of the Laws of 1896.

Took effect May 19, 1897.

(Amends building laws in relation to fireproof buildings.)

1897. * Chapter 672, p. 919, Vol. 2. — An act to amend chapter 410, of the Laws of 1882, entitled "An act to consolidate into one act and to declare the special and local laws affecting public interests in the city of New York," as amended by chapters 84 and 288, of the Laws of 1887, and by chapter 238, of the Laws of 1892, and by chapter 567, of the Laws of 1895, and otherwise, so as to provide for the improvement of tenement and lodging-houses.

Took effect May 27, 1897.

(Provides for window guards in tenement houses.)

1897. Chapter 724, p. 984, Vol. 2. — An act to amend chapter 410, of the Laws of 1882, entitled "An act to consolidate into one act and to declare the special and local laws affecting the public interests in the city of New York," relating to the erection of coverings over sidewalks, and inclosures around buildings for the protection of pedestrians.

Took effect May 22, 1897.

(Amends General Building Laws.)

1899. * Chapter 161, p. 313. — An act to repeal chapter 672, of the Laws of 1897, relative to window guards.

Took effect March 30, 1899.

(Repeals window guard provisions.)

1899. Chapter 646, p. 1429, Vol. 2. — An act to amend chapter 410, of the Laws of 1882, entitled "An act to consolidate into one act and to declare the special and local laws affecting the public interests in the city of New York," in relation to buildings in the county of New York.

Took effect May 25, 1899.

(Amends building laws in relation to bay windows.)

1899. The Building Code. — An ordinance adopted by the city of New York. Took effect December 20, 1899; authorized under the provisions of section 647 of the Greater New York Charter.

(A new General Building Law, repeals all previous State laws and local ordinances upon this subject.)

1900. Chapter 279, p. 620, Vol. 1. — An act appointing a commission to examine into the tenement-house question in cities of the first class, and to report to the next legislature a code of Tenement-House Laws.

Took effect April 4, 1900.

* **Laws marked thus contain provisions in reference to tenement houses.**

APPENDIX VII

RESULTS OF INVESTIGATIONS IN BUFFALO IN 1900

BY WILLIAM A. DOUGLAS AND WILLIAMS LANSING

APPENDIX VII

RESULTS OF INVESTIGATIONS IN BUFFALO IN 1900

BY WILLIAM A. DOUGLAS AND WILLIAMS LANSING

RESULTS OF INVESTIGATIONS IN BUFFALO IN 1900

In the investigations made by the Commission in Buffalo, three schedules were prepared, one having reference to the general conditions of the houses and grounds, called the "General Statistical Card"; one relating to the interior of the houses, called the "Interior Card"; and one relating to the condition of the separate apartments, known as the "Apartment Card." Copies of these schedules will be found in Appendix X. With these cards as the basis of their investigation, one inspector was detailed to examine the Italian District and one to examine the Polish District. The results of the inspection were noted on the cards as the investigations were made and turned in daily. From these cards have been prepared the tables below, which set forth the principal facts obtained. It has not, however, been deemed necessary or of value to tabulate all the items noted upon the inspection cards. The tables set out the information separately for the Italian and Polish Districts, as the conditions differ widely in the two localities. In the Italian District the examination has been confined practically to those houses which under the Buffalo ordinances are defined as tenement houses, viz. houses occupied as a dwelling by over four families or more living independently of one another and doing their cooking upon the premises, or by three or more above the second floor so living and cooking. The total number of such houses reported is 151, but from this number should be deducted 3 lodging houses. All percentages shown are with these lodging houses excluded.

In the investigation of the Polish District 197 houses were examined, and houses containing three or more families were included for the reason that the Poles live mostly in small, detached houses. It has not been attempted to report upon all houses of this class, for the reason that it would have been impossible, within the time and means at our disposal. The worst specimens are, however, included, and it is believed that the whole number reported upon exhibit fairly the conditions that exist in that section.

In the following table the facts as shown by the General Statistical and Interior Cards are summarized: —

Italian District

Number of houses	151
Controlled by —	
Owner	92
Percentage of same	61%
General lessee	29
Percentage of same	19%
Agent	30
Percentage of same	20%
Material of construction —	
Wood	33
Percentage of same	22%

Stone	8
Percentage of same	5%
Brick	110
Percentage of same	73%
Height of buildings —	
One story	1
Percentage of same	1%
Two stories	42
Percentage of same	28%
Over two stories and not more than three	71
Percentage of same	47%
Over three stories and not more than four	29
Percentage of same	19%
Five stories	8
Percentage of same	5%
Total number of apartments	1,573
Average number of apartments to tenement	10.63
Number of rooms	3,655
Average number of rooms to an apartment	2.3
Number of families	1,552
Total number of inhabitants	6,683
Average persons to apartment	4.74
Number of adults over 14 years of age	4,184
Percentage of same	63%
Children from 5 to 14 years	1,291
Percentage of same	19%
Children under 5	1,208
Percentage of same	18%
Vacant apartments	164
Percentage of same	10%
Vacant rooms	401
Percentage of same	11%
Number of houses with janitor	24
With night watchman	3
Paving of courts and yards —	
With stone	3
Percentage of same	2%
With brick	7
Percentage of same	5%
With plank	25
Percentage of same	17%
With cement	2
Percentage of same	1%
Not paved	77
Percentage of same	50%
Number of houses without courts	34
Percentage of same	25%
Courts drained	17
Drain trapped	17
Courts —	
Clean	87
Percentage of same	78%
Fair	10
Percentage of same	8%
Dirty	17
Percentage of same	14%
Tenements with outhouses used for storage, fuel, garbage, water-closets	96
Outhouses —	
Clean	77
Percentage of same	80%
Fair	15
Percentage of same	16%
Dirty	4
Percentage of same	4%

Outhouses whitewashed	1
Buildings with fire-escapes	19
Percentage of same	12%
Buildings with fire-escapes of iron	17
Buildings with fire-escapes of wood	2
Ladders connecting with roof	18
Fire-escapes encumbered	5
Tenements with animals on premises, all horses	12
Basements used for dwellings	23
Percentage of same	15%
Basements used for saloon	1
Basements used for kitchen	1
Tenements without cellars	22
Average width of public hallways	5.5 ft.
Public hallways	148
Dark	39
Percentage of same	25%
Fair	2
Percentage of same	1%
Light	107
Percentage of same	74%
Tenements with red light on each floor	5
With white light on each floor	79
With suitable fire gongs	31
With two means of egress	27
Tenements, front door locked at night	15
Number of tenements with private halls dirty	19
Percentage of same	13%
With halls fair	30
Percentage of same	20%
With halls clean	99
Percentage of same	67%
With odors in hall	30
Tenements with wood and iron stairs	4
Percentage of same	3%
With stone and wood stairs	2
Percentage of same	1%
With wooden stairs	142
Percentage of same	96%
Tenements with stairs dirty	14
Percentage of same	9%
With stairs fair	41
Percentage of same	27%
With stairs clean	93
Percentage of same	64%
Tenements with staircase to roof	30
Roof used to dry clothes	21
Chimneys —	
Plenty of chimneys, place for stove or fireplace for each apartment.	
City water —	
Furnished for every set of apartments	130
Percentage of same	88%
Not furnished	18
Percentage of same	12%
Water protected from freezing	1
Tenements with baths	4
Shower	1
Tubs	3
Number of water-closets	526
Privies	28
Kind of closets —	
Automatic	7
Tank	24
Plunger	6

Kind of closets (*continued*) —	
Hopper	124
Tenements without one water-closet for every family or fifteen persons	46
Condition of plumbing —	
Bad	10
Percentage of same	6%
Fair	4
Percentage of same	3%
Good	134
Percentage of same	91%
Number of tenements not whitewashed twice a year	133
Whitewashed twice a year	14
Facilities for washing and drying clothes —	
Without	7
Percentage of same	5%
Poor	19
Percentage of same	12%
Good	122
Percentage of same	83%
Garbage and ashes in wooden barrels	147
Place for garbage not provided	30
Business conducted on premises —	
Groceries	41
Saloons	19
Barber shops	9
Shoe shops	9
Undertaker	1
Fruit storage	2
Cigar factory	1
Milk depots	2
Miscellaneous	27
No business	67
Total rent ascertained for 147 tenements, per month	$8,258.75
Average monthly rental per tenement	55.80
Average monthly rental per apartment	5.32

Polish District

Total number of houses	197
Controlled by agent	13
Percentage of same	6%
Material of construction, wood	197
Height of buildings —	
One story	65
Percentage of same	33%
Over one story and less than two	31
Percentage of same	15.5%
Two stories	100
Percentage of same	51%
Three stories	1
Percentage of same	.5%
Number of apartments	873
Average number of apartments to tenement	4.4343
Number of rooms	2,188
Average number of rooms to apartment	2.5
Number of families	863
Total number of inhabitants	4,612
Average number of persons to apartment	5.5
Number of adults over fourteen	2,277
Children between ages of three and fourteen	1,394
Under five	941
Vacant apartments	33
Vacant rooms	76
Houses having janitor	1

Houses having courts or yards	197
Percentage of same	100%
Courts paved with stone	2
Percentage of same	1%
Courts paved with plank	21
Percentage of same	10%
Unpaved	174
Percentage of same	89%
Courts drained and trapped	2
Cleanliness of court —	
Clean	171
Percentage of same	87%
Fair	11
Percentage of same	6%
Dirty	15
Percentage of same	7%
Tenements with outhouses used for storage, fuel, garbage, water-closets	194
Cleanliness of outhouses —	
Clean	189
Percentage of same	96%
Fair	3
Percentage of same	1.5%
Dirty	5
Percentage of same	2.5%
Outhouses whitewashed	1
Fire-escapes	none
Tenements with animals on premises	10
Kinds of animals —	
Horses	6
Fowls	4
Basements used for dwelling	none
Cellars used for storage and fuel	12
Percentage of same	7%
Tenements without cellars	185
Percentage of same	93%
Average width of public hallways	5.46
Public hallways, dark	1
Percentage of same	.5%
Public hallways, light	196
Percentage of same	99.5%
Tenements with two means of egress	63
Front door locked at night	196
Tenements with halls dirty	6
Percentage of same	3%
Fair	1
Percentage of same	.5%
Clean	190
Percentage of same	96.5%
Tenements with odors in hall	2
Material of stairs —	
Wood	197
Percentage of same	100%
Tenements with stairs dirty	6
Percentage of same	3%
Fair	1
Percentage of same	.5%
Clean	190
Percentage of same	96.5%
Tenements with staircase to roof	1
Chimneys —	
Plenty of chimneys in each apartment.	
Location of water supply —	
In the yard	43
Percentage of same	22%

Location of water supply (*continued*) —	
In yard and house	101
Percentage of same	51%
In house	53
Percentage of same	27%
Water not furnished for every one family or set of apartments	1
Protected from freezing	none
Tenements with baths	1
Number of water-closets	219
Privies	132
Tenements with water-closets in house	6
Percentage of same	3%
In yards	191
Percentage of same	97%
Kind of closets —	
Fountain	2
Percentage of same	1%
Plunger	1
Percentage of same	.5%
Hopper	194
Percentage of same	98.5%
Tenements without at least 1 water-closet for every family or 15 persons	18
Percentage of same	10%
With water-closet for every family or 15 persons	179
Percentage of same	90%
Condition of plumbing —	
Good	189
Percentage of same	96%
Bad	8
Percentage of same	4%
Tenements whitewashed twice a year	none
Facilities for washing and drying clothes, with	196
Without	1
Garbage and ashes kept in wooden barrels in yard —	—
Business conducted on premises —	
Grocery	1
Percentage of same	.5%
Saloon	7
Percentage of same	.5%
No business	182
Percentage of same	92.5%
Miscellaneous	7
Percentage of same	3.5%
Total present rent ascertained from 189 tenements, per month	$2,681.60
Average rental per month per tenement	14.19
Average monthly rental per apartment	3.11

The following table contains a summary of facts relating to separate apartments: —

ITALIAN DISTRICT

Total number of houses	147
Total number of apartments	1,573
Apartments with windows opening on yard or court only	384
Percentage of apartments with windows opening on yard or court only	24%
Total number of rooms	3,655
Rooms reported dark	563
Percentage of dark rooms	15%
Rooms with fair light	93
Percentage of rooms with fair light	3%
Rooms well lighted	2,099
Percentage of rooms well lighted	82%

Rooms with bad ventilation	663
Percentage of rooms with bad ventilation	18%
Rooms with fair ventilation	356
Percentage of rooms with fair ventilation	10%
Rooms with good ventilation	2,636
Percentage of rooms with good ventilation	72%
Number of lodgers	439
Number of families with one or more lodgers	139
Percentage of families with lodgers	9%
Apartments where lodgers are separate from family	130
Apartments where lodgers are not separate	9
Number of apartments actually used for sleeping rooms	2,584
Percentage of rooms actually used for sleeping rooms	70%
Number of children attending school between ages of five and fourteen	1,114
Percentage of children attending school between ages of five and fourteen	86%
Number of children between ages of five and fourteen working	43
Manufacturing carried on on premises —	
Cigar making	3
Dressmaking	1
Tailor	1
Shoemaking	1
Apartments with sickness at time of report	42
Cases of tuberculosis	8
Epilepsy	1
Typhoid fever	1
Skin diseases	5
Number of apartments dirty	129
Percentage of dirty rooms	8%
Number of apartments fairly clean	231
Percentage of same	15%
Number of apartments clean	1,213
Percentage of same	77%
Number of families in which head of family is a laborer	989
Total amount of wages of families reported	$10,797.50
Average wages of family per week after deducting wages of families not ascertained	7.03
Average rent of apartments per month after deducting all apartments, the rent of which was not ascertained	4.63
Nationality of families —	
Italian	1,345
American	101
German	26
Irish	27
Canadian	20
English	10
Scotch	5
French	4
Russian	3
Austrian	1
Hungarian	1
Polish	2
Arabian	1
Syrian	6

Polish District

Total number of houses	197
Total number of apartments	873
Apartments with windows opening on yard or court only	493
Percentage of apartments with windows opening on yard or court only	56%
Total number of rooms	2,188
Rooms reported dark	16
Percentage of dark rooms, less than	19%

Rooms well lighted	2,172
Rooms with ventilation bad	15
Percentage of rooms with bad ventilation, less than	1%
Rooms with good ventilation	2,173
Number of lodgers	47
Number of families with one or more lodgers	30
Percentage of families which have lodgers	3%
Lodgers separated from families by partitions	47
Number of rooms actually used for sleeping	1,610
Percentage of rooms actually used as sleeping rooms	74%
Number of children attending school	951
Percentage of children attending school between ages of 5 and 14	68%
Number of children between ages of 5 and 14, working	46
Manufacturing carried on on premises —	
Dressmaking	1
Watchmaking	1
Shoemaking	1
Premises with sickness at present time, kind of disease not reported	25
Number of apartments dirty	42
Percentage of dirty apartments	5%
Number of apartments reported fairly clean	8
Percentage of fairly clean apartments	1%
Number of apartments clean	825
Percentage of apartments clean	94%
Number of families in which head of family is a laborer	543
Total amount of average weekly wages of families	$7,162.05
Average wages of family per week, after deducting all families whose average wages were not ascertained	8.56
Total amount of rent of apartments per month	$2,633.80
Average rent of apartments per month after deducting apartments the rent of which was not ascertained	3.46
Nationality of families —	
Polish	826
German	20
Italian	1
Russian Jews	8
Canadian	1
American	6
Hollander	1

It will be noticed that about 39 per cent of the tenements in the Italian District are controlled by agents or lessees, while less than 7 per cent are similarly controlled in the Polish District. This fact is at the bottom of many of the evils that prevail in the Italian Quarter. The owner rents the premises for a round sum to some one more or less enterprising whose whole object then is to secure as much rent as possible out of the tenant for the smallest possible amount of expense for repairs or proper sanitary provision. In this way the owner frequently gets a good return from property that otherwise would be wholly unproductive. In the Italian District, out of a total of 148 houses 27 per cent cover 100 per cent of the lot; 3 per cent cover 95 per cent of the lot; 6 per cent cover 90 per cent of the lot; 6 per cent cover 85 per cent of the lot; 11 per cent cover 80 per cent of the lot; 9 per cent cover 75 per cent of the lot, and 38 per cent cover 65 per cent or less of the lot.

In the Polish District, out of a total of 197 houses ½ of 1 per cent cover 100 per cent of the lot; 2 per cent cover 90 per cent of the lot; 4 per cent cover 80 per cent of the lot; 6 per cent cover 75 per cent of the lot; 6 per cent cover 70 per cent of the lot; 10 per cent cover 65 per cent of the lot, and 71½ per cent cover 60 per cent or less of the lot.

In the ordinances controlling tenement houses it is provided, that all such houses erected after passage of the act shall cover only 75 per cent of the lot, except in the case of a corner lot, when 90 per cent may be utilized. The high percentage of ground covered by so many of the Italian tenements is because nearly all these houses are old and were in existence before the ordinances were enacted.

In the Italian District 22 per cent of the houses are wood, 5 per cent stone, and 73 per cent of brick, while in the Polish District all are of wood. As to height of buildings, the Italian District shows more than two-thirds to be of 3 stories or less, the balance 5 stories and more than 3 stories. Of the 5-story houses there are only 8 reported. In the Polish District there is only 1 house reported more than 2 stories in height. The whole number of apartments in the Italian District is 1573, containing 3655 rooms, with an average of 10.63 apartments to a tenement, and an average of 2.3 rooms to an apartment. These apartments are inhabited by a total of 6683 persons, divided into 1552 families, showing an average to each apartment of 4.74 persons. Of this total population, 4184 appear to be Italian, with 2499 children under the age of 14 years.

Turning to the Polish District, we find the total apartments to be 873, containing 2188 rooms, with an average of 4.43 apartments to a tenement, and an average of 2.5 rooms to an apartment. The total population appears to be 4612, divided into 863 families, an average of 5.5 persons to each apartment. Of this total population 2277 are adults and 2333 are children under 14 years of age. These results show rather curiously that, though the Poles live in small and detached dwellings, yet that the overcrowding is greater by far than among the Italians, who live in the typical tenement houses. It also seems to indicate that there are a larger number of the Italians who are unmarried, as the number of children among the Poles is so much greater in proportion than among the Italians. In the Italian Quarter 24 out of 51 houses examined have janitors and 3 a night watchman. In the Polish Quarter only 1 janitor is reported, but this is because the ordinances require janitors only in dwellings having 8 families or more. It appears that 114 out of 148 houses in the Italian Quarter have courts, and of these 77 are paved, but only 17 are trapped and drained properly. Seventy-eight per cent of the courts are reported clean, 8 per cent fair, and 14 per cent dirty. In the Polish District, owing to the character of the houses, only 23 houses appear to have courts, 2 only of which are drained and trapped, but 87 per cent of the yards and courts are reported clean, 6 per cent fair, and 7 per cent dirty.

As to fire protection in the Italian District, 19 out of 148 houses only have fire-escapes, 17 of which are of iron, 2 of wood. Eighteen of these buildings have ladders connecting with roof. Five of the escapes are encumbered. In the Polish District there are no fire-escapes, as there is only 1 building more than 2 stories high. It should be noted that fire protection is a matter within the control of the Fire Department of the city of Buffalo, and the regulations governing that Department control the disposition of fire-escapes.

The keeping of animals on tenement premises does not seem to be a serious evil, as in the Italian Quarter there are only 12, all horses. In the Polish Quarter there are 10 cases, 6 having horses in barns on the premises, 4 having fowls in the yards.

Twenty-three basements in the Italian Quarter are occupied as dwellings, but under the definition of a basement in the Buffalo ordinances, more than one-half the height of said basement from floor to ceiling must be above the ground, so that there is rarely trouble for want of light or air. In the Polish Quarter no basements or cellars are used for residences.

It appears also that the average width of public hallways is 5.5 feet in the Italian Quarter, and about the same in the Polish Quarter. This seems to be a generous width, sufficient for light and ventilation, if properly arranged. Twenty-five per cent of these hallways in the Italian Quarter are dark, about 1 per cent fair, and the balance light. In the Polish District only 1 dark hallway is reported, the balance being all light.

The ordinances provide that in all tenement houses containing 8 or more families, and over 3 stories in height, red lights shall be maintained all night on every flight of stairs, and 1 or more gongs shall be so placed and be of such size and number as to give an alarm throughout the house in case of fire. As only 5 tenements in the Italian Quarter are reported as having such lights, it appears that the ordinance is not enforced. Seventy-nine houses, however, are reported as having white lights, and 21 houses as having suitable fire gongs. In the Polish Quarter no red lights or gongs are reported whatever.

Only 2 of the houses in the Italian District are reported as having 2 means of egress, and in 15 the front door is locked at night. In the Polish Quarter all the front doors seem to be locked at night, and 63 out of 197 have 2 means of egress. In the Italian District 19 of the halls are dirty, 30 fair, the balance, 89 in number, being clean. In the Polish Quarter 6 houses are reported dirty, 1 fair, and the balance clean.

In the Italian Quarter there are only 4 houses with wood and iron stairs, 2 of stone and wood, the balance, 142, having wooden stairs. In the Polish Quarter, of course, all the staircases are of wood. Fourteen of these staircases in the Italian Quarter are dirty, 41 fair, 93 clean. In the Polish Quarter 6 of the staircases are dirty, 1 fair, and the balance clean. In the Italian Quarter 30 houses have staircases to the roof and in 21 the roof is used to dry clothes. In the Polish Quarter the roofs are not used at all, and there are no staircases to the roof.

It appears that in both tenement sections the houses are furnished with plenty of chimneys, with places for stoves or fireplaces in each apartment.

The ordinances provide that city water be furnished for every family or set of apartments. In the Italian Quarter 18 houses have not water so furnished. In the Polish Quarter only 1 seems to be without sufficient provision of water. Practically, no provision is made for protecting the water from freezing, as a matter of fact, and in cold weather the water is let run. The Italians have 4 baths, in the 148 houses reported, 1 shower, the balance tubs. The Poles have 1.

In the Italian Quarter there are 536 water-closets, 28 privies, which, divided among the total population, would give 1 to every 12 persons, which is within the provisions of the ordinances, which provided one for every family or 15 persons. It appears, however, that actually there are 46 families without adequate provisions in this respect. In the Polish District, taking the whole number of water-closets and privies, there is 1 for every 13 persons. There are 18 cases where the provision is inadequate.

The condition of the plumbing is bad in 10 cases in the Italian Quarter, 4 fair, the balance good. In the Polish Quarter there are 8 bad cases, and the balance are reported good.

The ordinances of Buffalo require that all tenements be whitewashed twice a year. This is a provision which is almost universally not enforced in either the Italian or the Polish Quarter. The ordinances also provide that receptacles for garbage shall be of incombustible material. This also is not enforced, as all receptacles reported appear to be wooden barrels. In 30 cases in the Italian Quarter no space for garbage is provided on the lands of the owner of the building.

In the Italian Quarter a great variety of business seems to be carried on on the tenement house premises, mainly, however, on the ground floor, as many of the buildings have shops on this floor. It will be noticed, however, that there is only 1 cigar factory and 2 milk depots. Out of 148 houses 67 have no business carried on. In the Polish Quarter only 15 places are reported as carrying on business, 1 a grocery, 7 saloons, and 7 miscellaneous.

The total rent ascertained for 148 tenements in the Italian Quarter is $8258.75 per month, or an average monthly rental of $55.80 per tenement house, or an average monthly rental per family of $5.32. In the Polish Quarter the total present rent ascertained for 189 tenements per month is $2681.60, or an average rental per month per tenement house of $14.19, or an average monthly rental per apartment of $3.11, from which it appears that the average rental of inferior dwellings among the Italians is per apartment about 71 per cent higher than in the Polish District.

In the Italian District 24 per cent of the apartments have windows opening only on yards or courts, and of the total number of rooms reported 15 per cent are dark, 3 per cent with fair light, and 82 per cent with good light. In the Polish Quarter 50 per cent of the apartments have windows opening on yards or courts only. It must be understood, however, in this latter case, that yard or court is taken to be space between houses or in the rear of lots, usually ample. In the Polish Quarter there is less than 1 per cent of dark rooms; the balance are well lighted.

As to ventilation, in the Italian Quarter there are 18 per cent of the rooms with bad ventilation, 10 per cent with fair ventilation, 72 per cent with good ventilation. In the Polish Quarter, less than 1 per cent of the ventilation is bad; the balance is good.

It is not believed that these statistics as to lodgers are accurate, for the reason that it is almost impossible to ascertain their number. The situation as to lodgers varies from time to time, as at certain seasons of the year they are very much more numerous than at others. In addition, the families who take lodgers usually refuse to tell the truth about the number whom they entertain.

In the Italian District, 70 per cent of the rooms actually occupied are used as sleeping rooms, in the Polish District 74 per cent.

The percentage of children between the ages of 5 and 14 years attending school in the Italian District is 86; in the Polish District, 68. The number of children working between the ages of 5 and 14 in the Italian District is 43 per cent; in the Polish 46 per cent.

Very little manufacturing is carried on on the premises in either the Polish or Italian District. There appear to be 3 cases of cigar making in the former and none in the latter.

As to the matter of health, only 42 cases of contagious disease are reported in the Italian District out of a population of 6683, and of these 8 cases are reported as being tuberculosis. In the Polish District 25 cases are reported out of a total population of 4612, but among these there appear to be no cases of tuberculosis.

As to cleanliness of apartments in the Italian District, 8 per cent are dirty, 15 per cent are fairly clean, 77 per cent are clean. In the Polish Quarter about 5 per cent of the apartments are dirty, about 1 per cent fair, and 94 per cent clean. In 989 cases the head of the family, among the Italians, is a laborer. In 543 cases among the Poles the head of the family is a laborer. The total amount of weekly wages of families reported among the Italians is $10,797.50; and the average wages of each family per week, excluding those families whose wages are not ascertained, is $7.03 per week. The average rent of premises per month, excluding all apartments the rent of which was not ascertained, is $4.63. Among the Poles, the average wages of each family per week, excluding all families whose wages were not ascertained, is $8.56. The total amount of rent of apartments per month is $2633.80, and the average rent of apartments per month, excluding all apartments the rent of which is not ascertained, is $3.46, which indicates that the Poles, while earning considerably higher wages, pay a much less rent per month.

As to nationality, in the Polish Quarter, so-called, the bulk of the population is Polish, as in the Italian Quarter it is Italian, there being scattering families of almost every nationality, including a considerable number of Americans.

APPENDIX VIII

TESTIMONY OF BUILDING DEPARTMENT OFFICIALS IN RELATION TO THE NON-ENFORCEMENT OF THE TENEMENT HOUSE LAWS IN NEW YORK CITY

TESTIMONY OF BUILDING DEPARTMENT OFFICIALS IN RELATION TO THE NON-ENFORCEMENT OF THE TENEMENT HOUSE LAWS IN NEW YORK CITY

THE Commission held its sixth public meeting at the Assembly Room of the United Charities Building, 109 East 22d Street, New York, on December 10, 1900, at 2.30 P.M.

There were present the Chairman and members of the Commission.

The Chairman. — I will open this hearing of the Tenement House Commission, and there are just two or three words I wish to say in behalf of the Commission in opening it. The Commission, since it was appointed, has received the utmost courtesy from all the heads of our city departments. At an early period of our work we invited them to meet with us informally, and we discussed informally various questions, and particularly had the benefit of having, by informal discussion, suggestions from the different members of the city government, and I refer particularly to the members of the Department of Buildings, of the Department of Health, of the Fire Department, and also, though less concerned with our work, from members of the Police Department; and I will say that since that time every request that this Commission has made of any of the city departments has been cheerfully and promptly complied with, and all records and papers which we have asked to see have been promptly placed at our disposal.

We have made inspections of our own through our own inspectors, as it was our duty to do, and those inspections have developed a number of instances in which it seemed that the law had been violated, or else that discretion given under the laws had been unwisely used. We have thought that it was our duty under these circumstances to bring these matters to the attention of the heads of city departments by a hearing of this character, and accordingly they have been asked to come before us in the manner provided by law; that is, by the service of a subpœna, and in sending that subpœna we have sent a letter similar in form, I think, in every instance, and that letter I now read, from the one addressed to Mr. Brady of the Building Department, and I read it because it is intended to represent and does represent the attitude of the Commission in this matter. This is addressed to the Hon. Thomas J. Brady, President of the Board of Buildings, etc.

"It evidently becomes the duty of the Tenement House Commission to inquire in some degree into some instances of apparent neglect of duty on the part of persons connected with your department; and for that reason we have thought it preferable, both for you and for us, that you should be requested to attend before us by the service of a subpœna in the manner provided by the law under which we are acting. We would wish you to understand, however, that we recognize none the less the courtesy with which you have aided the Commission in the performance of their duty. We shall endeavor to send you either with this letter or later some memoranda which will call your attention to a number of subjects on which we seek information, so that you may have full opportunity to inform yourself about them."

And simultaneously with this letter, and if I understand rightly, enclosed in it, was a memorandum, which was intended to call attention to a number of subjects to which we wish to refer this afternoon.

In the division of labor which has been made among members of the Commission, the particular duties connected with this hearing have been undertaken by the Vice-Chairman, Mr. Cravath, and he will practically occupy the chair for the purposes of this meeting.

Mr. Cravath then took the chair.

TESTIMONY OF THOMAS J. BRADY

Commissioner of Buildings of the Boroughs of Manhattan and Bronx, and President of the Board of Buildings of Greater New York

Thomas J. Brady, being duly sworn, testified as follows:—

The Chairman.—What official position do you hold, Mr. Brady, under the city government?

Mr. Brady.—Commissioner of Buildings of the Boroughs of Manhattan and Bronx, and President of the Board of Buildings of Greater New York.

The Chairman.—You are the head of the Department of Buildings?

Mr. Brady.—Yes, sir.

The Chairman.—Will you briefly state the organization of that Department for the entire city, the manner in which the work is divided between heads and sub-heads, etc.?

Mr. Brady.—The Commissioners are coequal in the powers they represent. Commissioner Guilfoyle has sole administrative authority and appointing power for the Borough of Brooklyn. Commissioner Campbell has sole administrative power and appointing power for the Boroughs of Richmond and Queens. I have sole administrative power and appointing power for the Boroughs of Manhattan and Bronx. The three Commissioners meet and adopt rules for the government of Greater New York which are to be enforced uniformly in all boroughs. In each of the boroughs each Commissioner has the right to designate or appoint a Superintendent of Buildings. Each Commissioner has that as his individual right. The Superintendent's duties are to perform the duties specified by law, and act as Commissioner in the absence of the Commissioner. That will be the first Superintendent in the Boroughs of Manhattan and the Bronx. We have two separate superintendents. Mr. John A. Dooner is first Superintendent. Mr. Sylvester Murphy is second Superintendent. We have the bureaus in the Department divided into what are termed divisions. That is, the plan division, violation clerk's division, the fire-escape division, unsafe buildings division, and complaint division. The work assigned to each of these divisions are matters appertaining to what they are organized for. We have a corps of inspectors classified as construction inspectors, who are mechanics such as the law requires, either architects, civil engineers, masons, carpenters, or iron-workers. Those men have charge of the construction of buildings. We have a plumbing, lighting, and ventilation division where the inspectors are practical plumbers and sanitary engineers. Their duties are to inspect the construction and the progress of the work as to light, ventilation, plumbing, and drainage. We have a corps of engineers, most of them appointed by the title of inspectors, who are assigned to examining plans and report on the applications when made as to whether any infringement or infraction of the law is shown either by plan or specification, and their objections are founded on the plans as submitted, which are then returned to the office for disapproval, and by amending or correcting the mistakes that may have occurred in these plans, then the final approval for a permit is issued. Matters of alterations of buildings are adopted on a similar score. The plan division is the portion where applications are filed for a permit to either erect or alter a building. If it is a building that requires to be referred to the sanitary experts, such as a tenement house, lodging house, or class of building that would come under that section of the law, that goes to the sanitary examination, plumbing, light, and ventilation division. If there is no question as regards light or ventilation such as is required by law, as in an office building, warehouse, or stable, that goes direct to the construction engineers and is passed on by them as to the strength of material and all matters appertaining to the construction submitted. Any reports found on these are returned back to the plan desk, so that the architect can know on what grounds the plans have been disapproved. He is also forwarded a slip containing a memorandum of why the permit has been denied, and with that information the custom is that they call at the office, make a correction in them in what we term the form of amendment to their plan, and then the plan is finally acted upon and approved.

Questions as regards complaints from all sections of the city are received, whether anonymous or signed by any person, and are forwarded to the complaint desk, and through the complaint clerk assigned to the inspector of the district in which the complaint refers to. Thereupon it is investigated by the inspector and reports made back to the division of complaints. If it develops a case that should require a fire-escape, the case is made against the building where the cause of complaint is found warranted, and they are recorded at the fire-escape desk, or fire-escape division; notice is prepared and served on the owners. If it should be a violation of law other than the question of a fire-escape, it will go to the general violation division, there recorded and forwarded for prosecution. If it should be an unsafe case, it would be recorded in the unsafe division, and proper notice issued to the owners of the building.

The Chairman. — To whom do you forward these violations for prosecution?

Mr. Brady. — To the Corporation Counsel.

The Chairman. — You have no legal department of your own?

Mr. Brady. — No, sir.

The Chairman. — You simply have such counsel as the Corporation Counsel's office assigns to you?

Mr. Brady. — Yes, sir.

The Chairman. — I understand you, as President of the Board, have no jurisdiction in Brooklyn?

Mr. Brady. — No, sir, except in joint body by action of the Board.

The Chairman. — If, for instance, there were differences of opinion between you as Superintendent for New York, or as the Commissioner for New York, and the Commissioner for Brooklyn as to the construction of a law, that could only be settled by an appeal to the full Board?

Mr. Brady. — That could only be settled by an appeal to the full Board, or an opinion from the Corporation Counsel for an interpretation of the law.

The Chairman. — But the decision of the full Board upon any question is binding upon each of the three Commissioners?

Mr. Brady. — The majority is the way we rule.

The Chairman. — You have no separate department of your organization for tenement houses, have you?

Mr. Brady. — Except the division we term plumbing, light, and ventilation. They deal exclusively with the plans as filed for plumbing, drainage, light, and ventilation, and those are in a form of application that refers directly to tenement houses.

The Chairman. — And also to other classes of houses where the same questions arise?

Mr. Brady. — The same question does not arise in other classifications of buildings.

The Chairman. — So that the questions of light and ventilation refer almost exclusively to tenement houses, and therefore that work of the Department is almost entirely taken up with tenement house inspection?

Mr. Brady. — Yes, sir; in the examination of plans and issuing permits; but the inspectors on plumbing, light, drainage, and ventilation may measure the rooms, measure the size of the openings, measure the size of the courts and area of the lot covered, while the construction inspector, who is a mechanic, looks after the foundation, mason work, iron work, and all other matters pertaining to the construction.

The Chairman. — Then none of your inspectors in point of fact would give all their time to tenement houses; they would be called upon, also, to examine other buildings so far as they relate to their particular department?

Mr. Brady. — Yes, sir, but the plumbing, drainage, light, and ventilation would only refer to the tenement house section; their duties would not be applicable at all to examining the plumbing in other buildings because there would be no requirement as to light and ventilation under the statutes.

The Chairman. — How many inspectors have you altogether for the Boroughs of Manhattan and Bronx?

Mr. Brady. — I cannot recall that from memory at the present time.

The Chairman. — Approximately?

Mr. Brady. — Probably 160.

The Chairman. — Do you remember how many of these belong to the light and ventilation department, approximately?

Mr. Brady. — Probably fifty.

The Chairman. — And you think the principal work of those fifty is the inspection of tenement houses and tenement house plans?

Mr. Brady. — With the exception of the time they devote for the general work of plumbing.

The Chairman. — What proportion of the work of those fifty would be in connection with plumbing on other buildings than tenement houses?

Mr. Brady. — Every one of them, just according to the number of buildings that would be in that district.

The Chairman. — Can you give a rough estimate as to the relative distribution of their work between tenement houses and other buildings?

Mr. Brady. — No; it would be their entire duty to examine all classes of plumbing, so that if we had an office building or stable they would have to see that the plumbing was properly executed just as much as if it were a tenement house; and it depends on the district, how many buildings would be erected where plumbing would be used; those men would have to cover that district.

The Chairman. — And men having a tenement house district would have a great deal to do with tenement houses?

Mr. Brady. — More in certain sections of the city than in others.

The Chairman. — I understand you have no separate inspectors for light and ventilation?

Mr. Brady. — Yes, sir.

The Chairman. — The same inspector looks after ventilation, light, and plumbing and sanitary questions generally, so far as affecting that department?

Mr. Brady. — Yes, sir.

The Chairman. — Have you the full amount of inspectors allowed by law?

Mr. Brady. — Yes, sir.

The Chairman. — How is the number of inspectors for your Department determined?

Mr. Brady. — Altogether by the appropriation that we receive from the city government.

The Chairman. — You could have more inspectors if you had a larger appropriation?

Mr. Brady. — Yes, sir.

The Chairman. — Did you get in the last budget the full appropriation you asked for?

Mr. Brady. — No, sir; we were reduced.

The Chairman. — Do you remember what you asked and what you received?

Mr. Brady. — From 1898, the first reduction was about $45,000, commencing on the 1st of January, 1898. 1899 was continued by an additional reduction of about $10,000. In 1900, for the year 1901, there is a still further reduction of about $10,000. In all for the past three years we have been reduced $65,000 or $70,000 on the general appropriation.

The Chairman. — And in asking for that appropriation do you specify a specific sum for inspectors?

Mr. Brady. — Yes, sir; number of inspectors and the salaries.

The Chairman. — Do you remember to what extent your allowance for that appropriation for inspectors has been reduced?

Mr. Brady. — Probably ten or twelve inspectors.

The Chairman. — That is, say, about 8 per cent?

Mr. Brady. — I asked for the restoration of the $10,000 that was cut for the present year for the purpose of employing additional inspectors at an average of $1200 a year, which would employ eight. Some of the inspectors are employed for $1000 a year, so that would be eight or ten we are short this coming year.

The Chairman. — And you were short the same last year?

Mr Brady. — Short the same amount last year and a larger amount the year previous.

The Chairman. — So you now have, I should imagine from your figures, upward of twenty fewer inspectors than you have asked for?

Mr. Brady. — No; in some places we adopted a different theory of reducing salaries so as to keep the force intact as near as possible.

The Chairman. — You cannot state from memory any division of your light, ventilation, and plumbing inspectors between tenement house districts and other districts, can you? I am trying to get at what proportion of the force is available under your practice for tenement house inspection.

Mr. Brady. — No, I cannot, because they merge into each other.

The Chairman. — Can you, if we wish it, furnish a statement showing the districts into which you have divided the city and the number of light, ventilation, and plumbing inspectors for each district?

Mr. Brady. — Yes, sir, I can furnish that at any time.

The Chairman. — I will be obliged if you will furnish that in the next few days.

Mr. Brady. — I will see that it is done.

The Chairman. — Now we want your help, Mr. Brady, not only on questions involving the enforcement of law, but also to some extent on the questions we are considering in connection with the present law. One of the important subjects, as you know, treated of by the law now, is the percentage of the lot, particularly an inside lot, which may be covered by the tenement house?

Mr. Brady. — Yes, sir.

The Chairman. — Do you regard the present restrictions of the law adequate in that regard?

Mr. Brady. — I think they are satisfactory.

The Chairman. — You think they are satisfactory from a sanitary point of view?

Mr. Brady. — Yes, sir.

The Chairman. — What proportion of an inside lot do you understand may be covered now by a tenement house?

Mr. Brady. — Seventy-five per cent, the extreme.

The Chairman. — It is your opinion, then, that where a lot is built upon with tenement houses covering 75 per cent of an inside lot, and the maximum of a corner lot, which, I believe, is 92 per cent, that adequate provision is made for light, air, and ventilation?

Mr. Brady. — Yes, sir, if the plan is properly prepared, they can adopt the size of courts and shafts that will give proper ventilation. Some plans do not cover the full 75 per cent; some cover anything from 65 to 75.

The Chairman. — The limit is 75?

Mr. Brady. — Yes, sir; it was formerly 78 per cent.

The Chairman. — In your judgment is the law in respect to limiting tenement houses to 75 per cent of the lot being enforced?

Mr. Brady. — Yes.

The Chairman. — You think it is pretty generally?

Mr. Brady. — Yes, sir.

The Chairman. — Now as to air shafts; the present law, as I understand it is that air shafts must be at least 2 feet 4 inches in width?

Mr. Brady. — Where the building is not more than five stories high.

The Chairman. — Has your Department some discretionary power with reference to regulating the size and character of air shafts?

Mr. Brady. — Nothing less than 2 feet 4 inches in width, and we have the power where the building is increased in height to compel an increased area for the shaft, which we adopted by rule by the Board of Buildings, a building more than five stories in height must increase the width of the shaft at the narrowest point not less than 4 inches in addition.

The Chairman. — And you exercise the same care in enforcing the provisions of this rule as you do of the statutes?

Mr. Brady. — Yes, sir.

The Chairman. — You recognize the Building Code as having the same force on your Department as the statutes passed by the legislature, do you not?

Mr. Brady. — Yes, sir.

The Chairman. — And you draw no distinction between the enforcement of the Building Code and the general statutes?

Mr. Brady. — None at all. The Building Code is based on the section of the Charter authorizing the Municipal Assembly to adopt a Building Code, in consequence of the Boroughs of Queens and Richmond not having any building law.

The Chairman. — Did your Department pass on that Building Code before it was adopted?

Mr. Brady. — The three Commissioners of the Building Department to-day were members of the Building Code Commission.

The Chairman. — And does that Code represent the views of the three Commissioners?

Mr. Brady. — Yes, sir; at the time of the adoption of the Code on the 23d of December, 1898.

The Chairman. — What do you understand to be the minimum air shaft allowed under any conditions by the present law, or present Building Code?

Mr. Brady. — Twenty-five square feet of area, and for smaller buildings 10 square feet, but anything less than 25 square feet is not included in the area covered.

The Chairman. — The law allows less than 25 square feet in smaller buildings?

Mr. Brady. — Yes, sir.

The Chairman. — What do you mean by "smaller buildings"?

Mr. Brady. — Take a building that will not cover an extra depth of lot; three-story buildings and with maybe four or five rooms on a floor, the interior shaft lighting not more than two rooms, we make a concession, make that regulation to adapt itself to that class of buildings; whereas a five-story building with four or five families on a floor no consideration is given for less than 25 feet of the area covered.

The Chairman. — Do you mean to say that in the Boroughs of Manhattan and Bronx you permit in any building air shafts less than 25 feet in area?

Mr. Brady. — No, sir.

The Chairman. — You would not permit them here even in a small building?

Mr. Brady. — No, sir; we get 25 square feet as a rule in all plans.

The Chairman. — Is not the law mandatory that the minimum must be 25 square feet?

Mr. Brady. — No, sir; only they are not given consideration as to the area of the lot covered.

The Chairman. — Can you refer me to the law that permits air shafts smaller than 25 feet?

Mr. Brady. — The section of the law states that not less than 25 feet of the area shall be covered. It don't restrict a smaller shaft where we can get light and ventilation.

The Chairman. — It is permissible to have bedrooms open on these smaller shafts?

Mr. Brady. — Yes, sir; they very rarely occur, except in the alteration of old houses.

The Chairman. — But I understood you to have stated it is permissible?

Mr. Brady. — Yes, sir.

The Chairman. — You have stated where there were four or five rooms on a floor you permitted them to open on to these smaller shafts?

Mr. Brady. — Yes, sir; in special cases.

The Chairman. — Are the regulations in the various boroughs uniform?

Mr. Brady. — Yes, sir.

The Chairman. — Where they rest in the discretion of this Department?

Mr. Brady. — Yes, sir; and the regulations are prepared and based on the Code and Charter, and adopted by the Board making uniform rules and regulations for the entire city.

The Chairman. — So that if that regulation is enforced in the Borough of Manhattan it is also enforced in the Borough of Brooklyn?

Mr. Brady. — Yes, sir; as near as we can.

The Chairman. — I read you a regulation of the Building Department: "Except as hereinafter otherwise stated, every light and air shaft or court for habitable rooms must be at least 25 square feet in area up to and including five stories in height, and be increased five square feet in area for each additional story beyond the fifth." That is the regulation for all boroughs?

Mr. Brady. — Yes, sir.

The Chairman. — Does that regulation permit of any exceptions?

Mr. Brady. — Alterations.

The Chairman. — I mean new buildings?

Mr. Brady. — Well, it would be in buildings less than five stories in height.

The Chairman. — It does not say so. "Up to and including five stories in height."

Mr. Brady. — That is the question of the estimated area and making calculations of the lot area.

The Chairman. — No. "Except as hereinafter otherwise stated, every light and air shaft or court for habitable rooms must be at least 25 square feet in area up to and including five stories in height, and be increased five square feet in area for each additional story."

Mr. Brady. — Yes; except where there may be an alteration of any building.

The Chairman. — We are speaking about new buildings entirely.

Mr. Brady. — We do not allow that.

The Chairman. — So that there can be no question then in favor of an air shaft less than 25 square feet?

Mr. Brady. — No, sir.

The Chairman. — Now on the question of the requirements as to windows opening into the outer air, what is the practical construction of the law by the Building Department?

Mr. Brady. — We consider the open air an open court.

The Chairman. — So that if a court is enclosed on four sides it is not the outer air?

Mr. Brady. — It is the outer air unless it is enclosed on the roof.

The Chairman. — So that if you have an air shaft 25 square feet in area, 5 feet square, and a building five stories high, you consider windows on that shaft opening to the outer air?

Mr. Brady. — Yes, sir.

The Chairman. — Provided it is open at the top?

Mr. Brady. — Yes.

The Chairman. — If it is closed at the top you would not permit windows opening on that shaft?

Mr. Brady. — We do not have any closed shafts at all.

The Chairman. — You draw no distinction between air shafts closed on all sides and air shafts open on one side with reference to determining whether the outer air is in that shaft or not?

Mr. Brady. — We always try to adopt that form to get them to have currents of air through their shafts, but where the shaft is not enclosed at the top we consider it open air.

The Chairman. — On the question of ventilating halls and stairs, what do you understand the practical construction of the law to be by the Building Department?

Mr. Brady. — We have tenement houses with three or four families on a floor, which is practically dumb-bell shape, with court adjoining the stairways and windows opening into the open courts. Where there are tenement houses constructed with one family on each side of the hall and stairs located separately there is a width between the cylinders of the stairs, averaging 9 to 12 inches; it has a bulkhead on the roof and ventilating skylight which ventilates that hall to the roof, and the lower hall or main entrance hall direct to the street.

The Chairman. — In these cases you permit a hall that has no window opening into the outer air?

Mr. Brady. — There is no law against it.

The Chairman. — So it has no window at all?

Mr. Brady. — I speak of a tenement house five stories in height with a family each side of the hall, stairs located in the centre of the building. There is no law either by the Charter, Consolidation Act, or Code, making it compulsory to open that stair to an open window.

The Chairman. — Have you discretionary power to require a window in that case?

Mr. Brady. — No, sir; the rules govern that, and we believe in a ventilating skylight on the roof with bulkhead and main entrance hall direct to the street, which causes a current of air through every time the door is opened. We take the precaution of having fan-lights in the various apartments opening on these halls.

The Chairman. — I read from section 1320 of the Charter: "Every such house erected after May 7th, 1887, or converted, shall have the halls on each floor open directly to the external air, with suitable windows, and shall have no room or other obstruction at the end, unless sufficient light or ventilation is otherwise provided for in said halls, in a manner approved by the Department of Buildings." That is the provision of the law to which you refer?

Mr. Brady. — I refer to all the general provisions of the law. That is an amendment back in 1887. There have been many amendments made since that time.

The Chairman. — Does not that provision seem to be mandatory: "Every such house erected after May 7th, 1887, or converted, shall have the halls on each floor open directly to the external air, with suitable windows, and shall have no room or other obstruction at the end, unless sufficient light or ventilation is otherwise provided for in said halls, in a manner approved by the Department of Buildings"?

Mr. Brady. — That speaks of halls in every instance and not stairs, and the halls connected with the stairs from the main entrance from the street is to direct open air, with a bulkhead and ventilating skylight on the roof, which gives a ventilation to the interior stairs.

The Chairman. — The law says "shall have halls on each floor open directly to the external air with suitable windows." How can you comply with that law by simply providing a skylight above?

Mr. Brady. — We apply all the law of precedent, rule, and usage, and decisions of the court. A decision of the court has gone as far as the Court of Appeals holding that a skylight on the roof bulkhead is a window.

The Chairman. — How recently was that decision rendered?

Mr. Brady. — I cannot give you the date, but I can give you a statement by reference.

The Chairman. — Under the provision that the hall should not be obstructed by rooms at the end, what construction do you give to that in enforcing the law?

Mr. Brady. — We have no plans submitted of that class with very few exceptions, and, as I say, where we can get an open window to an open court on a dumb-bell shaped plan, we always get it.

The Chairman. — You do not require it invariably?

Mr. Brady. — We do on that class of buildings invariably.

The Chairman. — Would you in any case approve plans for a tenement house which provided for no windows either on the stairs or in the hall, not counting the skylight as a window?

Mr. Brady. — We have windows in the partitions.

The Chairman. — My question is, would you approve any tenement-house plan which provided for no windows connecting with the outer air in either the public halls or stairway well, not counting a skylight as a window?

Mr. Brady. — Yes, sir, in that class of buildings I have described.

The Chairman. — Describe again what that is.

Mr. Brady. — A building of the ordinary tenement house with one family on each side of the main stairway, with entrance from the street to the roof.

The Chairman. — Where do you get that definition?

Mr. Brady. —As I said before, by precedent of cases, rules established by the Board of Health which were established under the Consolidation Act since 1861, and by custom and practice and different decisions.

The Chairman. —Do you think custom, practice, and precedent authorize you to violate the law?

Mr. Brady. — Custom and practice, I believe, make law where law is based on section 661, which simply states that rules adopted by the Board of Health will be the law, and they have adopted those rules and they have become the law.

The Chairman. — Do the rules of the Board of Health authorize you to construct buildings prohibited by statute? Now it seems to me the construction you have spoken of is expressly prohibited by statute. Now do you regard the rules of the Board of Health and precedent as authorizing that?

Mr. Brady. — In addition to the decisions rendered in litigations.

The Chairman. — But we say there is no decision of that character.

Mr. Brady. — I cannot imagine there is no decision when I know there is, and I claim from my own experience and practice that a five-story building, with a family on a floor, a bulkhead on the roof and ventilating skylight is a direct ventilation for that hall.

The Chairman. — Do you permit that whether expressly authorized by law or not?

Mr. Brady. — Yes, sir; I would build a building of that kind for my own individual use if there was no building law in existence.

The Chairman. — Would that make the halls light?

Mr. Brady. — Yes, sir.

The Chairman. — How far down?

Mr. Brady. — With a cylinder from 9 to 12 inches in width and a bulkhead on the roof, skylight and transoms and windows in the partitions make that stairway practically light.

The Chairman. — How about the halls?

Mr. Brady. — The halls as well.

The Chairman. — How deep would the halls be from the entrance of the building to the point where they reach the stairs?

Mr. Brady. — That class of building averages about 65 feet. The stair well would take a run of about 15 feet and that would be located pretty nearly the centre of the building.

The Chairman. — So you think such a construction would provide adequate light and ventilation?

Mr. Brady. — Yes, sir.

The Chairman. — Will you send us a reference to the decision of the court on that subject.

Mr. Brady. — Yes, sir. I will have the Corporation Counsel hunt that up and send it to you.

The Chairman. — Now I read a provision of the statute with which you are familiar. First is the provision limiting tenement houses, or the proportion of an inside lot that may be covered by a tenement house, to 65 per cent. Then comes this language: "But where the light and ventilation of such tenement or lodging house are, in the opinion of the superintendent of buildings, materially improved, he may permit such tenement or lodging house to occupy an area not exceeding 75 per centum of the said lot, and in the same proportion if the lot be greater or less in size than 25 by 100 feet; but this provision shall not apply to corner lots, in which, however, no such building hereafter constructed, above the first story shall occupy more than 92 per centum of the area of a lot." That is the only provision of law defining the proportion of an inside lot that may be covered by a tenement house?

Mr. Brady. — Yes, sir.

The Chairman. — I wish you would explain upon what theory your Department have concluded that that permits 75 per cent to be occupied in any case, because I understand that to have been your practice.

Mr. Brady. — Yes; because we have succeeded in having the architects prepare improved plans, improving the method of lighting and ventilation in buildings from the time that requirement of law was established.

The Chairman. — You consider that the plans, then, that you approve as coming within the requirements of law as to light and ventilation, are materially improved?

Mr. Brady. — Over any of the old systems and customs. There is no comparison. The poorest class of tenement houses erected with the area of 75 per cent of the lot covered, is an advance and beneficial both to the occupants and for the rental qualities of the building over any of the old-style structures under the old form of shafts.

The Chairman. — Then this material improvement to which the statute refers, in your mind refers to the kind of buildings built some years ago?

Mr. Brady. — Certainly; that was the reason that statute was amended and gave that power at that time.

The Chairman. — Do you require architects' proposed plans now to state specifically the respects in which their plans are improved in light and ventilation?

Mr. Brady. — We make them give us the size of every shaft, make the calculations, and we have the plans before us and see that plan is based on the modern form of construction, and the improvements in comparison with the old plans originally adopted, and give them the right for 75 per cent to be covered.

The Chairman. — Do you take up in each case the consideration of the question whether you shall limit them to 65 per cent of the lot, or allow them to occupy 75 per cent?

Mr. Brady. — No; we make the rule 75 per cent.

The Chairman. — If that, then, be the requirement of law, the invariable practice of your Department is to now permit 75 per cent of inside lots to be occupied?

Mr. Brady. — Yes; unless there is something of a detrimental character in the plans submitted, and in those cases the stringent rule will be applied to prevent them getting more than 65 per cent.

The Chairman. — Is it a matter of frequent occurrence that you require them to cover less than 75 per cent?

Mr. Brady. — I can name many instances.

The Chairman. — How many in the past year have you had?

Mr. Brady. — I cannot recall from memory an individual case this present year. I can give you a case last year, and send the plans here of a seven-story building with thirteen families on a floor. The man could not build it. I restricted him to 65 per cent, and he could not plan his building to get in that thirteen families. He threatened mandamus proceedings, but failed to mandamus the Department, and no permit was ever issued for that and the plan was withdrawn.

The Chairman. — In what proportion of cases in the last year do you suppose less than 75 per cent of the lot was allowed to be covered?

Mr. Brady. — They figure as close to 75 as possible. In many instances it may be 73, 74, and 72, but they always average between 65 and 75; none beyond 75.

The Chairman. — You are very strict in enforcing the law in that regard?

Mr. Brady. — Seventy-five per cent is the ultimatum.

The Chairman. — You have no discretion to let them go beyond 75?

Mr. Brady. — No, sir; the discretion is vested in the Department between 65 and 75, and we use the discretion in the interest of the people.

The Chairman. — Do you carefully examine the building to know whether more than 75 per cent is covered?

Mr. Brady. — Yes, sir; the inspector's duties, of plumbing, light and ventilation, is to measure every shaft and see it conforms to the plans as approved, and a copy of the permit they carry with them.

The Chairman. — And they have to measure up the building area?

Mr. Brady. — Measure up the building as the work progresses, and certify to the fact of the size of these shafts, and they must be in conformity with the plan as approved.

The Chairman. — And is it your opinion that no buildings on inside lots, tenement houses, during your administration have covered more than 75 per cent of a lot?

Mr. Brady. — There have been attempts to violate the law in cases pending and some of them have been remedied.

The Chairman. — How can they be remedied after the building is built?

Mr. Brady. — We have taken in places and removed the building; removed portions of the building.

The Chairman. — How many such cases have you had?

Mr. Brady. — I could not say offhand; quite a number; many cases pending in court now.

The Chairman. — Do you think generally the requirements of the law and the Building Code are being enforced with reference to tenement houses?

Mr. Brady. — I believe it is as far as I know, and where it is not, it is reported and in the hands of the attorneys for prosecution.

The Chairman. — To what extent are violations actually prosecuted by the attorneys in court?

Mr. Brady. — The attorneys for the department are in court in every section of the city almost every day of the week.

The Chairman. — How many attorneys are assigned to that work?

Mr. Brady. — Mr. Otterbourg is the Assistant Corporation Counsel that is assigned, and there are four assigned to him to assist him.

The Chairman. — In point of fact do many of these prosecutions for violation ever come to trial?

Mr. Brady. — Yes, quite a number come to trial and a penalty is imposed.

The Chairman. — How many come to trial in the course of a year do you suppose?

Mr. Brady. — I consider a case comes to trial when the owner and the attorney are in court, whether they compromise or not, and most every case comes to trial by issue in court.

The Chairman. — How many violations were filed last year?

Mr. Brady. — Probably in the neighborhood of 11,000.

The Chairman. — Your report says 24,000 for the three boroughs. Your Department alone how many?

Mr. Brady. — Eleven to twelve thousand.

The Chairman. — How many of those were turned over to the legal department?

Mr. Brady. — Every one of them, unless remedied in 24 hours.

The Chairman. — How many actually come to trial in court?

Mr. Brady. — I could not answer that because I would have to give you that from the records of the Corporation Counsel.

The Chairman. — Do you think many have?

Mr. Brady. — Yes, sir.

The Chairman. — Fifty?

Mr. Brady. — Oh, yes, probably 500.

The Chairman. — Have you collected many penalties?

Mr. Brady. — No, sir.

The Chairman. — What is the total amount of penalties collected last year?

Mr. Brady. — I could not give you that offhand.

The Chairman. — One thousand dollars?

Mr. Brady. — No; more than that, because I get returns from the Corporation Counsel.

The Chairman. — I mean for violations now in the construction of new buildings?

Mr. Brady. — I could not form an opinion of it.

The Chairman. — Ten thousand dollars?

Mr. Brady. — No, sir. The law specifically states that the law is to be construed liberally in the interest of the people, and the disposition of the Department is not to collect penalties, but enforce a compliance without penalties.

The Chairman. — The amount collected is so small it makes no impression on you?

Mr. Brady. — Not at all.

The Chairman. — In how many cases have buildings been torn down and practically changed after completion because of violations in the last year, and which were not condemned as being unsafe?

Mr. Brady. — That would be impossible to answer without reference to the record. There was a building at 130th Street, I think, a violation of the plan as approved became unsafe and the building was removed.

The Chairman. — Can you mention any other case, confining yourself to the past year?

Mr. Brady. — I had men out Saturday afternoon after 2 o'clock tearing down a building erected in Hancock Street.

The Chairman. — Was it a recent building?

Mr. Brady. — Building had been in litigation for probably a year.

The Chairman. — That was unsafe?

Mr. Brady. — No; built in violation of law.

The Chairman. — Mention any other case.

Mr. Brady. — 125th Street and 7th Avenue. I spent all day Saturday tearing down a building erected contrary to law and without a permit.

The Chairman. — Have there been five cases in the past year?

Mr. Brady. — Yes, sir; more.

The Chairman. — Ten?

Mr. Brady. — I think more.

The Chairman. — Fifteen?

Mr. Brady. — I would not want to specify a limit.

The Chairman. — You think more than ten, but you are not certain beyond fifteen?

Mr. Brady. — I would not say as to the number. I can give you it by record. It will be useless to make statements as to the number without having some specific knowledge of it.

The Chairman. — Now, as Mr. De Forest stated in the preliminary statement to-night, this Commission have made a careful inspection of the tenement houses constructed during the past year, and in course of construction during the period of our examination, in all the boroughs. I will confine what I have now to say to the Borough of Manhattan, and I will read without going into too minute detail a summary of the result of these investigations. About 650 buildings were inspected in Manhattan; 317 of these were found to be better-class apartment houses, and 333 were found to be strictly tenement houses. Of these 333 tenement houses, only 15 tenement houses, or 4 per cent of all, were found where there were no violations of the tenement house law. In one house were found as many as 13 different violations of the law; in another house 9 different violations; in 7 houses 8 different violations in each; in 2 houses 7 different violations; in 21 houses 6 different violations; in 46 houses 5 different violations; in 57 houses 4 different violations; in 56 houses 3 different violations; in 74 houses 2 violations; and in 53 houses 1 violation each. Now what is the explanation as to the cause for that condition of affairs?

Mr. Brady. — We may have every one of those cases reported in our Department and in prosecution now.

The Chairman. — What good does it do when the buildings are built? Substantially all of these buildings are built. What is the use of the violation if it does not correct the evil?

Mr. Brady. — It does correct the evil.

The Chairman. — You say that during the past year you won't be certain of to exceed ten buildings that have been radically changed or torn down after completion?

Mr. Brady. — I did not say parts of buildings. When you speak about the removal of buildings I mean complete buildings.

The Chairman. — Torn down or radically changed?

Mr. Brady. — Or compliance with the order when first issued by the owner.

The Chairman. — I mean a violation after the building is completed. How many completed buildings have been torn down or radically changed at the instance of the Building Department during the past year? You thought ten, but were not willing to go to fifteen.

Mr. Brady. — That is true.

The Chairman. — Now, here we have 313 completed buildings containing this immense amount of violations, and you say you doubtless have violations pending?

Mr. Brady. — Yes, sir.

The Chairman. — On your own statement those violations cannot correct these evils?

Mr. Brady. — Yes, they can, as soon as we get the orders from the court. We cannot correct them until we do.

The Chairman. — You do not get the orders from the court?

Mr. Brady. — Yes, sir; and when we do we enforce them.

The Chairman. — How often do you apply for an injunction to stop a building?

Mr. Brady. — I suppose within the past year probably twenty or twenty-five times.

The Chairman. — Out of 11,000 violations filed?

Mr. Brady. — Yes, sir.

The Chairman. — And 333 tenement houses we find were built at least. It is not your practice to obtain injunctions when you find serious violations in a building?

Mr. Brady. — Yes, sir, always; when called to our attention at the office.

The Chairman. — What do you call serious violations?

Mr. Brady. — Well, anything that would tend to make a building unsafe.

The Chairman. — Say it covers more than 75 per cent of the lot. Would you call that serious?

Mr. Brady. — Yes, sir.

The Chairman. — Or had wooden stairs?

Mr. Brady. — The law allows them to have wooden stairs in slow-burning construction.

The Chairman. — If it covers more than 75 per cent, you would count that serious?

Mr. Brady. — Yes, sir.

The Chairman. — Have you had any building constructed in the past two years torn down because it covers more than 75 per cent of the lot?

Mr. Brady. — We have restrained them by injunction proceedings.

The Chairman. — Torn them down?

Mr. Brady. — We could not get an order from the court to do it.

The Chairman. — When a building is completed and covers more than 75 per cent of the lot, can that trouble be well remedied without tearing down the building?

Mr. Brady. — Yes, sir.

The Chairman. — In how many cases has that been done in point of fact?

Mr. Brady. — I cannot tell you.

The Chairman. — Don't you know that when a building has been completed and its occupation has been begun, that any radical changes are exceedingly rare?

Mr. Brady. — Yes, it is exceedingly rare.

The Chairman. — Whenever you find a building is covering more than 75 per cent of the lot, you then obtain injunctions?

Mr. Brady. — Not always.

The Chairman. — You stated it was your custom to.

Mr. Brady. — Yes, to obtain the injunction and have them remove the violation by tearing down the walls.

The Chairman. — You have the same means of preventing their doing it?

Mr. Brady. — Whenever we know it.

The Chairman. — You do know it, don't you?

Mr. Brady. — In what way? We know if the inspector reports the violation, and forward it to the attorney for prosecution.

The Chairman. — You have means of knowing whether any building covers more than 75 per cent of the lot?

Mr. Brady. — Not unless the inspector makes the report.

The Chairman. — You stated that inspectors do.

Mr. Brady. — They do where they discover violations of the law.

The Chairman. — It is not hard to discover whether a given building covers more than 75 per cent of the lot, is it?

Mr. Brady. — No, sir; it is simply a question of examination and measurement.

The Chairman. — So your inspectors do report violations of the law in the case of covering more than 75 per cent of the lot?

Mr. Brady. — Yes, sir.

The Chairman. — And you invariably act on the violation?

Mr. Brady. — That is the custom and rule of the Department.

The Chairman. — Now, Mr. Brady, from a tabulation of the reports of our inspectors, and their report is concurred in by at least two men, and many of them have been re-verified by some other member or employee of the Commission, we find this to be the case: out of 286 tenements inspected where this information was obtainable, 282, or 99 per cent, covered more than 65 per cent of the lots; 274 tenement houses, or 96 per cent, covered more than 70 per cent of the lots.

Mr. Brady. — There would be no violation as long as it did not exceed the 75 per cent, as long as the plans were approved for 75 per cent.

The Chairman. — Ninety-three tenement houses, or 32 per cent, cover exactly 75 per cent of the lot.

Mr. Brady. — That would be a compliance with the law.

The Chairman. — Eighty-eight tenement houses, or 31 per cent, covered more than 75 per cent of the lots, the extreme maximum authorized by law in any case.

Mr. Brady. — Those 31 may be in suit at the present time.

The Chairman. — Twenty-nine, or 10 per cent, covered 80 per cent of the lot or over.

Mr. Brady. — I do not know of one existing in New York.

The Chairman. — You do not know of one?

Mr. Brady. — No. I would like to have a copy of that report as a matter of courtesy to my Department, and if there is such a thing existing, that I may force the issues with the attorneys for the purpose of removing where they exceed the 75 per cent.

The Chairman. — In answer to my suggestion that 31 covered more than 75 per cent, you said probably violation proceedings had been instituted?

Mr. Brady. — Yes, sir.

The Chairman. — And you said a moment ago that you did not know of a single instance where a building was allowed to go up covering more than 75 per cent?

Mr. Brady. — Where we know it.

The Chairman. — You said you knew it in every case?

Mr. Brady. — We have means of knowing it just as any other person has, provided the inspectors and employees do their duty and report the cases.

The Chairman. — Your inspectors can find by measuring?

Mr. Brady. — Yes, sir.

The Chairman. — And if they do their duty, you know?

Mr. Brady. — If they do their duty, they make reports back to the Department.

The Chairman. — If you find a building and you see it does cover more than 75 per cent, the law furnishes adequate means to stop the construction of that building?

Mr. Brady. — Yes.

The Chairman. — So that there is no lack of legal aid?

Mr. Brady. — No, sir, except in the matter of the number of violations, the attorney simply takes the usual course of cases where you have not precedence.

The Chairman. — Yes, but you say in serious cases you insist on immediate enforcement of the law?

Mr. Brady. — We insist on immediate enforcement of the law whether a case of violation or mistake. Every one is forwarded to the attorney for prosecution and so indorsed.

The Chairman. — Assuming it to be a fact that 31 per cent of these tenement houses inspected by us do cover more than 75 per cent of the lot, what explanation would you make as to the cause of that condition of affairs?

Mr. Brady. — I would not give any cause unless I knew it to be a fact. I doubt the 31 per cent of that report, and for that reason I request the Committee to furnish me with a list of those places, and if they are not covered by violations and in suit at the present time, I will enforce them as soon as I know they exist.

The Chairman. — What good does a violation in suit do if the building goes up when you yourself have testified that it is exceedingly rare that a building once completed is radically changed or torn down?

Mr. Brady. — I cannot answer that question because we do not have the prosecution of cases. It is a separate and distinct branch of the city government that has the enforcement of these cases, and those people are not under my jurisdiction or control. They coöperate when I call their attention to them, and when a matter of that class is called to my attention, out of the eleven or twelve thousand cases that pass through the Department annually, I forward that with special directions for immediate prosecution.

The Chairman. — I am not questioning you try to do your duty, but if it is a fact that 31 per cent, or 21 per cent, or 11 per cent, of these 286 tenement houses cover more than 75 per cent of the lot, doesn't it mean that there is something wrong somewhere in the administration of the law, either among your inspectors or in your legal department?

Mr. Brady. — It may be.

The Chairman. — Doesn't it necessarily lead to that conclusion?

Mr. Brady. — If that was a fact, it certainly would look as if there is something wrong, and that is what I would like to know about myself.

The Chairman. — Then you concede if that is the condition of affairs, something must be wrong?

Mr. Brady. — I do not concede it. I state the knowledge of my Department, the records in the Department and the system we have. I do not think such a thing could exist without my knowledge.

The Chairman. — You do not know of a case where more than 75 per cent is covered?

Mr. Brady. — Yes, sir; I have one in my desk now, consulting with an attorney about the method of rectifying the case after the building being built and occupied.

The Chairman. — Is that the only case?

Mr. Brady. — The only one I recall now. The building is completed and occupied, and I have the papers on my desk to have signed for an injunction to restrain them from occupying that place until they correct it.

The Chairman. — Do you assure this Commission that in every case where we indicate to you that more than 75 per cent is covered by buildings erected in your time, you will enforce the law in that way?

Mr. Brady. — Yes, sir. I would request a list of these places that I may verify the statement and check such places and remove the violation.

The Chairman. — What is the law with reference to a proportion of the lot to be covered by a corner building?

Mr. Brady. — Ninety-two per cent.

The Chairman. — How about the proportion of the lot at the rear which must be left vacant?

Mr. Brady. — Five feet.

The Chairman. — Does that extend from the ground up, under the law in force since January 1, 1898?

Mr. Brady. — No, sir.

The Chairman. — Does not that apply to the ground?

Mr. Brady. — No, sir.

The Chairman. — Can you cover the entire lot on the ground?

Mr. Brady. — Yes, sir.

The Chairman. — Under what authority of law?

Mr. Brady. — Under the section of the Charter, about tenement houses, where there is another house on the rear end of the lot and another building on the front of the lot there must be from the ground up, but in the section of the Charter referring to the area of the lot, there is no specific space designated as to where the area is to be computed. Where we have business buildings for business purposes, and no person living in the basement or store floor, we sometimes have the shaft go to the second story.

The Chairman. — Isn't it a matter of fact that before the Charter was adopted the law permitted corner houses to cover the entire lot, so far as the first story?

Mr. Brady. — Yes, sir.

The Chairman. — Was not the law changed in that regard by the Charter? Don't you remember the change in that regard?

Mr. Brady. — No, sir, I do not recollect.

The Chairman. — That change was the omission of the words for exemption in favor of the first story, so that the law now reads, "No such building hereafter constructed above the first story shall occupy more than 92 per cent. of the area of the lot, and no such building shall come within 5 feet of the rear of such lot."

Mr. Brady. — It specifies there above the first story.

The Chairman. — No; that is omitted under the present law.

Mr. Brady. — I cannot speak about that without a comparison between the Charter and the section.

The Chairman, reading. — "But this provision" (of 75 per cent) "shall not apply to corner lots, in which, however, no such building hereafter constructed, above the first story shall occupy more than 92 per centum of the area of a lot," and "no such building shall come within 5 feet of the rear of said lot."

Mr. Brady. — It specifies there "above first story."

The Chairman. — "Above the first story" is not in that law.

Mr. Brady. — I do not know whether you are reading in the law now, or a quotation from some other place.

The Chairman. — I am reading from the Charter.

Mr. Brady. — The Charter is the law to-day.

The Chairman. — The words "above the first story" were omitted when the Charter was adopted.

Mr. Brady. — I do not recollect the question of the change between the Charter and what you have read there, but the words "first story" is the designated point for the area of the lot to be determined by.

The Chairman. — This is the law of 1895: "But this provision shall not apply to corner lots, in which, however, no such building hereafter constructed, above the first story shall occupy more than 92 per centum of the area of a lot." Now the Charter omitted the words "above the first story."

Mr. Brady. — I do not recall that.

The Chairman. — Then you do not know the laws in that regard?

Mr. Brady. — I do know the law fairly well.

The Chairman. — Do you still contend that the law now permits a corner tenement house to occupy the entire lot up to the first story?

Mr. Brady. — Yes, sir.

The Chairman. — Can there be any ambiguity about this provision of the law that "no such building hereafter constructed, above the first story shall occupy more than 92 per cent of the area of the lot," and "no such building shall come within five feet of the rear of said lot." Can there be any ambiguity about that?

Mr. Brady. — Yes, sir.

The Chairman. — What is it?

Mr. Brady. — That you can have a house not covering more than 92 per cent of the lot and simply take your computation at the level of the second tier of beams.

The Chairman. — But "no such building shall be."

Mr. Brady. — You have read "the first story" there several times.

The Chairman. — That refers to percentage. "No such building hereafter constructed, above the first story shall occupy more than 92 per cent of the area of the lot, and no such building shall come within 5 feet of the rear of said lot."

Mr. Brady. — You comply with the requirements so far as your area is concerned when you —

The Chairman. — Do you mean to say that law permits it?

Mr. Brady. — There is no prohibition.

The Chairman. — "And no such building shall come within 5 feet of the rear of said lot." Is not that a prohibition?

Mr. Brady. — Not on the first story, because it states in the former section on the level above the first story.

The Chairman. — When you consider that when that law was enacted they omitted the words "above the first story," why did they omit those words?

Mr. Brady. — I don't know that they are omitted except as you are reading at the present time.

The Chairman. — Have you ever applied to the Corporation Counsel for an opinion on that?

Mr. Brady. —Yes, sir.

The Chairman. — Did you get one?

Mr. Brady. — Yes, sir.

The Chairman. — Can you send us a copy of it?

Mr. Brady. — I do not know whether I have got it written. I have discussed that with the Assistant Corporation Counsel, and I believe I may find a written opinion in connection with it. If I have one I will furnish it to you with pleasure.

The Chairman. — I assume your Department does permit the corner tenement houses to occupy the entire lot?

Mr. Brady. — In some instances, where they apply for it.

The Chairman. — Where they do not apply for it?

Mr. Brady. — Then they do not want it.

The Chairman. — You never object to plans for corner tenement houses simply on the ground that the entire lot is occupied up to one story?

Mr. Brady. — No, sir; we would allow them to build it in that way where it would not exceed 92 per cent of the lot.

The Chairman. — Now about air shafts; do you express the same opinion with regard to the enforcement of the law with reference to air shafts that you do on other subjects?

Mr. Brady. — I don't know what you mean.

The Chairman. — Do you mean the law in reference to the size and character of the air shafts is being enforced?

Mr. Brady. — Yes, sir.

The Chairman. — Do you think the provision of the law requiring that there should be an additional 4 inches in width for stories above the fifth is being enforced?

Mr. Brady. — Yes, sir.

The Chairman. — Do you think the provision of the law in all boroughs requiring air shafts to be at least 25 feet in area is enforced?

Mr. Brady. — I cannot answer for the other boroughs.

The Chairman. — You think it is enforced in your borough?

Mr. Brady. —I believe it is and I presume it is in the other boroughs.

The Chairman. —Now what do you understand to be the practical enforcement of the law in this borough with respect to the fireproof character of stairs, floors, or halls; public halls and stair wells and enclosures?

Mr. Brady. — I believe the law is enforced.

The Chairman. — What is the practical enforcement you require as to that law, and do you require fireproof floorings in halls?

Mr. Brady. — Wherever the law requires it we do.

The Chairman. — Where does the law require it?

Mr. Brady. — Buildings more than five stories in height with more than three families on a floor.

The Chairman. — There you require it invariably?

Mr. Brady. — Yes, sir.

The Chairman. — Do you define wood a fireproof material?

Mr. Brady. — No, sir.

The Chairman. — Wood cannot under any conditions be a fireproof material?

Mr. Brady. — Yes, sir.

The Chairman. — If chemically treated?

Mr. Brady. — Yes, sir.

The Chairman. — What distinction do you draw between slow-burning and fireproof material?

Mr. Brady. — Fireproof material is usually burnt clay, iron construction, tile. Slow-burning construction may be studs filled in with mineral wool, brick with wire lath and plaster on the surface.

The Chairman. — Treated wood you would regard as fireproof or slow-burning?

Mr. Brady. — If properly treated, would be a fireproof material.

The Chairman. — What is the special provision regarding buildings over three stories and a cellar?

Mr. Brady. — Slow-burning construction for stairs and halls.

The Chairman. — In any case are untreated wood stairs permitted in tenement houses?

Mr. Brady. — Yes, sir.

The Chairman. — In what cases?

Mr. Brady. — Under five stories in height.

The Chairman. — As I understand the law, the stairs must be slow-burning material in such cases?

Mr. Brady. — They are if protected by wire lath and studs filled in with brick or mineral wool.

The Chairman. — We are speaking of the stair treads.

Mr. Brady. — When the surface of the stairs is protected by wire lath on the under side.

The Chairman. — When the risers are of wood?

Mr. Brady. — Yes, sir.

The Chairman. — That is the practical construction you give the law which requires that tenement house stairs shall be of fireproof or slow-burning material, that you permit the treads and risers of wood?

Mr. Brady. — Yes, sir.

The Chairman. — And whole stair structure of wood?

Mr. Brady. — Yes, sir.

The Chairman. — On what theory do you justify that?

Mr. Brady. — Because we adopt a system of wire lath and plaster boards and enclose them with brick and mineral wool.

The Chairman. — The law says the stairs must be fireproof.

Mr. Brady. — The halls and stairs are only part of the building.

The Chairman. — Where the law requires them to be slow-burning material?

Mr. Brady. — It is protected.

The Chairman. — Does the law give you discretion to use inflammable material because you think it is protected?

Mr. Brady. — Yes, sir, slow-burning.

The Chairman. — Untreated wood is inflammable?

Mr. Brady. — Yes, sir.

The Chairman. — Where do you get the discretion to permit that?

Mr. Brady. — The point I have explained to you, that plaster boards and wire lathing on the under side make it slow-burning because the fire will not penetrate to the risers or treads.

The Chairman, reading. — "Every tenement house hereafter constructed, or buildings hereafter converted to the purpose of a tenement house, exceeding three stories in height, or having a basement with three stories above the cellar, shall have the entrance hall and entire stairwell and stairs built of slow burning construction or fire-proof material?"

Mr. Brady. — Yes, sir.

The Chairman. — The expression "entire stairs" is pretty clear?

Mr. Brady. — Yes, sir.

The Chairman. — And yet you say under the law you have the discretion to permit the stairs to be built of wood?

Mr. Brady. — Yes, sir.

The Chairman. — And that allows you to have the stairs of public halls of wood too?

Mr. Brady. — For that class of building, between three and five stories in height.

The Chairman. — Notwithstanding the apparently mandatory provision of law that there must be a fireproof or slow-burning material?

Mr. Brady. — We apply the slow-burning material.

The Chairman. — What is slow-burning material?

Mr. Brady. — Wood may be made so by the manner in which it is treated.

The Chairman. — You have stated you do not require treatment?

Mr. Brady. — You can protect wood by mineral wool and if it is brick-filled with wire lath on the face.

The Chairman. — Does that prevent wood being inflammable?

Mr. Brady. — Yes, sir; makes it slow-burning and because there is no draft of air or opportunity for the combustion to start.

The Chairman. — You call wooden floors with no filling between the beams slow-burning?

Mr. Brady. — No, sir.

The Chairman. — Would you permit it if you found it out?

Mr. Brady. — No, sir; as far as the law is concerned in a three or five story building, yes.

The Chairman. — On what theory?

Mr. Brady. — Because the halls and stairs are protected by a form of construction with mineral wool, brick-filled partitions, wire lath, and plaster boards.

The Chairman. — In other words, because you think the surroundings are adequate protection, you go against express provisions of the law?

Mr. Brady. — It is a discretionary power vested in the Commissioner of Buildings to use slow-burning construction.

The Chairman. — Where do you find the discretionary power?

Mr. Brady. — Because it specifies slow-burning construction, which is a matter of difference of opinion; which can be made of various classes of material.

The Chairman. — Isn't it a fact that the law, before the Charter was adopted, gave the Superintendent of Buildings discretion in that regard?

Mr. Brady. — The law went into effect in April or May, 1895, and the words "slow-burning" came in there. Previous to that there was no requirement on that subject.

The Chairman. — Do you remember the provision of the law was "stairs built of such slow burning construction or fire proof material as the superintendent of buildings shall decide," and when the Charter was adopted the words "such as the superintendent of buildings" were omitted?

Mr. Brady. — No, sir, I do not.

The Chairman. — If you were told they were omitted, wouldn't you say the intention was to take away discretion from the Superintendent of Buildings?

Mr. Brady. — No, sir; because it would not be possible to tell what anybody meant by slow-burning construction, except by applying construction to the wood to make it burn slow, or prevent fire from reaching it.

The Chairman. — You admit ordinary untreated wood is inflammable?

Mr. Brady. — Yes, sir.

The Chairman. — And yet you permit its use in halls and stairs?

Mr. Brady. — Yes, sir; with a protection of wire lath and plaster boards and filled in with mineral wool and bricks.

A Commissioner. — Is it your theory that the fire occurs often underneath, and if the underneath portion is protected it will not spread?

Mr. Brady. — Yes, sir.

The Commissioner. — As a matter of fact does flooring of ordinary untreated wood burn quickly when it is on top of slow-combustion material?

Mr. Brady. — No, sir; it does not burn rapidly.

The Chairman. — Now, Mr. Brady, I find here an original amendment prepared by one of your inspectors, John A. Lee, a statement of objections, and here is the requirement as to a corner tenement house: "A five-foot space at the rear must exist from the ground up," and I understand that that same criticism occurs in a great many statements of objections?

Mr. Brady. — Yes, sir; we try to enforce that as far as we can approximately.

The Chairman. — You testified a few minutes ago that you never objected to a plan because the first story covered the entire lot, on a corner?

Mr. Brady. — We do object to plans at times, yet we have to modify and allow them to build on the full depth of the lot, and that was the question that came up, and I requested an opinion from the Corporation Counsel.

The Chairman. — You said a while ago you had no discretion, but were bound to permit a corner building to cover the entire lot on the first story if it was requested?

Mr. Brady. — If they file the plan that way, we do.

The Chairman. — Yes, but here are objections.

Mr. Brady. — It was a misunderstanding of the section of the Code that brought out the discussion between the Corporation Counsel and myself. That may be the case the question arose on.

The Chairman. — When did that discussion come up with the Corporation Counsel?

Mr. Brady. — I can't tell.

The Chairman. — About when?

Mr. Brady. — Within a year; between the first of last January and the present time.

The Chairman. — You don't remember about when it was?

Mr. Brady. — No; I think the weather was warm and it may have been in the spring.

The Chairman. — You will remember to give us that information if you have it?

Mr. Brady. — Yes, sir, certainly.

The Chairman. — Are there any conditions under the present law when rooms are lawful that do not have windows opening into the outer air in the new tenement houses; sleeping rooms or living rooms?

Mr. Brady. — No, sir.

The Chairman. — So that you would condemn any plan showing rooms having no windows except into some other room?

Mr. Brady. — No; condemn the plan if it shows rooms opening into other rooms unless it opens into external air.

The Chairman. — By "external air" you mean a shaft open at the top?

Mr. Brady. — Yes, sir.

The Chairman. — And over 25 square feet for the area of the shaft?

Mr. Brady. — Yes, sir.

The Chairman. — Now with a view to finding out ourselves, as far as we could from the records of your Department, about some of these buildings containing, as we find, anywhere from one to twenty violations of the building law, we have examined the records of your Department with respect to some specific buildings, and I will take them up — and I might say that the records were taken up from our own lists of violations without any particular order, but a dozen or fifteen were examined in the order they were found in our table by Mr. Stokes and one or two others representing the Commission. The first sample case here is that of a tenement house, northeast corner of Goerck and Rivington Streets. Our inspector, on July 21, found the following apparent violation of the law: Entire yard space was covered over on the first story. Now would you say that was permissible, that being a corner lot?

Mr. Brady. — Yes, sir.

The Chairman. — Above the first story yard space only 3 feet 7 inches instead of 5?

Mr. Brady. — That would be a violation of law.

The Chairman. — Why wasn't that building stopped?

Mr. Brady. — I cannot tell.

The Chairman. — Do you think such cases as that are frequent?

Mr. Brady. — No, sir; I think they are rare.

The Chairman. — There is one room containing only 400 cubic feet of air, and there are three dark rooms back of the store with no window of any kind to the outer air. Would this be permitted?

Mr. Brady. — No, sir, not if they were living rooms.

The Chairman. — An examination of your records shows the following facts: That the original plans show a yard space of only 3 feet deep. The Department examiners disapproved the plans of December 22, 1899, with the following objection, "There must be five feet at rear." On June 9, the architect filed the following amendment: "There will be five-foot space at rear." Now what I want to call attention to there, is that your objection was made December 22, and the architect filed no amendment until June 9, and in the meantime the building was built. Now how could that happen under the proper administration of the Department?

Mr. Brady. — When he commenced the work he could make an application to erect the building to-day, and not start for twelve months.

The Chairman. — In point of fact, that building was then nearly completed on July 31, and it must have been well advanced on June 9?

Mr. Brady. — I cannot answer that without making an investigation.

The Chairman. — That would be some defect in the administration of the Department?

Mr. Brady. — If such a thing occurred, yes.

The Chairman. — The plan shows three dark rooms back of the store on the first floor. The Department examiners on June 11 disapproved the plan with the following objections — almost six months after the plans had been filed, and when the building was well toward completion — "Rooms marked X at first floor are not provided with windows to the external air." On June 12 the architect amended his plans: "Rooms marked thus (x) are dispensed with." Also on June 11 the Building Department examiners disapproved the plan for the further following reasons, "The five foot space at the rear must extend from the ground up." That was in June?

Mr. Brady. — Yes, sir.

The Chairman. — Had you then received the opinion of the Corporation Counsel?

Mr. Brady. — I could not exactly say the date. As I said before, it was a discussion that arose on the point of law which I discussed with Mr. Otterbourg, and I may have a written opinion which I will forward to this Commission.

The Chairman. — On June 12, the architect requested a modification of this law, and this objection was endorsed: "Objection waived. Application filed December 22, 1899." So that you decided to waive that objection?

Mr. Brady. — Any building plans filed previous to the adoption of the Code had to be treated as filed previous to the adoption of the Code.

The Chairman. — This is under the Charter, and not under the Code?

Mr. Brady. — If it was an objection that was raised before that section of the Code, they would have the right to have an opportunity to follow the old law if it was filed previous to the 23d of December.

The Chairman. — These objections do not come under the Code at all, but are under the Charter?

Mr. Brady. — There are some that come under the Code.

The Chairman. — You do not pretend that the provision as to whether five feet must be left at the rear of a corner lot is a provision of the Code?

Mr. Brady. — No, sir.

The Chairman. — Another one. December 22d the plan examiners disapproved the plan with the following objection, "There must be a clear space of ten feet in the rear of that portion of the building in excess of twenty-five feet, or in lieu thereof, the five foot space must extend to the first interior room." On June 11th, when the architect amended his plan, he made no answers on this point, and yet the building was going ahead. Should not action have been taken there?

Mr. Brady. — There may have been action taken.

The Chairman. — We find the building is completed with that defect embodied.

Mr. Brady. — There may be cases pending in court.

The Chairman. — What good does it do to have cases in court and buildings completed involving these defects, when you have the power to stop the construction of the building in forty-eight hours if you choose?

Mr. Brady. — When we take 11,000 cases, one violation is as important as the other, and the attorney is the best judge as to the course of prosecution. They are referred direct to him for prosecution.

The Chairman. — You said some time ago that where the violation was serious, you saw to it that the building was stopped?

Mr. Brady. — Where it was called to my attention.

The Chairman. — Then it is not the custom of your department to pick out the serious violations and see that they are enforced?

Mr. Brady. — Yes, sir. Where they see an important case they call it to my personal attention, and while that case might be record No. 9560, it might be prosecuted in advance of the case that might be numbered 999 the same year.

The Chairman. — And would not you account this to be a serious case?

Mr. Brady. — I do not know the individual cases because I do not handle them. It is impossible.

The Chairman. — Assuming the fact to be that only three feet and some inches were left at the rear, would you count that a serious case?

Mr. Brady. — Yes, sir; and would call it to the attention of the attorney for additional prosecution.

The Chairman. — And if you found that a building had been completed without that defect being corrected?

Mr. Brady. — I would take steps to remove the encroachment.

A Commissioner. — This plan was disapproved in the first instance, I understand, by the examiner of plans?

Mr. Brady. — Yes, sir.

The Commissioner. — Then could the building go ahead without a permit being issued?

Mr. Brady. — No, sir; the first step would be a violation for proceeding without having plans approved, and that would be forwarded to the attorney for prosecution, and that is a violation that is occurring every day.

The Commissioner. — I should like to know if it appeared in this case whether the building went ahead without a permit or with a permit?

The Chairman. — The records of the Department show the plans were not approved until June 12th.

The Commissioner. — The building went up, in fact, without a permit?

The Chairman. — And early in July it was substantially complete, thus showing that it must have been proceeding on the original plan filed in December without waiting for a permit from the Building Department.

Mr. Brady. — In the natural course of events I will state now that I believe if you look back to the records you will find a violation for proceeding without a permit.

The Chairman. — Does it not happen in the majority of cases that the buildings go ahead, notwithstanding the violation having been filed?

Mr. Brady. — No, sir.

The Chairman. — You say 11,000 violations were filed last year in this borough alone?

Mr. Brady. — Yes, sir.

The Chairman. — The building stopped 11,000 times?

Mr. Brady. — No; many of them were removed by amendment of architects.

The Chairman. — Don't you know it to be a fact that builders do not stop buildings because violations are filed?

Mr. Brady. — As a rule they do not. They try to push ahead with their work.

The Chairman. — And as a rule they do in fact push ahead with their work?

Mr. Brady. — Yes, sir.

The Chairman. — And frequently sell their buildings with violations on them?

Mr. Brady. — Yes, sir.

The Chairman. — So as a rule you do not succeed in stopping the erection of buildings because violations have been filed?

Mr. Brady. — Those violations are technical violations not affecting the stability of the building itself.

The Chairman. — We are limiting our discussion to important violations.

Mr. Brady. — We established a system that buildings may be sold with violations pending. Many of them are sold in that way, and many times the attorneys in passing title send to the Department for a search to know whether there is any violation pending against the property or not, and we make a return on them the same as the County Clerk does, and we have an examination of the building made at the time of that examination, and many times it interferes with the transfers of property and it compels them to make corrections in the buildings.

The Chairman. — What good does the filing of violations do to the number of 11,000, which indicates great industry on the part of a certain division of your Department, if, as we find to be the case, it is the rule among builders to go ahead with their tenement houses without paying attention to those violations?

Mr. Brady. — They do not go ahead without paying attention to them. We notify their architects that they haven't a permit. Out of 11,000 cases you might find 1000 cases of these violations for starting without a permit, and then the approval of the plan will remove that violation without suit.

The Chairman. — You recognize that many tenement houses are started and carried on some distance without a permit?

Mr. Brady. — There may be some instances to the point, but they do not go very far.

The Chairman. — We find a great many instances.

Mr. Brady. — We do not find many instances. We find some and then we stop them.

The Chairman. — What do you do when you find a building going ahead without a permit?

Mr. Brady. — Serve notice on the owner and architect that they are proceeding without a permit and send it to the attorney for prosecution.

The Chairman. — Then your responsibility ends?

Mr. Brady. — No, sir; because we find if they do not make their returns quarterly of violations received, dismissed and removed.

The Chairman. — Don't these proceedings to enforce violations drag along for months in the attorney's office?

Mr. Brady. — Yes, sir.

The Chairman. — Is it not a matter of frequent occurrence that a tenement house subject to numerous violations in the hands of attorney for prosecution, is carried to completion?

Mr. Brady. — Not numerous; very rare.

The Chairman. —We find a great many such cases. We find as a matter of fact but a small percentage of the buildings getting to completion without one or more violations of law, and violations of law that are not changed, when they are completed.

Mr. Brady. — I cannot say that because I would not discuss a problematic case. If you give me a specific case, I will answer that. There might be a difference of opinion between your inspectors making an inspection, and those authorized and organized by law to make those inspections.

The Chairman. — I have given you a specific case.

Mr. Brady. — I have told you I cannot answer that without referring to books that will refresh my memory.

The Chairman. — We understand you will enforce all these violations we call your attention to?

Mr. Brady. —Yes, sir.

The Chairman. —Now, in the same record, "There must be a clear space of 10 feet in the rear of that portion of the building in excess of 25 feet or in lieu thereof the 5-foot space must extend to the first interior room." On June 11, when the architect amended his plan, he made no answers on this point. On June 12 the Department examiners still disapproved the plan with the following notes, or objection, "Not removed." On the same day the architect asked for a modification in this respect, "As the building is sufficiently ventilated," and the plans are indorsed on that day, "Modification granted." Signed "W. J. Carey." Also "John A. Dooner" and "plans approved."

Mr. Brady. — Yes, sir.

The Chairman. — Now had you any right to grant the modification?

Mr. Brady. — Yes, sir.

The Chairman. — On what theory? Remember this was not on a corner lot.

Mr. Brady. —We have that under the rules established under section 661, Consolidation Act, transferred to us from the Board of Health.

The Chairman. — That has been repealed by the Charter. Did you have any discretion in this case to permit the portion of that building on an inside lot to extend further back than to within 10 feet of the rear of the lot?

Mr. Brady. — Yes, sir; as long as it was one individual building and ample light, air, and ventilation were secured.

The Chairman. — You stated a few moments ago that the provision of law that a building could not cover more than 75 per cent of an inside lot was mandatory and you had no discretion?

Mr. Brady. — You take those irregular buildings you describe, you have a plan of building to get a return from that piece of land, and if a proper plan is submitted that shows proper light and ventilation, the Department uses its best discretion to grant the permit to improve the property.

The Chairman. — Is not that a case where you exercise a discretion the law does not confer?

Mr. Brady. — No, sir; we are advised we have that discretionary power.

The Chairman. — If you objected to it in the first place, why did you finally approve it without having changes made?

Mr. Brady. — Because the examiners, if they were given the right to change and modify the rules or the law without a reference back to some person in authority, we would have no rules or regulations, and when an application would come back to Mr. Dooner acting as Commissioner he has the authority to vary or change that with my knowledge or consent.

The Chairman. — Then you do not stand by your original testimony that in no case can a tenement house cover more than 75 per cent of an inside lot?

Mr. Brady. — I do not consider that an inside lot. That is a peculiar shaped lot on a corner.

The Chairman. — 176 and 178 Eldridge Street. This building was examined on August 16th by inspectors. They found the following apparent violations of the law: The dumb-waiter doors not self-closing. The law requires them to be?

Mr. Brady. — Yes, sir.

The Chairman. — Do you attempt to enforce the law in that regard?

Mr. Brady. — Yes, sir.

The Chairman. — Don't you know as a matter of fact in a large number of cases they are not?

Mr. Brady. — The original law for the dumb-waiter shaft did not consider anything about a door at all, and they were built with wooden doors originally, and I finally succeeded in getting an iron door placed on the dumb-waiter shaft, and in the cellar we forced the matter by making it mandatory to have them self-closing, but in the upper floors there were iron doors in compliance with the law.

The Chairman. — Does not the Code require them to be self-closing on all floors?

Mr. Brady. — No, sir.

The Chairman. — The report also says the first tier of beams over the cellar is constructed of wood instead of iron with fireproof flooring. Was that permissible under the law on a seven-story building?

Mr. Brady. — No, sir.

The Chairman. — If they were there, that was a clear violation of law?

Mr. Brady. — Yes, sir.

The Chairman. — The violation was filed early in the construction of that building. Why was not that enforced?

Mr. Brady. — I do not know whether there was a violation.

The Chairman. — A violation was filed and is still pending, but yet that building is completed and occupied. Isn't there some defect in the administration of the law there?

Mr. Brady. — There may be delay, as far as the attorney is concerned.

The Chairman. — What good did it do to file a violation on that building by an objection to the cellar beams if the building isn't stopped and is allowed to be completed and occupied?

Mr. Brady. — Is that the building that was the question of dispute that the tier of beams was placed in the second story instead of the first?

The Chairman. — I don't know about that.

Mr. Brady. — I think you will find there was a tier of iron beams, and it was a dispute between the owner on the intent of the law as to the placing of the iron beams.

The Chairman. — What do you consider the first tier of beams?

Mr. Brady. — Above the sidewalk.

The Chairman. — It must be above the level of the sidewalk?

Mr. Brady. — Yes, sir.

The Chairman. — You require iron beams above the cellar?

Mr. Brady. — Yes, sir.

The Chairman. — The beams in this case were above the cellar, and being of wood they were clearly a violation of law?

Mr. Brady. — Yes, sir.

The Chairman. — But you did file an objection, but it has not been enforced. Now do you suppose you will compel them to substitute iron beams?

Mr. Brady. — No, sir.

The Chairman. — Why not?

Mr. Brady. — I think if I recall that plan —

The Chairman. — I am assuming it is a clear violation of the law, and the wooden beams are found above the cellar instead of iron beams, and a violation is pending. Do you expect the result of that violation will be to compel the substitution of iron beams in the completed building?

Mr. Brady. — No, sir. The plan, if I recollect that individual case, was not to have any cellar and that there was no cellar there, and that the beams put in that place were simply sleepers, and that the first tier of beams in the building, which would be second floor beams, was above the street level, and that it was a question of dispute whether that was a proper location or not. They excavated a part of the cellar to use it for coal-bins, and there was a question of personal opinion, when the change was made in the tenement house law to compel them to put in the first tier of beams of iron, and I advocate the placing of the first tier of beams in the second floor, and therefore protect the inmates of tenement houses above the store floor, and I consider to-day it is dangerous to have the first tier of beams on the level of the first floor; and all these small tenement house stores, where they have kerosene oil, wood, groceries, and all that, are above the tier of iron beams, and the under portion is unprotected by wooden beams.

The Chairman. — Yes, but that does not make any less mandatory the requirement of the law that the beams above the cellar shall be of iron?

Mr. Brady. — Above the cellar they should be.

The Chairman. — If in point of fact there is a cellar?

Mr. Brady. — I think you will find that the owner of this building or the architect filled in these cellars or excavations they had there.

The Chairman. — That may have been done since our inspector saw it.

Mr. Brady. — I think you will find something of the kind.

The Chairman. — That is not the only case. If you find a building completed within the last year, having a cellar, and with wooden beams instead of iron above the cellar, and a violation had been filed while the building was in course of construction, what would you do?

Mr. Brady. — I would assist the owner to keep the beams on the level of the first story because I think it is where they should be, and modify the law by an act of the Board of Examiners or Board of Buildings.

The Chairman. — Can they modify the law?

Mr. Brady. — Yes, sir.

The Chairman. — You think they can modify a mandatory act of the legislature?

Mr. Brady. — Yes, sir.

The Chairman. — Would you consider they should in a case like that?

Mr. Brady. — I would vote for it as a member of the Board.

The Chairman. — Would not the thing to have done be to have prevented the erection of that building before it went beyond the cellar floor?

Mr. Brady. — We would have to know it first. Now they filled in that excavation that they had for the cellar, and then the iron beams were the first tier of iron beams in compliance with the law.

The Chairman. — 219 Division Street. This building was inspected August 2, by inspectors who reported the following apparent violations of the laws: "Seven stories; cellar; first violation that the stairs were located in the centre of the building without having any window opening to the outer air." Was that a violation?

Mr. Brady. — No, sir.

The Chairman. — Why not?

Mr. Brady. — There is no mandatory provision of law to compel the stairs to be opened to the open air.

The Chairman. — Also that the air shafts were not increased in width above the fifth story, the building being a seven-story building. Was that a violation?

Mr. Brady. — It would be a violation if the shaft had not been increased in proportion to the height of the building.

The Chairman. — "That the floors of the public halls were made of wood instead of iron or other fireproof material." In a seven-story building was that a violation of law?

Mr. Brady. — That would be a violation of law.

The Chairman. — "That the stairs were constructed of wood and enclosed by wooden partitions." Is that a violation of law?

Mr. Brady. — Yes, sir.

The Chairman. — "That the stairs from the basement to the first floor were located inside of the building and were not enclosed with brick walls or provided with self-closing fireproof doors top and bottom, but were built of wood." Would that be a violation of law?

Mr. Brady. — Yes, sir.

The Chairman. — "That the dumb-waiter shaft was apparently constructed of wood although it extended through the roof, instead of being fireproof." Would that be a violation of law?

Mr. Brady. — Yes, sir.

The Chairman. — "That it was enclosed in the cellar with wooden partitions instead of brick walls and has no door." Would that be a violation?

Mr. Brady. — Yes, sir.

The Chairman. — "That the dumb-waiter doors at each story were not self-closing." Is that a violation?

Mr. Brady. — Yes, sir.

The Chairman. — "That the first tier of beams was of wood instead of iron; that the floors of the water-closet compartments were of wood instead of being waterproof." Would this be a violation?

Mr. Brady. — Yes, sir.

The Chairman. — "The examination of the Building Department's records show the following facts: the application states that the building is to be six stories and basement high; also states that the first tier of beams is to be 3″ by 10″ spruce beams. Application was filed June 28, '99, and July 25th, the following objections from the point of view of construction were made; the connecting hallway from the stairs to the street on the first story should be enclosed with brick walls." Why was no objection made to the first tier of beams being spruce?

Mr. Brady. — I do not know that there was not.

The Chairman. — Our examination shows none was made. There are the records.

Mr. Brady. — This calls for a building six-story and basement. You say it is seven-story.

The Chairman. — Yes; in point of fact.

Mr. Brady. — These records say six-story and basement.

The Chairman. — Should not the first tier of beams have been of iron then?

Mr. Brady. — Yes, sir.

The Chairman. — Was there any objection to the plan in that regard?

Mr. Brady. — Original application calls for first tier of beams 3″ by 10″ spruce; second tier 8 inch, —

The Chairman. — We are talking about the first-tier beams.

Mr. Brady. — The law designates the iron beams are to be first-tier beams.

The Chairman. — Where there is a store they both have to be iron?

Mr. Brady. — Not until the adoption of the Code, December 23, 1899, and that plan was fully six months previous to the adoption of the Code.

The Chairman. — Don't you think the first tier of beams still should have been fireproof?

Mr. Brady. — Yes, sir.

The Chairman. — But that objection was not made?

Mr. Brady. — That might have been an oversight made by the examiner.

The Chairman. — You would account that a serious oversight?

Mr. Brady. — I would; serious oversight by simply misplacing the tier of beams, instead of the first to the second-story level, and I consider a benefit to the building by the mistake occurring, personally.

The Chairman. — How do you account for the stairs being of wood and halls of wood; stairs of wood, a seven-story building when the plans call for a six-story building?

Mr. Brady. — Our plans will show that the plan was for a dumb-waiter shaft fireproof. It shows mason work.

The Chairman. — How did it come about? The plans show that the building was not built in accordance with them.

Mr. Brady. — The explanation which I have stated before, if the inspectors outside do not carry out their duty and enforce the law when they have a copy of these plans, it is their fault and not the fault of the administration of the Department.

The Chairman. — Then you attribute these numerous violations we have found to the fault of the inspectors, do you?

Mr. Brady. — In many instances, yes, sir.

The Chairman. — Are your inspectors an efficient body of men?

Mr. Brady. — We have occasion to dismiss quite a number for being inefficient and careless.

The Chairman. — Has it been your experience that there are a great many oversights and mistakes?

Mr. Brady. — I guess within three years I have dismissed probably one hundred inspectors for just such work as that.

The Chairman. — Out of a total of 160 employed?

Mr. Brady. — About that, yes, sir; practically a change of the corps.

The Chairman. — Do you think you have increased efficiency?

Mr. Brady. — Well, until we detect them in wrong-doing we have to give them the benefit of the doubt and say they are doing their duty.

The Chairman. — What methods do you adopt to determine whether your inspectors are making correct reports?

Mr. Brady. — We have special inspectors over them.

The Chairman. — Now, we have a number of these special cases, and those I have given have illustrated the history of the number of cases we have examined. Assuming that the conclusions which our inspectors have reached are correct as to the great number of violations of the tenement house law by the buildings constructed during the past year, I understand that you ascribe the trouble first to inadequate inspection?

Mr. Brady. — Yes, sir.

The Chairman. — The faults of the inspectors?

Mr. Brady. — Yes, sir.

The Chairman. — And second to delays in enforcing the law with the legal department with which you have to deal?

Mr. Brady. — Yes. I do not place the entire responsibility on the legal department because I state here publicly that with the volume of business the attorneys have to handle, it is a practical impossibility for them to try 11,000 cases in the district courts of the city of New York.

The Chairman. — How about these important cases? Could they have been tried?

Mr. Brady. — Yes; where a case of a special class or character is called to my attention injunction proceedings are begun and followed up to the extent of often removing the building.

The Chairman. — But you think a serious difficulty is the practical one of enforcing the great number of violations that you have to file?

Mr. Brady. — Yes, sir.

The Chairman. — Do you think your force of inspectors is adequate, especially on light, ventilation, and plumbing?

Mr. Brady. — No, sir; I think we ought to have more.

The Chairman. — How many more?

Mr. Brady. — I think for the Boroughs of Manhattan and the Bronx if they were increased 25 inspectors we would not have any too many.

The Chairman. — Do you think with 25 additional inspectors the work would be thoroughly done?

Mr. Brady. — It would be a decided improvement and it would be more opportunity to detect the inspectors in any wrong-doing.

The Chairman. — Do you depend upon one inspector for each building or do you have a system of checking?

Mr. Brady. — We have a system of checking their work by sending another.

The Chairman. — Regularly or in isolated cases?

Mr. Brady. — No, sir; regularly. The district inspector has a territory known as his building district, and the general inspector is like a roundsman. He has a larger territory; he goes over three or four districts, depending on the amount of building operations going on in that section. We shift the general inspectors so that they do not become too familiar with the district inspectors.

The Chairman. — Don't you think that the fact that the builders of tenement houses do so frequently go ahead with their buildings without having received a permit, or after violations have been filed, which I understand would have the same effect, indicates a lack of proper fear on their part of the public authorities?

Mr. Brady. — Well, they get advice from attorneys and there is a difference of opinion in law, and they are ready to give us a fight in the legal department, and they are encouraged by their attorneys to proceed, and they have every excuse to proceed and take the chance.

The Chairman. — Ought it not to be by correcting the administration of the law, or correcting the law so that no one would dare construct a tenement house without first receiving a permit from your department?

Mr. Brady. — That is the law to-day.

The Chairman. — Then, if they do commence, it is due to the lack of enforcement of the law, or to the lack of proper machinery to enforce the law?

Mr. Brady. — No; in many instances an architect files a plan and the owner starts to put up his building and gets notice that the plans are not prepared in accordance with the law, and the architect as his representative calls at the Department and makes an amendment and complies with the requirement of law and the permit is issued and that removes the original violation.

The Chairman. — Don't you think it is your duty to stop the erection of tenement houses until you know the plans have been approved and permits issued for the building?

Mr. Brady. — Yes, sir, and we do.

The Chairman. — You practically stop it in very few cases. We find, and I think you practically concede, that the custom is to go ahead even though a permit has not been granted, and trust to adjusting the difficulties before the building gets too far?

Mr. Brady. — No; I think there are cases of that kind.

The Chairman. — They are rather frequent, are they not?

Mr. Brady. — No, sir.

The Chairman. — Our investigations show they are very frequent.

Mr. Brady. — Our investigations every day show that they are very infrequent.

Mr. De Forest. — Considering the point of view of good practice, I mean what the law should be, with your large experience, is it not essential that tenement houses should not be commenced until after the plans for them have been approved by the Department?

Mr. Brady. — Yes, sir.

Mr. De Forest. — Now, with your experience, what do you think ought to be done to secure that result ? If you had full power to legislate and do anything, what would you do to produce that result?

Mr. Brady. — Impose a penalty; the full penalty of law for proceeding without the plan being approved, and not allow them to come back and amend the law, which with custom and habit has grown to be usage.

Mr. De Forest. — You mean not to allow them to come back and amend the plans?

Mr. Brady. — Not to allow them to take advantage by amending the plans to waive that prosecution. The mere fact that they start without a permit would carry with it a penalty which could not be removed or dismissed in court. In other words to make that clear: If you go into court with a notice of a violation for a man commencing the construction of a building without having a permit, forthwith they will produce a certified copy that a permit is in existence, and that the statute says that the law shall be liberal; that the intent of the law shall be complied with; in 99 times out of 100 the judge will dismiss that without costs, and it falls into disuse. Sometimes, filing the violation enforces them to correct their plans and specifications up to that point. If the first section of the law carried with it a penalty of $250, and it was mandatory on the judges to do that, and that even the Commissioner of Buildings would not have the right to remove, repeal, or remit, that would have a tendency to prevent that mistake occurring as often as it does.

Mr. De Forest. — You think that if a penalty were enforced when buildings were commenced without having a permit, quite regardless of whether or not a permit were subsequently granted, such action would effectually prevent what seems to be to a certain extent the practice now of commencing without reference to the time of getting a permit?

Mr. Brady. — Yes; they would be afraid of the penalty of $250 and would wait a few days.

Mr. De Forest. — Do you think that $250 would be a serious enough penalty to accomplish that result?

Mr. Brady. — I think so. I don't believe they would want to do it a second time.

Mr. De Forest. — Now take the same question in reference to what you would call a serious violation, for instance, the occupation of more than 75 per cent of the lot area. Take cases in which, though the plans filed in your Department which have been approved show that the buildings only occupied 75 per cent, the builder goes ahead and occupies more and that is brought to your attention, or of your Department, because I know you cannot personally look at everything in the vast amount of detail you have, and that is brought to the attention of the Department. What, in your opinion, should be the law, and what action should be taken under it to secure a cessation of work in the building at that point, and the immediate remedy of that violation before the building goes up?

Mr. Brady. — We have that right by injunction at the present time; but where these important violations come there, with the large number of violations I have explained, they are received by a clerk, prepared for a violation of a certain section of the Code, docketed, recorded, notice served on the owners, and with compliance within the coming forty-eight hours there is no penalty, and that whole raft of violations is in constant transition to the attorney's office; and if the attorneys themselves, recognizing the importance of the violations when they are assigned to the attorneys, were to use some personal judgment, knowing the effect and the hardship, to remove a violation providing the buildings were complete, and prepare injunction proceedings, it would be merely a matter of signing an application for an injunction order.

A Commissioner. — Isn't it in the power of the police to immediately stop a violation by preventing a cart from crossing the sidewalk?

Mr. Brady. — No; because the Highway Department issues a permit on an application for excavation of the lot, or for dumping material in the street, and while they have a permit in compliance with regulations of the Highway Department, that cart has a right to cross the street and a policeman has no right to interfere.

The Commissioner. — But supposing the Highway Department had no legal authority to issue a permit to cross the sidewalk to begin the erection of a building until the Building Department had certified that the plans had been approved, then it would not need an injunction. You could at once notify the police that no permit had been issued for such a building, or that it had been revoked, and immediately it would stop?

Mr. Brady. — Yes, sir.

The Chairman. — Is not that a simpler and shorter way than injunctions?

Mr. Brady. — Yes. I did advocate some years ago taking the power from the Department of Public Works prior to the organization of Greater New York; that a building permit issued by the Building Department carried with it the right to place material on the street in accordance with the ordinances in existence and thereby preventing them even excavating or delivering material until the permit was secured, but that failed of passage. Now if that power was conferred on the Building Department, the mere matter of revoking a permit and calling on the police to arrest any persons attempting to dump material on the street would have the same effect as injunctions.

The Commissioner. — Suppose it came to your personal knowledge that an inside tenement house was being built, say covering 80 per cent of the lot, and you knew that those were the facts, what steps would you personally take to stop that building being built? When it was a question of knowledge, could you not stop that?

Mr. Brady. — By injunction proceedings only.

The Chairman. — You get an injunction *ex parte*?

Mr. Brady. — Yes, sir.

The Commissioner. — That does not take long?

Mr. Brady. — No; it is a mere matter of the preparation of papers. The order is always granted and a special day set for a hearing.

The Chairman. — Your right to an injunction where the builder has no permit has not been questioned?

Mr. Brady. — No. If we were to adopt the practice of preparing injunction orders in every case, we would want a corps equal to our inspectors in number. I think the suggestion of placing of the material on the street in accordance with the ordinances, and the right of crossing the street for excavation centred with the Building Department, that would stop them having the material and they could not build; and if we had the right to call the assistance of a policeman to arrest a builder that would deliver material after his permit was revoked, that would end it. Now the

Highway Department issues a permit for material to be delivered at the building and it has to be renewed every thirty days. If a builder fails to have the permit renewed within thirty days, that is read off in the station houses, and the officer on post is authorized to arrest that man for placing any material there. It is an incumbrance on the highway without authority, and if we had the permit revoked and they couldn't use the material to build, they couldn't build. If you arrested the man that was going to deliver the material, that would stop the material being brought there. But so far as all that is concerned the penalties, if enforced, would fall upon the poor unfortunate man trying to earn a dollar in the pursuit of his daily toil, and I never was interested in trying to arrest a man in that way. It would be the poor truck driver that would pay the penalty instead of the owner. So that a penalty of $250 on the owner, and no remission, where it would be compulsory on the court to impose that penalty irrespective of it being removed by the issuing of the permit, that would touch the owner, the responsible party, and compel them to live up to the law, and if compelled to pay $250 for removal of the violation or a penalty for violating the law, they would not forget it when starting the next building. That would correct that to a great extent.

A Commissioner. — Do you think the failure to prevent tenement houses being finished that have violations on them lies with the fact that you have not enough inspectors?

Mr. Brady. — I would suggest more inspectors and clerical help.

The Chairman. — Does not the law now provide a penalty of $50?

Mr. Brady. — Yes.

The Chairman. — And $250 if not removed in a certain time?

Mr. Brady. — Yes, sir.

The Chairman. — Then you have $300 penalty?

Mr. Brady. — No.

The Chairman. — You can collect the $50 anyhow?

Mr. Brady. — Yes.

The Chairman. — As a point of fact, you have not deemed it practicable to enforce those penalties?

Mr. Brady. — No, sir; because we went into court for commencing a building without a permit, and the defendant produces the permit, and they say it is a technical violation and the defendant is pounded and they dismiss it. After the permit is issued, it remedies the violation of its own force and effect.

The Chairman. — We will instruct the Secretary to give you the particulars of each of these cases spoken of to-day, so that you can give any explanation you wish to us and enforce the law if you find our inspectors are right in their conclusion that those violations are occurring.

Mr. Brady. — I will be happy to look into them, and if I find it is a violation of law, we will take the necessary steps to have them corrected.

Mr. De Forest. — Do you think tenement houses should be permitted to be occupied that have three or four violations pending, or do you not think that some provision of law by which they should not be occupied so long as violations were pending, would prevent violations, or if there were violations pending, lead to their being removed?

Mr. Brady. — That might be a hardship in many instances, and give an oppressive power to inspectors. There are two sides to everything, and if an inspector gets too much power and finds a technical violation, and you cannot occupy that building, it gives him an awful power over the owner.

Mr. De Forest. — And might be abused?

Mr. Brady. — Yes; and I would be afraid to trust it to the average man who would be there.

Mr. De Forest. — Do I understand you to say that the Board of Examiners have power to modify or change the tenement house laws?

Mr. Brady. — Not the tenement house laws. Laws relating to the construction of buildings, but not as regards light and ventilation. I have always held and ruled in the Department that the Board of Examiners should not vary or change the area of the lot covered by tenement houses, and I hold to-day in the matter of the Code that where there is no restriction about percentage of a lot covered by a hotel, and in the adoption of the Code that placed restrictions of 90 per cent to be covered by a hotel and 2½ per cent for each additional story, a case is now pending on my desk where a building is sixteen stories high, and therefore under the Code passed last September, it requires 37½ per cent of the lot on Broadway to be left vacant. Now picture the hardship it is to the owner of that valuable land, and in that instance, it being the requirement of the Code, that the Board of Buildings would have a right to vary that as a practical question.

Mr. De Forest. — I am distinguishing between the provisions of the Building Code and matters of positive law; say the tenement house law as it stands; do I understand that in your opinion and practice the Board of Examiners have power to modify that?

Mr. Brady. — Where it becomes a question of construction, but I have always ruled we have no right to interfere with light and ventilation.

Mr. De Forest. — And you would rule whenever it did affect questions of construction, the power did exist in the Board of Examiners to modify the law?

Mr. Brady. — To vary or modify the law.

Mr. De Forest. — That is a power that has been exercised?

Mr. Brady. — Yes, sir.

Mr. De Forest. — Frequently?

Mr. Brady. — Yes, sir; custom and habit for years.

A Commissioner. — What do you think of the proposition that no building shall be legally supposed to be finished until the owner has received from your Department a certificate saying that his building is built according to law?

Mr. Brady. — They can make that mandatory. I don't know what effect it would have, because any person can get that certificate on the completion of a building now.

The Commissioner. — Does the Department furnish it?

Mr. Brady. — Yes, sir.

The Commissioner. — That would be a guarantee that the building was built according to law, and the character of the work was according to law?

Mr. Brady. — Yes, sir; we issue such certificates.

Mr. De Forest. — Suppose in the case of a tenement house, occupation of it were not to be permitted until a certificate of that kind were received from your Department, would that be in your opinion a proper means of having the law enforced, and providing that it should be enforced?

Mr. Brady. — There is a certificate filed by the inspector in the Department that it is completed in accordance with the plans and specifications filed in such and such a manner. That is a matter of public record. The original application so certifies, and if there is any violation of law pending, it is under the heading of remarks written in the report, so that reference on inquiry from any person will show whether there has been any violation or not. Then by tracing to the violation department you will see by what method these violations have been remedied, and if you make it a mandatory matter on the owners of the building, inspectors might report some technical violation, and fail to issue that certificate or make that report, detrimental to the owner. There would be a severe temptation.

Mr. De Forest. — I know we have had a number, — perhaps a small number, — of cases of violation reinspected recently, and I think the list is a comparatively small one. If we were able to furnish you with a list of houses by to-morrow morning, say at ten o'clock, would it be possible for you at the opening of our session in the afternoon to give us a list of the violations which have been filed say in ten or twenty instances?

Mr. Brady. — For to-morrow?

Mr. De Forest. — Yes.

Mr. Brady. — Hardly. I would the following day.

Mr. De Forest. — I want to know first what violations there are and what disposition has been made of them?

Mr. Brady. — Yes, sir, I can do that.

A Commissioner. — In your opinion would a separate legal department of the Building Department, apart from the Corporation Counsel's office, facilitate the enforcement of the law if you had a special bureau?

Mr. Brady. — I think it would. We did have that from 1892 to 1899, until the consolidation of the Greater New York, and the attorneys there were direct appointees of the Building Department, and we had no hesitation of calling them to account. To-day, if you want to call them to account for dereliction, it is a complaint to the Corporation Counsel.

The Chairman. — How large a force did you have when you had your own legal department?

Mr. Brady. — Mr. Otterbourg, Mr. Gleason, Mr. Chambers, and Mr. Parmenter as attorneys, with a corps of clerks and assistants.

LETTER SENT TO THE COMMISSIONER OF BUILDINGS, December 11, 1900

105 East 22d Street, New York.

Hon. Thomas J. Brady, Commissioner of Buildings, 220 Fourth Avenue, City.

Dear Sir: In compliance with your request made yesterday at the public hearing of the Tenement House Commission, I beg to send herewith a list of a *few* of the new tenement houses inspected by our inspectors, in which violations of the different provisions of the tenement house law were found. This list includes ten different buildings, and covers thirty-seven violations.

The Commission will greatly appreciate it if you can send to them by *2.30 to-day*, a statement of what violations the records of your Department show for these buildings; when such violations were filed; what they consist in; and what disposition has been made of them. They will also be glad to have from you, at a later date, a report as to whether upon inspection you find the statements of the inspectors of the Commission correct.

Yours truly,

(Sgd.) LAWRENCE VEILLER, *Secretary*.

N. E. cor. Goerck & Rivington Streets.

1. The yard space is only 3 feet 7 inches instead of 5 feet (Charter, Sec. 1318).
2. Also there are two dark rooms back of store with no windows to the outer air (Charter, Sec. 1318).

N. W. cor. Rutgers Street & East Broadway.

1. The yard space is only 3 feet instead of 5 feet (Charter, Sec. 1318).
2. The air shaft is covered over by a skylight (Charter, Sec. 1318).
3. The building occupies 100 per cent of the lot on the ground, and 94 per cent at the second tier of beams instead of 92 per cent. (The shaft being less than 25 square feet does not count as unoccupied area.) (Charter, Sec. 1318.)
4. This shaft less than 25 square feet lights and ventilates a bedroom — contrary to the law and regulations (Regulations Department of Buildings).
5. The building is six stories and cellar. The floors of the public halls are of wood instead of iron and fireproof material (Charter, Sec. 1318, & Code, Sec. 53).
6. The stairs are wood instead of fireproof material (Charter, Sec. 1318, & Code, Sec. 53).
7. The stairs are enclosed with wooden stud partitions instead of brick walls (Charter, Sec. 1318, & Code, Sec. 53).
8. There is no door to the dumb-waiter shaft in the cellar (Code, Sec. 97).

219 *Division Street.*

1. The building is seven stories and cellar; the floors of the public halls are wood instead of iron and fireproof material (Charter, Sec. 1318, & Code, Sec. 53).
2. The stairs are wood instead of fireproof (Charter, Sec. 1318, & Code, Sec. 53).
3. The stairs are enclosed by stud partitions instead of brick walls (Charter, Sec. 1318, & Code, Sec. 53).
4. The *cellar* stairs are located inside of the building, are of wood, and are enclosed at top by plaster partitions; at bottom not enclosed at all, instead of being enclosed with brick walls with fireproof self-closing doors at the top and bottom (Charter, Sec. 1318).
5. The dumb-waiter shaft is constructed of boards in the cellar, and of wooden studs and lath and plaster throughout the building. In the cellar there is a large opening to this shaft, but no door (Code, Sec. 97).

6. The first tier of beams is wood, instead of iron and fireproof flooring (Code, Sec. 53).

7. The *floors* of the water-closet compartment are not waterproof, but wood (Charter, Sec. 1318).

129 *East Broadway.*

1. This building occupies 96½ per cent of the lot instead of 65 per cent (at the first tier of beams). (Charter, Sec. 1318.)

2. There is no yard space of 10 feet at the ground floor, as required by law (Charter, Sec. 1318).

3. One shaft is only 2 feet 2 inches wide instead of 2 feet 4 inches, and does not increase in width above the fifth story as required (Charter, Sec. 1318, & Regulations).

215 *Thompson Street.*

1. Eighty-three per cent of the lot is occupied instead of 65 per cent (Charter, Sec. 1318).

2. The shafts do not widen above the fifth story (Building Department Regulations).

3. The dumb-waiter doors are not self-closing (Code, Sec. 97).

131 *Thompson Street.*

1. Percentage of lot occupied 84 per cent instead of 65 per cent (Charter, Sec. 1318).

2. Shafts are not increased in width above fifth story (Regulations of Building Department).

384–390 *East 10th Street* (4 buildings).

1. Yard is only 9 feet 6 inches instead of 10 feet (Sec. 1318).

2. Buildings occupy 83½ per cent of the lot instead of 65 per cent (Charter, Sec. 1318).

3. Shafts not increased in width above the fifth story (Regulations of Building Department).

10 Buildings — 37 Violations.

SECOND LETTER SENT TO THE COMMISSIONER OF BUILDINGS,

January 23, 1901

105 East 22d Street, New York.

Hon. Thomas J. Brady, Commissioner of Buildings, 220 Fourth Avenue, New York.

My Dear Sir: At the public hearing given by the Tenement House Commission on December 10, you were asked whether it would be possible for you at the opening of the session of the Commission on the following day, to give them a list of the violations which had been filed in ten or twenty instances if a list of the houses were furnished to you on the following morning. You replied that you could hardly do that for the next day, but would on the day after. On the next day, December 11, our Secretary sent you a list of some new tenement houses in which violations of different provisions of the Tenement House Law were found. This list included ten different buildings and covered thirty-seven violations. Our Secretary asked you to send to the Commission a statement of what violations the records of your Department showed for these buildings, when such violations were filed, what they consisted in, and what disposition had been made of them. Up to the present date no information has been received from you on this subject. Our Secretary also stated that the Commission would be glad to have from you at a later date a report as to whether upon inspection you found the statements of the inspectors of the Commission correct, in the particulars called to your attention at the hearing. We are also without information from you on this subject. You will oblige the Commission very much by letting us have this information within the current week. We wish to use it in connection with our report. We wish to do no injustice to your Department, and therefore particularly wish to have the investigations of our inspectors checked by your subsequent investigations.

Respectfully yours,
(Sgd.) Robert W. De Forest, *Chairman.*

At the time of making this report no answer to these communications had been received from the Commissioner of Buildings.

TESTIMONY OF JOHN A. DOONER

Superintendent of Buildings for the Boroughs of Manhattan and Bronx

December 10, 1900.

John A. Dooner, being duly sworn, testified as follows: —

The Chairman. — What is your position?

Mr. Dooner. — Superintendent of Buildings and acting Commissioner in the absence of the Commissioner.

The Chairman. — You are the chief official in that Department for Manhattan and the Bronx under Mr. Brady?

Mr. Dooner. — Yes, sir.

The Chairman. — The immediate supervision of the Department is yours, then?

Mr. Dooner. — Partly so.

The Chairman. — You have heard Mr. Brady's testimony?

Mr. Dooner. — Yes, sir.

The Chairman. — Is it your belief that but few buildings have been built in the past year, tenement houses, which cover more than 75 per cent of the lot?

Mr. Dooner. — I do not know of any which covers more.

The Chairman. — If you find by investigating a list furnished by us that there were a considerable number which cover more, would your conclusion be that there was some defect in the administration of your Department?

Mr. Dooner. — I would report it to the Commissioner.

The Chairman. — It ought to be possible with the force at your disposal to find out any case where more than 75 per cent of the lot is covered?

Mr. Dooner. — Yes, sir.

The Chairman. — What do you understand the law to be with reference to a tenement house on a corner lot? That the law permits that the first story may cover the entire lot?

Mr. Dooner. — Yes, sir.

The Chairman. — And you have enforced that law with that construction, have you?

Mr. Dooner. — Yes, sir.

The Chairman. — Do you personally examine buildings?

Mr. Dooner. — Sometimes.

The Chairman. — In what cases do you examine buildings?

Mr. Dooner. — An unsafe building, or where I am going along a street I make an examination of it.

The Chairman. — The regular routine examinations of new buildings are examinations made by any one in your Department except the district inspector?

Mr. Dooner. — The special inspector examines them.

The Chairman. — Do regular inspectors examine them?

Mr. Dooner. — Yes, sir.

The Chairman. — But in an ordinary case no one but those two inspectors examine a tenement house?

Mr. Dooner. — This is all, sir.

The Chairman. — Do you think it is a fact that the tenement houses erected during the past year are in your opinion substantially free from the violation of the tenement house laws?

Mr. Dooner. — I do not say that they all are.

The Chairman. — Are there not a great many violations pending and undisposed of as to buildings which have been completed?

Mr. Dooner. — Yes, sir.

The Chairman. — What will be the fate of those violations in the ordinary course?

Mr. Dooner. — Sent to the attorney for prosecution.

The Chairman. — What will be their fate there?

Mr. Dooner. — I do not know anything about the attorney's office; I have no jurisdiction.

The Chairman. — Your interest ceases after the violation is turned over to the attorney?

Mr. Dooner. — Yes, sir.

The Chairman. — Have there been any substantial number of cases in the past year or two where buildings, having been completed, have been torn down or substantially changed because of a failure to comply with the law?

Mr. Dooner. — Some.

The Chairman. — How many cases do you suppose?

Mr. Dooner. — I couldn't judge; maybe ten.

The Chairman. — During the past year or two?

Mr. Dooner. — There might have been ten or twenty.

The Chairman. — Have there been any cases where a recently constructed building has been torn down?

Mr. Dooner. — Yes, sir.

The Chairman. — How many?

Mr. Dooner. — Tore down one Saturday.

The Chairman. — Was that because of inadequate light and ventilation, or because it was unsafe?

Mr. Dooner. — It was not unsafe; built contrary to law.

The Chairman. — What was that particularly?

Mr. Dooner. — A wooden structure built 18 feet high.

The Chairman. — Has any brick building been torn down, constructed in the past year or two?

Mr. Dooner. — Yes, sir.

The Chairman. — For what offence?

Mr. Dooner. — Being unsafe and covering more than the law requires.

The Chairman. — In how many cases have they been torn down for that reason?

Mr. Dooner. — I couldn't recollect how many.

The Chairman. — Five cases?

Mr. Dooner. — Yes; I should judge more than that.

The Chairman. — Will you furnish us with a list of such cases?

Mr. Dooner. — I will, with the permission of the Commissioner.

The Chairman. — We will write you a letter to-morrow asking for a list, asking for all cases where buildings constructed in the past two years have been torn down or radically modified because they covered more than the proportion of the lot authorized by law.

Mr. Dooner. — You had better ask that of the Commissioner.

The Chairman. — If we brought to your attention twenty or thirty cases of buildings constructed on inside lots in the past year, covering more than 75 per cent of the lot, what action would you recommend?

Mr. Dooner. — To be sent immediately for correction.

The Chairman. — Is it possible to correct that without substantially tearing down the building?

Mr. Dooner. — Sometimes they can, yes.

The Chairman. — The building has to be radically changed?

Mr. Dooner. — No, according to what it is.

The Chairman. — If the fault is it covers more than 75 per cent of an inside lot?

Mr. Dooner. — They can easily remedy it.

The Chairman. — In what way?

Mr. Dooner. — What way do you say the building would cover? Do you say it is the light shaft?

The Chairman. — Yes.

Mr. Dooner. — Take down the shaft and rebuild it.

The Chairman. — That would be taking down the whole wall?

Mr. Dooner. — No, sir.

The Chairman. — On one side of the shaft?

Mr. Dooner. — Only take down the shaft.

The Chairman. — What is a shaft?

Mr. Dooner. — The shaft is the place where the light shaft is built.

The Chairman. — Which is surrounded by walls?

Mr. Dooner. — There is only one wall in it.

The Chairman. — You have to take down that wall?

Mr. Dooner. — Yes, sir.

The Chairman. — Where the defect is that more than 75 per cent is covered, a building must be torn down or radically changed to comply with the law?

Mr. Dooner. — It can be changed by taking down that light shaft.

The Chairman. — Have you ever knowingly permitted buildings to be completed where you knew their completion involved serious violations of the law?

Mr. Dooner. — Not as I know of.

The Chairman. — If you find that a given building does involve the violation of the law, tell us what your duty is?

Mr. Dooner. — The chief inspector should report to me.

The Chairman. — When he reports a building is going up involving serious violations of the law, what steps do you take?

Mr. Dooner. — Report it to the Commissioner.

The Chairman. — What next?

Mr. Dooner. — Goes to the attorney for prosecution.

The Chairman. — And then your responsibility ends?

Mr. Dooner. — Yes, sir.

The Chairman. — Do you remember the case of a building 262 and 264 West 144th Street regarding which Mr. Andrus called on you on behalf of Mr. Brown?

Mr. Dooner. — No, I don't recollect it. Do you mean Norman Andrews?

The Chairman. — Yes.

Mr. Dooner. — With respect to a frame building?

The Chairman. — With reference to some building on 144th Street. Mr. Charles Andrus. Do you know him?

Mr. Dooner. — Yes, sir.

The Chairman. — And he called upon you with reference to it and called your attention to the fact that they were violating the law?

Mr. Dooner. — In what way do you mean?

The Chairman. — I am not trying to criticise you, but to find what we deem to be defects in the present mode of enforcing the law. Our information is that a great many violations were filed against these particular buildings, and they were going up notwithstanding those violations, and that Mr. Andrus called upon you. Do you remember that incident?

Mr. Dooner. — Mr. Andrus was in there to-day with respect to a frame building.

The Chairman. — This was some time ago; the buildings are now completed and occupied.

Mr. Dooner. — I do not recollect it.

The Chairman. — Do you remember the instance of causing the erection of these buildings to be stopped temporarily on Mr. Andrus' complaint?

Mr. Dooner. — I don't recollect that.

The Chairman. — What is your personal view as to the advisability of the present provision of the law permitting 75 per cent of the lot to be covered by tenement houses?

Mr. Dooner. — I think 75 per cent is a fair rate for tenement houses.

The Chairman. — Do you think the tenement houses now being constructed covering that proportion of the lot are sanitary?

Mr. Dooner. — Yes, sir.

The Chairman. — And are adequately provided with light and air?

Mr. Dooner. — Yes, sir; according to the rules and regulations of the Department.

The Chairman. — I am leaving that out of consideration. You have some views about tenement houses, do you not?

Mr. Dooner. — I have built a good many of them.

The Chairman. — And you have had to do with a great many of them in your present official capacity?

Mr. Dooner. — Yes, sir.

The Chairman. — Is it your judgment, apart from the requirement of the law, that the ordinary tenement house built at the present day under the requirements of the law, covering 75 per cent of the lot is adequately provided with light and air?

Mr. Dooner. — It is, sir; that is my opinion.

The Chairman. — You think there can be no substantial improvement in the type of tenement houses now built?

Mr. Dooner. — No, sir, I do not.

The Chairman. — And are you familiar with the tenement houses now being built in Brooklyn?

Mr. Dooner. — No, sir, I am not.

The Chairman. — On the question of air shafts, do you think that in any building living rooms should be allowed to receive their only light and air from air shafts less than 25 square feet?

Mr. Dooner. — Well, yes; 25 feet is reasonable enough.

The Chairman. — You think that should be the minimum, do you not?

Mr. Dooner. — Yes, sir.

The Chairman. — You do not regard it good practice to have bedrooms in any building which receive their only light and air from air shafts 15 or 20 feet in area?

Mr. Dooner. — Well, it is according to the size of the building.

The Chairman. — Should in any case air shafts on which bedrooms depend for their only supply of light and air be covered at the top?

Mr. Dooner. — They should be open.

The Chairman. — And if they are covered at the top you regard their condition as unsanitary?

Mr. Dooner. — Yes, sir.

The Chairman. — So far as your observation extends, has the law that requires air shafts to widen four inches over every story beyond five, been enforced?

Mr. Dooner. — Yes, so far as I know.

The Chairman.—I will read to you the same summary of the results of this investigation I read to Mr. Brady. Out of 286 tenements inspected where this information was obtainable, 282, or 99 per cent, covered more than 65 per cent of the lot; 274 tenement houses, or 96 per cent of them, covered more than 70 per cent of the lot; 93 tenement houses, or 32 per cent, covered exactly 75 per cent of the lot; and 88 tenement houses, or 31 per cent, covered more than 75 per cent of the lot, the extreme maximum authorized by law in any case. And 29 tenements, or 10 per cent, covered 80 per cent of the lot and over. Would it be a surprise to you to find that condition of affairs existed?

Mr. Dooner. — Yes, sir.

The Chairman. — You personally know of no cases of recently completed tenement houses covering more than 75 per cent of an inside lot?

Mr. Dooner. — I do not.

The Chairman. — Except the one that you speak of where the building was torn down?

Mr. Dooner. — That was torn down.

The Chairman. — Why was that, instead of being modified?

Mr. Dooner. — Because it was a foot over the line.

The Chairman. — Over what line?

Mr. Dooner. — Their own line; it encroached a foot on another man's property.

The Chairman. — And for that reason you ordered it torn down?

Mr. Dooner. — No, sir; there was another difference; they made a false affidavit.

The Chairman. — What percentage of the lot did that building cover?

Mr. Dooner. — Ninety-five per cent.

The Chairman. — How do you account for that building being built without having been stopped?

Mr. Dooner. — Because they took five feet of another man's lot and put it on their survey.

The Chairman. — That didn't make it cover 95 per cent?

Mr. Dooner. — It did when they set back on another man's lot.

The Chairman. — By taking five feet from another man's lot you don't increase the proportion of your own lot?

Mr. Dooner. — He swore it was his lot.

The Chairman. — And that building was completely torn down?

Mr. Dooner. — Yes, sir.

The Chairman. — Now, coming back to that subject again, is that the only case you know of where a building has been torn down because it covers more than a proper proportion of the lot?

Mr. Dooner. — No; I know of more, but I couldn't tell you just where, now.

The Chairman. — Don't you remember any specific instance?

Mr. Dooner. — I know there is some.

The Chairman. — Have you had more cases within the past two years?

Mr. Dooner. — I should judge we had ten cases; perhaps more.

The Chairman. — Where the building has been completely torn down for that reason?

Mr. Dooner. — Oh, no; not completely.

The Chairman. — Portions taken down?

Mr. Dooner. — Yes, sir.

The Chairman. — If you found that a building had been completed within the last year seven stories high without the air-shaft being wider than 2 feet 4 inches above the fifth story, what course would your Department pursue?

Mr. Dooner. — Send it to the attorney.

The Chairman. — You would endeavor to push it to a decision and have the air shaft widened?

Mr. Dooner. — Yes, sir.

The Chairman. — Do you know of any cases within the past two years when completed buildings have been so changed as to widen the air shaft above the fifth story?

Mr. Dooner. — Not above the fifth story; they have got to widen them below.

The Chairman. — Assuming they are wide enough below, but not widened above the fifth story, has any such change been required?

Mr. Dooner. — They couldn't widen them on the fifth story, because the walls are only 12 inches thick.

The Chairman. — Have you compelled them to widen clear to the bottom because of that?

Mr. Dooner. — Might let them set off on the outside of the wall instead of the inside.

The Chairman. — Have there been any changes in buildings constructed in the past two years where you have required the entire shaft to be widened?

Mr. Dooner. — No.

The Chairman. — Your Department has to do with recommending fire-escapes for old buildings?

Mr. Dooner. — Yes, sir, where there is three families or more.

The Chairman. — Have you inspectors regularly employed in that department of your work?

Mr. Dooner. — Yes, sir.

The Chairman. — How many?

Mr. Dooner. — One.

The Chairman. — He does nothing else but look after fire-escapes?

Mr. Dooner. — That is all.

The Chairman. — Are there any tenement houses in the Borough of Manhattan that have no fire-escapes?

Mr. Dooner. — I should judge there is.

The Chairman. — How does that happen to be?

Mr. Dooner. — May be violations. I know there were six or seven thousand violations for fire-escapes.

The Chairman. — To what extent have those been carried to a conclusion?

Mr. Dooner. — There is a great many of them putting them up.

The Chairman. — You think there is a large number where there are no fire-escapes at all?

Mr. Dooner. — Yes, sir.

The Chairman. — That has been so for some time?

Mr. Dooner. — Yes, sir.

The Chairman. — How long has your Department been enforcing the law in that regard?

Mr. Dooner. — Started on the block system about two years ago.

The Chairman. — Now, isn't there something wrong in the administration of the law that there should still be so many tenement houses entirely without fire-escapes?

Mr. Dooner. — I think our Department since I came into it has put more fire-escapes on than in the history of the Department.

The Chairman. — Why should not they universally have fire-escapes?

Mr. Dooner. — Under the Code a tenement house is a three-family house.

The Chairman. — The law is mandatory?

Mr. Dooner. — Yes, sir.

The Chairman. — What was the fate of these owners of the numerous tenement houses which have continued all this time without fire-escapes; do they go unpunished?

Mr. Dooner. — There is no fire-escape on a five-story building in New York that is not put up.

The Chairman. — There are some four-story tenement houses?

Mr. Dooner. — Some four, three, and two stories.

The Chairman. — And a great many of those are occupied by more than one family on a floor?

Mr. Dooner. — Yes, sir.

The Chairman. — Those buildings should have fire-escapes?

Mr. Dooner. — Yes, sir.

The Chairman. — Why don't you force them to?

Mr. Dooner. — That is for the attorneys to take care of. We send them to the attorneys for prosecution.

The Chairman. — Have you turned over to the Legal Department all the cases you found where, in a reasonable time, your requirements have not been complied with?

Mr. Dooner. — Yes, sir; we give them a reasonable time.

The Chairman. — Do you file violations in every case?

Mr. Dooner. — Yes, sir.

The Chairman. — How many years has the law requiring tenement houses to have fire-escapes been in force?

Mr. Dooner. — Since I have been in the Department.

The Chairman. — And for some years before, was it not?

Mr. Dooner. — Yes.

The Chairman. — Doesn't it seem to you there is some fault somewhere in the administration of the law, or in the law itself, if after that law has been in force several years you see so many tenement houses without fire-escapes?

Mr. Dooner. — Well, we would not have known that, only I took up the block system and examined every house on Manhattan Island and the Bronx, something that was never done in the history of the Department before. Every house has been examined, and where they needed fire-escapes the violation was made.

The Chairman. — I have no doubt your Department, so far as the inspection is concerned, has done its duty, but isn't there something wrong that so many of these buildings have not received fire-escapes?

Mr. Dooner. — Take 11,000 violations and 7000 or 8000 thousand fire-escape notices, and unsafe buildings, we haven't enough attorneys to carry them on. It would take all of the courts in New York to attend to it.

The Chairman. — If you had more lawyers, you could accomplish more?

Mr. Dooner. — Then it would take up all the time of the courts.

The Chairman. — You regard the equipment of these buildings with fire-escapes as an important thing for the safety of their inmates?

Mr. Dooner. — Yes, sir.

The Chairman. — And the tenement houses without fire-escapes are a serious menace to their inmates?

Mr. Dooner. — Yes, sir. I don't know of one in the city of New York, five-story tenement house.

The Chairman. — Four-story?

Mr. Dooner. — Yes, sir.

The Chairman. — Their inmates are in a dangerous condition?

Mr. Dooner. — Yes, sir.

The Chairman. — How is it you have been able to compel every five-story tenement house to provide fire-escapes and have not been able to compel four-story ones?

Mr. Dooner. — Because the four-story ones have been changed, the occupancy of the building. Sometimes it is a boarding house, which the law does not require, unless it has fifteen sleeping rooms. Then they change them into a tenement house, and then it is time to put a fire-escape on.

The Chairman. — No matter how recently the building has been changed, the law is still mandatory?

Mr. Dooner. — Yes, sir.

The Chairman. — If you have been able to enforce the law as to five-story buildings, why cannot you enforce it as to four stories?

Mr. Dooner. — We do the best we can.

The Chairman. — You say you do with perfect success as to the five stories?

Mr. Dooner. — I do not know of one without them at this time.

The Chairman. — Why can't you do the same as to the four-story buildings?

Mr. Dooner. — We do.

The Chairman. — You said a moment ago you cannot get enough lawyers and courts to enforce the law against these violations?

Mr. Dooner. — That is with the Corporation Counsel's office.

The Chairman. — Do you understand that the law permits in any instance living rooms which have no windows which do not open into the outer air, either into an air shaft or street?

Mr. Dooner. — I don't know of any.

The Chairman. — It is not lawful to have a sleeping room which receives its only light and ventilation from another living room?

Mr. Dooner. — No, sir; it may be in old houses, but not in new ones. I don't know of any.

The Chairman. — So that if you saw that buildings were being built in any part of Greater New York with such rooms, would you say the law was being violated?

Mr. Dooner. — Yes, sir.

A Commissioner. — You speak about light shafts being 2 feet 4 in width where the building is not over five stories. Now, when a building is six or seven stories they are to be widened 4 inches for each story?

Mr. Dooner. — Yes, sir.

The Commissioner. — How can that be executed; how do they manage to widen the shaft?

Mr. Dooner. — They start from the bottom. If the wall is 2 feet thick and the first story 20 inches, they can cut 4 inches off on each of these stories, as they generally do, on the outside of the light shaft, and that keeps increasing the air shaft.

The Commissioner. — They carry the wall up on the inside?

Mr. Dooner. — Yes, sir.

The Commissioner. — And rack off the 4 inches from the outside?

Mr. Dooner. — On the outside.

The Commissioner. — The reason I asked it was that it struck me that once the shaft was run up, if there was a violation, they couldn't do anything unless they tore the wall down altogether?

Mr. Dooner. — That is the only thing they can do, tear it down to where the set-off is. They generally set-off on the outside.

The Commissioner. — You made the remark that they could enlarge the percentage left for air and light by simply removing the wall of the shaft. In that case would not it cut off the rooms of the house?

Mr. Dooner. — No; suppose they are only 4 inches off, he has only to shore up the beams, take the wall down, and set it back 4 inches.

The Commissioner. — The amount of 4 inches I do not suppose there would be any question raised; but I mean in a building covering 80 per cent of the lot, how could that be done without tearing down the whole wall and cutting in on the rooms?

Mr. Dooner. — If the shaft would be only 4 inches out of the way, they would take down the shaft and move it in 4 inches. They would cut back to the rear.

The Commissioner. — Do they do that?

Mr. Dooner. — Yes, we have had it done in Division Street; when I made a case in Division or West Broadway. I am pretty sure on one case I had them cut down in the rear.

The Commissioner. – If these walls in many of these houses could be built up with good material, good mortar and such as that, would you give your opinion as to whether they might not be built lighter than they are; not occupy so much room?

Mr. Dooner. — I do not think any wall in a tenement house should be lighter than 12 inches.

The Commissioner. — No, but when they start the walls to have them 20 inches?

Mr. Dooner. — I think a tenement house wall should be built 20 inches, second story 15 inches, and the rest 12.

The Commissioner. — That is what there is now, but there is so much inferior material used; but if it was built up of good cement mortar, don't you think it would accomplish the result?

Mr. Dooner. — A 12-inch wall of cement mortar would do all the way up in my opinion.

The Commissioner. — And in that way they would save so much room?

Mr. Dooner. — Yes, sir.

The Commissioner. — That means for a five-story house?

Mr. Dooner. — Yes, sir; in fact, any building. If I had my way, I wouldn't allow any lime to be used in any building in the city of New York; nothing but cement. It don't cost much more.

A Commissioner. — Now, as a matter of fact, buildings do seem to be completed with violations on the buildings. What is your remedy to stop that?

Mr. Dooner. — They ought to be prosecuted.

The Commissioner. — Prosecute whom?

Mr. Dooner. — Prosecute the owner.

The Commissioner. — Fine him?

Mr. Dooner. — Yes, sir.

The Commissioner. — Is that the remedy you would suggest to stop that?

Mr. Dooner. — Yes, sir, I would fine the owner.

The Commissioner. — Isn't it possible by the machinery of your Department to finally stop a building being built when important violations are on the building?

Mr. Dooner. — Yes, if they draw it to my attention.

The Commissioner. — What would you do?

Mr. Dooner. — I would take it in to the Commissioner, have the Commissioner get ready, and have the attorneys get an injunction.

The Commissioner. — That is the only remedy you have?

Mr. Dooner. — Yes, sir.

The Chairman. — Don't you think there should be some way by which buildings cannot be started until they get permits from your Department?

Mr. Dooner. — The only way you can do that is to begin with the excavation. A man should not excavate unless he had a permit from the Department of Buildings.

The Chairman. — You would favor that?

Mr. Dooner. — Yes, sir. I think everything in reference to a building should come under the Building Department, such as a permit for putting material on the street, and for crossing the sidewalk. I think that is the only way to remedy it.

The Commissioner. — How has it happened that a number of these buildings have been finished notwithstanding the fact that violations have been on them?

Mr. Dooner. — That I couldn't answer. They may be in court and may be in process of suit. The case we tore down Saturday was over a year in court.

TESTIMONY OF JOHN GUILFOYLE

COMMISSIONER OF BUILDINGS FOR THE BOROUGH OF BROOKLYN

DECEMBER 10, 1900.

JOHN GUILFOYLE, being duly sworn, testified as follows: —

The Chairman. — What is your official position?

Mr. Guilfoyle. — Commissioner of Buildings, Borough of Brooklyn.

The Chairman. — How long have you held that position?

Mr. Guilfoyle. — June 3, 1898.

The Chairman. — What is your occupation apart from that?

Mr. Guilfoyle. — Builder twenty-two years.

The Chairman. — What have you to say with reference to the enforcement of the law in Brooklyn with reference to fire-escapes on tenement houses?

Mr. Guilfoyle. — I think they ought to be on all tenement houses. I don't know of any tenement houses it is not on.

The Chairman. — You don't know of any tenement houses in Brooklyn not provided with fire-escapes?

Mr. Guilfoyle. — No, sir.

The Chairman. — What do you define a tenement house to be?

Mr. Guilfoyle. — A three-family house.

The Chairman. — So you think the law in Brooklyn has been generally enforced in that regard?

Mr. Guilfoyle. — I do; yes, sir.

The Chairman. — Now, if we tell you that of 661 tenement houses examined in Brooklyn it was found 283 were without fire-escapes of any kind whatsoever, would you be surprised at that information?

Mr. Guilfoyle. — Yes, sir, I would.

The Chairman. — You don't know one?

Mr. Guilfoyle. — No, sir, I do not.

The Chairman. — Would you also be surprised to learn that of that number 244 were wooden tenement houses where the chance of escape in case of fire is much less than in big buildings?

Mr. Guilfoyle. — Yes, sir.

The Chairman. — Have you had a thorough inspection of Brooklyn made with a view to finding whether the fire-escape law had been enforced?

Mr. Guilfoyle. — I give my men weekly lectures governing all those things, and insist that the law should be carried out in every particular.

The Chairman. — Have you adopted the block system?

Mr. Guilfoyle. — Yes, sir.

The Chairman. — And you have gone through the form of making a complete inspection in that regard?

Mr. Guilfoyle. — Yes, sir.

The Chairman. — And your reports show that the tenement houses are supplied with fire-escapes?

Mr. Guilfoyle. — Yes, sir.

The Chairman. — If it is a fact that 283 tenement houses in Brooklyn are without fire-escapes, what is your conclusion as to the manner in which the law is being enforced in Brooklyn?

Mr. Guilfoyle. — I do not think the men would be doing their duty.

The Chairman. — It would show a very hopeless breach of duty on their part?

Mr. Guilfoyle. — No question about that.

The Chairman. — To have led you into supposing they had all been supplied with fire-escapes?

Mr. Guilfoyle. — Yes, sir; I do not believe that report is correct.

The Chairman. — We will send you a list of these 283 houses.

Mr. Guilfoyle. — All right, sir; notwithstanding I say that there may be violations upon all of these things.

The Chairman. — Your statement was that so far as you knew there was not a tenement house in Brooklyn without fire-escapes?

Mr. Guilfoyle. — Without violations on them, I said.

The Chairman. — No; you did not say that.

Mr. Guilfoyle. — It is supposed without a violation.

The Chairman. — Do you think there are many which are not provided with fire-escapes?

Mr. Guilfoyle. — I do not think there is one. They have fire-escapes or violations upon them.

The Chairman. — What proportion has fire-escapes and what has violations?

Mr. Guilfoyle. — I could not say.

The Chairman. — Do you think there are many not provided with fire-escapes? You said a moment ago there were none.

Mr. Guilfoyle. — I have got only 176 violations of fire-escapes in Brooklyn to-day; 440 of the total, and 264 remedied, and I have been insisting from day to day to get those tried.

The Chairman. — Then your own records show 176 are subject to violations?

Mr. Guilfoyle. — Yes, sir.

The Chairman. — So you correct your testimony of a few moments ago that you know of no tenement houses not provided with fire-escapes?

Mr. Guilfoyle. — Oh, yes; no tenement house is not provided with fire-escapes to-day that has not a violation on it.

The Chairman. — Our examination shows that of the 661 tenement houses in the seventeenth ward alone, and I understand that ward represents but a portion, and not a large portion of the tenement house district of your city, 283 were entirely without fire-escapes of any kind. You have heard the testimony of the Commissioner and Superintendent Dooner with reference to the requirement of law to the effect that no living rooms should be without windows opening to the outer air. You have the same understanding of the law?

Mr. Guilfoyle. — Yes, sir, or on a court or light shaft.

The Chairman. — You enforce that law in that regard in the same way in Brooklyn?

Mr. Guilfoyle. — Yes, sir.

The Chairman. — Is it lawful in your judgment to count as the outer air a light shaft with a roof or skylight on top?

Mr. Guilfoyle. — Yes, sir.

The Chairman. — You differ with Commissioner Brady and Superintendent Dooner in that regard?

Mr. Guilfoyle. — Yes, sir, because they do not have any 10-foot light shafts here, I understand. All their buildings are over five stories generally.

The Chairman. — What is a 10-foot light shaft?

Mr. Guilfoyle. — Ten square feet.

The Chairman. — You say it is lawful to allow bedrooms or living rooms which depend for their only light and ventilation upon windows opening into 10-foot air shafts roofed over at the top?

Mr. Guilfoyle. — Yes, sir.

The Chairman. — Do you recognize that is exactly contrary to the testimony of both Commissioner Brady and Superintendent Dooner?

Mr. Guilfoyle. — I do not know that.

The Chairman. — You heard their testimony?

Mr. Guilfoyle. — I did not recognize that part of it.

The Chairman. — You do permit generally in Brooklyn living rooms built with windows opening into these 10-foot air shafts.

Mr. Guilfoyle. — Yes, sir; always did; always has been so.

The Chairman. — Does the law permit that now?

Mr. Guilfoyle. — Yes, sir, in buildings under five stories.

The Chairman. — Where is it in the law?

Mr. Guilfoyle. — It states that the light shaft for a building over five stories and basement must be at least 25 feet area of light shaft.

The Chairman. — I know; but I am speaking of the other provision of law that living rooms shall be provided with windows opening into the outer air, and can you consider a 10-foot light shaft closed at the top an opening into the air?

Mr. Guilfoyle. — It has a skylight on it and ventilation is ample.

The Chairman. — "Except as hereinafter otherwise stated every light and air shaft or court for habitable rooms must be twenty-five square feet in area up to and including five stories in height." Is not that provision of the law clear?

Mr. Guilfoyle. — Yes; we have taken that to mean a five-story and over.

The Chairman. — " Up to and including; except as hereinafter otherwise stated every light and air shaft or court for habitable rooms must be at least twenty-five square feet in area up to and including five stories in height." Does not that clearly include a three-story building?

Mr. Guilfoyle. — Yes; but the shaft provision was by the Board of Buildings, and their rules for light and ventilation allowed for 10-foot light shafts.

The Chairman. — Do you think that contemplates changes by the Board?

Mr. Guilfoyle. — No, I don't suppose it does.

The Chairman. — Don't you know the law to be clear that such air shafts as you permit in Brooklyn are not authorized by the statutes of the State?

Mr. Guilfoyle. — No, I do not know that. I supposed it was allowed by the Department.

The Chairman. — It has been allowed by your Department?

Mr. Guilfoyle. — Yes, sir.

A Commissioner. — Do you allow new buildings to have 10-foot shafts?

Mr. Guilfoyle. — No, sir; frame buildings less than 65 per cent.

The Chairman. — You do allow new buildings less than five stories high to be equipped with these 10-foot air shafts roofed over?

Mr. Guilfoyle. — In small frame buildings less than 65 per cent of the lot.

The Chairman. — You mean covering less than 65 per cent of the lot?

Mr. Guilfoyle. — Yes, sir.

The Chairman. — Here is what we find in the Borough of Brooklyn in that regard: In thirty-four new tenement houses there were rooms which had no windows to the outer air and opened solely on small interior shafts. In thirty-eight cases examined at random 94 per cent had such windows. Won't you look up the law and see about that?

Mr. Guilfoyle. — Covering less than 65 per cent of the lot?

The Chairman. — I do not know whether that is the fact, but the law makes no provision of that kind. You know the language of the statute which says where the house covers less than 65 per cent of the lot?

Mr. Guilfoyle. — It is the rules of the Board.

The Chairman. — You know the rules of the Board cannot change the law?

Mr. Guilfoyle. — Certainly.

The Chairman. — If you find on examination that there is no law authorizing such air shafts, and conclude, as I think you will, that the Board cannot go against the law, will you stop the use of such air shafts in Brooklyn?

Mr. Guilfoyle. — Certainly.

The Chairman. — Do you permit in Brooklyn rooms which have no means of light and ventilation except a door, transom, or window connecting with an adjoining room?

Mr. Guilfoyle. — Yes, sir.

The Chairman. — Do you regard that as lawful?

Mr. Guilfoyle. —Yes, sir.

The Chairman. — Explain on what theory.

Mr. Guilfoyle. — That is, where it comes to two families on a floor we have allowed it.

The Chairman. — Where do you find it in the law?

Mr. Guilfoyle. — I cannot give you the section just now.

The Chairman. — Do you permit in any case rooms which have no windows into the air shafts, or certainly which depend entirely upon an adjoining room for their light and air, Mr. Dooner?

Mr. Dooner. — No, sir, we do not.

The Chairman. —Your view is the law does not permit it?

Mr. Dooner. — No, sir. If it opens on to a hall, it is all right.

The Chairman. — If it gets its only light and ventilation from the hall is it all right?

Mr. Dooner. — Cannot get it there.

The Chairman. — Isn't the law mandatory that every room shall have an opening into the outer air?

Mr. Guilfoyle. — It is when the hall is covered by a skylight over the stairs.

The Chairman. — You define that to be the outer air?

Mr. Guilfoyle. — Yes, sir.

The Chairman. — So that the theory on which you decide rooms having no means of light and ventilation except an opening into an adjacent hall is that the hall is the outer air because it has the skylight above?

Mr. Guilfoyle. — Yes, sir.

A Commissioner. — With louvres, you mean?

Mr. Guilfoyle. — Yes, sir.

The Commissioner. — The whole secret being the louvre?

Mr. Guilfoyle. — Yes, sir.

The Chairman. — If the only means of light and ventilation was through another bedroom?

Mr. Guilfoyle. — It is not proper ventilation.

A Commissioner. — In these decisions are you following the steps of your predecessor?

Mr. Guilfoyle. — Yes, sir, in many cases.

The Commissioner. — And the custom of the Department?

Mr. Guilfoyle. — Yes, sir.

Mr. De Forest. — Are not you the first Commissioner under Greater New York?

Mr. Guilfoyle. — No, sir; the second.

A Commissioner. — Would you allow a four-story building to be built with a covered court with rooms opening on to it?

Mr. Guilfoyle. — Two rooms on each story.

The Commissioner. — But not five stories?

Mr. Guilfoyle. — No, sir.

The Commissioner. — You draw the limit between four and five as an arbitrary limit yourself?

Mr. Guilfoyle. — Yes, sir.

The Commissioner. — How many inspectors have you in your Department?

Mr. Guilfoyle. — Sixty.

The Commissioner. — Do you consider them ample to do the work?

Mr. Guilfoyle. — No, sir, I do not.

The Commissioner. — How many do you feel you should have?

Mr. Guilfoyle. — I ought to have a dozen more.

The Chairman. — Do you permit dumb-waiter shafts constructed of wood?

Mr. Guilfoyle. — No, sir; we have none.

The Chairman. — Our inspectors report that out of 83 buildings 22 buildings were supplied with dumb-waiter shafts constructed of wood.

Mr. Guilfoyle. — I had a case of a man named Hatch where I got an injunction restraining him from going ahead with five buildings he had. He vacated the injunction and then we commenced suit. I pressed it, because I had some four hundred cases pending in the same way on dumb-waiter shafts. I forced this to the Supreme Court and we got a decision from the Supreme Court, and this man got a stay compelling me not to touch the building, and in the meantime he had let the whole five. I was trying to stop the tenants going in there. He got a stay and the thing has been dragging along for the last four months, and I have asked for the last three weeks to get that case from the Appellate Division. He appealed from the decision of the Supreme Court to the Appellate Division and I have thirty-two cases against him in the same way.

The Chairman. — Who is your attorney in that case?

Mr. Guilfoyle. — No attorney assigned to the Building Department. We have one man there as counsel from the Corporation Counsel, but nobody is assigned there.

The Chairman. — You have got them yourself?

Mr. Guilfoyle. — I have exceeded my authority in going to the Supreme Court and asking to have that carried out.

The Chairman. — Your troubles are due largely to a lack of legal help?

Mr. Guilfoyle. — There is no question about that.

The Chairman. — Have you enough inspectors?

Mr. Guilfoyle. — No, sir. I have one plan examiner only.

The Chairman. — If I tell you out of 83 buildings we find 22 buildings with dumb-waiter shafts constructed of wood, what would you say?

Mr. Guilfoyle. — It would not surprise me at all. I propose to take them all out if I get this decision.

The Chairman. — I understood you to say you had none?

Mr. Guilfoyle. — The way you asked me the wooden shafts, I suppose you meant boarded right up, wooden sides lathed and plaster. That is the one I am fighting on now. They got a stay, and when I told the counsel I was going to go to the judges he thought I was exceeding my authority.

The Chairman. — How many inspectors have you?

Mr. Guilfoyle. — Sixty.

The Chairman. — How many do you think you ought to have?

Mr. Guilfoyle. — Seventy-five easy. I have a man covering eight square miles of a district; impossible for him to cover it.

The Chairman. — Do you feel at the present time that laws with reference to tenement houses are being adequately enforced in Brooklyn?

Mr. Guilfoyle. — I do.

The Chairman. — Are the results satisfactory to you?

Mr. Guilfoyle. — As a rule, yes, sir. A large percentage of our tenement houses in Brooklyn do not exceed 65 to 70 per cent of the lot, and they don't exceed in any case — I don't suppose we have a six-story tenement house in Brooklyn.

A Commissioner. — Don't you think that those small shafts with covered roofs are unsanitary?

Mr. Guilfoyle. — I don't know. I understood some of them were left open. We had a case where a man had a 25-foot light shaft, but covered it over, and under the ruling we had in the Department we would allow him a 10-foot light shaft in that building, and if he put it in he could cover it and put a louvre skylight on, and in the same way we permitted the 25, and for that reason we permitted him to cover them. We have a case to-day where there is a five-story building, four of them together joined on the same plot, where the light shaft is in the centre, and a communication from each floor is by an iron balcony against the light shaft, and all the cold weather comes down on these platforms and goes in the adjoining houses. They had asked me to allow them to cover it over, but I would not. I didn't think they had any right to be built in that way in the first place.

The Commissioner. — Don't you think the 10-foot light shafts are too small for the rooms to open into?

Mr. Guilfoyle. — Not where there is only two rooms to open in it.

The Chairman. — Why are they necessary in Brooklyn? These small light shafts are not permitted in New York under any conditions.

Mr. Guilfoyle. — We have been going right along there for years on that condition.

The Chairman. — I understand in New York in no case will they permit a light shaft less than 25 feet in area unless where it is confined to water-closets. Is there any reason why you do that in Brooklyn?

Mr. Guilfoyle. — No, sir.

The Chairman. — Do you think you had better make a radical change in that regard?

Mr. Guilfoyle. — Yes.

The Chairman. — Do you think 25-foot tenement houses covering 75 per cent of the lot, that a number of those tenement houses in a row can be adequately supplied with light and air?

Mr. Guilfoyle. — Yes, sir.

The Chairman. — Do you think that the tenement houses now being built on 25-foot lots covering 75 per cent are in point of fact adequately supplied with light and air?

Mr. Guilfoyle. — I do, yes, sir, where they do not run over four or five stories high.

The Chairman. — Where they are six or seven?

Mr. Guilfoyle. — I don't think they can be.

The Chairman. — Then you would say if a tenement house exceeds five stories, it should not cover 75 per cent?

Mr. Guilfoyle. — Yes, sir, because you ought to get the light from the front or rear somewhere.

Mr. De Forest. — Suppose it exceeds four stories?

Mr. Guilfoyle. — No; four stories I would allow.

Mr. De Forest. — Anything over four stories you would not?

Mr. Guilfoyle. — No, sir; you have too many rooms on a story then.

A Commissioner. — Don't you think there would be overcrowding; get too many people on the same area, I mean?

Mr. Guilfoyle. — That depends on the size of the rooms.

TESTIMONY OF DANIEL CAMPBELL

Commissioner of Buildings for the Boroughs of Richmond and Queens

December 10, 1900.

Daniel Campbell, being duly sworn, testified as follows: —

The Chairman. — You are the Superintendent of Buildings of the Boroughs of Richmond and Queens?

Mr. Campbell. — Yes, sir.

The Chairman. — And a member of the Board?

Mr. Campbell. — Yes, sir.

The Chairman. — What is the present condition of the enforcement of the law with reference to fire-escapes on tenement houses in those boroughs, so far as your observation has extended?

Mr. Campbell. — There are a great many houses that have no fire-escapes, but we are serving notice to have them put on, and we have served a number of notices of violations.

The Chairman. — What proportion do you think of the tenement houses in Richmond and Queens have fire-escapes?

Mr. Campbell. — Well, I suppose 25 per cent.

The Chairman. — And 75 per cent have not?

Mr. Campbell. — Yes, sir. Excuse me. You understand that this law in relation to fire-escapes has been enforced since 1867 in Brooklyn and New York, and only since 1898 in Queens, so that we have done pretty well in comparison.

The Chairman. — And you think that 25 per cent are now equipped with fire-escapes?

Mr. Campbell. — Yes, sir.

The Chairman. — Have you filed violations against the remaining 75?

Mr. Campbell. — I do not know that I have against the whole of them; but I would like to qualify that further, that very few of these houses are four stories in height. The majority of them are three stories in height, and some of them are two stories in height.

The Chairman. — You recognize that the law is mandatory that all buildings occupied by more than three families shall have fire-escapes?

Mr. Campbell. — Yes, sir.

The Chairman. — And you think 75 per cent of the buildings coming within that class are not yet provided with them?

Mr. Campbell. — That is a broad guess. It is rather less than that.

The Chairman. — Have you any lawyers assigned to your Department?

Mr. Campbell. — Not since we started.

The Chairman. — What do you do when you have violations to enforce?

Mr. Campbell. — Send them to the Corporation Counsel, but we have not sent many.

The Chairman. — Have you had any difficulty in buildings constructed during your administration in complying with the law?

Mr. Campbell. — We have had very little. That is, where people, from ignorance I might say almost, of the law, went ahead and did something that is not in compliance with the law, we have notified, and they generally rectify that.

The Chairman. — Do you have the same difficulty that we have spoken of in connection with defective or small air shafts less than 25 square feet in area and covered at the top?

Mr. Campbell. — Yes, sir.

The Chairman. — Are you permitting them?

Mr. Campbell. — Yes, sir.

The Chairman. — Do you think that is authorized by law?

Mr. Campbell. — Well, I might say that I think it is not prevented by law.

The Chairman. — You think the law permits it, do you?

Mr. Campbell. — Yes, sir.

The Chairman. — Haven't you in mind the provision which says, "That no air shaft shall be less than 25 square feet in area on which habitable rooms open"?

Mr. Campbell. — The law also says in speaking of air shafts that no air shafts over 10 feet shall be covered, so it must be intended that there shall be air shafts which are 10 feet.

The Chairman. — The law says air shafts on which habitable rooms open shall not be less than 25 feet. We know there may be those on which water-closets open that may be smaller.

Mr. Campbell. — I do not know that I have approved any plans where rooms open only in such air shafts of less than 25 square feet. They opened into rooms which did open into the external air.

The Chairman. — You have approved plans permitting living rooms which received their light and ventilation only from an adjoining living room?

Mr. Campbell. — And an air shaft or hall.

The Chairman. — Do you think that is permitted by the law?

Mr. Campbell. — Yes, sir.

The Chairman. — You had better study your law, I think, Mr. Campbell. We think you will find that such rooms are not permitted. Have you enough inspectors?

Mr. Campbell. — No, sir.

The Chairman. — How many have you for the two boroughs?

Mr. Campbell. — Eight.

The Chairman. — How many ought you to have?

Mr. Campbell. — I asked for sixteen.

The Chairman. — Do you think you could do your work well with sixteen?

Mr. Campbell. — I think we could.

The Chairman. — But it is not being adequately done now with eight?

Mr. Campbell. — No, sir, it is not.

Mr. Guilfoyle. — You asked me for a case of authority I got for these dark bedrooms. I have a memorandum here covering that. Dark bedrooms have been allowed in a few instances in this Department when the architect has made a demand under Section 1319 of the Charter. Assistant Corporation Counsel Courtney rendered a decision that this should be granted, as this section followed 1318, which section requires air shafts. He is also sustained in his decision by another Corporation Counsel, who rendered a decision that this section, being more liberal to builders, must be followed.

The Chairman. — We understand there is a conflict between your Department and the Department here in New York.

The Commission then adjourned to meet on Tuesday afternoon, December 11th, 1900, at 2.30 P.M.

TESTIMONY OF EUGENE OTTERBOURG

Assistant Corporation Counsel assigned to the Department of Buildings, for the Boroughs of Manhattan and Bronx

December 11, 1900.

Eugene Otterbourg, being duly sworn, testified as follows: —

The Chairman. — What is your official position under the city government, Mr. Otterbourg?

Mr. Otterbourg. — Assistant Corporation Counsel.

The Chairman. — And how long have you held that position?

Mr. Otterbourg. — Since February 1, 1898.

The Chairman. — What had been your position prior to that time?

Mr. Otterbourg. — Attorney and Counsellor at Law. I was attorney to the Department of Buildings in 1892, and for several years thereafter.

The Chairman. — Continuously from then until now?

Mr. Otterbourg. — No, sir; I have had three successors in the interim between 1895 and 1898.

The Chairman. — Since you have been connected with the office of the Corporation Counsel have you had any special relations to the Building Department, and if so, what?

Mr. Otterbourg. — I have been one of six attorneys assigned to the Building Department for the Boroughs of Manhattan and Bronx.

The Chairman. — So that your principal time has been devoted to the work of that Department?

Mr. Otterbourg. — Mainly.

The Chairman. — You have had charge of that work, have you not?

Mr. Otterbourg. — I am one of six attorneys there.

The Chairman. — You have been the assistant in charge of that work?

Mr. Otterbourg. — Well, you might put it in that way.

The Chairman. — Where is your office, with the Corporation Counsel, or in the same building with the Department of Buildings?

Mr. Otterbourg. — We have office accommodations in the Department of Buildings.

The Chairman. — And that is true of the other six associated with you?

Mr. Otterbourg. — The other five.

The Chairman. — The Superintendent of Buildings, Mr. Brady, or the Commissioner, testified yesterday during the past year about 11,000 violations of the building law had been filed in the Boroughs of Manhattan and Bronx, and both he and Superintendent Dooner testified that these violations, having been filed and turned over to you, their responsibility ceased. Will you state, according to the best of your recollection, what proportion of the violations received by the Corporation Counsel during the past year were ever prosecuted?

Mr. Otterbourg. — Do you mean this year, 1900?

The Chairman. — Yes.

Mr. Otterbourg. — The subpœna to attend here to-day was received by me about half-past eleven, and it requested certain information which I have endeavored to secure, and the time being quite limited I will have to rely for the statistics upon the information furnished to me by the chief clerk of the department of my division. It appears from his report to me that the cases received of so-called violations since January 1st, 1900, were 10,454; that there were disposed of violations subsequent to their having been certified to the Corporation Counsel this year, 8042. That in relation thereto there were written letters 3383. Notices issued, 16,429. This of course is exclusive of considerable other legal work at the attorney's office.

The Chairman. — The difference between the number of violations received and those disposed of represents those which are still pending?

Mr. Otterbourg. — No, sir. There are more pending. I simply give the figures of those received this year and disposed of this year, because there is an accumulation of cases for years past.

The Chairman. — What do you mean by "violations disposed of"; what kind of disposition have you in mind?

Mr. Otterbourg. — That means that according to the certification by the Department of Buildings to the Corporation Counsel's office the law in those 8042 cases has been complied with subsequent to the certification thereof to the Corporation Counsel's office.

The Chairman. — Now, roughly, how many of these violations have reached a trial in open court?

Mr. Otterbourg. — From the papers submitted to me by the clerk it appears that there were 362 actions for penalties instituted during this year.

The Chairman. — Actions for penalties?

Mr. Otterbourg. — Yes, sir.

Mr. De Forest. — Of cases received during the current year or of cases received prior to that?

Mr. Otterbourg. — The memorandum does not specify that.

The Chairman. — That represents the total number of proceedings instituted by your office this year, approximately?

Mr. Otterbourg. — Well, no, sir. The operations of the Department involve proceedings by correspondence.

The Chairman. — No; I mean proceedings in court.

Mr. Otterbourg. — Oh, in court. That is the number of proceedings instituted in municipal courts. His memorandum says that there were cases in courts of record for the year 1900, 102.

The Chairman. — On what basis are the cases divided between courts of record and municipal courts; what classes of cases go into one court and what into the other?

Mr. Otterbourg. — I personally attend to all the matters in courts of record, the argument thereof, and trial, and they relate to mandamus proceedings, injunctions, certiorari to the Appellate Division, and orders to remove violations of the building laws.

The Chairman. — The suits for penalties are brought in the municipal courts?

Mr. Otterbourg. — Yes, sir. Litigations against the city for damages. One very large case involving a very large amount of contracts, and against the city for operations in connection with the fire at the Windsor Hotel. All these classes of cases are included in these 102 cases. The 362 cases are limited to actions for the collection of penalties.

The Chairman. — What proportion of that 102 cases in courts of record are cases where the city is defendant, roughly speaking?

Mr. Otterbourg. — I should not like to guess at it. There have been very many certioraris. I remember I think perhaps three or four attempts at mandamus, to mandamus the Commissioner of Buildings. I remember an action for damages involving about $70,000; on the Windsor fire case, involving a claim for $106,000.

The Chairman. — Would you say that one-half of these 102 cases are cases where the city is defendant?

Mr. Otterbourg. — No, sir.

The Chairman. — Would you say one-quarter? We want a rough idea?

Mr. Otterbourg. — Well, I should think perhaps a quarter would cover the number.

The Chairman. — Would the remaining cases cover cases in courts of record to enforce the building laws in one manner and another?

Mr. Otterbourg. — Yes, sir.

The Chairman. — How many cases, in courts of record in which you are seeking to enforce the building laws, have been tried during the present year?

Mr. Otterbourg. — Do you include in the trial, arguments on mandamus and certiorari and injunctions?

The Chairman. — Yes; I would count that a trial. That is, how many of these cases have reached the stage of an actual contest in court, in which a controverted question was submitted to the court?

Mr. Otterbourg. — One of the difficulties in answering that question is this; that in these unsafe proceedings, which are amongst the most important cases that come under my observation, very often, in most cases indeed, upon the defendants and their attorneys, generally leading representatives of the bar, becoming familiar with the law and being informed right at the Supreme Court of their rights, even after judgments, they do not resist. Yet we have to submit findings of fact and law, and it is practically a trial. Taking those all in, I should say that they have practically all been tried.

The Chairman. — I imagine that of the 75 cases, taking a rough estimate, in which the city is enforcing the building law, a large proportion of those cases are cases against unsafe buildings, are they not?

Mr. Otterbourg. — In the courts of record?

The Chairman. — Yes.

Mr. Otterbourg. — Yes, sir.

The Chairman. — Now, in how many cases during the past year have you obtained injunctions against the completion of buildings because of violations of the laws affecting light and ventilation?

Mr. Otterbourg. — I have obtained injunctions in two cases relating to light and ventilation in a tenement house, and obtained orders to remove, and injunctions in several other cases involving in a sense light and ventilation, but not being directly against a tenement house.

The Chairman. — There are two cases in which you have interrupted by injunction the erection of tenement houses during this year?

Mr. Otterbourg. — Interfered; disturbed the conditions.

The Chairman. — And the record for the year before would be substantially the same?

Mr. Otterbourg. — I could not recall. I really could not state without having the record looked into.

The Chairman. — In point of fact, there are not many cases in which the remedy of injunction is resorted to in connection with enforcing the light and ventilation laws in the building of tenement houses?

Mr. Otterbourg. — There are not.

The Chairman. — Have you a reason for that?

Mr. Otterbourg. — As far as the Corporation Counsel's office is concerned, they cannot take any action in relation to an application for an injunction involving the light and ventilation of tenement houses unless so requested by special direction of the Commissioner of Buildings. The power and jurisdiction is with the Department of Buildings. In every case in which I have been requested to secure an injunction I have secured it.

The Chairman. — The testimony yesterday was that the Building Department would turn over these violations of light and ventilation laws to the Law Department, and their responsibility ended; and they said, if those violations did not ripen into injunctions or judgments in some other form, it was the fault of that Department and not of theirs. That is not your view, I take it?

Mr. Otterbourg. — The shifting of official responsibility is quite a science. A distinction should be drawn, and perhaps the lay gentleman who testified did not distinguish between a penalty and an action for a penalty and other proceedings in relation to violations of that nature.

The Chairman. — That is, I take it, the policy of your Department has been necessarily that you did not apply for injunctions unless you have been instructed to?

Mr. Otterbourg. — I have no right to.

The Chairman. — And unless evidence to support the application was specifically furnished by that Department?

Mr. Otterbourg. — I would not have the evidence otherwise.

The Chairman. — What amount have you collected by way of penalties for a failure to comply with building laws during the past year, Mr. Otterbourg?

Mr. Otterbourg. — I have not charge of the actions for collection of penalties, so that I personally have not collected any.

The Chairman. — When I say "you" I mean you and your associates.

Mr. Otterbourg. — According to the statement of the chief clerk, judgments for penalties in 1900 were obtained in four cases. The judgments were vacated on motion of the defendants on various grounds. In this connection I will state that there has been a decision some years ago to the effect that it was neither for the interest of the city nor the desire of the Department to insist upon penalties, even if they are technically entitled to them, when the purpose for which they are imposed has been fully effected, and that has been practically the policy of the Department in relation to that matter.

The Chairman. — By whom was that decision?

Mr. Otterbourg. — This was by Mr. Justice Parker.

The Chairman. — Sitting where?

Mr. Otterbourg. — Sitting in one of the district courts, but for the purpose of this issue the Court of Appeals, in view of the fact that all actions for penalties under the Charter must be brought in the municipal court.

The Chairman. — Is this Justice Parker of the Supreme Court?

Mr. Otterbourg. — No, sir; District Court Judge. That has been the general policy of the Department of Buildings before the Charter and since the Charter. Throughout all its various administrations it has been not to collect penalties, and the law practically provides that way. It authorizes an action for the recovery of a penalty and then says that, if an effort is made within ten days toward the removal of the violation, if it is commenced within ten days, the action should cease. It may commence within ten days and continue ten months; and finally permits the Commissioner of Buildings to remit the penalty, always provided, however, that the violation of law has been removed. So that, in these 8042 cases which were disposed of, if there had been penalties in each one under the policy of the Department, they would not have been collected, and the system is that when the violation, according to the Department, has been complied with, or removed, the case is recalled from the attorney's office, and the recall is really a stoppage to all legal proceedings in relation to the case.

The Chairman. — The experience of yourself and associates with respect to the number of injunctions obtained and judgments for penalties entered this year substantially indicates your experience for the year before, does it not?

Mr. Otterbourg. — Oh, it may be fair to say that this is about the average.

The Chairman. — In the cases where you have attempted to enjoin the continuation of the erection of tenement houses because of violations of the Building Law, have you had any trouble in getting injunctions?

Mr. Otterbourg. — Not at all, sir. I have succeeded in enforcing every law I have ever undertaken to enforce.

The Chairman. — If you are notified on one day that a given tenement house has been started without a permit from the Building Department, how long would it take you to obtain an injunction against that building?

Mr. Otterbourg. — That would depend upon the conditions of the particular case; each case has its history.

The Chairman. — I say without a permit, where the builder has received no permit for the construction of the building. Is that itself a ground for obtaining an injunction?

Mr. Otterbourg. — I could obtain an injunction for that.

The Chairman. — You could apply *ex parte* for an injunction?

Mr. Otterbourg. — Yes, sir.

The Chairman. — And then the burden would be on the defendant to show that a permit has been arbitrarily withheld?

Mr. Otterbourg. — Yes, sir; but the law requires notice of violation to be served; and in many instances the service is not just correct, and in other instances there has been a conveyance — further conveyance of the title to the property, and we have to make a search to get the right party and that sometimes causes delay. If everything is in proper condition, I can get it within twenty-four hours.

The Chairman. — We have found numerous cases where buildings were carried well on toward completion, and in many cases completed during this year, without a permit ever having been obtained for their erection, and when they were subject to numerous violations. If that state of affairs had been brought to your attention, you could have readily obtained an injunction against the completion of that building?

Mr. Otterbourg. — If I had been requested to obtain an injunction.

The Chairman. — If you had been requested by the Department of Buildings and had been furnished with evidence that no permit had been obtained, and that violations were pending, and that Mr. So-and-So was the owner, then you could readily obtain an injunction *ex parte*, could you not?

Mr. Otterbourg. — That is not the situation exactly in the very class of cases you speak of. The violation may have been certified to the Corporation Counsel, showing that operations were commenced before the approval of the plans, and in that case may have been assigned to one of the assistants for the purpose of collecting a penalty. The law says that an application for an injunction must be made upon the affidavit of the Commissioner of Buildings and can be applied for in his discretion. *Non constat* that a violation may have been certified to the Corporation Counsel's office, unless a request was made for an injunction, I would not obtain one.

The Chairman. — If a request were made, it would be a comparatively simple matter to get it?

Mr. Otterbourg. — It would if the conditions I have specified were not existent in that particular case.

The Chairman. — We all agree, including the representatives of the Building Department, that the present condition of affairs, under which buildings are frequently, and I might say habitually, begun, and even carried well towards completion, without a permit from the Building Department, and when they are subject to violations, is an exceedingly bad one. Now what suggestions have you to make, based on your long experience, with reference to the best means of remedying that condition of affairs?

Mr. Otterbourg. — I would be pleased to have the Commission read, at its leisure, an article which I prepared in relation to that question, published in the *Record and Guide* on May 12, 1900, which fully expresses my views; and since having received the subpœna this morning I have dictated to the stenographer a few memoranda in relation to the recommendations, which I will be pleased to submit if requested.

The Chairman. — We do request you to submit them, and will be very glad to have them.

Mr. Otterbourg. — I would suggest that architects, engineers, or builders should be examined as to their competency by proper authority, licensed and registered, and the license be subject to revocation so that we would know whom to hold responsible for violations being committed, without searching for owners who may be travelling all through the world, for agents whose relations to the owner we could not prove without considerable loss of time.

Now, if we had a responsible architect, engineer, or builder with a license, so that a man would have something to lose if he violated the law, why, that would be practically a building department right at that building, and it would reduce, in my opinion, the so-called violations to a very large degree.

I think that the names of owners and notice of transfers in relation to tenement houses should be filed and given to the Department of Buildings the same as the Board of Health. Some years ago I inaugurated a system of search cards in connection with the operations of a Title Guarantee Company, which facilitates our obtaining the record of the owners of premises. It is very difficult to ascertain the names of owners in any one block in the city of New York; and very often a record owner is not the owner in fact, because there are so many so-called dummies used; and the real title, or return deed, is in the safe of the actual owner, and yet the dummy has the title of record. So that in many cases I have had in courts of record I have had to bring actions and make parties defendant the real owner, and the supposed owner to the best of our information and belief.

I think that violations should not be certified to the Corporation Counsel unless it is intended to collect a penalty; and they should not be certified until after a reasonable time has been given to offer whatever amendments the law may direct in relation to the plans. The plans should be complete in fact and in law before the operation commences, because the violation being certified and subsequently amended, causes the violation to be so much in motion it is almost impossible under the rules of the Code of Civil Procedure to secure any satisfactory result.

I think that the law should provide for a criminal prosecution in cases of material violations of the building laws. It did so provide before 1892, but about that year was amended. A man who commences the construction of a building without having a permit, if then and there arrested by the officer on the post, it would enforce the law much quicker than could the Supreme Court of the State of New York; and there certainly can be no excuse for a man commencing the construction of a building without having his permit; and the man who deliberately constructs beyond the area that he has the right to construct a building, should then and there be arrested, and that would stop that operation. So that there ought to be a way of summary prosecution, and we should not be relegated to the slow procedure of a civil action, which involves many delays and is not at all satisfactory in cases of this kind.

I think that all penalties when once incurred should not be remitted, except with the concurrence of the Corporation Counsel.

I think that the clerks and stenographers of the attorney's office connected with the Department of Buildings should be transferred to the law department pay-roll. Under the law of 1892 the then superintendent of Buildings had the power to appoint his own attorney, and then the law office was organized under that law. Just prior to the Charter becoming operative, and under its provisions, the mayors of the three cities met and assigned the different officials to the new departments created under the Charter, and so it happened that the clerks and stenographers connected with the attorney's office in the Building Department remained in the Building Department, and were not transferred to the Corporation Counsel's office; and it would facilitate the law business very much to have those employees directly under the jurisdiction of the Corporation Counsel.

I think — and this is very important to my mind — that a building should not be occupied until certified to as conforming to the law, and consent to turn on water not to be given before that. That would be more powerful than a Court of Appeals and all the other courts put together in removing the violation, because if a man could not occupy the premises until he had a certificate to that effect, the authorities or the officers in authority would have to go on record certifying that the law has been complied with; and if it is not, the man should be prohibited from prosecuting his interests as he sees fit.

I think the tenement house law should be codified, and building laws amended so as not to require application for removal of violations to be made upon the affidavit of the Commissioner of Buildings. From the nature of things, it is impossible for the Commissioner of Buildings to be personally cognizant of all the conditions of the various buildings, and every lawyer will know that his affidavit required under the statute would have to be on information and belief and required to be corroborated by half a dozen other affidavits, which causes considerable delay in making the necessary applications for the removal of violations.

I think that a violation filed by an inspector, if intended to be prosecuted, should be verified and constitute the issue to be presented to the Court, assimilating the procedure somewhat to the procedure in relation to unsafe building cases which, as I have already stated, are of the most important certified to the Corporation's Counsel's office from the Department of Buildings, and in such cases I am quite certain in 98 per cent we secure a precept and order from the Supreme Court within twenty-four hours. If a violation is carefully specified by an inspector who understands his duty, that ought to be the complaint, and we ought to be able to take it right to court.

The Chairman. — Let me ask if during the past year you had received an average of ten requests a month for injunctions against the construction of tenement houses for which no permits have been issued, would your associates and yourself have had any difficulty in finding time to obtain those injunctions?

Mr. Otterbourg. — No, sir.

The Chairman. — Say there had been twenty a month, could you?

Mr. Otterbourg. — It would depend somewhat on the conditions of the particular case and nature of the violations.

The Chairman. — Taking the average case?

Mr. Otterbourg. — An average case requires the examination of the plans and specifications that it would take rather a clear-headed gentleman of considerable experience a day or two to comprehend.

The Chairman. — You could have cared for ten a month?

Mr. Otterbourg. — Oh, I could get twenty a month if the papers were in condition and the conditions were not extraordinary. Of course, I have a great deal of other business to attend to there, but I would get them.

The Chairman. — You mean you personally could?

Mr. Otterbourg. — The way the office is organized, I have one gentleman whose time is particularly devoted toward assisting in the preparation of this class of cases, and with his assistance I could get them.

I think that a *lis pendens* should be filed in the discretion of the Corporation Counsel. It is now in the discretion of the Building Department. It is quite an absurd provision, to my mind, because with the litigation in the hands of the Corporation Counsel the power to file *lis pendens* should be, as in every other case involving legal procedure.

Mr. De Forest. — Why should not it be filed as a matter of course and not in the discretion of anybody?

Mr. Otterbourg. — Perhaps it could be filed as a matter of course excepting if the violation is technical, the consequences are very serious. It gives a black eye to the premises for the time being, interferes with the financial operations in relation to building loans, interferes with the passage of titles. If the violation is serious, by all means, but if technical it should not be; and in that connection I would suggest that the law should do away with the necessity of the city of New York paying its own County Clerk for filing these *lis pendens*, because otherwise the attorney having charge of the matter could spend $5000 or $10,000 a year in filing these *lis pendens* and then await the operations of the Finance Department, before he could have a return of his money, and it would depend upon his financial condition whether he could afford to do that.

I think — and this is very important — a law should be enacted to make the expenditures incurred by the city of New York in connection with the removal of violations and protection of unsafe buildings a lien thereon, similiar to a tax lien, with the provision that after such lien the mortgagees shall have a right to institute foreclosure proceedings. As the law stands now the responsibility on the part of the city for the removal of any violations while under the law as provided it shall be a lien on the property, is a lien subsequent to so many mortgages, more particularly when it is one of these Building Loan Associations, that you cannot recover the money, and the city of New York loses thousands of dollars, and the head of the Department often hesitates in any prosecution involving the expenditure of money, because he cannot get it back.

These recommendations were hurriedly prepared, but I will leave them with you if you desire.

The Chairman. — Would you leave them with us?

Mr. Otterbourg. — I think, in the main, in addition to that report or article that I prepared for the *Record and Guide*, they are fairly explicit.

The Chairman. — We are obliged to you for your suggestions, some of which are very valuable, and if any more occur to you will you reduce them to writing and send them to our secretary?

Mr. Otterbourg. — I will.

Mr. De Forest. — In how many cases has the Department requested you to apply for an injunction to prevent the erection of buildings in the past year? When I say you, I mean you or your associates who are acting for the Building Department.

Mr. Otterbourg. — Well, there have been injunctions against the use of premises, or rather applications for the removal of constructions other than tenement houses. If you limit the question to tenement houses, I now only recall two cases.

Mr. De Forest. — I limit the question to tenement houses.

Mr. Otterbourg. — There are several cases, too, that I recall now that are prepared for an injunction and are under consideration by the Department.

Mr. De Forest. — But only in two cases have you been requested as yet to bring injunction proceedings for tenement houses during the past year?

Mr. Otterbourg. — Yes, sir.

Mr. De Forest. — Am I correct in understanding that only in four cases during the past year have judgments been rendered imposing penalties?

Mr. Otterbourg. — That is the record of the clerk.

The Chairman. — Those were in default, I infer, from the fact that they were subsequently vacated?

Mr. Otterbourg. — I really do not know.

The Chairman. — That must be so if finally vacated on motion?

Mr. Otterbourg. — No, not necessarily, because the papers may not have been properly served. I do not know whether they were by default or not. You would have to inquire from the particular attorney in each case. His name can be had at the Corporation Counsel's office. I have not had charge of any of these cases for the recovery of penalties.

The Chairman. — Have you rendered any opinion to the Building Department as to whether under the Charter a corner tenement house may lawfully cover the entire lot for the first story?

Mr. Otterbourg. — Well, in that connection I desire to have the ruling of the Commissioner in this view, with which you are undoubtedly familiar under Section 835 of the Code of Civil Procedure. An attorney and counsellor at law should not be allowed to disclose communications made by his clients to him, or advice given thereon in the course of his professional employment, and it has been held that advice —

The Chairman. — I will interrupt you to say we won't compel you to answer that question unless you feel free to.

Mr. Otterbourg. — While I did not attend the hearing yesterday I do not know what has been testified to, and I do not know but the privilege has been waived. I have nothing to conceal in the matter, but I was not here and do not know what the legal position is.

The Chairman. — Then you had rather not answer that question?

Mr. Otterbourg. — I do not say that.

The Chairman. — My recollection is that Mr. Brady stated in substance that his understanding of the law — and he thought he had had advice of the Corporation Counsel — was that under the Charter a corner tenement might cover the entire lot for the first story?

Mr. Otterbourg. — Well, I will answer the question in this way for the present, that the communication received from your honored Chairman by me this day asked me to bring a copy of an opinion to that effect, and I would state that I have no such copy under my control or in my possession.

The Chairman. — There was a controversy yesterday, or discussion yesterday, as to whether under the present condition of the law it was lawful to permit tenement houses having living rooms provided with no windows except windows opening into a hall, which hall was connected with the stair well, with a louvre and skylight at the top; in other words, whether the hall could be counted as the outside air. Do you mind saying whether you have rendered an opinion on that subject?

Mr. Otterbourg. — Well, I was spoken to in relation to that subject yesterday for the first time.

The Chairman. — For the first time?

Mr. Otterbourg. — Yes; and I did call the attention of the Commissioner to a case now pending in the Court of Appeals — I do not know whether you are familiar with that — involving the very question. Judge Gray of the Court of Appeals granted leave to appeal to that court chiefly upon the question whether a skylight in a roof is a window opening outside from a hallway two floors below, which enables the sun's rays to enter through the opening between the banisters, and I have prepared a memorandum of the case having been referred to in that communication.

The Chairman. — What is the decision of the court below?

Mr. Otterbourg. — It is entitled, "Is a skylight a hall window," and says about a year ago Charlotte Lendle, represented by Clarence E. Lexow, recovered a verdict for $2750 against the owners of the tenement house No. 541 West 48th Street, for breaking two ribs and sustaining other injuries by falling down stairs. She claimed that she tripped upon a torn rubber pad; that the hall was entirely dark and that it was after sunset.

Her husband also shortly afterward got a verdict for $500 for loss of her services. The Appellate Division unanimously affirmed both judgments, and refused leave to William Blakie, counsel for the defendant, to appeal from either. Associate Judge Gray of the Court of Appeals has just granted leave to appeal to that court in both cases, chiefly upon the question whether the skylight in the roof is a window opening outside from a hallway two floors below, which enables the sun's rays to enter through the opening between the banisters. This case is of interest to the many owners of tenements and apartments in this city because Chapter 567 of the laws of 1895 requires them to burn lights from 8 A.M. to 10 P.M. every day, in all such halls as have no windows opening to the outside, or which are not otherwise sufficiently lighted, and because the present question has never been passed upon by the Court of Appeals.

The Chairman. — Do you object to saying whether in your opinion it is lawful, under the Charter, to cover an entire corner lot with the first story of a tenement house?

Mr. Otterbourg. — I think counsel to the Commission can answer that question as well as I can.

The Chairman. — We ask you that because there has apparently been a real controversy on that point, and these questions are new to us and they are very familiar ones to you.

Mr. Otterbourg. — The matter has been somewhat involved because there have been a few words omitted in the Charter provision in relation to that particular question as compared to the law in force prior to the Charter, and it may be that the Department has been misled in that way. In fact the laws in relation to the Building Department are in many ways so confusing that the head of the Department ought to be a lawyer instead of a builder to properly administer the affairs.

The Chairman. — We would be glad if, after conferring with Mr. Brady, you would send us, if he is willing, any opinions that have been rendered on either of these questions; and if no opinions have been rendered, to state the fact to us.

Mr. Otterbourg. — I would state here that whatever opinions have been rendered in writing of course are in the possession of the Commissoner, and he is at liberty to use them in any way that he deems proper, and I should be very happy to have him do so; and I should be glad to assist this Commission in any way, but I feel convinced that the Commission will appreciate my position under the law.

The Chairman. — We think your position is a correct one.

Mr. Otterbourg. — I am compelled to hold my tongue unless you get your information from the Commissioner, or through me with his consent; so I would suggest that you make that request to the Commissioner.

The Chairman. — We withdraw that request and will make it to the Commissioner directly. We are very much obliged to you and hope you will not hesitate to send us any other suggestions which you may have.

Memorandum submitted by Mr. Otterbourg

Architect, engineer or builder should be examined as to their competency by proper authority and licensed and registered, and license subject to revocation.

Name of owners and notice of transfers in relation to tenement houses to be filed and given to the Department of Buildings same as the Board of Health.

Criminal Prosecution

Violations not to be certified to the Corporation Counsel unless it is intended to collect penalty, etc. (and plans not to be subject to amendment thereafter).

Penalty not to be remitted excepting with the concurrence of the Corporation Counsel.

Clerks and stenographers in attorney's office to be transferred to the Law Department pay-roll.

Buildings not to be occupied until certified to as conforming to the law, and consent to turn on water not to be given before that.

Tenement house laws codified and building laws amended so as not to require application for removal of violations to be made upon the affidavit of the Commissioner of Buildings.

The violation filed by the inspector, if intended to prosecute, should be verified, and constitute the issue to be presented to the Court.

Lis pendens to be filed in the discretion of the Corporation Counsel, and a law enacted doing away with the necessity of paying County Clerk for recording same.

Law enacted to make expenditures incurred by the city of New York, in connection with the removal of violations and protection of unsafe buildings, a lien thereon similar to the tax lien, with a provision that after such lien the mortgagees shall have the right to institute foreclosure proceedings.

APPENDIX IX

TENEMENT HOUSE RENTALS

BY LAWRENCE VEILLER

TENEMENT HOUSE RENTALS

Rents in tenement houses vary so much in different parts of the city, and in fact in different parts of the same house, that no general statement can be made in regard to this subject.

Investigation shows not only that rents vary in different wards, but also that in the same house the rents in the front apartments are nearly always higher than rents in the rear apartments, and that in some cases the rents on one side of the house are greater than the rents on the other side of the house, depending on the situation of the adjoining property; also, that the higher up one goes the less the rents become.

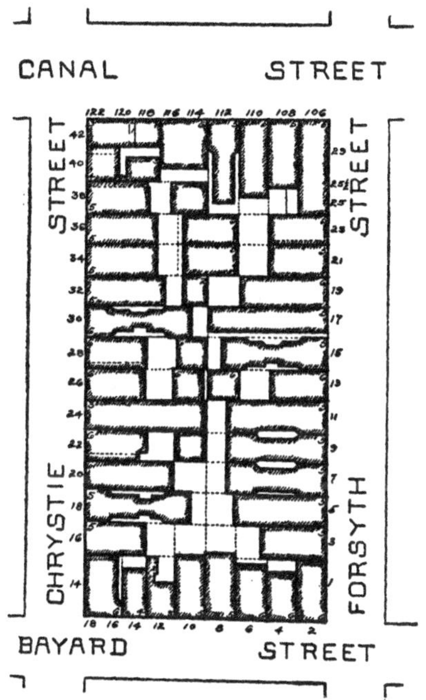

The following statement of the rents in one tenement house block located on the lower East Side at Chrystie, Forsyth, Canal, and Bayard Streets indicates what the prevailing rents were on January 1, 1900, in this portion of the city, in the various kinds of tenement houses in this block, and in the different parts of each house. A ground plan of the block, showing the types of houses, is shown in the accompanying illustration. Further information in regard to this particular block will be found on page 112 of Vol. I.

---

1 Forsyth Street and 2 Bayard
(Corner building)

Liquor saloon	$140.00 per month
First Floor:	
Three rooms facing Forsyth	15.00 per month
Five rooms facing Forsyth and Bayard	23.00 per month
Second Floor:	
Two rooms facing Forsyth	8.00 per month
Two rooms facing Forsyth and Bayard	10.00 per month
Four rooms facing Bayard	15.00 per month

Third Floor:

Two rooms facing Forsyth	$8.00 per month
Two rooms facing Bayard	8.00 per month
Two rooms facing Bayard and Forsyth	9.00 per month
Two rooms facing back yard	7.00 per month

Fourth Floor:

Two rooms facing Bayard	7.00 per month
Two rooms facing Forsyth	7.00 per month
Two rooms facing Bayard and Forsyth	8.00 per month
Two rooms facing back yard	6.00 per month

Fifth Floor:

Two rooms facing Bayard	7.00 per month
Two rooms facing Forsyth	7.00 per month
Two rooms facing Bayard and Forsyth	7.00 per month
Two rooms facing back yard	5.00 per month

3 Forsyth Street

Delicatessen store — two rooms and cellar	$42.00 per month
Crockery store and cellar	42.00 per month

First Floor:

Two rooms, front, right	9.50 per month
Two rooms, front, left	9.50 per month
Two rooms, back, left	9.00 per month
Two rooms, back, right	9.00 per month

Second Floor:

Two rooms, front, right	9.00 per month
Two rooms, front, left	9.00 per month
Two rooms, back, left	8.00 per month
Two rooms, back, right	8.00 per month

Third Floor:

Two rooms, front, right	8.50 per month
Two rooms, front, left	8.50 per month
Two rooms, back, left	8.00 per month
Two rooms, back, right	8.00 per month

Fourth Floor:

Two rooms, front, right	8.00 per month
Two rooms, front, left	8.00 per month
Two rooms, back, left	7.50 per month
Two rooms, back, right	7.50 per month

5 Forsyth Street

Two stores and cellars, approximately	$70.00 per month

First Floor:

Three rooms, front, right	13.00 per month
Three rooms, front, left	13.00 per month
Three rooms, back, left	12.00 per month
Three rooms, back, right	13.00 per month

Second Floor:

Three rooms, front, right	12.00 per month
Three rooms, front, left	12.00 per month
Three rooms, back, left	11.00 per month
Three rooms, back, right	12.00 per month

Third Floor:

Three rooms, front, right	$11.00 per month
Three rooms, front, left	11.00 per month
Three rooms, back, left	10.00 per month
Three rooms, back, right	11.00 per month

Fourth Floor:

Three rooms, front, right	10.00 per month
Three rooms, front, left	10.00 per month
Three rooms, back, left	9.50 per month
Three rooms, back, right	10.00 per month

7 Forsyth Street

Barber shop	$25.00 per month
Cellar	10.00 per month
Grocery — two rooms and cellar	35.00 per month

First Floor:

Four rooms, front, right	14.00 per month
Four rooms, front, left	13.00 per month
Three rooms, back, left	11.50 per month
Four rooms, back, right	13.00 per month

Second Floor:

Four rooms, front, right	13.00 per month
Four rooms, front, left	12.00 per month
Three rooms, back, left	11.00 per month
Four rooms, back, right	13.00 per month

Third Floor:

Four rooms, front, right	12.50 per month
Four rooms, front, left	12.50 per month
Three rooms, back, left	10.00 per month
Four rooms, back, right	12.00 per month

Fourth Floor:

Four rooms, front, right	12.00 per month
Four rooms, front, left	11.00 per month
Three rooms, back, left	9.50 per month
Four rooms, back, right	12.00 per month

9 Forsyth Street

Right, hairdresser — three rooms	$35.00 per month
Left, laundry	35.00 per month
Left, stand	5.00 per month
Right, cellar	12.00 per month

First Floor:

Four rooms, front, right	14.00 per month
Four rooms, front, left	14.00 per month
Three rooms, back, left	12.00 per month
Four rooms, back, right	14.00 per month

Second Floor:

Four rooms, front, right	14.00 per month
Four rooms, front, left	14.00 per month
Three rooms, back, left	11.00 per month
Four rooms, back, right	13.00 per month

Third Floor:

Four rooms, front, right	$13.00 per month
Four rooms, front, left	13.00 per month
Three rooms, back, left	10.50 per month
Four rooms, back, right	13.50 per month

Fourth Floor:

Four rooms, front, right	12.00 per month
Four rooms, front, left	12.00 per month
Three rooms, back, left	9.00 per month
Four rooms, back, right	11.50 per month

11 Forsyth Street

Right, butcher store — two rooms	$45.00 per month
Right, cellar	8.00 per month
Left, grocery and three rooms	45.00 per month
Left, coal cellar	9.00 per month

First Floor:

Four rooms, front, right	13.00 per month
Four rooms, front, left	14.00 per month
Four rooms, back, left	13.00 per month
Three rooms, back, right	11.00 per month

Second Floor:

Four rooms, front, right	13.50 per month
Four rooms, front, left	14.00 per month
Four rooms, back, left	13.00 per month
Three rooms, back, right	11.00 per month

Third Floor:

Four rooms, front, right	12.00 per month
Four rooms, front, left	13.00 per month
Four rooms, back, left	12.00 per month
Three rooms, back, right	10.50 per month

Fourth Floor:

Four rooms, front, right	11.00 per month
Four rooms, front, left	12.00 per month
Four rooms, back, left	11.50 per month
Three rooms, back, right	9.50 per month

13 Forsyth Street

Right, cloak shop and two rooms	$28.00 per month
Right, cellar — glass store	19.00 per month
Left, butcher shop and two rooms	30.00 per month
Left, cellar — vegetables	15.00 per month

First Floor:

Two rooms, front, right	7.50 per month
Two rooms, front, left	7.50 per month
Two rooms, back, left	7.50 per month
Two rooms, back, right	7.50 per month

Second Floor:

Two rooms, front, right	7.50 per month
Two rooms, front, left	7.50 per month
Two rooms, back, left	7.00 per month
Two rooms, back, right	7.00 per month

THIRD FLOOR:

Two rooms, front, right	$7.00 per month
Two rooms, front, left	7.00 per month
Two rooms, back, left	6.50 per month
Two rooms, back, right	6.50 per month

FOURTH FLOOR:

Two rooms, front, right	6.50 per month
Two rooms, front, left	6.50 per month
Two rooms, back, left	6.00 per month
Two rooms, back, right	6.00 per month

FIFTH FLOOR:

Two rooms, front, right	6.00 per month
Two rooms, front, left	6.00 per month
Two rooms, back, left	6.00 per month
Two rooms, back, right	6.00 per month

Rear House of 13 Forsyth Street

FIRST FLOOR:

Two rooms, right	$6.50 per month
Two rooms, left	6.50 per month

SECOND FLOOR:

Two rooms, right	6.50 per month
Two rooms, left	6.50 per month

THIRD FLOOR:

Two rooms, right	6.00 per month
Two rooms, left	6.00 per month

FOURTH FLOOR:

Two rooms, right	5.50 per month
Two rooms, left	5.50 per month

FIFTH FLOOR:

Two rooms, right	5.00 per month
Two rooms, left	5.00 per month

15 Forsyth Street

Right, candy store and two rooms	$32.00 per month
Left, milk store, three rooms and cellar	45.00 per month

FIRST FLOOR:

Four rooms, front, right	18.00 per month
Four rooms, front, left	18.00 per month
Three rooms, back, left	14.00 per month
Three rooms, back, right	13.00 per month

SECOND FLOOR:

Four rooms, front, right	17.00 per month
Four rooms, front, left	17.00 per month
Three rooms, back, left	13.50 per month
Three rooms, back, right	13.50 per month

THIRD FLOOR:

Four rooms, front, right	16.00 per month
Four rooms, front, left	16.00 per month
Three rooms, back, left	13.00 per month
Three rooms, back, right	13.00 per month

Fourth Floor:

Four rooms, front, right	$15.00 per month
Four rooms, front, left	15.00 per month
Three rooms, back, left	12.50 per month
Three rooms, back, right	12.50 per month

Fifth Floor:

Four rooms, front, right	14.00 per month
Four rooms, front, left	14.00 per month
Three rooms, back, left	11.50 per month
Three rooms, back, right	11.50 per month

17 Forsyth Street

(Divided in five parts, with five different entrances)

FRONT PART

(Facing Forsyth Street, all others facing narrow courtyard)

First Floor (ground floor — belongs to store below):

Right, shoe store and two rooms	$35.00 per month
Left, coffee store and cellar	35.00 per month

Second Floor:

Three rooms . . . . 10.00 per month

Third Floor:

Three rooms . . . . 10.00 per month

Fourth Floor:

Three rooms . . . . 9.00 per month

SECOND PART

First Floor (ground floor):

Three rooms . . . . 7.00 per month

Second Floor:

Three rooms . . . . 7.00 per month

Third Floor:

Three rooms . . . . 7.50 per month

Fourth Floor:

Three rooms . . . . 7.00 per month

THIRD PART

First Floor (ground floor):

Three rooms . . . . 7.50 per month

Second Floor:

Three rooms . . . . 7.00 per month

Third Floor:

Three rooms . . . . 7.00 per month

Fourth Floor:

Three rooms . . . . 7.50 per month

FOURTH PART

First Floor (ground floor):

Three rooms . . . . 7.50 per month

Second Floor:

Three rooms . . . . $7.50 per month

Third Floor:

Three rooms . . . . 7.50 per month

Fourth Floor:

Three rooms . . . . 7.50 per month

FIFTH PART

First Floor (ground floor):

Three rooms . . . . 7.00 per month

Second Floor:

Three rooms . . . . 7.50 per month

Third Floor:

Three rooms . . . . 7.50 per month

Fourth Floor:

Three rooms . . . . 7.50 per month

19 Forsyth Street

Right, restaurant and three rooms . . . . $42.00 per month
Left, grocery — cellar and three rooms . . . 40.00 per month

First Floor:

Three rooms, front, right . . . . 12.50 per month
Three rooms, front, left . . . . 13.00 per month
Three rooms, back, left . . . . 12.00 per month
Three rooms, back, right . . . . 12.50 per month

Second Floor:

Three rooms, front, right . . . . 13.00 per month
Three rooms, front, left . . . . 12.50 per month
Three rooms, back, left . . . . 12.00 per month
Three rooms, back, right . . . . 12.50 per month

Third Floor:

Three rooms, front, right . . . . 12.00 per month
Three rooms, front, left . . . . 12.00 per month
Three rooms, back, left . . . . 11.50 per month
Three rooms, back, right . . . . 11.50 per month

Fourth Floor:

Three rooms, front, right . . . . 11.00 per month
Three rooms, front, left . . . . 11.00 per month
Three rooms, back, left . . . . 10.50 per month
Three rooms, back, right . . . . 10.50 per month

21 Forsyth Street

Right, grocery — two rooms and cellar . . . . $37.50 per month
Left, candy store — two rooms and cellar . . . 28.00 per month

First Floor:

Four rooms, front and back, left . . . . . . 17.00 per month
Two rooms, front, right . . . . 9.00 per month
Two rooms, back, right . . . . 8.50 per month

Second Floor:

Two rooms, front, right	$8.50 per month
Two rooms, front, left	8.50 per month
Two rooms, back, left	8.00 per month
Two rooms, back, right	8.00 per month

Third Floor:

Two rooms, front, right	8.00 per month
Two rooms, front, left	8.00 per month
Two rooms, back, left	7.00 per month
Two rooms, back, right	7.00 per month

Fourth Floor:

Two rooms, front, right	7.50 per month
Two rooms, front, left	7.50 per month
Two rooms, back, left	7.00 per month
Two rooms, back, right	7.00 per month

Rear House of 21 Forsyth Street

First Floor (ground floor):

Two rooms, front, right	$6.00 per month
Two rooms, front, left	6.00 per month
Two rooms, back, left	5.00 per month
Two rooms, back, right	6.00 per month

Second Floor:

Two rooms, front, right	7.00 per month
Two rooms, front, left	7.00 per month
Two rooms, back, left	7.00 per month
Two rooms, back, right	7.00 per month

Third Floor:

Two rooms, front, right	7.00 per month
Two rooms, front, left	7.00 per month
Two rooms, back, left	6.50 per month
Two rooms, back, right	6.50 per month

Fourth Floor:

Two rooms, front, right	6.50 per month
Two rooms, front, left	6.50 per month
Two rooms, back, left	6.00 per month
Two rooms, back, right	6.00 per month

23 Forsyth Street

Ground floor, temporary cart storage — including cellar	$70.00 per month

First Floor:

Three rooms, front and back, right	13.50 per month
Two rooms, front and back, left	9.50 per month
Two rooms, front and back, left	9.50 per month

Second Floor:

Two rooms, front, right	9.50 per month
Two rooms, front, left	9.50 per month
Two rooms, back, left	8.50 per month
Two rooms, back, right	8.50 per month

THIRD FLOOR:

Two rooms, front, right	$8.00 per month
Two rooms, front, left	8.00 per month
Two rooms, back, left	7.50 per month
Two rooms, back, right	7.50 per month

FOURTH FLOOR:

Two rooms, front, right	7.50 per month
Two rooms, front, left	7.50 per month
Two rooms, back, left	7.00 per month
Two rooms, back, right	7.00 per month

Rear House of 23 Forsyth Street

FIRST FLOOR (ground floor):

Two rooms, front, right	$6.50 per month
Two rooms, front, left	6.50 per month
Two rooms, back, left	6.00 per month
Two rooms, back, right	6.00 per month

SECOND FLOOR:

Two rooms, front, right	8.00 per month
Two rooms, front, left	8.00 per month
Two rooms, back, left	7.50 per month
Two rooms, back, right	7.50 per month

THIRD FLOOR:

Two rooms, front, right	8.00 per month
Two rooms, front, left	8.00 per month
Two rooms, back, left	7.50 per month
Two rooms, back, right	7.50 per month

FOURTH FLOOR:

Two rooms, front, right	7.50 per month
Two rooms, front, left	7.50 per month
Two rooms, back, left	7.00 per month
Two rooms, back, right	7.00 per month

FIFTH FLOOR:

Two rooms, front, right	6.50 per month
Two rooms, front, left	6.50 per month
Two rooms, back, left	6.50 per month
Two rooms, back, right	6.50 per month

Corner Building, 25–27 Forsyth Street and 106 Canal

25–27 Forsyth Street, undertaker's store and cellar	$25.00 per month
Corner store, wholesale fancy goods	175.00 per month

FIRST FLOOR:

Three rooms facing Forsyth and Canal	16.00 per month
Three rooms facing Canal	14.00 per month
Three rooms facing Forsyth	15.00 per month
Three rooms facing rear	11.00 per month

SECOND FLOOR:

Three rooms facing Canal and Forsyth	15.00 per month
Three rooms facing Canal	13.00 per month
Three rooms facing Forsyth	14.00 per month
Three rooms facing rear	12.00 per month

THIRD FLOOR:

Three rooms facing Forsyth and Canal	$14.00 per month
Three rooms facing Canal	13.00 per month
Six rooms facing Canal and rear	23.00 per month

FOURTH FLOOR:

Three rooms facing Canal and Forsyth	13.00 per month
Three rooms facing Forsyth	12.00 per month
Three rooms facing Canal	12.00 per month
Three rooms facing rear	10.00 per month

108 Canal Street

Right, dry goods store and basement	$60.00 per month
Left, milk store	60.00 per month

FIRST FLOOR:

Four rooms, front and back, right	19.00 per month
Four rooms, front and back, left	19.00 per month

SECOND FLOOR:

Four rooms, front and back, right	19.00 per month
Four rooms, front and back, left	19.00 per month

THIRD FLOOR:

Four rooms, front and back, right	18.00 per month
Four rooms, front and back, left	18.00 per month

FOURTH FLOOR:

Four rooms, front and back, right	16.00 per month
Four rooms, front and back, left	16.00 per month

110 Canal Street

Right, dry goods store and cellar	$60.00 per month
Left, jeweller's store and cellar	60.00 per month

FIRST FLOOR:

Five rooms, front and back, right	22.00 per month
Five rooms, front and back, left	22.00 per month

SECOND FLOOR:

Five rooms, front and back, right	21.00 per month
Five rooms, front and back, left	21.00 per month

THIRD FLOOR:

Five rooms, front and back, right	20.00 per month
Five rooms, front and back, left	20.00 per month

FOURTH FLOOR:

Five rooms, front and back, right	19.00 per month
Five rooms, front and back, left	19.00 per month

112 Canal Street

Right, cutlery store and cellar and one room	$65.00 per month
Left, clothing store and cellar	50.00 per month

FIRST FLOOR:

Four rooms, front, right	14.00 per month
Four rooms, front, left	14.00 per month
Four rooms back, right and left	11.00 per month

Second Floor:

Four rooms, front, right	$14.00 per month
Four rooms, front, left	14.00 per month
Four rooms, back, right and left	12.00 per month

Third Floor:

Four rooms, front, right	13.00 per month
Four rooms, front, left	12.50 per month
Four rooms, back, right and left	11.00 per month

Fourth Floor:

Four rooms, front, right	12.00 per month
Four rooms, front, left	12.00 per month
Four rooms, back, right and left	10.00 per month

114–116 Canal Street

114–116, wholesale jewelry	$1600 per year
114, dry goods, first floor and cellar	1650 per year

First Floor:

Store rooms — rent not ascertained

Second Floor:

Five rooms, front and back, right	27.00 per month
Five rooms, front and back, left	25.00 per month

Third Floor:

Five rooms, front and back, right	27.00 per month
Five rooms, front and back, left	25.00 per month

Fourth Floor:

Five rooms, front and back, right	23.00 per month
Five rooms, front and back, left	23.00 per month

Fifth Floor:

Five rooms, front and back, right	20.00 per month
Five rooms, front and back, left	20.00 per month

118 Canal Street

Store only — rent not ascertained.

120 Canal Street

Hotel — (corner building) — rent not ascertained.

40 Chrystie Street

First Floor:

Three rooms, front and back, right	$10.00 per month
Three rooms, front and back, left	10.00 per month

Second Floor:

Three rooms, front and back, right	10.00 per month
Three rooms, front and back, left	10.00 per month

Third Floor:

Three rooms, front and back, right	9.00 per month
Three rooms, front and back, left	9.00 per month

Rear House of 40 Chrystie Street

First Floor:

One room adjoining store in front — rent not ascertained.

Second Floor:

Two rooms . . . . $5.00 per month

Third Floor:

Two rooms . . . . 5.00 per month

38 Chrystie Street

Dairy, approximately . . . . $60.00 per month

First Floor:

Four rooms, front and back, right . . . . . 18.00 per month
Four rooms, front and back, left . . . . . 18.00 per month

Second Floor:

Four rooms, front and back, right . . . . . 18.00 per month
Four rooms, front and back, left . . . . . 18.00 per month

Third Floor:

Four rooms, front and back, right . . . . . 16.00 per month
Four rooms, front and back, left . . . . . 16.00 per month

Fourth Floor:

Four rooms, front and back, right . . . . . 14.00 per month
Four rooms, front and back, left . . . . . 14.00 per month

36 Chrystie Street

Saloon entire ground floor . . . . $60.00 per month

First Floor:

Three rooms, front, right . . . . 12.00 per month
Three rooms, front, left . . . . 12.00 per month
Two rooms, back, left . . . . 9.00 per month
Two rooms, back, right . . . . 9.00 per month

Second Floor:

Three rooms, front, right . . . . 11.50 per month
Three rooms, front, left . . . . 11.50 per month
Two rooms, back, left . . . . 8.50 per month
Two rooms, back, right . . . . 8.50 per month

Third Floor:

Three rooms, front, right . . . . 11.00 per month
Three rooms, front, left . . . . 11.00 per month
Two rooms, back, left . . . . 8.00 per month
Two rooms, back, right . . . . 8.00 per month

Fourth Floor:

Three rooms, front, right . . . . 10.50 per month
Three rooms, front, left . . . . 10.50 per month
Two rooms, back, left . . . . 7.50 per month
Two rooms, back, right . . . . 7.50 per month

34 Chrystie Street

Right, butcher shop and two rooms . . . . $32.00 per month
Right, cellar, ironware . . . . 8.00 per month
Left, grocery — two rooms and cellar . . . . 37.50 per month

First Floor:	
Three rooms, front, right	$11.00 per month
Three rooms, front, left	11.00 per month
Two rooms, back, left	8.00 per month
Two rooms, back, right	8.00 per month
Second Floor:	
Three rooms, front, right	10.50 per month
Three rooms, front, left	10.50 per month
Two rooms, back, left	8.00 per month
Two rooms, back, right	8.00 per month
Third Floor:	
Three rooms, front, right	10.50 per month
Three rooms, front, left	10.50 per month
Two rooms, back, left	7.50 per month
Two rooms, back, right	7.50 per month
Fourth Floor:	
Three rooms, front, right	9.50 per month
Three rooms, front, left	9.50 per month
Two rooms, back, left	7.00 per month
Two rooms, back, right	7.00 per month

32 Chrystie Street

Right, trimming store — three rooms and cellar	$32.00 per month
Left, trimming store — three rooms and cellar	32.00 per month
First Floor:	
Five rooms, front, right and left	20.00 per month
Five rooms, back, right and left	20.00 per month
Second Floor:	
Three rooms, front, right	11.00 per month
Three rooms, front, left	10.50 per month
Two rooms, back, left	7.50 per month
Two rooms, back, right	8.00 per month
Third Floor:	
Three rooms, front, right	11.50 per month
Three rooms, front, left	10.50 per month
Two rooms, back, left	7.50 per month
Two rooms, back, right	8.00 per month
Fourth Floor:	
Three rooms, front, right	10.00 per month
Three rooms, front, left	9.50 per month
Two rooms, back, left	7.00 per month
Two rooms, back, right	7.50 per month

30 Chrystie Street

Building in process of construction.

28 Chrystie Street

Grocery — three rooms and cellar	$33.00 per month
First Floor:	
Two rooms, front, right	8.00 per month
Two rooms, front, left	8.50 per month
Two rooms, back, left	7.50 per month
Two rooms, back, right	8.00 per month

Second Floor:

Two rooms, front, right	$7.50 per month
Two rooms, front, left	7.50 per month
Two rooms, back, left	7.00 per month
Two rooms, back, right	7.00 per month

Third Floor:

Six rooms, front, right and left, and back, right	20.00 per month
Two rooms, back, left	6.00 per month

Fourth Floor:

Two rooms, front, right	6.50 per month
Two rooms, front, left	6.50 per month
Two rooms, back, left	6.00 per month
Two rooms, back, right	6.00 per month

Fifth Floor:

Two rooms, front, right	6.00 per month
Two rooms, front, left	6.00 per month
Two rooms, back, left	5.50 per month
Two rooms, back, right	5.50 per month

Rear House of 28 Chrystie Street

First Floor (ground floor):

Two rooms, right	$6.00 per month
Two rooms, left	6.00 per month

Second Floor:

Two rooms, right	6.00 per month
Two rooms, left	6.00 per month

Third Floor:

Two rooms, right	6.00 per month
Two rooms, left	6.00 per month

Fourth Floor:

Two rooms, right	6.00 per month
Two rooms, left	6.00 per month

Fifth Floor:

Two rooms, right	6.00 per month
Two rooms, left	5.50 per month

Sixth Floor:

Two rooms, right	5.00 per month
Two rooms, left	5.00 per month

26 Chrystie Street

Right, store — three rooms and cellar	$35.00 per month
Left, vacant, no cellar	25.00 per month

First Floor:

Two rooms, front, right	8.50 per month
Two rooms, front, left	8.50 per month
Two rooms, back, left	8.00 per month
Two rooms, back, right	8.00 per month

Second Floor:

Two rooms, front, right	8.00 per month
Two rooms, front, left	8.00 per month
Two rooms, back, left	7.50 per month
Two rooms, back, right	7.50 per month

THIRD FLOOR:

Two rooms, front, right	$7.50 per month
Two rooms, front, left	7.50 per month
Two rooms, back, left	7.00 per month
Two rooms, back, right	7.00 per month

FOURTH FLOOR:

Two rooms, front, right	7.00 per month
Two rooms, front, left	7.00 per month
Two rooms, back, left	6.50 per month
Two rooms, back, right	6.50 per month

FIFTH FLOOR:

Two rooms, front, right	6.00 per month
Two rooms, front, left	6.00 per month
Two rooms, back, left	6.00 per month
Two rooms, back, right	6.00 per month

Rear Building of 26 Chrystie Street

FIRST FLOOR (ground floor):

Two rooms, right	$5.00 per month
Two rooms, left	5.00 per month

SECOND FLOOR:

Two rooms, right	7.00 per month
Two rooms, left	7.00 per month

THIRD FLOOR:

Two rooms, right	6.50 per month
Two rooms, left	6.50 per month

FOURTH FLOOR:

Two rooms, right	6.50 per month
Two rooms, left	6.50 per month

FIFTH FLOOR:

Two rooms, right	6.50 per month
Two rooms, left	6.50 per month

SIXTH FLOOR:

Two rooms, right	5.50 per month
Two rooms, left	5.50 per month

24 Chrystie Street

Picture frame store — full floor	$50.00 per month
First and second floors, synagogue.	

22 Chrystie Street

Grocery — one room	$35.00 per month
Basement, right	10.00 per month
Basement, left	12.00 per month

FIRST FLOOR:

Four rooms, front and back, right	15.00 per month
Four rooms, front and back, left	15.00 per month

SECOND FLOOR:

Four rooms, front and back, right	15.00 per month
Four rooms, front and back, left	15.00 per month

Third Floor:	
Four rooms, front and back, right	$14.00 per month
Four rooms, front and back, left	13.00 per month
Fourth Floor:	
Four rooms, front and back, right	14.00 per month
Four rooms, front and back, left	13.00 per month
Fifth Floor:	
Four rooms, front and back, right	12.00 per month
Four rooms, front and back, left	11.00 per month

Rear Building of 22 Chrystie Street

First Floor (ground floor):	
Two rooms, right	$5.00 per month
Two rooms, left	5.00 per month
Second Floor:	
Two rooms, right	7.50 per month
Two rooms, left	7.50 per month
Third Floor:	
Two rooms, right	7.50 per month
Two rooms, left	7.50 per month
Fourth Floor:	
Two rooms, right	7.00 per month
Two rooms, left	7.00 per month
Fifth Floor:	
Two rooms, right	7.00 per month
Two rooms, left	7.00 per month

20 Chrystie Street

Right, grocery and four rooms	$34.00 per month
Cellar under store	8.00 per month
Left, butcher's store — four rooms	35.00 per month
Cellar under store	8.00 per month
First Floor:	
Three rooms, front, right	13.00 per month
Three rooms, front, left	13.00 per month
Three rooms, back, left	13.00 per month
Three rooms, back, right	12.00 per month
Second Floor:	
Three rooms, front, right	12.00 per month
Three rooms, front, left	12.00 per month
Three rooms, back, left	13.00 per month
Three rooms, back, right	13.00 per month
Third Floor:	
Three rooms, front, right	12.00 per month
Three rooms, front, left	12.00 per month
Three rooms, back, left	12.00 per month
Three rooms, back, right	12.00 per month
Fourth Floor:	
Three rooms, front, right	11.00 per month
Three rooms, front, left	11.00 per month
Three rooms, back, left	11.00 per month
Three rooms, back, right	11.00 per month

Fifth Floor:

Three rooms, front, right	$10.00 per month
Three rooms, front, left	10.00 per month
Three rooms, back, left	10.00 per month
Three rooms, back, right	10.00 per month

18 Chrystie Street

Right, trimmings store — four rooms	$37.00 per month
Left, lunch room	37.00 per month
Cellar	8.00 per month
First Floor:	
Four rooms, front, right	17.00 per month
Four rooms, front, left	16.50 per month
Three rooms, back, left	13.00 per month
Three rooms, back, right	14.00 per month
Second Floor:	
Four rooms, front, right	16.50 per month
Four rooms, front, left	16.00 per month
Three rooms, back, left	12.50 per month
Three rooms, back, right	13.50 per month
Third Floor:	
Four rooms, front, right	16.00 per month
Four rooms, front, left	15.50 per month
Three rooms, back, left	12.00 per month
Three rooms, back, right	13.00 per month
Fourth Floor:	
Four rooms, front, right	15.50 per month
Four rooms, front, left	15.00 per month
Four rooms, back, left	11.50 per month
Four rooms, back, right	12.50 per month

16 Chrystie Street

Chair-seats store — one room	$25.00 per month
Clothing store — two rooms	25.00 per month
First Floor (a few steps up from street):	
Two rooms, front, right	8.50 per month
Two rooms, front, left	8.50 per month
Two rooms, back, left	8.00 per month
Two rooms, back, right	8.00 per month
Second Floor:	
Two rooms, front, right	9.50 per month
Two rooms, front, left	9.50 per month
Two rooms, back, left	9.00 per month
Two rooms, back, right	9.00 per month
Third Floor:	
Two rooms, front, right	8.50 per month
Two rooms, front, left	8.00 per month
Two rooms, back, left	8.00 per month
Two rooms, back, right	7.50 per month
Fourth Floor:	
Two rooms, front, right	8.00 per month
Two rooms, front, left	8.00 per month
Two rooms, back, left	7.50 per month
Two rooms, back, right	7.00 per month

14 Chrystie Street and 16 Bayard

(Corner building)

Drug store (corner)	$50.00 per month
14 Chrystie Street:	
Right, laundry	20.00 per month
Left, laundry	20.00 per month
16 Bayard Street:	
Right, dry goods store	40.00 per month
Left, jeweller's store	25.00 per month
First Floor:	
Five rooms, right, facing Chrystie and Bayard	22.00 per month
Five rooms, left, facing Chrystie	18.00 per month
Second Floor:	
Three rooms facing Chrystie and Bayard	12.00 per month
Three rooms facing Bayard	9.00 per month
Three rooms facing Chrystie	11.00 per month
Three rooms facing rear	7.00 per month
Third Floor:	
Three rooms facing Chrystie and Bayard	12.00 per month
Three rooms facing Chrystie	10.50 per month
Three rooms facing Bayard	9.00 per month
Three rooms facing rear	8.00 per month
Fourth Floor:	
Three rooms facing Chrystie and Bayard	11.00 per month
Three rooms facing Chrystie	10.00 per month
Three rooms facing Bayard	9.00 per month
Three rooms facing rear	8.00 per month
Fifth Floor:	
Three rooms facing Chrystie and Bayard	10.00 per month
Three rooms facing Chrystie	9.00 per month
Three rooms facing Bayard	9.00 per month
Three rooms facing rear	8.00 per month

14 Bayard Street

Store	$50.00 per month
First Floor:	
Three rooms, front	12.00 per month
Three rooms, back	11.00 per month
Second Floor:	
Three rooms, front	11.00 per month
Three rooms, back	10.00 per month
Third Floor:	
Three rooms, front	10.00 per month
Three rooms, back	9.50 per month

12 Bayard Street

Two-story private house, belonging to people in store below

10 Bayard Street

Picture frame store — both sides, including cellar $105.00 per month

First Floor:

Four rooms, front and back, right	$16.00 per month
Four rooms, front and back, left	16.00 per month

Second Floor:

Four rooms, front and back, right	15.50 per month
Four rooms, front and back, left	15.50 per month

Third Floor:

Four rooms, front and back, right	15.00 per month
Four rooms, front and back, left	15.00 per month

8 Bayard Street

Right, book store with two rooms in back	$45.00 per month
Left, grocery	45.00 per month

First Floor:

Two rooms, front, right	10.00 per month
Two rooms, front, left	10.00 per month
Two rooms, back, left	9.50 per month
Two rooms, back, right	9.50 per month

Second Floor:

Two rooms, front, right	9.50 per month
Two rooms, front, left	9.50 per month
Two rooms, back, left	9.00 per month
Two rooms, back, right	9.00 per month

Third Floor:

Two rooms, front, right	9.00 per month
Two rooms, front, left	9.00 per month
Two rooms, back, left	8.50 per month
Two rooms, back, right	8.50 per month

Fourth Floor:

Two rooms, front, right	8.00 per month
Two rooms, front, left	8.00 per month
Two rooms, back, left	7.50 per month
Two rooms, back, right	7.50 per month

6 Bayard Street

Butcher's store and cellar, right (including cellar)	$40.00 per month
Dry goods store and one room, back, left	32.00 per month
Cellar	8.00 per month

First Floor:

Two rooms, front, right	8.50 per month
Two rooms, front, left	8.50 per month
Two rooms, back, left	7.50 per month
Two rooms, back, right	7.50 per month

Second Floor:

Two rooms, front, right	8.00 per month
Two rooms, front, left	8.00 per month
Two rooms, back, left	8.00 per month
Two rooms, back, right	7.00 per month

Third Floor:

Two rooms, front, right	7.50 per month
Two rooms, front, left	7.50 per month
Two rooms, back, left	6.00 per month
Two rooms, back, right	6.00 per month

4 Bayard Street

Grocery store, both sides — cellar and three rooms	$90.00 per month
First Floor:	
Three rooms, front	12.00 per month
Three rooms, back	12.00 per month
Second Floor:	
Three rooms, front	11.00 per month
Three rooms, back	11.00 per month
Third Floor:	
Three rooms, front	11.00 per month
Three rooms, back	11.00 per month
Fourth Floor:	
Three rooms, front	10.00 per month
Three rooms, back	10.00 per month
Fifth Floor:	
Three rooms, front	9.00 per month
Three rooms, back	9.00 per month

Total monthly rent paid for the block for living purposes (excluding stores and shops)	$6,457
Total monthly rent of stores and shops	3,040
Total monthly rental of both stores and apartments	$9,497
Total annual rental	$113,964

APPENDIX X

SCHEDULES, FORMS, AND BLANKS USED IN THE INVESTIGATIONS OF THE COMMISSION

SCHEDULES, FORMS, AND BLANKS USED IN THE INVESTIGATIONS OF THE COMMISSION

CIRCULAR LETTER SENT OUT TO THE PUBLIC, ASKING ADVICE ON THE PARTICULAR POINTS MENTIONED

105 East 22d Street,
New York, June 13, 1900.

The members of the Tenement House Commission, appointed under Chapter 279 of the laws of 1900, wish to obtain your suggestions and advice, and that of others who are especially familiar with tenement house problems, to aid them in the performance of their duties. After consultation with some of those whose advice we seek, we have determined that it would presumably be more satisfactory to you and others to present your views in writing, than to give oral testimony before the Commission; at least at this stage of the Commission's work. The duty of the Commission is "to make a careful examination into the tenement houses in cities of the first class, their condition as to construction, healthfulness, safety, rentals and the effect of tenement house life on the health, education, savings and morals of those who live in tenement houses, and all other phases of the so-called tenement house question in these cities, that can affect the public welfare." The practical questions to which your attention is chiefly directed, and on which we desire a full expression of opinion, are as follows:

I. *Tenements hereafter to be built.* What changes in law are desirable from all points of view to secure the best type of tenement houses in the future, and to insure their proper regulation?

II. *Existing tenements.* What changes are desirable in their regulation?

III. *The enforcement of existing tenement house laws.*

A list of questions is enclosed herewith, intended to point out some of the more important subjects of actual or possible regulation in the expectation that these questions will be helpful to you in giving your views. We do not necessarily ask you to answer all these questions, but only those on which you have an opinion. Least of all do we wish to limit your suggestions to the points covered by the questions, for they by no means include all the subjects which we have under consideration. Should you prefer to express your views orally, we would ask you to so notify us, in which case we shall ask you to attend some of the public hearings which will be held in the future. Your answers should be sent to the secretary, Mr. Lawrence Veiller, at the above address, if possible before July 15th. — Respectfully yours,

(Sgd.) Robert W. De Forest, *Chairman.*
(Sgd.) Lawrence Veiller, *Secretary.*

POINTS ABOUT WHICH INFORMATION IS DESIRED IN REFERENCE TO TENEMENT HOUSES

These questions are not in any way intended to express the views of the members of the Commission, nor does the Commission wish to be understood as being committed to any definite decision in any of the matters here mentioned.

1. What should be the minimum percentage of a lot (whatever its size) which should be left unbuilt upon for purposes of light and air?

 a. On an interior lot? (The present law permits 65 per cent. of the lot to be built upon, but gives the Building Commissioner discretion to permit 75 per cent. to be built upon.)

b. On a corner lot? (The present law permits 92 per cent. of the lot to be built upon.)

2. What should be the minimum size of all "air shafts"?

a. Should there be a minimum width as well as a minimum area? (The present regulations permit shafts only *28 inches wide.*)

b. When "air shafts" are increased in length, shall they be increased proportionately in width? (The present law does not require it.)

c. What relation should exist between the size of air shaft and height of building?

d. What relation should the size of an "air shaft" or court bear to the number and size of rooms opening upon it?

3. Should all "air shafts" or courts be open to the outer air at one side? (The present law does not require it.)

a. Under what conditions should closed courts or shafts be permitted?

4. What should be the maximum height of new tenement houses? (The law allows 85 feet — 7 stories and basement — when the first two floors are fireproof, and 150 feet — 12 stories — when fireproof throughout.)

a. When fireproof?

b. When not fireproof?

c. If provided with elevators?

d. In relation to the size of courts or "air shafts"?

5. How should overcrowding be prevented?

a. By limiting the number of persons who are permitted to occupy a given cubical space in a house?

b. By limiting the number of persons who are permitted to occupy a given area? Or,

c. By limiting the height of tenement houses, and permitting only a certain area of land to be covered, thus limiting the accommodations to a certain number of people?

6. Are the present laws in regard to fire construction adequate?

a. Should all new tenement houses be fireproof throughout?

b. If not, what form of construction is adequate?

c. Should stairs be permitted to open upon the air shafts?

d. Should not all shafts in such buildings, including dumb-waiter shafts, be fireproof?

7. Are the present laws in reference to fire-escapes for tenements adequate? (At present the Commissioner of Buildings has full power to decide what kind of fire-escape shall be erected.)

a. On tenement houses should vertical ladders be permitted, or should stairs with hand-rails be required?

b. What method can be adopted to prevent obstruction of fire-escapes?

8. Should owners of tenement houses be compelled by law to provide bathing facilities for the tenants?

a. If so, to what extent and in what manner?

9. Shall it be compulsory to have a private water-closet for each set of rooms or family? (The present law allows one water-closet to every two families.)
   a. Shall water-closets be allowed to ventilate upon the same shaft as bedrooms?
   b. Shall they be located in the common hallway, as permitted by the present law?

10. Shall all the existing backyard privy vaults, sinks, etc., be removed by a certain date? (This was required by the law of 1887, but was repealed by the Charter.)

11. Common hallways in new tenement houses.
   a. What should be the minimum width?
   b. Are the present hallways light enough? If not, what method should be adopted to light them?
   c. How should hallways be ventilated?
   d. Should hallways have windows opening directly on the outer air? (At present most public hallways receive their only light and air from windows opening on the stairs.)

12. Common hallways in old buildings.
   a. How should such hallways be lighted?
   b. How should they be ventilated?

13. Is the space left vacant at the rear of new tenement houses sufficient? (Under the present law on interior lots a space of 10 feet is required to be left, and on corner lots a space of 5 feet.)

14. What action should be taken in reference to the existing unsanitary tenement houses in this city?
   a. Are the present powers of the Board of Health in this respect sufficient?
   b. Should the work of condemning unsanitary property and building model tenements undertaken on such a large scale by European cities be followed in New York?

15. Should the definition of a tenement house as a house occupied by three families or more be changed?
   a. Should the tenement house law apply to flats and apartment houses as well as to tenements? (It does at present.)
   b. If not, mention provisions of the present tenement house law from which apartments and flat houses should be exempt.

16. In general, what practical suggestions have you to make to the Commission with regard to its work?

These questions are intended to draw attention to particular points of possible tenement house regulation, and to elicit opinions on as many of them as possible.

Signature...

Address...

Date.........................

SCHEDULES USED IN BUFFALO INVESTIGATION

GENERAL STATISTICAL CARD

INSPECTOR --

Date --

Street -------------------- No. ---------- Ward ---------- District -------

Owner ---------------------------- Address ----------------------

Agent ---------------------------- Address ----------------------

General lessee ---------------------- Address ----------------------

Condition of street --

Paved and how ---------------------------- Sewer ----------------

Lodging house --

Size of lot --

Width of building --

Depth of building --

Percentage of lot covered --

No. of stories --

Total number of apartments --

Total number of rooms --

Total number of families --

Total number of inhabitants --

Total number of adults (over 14) --

Total number of children (5–14) --

Total number of children under 5 --

Number of vacant apartments --

Number of vacant rooms --

Janitor --

Capable --

What does he do? --

Night watchman --

Yards or courts. — Size ____________________

How paved ____________________

Drained ____________________

Is drain trapped? ____________________

Cleanliness ____________________

Outhouses. — No. ____________________

What used for ____________________

Whitewashed ____________________

Cleanliness ____________________

Fire-escapes. — No. ____________________

Iron or wood ____________________

Where located ____________________

Are there connecting ladders? ____________________

Are balconies incumbered or kept clear? ____________________

Animals on Premises. — No. ____________________

Kind ____________________

Where kept ____________________

Photo desirable ____________________ Photo No. ____________________

INTERIOR CARD

Street ______________________________ **No.** ____________

Cellar or Basement. — Material of floor ______________________________

Floor water-tight ______________________________

Height ________________ Height of ceiling above sidewalk ____________

How ventilated ______________________________

Used for what purpose ______________________________

Inhabited for dwelling ______________________________

Public Hallways. — Width of ______________________________

Light or dark, how lighted ______________________________

Is there a red light on every flight of stairs at night? ____________________

Are suitable fire gongs furnished? ______________________________

Are there two independent means of egress each accessible from each apartment?

____

Locked front door or not ______________________________

How ventilated ______________________________

No. of families using hall of each floor ______________________________

Cleanliness ______________________________

Odors ______________________________

Stairs. — Construction of ______________________________

Cleanliness ______________________________

Roof. — Staircase to roof ______________________________

Size of scuttle ______________________ Is roof used? ________________

What for ______________________________

Scuttle left unlocked ______________________________

Chimneys. — No. __________ Do they run through every floor? ______________

Is there fireplace or place for stove for each family set of apartments? __________

Water Supply. — Location of (hall, cellar, kitchen, yard) ____________________

____

Is there city water for every one or more families or set of apartments? __________

How protected from freezing ______________________________

Baths. — No. .... Location ....

Kind ....

Water-closets. — No. .... No. privies ....

Where located ....

How constructed ....

Is at least one water-closet furnished for every three families or fifteen persons?

....

Condition of plumbing ....

How ventilated ....

Cesspool .... Where located ....

Are walls and ceilings whitewashed twice a year? ....

Facilities for washing and drying clothes ....

What is done with garbage and ashes? ....

Is space for deposit of garbage provided on land of owner? ....

What business conducted on premises ....

Rent of whole house ....

APARTMENT CARD

Street ____________________ **No.** ________

Location of Apartment ____________________

No. of rooms ____________________

Size of each ____________________

Height of rooms ____________________

No. of windows in each ____________________

Windows open on what ____________________

Rooms light or dark ____________________

Kitchen ____________________

Parlor ____________________

Bedrooms ____________________

Source of light (street, yard, air shaft, own lot or adjoining premises) ________

____

Ventilation ____________________

Kitchen ____________________

Parlor ____________________

Bedrooms ____________________

No. of families occupying apartment ____________________

No. of people occupying apartment ____________________

No. and sex of adults (over 14 years) ____________________

No. and sex of children (5–14 years) ____________________

No. and sex of children under 5 ____________________

No. of lodgers ____________________

Are lodgers separated from family at night, and how? ____________________

No. of rooms actually used for sleeping ____________________

No. of children at school ____________________

No., age and sex of children working ____________________

Any manufacturing carried on in rooms ____________________

If so, what? ____________________

Nationality ____________________

Sickness at present time ....

Cleanliness of rooms ....

Occupation, head of family ....

Average weekly wages of family ....

Rent of apartment ....

REMARKS

....

....

....

SCHEDULES USED IN NEW YORK

FIRE-ESCAPE BLANK

Street ____________________

No. ____________________

Stories ____________________

Material ____________________

No. families on each floor ____________________

No. balconies front and rear ____________________

Do they take in one window of each apartment? ____________________

How connected (vertical ladders or stairs)? ____________________

Floor slats — wood or iron ____________________

Balconies encumbered ____________________

Remarks: ____________________

Signature ____________________

Address ____________________

Date ____________________

(Make same record for rear buildings.)

BACK-TO-BACK TENEMENTS

Street...

No...

Stories...

Abuts,

Street...

No...

Stories...

Space between bldgs...

No. windows opening on such space } ....

Remarks:...

Date...

Signature...

Address...

NEW TENEMENTS

BUILDINGS IN COURSE OF CONSTRUCTION

Street --

No. --

Date and Hour of Inspection --

Condition of work at time of inspection --

a. Height of buildings. Stories --

b. Diagram of lot showing outline of second or typical floor with dimensions of back yard, courts, air shafts and halls. Indicate thickness of walls and height of ceiling.

c. Percentage of lot occupied. (Corner buildings to be measured at second tier of beams — interior buildings at first tier.) ----------------------------

2. Shafts or Courts.

a. Width of shaft above fifth story at each floor ------------------------

3. Cellar and Basement.

a. If basement is to be occupied as dwelling, give :

1. Number of rooms --
2. Height of rooms --
3. Do all windows of exterior rooms open on to an area the full width of building, 2 feet 6 inches wide, and extending 6 inches below the basement floor? --
4. Is such area properly drained? --------------------------------
5. Height of ceiling of living rooms above curb ----------------------

b. Is there an entrance to basement from the street? ----------------------

c. Is the cellar floor concreted? --

4. Public Halls.

a. Are floors made of iron and fireproof material? ----------------------

If not, how are they constructed? ----------------------------------

5. Stairs.

a. Of what material constructed --

b. How enclosed --

c. Are stairs from basement to first story inside building? ------------------

If so, are they enclosed with brick walls and provided with self-closing fireproof doors top and bottom? ----------------------------------

d. If located under first story stairs, is soffit of latter protected by fireproof material? -------------- What? ----------------------------------

6. Dumb-waiter and Elevator Shafts.

a. How enclosed ________________

b. Extend through how many stories ________________

c. Is there an elevator or dumb-waiter in cellar? ________________ If so, is it enclosed with fireproof walls and self-closing fireproof doors at all openings? ________________

d. Are there self-closing fireproof doors at each story? ________________

7. Rooms.

a. Are there any rooms having a cubage less than 600 feet? ________________ If so, state how many and give dimensions ________________

8. First Tier of Beams.

a. Iron or wood ________ Depth of beams ______ Distance on centres ______

b. Are bottoms, flanges and all exposed portions protected? ________________ How? ________________

9. Second Tier of Beams.

a. If store on first floor, give same data as in "8" ________________

10. Water-closets, etc.

a. Number of families per water-closet ________________

b. W. C. compartments. How ventilated ________________ (Window to outer air or ventilating flue) ________________

c. Are floors waterproof? ________________

d. Character and position of fresh air inlet ________________

11. Flues.

How lined ________________

12. Materials & Workmanship.

a. Materials, character of ________________

b. Workmanship, character of ________________

____

13. Remarks ________________________________

____

____

____

Signature ________________________________

Signature ________________________________

OLD BUILDINGS

Street ____________________

Number ____________________

Date of inspection ____________________

When built ____________________

Material of which building is built ____________________

Height ____________________

No. of families ____________________

Diagram of lot, showing plan of typical floor with dimensions of back yard, courts and air shafts.

1. Basement and Cellar Rooms. If used for dwelling give

a. Permit for occupancy from Board of Health____________________

b. Height of____________________

c. Height of ceiling above curb____________________

d. Is there an open area the full width of building, 2 feet 6 inches wide, in front of room, and 6 inches below level of cellar floor?____________________

____

e. Is such area properly drained?____________________

f. What water-closet accommodations, and where located?____________________

____

g. Have all rooms windows at least 9 sq. ft., opening to outer air?____________________

____

h. Is cellar floor water-tight?__________How?____________________

i. Is ceiling plastered?____________________

j. Walls and ceilings, how recently whitewashed?____________________

2. Halls.

a. How lighted?____________________

b. Are they light or dark?____________________

c. If there are no windows opening to outer air, is there a light burning on each floor?____________________

d. How are halls ventilated?____________________

e. Is there a ventilator in roof?__________Construction and dimensions of same ____________________

3. Sleeping Rooms.

a. Have they windows opening to outer air?____________________

b. If not, have they transoms to outer room and to hall?____________________

____

4. Water-closets.

a. Where located ? ....

b. Kind and no. ....

(Privies, school sinks or water-closets) ....

c. Is there a sewer connection ? ....

d. Is there a sewer in the street ? ....

e. Number of families per water-closet ....

5. Water.

a. Where supplied ....

6. Bakeries.

a. Where located ....

b. Any opening from bakery to other parts of the house, and what ....

....

c. Ceilings and side walls, how constructed ....

d. Cleanliness of ....

7. Cleanliness of Building. Yard. Halls. Rooms.

....

....

8. Remarks.

....

....

Signature ....

Address ....

SANITARY INSPECTION,
TENEMENT HOUSE COMMISSION,
1900.

Pg. 1.

BUILT______________

Record No.______________

APARTMENTS

Street______________No.__________Near______________{St. Ave.

No. of stories__________Date of inspection______________1900

Hour__________{A. M. P. M. Inspector______________

No. of buildings in row of which this is typical ______________

First Floor.

Used for what business ______________and______________

Any special fixtures ______________

Apartments.

No. of apartments on each floor ______________ Total no. __________

No. of people on each floor ______________

Each apartment has how many rooms ______________

Sinks in Apartments.

Location ______________

Material ______________

Condition of sink ______________

" " floor and woodwork ______________

Enclosed in woodwork ______________

Sink waste, free or choked ______________

" drain boards, condition ______________

Cold and hot water faucets ______________

Does water run freely on top floor ?______________

Sink Trap.

Size __________ Material __________ Condition __________

Sink Trap Vent.

Size __________ Material __________ Condition __________

Wash Tubs in Apartments.

Number______________ Location______________

Material______________ Condition______________

Covers — open or closed ____________

Tubs filled or empty ____________

Hot and cold water faucets ____________

Condition of floor and woodwork ____________

Wash Tubs Trap.

Size ________ Material ________ Condition ________

Wash Tubs Trap Vent.

Size ________ Material ________ Condition ________

Bath Tub.

Describe ____________

____

Light and ventilation of bath compartment ____________

Stove Heated Boiler.

Sediment ends where ____________

Water-closets in Apartment ____________(see special card)

Any Other Fixtures

Describe : ____________

____

Ice Box.

Location and condition ____________

Drip, how disposed of ____________

Is safe waste trapped ? ____________

Condition of floor ____________

Are Clothes dried in Apartment ; what Rooms ?

____

Soil, Waste or Vent Pipes in Apartments.

Visible in apartment or concealed ____________

No. of soil ________ Material ________ Condition ________

No. of waste ________ " ________ " ________

No. of vent ________ " ________ " ________

Joints in Soil, Waste and Vent Pipes.

Material ________ Condition ________

Remarks : ____________

____

Official Inspection of Building.

When and by whom ____________

SANITARY INSPECTION,
TENEMENT HOUSE COMMISSION,
1900.

Pg. 2.

BUILT..........................

Record No...........................

CELLAR, YARDS, HALLS, ROOF, CESSPOOLS, SOIL

Street.......................No.......... Near........................ { St. / Ave.

No. of stories............... Date of inspection.............................1900

Hour.................. { A. M. / P. M. Inspector..

CELLAR.

Used for what purpose ....

Closed or open stairs or shafts from cellar to upper floors ....

....

Light by day ....

" " night ....

Ventilation ....

Condition of Cellar.

Clean or dirty ....

Rubbish or fœcal matter ....

Whitewashed ....

Kind of Cellar Floor and Condition.

Earth. Cement. Stone ....

Waterproofed. How ....

Damp, wet or dry ....

Ceiling of Cellar.

Material. Fireproof ....

Sound or broken ....

Openings into pipe chases or flues ....

Cellar Floor Drain.

How connected ....

Evidence of under-drains. How connected ....

Blind drains. Condition ....

Main Drain.

Above or below floor ....

Material and quality ____________________
Size ____________________
How supported ____________________
Patched or sound ____________________
Kind and condition of joints ____________________
Number of free openings in drains ____________________
Any odor from drains ____________________
Steam or other drips, connecting with drains where ____________________
Cleanouts on drains — kind and no. ____________________

House Trap.

Location ____________________ Accessible ____________________
Kind of cleanout covers ____________________

Fresh Air Inlet.

Size ____________________
Ends, where and how ____________________
Free or choked ____________________

Number and Sizes of Connecting Drains in Cellar.

No. of soil pipes	____	Size	____	Material	____
" waste pipes	____	"	____	"	____
" vent pipes	____	"	____	"	____

No. of Visible Traps in Cellar for

Leaders ____________________
Yard, court or area drains ____________________

Sink or Other Fixture in Cellar.

No. and kind ____________________
Material and condition ____________________
Trapped and vented ____________________
How supplied with water ____________________
Drips or safe wastes over sink. Flap valves ____________________

Water Service in Cellar.

Size of house mains and material ____________________
Meter, what kind ____________________
Supply to house tank, direct or pump ____________________ Size ____________________
Controlled by whom ____________________
Pump — Kind. Size. Condition ____________________
Direct supply, to what floors ____________________
Tank supply, " " " ____________________

Rubbish Bins.

Location. Material. Condition ____________________

SANITARY INSPECTION,
TENEMENT HOUSE COMMISSION,
1900.

Pg. 3.

BUILT............................

Record No.............................

CELLAR, YARDS, HALLS, ROOF, CESSPOOLS, SOIL

Street............................No..................Near............................ { St. / Ave.

No. of stories...............Date of inspection..1900.

Hour.......................{ A.M. / P.M. Inspector..

FRONT AND BACK YARDS, COURTS, AREAS, LIGHT SHAFTS.

Condition ....

Paved. Material ....

Will surface drain ?..

Provision for Drainage, Back Yards and Courts.

Iron cesspools ....

Mason's traps ....

Blind drains ....

Trapped ....

Leaders.

No. and location. Inside or outside ....

Material ....

Trapped ....

Condition ....

Used for soil or vent pipes ....

Are soil, waste or vent pipes used for leaders ?...................................

Hydrant in Yard.

Location ....

Used by how many families ....

" " " people ....

Is hydrant water used for drinking ?..

Pump or Well in Yard.

Location ....

How near privies ....

Condition --

Used by how many families --

" " " people --

Is water used for drinking? --

Garbage Cans.

Location and condition --

CESSPOOL.

No. and location --

Dimensions------------------------- x ------------------------- deep

How far from building --

" " " pump or well --

Nature of surrounding soil --

Material of walls --

Tight or leaching --

Overflow delivers where --

Ventilated --

Provision for emptying --

Emptied how often and how --

Disinfected how often and how --

Receives what drainage --

HALLS.

Do water-closets open on halls? -------------------------(see special card)

Public Sinks in Halls.

Number. Location ---------------------------- Total no. -----------

Used by how many families --

" " " people --

Material of sink --

Used for fœcal matter or urine --

Cased or free --

Trap material. Size. Condition --

Vent " " " --

Any odor at sink --

Is sink well lighted? --

Condition of floors and walls --

Sanitary Inspection,
Tenement House Commission,
1900.

Pg. 4.

BUILT.........................

Record No.........................

CELLAR, YARDS, HALLS, ROOF, CESSPOOLS, SOIL

Street....................No............Near.................... { St. / Ave.

No. of stories............Date of inspection....................1900

Hour.................{ A.M. / P.M. Inspector....................

HALLS — (Continued).

Water Supply for Hall Fixtures.

Street supply. What floors ....

Deficient supply, on what floors ....

Pump at fixtures, what floors ....

Tank supply. What floors ....

Other Fixtures in Halls.

Describe:....................

....

ROOF.

Condition of roof. Any fœcal matter ....

Roof drains where ....

Condition of gutters ....

Are leader connections free ....

Soil Waste and Vent Pipes above Roof.

	No.	Size	Material
Soil	....	....	....
Waste	"	"	" ....
Vent	"	"	" ....

Wire globe cages or caps ....

Open how high above roof ....

Open less than 20 ft. from windows or ventilators ....

Roof Tank.

Location ....

Material ....

Dimensions inside ______________________________

Capacity in U. S. gallons ______________________________

Tight or leaking ______________________________

Cover. Material ______________________________

Tank, how full ______________________________

" " supplied ______________ ball cock ______________ pump ________

" frost proofed ______________________________

" supplies what floors ______________________________

" water used for drinking ______________________________

" overflow ends where ______________________________

" " trapped ______________________________

" clean or dirty ______________________________

" draw-off ends where ______________________________

Do drain vents open near tank? ______________________________

Provision for Drying Clothes.

Back yard ______________________ Back yard poles ______________________

Roof lines ______________________ In air shaft ______________________

SOIL.

Character of ground shown by Viele's map ______________________________

Over water course ______________________________

" marsh ______________________________

" made land ______________________________

REMARKS: ______________________________

____

____

____

LAWS.

Do plumbing and drainage conform with laws in force at time building was built? ______________________________

What violations? ______________________________

____

____

Sanitary Inspection,
Tenement House Commission,
1900.

Pg. 5.

BUILT____________________

Record No.____________________

WATER-CLOSET ACCOMMODATIONS. PIPES

Street____________No.__________Near____________{St. / Ave.}

No. of stories__________Date of inspection____________________1900

Hour __________{A. M. / P. M.} Inspector____________________

No. and Kind of Fixtures. **Location.**

Privy vault ______________ ______________

School sink or latrine ______________ ______________

Water-closets ______________ ______________

Sewer or cesspool disposal ______________ ______________

Each Fixture used by how Many:

Families ______________ Total no. of families ______________

People ______________ Total no. of people ______________

Buildings in Back Yard.

No., material of structure; size, condition ______________

How far from other buildings ______________

Used separately or in common ______________

No. of compartments and condition ______________

Locked or open ______________

Separate buildings or compartments for sexes ______________

Building, how lighted by day ______________

" " " " night ______________

" " ventilated ______________

Kind of floor and condition ______________

No. and kind of seats and condition ______________

Cased with wood below seats ______________

Remarks: ______________

____

Privy Vault and Location ____________

Size and material of vault ______ x ______ x ______ deep ______

Water-tight or leaching ____________

Is overflow connected to sewer or cesspool? ____________

" trapped? ____________

Vault, how full ____________

Provision for flushing ____________

" " emptying ____________

Emptied, how often ____________

Apparatus used for emptying ____________

Provision for disinfecting ____________

Disinfected, how often ____________

Condition ____________

Odor ____________

Remarks: ____________

____

School Sink or Latrine and Location ____________

No. ______ Material ______ Above or below floor ______

Size and how full ____________

Outlet plugged or open ____________

Who operates plug, and how often? ____________

Sewer or cesspool connected ____________

Is fixture trapped? ____________

Provision for flushing ____________

Water, how connected ____________

Condition of fixture ____________

Remarks: ____________

____

SANITARY INSPECTION,
TENEMENT HOUSE COMMISSION,
1900.

Pg. 6.

BUILT..............................

Record No..............................

WATER-CLOSET ACCOMMODATIONS. PIPES

Street..............................No..............................Near..............................{St. / Ave.}

No. of stories..............................Date of inspection..............................1900

Hour..............................{A. M. / P. M.} Inspector..............................

Water-closets — Location and No.

In yard ....
" cellar ....
" halls ....
" apartments ....

W. C. Compartment.

Has compartment window to outer air, court, light shaft, light well, hall, cellar, or apartment; specify ? ....
Well lighted ....
How lighted at night ....
Has compartment ventilation flue ?.............................. Size ....
United or individual vent flues ....
Material of floor and condition ....
" " walls " " ....
Floor slab or safe. Material. Wet or dry ....
Is there a safe waste ?..............................

Type of Closet and How Trapped.

Pan .... Syphon ....
Wash out .... Long hopper ....
Wash down .... Short hopper ....
Other type ....

Material of Bowl and Condition.

Earthenware ....

Enameled iron ______

Iron ______

Connected earthenware vent horn, cracked or broken ______

Washered coupling on vent ______

Vented from below floor ______

Floor plate ______

Drip pan. Condition ______

Material and condition of seat ______

Is fixture cased in wood or stone? Condition ______

Closet, How Flushed.

Individual tank ______

Automatic " ______

Direct from water pipe ______

Water from house tank or street pressure ______

Is there sufficient flush on all floors? ______

Deficient flush, on what floors ______

Tanks out of order ______

Odor ______

What disinfectants used ______

Remarks: ______

______

Soil, Waste and Vent Pipes.

Soil, No. ______ Size ______ Material ______

Waste, No. ______ " ______ " ______

Vent, No. ______ " ______ " ______

Exposed or cased ______

Patched, and how ______

Are openings about pipes sealed at floors? ______

Joints.

Kind and condition of joints ______

Remarks: ______

______

SANITARY INSPECTION,
TENEMENT HOUSE COMMISSION,
1900.

Pg. 7.

BUILT..................................

Record No..................................

Street.................... No.............. Near.................... { St. / Ave.

Builder ....

Owner ....

Plumber ....

Are plans now on file in Bldg. Dept.? ....

Plans approved by ....

Violations filed ....

" removed ....

Recorded date of water-test by Dept. ....

" " " final test " " ....

Deaths .... in .... years ....

Contagious diseases reported. No. in.............. " ....

What diseases ....

....

....

....

Death rate of building ....

" " block ....

Sick rate of building ....

" " block ....

SMOKE TEST

Applied. Date .... 1900. Hour ....

By..................................

Machine attached to ....

noke returned through..................................

....

ipes choked ....

ntrapped ....

....

Leaks disclosed and location ....

....

....

....

....

Total number of leaks ....

Remarks: ....

....

FREE OPENINGS FOR ESCAPE OF DRAIN AIR TO BUILDING

Disclosed by inspection (enumerate) ....

....

....

....

....

Total number of openings ....

TRAP SYPHONAGE

Any evidence of trap syphonage. Where ....

....

....

....

....

....

....

....

....

INDEX

INDEX

(Figures refer to Pages)

MUNICIPAL ENGINEERING AND SANITATION

By M. N. Baker, Ph.B.

Associate Editor of Engineering News

12mo Half Leather $1.25 net

"It is designed to be a review of the whole field of municipal engineering and sanitation rather than an exhaustive study of one or a few branches of the subject. The most vital points, however, under each class of activities and interests have been dwelt upon, the underlying principles stated, and in many instances details from actual practice given," says the author. Among the practical questions discussed are: Ways and means of communication, municipal supplies, collection and disposal of waste, recreation and art, administration, finance and public policy. It is a volume which must appeal to all classes interested in any degree in municipal affairs.

"Full of significant facts and judicial comments. The subjects covered include the building, repairing, and cleaning of streets, the construction of subways, the elimination of grade crossings, the management of water-works, the purification of water supplies, ice supplies, and milk supplies, the disposal of sewage and garbage, the protection of property from fire, the protection of health by plumbing regulations, the protection of comfort by smoke abatement and the suppression of noises, and, finally, a series of problems connected with the administration of various public works having an engineering or sanitation side. That which most impresses the reader is the wide range of observation from which Mr. Baker speaks. . . . The reports of foreign engineers upon experiments abroad are also frequently used, but the work is better for American readers because American experience is kept constantly in the foreground." — *The Outlook.*

PRINCIPLES OF SANITARY SCIENCE

AND THE PUBLIC HEALTH

With Special Reference to the Causation and Prevention of Infectious Diseases

By William T. Sedgwick, Ph.D.

Cloth 8vo $3.00 net

"The present volume is the direct outgrowth of a course of lectures on Sanitary Science and the Public Health given for several years by the author to certain senior students — chiefly engineers, biologists, chemists, and architects — of the Massachusetts Institute of Technology, and it has been prepared primarily for their use. It is believed, however, that a larger circle of students, and some physicians, publicists, and general readers may be glad to have access to the same material. If any apology is required for the occasional use of examples drawn from the author's personal experience, chiefly in Massachusetts, it may be said that these have been referred to, not because the author regards them as of paramount importance, but because he has preferred to deal as far as possible at first hand with matters within his own knowledge rather than to depend upon the digests or even the original reports of others." — *From the Author's Preface.*

THE MACMILLAN COMPANY

66 FIFTH AVENUE, NEW YORK

www.ingramcontent.com/pod-product-compliance
Lightning Source LLC
LaVergne TN
LVHW011252110826
845149LV00001B/113

* 9 7 8 1 4 1 8 1 8 8 9 3 1 *